Making Sense

Making Sense

Essays on Art, Science, and Culture

Second Edition

Bob Coleman
University of South Alabama

Rebecca Brittenham
Indiana University–South Bend

Scott Campbell
University of Connecticut

Stephanie Girard
Spring Hill College

Houghton Mifflin Company   Boston   New York

Publisher: Patricia A. Coryell
Executive Editor: Suzanne Phelps Weir
Development Manager: Sarah Helyar Smith
Assistant Editor: Anne Leung
Project Editor: Shelley Dickerson
Senior Manufacturing Coordinator: Marie Barnes
Senior Marketing Manager: Cindy Graff Cohen
Marketing Associate: Wendy Thayer

Cover image: © Beth Caspar: Structure in Nature (Earth). Linocut 42"x 42". 1999.

Acknowledgements appear on pages 686–688, which constitutes an extension of the copyright page.

Printed in the U.S.A.

Library of Congress Control Number: 2003115598

ISBN: 0-618-44135-2

3 4 5 6 7 8 9-FFG-10 09 08 07 06

Contents

"I think that using art to provoke uncertainty is what great writing and inspired images do most brilliantly. Art should provoke more questions than answers and, most of all, should make us think about what we rarely want to think about at all."

"*Nepantla* is the Nahuatl word for an in-between state, that uncertain terrain one crosses when moving from one place to another, when changing from one class, race, or gender position to another, when traveling from the present identity into a new identity."

"What is true of art is true of serious reading as well. Fewer and fewer people, it seems, have the leisure or the inclination to undertake it. And true reading is hard. Unless we are practiced, we do not just crack the covers and slip into an alternate world. We do not get swept up as readily as we might be by the big-screen excitements of film. But if we do read perseveringly we make available to ourselves, in a most portable form, an ulterior existence."

"How do we define class? Is it a matter of values, lifestyles, taste? Is it the kind of work you do, your relationship to the means of production? Is it a matter of how much money you earn? Are we allowed to choose?"

separates you from your past, this is precisely what will happen. It is important to stand firm in the conviction that nothing can truly separate us from our pasts when we nurture and cherish that connection."

"Discussion, argument, legal actions, and decrees replace shoot-outs. Finding a better way to live and to manage environmental issues such as land use rests on language, on the use of language to discover, initiate, persuade, understand, anger, conciliate: on rhetoric."

"In a democracy, only informed debate by an educated citizenry can make the mature decisions about a technology so powerful that we can dream of controlling life itself."

"I conclude that we need a new vocabulary and new concepts for analyzing events like the discovery of oxygen. Though undoubtedly correct, the sentence 'Oxygen was discovered' misleads by suggesting that discovering something is a single simple act unequivocally attributable, if only we knew enough, to an individual and an instant in time."

"Since the public no longer participates in debates on national issues, it has no reason to inform itself about civic affairs. It is the decay of public debate, not the school system (bad as it is), that makes the public ill informed, notwithstanding the wonders of the age of information. When debate becomes a lost art, information, even though it may be readily available, makes no impression."

"For the first time in our tradition, the ordinary ways in which individuals create and share culture fall within the reach of the regulation of the law, which has expanded to draw within its control a vast amount of culture and creativity that it never reached before. The technology that preserved the balance of our history—between uses of our culture that were free and uses of our culture that were only upon permission—has been undone. The consequence is that we are less and less a free culture, more and more a permission culture."

"In our social anthropological research we are uncovering another picture of what science literacy might consist of by asking nonscientists, at all educational levels and from a variety of ethnic and socioeconomic settings, to tell us in their own terms what they know about health and their bodies, in particular about immunity and the immune system."

"If people failed to UNDERSTAND comics, it was because they defined what comics could be too narrowly."

"Photography implies that we know about the world if we accept it as the camera records it. But this is the opposite of understanding, which starts from *not* accepting the world as it looks. All possibility of understanding is rooted in the ability to say no. Strictly speaking, one never understands anything from a photograph."

"The incommunicability of the experience of the Vietnam veterans has been a primary narrative in Vietnam War representation. This silence has been depicted as a consequence of an inconceivable kind of war, one that fit no prior images of war, one that the American public would refuse to believe. The importance of the Vietnam Veterans memorial lies in its communicability, which in effect has mollified the incommunicability of the veterans' experience."

"Buffalo Bill was a person who inspired other people. What they saw in him was an aspect of themselves. It really doesn't matter whether Cody was as great as people thought him or not, because what they were responding to when he rode into the arena, erect and resplendent on his charger, was something intangible, not the man himself, but a possible way of being."

"If the symbols of science are being used to endorse or legitimize certain values and meanings but not the values and meanings of science, then to what exactly do these symbols refer? What do the symbols of science convey, if not the content of science? What are the nonscientific ideas that are being expressed by means of scientific symbols?"

"None of the historians had ever learned our mother tongue. They had all been content to read what Europeans and Americans had written. But why did scholars, presumably well-trained and thoughtful, neglect our language? Not merely a passageway to knowledge, language is a form of knowing by itself."

"What do the words 'reality' and 'real' mean? Although philosophers do not find it easy to agree on an answer, ordinary thinking people have little difficulty using these words in everyday talk, often in conjunction with their opposites, 'fantasy' and 'unreal.' Such talk, when looked at closely, shows how the meaning of 'real' shifts, even radically, as the context changes."

"But even when women felt free to experiment with soft mastery, they faced a special conflict. Tinkering required a close encounter with the computer. But this violated a cultural taboo about being involved with 'machines' that fell particularly harshly on women. When I was a young girl, I assembled the materials to build a crystal radio. My mother, usually encouraging, said, 'Don't touch it, you'll get a shock.' Her, tone, however, did not communicate fear for my safety, but distaste."

SUSAN WILLIS, "Disney World: Public Use/Private State"   *582*

> "What's most interesting about Disney World is what's not there. Intimacy is not in the program even though the architecture includes several secluded nooks, gazebos, and patios. During my five-day stay, I saw only one kiss— and this a husbandly peck on the cheek. Eruptions of imaginative play are just as rare."

JEANETTE WINTERSON, "Imagination and Reality"   *597*

> "We have to admit that the arts stimulate and satisfy a part of our nature that would otherwise be left untouched and that the emotions art arouses in us are of a different order to those aroused by experience of any other kind."

Part III: Assignment Sequences   *611*

Preface

Whatever the topic—borders, "Blaxicans," or Buffalo Bill; dream houses, comics, or intellectual property rights—the essays in *Making Sense: Constructing Knowledge in the Arts and Sciences* challenge students (and their instructors) to reconsider both what they know and what they'd like to learn. We recognize that students in composition courses are rarely, if ever, a homogeneous group and we hope that the mix of topics, approaches, themes, and disciplines will appeal equally to chemists and composers, engineers and English majors.

One of our goals for this book is for students to develop an appreciation of academic disciplines as more than a shared subject and set of texts. We want them to see that disciplines are also common habits of mind: shared ways of thinking, writing, and speaking about that subject, those texts, and the ideas that animate them.

Principles for Selecting the Readings

To achieve that goal, we have selected our readings and designed our teaching apparatus around three basic principles. First, we believe that students benefit from seeing strong examples of how writers "make sense" of the world through writing and how they position themselves relative to their subjects and imagined audiences. So, we selected essays that share an exploratory, testing quality that characterizes good expository writing. We do not think of the selections as authoritative sources to be endorsed or "primary" texts to be analyzed and commented upon by a "secondary" text (the student's writing). Instead, we see these texts as invitations to a complex intellectual inquiry that goes beyond summarizing positions and choosing sides. *Making Sense* sees students as active peers and producers, not simply inheritors.

A second principle guiding the book is our commitment to writing as an engagement with other writers' texts and ideas. *Making Sense* makes linking, connecting, and building its top priorities. To that end, we have created an apparatus that asks students to be aware of what they already know or think they know about a subject or author, before they read the text. The questions that follow the text to help students develop their reading skills by identifying key words or ideas, thinking through evidence and examples, and recognizing how the author uses the work of others to make his or her point. Because we believe that the readings are the strongest feature of *Making Sense*, we have designed the post-reading questions to offer students opportunities and strategies for digging deeper and learning more about how the texts work both as individual pieces of writing and as part of *Making Sense* and the world of texts beyond it.

The final principle underlying *Making Sense* is our belief that students learn more and retain what they learn more easily when they can see relationships between what they know, what they are learning, and how this knowledge relates to the world they live in. Above all else, *Making Sense* is a collection of readings designed to help beginning writers make connections between academic inquiry and their own interests and experience. While we expect our writing courses to pursue scholarly, academic goals, we see no need to unduly mark writing as either "creative/exploratory" or "rigorous/academic." *Making Sense* is built with the understanding that academic work *is* exploratory and creative. Students will benefit from seeing the rich interaction between "real lives" and academic work that animates these essays.

In these three principles students can find something we call the "making sense" moment—the moment when a writer finds a place in a discussion and a purpose for advancing that discussion. This moment is also the moment of interface between students at the beginnings of their academic careers and those of us facilitating these moments. In sum, we see *Making Sense* as fostering an awareness of the existing, evolving community of writers/thinkers and offering an invitation to students to consider and articulate their place in this community, to think *through* these ongoing exchanges.

What's New in the Second Edition

This second edition of *Making Sense* is, as they say, new and improved. We've learned from our experiences in teaching the book as well as those shared with us by teachers and students. The result is a stronger, more engaging book that builds on the strengths of the previous edition, while introducing new texts and new features that will appeal to composition instructors and students alike.

- **New readings and images.** We have added new readings, such as Dorothy Allison, "This is Our World"; bell hooks, "keeping close to home: class and education"; Lawrence Lessig, "Introduction" to *Free Culture;* and Marita Sturken, "The Wall, the Screen, and the Image: The Vietnam Veterans Memorial." The Dorothy Allison essay has been illustrated with two Depression-era photos and the Marita Sturken essay on the Vietnam Memorial includes four photographs by the author. Four new images have been added to Gloria Anzaldúa's essay on border artists and three new advertisements to Stuart Ewen's essay on consumer style.

- **Introduction.** We have written a new and more inviting Introduction that asks students to see writing and drafting as a form of tinkering, a continuous process of learning rules from models and applying them to new tasks. To help them start tinkering, we've included a section on analyzing a writing task in rhetorical terms.

- **New pre-reading questions.** The new set of pre-reading questions for each reading, *What Do You Know? What Do You Expect to Discover?*, uncovers the knowledge and ideas that students already have about the topic so they can move with more confidence into their reading of the text. These questions help students anticipate key ideas and develop their own framework for understanding the reading.

- **Updated post-reading questions.** We have retitled, updated, and revised the post-reading questions. Because we don't expect instructors to use every question we've written, we have included a mix of questions that can stand alone and questions that build on previous answers. These sections are now arranged in the following four categories:

  Reading, Rereading, and Analysis—This section focuses on the process and techniques of textual analysis, while adding more suggestions for group activities.

  Responding through Writing: Building an Interpretation—New and revised questions in this section build on previous responses to encourage students to construct their own positions on the subject.

  Going Further: Learning from Other Sources—These questions invite students to connect their readings to the world outside the text. By conducting research in the library or on the Internet, students can learn to challenge the essay's themes and arguments or to follow up on their own responses.

  Applying What You've Learned—Questions in this section ask students to develop and demonstrate an understanding of one text by applying its terms, approach, or argument to another.

- **Assignment sequences.** We have added 10 new assignment sequences to bring the total to 25. And, we have created two new appendices where you will find "Making Sense through Research" and a collection of five essays on "Writing in the Disciplines."

Keeping the Best of the First Edition

We have retained the following features that continue to distinguish *Making Sense*:

- **Intriguing authors.** The authors in *Making Sense* include familiar scholarly names like Nancy Sommers, Sherry Turkle,

Thomas Kuhn, and Jane Tompkins; famous popular authors like Walter Mosley, Dorothy Allison, and Richard Florida; and less well-known but equally accessible writers like Arlie Russell Hochschild, Witold Rybczynski, and Marita Sturken.

- **Flexible organization.** *Making Sense* can be easily adapted for courses organized by theme, discipline, or argumentative approach. The alternative thematic and disciplinary tables of contents and our links between essays throughout the book are designed to provide examples of the many possible course designs to which the book can be adapted.

- **Cross-disciplinary selections.** The writers in this collection, from whatever their "home" discipline, write to readers beyond their discipline's borders in readable, understandable language. Their essays demonstrate the many ways that arguments can be made and supported in order to make sense to particular audiences.

- **Variety in the length and complexity of readings.** *Making Sense* offers essays that vary in length and difficulty. The variety in length and complexity gives each teacher latitude in developing the course best suited to the students in a particular class. It also gives students a more authentic portrayal of academic writing, which does indeed come in all shapes and sizes.

- **Engaging questions.** Questions that precede and follow the readings are not of the yes/no, right/wrong variety; instead they are designed to open up discussion, to provoke responses, and to suggest a variety of ways to make sense of the essay.

- **Headnotes.** Each essay is introduced with a brief headnote providing biographical information about the author and including, where necessary, an explanation of important terms or concepts.

- **Assignment Sequences.** The 25 assignment sequences invite students to practice revision: Instead of reading one essay, writing a paper on it (and often tossing that paper out once it has been "finished" and graded), and then moving on to completely fresh ground, students responding to sequenced assignments are encouraged to revisit their own earlier papers just as they revisit essays they have already read and written about. Sequencing makes particular sense within scholarly communities where essays are rarely limited to an engagement with a single writer and where the conventions of citation, allusion, and footnoting demand that each new conversation make reference to traditions of thought and ongoing conversations.

Supplements for Students

Making Sense Student Web site

The student Web site offers both links to additional information on the authors and topics included in *Making Sense* and supplemental images that expand or develop the visual component of the essays.

SMARTHINKING™

This online tutoring service links students to a unique Web-based writing center staffed by experienced composition instructors. Students can communicate in real time through one-on-one tutoring sessions, or they can submit papers for quick, personalized feedback and suggestions. For more information, please visit http://www.smarthinking.com/houghton.html.

e-Exercises

Also available on the Houghton Mifflin Web site are over 700 self-quizzes covering punctuation and mechanics, parts of speech, sentence problems, and style.

Supplements for Instructors

Instructor's Resource Manual

A separate Instructor's Resource Manual includes teaching tips and strategies for making the best use of *Making Sense* based on the editors' own experiences in using these essays in composition classrooms at Indiana University at South Bend, the University of South Alabama, Rutgers University, and Stony Brook University. The entries provided for each essay include a list of critical vocabulary, suggestions for points of entry and emphasis, a discussion of student responses to the essay, and advice on linking essays in sequences. We also identify selections that work well at the beginning of the semester or the beginning of the sequence.

For the second edition of the manual, we have added a section specifically designed to help Teaching Assistants use *Making Sense*.

Making Sense Instructor Web site

Houghton Mifflin hosts a companion Web site where instructors will find links to visual and other instructional aids that can be either presented directly in the classroom or assigned for students to find through Internet searching. We invite instructors to submit their own syllabi and assignments for posting to the site. With your help, we hope to expand the site over time and increase its utility as a pedagogical resource and an online community. The Web site will also include information about the editors and an email address where you can send us your comments, questions, and ideas.

WriteSpace™

For adopters seeking the latest technology writing tools for their students and a powerful, customizable classroom management program for themselves for either traditional or distance-learning courses, the second edition of *Making Sense* can be packaged with student passkeys to an exciting new online writing program, WriteSpace. Powered by Blackboard™, this complete electronic writing program includes an extensive array of writing learning modules and assignments; more than 2,000 grammar and writing exercises; a series of diagnostic tests; and access to an easy-to-search digital handbook, Ann Raimes' *Keys for Writers*. In addition, students are one click away from the SMARTHINKING™ Online Writing Lab for online tutoring with qualified instructors. To learn more about WriteSpace, visit http://www.eduspace.

Acknowledgments

We would like to thank the following reviewers of *Making Sense* for their helpful reading of the manuscript at various stages. Their ideas and suggestions were extremely valuable in the development of this book.

> Valerie K. Anderson, York College of the City University of New York
>
> Polly Buckingham, Eastern Washington University
>
> Janice Chernekoff, Kutztown University of Pennsylvania
>
> Kathleen Kelly, Northeastern University
>
> Michael Kula, Carroll College
>
> Thomas Peele, Boise State University
>
> Marilyn M. Robitaille, Tarleton State University
>
> Susan Ryan, University of Louisville
>
> Nancy K. Salter, Eastern Connecticut State University
>
> Rebecca Shapiro, St. Thomas Aquinas College
>
> Alan Tessaro, University of Missouri–St. Louis

Laura Kuske von Wallmenich, Alma College

Alida Young, Boston University

Our thanks go to Suzanne Phelps Weir, Laura Barthule and Martha Bustin, Anne Leung and Sarah Smith, Carla Thompson, Shelley Dickerson, and the staff at Houghton Mifflin for making this book possible. We also thank good friends and indirect contributors: Jonathan Nashel, Anne Wettersten, Claire Berardini, Dawn Scorzewski, Hildegard Hoeller, Alec Marsh, Jim Albrecht, Joe Thomas, Shevaun Watson, and Martha Patterson. We are particularly grateful to our students and colleagues at Indiana University, South Bend, the University of South Alabama (especially Sue Walker, Jean McIver, Larry Beason, Becky McLaughlin, Ellen Harrington, Bruce Alford, Cris Hollingsworth, Pat Cesarini, Tom West, Deidre Dowling, Lauren Murphey, Andy Pigott, Kathy White, and Georgia Godwin), Stony Brook University (especially Wilbur Farley, Richard Buch, Kathleen Kern, Gabriel Brownstein, and Anne Beaufort), Spring Hill College (especially Noreen Carrocci, Michael Kaffer, Margaret Davis, and John Hafner), the University of Connecticut (especially Tom Recchio and Sarah Winter), Long Island University (especially Tom Kerr, Harriet Malinowitz, Deborah Mutnick, and Patricia Stephens), Montclair State University (especially Janet Cutler, Jim Nash, and Tom Benediktsson), and Rutgers University (especially Ron Christ, Barry Qualls, Michael McKeon, Carol Smith, Marianne DeKoven, Bill Galperin, Hugh English, Suzanne Diamond, Judy Karwowski, Susan Mayer, Michael Goeller, Kurt Spellmeyer, and Richard Miller). We are especially grateful to Tam Mai, for allowing us to include her student essay, and to the contributors to "Writing in the Disciplines":

Barbara Scofield, University of Texas at the Permian Basin

Steven Gerencser, Indiana University, South Bend

Ann Grens, Deborah Marr, Andrew Schnabel, Indiana University, South Bend

Kent McClelland, Grinnell College

Heide R. Lomangino, University of South Alabama

Final Note

The editors of *Making Sense* recognize that controversies within composition studies, departments of English, divisions of Humanities, and universities as a whole are signs of a fundamental shift in ways of defining what it means to have a college education. Increasingly, students are vocationally oriented, pursuing not an education but a career. Simultaneously, however, business and industry executives are searching for employees who combine specialized knowledge with excellent writing and oral communication skills, employees who are flexible and able to change as the organization changes. And, notwithstanding these pressures, many students (and educators) still want college work to inspire and inform the life outside and beyond professional employment. In an effort to respond to these conflicting needs, we have created a composition reader that not only challenges students to examine and investigate ideas circulating in the world around them but also to reflect on their role in building on these ideas.

We welcome your feedback on how you have chosen to use *Making Sense* in your courses. Please send us your syllabi, your assignments, and your comments through our companion website at http://college.hmco.com.

B. C.
R. B.
S. C.
S. G.

Thematic Table of Contents

List of Figures and Illustrations

Part I

Making Sense

Introduction

It could be a math problem, a poem, a carburetor that won't work, or an error in the computer code you're using to build your own video game. You stare and stare at it, but you have no idea how to fix it. A friend, a teacher, a mechanic, or a younger brother looks at it and offers a solution. To persuade you that it's the right solution, he or she points to the evidence, gives you examples of similar situations, reads to you from the owner's manual (or the textbook, the dictionary, or the literary handbook), and shows how all these facts, examples, and evidence add up. If it all seems to fit together, you're very likely to say, "That makes sense!"

When a solution makes sense to us, it follows the rules we've learned from experience and it builds on knowledge we already have. For centuries, writing has been used to make sense of our world and ourselves, by helping us to learn what we think. Most of us are messy thinkers. Ideas, feelings, and memories tumble together in our heads until we give them order and meaning by putting them into words and sentences. We can, of course, say those sentences out loud, but unless we have a really good memory or recording equipment, they won't last and they won't travel, at least not in the same form.

Most of us are also messy talkers. In conversation, we don't worry too much about making ourselves understood. We usually know our listeners, speak their language—sometimes with the same accent—and share their assumptions about how things work. We also know that they are right there—across the table, on the phone, or in the chat room—and they can ask us questions if they don't understand something we say. When we write, however, our readers are not usually in the room with us. Their absence means that we need to anticipate their questions and potential objections by writing as clearly and persuasively as we can. Thinking about the possible needs of readers can help us as writers to clean up messy thinking, fill in gaps, offer examples, and discover what we really know and what we really think.

Unlike talking, writing allows us to see our words. Whether they're written on paper or on the computer screen, our words are now separate from us. They are objects. We can move them around, like blocks or puzzle pieces, and test out the new meanings generated from each new position until we find one that makes sense. When we begin to see the pattern or sense emerging from the words, we know that we are that much closer to finding a solution to the math problem, a meaning for the poem, or the correct code for the video game.

Admittedly, the carburetor probably can't be fixed by writing. Reading a page or two in the car-repair book might help, but you—or your mechanic—are most likely to fix it by tinkering, which is a kind of trial and error with tools. In other words, you make a few adjustments and then test them out until you find the right ones. Tinkering, or "bricolage" as Sherry Turkle calls it in her essay, "The Triumph of Tinkering" (see page 569), is actually much like writing. Some writers use the strategy described above: They begin by collecting ideas, quotations, or phrases that they know they want to use and then "tinker" with them until they have a rough draft. Other writers prefer to begin with a very structured outline of what they want to say and then fill it in step-by-step in order. Still other writers use some combination of the two strategies. None of those strategies is right or wrong. Good writers learn to use the strategy that makes the most sense to them.

We chose the Turkle essay and other readings in this book because they made sense to us. They made us look at events and facts in a new way. They made us interested in subjects we don't often read about, such as the Buffalo Bill Museum, the history of science, copyright law, and Chicana artists. They gave us tools we could use to make sense of other events, other facts, and other texts.

We also picked these readings because they're well written and can be read by the average person. That is not to say, however, that the average person can understand them completely after one reading. These are essays that are worth reading more than once. We've read them often and yet, each time we read them, we learn something new or see some connection that we missed before.

We hope that these texts will teach you something new about the world and about yourselves. We hope that they will be models of good writing that you can come back to again and again.

How to Use This Book

By the time you read this book, you will have accumulated a variety of experiences through interactions with friends, family, and the world around you. Those experiences, together with the facts that you've learned through your formal education, provide a framework for understanding new information. That framework, however, is frequently invisible to us. We don't know that it's there; we just know that some things make sense to us and some don't.

As composition teachers and editors of this book, we think it's important for you to see that framework and to give yourself credit for what you already know. To help you do that, we've included a set of questions before each reading. These questions, together with some brief information about the author and some suggested sources to pursue if you'd like to learn more about the author or his or her subject, are designed to help you discover what's new and interesting in these essays by connecting it to what you already know.

We want you to be ready to listen to these authors and to decide for yourself if what they say makes sense to you. As we explain in Chapter 1, "Making Sense Through Reading," you may want to mark your book as you read. You don't have to say anything profound or worry about anyone else reading your marks. These marks are for you. They can help you to go to a definition, an example, or a passage you particularly like or one that didn't make sense to you. When you reread the essay, you can focus on the words you've marked. You can even quote them in your paper.

When you finish your first reading of an essay, you may need some ideas on how to start talking or writing about it. The questions that follow the readings are designed to stimulate your thinking. They are divided into four sections:

1. **Reading, Rereading, and Analysis.** Questions or prompts in this section are designed to help you recognize key concepts and how they might apply to situations or examples different from the ones the author chose to use. You may be asked to draw a diagram, make a list, or work in a group to come up with questions of your own.

2. **Responding Through Writing: Building an Interpretation.** These questions were written to help you begin tinkering with the essay—that is, learning what you think about it through writing. As the section title suggests, we hope that you will use the answers or ideas generated in response to the other questions to build your own interpretation of the essay.

3. **Going Further: Learning from Other Sources.** These suggestions for researching concepts, examples, or individuals discussed in the essays are meant to help you develop your ability to find and evaluate information in the library or on the Internet.

4. **Making Connections: Applying What You've Learned.** As we mentioned earlier, everything you read and experience adds to the store of knowledge you bring to a new reading, whether it's a text you haven't read before or one that you're reading again. In this section, we suggest ways in which you might connect what you've learned from reading and writing about one essay to reading and writing about another. What we hope

you will learn from these assignments is how ideas associated with one discipline or field of study can help you to understand another.

However you choose to use this book, we hope that one of the things you will "get" from it is a set of strategies for writing about and making sense of the world and your place in it.

Analyzing a Writing Task

Good writers know the importance of matching a writing strategy to a specific writing task. Once we discover the solution or interpretation that makes sense to us, we may want to communicate it to someone else. The following questions can help you decide what strategies to use to achieve the effects you want.

Purpose: Why are you speaking or writing? What do you want to accomplish? Do you want to persuade your audience to take a particular action, to understand your position on a complex issue, or to see you in a different way? Are you responding to someone else or initiating a conversation? Are you being funny, serious, or ironic? If you are writing in response to an assigned question, you might analyze the assignment to see what sense of purpose it implies. Look for action verbs, such as explain, describe, examine, analyze, or respond.

Persona: What role are you being asked to play? What is the source of your authority as a writer or a speaker? Do you have some knowledge, derived through research, reading, or experience, that helps you to speak confidently on the topic? Do you have a unique perspective on the topic that you want to share with your audience, or a set of questions you want to ask them? When you respond to the writing prompts included in *Making Sense,* you are playing the role of a reader who is responding to the text or analyzing it. You are the one making sense of a particular reading, creating a unique connection between readings, or showing how one theme links several writers' perspectives.

Audience: To whom are you speaking or writing? It could be an individual you know well or someone you don't know at all; it could be a large group such as a lecture audience or the readers of a newspaper or magazine; or it could be a small group of people whom you can assume share your views and opinions, such as members of your class. In each of these cases, you will need either to adapt your language and your argument to the expectations of the audience, or to understand the consequences of not satisfying those expectations.

Argument: How can you achieve your purpose? Should you present evidence and demonstrate how it can be interpreted, or should you offer examples? Should you appeal to your audience's emotions, their intelligence, or their perceived self-interests? In what order should you present your ideas to make them most effective?

Although purpose, persona, audience, and argument are not the only terms that can be used to define a communication situation, they are the terms that we have found useful in our thinking and writing both in and out of the classroom.

Another virtue of these terms is that we can apply them as readers; that is, we can look for the words and phrases that signal what the author is trying to achieve (purpose), what qualifications the author has to speak on the subject (persona), for whom the author is writing (audience), and how the author presents his or her information (argument).

Chapter 1

Making Sense Through Reading

IT IS NO SECRET THAT texts of all types surround us: labels on clothing, billboards, signs in front of businesses, words and numbers on calendars, the headlines and print of newspapers, e-mail and Internet pop-ups, and the words on the pages of books. Although it is true that we increasingly live in a highly visual culture, it is also true that the literacy we associate with print culture continues to structure our daily lives in the most profound ways. The term "reading" thus describes activities ranging from close, analytical work with sentences and paragraphs to the larger ways in which we evaluate and process words and images to make sense of the world.

In an essay included in this collection, Sven Birkerts contrasts the "intensive," careful reading of earlier centuries, when any scrap of print was rare and thus deeply valued, with the "extensive," shallow reading skills we use now to sift through the constant bombardment of texts we see every day (p. 71). Unlike Birkerts, who sees these two types of reading as polar opposites, we believe that the reading skills we use every day can be focused and combined with more detailed, analytical skills to get the most out of the scholarly texts assembled here. By becoming mindful and deliberate about the choices we are already making to sift the important from the unimportant, to factor visual impressions in with language, to use what we already know as a way to make sense of the unfamiliar, we can learn to take advantage of the training contemporary life has already provided us with.

We also believe that there is an intimate relationship between developing and strengthening reading skills and developing and strengthening writing abilities. Reading and writing are not two discrete or separate subjects—one taught by literature professors and the other taught by rhetoric and composition specialists. Instruction in reading, a type of consumption, and in writing, a type of production, is arguably at the structural core of college and university education. Engaged, critical reading involves pausing to write and think about ideas as we read, talking about ideas with others, and returning to reread, question, respond, and write again. Through such instruction we learn to make sense and to determine what doesn't make sense given the evidence at hand.

Although there is no set formula for reading well, in each of the three sections of this chapter we offer a series of techniques for using and building on the reading skills you already have so that you may become a stronger, more engaged, and more analytical reader.

- Section 1, Finding a Point of Connection, focuses on making the initial acquaintance of a reading, on finding ways to connect the words and images in this book with the knowledge, experiences, and skills you already possess.

- Section 2, Reading Comprehension, identifies a series of techniques for improving your reading comprehension, for deepening and intensifying your reading focus.
- Section 3, Reading Visual Texts, offers specific advice for reading images, advertisements, photographs, paintings, and drawings in the context of their function as subjects for analysis or illustration.

Finding a Point of Connection

Some of the writers in this collection will do everything they can, from the first sentence on, to pull you into a reading. Listen to Annie Dillard, for example: "When I was six or seven years old, growing up in Pittsburgh, I used to take a precious penny of my own and hide it for someone else to find" (p. 111). Other writers are so anxious to dig into a specialized topic that they may come across as less approachable: "My object in this article is to isolate and illuminate one small part of what I take to be a continuing historiographic revolution in the study of science" (Kuhn, p. 289). Yet every essay will have its points of accessibility, places where the writer reaches out to make contact with you, finds a way to draw you in. When approaching these essays in search of those moments of accessibility, keep the following three techniques in mind.

Just Dive In

No one, least of all their authors, ever intended the essays in this book to be understood after one reading. These are rich, scholarly essays whose writers want to intrigue you; even more than giving you information, they will be doing their level best to get you thinking and asking questions. On a first reading, simply let the sentences and paragraphs slide through your mind, keeping your eye on the examples, picking up an interesting idea here and there, letting your eyes and ears adjust to the writer's voice, and ignoring the parts you don't understand. In this sense, you are bringing to an essay the "extensive" reading skills you use every day to sort through all the texts you encounter: advertisements, newspaper headlines, e-mail.

Use the following strategies to connect to an essay the first time you read it.

- Pay attention to things that seem interesting or important; overlook the rest.
- Look through the illustrations before beginning an essay and start by reading the text that surrounds a particular illustration.

- Skim through the essay looking for interesting examples or anecdotes.
- Find one or two points of connection in the essay, one or two places that speak to you and that you can circle or highlight or respond to in the margins of the page.
- Leave question marks along the way just to remind yourself of points you found puzzling, and checkmarks to indicate points that seemed interesting and worth going back to.

Use the Pleasure Principle

You may be working your way through a six-course meal, but there's no one to stop you from dipping into the dessert first. As you read, especially the first time, pay attention to the things that interest or delight you, that get you thinking. A reader perusing the essay by Nancy Sommers may focus at the point where one of Sommers's students analyzes a joke about a canary. Another reader may be intrigued by places in "Designs for Escape" (p. 427) where the writer fantasizes about creating the perfect vacation cottage.

When you pick up an essay for the first time, you are holding all the potential for hilarity, boredom, polite interest, or the love affair of a lifetime that you might have when first meeting a person, and, as in any first encounter, it helps to be as tolerant and open-minded as possible. It helps simply to listen, to ask questions, to wait for your new acquaintance to stumble on a point of commonality, a shared interest. Finding some moment like that often marks the turning point between the first pleasure-seeking test-run reading of an essay and the second reading, when you might begin by ignoring the introductory and surrounding material and move directly to the passage or two that piqued your interest the first time around. In this sense, you are already beginning to combine "extensive" reading skills with more focused, "intensive" reading of particular sections.

When the topic of the essay is completely new, that moment of intensive connection may emerge not from previous knowledge but from just a spark of interest when the writer launches into an idea or example that seems accessible, intriguing, worth hearing more about. For example, in responding to the Kuhn essay quoted earlier one reader described feeling a little left out until page 293, when Kuhn began telling the story of the first scientist who discovered the X-ray. Something about an image of the scientist Roentgen holed up in his laboratory for "seven hectic weeks" trying desperately to track down why his cathode-ray tube was glowing caught that reader's attention and helped her make sense of that one aspect of Kuhn's essay. Sometimes such moments leap out at you and sometimes they have to be searched out, but often they will be the moments you end up writing about, remembering, referring to in discussions, and using in later papers. During a second reading, it can be useful to list those moments on a separate sheet of paper, noting the page numbers and jotting down a sentence or two about what the writer is saying and how you respond to it. Keep in mind that the moments that puzzle you the most or when you violently disagree with something the writer has said are also often immensely valuable in helping you to develop an interpretation of the essay.

Discuss, Take Notes, Reread; Discuss, Take Notes, Reread

If you appear in class after an initial reading with just a few sections marked, just a few questions or comments written down, you will be ready for a discussion no matter how much of the essay still remains a puzzle. Discussion is a crucial stage of reading, because it allows you to combine what you've learned so far with the discoveries other readers have made. Your few points of connection to a reading become exponentially expanded through the radius of connections provided by every member of a discussion group no matter how preliminary or flawed their responses might be. You will improve your understanding of particular moments in the reading not only by hearing what other readers have to say and by testing your ideas against theirs but also through the sheer act of putting your own uncertain reactions or nebulous thoughts into words. Every note you take, every response you hear or articulate for others, every piece of an essay you reread to test or develop your understanding of it becomes one more point of connection between you and the writer of that essay. Rereading is also crucial, partly because each time you read a text, it is a different experience. You are not the same reader you were before. The first time you reread a text, you know how it ends or where it leads, and that knowledge helps you to notice and appreciate details and ideas you may have missed. With each subsequent reading, you bring new expectations, new ideas, and new contexts for understanding.

Reading Comprehension: Getting the Larger Picture

Once you have made the acquaintance of an essay, jumped in, identified a few places of interest, begun to discuss it with others, and perhaps written about the particular moments that struck you one way or another, you are on your way to understanding the essay. As you start on a second or third reading, use the following techniques to deepen your understanding of the essay.

Use the Parts to Make Sense of the Whole

Piece together the parts of the essay that made sense to you; then go back to see how those parts fit into the essay as whole. How does the claim a writer makes on the essay's second page connect to or conflict with something he or she says six pages later? In particular, keep an eye out for the examples a writer uses, the stories he or she tells as a way to convey a particular idea or make a point. For instance, in "The Triumph of Tinkering" (p. 569), the author wants to make a point about the different styles and approaches men and women bring to computer programming, but she does so through a series of examples from her own experience, from students she has known, from various writers she has read. You will hear about Lisa, who turns to poetry to express her frustration with the rule-bound study of computer programming; about Robin the pianist, who is told that manipulating computer code like musical notes is a "waste of time"; about the author, Sherry Turkle, herself as a college student finding strategies to cover up for her intuitive way of organizing and writing an essay. By tracking what Turkle does with several of those examples, you will arrive at a clearer and more nuanced view of what she is trying to do in the essay as a whole.

Identify and Define Key Terms

Every writer has a few important concepts that he or she wants to focus on in a particular essay. Often those concepts will appear in the title of the essay, will be carefully defined by the writer, or will be repeated throughout the essay. By zeroing in on this kind of signal, you can often cut to the core of an essay and discover what the writer most wants to accomplish. In one essay in this book, Richard Rodriguez uses his title, "'Blaxicans' and Other Reinvented Americans" (p. 420), to introduce the made-up term "Blaxicans" and the concept of composite cultural and ethnic identity that will be the key topic of the essay. Walker Percy, another writer you will encounter in this book, does not use his key term "symbolic complex" in the title of his essay, but he does slow down to define that term carefully and to offer examples that help his reader understand what he means by it.

Read Closely

Close reading is an enormously useful way to begin the work of rereading and analysis. Pay attention to sentences in the essay that seemed particularly dense or confusing the first time through. Zoom in to focus on the specifics of the writer's language. For instance, when reading Marita Sturken's essay on the Vietnam memorial included in this book, you might pause when she says, "A singular, sanctioned history of the Vietnam War has not coalesced, in part because of the disruption of the standard narratives of American imperialism, technology, and masculinity that the war's loss represented" (p. 487). What a wonderfully rich sentence! It's a sentence worth paying attention to, worth going over in a discussion with classmates, worth writing about. What does she mean by "sanctioned history," and what are those "standard narratives" she lists? What was "disrupted" and why? The clues that will help you to unpack that sentence are strewn throughout the essay.

Highlight Key Phrases

Writers often spend hours thinking about the particular words they might use and the implications of those words. By paying attention to those words, you will gain the most accurate and nuanced understanding of what makes that writer tick. As you read, highlight phrases you might include in your paper. By quoting and responding to the specifics of a writer's language when you write about an essay, you demonstrate your skill and accuracy as a reader and you provide evidence for your own interpretation, whether you end up endorsing the writer's view or tearing it to shreds.

Use Outlines

Whereas close reading zooms in to focus on particular moments in an essay, outlining involves stepping back to see a diagram of the essay as a whole. Especially once you have explored some of the finer points and examples in an essay, outlining provides a valuable way to put those various parts together, to get a sense of each move in the writer's argument and how it contributes to the whole. Think of an outline as a map leading you or other readers to the key points of the essay. One method of outlining involves simply creating a paragraph-by-paragraph list of the key points as you reread the essay.

The following tips will help you create and use such an outline.

- Wherever possible, note the paragraphs absolutely crucial to the meaning and purpose of the essay, and note the paragraphs that are subordinate, the ones that merely add further illustration or complexity to a previously made point.

- Look beyond the paragraph structure of the essay to consider the distinct points a writer makes. For example, a writer may use three paragraphs and three separate examples to make one larger point or a series of closely related points.

- When an essay seems meaningfully divided into sections and subsections, use those divisions to structure your outline, and add numbered and bulleted lists that help to define the relationships between the various parts.

- Compare your outline with those made by other students in the class. In particular, identify and discuss the differences in your outlines—the key points one reader may have noted that another overlooked, contradictory views of the writer's main point, and differing views on the relative importance of particular points. There is no single correct outline. Like any map, an outline will vary according to the perspective and focus of its creator. However, such discussions can improve the relative accuracy of an outline, its sensitivity to the priorities and purposes of an essay, and its ability to expose the skeletal structure of an essay in a way that numerous readers can understand.

- Consider what your outline reveals about the writer's overall purpose and message. For instance, one essay you will encounter in this collection, Gloria Anzaldúa's "Chicana Artists: Exploring *Nepantla, el Lugar de la Frontera*" (p. 55), can at first appear to be merely a series of examples and experiences the writer has strung together. Yet, after you have outlined each of her key points, you will see that the essay is focused on the issue of borderlands and on the complex identities of people who occupy those places where borders overlap.

Although we are not always aware of it, the appearance of a written text provides us with important information even before we read the first word. We recognize the visual patterns that distinguish a poem from an essay, a play from a short story, a newspaper article from a college composition assignment. Perhaps less obviously, we also understand the visual separations of paragraphs as indicating a shift in topic or a further stage in an argument. We expect to see these patterns, and when we don't we are forced to pay attention, to ask why the author isn't following the conventions. Sometimes the author has made a mistake, but sometimes he or she knows that deviating from the pattern will get your attention and make you look more closely at what's on the page.

Reading Visual Texts

Just as your first look at the printed page tells you what kind of written text you are about to read, your first glance at a visual image tells you something about what kind of image it is. For example, look at the image of tree roots reproduced in Annie Dillard's essay, "Seeing," in this collection (p. 113). How does it compare with other photographs, drawings, paintings, or visual images that you've seen? The caption tells us it was created by Ansel Adams, who gave it the title *Roots, Foster Gardens, Honolulu, Hawaii, 1948.* You might recognize the name Ansel Adams from posters, calendars, and books that

FIGURE 1 Ansel Adams, *Roots. Foster Gardens, Honolulu, Hawaii,* 1948. 7½ × 6 ³⁄₁₆ in. Collection of Marjorie and Leonard Vernon, Los Angeles. (© Ansel Adams Publishing Rights Trust/CORBIS.)

reproduce his photographs of the American West. If you don't, you can do some quick Internet research, which will reveal that Adams was a famous photographer and conservationist who took many of his photographs in U.S. national parks (see <http://www.zpub.com/sf/history/adams.html>).

Next, consider what catches your eye. Where do you find yourself looking first? Our first inclination is usually to find the center of the image, to look where the painter or the photographer seems to be directing us. In Adams's photograph, your eyes may be drawn upward until they settle on the tuft of grass to the upper left of center. If you're looking at Jimmy Stewart and his camera in Susan Sontag's essay, "In Plato's Cave" (p. 467), you might be drawn to Stewart's eyes or to the camera itself. In either case, the spot you choose to focus on will become the part around which you organize the other elements in the image.

Now that you've found your focus or center, you can begin reading the image in more detail. What is the image doing? Is it recording or commemorating an event? Is it explaining a process or an idea? Is it inviting us to respond to it as an art object? Or is it, like Stewart and his camera, asking us to step into the story and learn more? Although the Stewart image looks like a photograph, the caption tells us that it is a still image from the film *Rear Window*, directed by Alfred Hitchcock. This information helps us to think about the image's purpose. Knowing the plot of the movie provides a context for understanding the image, but it's not completely necessary. The size of the camera, its somewhat aggressive positioning toward the viewer, the image reflected in its lens, the deeply shadowed background, and the look in Stewart's eyes, all convey the sense of foreboding and mystery that characterizes the movie. Decoding the relationships between the photograph's various elements can help you to form your own interpretation, which you can then compare with those offered by critics such as Susan Sontag, who gives her own reading of the Stewart image on page 474.

FIGURE 2 Jimmy Stewart as L. B. Jeffries in *Rear Window*, directed by Alfred Hitchcock. (© Bettmann/CORBIS.)

FIGURE 3 Yolanda Lopez, *Portrait of the Artist as the Virgin of Guadalupe,* 1978. Oil pastel on paper.

Just as a written text can refer to other texts through quotation or allusion, a visual image can refer its viewer to other images or texts. For example, Yolanda Lopez's *Portrait of the Artist as the Virgin of Guadalupe,* reproduced in Gloria Anzaldúa's "Chicana Artists: Exploring *Nepantla, el Lugar de la Frontera*" (p. 55), asks the viewer to position the image in two different contexts. The first is the genre of the self-portrait, and the second is the iconography of the Virgin of Guadalupe. Those two contexts help us to see the figure in the painting as a reimagining of the relationship between the artist, the viewer, and the Virgin.

These references beyond the frame of the image are especially frequent in advertising. We know that, at a very basic level, the purpose of advertising is to sell a product or a service. To analyze an advertising image, then, you want to begin with the techniques described above:

- Determine the context of the image. Where was it first printed or shown?

- Identify its category and the conventions of that category. How does it compare with other advertisements you've seen for the same product or others?

- Find the focus. What catches your eye at first glance?

- Relate the other elements of the advertisement to the focus point. If there is written text, does it explain, comment on, or praise the item being sold?

- Define the allusions or cultural references. Does the image imitate or parody another, more familiar image? Does it include a famous person, character, or location? What metaphors, metonymies, or symbols are indicated?

Then you may want to ask a few more-specific questions:

- Who is the target audience? Advertisers frequently segment audiences by demographic categories, including age, gender, race, and economic status. Use the answers to the questions above to help you determine the audience.

- What strategies does the advertisement use to persuade you to buy the product or use the service? Does the advertiser appear to have purposes other than those? What kinds of responses does the advertisement appear to provoke or attempt to provoke?

Those are only a few of the strategies you can use to read advertisements and other visual texts. As you become more aware of how both you and the creator of the image are using those strategies, you will become a more savvy reader of visual texts.

Chapter 2

Making Sense Through Writing

Writing as Interpretation and Analysis

As you read, discuss, and write about a text, you may gain fresh insights on the subjects it covers or discover new ways of understanding and explaining it. The writing you do to articulate those insights and discoveries is called interpretation. The two processes of interpretive writing and reading are intrinsically related. Writing about an essay guarantees a better understanding of it, and careful, analytic reading provides the strongest possible basis for a piece of interpretive writing. There is no set formula for good writing, but the following suggestions will help you develop your initial responses to readings into more thoughtful, evidence-based arguments.

Use Writing to Investigate a Text

When approaching a new topic or reading, use writing to document what you already know and to tease out what there is to learn.

- Jot down notes as you read; pause momentarily to write about a particularly intriguing passage or to pose a series of questions about a puzzling one.
- Test your comprehension by closing the book and summarizing a paragraph you have just read.
- Keep a reading journal in which you work through your responses to various essays or to particular points in one essay.

Such techniques help you to assess and improve your reading comprehension and to connect new information to knowledge you already possess and experiences you've had. For example, you may never have thought much about a biomolecular revolution before reading Michio Kaku's "Second Thoughts: The Genetics of a Brave New World?" (p. 264). Jotting down your ideas and questions about cloning, bioengineered food, and other issues Kaku raises will help you both to organize and think through those ideas and to remember and make sense of what you are reading.

Used in this way, writing becomes a form of investigation or a means of discovery rather than simply an articulation of ideas that are already in your head. Many times writers report a kind of magic emergence on paper of an idea they were not yet aware of. There is really no magic involved, unless we allow for the magic made possible by a learned trust in the power of writing to make evident something that was unclear or to conjure up a rich vein of meaning from half-conscious fragments just when you feel you've run dry.

Writing as investigation can be particularly fruitful if you target an especially dense or interesting passage in a reading and slow down to write extensively about that passage. For instance, during a targeted rereading of the Kaku essay mentioned earlier, a reader might focus on his concluding sentence: "In a democracy, what is decisive is informed debate by an enlightened electorate." A journal entry about that sentence might look something like this:

> What does he mean by an "enlightened electorate"? With fewer people voting in national elections today than a generation ago, do we have a less "enlightened" electorate, less of a democracy? What does he mean by "informed" vs. uninformed debate? What are his assumptions about democracy?

Writing about any one of those questions in relation to one or more of Kaku's examples and perhaps in relation to his or her own knowledge and experiences would help a reader to generate a substantial interpretive response to the essay, which could very possibly become the basis for a draft. Such writing would also prepare that reader for class discussions, group assignments, or in-class writing.

Embrace Your Explanatory Powers

Most of your job as an interpreter is simply to explain the meaning of a text or some part of a text. There are all kinds of wonderful words to describe the nuances of this activity—unpack, gloss, explicate, review, describe, summarize, analyze—but it helps to keep this larger role clearly in mind. Imagine readers who are somewhat perplexed by a particular essay or image, have overlooked or forgotten the details of it, or are a little bored or put off by it. Your job is to make some part of that essay or image clearer to those readers, to remind them of important details they may have missed, and to reconnect them with some aspect of the essay or image, get them thinking about it in a slightly new way. The following three strategies may help you to think through your role as explainer.

ZOOM IN, PAN OUT: QUOTE, PARAPHRASE, SUMMARIZE, AND ANALYZE   As you explain a text, you are aiming for a balance: You want to account for the original writer's ideas with enough accuracy and detail to be convincing while avoiding an overly close or long-winded restatement of the original essay. The key methods used to explain a text are quotation, paraphrase, summary, and analysis. When you quote a text, you are as close to it as you can be. When you paraphrase, you take a step away by restating the writer's ideas in your own words. When you summarize, you gain more distance by condensing a paragraph or more from the original work into a pithy sentence or two of your own. When you analyze, you achieve an ideal balance by focusing on crucial details of the original writer's work—often paying attention to particular words and phrases—while using your own perspective or an idea from another text to help you shed some fresh light on the original writer's work. You might profitably combine all those techniques in a single paragraph, using one to enhance or lead into the other. For example, to explain Sven Birkerts's ideas in "The Owl Has Flown"—an essay described in the previous chapter—a writer might lead in with a brief summary of the work as a whole as a way to orient the reader, supply some context, and set up a direct quotation:

> In "The Owl Has Flown," Sven Birkerts gives a history of reading in order to argue that by learning to read widely and shallowly as a way to keep up with all the texts and technological data that bombard us, we have lost "the very paradigm of depth. A sense of the deep and natural connectedness of things is a function of vertical consciousness. Its apotheosis is what was once called wisdom. Wisdom: the knowing not of facts but of truths about human nature and the processes of life" (p. 71).

At this point, the writer has panned out to give us a larger glimpse of the Birkerts essay and then zoomed in to give us a close-up of Birkerts's own words. To explain the quotation, the writer might employ paraphrase to ease readers into the complexity of its vocabulary and sentence structure and help them focus on the concept of "wisdom":

> In particular, Birkerts mourns the loss of wisdom, which he defines as the glorified essence of depth, an awareness of core truths as opposed to the accumulation of trivial factual knowledge.

Notice how this paraphrase merely steers readers back into the quotation. The slightly different wording helps readers get a handle on some fairly complex ideas. From there, the writer could move into a more detailed analysis of Birkerts's language and its implications:

> The fact that Birkerts uses words such as "natural connectedness" and "the processes of life" also tends to glorify this idea of "depth" and give it a significance that transcends history. He conjures up the image of the guru on the mountain who achieves wisdom through a silent contemplation of the universe or of a few ancient texts. By implication, shallow, factual reading is unnatural and out of touch with our core humanity. Yet think of the scientist scanning screen after screen of flickering factual data to find a cure for cancer or a treatment for schizophrenia. Does that scientist lack wisdom? Is that person out of touch with "the processes of life"?

Here the writer launches into a fundamental disagreement with Birkerts, helps us to see that some of Birkerts's ideas are debatable, and prods us to consider the idea of "depth" from more than one angle. Because the writer has built up to this moment by carefully demonstrating a detailed understanding of Birkerts—using quotation, summary, and paraphrase to win our trust—he or she has established a solid basis from which to question or contradict Birkerts.

Analysis does not have to involve disagreement. A writer might fully support the claims an essay makes and still zoom in to provide a fresh perspective. In the previous example, the writer might have taken the analysis in a different direction by showing how Birkerts's ideas applied in a contemporary case. The writer might have argued, for instance, that the social anthropologists in "Scientific Literacy, What It Is, Why It's Important, and Why Scientists Think We Don't Have It" (p. 330), who take the trouble to study how nonscientists really think and talk about their own immune systems and about diseases such as AIDS, are putting Birkerts's concept of "wisdom" into practice by seeking to learn and communicate core truths about these natural processes rather than bewildering people with scientific jargon or overwhelming them with data.

DRAMATIZE YOUR VOICE Like most writers getting their initial thoughts down and churning out the early drafts of papers, you may feel unsure of what you have to say and hesitant about your authority to say it. However, the persona that shows up on the page need not reflect that uncertainty. In fact, within the confines of your own writing, you have the license to speak with complete authority, to dramatize what you would like to sound like, to speak with far more assurance than you may feel. After all, as an interpreter, you are bringing to bear a unique perspective, a set of experiences, questions, and attitudes that no one else can replicate. You are the one making sense of a particular reading, creating a unique connection between readings, or showing how one theme links several writers' ideas. Rather than advertising any hesitancy you might have about that role by, for example, repeating "I think" or "In my opinion" or allowing uncertainty to prevent you from expressing an idea, try hamming up the persona. Try out the voice of a storyteller using an experience or an example to engage an audience's interest and trust; try out the voice of a lecturer making a risky claim to capture the attention of a large group; try out the voice of a lawyer persuading a jury to share his or her view of the case by boldly presenting an argument and marshaling the evidence to back it up.

This willingness to dramatize yourself, to play up your explanatory role, goes hand in hand with developing an actual sense of purpose as you write and revise a paper. Your overt purpose in a classroom setting may be simply to complete an assignment and get a grade, but as a writer you want to instill a sense of urgency in the paper, a sense of something important at stake. Focusing on explanation as your goal, imagining yourself helping a reader to understand a complex topic in a slightly new way or persuading a reader to share your position on an issue, can help you infuse the paper with an internal sense of purpose. In a way, you are dramatizing the paper's function for your readers—letting them know what is interesting about the topic and why it matters. The five anthropologists who wrote "Scientific Literacy, What It Is, Why It's Important, and Why Scientists Think We Don't Have It" probably had their own professional goals in mind—to add a publication to their vitae, to get jobs or promotions, to gain respect in their field. They researched and wrote the article as a group, so the challenges of creating a unified persona must have been imposing. Yet they infuse the paper with an internal sense of urgency; they help us think about scientific literacy in a new way and convince us that listening to how ordinary people think and talk about their experiences and their bodies is just as crucial as scientific research and data. They create an embodied voice for the paper, a group persona whose excitement about the topic gains our attention: "The amazing world of the immune system is not separated from us; rather, 'it is us.' To know about it gives us a sense of a powerful self" (p. 332).

KEEP YOUR AUDIENCE IN MIND   The audience you write for affects how and what you write. A paper written for a college course—no matter what grade it received—will require substantial revision before it can be published in a national magazine. Similarly, a paper written for a history class will emphasize different facts and details than a paper on the same topic written for a political science or literature class. Different audiences have different expectations. Defining those expectations is an important part of the writing process.

When considering your audience it will help to ask the following questions:

- **Who will be reading this?** Imagine a reader who will benefit from the explanations and analysis you have to give. In most classroom settings, it helps to see the other members of the class as your audience.

- **How much does my reader need to know?** What level of assumed familiarity can I predict? Keeping an image of your readers firmly in mind may help you decide how much to quote, when to summarize, how much context to provide, or how detailed your explanation needs to be.

- **What vocabulary and sentence structures will be most appropriate in this setting and most effective in reaching this audience?** Sherry Turkle and Thomas Kuhn probably used this kind of audience measure to maintain an appropriate professionalism (among other things, they both risk using the first-person "I," which is banned in some scholarly settings) but also to avoid highly specialized programming or scientific jargon in their respective essays, "The Triumph of Tinkering" and "The Historical Structure of Scientific Discovery." Similarly, if you are writing in a classroom setting, notice the word choices and sentence structures used in the class readings and in other students' papers and ask the teacher for additional guidelines. These strategies will help you to develop an approach that is professional but not stilted.

Take Charge of Your Writing Process

An exercise guru from the 1990s used to screech at key moments in his body-shaping routine, "If you don't squeeze it, no one will squeeze it for you." That advice is true of the writing process, and the analogy to muscle development is more apt than it might seem. Over time, the repetitive practice of writing, reading, revising, rereading, and revising will improve your skills as a writer. Just as the continuous practice of weight lifting gradually teaches you how to identify and focus on particular muscle groups, the regular practice of writing can teach you to become more conscious and more in control of the various stages of your writing process.

You can enhance that learning curve just as a weight lifter does by focusing on particular parts of the process, becoming aware of the techniques you are using, reminding yourself of how you worked through the stages in drafts of previous papers, allowing yourself the time to rework and revise. Writers at every level of expertise still hit blocks and get frustrated; they struggle to generate ideas and to get words on the page. The advantage experienced writers have is that they recognize these challenges as part of a process they have worked through before; they have strategies at hand to help them slog through the tough parts, and they have a learned trust in what they can produce. The following strategies may help you to become more conscious of your writing process and more skilled at pushing a piece through the various stages of construction and revision.

Analyze the Assignment

As a college student, you will be asked to read and write in a variety of contexts. The types of reading and writing required in those contexts can often seem radically different from one another. For example, your biology lab report about experiments with single-cell organisms will look different from your economics paper on John

Maynard Keynes's monetary theories. An engineering assignment that asks you to research and write a solution for a hypothetical bridge-construction problem will require different writing than a two-part sociology assignment that asks you to summarize major research studies of deviancy and, then, to write a longer essay that assesses their strengths and weaknesses. Such writing assignments are a normal part of college just as writing an analysis of punctuation in an Emily Dickinson poem or of representations of race in a Toni Morrison novel is standard fare in many literature classes.

Making sense of an assignment begins with reviewing and deciphering the instructions, whether verbal or written. What are you being asked to do? Identifying the verbs in an assignment will help you to know where to begin. For example, you may be asked to *summarize,* to write a brief account of a text's main arguments or ideas. Such assignments give you the opportunity to show that you can identify the writer's key points in your reading. You may be asked to move beyond summary to *analyze* a specific claim a writer makes or to link a key concept from one essay to examples or ideas in another. You may be asked to *compare, contrast, describe,* or *put into your own words.* Phrases such as those will give you clues about the intended purpose of the paper, whether your goal is primarily to explain the readings or to persuade your audience to adopt a perspective or take a particular action.

Avoid the Blank Page: Prewriting Strategies

Writing about what you read—whether in a journal or on index cards or even on scraps of paper—is one of many prewriting strategies that can help you generate ideas about a topic or develop interpretations of a particular essay. Other common prewriting strategies include freewriting and brainstorming. In freewriting, you put your ideas on paper without worrying about grammar, spelling, or organization. The point is to begin thinking through writing without concerning yourself with what the end product will look like. Just write for approximately fifteen minutes and then look over what you have written. Your initial thoughts and connections in the freewriting can now become the basis for your rough draft. Brainstorming is another prewriting strategy, one with which you are probably already familiar. In brainstorming, you write down a key word or a key idea and then make lists of connections—examples and details that illustrate the word or idea or examples and details that go against it. Freewriting and brainstorming help you generate ideas about a key term or quotation in your reading. For instance, after reading Witold Rybczynski's "Designs for Escape" (p. 427), you might find it useful to freewrite about the idea of "escape" or to brainstorm about the word "rustic" or about what your "dream house" would be.

Use Outlining as a Map for Drafting and Revision

Just as outlining provides a wonderful tool for reading, it can also be a valuable spur to drafting and revision. Outlines are useful at the beginning of the writing process, when you sketch out a list of points you want to include in a draft. They help along the way to keep a tally of the brilliant ideas and potential sidetracks that occur to you as you are writing; and they are key to piecing together a line of argument in a later draft that still seems to lack one.

The key to effective outlining is to be honest about what is and isn't there—allow the outline to reveal missing pieces, gaps, and faulty relationships—and to remain open to radically changing the outline and the paper. In fact, outlining can be one of the most helpful tools when revising, for reexamining or reconsidering what you have written to develop explanations and to improve the organization of your evidence. As you read through your draft, try listing the main points and write a sentence or two describing the key relationships between the main sections and the subsections; use the act of outlining to help you piece together the relationships between your ideas, the internal logic of your argument. It can be enormously helpful to have other readers outline a draft for you, because they can often spot missing pieces or confusing points—ideas you have in mind that may not have made it to the page.

Take Charge of Peer Review and Make Use of Conferences

In composition courses, you typically read your peers' rough drafts. Some people are understandably shy about letting others read what they have written, whether it's a rough draft or a final draft. Keep in mind that no one expects you to be *the* authority. You and your classmates are working together to enhance your reading and writing skills. The following tips will help you give the most effective feedback during peer review.

- When you are uncertain about a claim made or an explanation given in a peer's rough draft, make a note in the margin or on a sheet of paper, asking the writer how else the idea might be explained or how else the claim might be made or supported.

- After reading the entire rough draft, write a summary or an outline of the main points of the rough draft. If your summary is at odds with what the writer sought to convey, then the writer can reexamine the draft to see if the main arguments are clearly stated and developed.

- Give specific and detailed suggestions, not general comments such as "looks great" or "some words are misspelled." Examples of specific advice include indicating where in the draft the writer might add a quotation, and why, and explaining why the writer might need to follow a quotation with a discussion of keywords or key phrases in the quotation.

As you move from a rough draft or drafts toward a final draft, you should also consider your instructor's role in the revision process. Do not be afraid to talk to your instructors in class and during office hours about your assignments. It is important to talk regularly with your instructor about your writing. Undoubtedly, she will provide you with written feedback on your essays, but if you do not see her to discuss questions you have about what she has written or questions you have about the essays you are reading, then your instructor will assume that you understand her comments and that all is going well. It has been our experience that students who talk with us about their writing are engaged and likely to improve their writing over the course of the term.

Polish the Final Product

Editing—working at the sentence level to improve clarity and flow, focusing on word choices, grammar, and punctuation—becomes more crucial at the later stages of revision when the deeper structural changes have already been made. Your hard work culminates in the final draft. You want it to look good and to make you look good. A reader's first impression is visual.

- Use clean, good-quality paper, dark ink, and a standard font, such as 12-point Times New Roman.
- Give your paper a title and assign it page numbers.
- Recheck the instructions your teacher has given you to be sure that you have included the information she needs in the place where she expects to find it.
- Proofread your paper to check for spelling errors, typing mistakes, and missing or incorrect citations. Proofread also for grammar and style.
- Double-check how you have developed your argument: Be sure that you have used appropriate and credible evidence, and that you have fairly considered alternative positions to your argument.
- Make any corrections and reprint your final document.

Following those steps will help you to present a paper that creates a good first impression. A reader who can focus on understanding your ideas without being distracted by errors or problems of presentation is more likely to be persuaded by your argument.

Making Sense Through Argument

We use the term "argument" throughout this book to refer to the purposeful structure that shapes, organizes, and drives an essay. Arguments can take many forms, but at the most basic level each argument presents and demonstrates a thesis which may also be called a "claim" or "debatable proposition" that the writer seeks to prove. Unlike an opinion, an argument is based on evidence and examples. Unlike a fact, an argument is not something settled and unchangeable. An argument signals a particular perspective on an issue. We know that people often do not see eye to eye, so we should not be surprised that other perspectives exist that challenge our own, particularly on issues we feel strongly about. We always want to think about how our own argument stacks up against competing arguments.

Finding a Position

The essays in *Making Sense* present engaging arguments; indeed, the writers want us to understand what they know or what they preach. These arguments will give you wonderful opportunities to examine and test the writers' and your own reading, writing, and critical-thinking skills. You can compare a writer's argument about a given topic with your own understanding of it. If you think that the writer's analysis makes sense, then think about how and why her writing is persuasive. How does the writer use evidence, and what other evidence might you have used? If you disagree with the writer's analysis or if you decide that a part of the argument is not convincing, then think about how you would explain your disagreement or your questions to your classmates and instructor.

For example, having read the Sven Birkerts essay, "The Owl Has Flown," you might be asked to analyze Birkerts's argument about the loss of wisdom in our contemporary, technological world. Birkerts's essay is an argument because he makes a claim about wisdom that he knows is debatable. To persuade readers to accept his claim as accurate, he presents and interprets evidence. Your job as a reader and a writer is to assess the validity or the persuasiveness of Birkerts's argument. You might begin by summarizing for yourself Birkerts's main ideas about "wisdom" and by defining his key terminology, such as "vertical" and "horizontal" consciousness. Next, you might test Birkerts's ideas against evidence and examples you find in other essays you have read and in other classes you have taken or are taking. If you decide that Birkerts makes sense, then you can use the evidence and examples you collected to help you develop and argue a thesis. If you conclude, however, that Birkerts's analysis does not make sense or that parts of his analysis are questionable, then you can use your evidence and examples to support an anti-Birkerts argument.

Whichever position you take, if you imagine your reader as someone who is skeptical of your thesis, then you can present evidence both to support your interpretation and to counter or call into question opposing or alternative perspectives.

Changing Your Mind

Changing your mind about an idea, an issue, or an argument is not a bad thing. It is not unusual for a writer to begin writing a paper with one belief, only to end up with the opposite belief after writing two or three drafts. Is the writer a hypocrite? Of course not! Transforming our ideas is crucial to learning.

Determining What Counts as Evidence

Evidence, together with your interpretation of it, supports your thesis and helps persuade the reader that your argument is valid. Different disciplines rely upon different types of evidence. In your composition class, quoting and discussing key sentences and passages from the assigned reading are important. Likewise, specific examples from the essays and your own experience count as evidence, as does data collected through research. If your instructor asked you to write an analysis of Susan Willis's essay, "Disney World: Public Use/Private State," then you would quote and discuss key sentences from Willis's text as specific examples of your argument or thesis.

Quoting from a text and discussing the significance of what you quote help you demonstrate for your reader how careful a reader you are and how insightful a writer you are. Because some quotations can be interpreted in several ways and some can be difficult to understand, you can help your reader see how they support your larger argument by providing a specific analysis or a close reading of keywords or key phrases in the quotations. In close reading you do not restate the quotation; rather, you discuss the significances you see in the quotation's keywords and key phrases. For example, you might want to show how a key phrase from Willis, such as "erasure of spontaneity," connects to another keyword or key idea in her essay or someone else's. In this way, your close reading of quotations will help you connect specific textual evidence with your essay's larger argument or thesis.

Discussing specific examples from the assigned reading can also help you support your claims and, thereby, develop your argument. In the Willis essay, there are a variety of examples one might want to discuss, including her contrast between the artificial and the natural and her discussion of conformity and consumption at Disney. It has been our experience that many students are very fond of Disney World and are troubled by some of Willis's criticisms of the theme park. To challenge Willis's argument that Disney erases spontaneity and implicitly outlaws play at its park, many students combine evidence from their own personal experiences at Disney World with evidence from Willis's text and from library and Internet research to corroborate or support their misgivings about it.

Combining the Elements

Take a look at the following sample essay by Tam Mai, a student at the University of South Alabama. Tam used the processes described in these two chapters—critical reading, freewriting, outlining, peer review, and attention to audience and argument—to create this wonderful essay. She started by deciphering the assignment, which asked students to use Turkle's ideas of "tinkering" and "hard" and "soft" programming styles from her essay, "The Triumph of Tinkering" (p. 567), to frame an analysis of Susan Willis's argument about conformity in her essay, "Disney World: Public Use/Private State" (p. 585). To prepare, Tam read Turkle's and Willis's essays more than once so that she could think carefully about their arguments. She wrote a rough draft that several of her peers read in class. They wrote specific revision advice for her. Tam then continued to work diligently to produce a final draft. In the margins you will see annotations—commentary about Tam's writing.

"Ungenerous" is well chosen, and this entire opening has great energy and purpose. But do you think that it's quite fair to call Willis's essay "vindictive bashing"? If so, you might show us an example of this.

I see you're not "siding" with either Disney or Willis at this point, which is probably best for your exploration of this topic, but your thesis that "both conformity and spontaneity do serve purposes" may come too soon and may be too "safe."

Here you smartly turn to Turkle's essay for a critical term, "hard programming," to frame your analysis of Willis's argument. Seeing Disney through this frame helps remove the "magic" from the theme park.

Mai   1

Disney World: Utopia?

Tam Mai

Ask any young child where heaven is, and he or she will likely answer Disney World. Making a pilgrimage to this amusement mecca means a chance to meet the cartoon celebrities who seem to have a permanent address there. It means a chance for fun and games all day. Even adults find themselves having a good time when they step on the Space Mountain ride or take a picture with Mickey Mouse. Hence, it seems ungenerous for a professional writer such as Susan Willis to devote a critical essay, "Disney World: Public Use/Private State," to the vindictive bashing of this wonderful place. However, Willis is only using Disney World to get her readers to think about larger issues about conformity and spontaneity in our culture and to think about what these terms mean. While she has a justly dismal outlook on our conformist society, both conformity and spontaneity do serve purposes, fulfill human needs, and are necessary and inevitable parts of our society.

To better understand Willis's arguments about conformity and spontaneity, it is helpful to consider Sherry Turkle's concept of "hard programming" from "The Triumph of Tinkering." According to Turkle, "hard programming" describes any system or methodology that is structured and rule driven (554). Those in charge of Disney World certainly offer an experience that is hard programmed. They do not gamble with its fantasy-land image, but instead have a set of highly structured plans for every event and aspect of the park. Everything, from the rides to the parades to the seemingly spontaneous humor of the tour guides, has been carefully scripted, rehearsed, and scheduled so that all will go smoothly, like parts of a well-oiled machine.

Tourists to Disney readily surrender their worldly cares to the enjoyment of the scheduled program and the Disney formula. They ride the rides at the set times, take pictures at the appropriate posts, and buy as much Disney memorabilia as possible, just as intended. They conform to these established routines in order to get the most "amusement" from the Disney World experience; after all, that is what they have paid monstrously high admission and hotel prices for. In fact, every tourist gives up his or her right to spontaneous play and free exploration when purchasing a ticket to the theme park. "Amusement is the negation of play," Willis declares. Why play at Disney when we can do that at home? We come to Disney to be amused!

"Conformity" is the key word both from the Disney Corporation's perspective and from the tourists' point of view. For those at Disney offering the experience, it is easy to understand why conformity is encouraged at this amusement haven: conformity maximizes profit. Everything at Disney, from tickets to bottled water, is overpriced. But why, one might ask, would a person want to subject himself or herself to an economic predator disguised as a harmless theme park? Disney provides a

Look again at Willis's quotation: You've excised a key term and not cited the page.

Why indeed? Great question.

Mai   3

much desired escape from the monotony of daily life. From the moment visitors deposit their luggage in their hotels to the moment they wistfully leave Disney, everything is programmed for them. For a few days, they do not have to worry about any business rivalries or life-affecting decisions. It is liberating to be able, for a while, not to have to think, use one's judgment, or care about personal problems. Yet many fail to realize the price of such paradoxical escape. It is ironic to try to escape from the materialistic nature of daily life to the equally profit-driven and rules-governed operations at Disney World.

Are these your ideas or Willis's? Doesn't she offer some similar comments? Should you draw on those here?

Disney's conformist strategy would not work unless the impulse to conform did not already exist in our minds. If amusement and escape from daily monotony are the goals for some Disney tourists, then for others the trip is perhaps taken out of conformity and because it is "the thing to do." Disney World is not any ordinary theme park—it is an icon of American popular culture. Disney logos are in every corner of the United States, and most people have either gone to Disney World at least once or hope to go some day. The pilgrimage to Disney can also stem from the desire to declare or affirm our social status. As Willis puts it, Disney's wholly themed environments target the "predominantly white, middle-class families" (589).

Your point is excellent, but can you say a little more about how this quotation from Willis fits?

Our lack of spontaneity in real life results because we feel we need to be conformists. In the family, the basic unit of society, we are trained from an early age to follow a set of moral, ethical, and legal rules. Most of us conscientiously go to school not out of the desire to learn, but out of the need to be like everybody else—that is, to have an education and a career. Eating, working, schooling, and sleeping are part of our daily routine. We usually do not deviate from this habitual schedule because it is comfortable. We wear clothing that is emblematic of our social status and in various ways hope to impress others. We are a culture of conformists. Even people who stray from the norms often quickly find their acts of originality trapped in the wheels of economic conformity, as whatever is the latest new trend soon becomes the norm.

In real life, this lack of value placed on spontaneity poses a threat, and that is the threat of no progress. Without spontaneity there is no tinkering. Children, Sherry Turkle suggests, learn through physically manipulating objects—tinkering and playing with the objects at their disposal. While rearranging what they know into something completely new, people learn the art of negotiation and compromise; they learn what works and what doesn't work. Similarly a tinkerer in any discipline is an inventor of sorts, playing around with the materials at hand, not knowing what each new combination might bring. A tinkerer arranges, rearranges, all the while feeling his or her way through discovery. For instance, the discovery of penicillin, the wonder drug, is a product of unplanned, spontaneous actions. Such style of "play," which Turkle calls "soft programming," permits room for flexibility. Spontaneity can lead to progress because it allows latitude for new discoveries.

Your return to Turkle here is crucial. Can you tell us more about why you think Willis and Turkle connect so well? Are you arguing that Disney functions like a programmed computer?

Mai   5

That is not to say, however, that conformity is bad. We expect, as an organized society, that certain conventions should be followed. Humans have to follow legal conventions or else chaos will result and criminals run amok. Consider serial killer Ted Bundy's criminal acts. His nonconformity did not promote progress or benefit human endeavors in any way. We also expect priests to act with dignity and doctors to behave with compassion. If every child ran wild at Disney World, everybody's enjoyment would be ruined. Thus, this positive aspect of conformity complicates Willis's negative critique of our conformist society. Neither the "soft," flexible, creative, playful, spontaneous approach in our society nor the "hard," rule-driven, conformist approach seems to be better than the other. Both have their places. Our society is increasingly conforming, but it is also increasingly spontaneous, as Sherry Turkle observes in her essay about our growing acceptance of the bricolage, "soft" programming style.

Would Willis agree that our society is "increasingly spontaneous"? Your conclusion works so hard for a balance that it seems to underplay Willis's sustained challenge to Disney, a difference hinted at in your more critical first paragraph. I think you share Turkle's optimism, but, in further revision, you might seek to more thoroughly engage with Willis's claims.

Tam—

This is an excellent paper because your thoughtful connections between Willis and Turkle help you accomplish something much more satisfying than a simple condemnation (or celebration) of Disney World. You have a very strong grasp on the ideas at play here, and your writing is both lively and purposeful.

Your thesis that "conformity and spontaneity do serve purposes" enables you to complicate, as you say, Willis's "negative critique of our conformist society." Recognizing such a complication results from your careful reflection on both Willis's and Turkle's arguments.

If you were to continue revising this paper, I would recommend turning more directly to the texts themselves, and especially to Willis, who really isn't given much room here for what is her rather complex set of ideas. You might find that Willis is more sympathetic with what you call the "desired escape from the monotony of daily life" than you suggest. I'd be curious to hear more about this part of your paper.

Part II

Essays

＊

DOROTHY ALLISON

Dorothy Allison (b. 1949) once told an interviewer, "Storytelling can be a strategy to make sense of your life. It's what I've done." She began life as the daughter of an unwed, fifteen-year-old waitress in Greenville, South Carolina, and became the best-selling author of *Bastard Out of Carolina*. It took her ten years to write the semiautobiographical novel that turns her early life of rural poverty and sexual abuse into "a heroic story about a young girl who faces down a monster." In addition to *Bastard* and her second novel, *Cavedweller*, Allison has published poetry, short stories, essays, an autobiography, and numerous articles and reviews. Today, Allison lectures, teaches, writes, and serves on the advisory boards of the National Coalition Against Censorship and Feminists for Free Expression.

> **For more information about these organizations, see <http://www.ncac.org/> and <http://www.ffeusa.org/>, respectively.**

WHAT DO YOU KNOW? WHAT DO YOU EXPECT TO DISCOVER?

Before reading the essay, take a moment to consider the following questions

1. How do you define "art"? What is its purpose? Who decides what art is "good" and what art is not?

2. Allison describes several of her own encounters with art. Write a brief account of one moment when you were surprised by or deeply affected by visual art, music, writing, or performance.

3. Think of a topic that causes arguments or disagreements. How might art be used to bring the two sides to a new understanding?

This Is Our World

The first painting I ever saw up close was at a Baptist church when I was seven years old. It was a few weeks before my mama was to be baptized. From it, I took the notion that art should surprise and astonish, and hopefully make you think something you had not thought until you saw it. The painting was a mural of Jesus at the Jordan River done on the wall behind the baptismal font. The font itself was a remarkable creation—a swimming pool with one glass side set into the wall above and behind the pulpit so that ordinarily you could not tell the font was there, seeing only the painting of Jesus. When the tank was flooded with water, little lights along the bottom came on, and anyone who stepped down the steps seemed to be walking past Jesus himself and descending into the Jordan River. Watching baptisms in that tank was like watching movies at the drive-in, my cousins had told me. From the moment the deacon walked us around the church, I knew what my cousin had meant. I could not take my eyes off the painting or the glass-fronted tank. It looked every moment as if Jesus were about to come alive, as if he were about to step out onto the water of the river. I think the way I stared at the painting made the deacon nervous.

The deacon boasted to my mama that there was nothing like that baptismal font in the whole state of South Carolina. It had been designed, he told her, by a nephew of the minister—a boy who had gone on to build a shopping center out in New Mexico. My mama was not sure that someone who built shopping centers was the kind of person who should have been designing baptismal fonts, and she was even more uncertain about the steep steps by Jesus' left hip. She asked the man to let her practice going up and down, but he warned her it would be different once the water poured in.

"It's quite safe though," he told her. "The water will hold you up. You won't fall."

I kept my attention on the painting of Jesus. He was much larger than I was, a little bit more than life-size, but the thick layer of shellac applied to protect the image acted like a magnifying glass, making him seem larger still. It was Jesus himself that fascinated me, though. He was all rouged and pale and pouty as Elvis Presley. This was not my idea of the son of God, but I liked it. I liked it a lot.

"Jesus looks like a girl," I told my mama.

She looked up at the painted face. A little blush appeared on her cheekbones, and she looked as if she would have smiled if the deacon were not frowning so determinedly. "It's just the eyelashes," she said.

The deacon nodded. They climbed back up the stairs. I stepped over close to Jesus and put my hand on the painted robe. The painting was sweaty and cool, slightly oily under my fingers.

"I liked that Jesus," I told my mama as we walked out of the church. "I wish we had something like that." To her credit, Mama did not laugh.

"If you want a picture of Jesus," she said, "we'll get you one. They have them in nice frames at Sears." I sighed. That was not what I had in mind. What I wanted was a life-size, sweaty painting, one in which Jesus looked as hopeful as a young girl—something other-worldly and peculiar, but kind of wonderful at the same time. After that, every time we went to church I asked to go up to see the paint-ing, but the baptismal font was locked tight when not in use.

The Sunday Mama was to be baptized, I watched the minister step down into that pool past the Son of God. The preacher's gown was tailored with little weights carefully sewn into the hem to keep it from rising up in the water. The water pushed up at the fabric while the weights tugged it down. Once the minister was all the way down into the tank, the robe floated up a bit so that it seemed to have a shirred ruffle all along the bottom. That was almost enough to pull my eyes away from the face of Jesus, but not quite. With the lights on in the bottom of the tank, the eyes of the painting seemed to move and shine. I tried to point it out to my sisters, but they were uninter-ested. All they wanted to see was Mama.

Mama was to be baptized last, after three little boys, and their gowns had not had any weights attached. The white robes floated up around their necks so that their skinny boy bodies and white cotton underwear were perfectly visible to the congregation. The water that came up above the hips of the minister lapped their shoulders, and the shortest of the boys seemed panicky at the prospect of gulping water, no matter how holy. He paddled furiously to keep above the water's surface. The water started to rock violently at his struggles, sweeping the other boys off their feet. All of them pumped their knees to stay upright and the minister, realizing how the scene must appear to the congregation below, speeded up the baptismal process, praying over and dunking the boys at high speed.

Around me the congregation shifted in their seats. My little sister slid forward off the pew, and I quickly grabbed her around the waist and barely stopped myself from laughing out loud. A titter from the back of the church indicated that other people were having the same difficulty keeping from laughing. Other people shifted irritably and glared at the noisemakers. It was clear that no matter the provoca-tion, we were to pretend nothing funny was happening. The minister frowned more fiercely and prayed louder. My mama's friend Louise, sitting at our left, whispered a soft "Look at that" and we all looked up in awe. One of the hastily blessed boys had dog-paddled over to the glass and was staring out at us, eyes wide and his hands pressed flat to the glass. He looked as if he hoped someone would rescue him. It was too much for me. I began to giggle helplessly, and not a few of the people around me joined in. Impatiently the minister hooked the boy's robe, pulled him back, and pushed him toward the stairs.

My mama, just visible on the staircase, hesitated briefly as the sodden boy climbed up past her. Then she set her lips tightly together, and reached down and pressed her robe to her thighs. She came down the steps slowly, holding down the skirt as she did so, giving one stern glance to the two boys climbing past her up the steps, and then turning her face deliberately up to the painting of Jesus. Every move she made communicated resolution and faith, and the congregation stilled in respect. She was baptized looking up stubbornly, both hands holding down that cotton robe while below, I fought so hard not to giggle, tears spilled down my face.

Over the pool, the face of Jesus watched solemnly with his pink, painted cheeks and thick, dark lashes. For all the absurdity of the event, his face seemed to me startlingly compassionate and wise. That face understood fidgety boys and stubborn women. It made me want the painting even more, and to this day I remember it with longing. It had the weight of art, that face. It had what I am sure art is supposed to have—the power to provoke, the authority of a heartfelt vision.

I imagine the artist who painted the baptismal font in that Baptist church so long ago was a man who did not think himself much of an artist. I have seen paintings like his many times since, so perhaps he worked from a model. Maybe he traced that face off another he had seen in some other church. For a while, I tried to imagine him a character out of a Flannery O'Connor short story, a man who traveled around the South in the fifties painting Jesus wherever he was needed, giving the Son of God the long lashes and pink cheeks of a young girl. He would be the kind of man who would see nothing blasphemous in painting eyes that followed the congregation as they moved up to the pulpit to receive a blessing and back to the pews to sit chastened and still for the benediction. Perhaps he had no sense of humor, or perhaps he had one too refined for intimidation. In my version of the story, he would have a case of whiskey in his van, right behind the gallon containers of shellac and buried notebooks of his own sketches. Sometimes, he would read thick journals of art criticism while sitting up late in cheap hotel rooms and then get roaring drunk and curse his fate.

"What I do is wallpaper," he would complain. "Just wallpaper." But the work he so despised would grow more and more famous as time passed. After his death, one of those journals would publish a careful consideration of his murals, calling him a gifted primitive.

Dealers would offer little churches large sums to take down his walls and sell them as installations to collectors. Maybe some of the churches would refuse to sell, but grow uncomfortable with the secular popularity of the paintings. Still, somewhere there would be a little girl like the girl I had been, a girl who would dream of putting her hand on the cool, sweaty painting while the Son of God blinked down at her in genuine sympathy. Is it a sin, she would wonder, to put together the sacred and the absurd? I would not answer her question, of course. I would leave it, like the art, to make everyone a little nervous and unsure.

FIGURE 1 Wright Morris, *Uncle Harry, Home Place, Norfolk, Nebraska,* 1947. (Center for Creative Photography.)

FIGURE 2 Dorothea Lange, *Jobless on Edge of Pea Field, 1937.* (Courtesy of Dorthea Lange Collection, Oakland Museum of California.)

I love black-and-white photographs, and I always have. I have cut photographs out of magazines to paste in books of my own, bought albums at yard sales, and kept collections that had one or two images I wanted near me always. Those pictures tell me stories—my own and others, scary stories sometimes, but more often simply everyday stories, what happened in that place at that time to those people. The pictures I collect leave me to puzzle out what I think about it later. Sometimes, I imagine my own life as a series of snapshots taken by some omniscient artist who is just keeping track—not interfering or saying anything, just capturing the moment for me to look back at it again later. The eye of God, as expressed in a Dorothea Lange or Wright Morris. This is the way it is, the photograph says, and I nod my head in appreciation. The power of art is in that nod of appreciation, though sometimes I puzzle nothing out, and the nod is more a shrug. No, I do not understand this one, but I see it. I take it in. I will think about it. If I sit with this image long enough, this story, I have the hope of understanding something I did not understand before. And that, too, is art, the best art.

My friend Jackie used to call my photographs sentimental. I had pinned them up all over the walls of my apartment, and Jackie liked a few of them but thought on the whole they were better suited to being tucked away in a book. On her walls, she had half a dozen bright prints in bottle-cap metal frames, most of them bought from Puerto Rican artists at street sales when she was working as a taxi driver and always had cash in her pockets. I thought her prints garish and told her so when she made fun of my photographs.

"They remind me of my mama," she told me. I had only seen one photograph of Jackie's mother, a wide-faced Italian matron from Queens with thick, black eyebrows and a perpetual squint.

"She liked bright colors?" I asked.

Jackie nodded. "And stuff you could buy on the street. She was always buying stuff off tables on the street, saying that was the best stuff. Best prices. Cheap skirts that lost their dye after a couple of washes, shoes with cardboard insoles, those funky little icons, weeping saints and long-faced Madonnas. She liked stuff to be really colorful. She painted all the ceilings in our apartment red and white. Red-red and white-white. Like blood on bone."

I looked up at my ceiling. The high tin ceiling was uniformly bloody when I moved in, with paint put on so thick, I could chip it off in lumps. I had climbed on stacks of boxes to paint it all cream white and pale blue.

"The Virgin's colors," Jackie told me. "You should put gold roses on the door posts."

"I'm no artist," I told her.

"I am," Jackie laughed. She took out a pencil and sketched a leafy vine above two of my framed photographs. She was good. It looked as if the frames were pinned to the vine. "I'll do it all," she said, looking at me to see if I was upset.

"Do it," I told her.

Jackie drew lilies and potato vines up the hall while I made tea and admired the details. Around the front door she put the Virgin's roses and curious little circles with crosses entwined in the middle. "It's beautiful," I told her.

"A blessing," she told me. "Like a bit of magic. My mama magic." Her face was so serious, I brought back a dish of salt and water, and we blessed the entrance. "Now the devil will pass you by," she promised me.

I laughed, but almost believed.

For a few months last spring I kept seeing an ad in all the magazines that showed a small child high in the air dropping toward the upraised arms of a waiting figure below. The image was grainy and distant. I could not tell if the child was laughing or crying. The copy at the bottom of the page read: "Your father always caught you."

"Look at this," I insisted the first time I saw the ad. "Will you look at this?"

A friend of mine took the magazine, looked at the ad, and then up into my shocked and horrified face.

"They don't mean it that way," she said.

I looked at the ad again. They didn't mean it that way? They meant it innocently? I shuddered. It was supposed to make you feel safe, maybe make you buy insurance or something. It did not make me feel safe. I dreamed about the picture, and it was not a good dream.

I wonder how many other people see that ad the way I do. I wonder how many other people look at the constant images of happy families and make wry faces at most of them. It's as if all the illustrators have television sitcom imaginations. I do not believe in those families. I believe in the exhausted mothers, frightened children, numb and stubborn men. I believe in hard-pressed families, the child huddled in fear with his face hidden, the father and mother confronting each other with their emotions hidden, dispassionate passionate faces, and the unsettling sense of risk in the baby held close to that man's chest. These images make sense to me. They are about the world I know, the stories I tell. When they are accompanied by wry titles or copy that is slightly absurd or unexpected, I grin and know that I will puzzle it out later, sometimes a lot later.

I think that using art to provoke uncertainty is what great writing and inspired images do most brilliantly. Art should provoke more questions than answers and, most of all, should make us think about what we rarely want to think about at all. Sitting down to write a novel, I refuse to consider if my work is seen as difficult or inappropriate or provocative. I choose my subjects to force the congregation to look at what they try so stubbornly to pretend is not happening at all, deliberately combining the horribly serious with the absurd or funny, because I know that if I am to reach my audience I must first seduce their attention and draw them into the world of my imagination. I know that I have to lay out my stories, my difficult people, each story layering on top of the one before it with care and craft, until my audience sees something they had not expected. Frailty— stubborn, human frailty—that is what I work to showcase. The wonder and astonishment of the despised and ignored, that is what I hope to find in art and in the books I write—my secret self, my vulnerable and embattled heart, the child I was and the woman I have become, not Jesus at the Jordan but a woman with only her stubborn memories and passionate convictions to redeem her.

"You write such mean stories," a friend once told me. "Raped girls, brutal fathers, faithless mothers, and untrustworthy lovers—meaner than the world really is, don't you think?"

I just looked at her. Meaner than the world really is? No. I thought about showing her the box under my desk where I keep my clippings. Newspaper stories and black-and-white images—the woman who drowned her children, the man who shot first the babies in her arms and then his wife, the teenage boys who led the three-year-old away along the train track, the homeless family recovering from frostbite with their eyes glazed and indifferent while the doctor scowled over their shoulders. The world is meaner than we admit, larger, and more astonishing. Strength appears in the most desperate figures, tragedy when we have no reason to expect it. Yes, some of my stories are fearful but not as cruel as what I see in the world. I believe in redemption, just as I believe in the nobility of the despised, the dignity of the outcast, the intrinsic honor among misfits, pariahs, and queers. Artists—those of us who stand outside the city gates and look back at a society that tries to ignore us—we have an angle of vision denied to whole sectors of the sheltered and indifferent population within. It is our curse and our prize, and for everyone who will tell us our work is mean or fearful or unreal, there is another who will embrace us and say with tears in their eyes how wonderful it is to finally feel as if someone else has seen their truth and shown it in some part as it should be known.

"My story," they say. "You told my story. That is me, mine, us." And it is.

We are not the same. We are a nation of nations. Regions, social classes, economic circumstances, ethical systems, and political convictions—all separate us even as we pretend they do not. Art makes that plain. Those of us who have read the same books, eaten the same kinds of food as children, watched the same television shows, and listened to the same music, we believe ourselves part of the same nation—and we are continually startled to discover that our versions of reality do not match. If we were more the same, would we not see the same thing when we look at a painting? But what is it we see when we look at a work of art? What is it we fear will be revealed? The artist waits for us to say. It does not matter that each of us sees something slightly different. Most of us, confronted with the artist's creation, hesitate, stammer, or politely deflect the question of what it means to us. Even those of us from the same background, same region, same general economic and social class, come to "art" uncertain, suspicious, not wanting to embarrass ourselves by revealing what the work

provokes in us. In fact, sometimes we are not sure. If we were to reveal what we see in each painting, sculpture, installation, or little
book, we would run the risk of exposing our secret selves, what we
know and what we fear we do not know, and of course incidentally
what it is we truly fear. Art is the Rorschach test for all of us, the protective hologram of our secret lives. Our emotional and intellectual
lives are laid bare. Do you like hologram roses? Big, bold, brightly
painted canvases? Representational art? Little boxes with tiny figures
posed precisely? Do you dare say what it is you like?

For those of us born into poor and working-class families, these
are not simple questions. For those of us who grew up hiding what
our home life was like, the fear is omnipresent—particularly when
that home life was scarred by physical and emotional violence. We
know if we say anything about what we see in a work of art we will
reveal more about ourselves than the artist. What do you see in this
painting, in that one? I see a little girl, terrified, holding together the
torn remnants of her clothing. I see a child, looking back at the
mother for help and finding none. I see a mother, bruised and exhausted, unable to look up for help, unable to believe anyone in the
world will help her. I see a man with his fists raised, hating himself
but making those fists tighter all the time. I see a little girl, uncertain
and angry, looking down at her own body with hatred and contempt.
I see that all the time, even when no one else sees what I see. I know I
am not supposed to mention what it is I see. Perhaps no one else is
seeing what I see. If they are, I am pretty sure there is some cryptic
covenant that requires that we will not say what we see. Even when
looking at an image of a terrified child, we know that to mention why
that child might be so frightened would be a breach of social etiquette. The world requires that such children not be mentioned, even
when so many of us are looking directly at her.

There seems to be a tacit agreement about what it is not polite to
mention, what it is not appropriate to portray. For some of us, that
polite behavior is set so deeply we truly do not see what seems outside that tacit agreement. We have lost the imagination for what our
real lives have been or continue to be, what happens when we go
home and close the door on the outside world. Since so many would
like us to never mention anything unsettling anyway, the impulse to
be quiet, the impulse to deny and pretend, becomes very strong. But
the artist knows all about that impulse. The artist knows that it must
be resisted. Art is not meant to be polite, secret, coded, or timid. Art
is the sphere in which that impulse to hide and lie is the most dangerous. In art, transgression is holy, revelation a sacrament, and pursuing one's personal truth the only sure validation.

Does it matter if our art is canonized, if we become rich and successful, lauded and admired? Does it make any difference if our pic-

tures become popular, our books made into movies, our creations win awards? What if we are the ones who wind up going from town to town with our notebooks, our dusty boxes of prints or Xeroxed sheets of music, never acknowledged, never paid for our work? As artists, we know how easily we could become a Flannery O'Connor character, reading those journals of criticism and burying our faces in our hands, staggering under the weight of what we see that the world does not. As artists, we also know that neither worldly praise nor critical disdain will ultimately prove the worth of our work.

Some nights I think of that sweating, girlish Jesus above my mother's determined features, those hands outspread to cast benediction on those giggling uncertain boys, me in the congregation struck full of wonder and love and helpless laughter. If no one else ever wept at that image, I did. I wished the artist who painted that image knew how powerfully it touched me, that after all these years his art still lives inside me. If I can wish for anything for my art, that is what I want—to live in some child forever—and if I can demand anything of other artists, it is that they attempt as much.

READING, REREADING, AND ANALYSIS

1. Why do you think Allison titles this piece "This Is Our World"? What significance does the phrase have here?

2. Write a couple of paragraphs describing the connection you see between Allison's account of her childhood experience with the painted baptismal font and her arguments about art that come later.

3. Mark all the appearances of the word "belief" and all its variations in Allison's essay. Why might she use this word so frequently?

RESPONDING THROUGH WRITING:
BUILDING AN INTERPRETATION

4. Allison claims that art should "provoke uncertainty." Using an example of your own as a "test case" (and perhaps drawing on your answer to question 2), write a paper that defends or challenges Allison's ideas about art. Must art be unsettling to be successful?

5. Allison implies throughout her essay that we protect ourselves from admitting our true feelings about many things in life, including art. On page 50, she even says, "Do you dare say what it is you

like?" Write an essay that explores this tendency to be secretive or guarded about our strongest feelings. What makes people protect themselves in this way, and how does the art that Allison champions help to remedy this situation?

6. Allison does not consider all imaginative work to be art. For example, she scorns the "television sitcom imaginations" of the illustrators who make magazine advertisements. What might she mean by that? Write an essay that looks closely at Allison's value judgments. What do you see as her criteria for evaluating art? Can you think of exceptions or challenges to her judgments?

GOING FURTHER: LEARNING FROM OTHER SOURCES

7. Choose an online bookstore, such as Amazon or another site with commentary or reviews on it, and search for one of Allison's books. What do her readers say about her work? Using Allison's statements about what she *wants* her books to accomplish as a reference, write about the responses her books actually bring out. Do these readers share her views about what art should do? Do they think that Allison has achieved her goal?

8. Using your library's academic databases, look into the recent writing about "popular art" or "populist art" or "popular culture." What issues and questions do you see emerging that might relate to Allison's essay? Is "traditional" or "high" art threatened by the rising interest in these popular art forms? Is the definition of art changing?

APPLYING WHAT YOU'VE LEARNED

9. Consider Scott McCloud's comic chapter, "Setting the Record Straight," as a work of art in the terms of Allison's essay. Does thinking about comics as art change your experience of reading them? What do you think McCloud's goals are for his work? Would he agree with Allison's ideas about what art can and should do?

10. Allison argues, in part, that art gets its importance from the fact that "our versions of reality do not match" (p. 49). On the basis of your reading of Jeanette Winterson's "Imagination and Reality," decide how Winterson might respond to that statement. Would she agree? Write a paper that examines both the important differences in the approaches and outlooks of the two writers and the possibility of common ground.

11. Allison shares Christopher Lasch's excitement about the good things that can come from confrontation and debate. Look closely at Lasch's "The Lost Art of Argument," and write an essay that answers one of the following questions: How well would the "art" of argument Lasch celebrates fit Allison's definitions of art? How well would the art that Allison celebrates fits Lasch's definitions of "argument"? In either paper, be sure to develop the consequences or implications of the relationship you set up.

GLORIA ANZALDÚA

Gloria Anzaldúa (1942–2004), a Chicana feminist activist and educator, grew up in the borderlands of South Texas. As a young girl, she worked with migrant Chicano field laborers in Arkansas. She turned to reading as an escape, eventually earning an M.A. in English from the University of Texas in Austin. Through poetry, fiction, children's books, and cultural criticism, Anzaldúa explored her interests in her own and other cultures. She won numerous awards for her experimental style of writing. Her book, *Borderlands/La Frontera: The New Mestiza* (1987), weaves Spanish and English poetry, memoir, and historical analysis into an extended exploration of multicultural identity. The following essay was first published in the NACLA Report on the Americas, July/August 1993.

> For more information on Chicana life, literature, and art, see <http://www.chicanas.com/>.

WHAT DO YOU KNOW? WHAT DO YOU EXPECT TO DISCOVER?

Before reading the essay, take a moment to consider the following questions.

1. What topics does Anzaldúa's biography suggest she is interested in? What do you know about those topics? Knowledge can come from personal experience, stories you've heard, other classes you've taken, or other reading you've done.

2. What does her title lead you to expect from her essay? Look closely at each word. Circle keywords. Use a dictionary to define or translate the words you don't recognize.

3. Anzaldúa describes a visit to a museum. Consider your own visits to museums or similar places. What did you see or feel or learn while you were there? Given your own experience, what do you expect Anazaldúa to describe?

❀

Chicana Artists:
Exploring Nepantla, el Lugar
de la Frontera

I stop before the dismembered body of *la diosa de la luna,*
Coyolxauhqui, daughter of Coatlicue. The warrior goddess' eyes
are closed, she has bells on her cheeks, and her head is in the form of
a snail design. She was decapitated by her brother, Huitzilopochtle,
the Left-Handed Hummingbird. Her bones jut from their sockets. I
stare at the huge round stone of *la diosa.* She seems to be pushing at
the restraining orb of the moon. Though I sense a latent whirlwind of
energy, I also sense a timeless stillness—one patiently waiting to ex-
plode into activity.

Here before my eyes, on the opening day of the "Aztec: The World

FIGURE 3 *La Diosa de la Luna* (© Bettman/CORBIS.)

of Moctezuma" exhibition at the Denver Museum of Natural History, is the culture of *nuestros antepasados indígenas*. I ask myself, What does it mean to me *esta jotita,* this queer Chicana, this *mexicatejana* to enter a museum and look at indigenous objects that were once used by my ancestors? Will I find my historical Indian identity here at this museum among the ancient artifacts and their *mestisaje lineage*?

As I pull out a pad to take notes on the clay, stone, jade, bone, feather, straw, and cloth artifacts, I am disconcerted with the knowledge that I am passively consuming and appropriating an indigenous culture. I arrive at the serpentine base of a reconstructed 16-foot temple where the Aztecs flung down human sacrifices, leaving bloodied steps. Around me I hear the censorious, culturally ignorant words of the Whites who, while horrified by the bloodthirsty Aztecs, gape in vicarious wonder and voraciously consume the exoticized images. Though I too am a gaping consumer, I feel that these artworks are part of my legacy—my appropriation differs from the misappropriation by "outsiders."

I am again struck by how much Chicana artists and writers feel the impact of ancient Mexican art forms, foods, and customs. *Sus símbolos y metáforas todavía viven en la gente chicana/mexicana.* This sense of connection and community compels Chicana writers/artists to delve into, sift through, and rework native imagery. We consistently reflect back these images in revitalized and modernized versions in theater, film, performance art, painting, dance, sculpture, and literature. *La negación sistemática de la cultura mexicana-chicana en los Estados Unidos impide su desarrollo haciéndolo este un acto de colonización.* As a people who have been stripped of our history, language, identity and pride, we attempt again and again to find what we have lost by imaginatively digging into our cultural roots and making art out of our findings.

I recall Yolanda López' *Portrait of the Artist as the Virgin of Guadalupe* (1978), which depicts a Chicana/*mexicana* woman emerging and running from the oval halo of rays that looks to me like thorns, with the mantle of the traditional *virgen* in one hand and a serpent in the other. She wears running shoes, has short hair, and her legs are bare and look powerful—a very dykey-looking woman. *Portrait* represents the cultural rebirth of the Chicana struggling to free herself from oppressive gender roles.[1]

I remember visiting Chicana *tejana* artist Santa Barraza in her Austin studio in the mid 1970s and talking about the merger and appropriation of cultural symbols and techniques by artists in search of their spiritual and cultural roots. As I walked around her studio, I was amazed at the vivid *Virgen de Guadalupe* iconography on her walls and on the drawings strewn on tables and shelves.

La gente chicana tiene tres madres. All three are mediators: *Guadalupe,* the virgin mother who has not abandoned us, *la Chingada (Malinche),* the raped mother whom we have abandoned, and *la*

FIGURE 4 Yolanda Lopez, *Portrait of the Artist as the Virgin of Guadalupe*, 1978. Oil pastel on paper.

Llorona, the mother who seeks her lost children and is a combination of the other two. *Guadalupe* has been used by the Church to mete out institutionalized oppression: to placate the Indians and *mexicanos* and Chicanos. In part, the true identity of all three has been sub-verted—*Guadalupe to* make us docile and enduring, *la Chingada* to make us ashamed of our Indian side, and *la Llorona* to make us long-suffering people. This obscuring has encouraged the *virgen/puta* di-chotomy. The three *madres* are cultural figures that Chicana writers and artists "reread" in our works.

Now, 16 years later, Barraza is focusing on interpretations of Pre-

FIGURE 5 Santa Barazza, *La Lupe—Tejana* 1995, oil on canvas, 30" × 50" size.

Columbian codices as a reclamation of cultural and historical mestiza identity. Her "codices" are edged with *milagros* and *ex votos*.[2] Using the folk-art format, Barraza is now painting tin testimonials known as *retablos*. These are traditional popular miracle paintings on metal, a medium introduced to colonial Mexico by the Spaniards. One of her devotional *retablos* is of *la Malinche,* made with *maguey.* (The *maguey* cactus is Barraza's symbol of rebirth.) Like that of many Chicana artists, her work, she says, explores indigenous Mexican "symbols and myths in a historical and contemporary context as a mechanism of resistance to oppression and assimilation."[3]

I wonder about the genesis of *el arte de la frontera.* Border art remembers its roots—sacred and folk art are often still one and the same. I recall the *nichos* (niches or recessed areas) and *retablos* that I had recently seen in several galleries and museums. The *retablos* are placed inside open boxes made of wood, tin, or cardboard. The *cajitas* contain three dimensional figures such as *la virgen,* photos of ancestors, candles, and sprigs of herbs tied together. They are actually tiny installations. I make mine out of cigar boxes or vegetable crates that I find discarded on the street before garbage pickups. The *retablos* range from the strictly traditional to modern, more abstract forms. Santa Barraza, Yolanda López, Marcia Gómez, Carmen Lomas Garza and other Chicana artists connect their art to everyday life, instilling both with political, sacred and aesthetic values. *Haciendo tortillas* becomes a sacred ritual in literary, visual, and performance arts.[4]

Border art, in critiquing old, traditional, and erroneous representations of the Mexico–United States border, attempts to represent the "real world" *de la gente* going about their daily lives. But it renders that world and its people in more than mere surface slices of life. If one looks beyond the tangible, one sees a connection to the spirit world, to the underworld, and to other realities. In the "old world," art was/is functional and sacred as well as aesthetic. When folk and fine art separated, the *metate* (a flat porous volcanic stone with rolling pin used to make corn tortillas) and the *huipil* (a Guatemalan blouse) were put in museums by Western curators of art.[5]

I come to a glass case where the skeleton of a jaguar with a stone in its open mouth nestles on cloth. The stone represents the heart. My thoughts trace the jaguar's spiritual and religious symbolism from its Olmec origins to present-day jaguar masks worn by people who no longer know that the jaguar was connected to rain, who no longer remember that Tlaloc and the jaguar and the serpent and rain are tightly intertwined.[6] Through the centuries a culture touches and influences another, passing on its metaphors and its gods before it dies. (Metaphors *are* gods.) The new culture adopts, modifies, and enriches these images, and it, in turn, passes them on changed. The process is repeated until the original meanings of images are pushed into the

FIGURE 6 Santa Barazza, *La Malinche*, 1991 oils and enamels on metal, 8"×9" size.

unconscious. What surfaces are images more significant to the prevailing culture and era. The artist on some level, however, still connects to that unconscious reservoir of meaning, connects to that *nepantla* state of transition between time periods, and the border between cultures.

Nepantla is the Nahuatl word for an in-between state, that uncertain terrain one crosses when moving from one place to another, when changing from one class, race, or gender position to another, when traveling from the present identity into a new identity. The Mexican immigrant at the moment of crossing the barbed-wire fence into the hostile "paradise" of *el norte*, the United States, is caught in

FIGURE 7 *Camas para suenos (Beds for Dreaming)* by Carmen Lomas Garza

a state of *nepantla*. Others who find themselves in this bewildering transitional space may be those people caught in the midst of denying their projected/assumed heterosexual identity and coming out, presenting and voicing their lesbian, gay, bi-, or transsexual selves. Crossing class lines—especially from working class to middle classness and privilege—can be just as disorienting. The marginalized, starving Chicana artist who suddenly finds her work exhibited in mainstream museums, or being sold for thousands of dollars in prestigious galleries, as well as the once-neglected writer whose work is on every professor's syllabus for a time inhabit *nepantla.* For women artists, *nepantla* is a constant state; dislocation is the norm. Chicana artists are engaged in "reading" that *nepantla,* that border.

I think of the borderlands as Jorge Luis Borges' *Aleph,* the one spot on earth which contains all other places within it. All people in it, whether natives or immigrants, colored or white, queer or hetero-sexual, from this side of the border or *del otro lado,* are *personas del lugar,* local people—all of whom relate to the border and to *nepantla* in different ways.

The border is a historical and metaphorical site, *un sitio ocupado,* an occupied borderland where individual artists and collaborating groups transform space, and the two home territories, Mexico and the United States, become one. Border art deals with shifting identities, bor-der crossings, and hybridism. But there are other borders besides the ac-tual Mexico/US *frontera.* Chilean-born artist Juan Davila's *Wuthering Heights* (1990) oil painting depicts Juanito Leguna, a half-caste, mixed breed transvestite. Juanito's body is a simulacrum parading as the phal-lic mother with hairy chest and hanging tits.[7] Another Latino artist, Rafael Barajas (who signs his work as "El Fisgón"), has a mixed-media piece entitled *Pero eso si . . . soy muy macho* (1989). It shows a Mexi-can male wearing the proverbial sombrero taking a siesta against the traditional cactus, tequila bottle on the ground, gunbelt hanging from a nopal branch. But the leg sticking out from beneath the sarape-like mantle is wearing a highheeled shoe, pantyhose, and a garter belt. It suggests another kind of border crossing—gender-bending.[8]

According to anthropologist Edward Hall, early in life we be-come oriented to space in a way that is tied to survival and sanity. When we become disoriented from that sense of space we fall in dan-ger of becoming psychotic.[9] I question this—to be disoriented in space is the "normal" way of being for us mestizas living in the border-lands. It is the sane way of coping with the accelerated pace of this complex, interdependent, and multicultural planet. To be disoriented in space is to be *en nepantla,* to experience bouts of disassociation of identity, identity breakdowns and buildups. The border is in a con-stant *nepantla* state, and it is an analog of the planet.

This is why the border is a persistent metaphor in *el arte de la frontera,* an art that deals with such themes as identity, border cross-ings, and hybrid imagery. The Mexico–United States border is a site where many different cultures "touch" each other and the permeable, flexible, and ambiguous shifting grounds lend themselves to hybrid images. The border is the locus of resistance, of rupture, of implosion and explosion, and of putting together the fragments and creating a new assemblage. Border artists *cambian el punto de referencia.* By disrupting the neat separations between cultures, they create a culture mix, *una mestizada* in their artworks. Each artist locates herself in this border *"lugar"* and tears apart then rebuilds the "place" itself. "Imagenes de la Frontera" was the title of the Centro Cultural Tijuana's June 1992 exhibition.[10] Malaquís Montoya's Frontera Series and Irene Pérez' Dos Mundos monoprint are examples of the multi-subjectivity, split-subjectivity, and refusal-to-be-split themes of the border artist creating a counter-art.

The *nepantla* state is the natural habitat of women artists, most specifically for the mestiza border artists who partake of the traditions of two or more worlds and who may be binational. They thus create a new artistic space—a border mestizo culture. Beware of *el romance del mestizaje,* I hear myself saying silently. *Puede ser una ficción.* But I and other writers/artists of *la frontera* have invested ourselves in it. *Mestizaje,* not Chicanismo, is the reality of our lives. *Mestizaje* is at the heart of our art. We bleed in *mestizaje,* we eat and sweat and cry in *mestizaje.* But the Chicana is inside the mestiza.

There are many obstacles and dangers in crossing into *nepantla.* Popular culture and the dominant art institutions threaten border artists from the outside with appropriation. "Outsiders" jump on the border artists' bandwagon and work their territory. The present unparalleled economic depression in the arts gutted by government funding cutbacks threatens *los artistas de la frontera.* Sponsoring corporations that judge projects by "family values" criteria force multicultural artists to hang tough and brave out financial and professional instability.

I walk into the Aztec Museum shop and see feathers, paper flowers, and ceramic statues of fertility goddesses selling for ten times what they sell for in Mexico. Border art is becoming trendy in these neo-colonial times that encourage art tourism and pop-culture ripoffs. Of course, there is nothing new about colonizing, commercializing, and consuming the art of ethnic people (and of queer writers and artists) except that now it is being misappropriated by pop culture. Diversity is being sold on TV, billboards, fashion runways, department-store windows, and, yes, airport corridors and "regional" stores where you can take home a jar of Tex-Mex *picante* sauce along with Navaho artist R. C. Gorman's "Saguaro" or Robert Arnold's "Chili Dog," and drink a margarita at Rosie's Cantina.

I touch the armadillo pendant hanging from my neck and think, *frontera* artists have to grow protective shells. We enter the silence, go inward, attend to feelings and to that inner *cenote,* the creative reservoir where earth, female, and water energies merge. We surrender to the rhythm and the grace of our artworks. Through our artworks we cross the border into other subjective levels of awareness, shift into different and new terrains of *mestizaje.* Some of us have a highly developed *facultad* and many intuit what lies ahead. Yet the political climate does not allow us to withdraw completely. In fact, border artists are engaged artists. Most of us are politically active in our communities. If disconnected from *la gente,* border artists would wither in isolation. The community feeds our spirits and the responses from our "readers" inspire us to continue struggling with our art and aesthetic interventions that subvert cultural genocide. Border art challenges and subverts the imperialism of the United States, and combats assimilation by either the United States or Mexico, yet it acknowledges its affinities to both cultures.[11]

"Chicana" artist, "border" artist. These are adjectives labeling identities. Labeling creates expectations. White poets don't write "white" in front of their names, nor are they referred to as white by others. Is "border" artist just another label that strips legitimacy from the artist, signaling that she is inferior to the adjectiveless artist, a label designating that she is only capable of handling ethnic, folk, and regional subjects and art forms? Yet the dominant culture consumes, swallows whole the ethnic artist, sucks out her vitality, and then spits out the hollow husk along with its labels (such as Hispanic). The dominant culture shapes the ethnic artist's identity if she does not scream loud enough and fight long enough to name herself. Until we live in a society where all people are more or less equal, we need these labels to resist the pressure to assimilate.

Artistic ideas that have been incubating and developing at their own speed have come into their season—now is the time of border art. Border *arte* is an art that supersedes the pictorial. It depicts both the soul *del artista* and the soul *del pueblo.* It deals with who tells the stories and what stories and histories are told. I call this form of visual narrative *autohistoria.* This form goes beyond the traditional self-portrait or autobiography; in telling the writer/artist's personal story, it also includes the artist's cultural history. The *retablos* I make are not just representations of myself, they are representations of Chicana culture. *El arte de la frontera* is community and academically based— many Chicana artists have M.A.s and Ph.D.s and hold precarious teaching positions on the fringes of universities. They are overworked, overlooked, passed over for tenure, and denied the support they deserve. To make, exhibit, and sell their artwork, and to survive, *los artistas* have had to band together collectively.[12]

I cross the exhibit room. Codices hang on the walls. I stare at the hieroglyphics. The ways of a people, their history and culture put on paper beaten from maguey leaves. Faint traces of red, blue, and black ink left by their artists, writers, and scholars. The past is hanging behind glass. We, the viewers in the present, walk around and around the glassboxed past. I wonder who I used to be, I wonder who I am. The border artist constantly reinvents herself. Through art she is able to reread, reinterpret, re-envision and reconstruct her culture's present as well as its past. This capacity to construct meaning and culture privileges the artist. As cultural icons for her ethnic communities, she is highly visible.

But there are drawbacks to having artistic and cultural power—the relentless pressure to produce, being put in the position of representing her entire *pueblo* and carrying all the ethnic culture's baggage on her *espalda* while trying to survive in a gringo world. Power and the seeking of greater power may create a self-centered ego or a fake public image, one the artist thinks will make her acceptable to her audience. It may encourage self-serving hustling—all artists have to sell themselves in order to get grants, get published, secure exhibit spaces, and get good reviews. But for some, the hustling outdoes the art-making.

The Chicana border writer/artist has finally come to market. The problem now is how to resist corporate culture while asking for and securing its patronage; how to get the dollars without resorting to "mainstreaming" the work. Is the border artist complicit in the appropriation of her art by the dominant art dealers? And if so, does this constitute a self-imposed imperialism? The artist, in making *plata* from the sale of her sculpture, "makes it." Money means power. The access to privilege that comes with the bucks and the recognition can turn the artist on her ear in a *nepantla* spin.

Finally, I find myself before the reconstructed statue of the newly unearthed *el dios murciélago*, the bat god with his big ears, fangs, and protruding tongue representing the vampire bat associated with night, blood sacrifice, and death. I make an instantaneous association of the bat man with the stage of border artists—the dark cave of creativity where they hang upside down, turning the self upside down in order to see from another point of view, one that brings a new state of understanding. Or it may mean transposing the former self onto a new one—the death of the old self and the old ways, breaking down former notions of who you are. Night fear, *susto,* when every button is pushed. The border person constantly moves through that birth canal, *nepantla.* If you stay too long in *nepantla* you are in danger of being blocked, resulting in a breech birth or being stillborn.

I wonder what meaning this bat figure will have for other Chicanas, what artistic symbol they will make of it and what political struggle it will represent. Perhaps the *murciélago* questions the viewer's unconscious collective and personal identity and its ties to her ancestors, *los muertos.* In border art there is always the specter of death in the background. Often *las calaveras* (skeletons and skulls) take a prominent position—and not just on *el día de los muertos* (November 2). *De la tierra nacemos,* from earth we are born, *a la tierra regresaremos,* to earth we shall return, *a dar lo que ella nos dió,* to give back to her what she has given. Yes, I say to myself, the earth eats the dead, *la tierra se come los muertos.*

I walk out of the Aztec exhibit hall. It is September 28, *mi cumpleaños.* I seek out the table with the computer, key in my birth-date and there on the screen is my Aztec birth year and ritual day name: 8 Rabbit, 12 Skull. In that culture I would have been named Matlactli Omome Mizuitzli. I stick my chart under the rotating rubber stamps, press down, pull it out and stare at the imprint of the rabbit (symbol of fear and of running scared) pictograph and then of the skull (night, blood sacrifice, and death). Very appropriate symbols in my life, I mutter. It's so *raza. ¿y qué?*

I ask myself, What direction will *el arte fronterizo* take in the future? The multi-subjectivity and split-subjectivity of the border artist creating various counter arts will continue, but with a parallel movement where a polarized us/them, insiders/outsiders culture clash is not the main struggle, where a refusal to be split will be a given. We are both *nos* (us) and *otras* (others)—*nos/otras.*

My mind reviews image after image. Something about who and what I am and the 200 "artifacts" I have just seen does not feel right. I pull out my "birth chart." Yes, cultural roots are important *but I was not born at Tenochitlán in the ancient past nor in an Aztec village in modern times. I was born and live in that in-between space,* nepantla, *the borderlands.* Hay muchas razas *running in my veins,* mescladas dentro de mi, otras culturas *that my body lives in and out of.* Mi cuerpo vive dentro y fuera de otras culturas *and a white man who constantly whispers inside my skull. For me, being Chicana is not enough. It is only one of my multiple identities. Along with other* border gente, *it is at this site and time,* en este tiempo y lugar *where and when, I create my identity* con mi arte.

1993

Notes

I thank Dianna Williamson and Clarisa Rojas, my literary assistants, for their invaluable and incisive critical comments, and Deidre McFadyen.
  1. See Amalia Mesa-Bains, *"El Mundo Femenino:* Chicana Artists of the Movement—A Commentary on Development and Production," in Richard Griswold Del Castillo, Teresa McKenna, and Yvonne Yarbo Bejarano (eds), *CARA, Chicano Art: Resistance and Affirmation* (Los Angeles: Wight Gallery, University of California, 1991).
  2. See Luz María and Ellen J. Stekert's untitled art catalog essay in *Santa Barraza,* March 8–April 11, 1992, La Raza/Galería Posada, Sacramento, CA.
  3. Quoted in Jennifer Heath's "Women Artists of Color Share World of Struggle," *Sunday Camera,* March 8, 1992, p. 9C.
  4. See Carmen Lomas Garza's children's bilingual book, *Family Pictures/Cuadros de familia* (San Francisco: Children's Book Press, 1990), in particular *"Camas para sonar/*Beds for Dreaming."
  5. The Maya huipiles are large rectangular blouses which describe the Maya cosmos. They portray the world as a diamond. The four sides of the diamond represent the boundaries of space and time; the smaller diamonds at each corner, the cardinal points. The weaver maps the heavens and underworld.

6. Roberta H. Markman and Peter T. Markman (eds), *Masks of the Spirit: Image and Metaphor in Mesoamerica* (Berkeley: University of California Press, 1989).

7. See Guy Brett, *Transcontinental: An Investigation of Reality* (London: Verso, 1990).

8. See *ex profeso, recuento de afinidades colectiva plástica contemporánea: imágenes: gay-lésbicas-éroticas* put together by Circulo Cultural Gay in Mexico City and exhibited at Museuo Universitario del Chope during Gay Cultural Week, June 14–23, 1989.

9. The exact quote is: "We have an internalization of fixed space learned early in life. One's orientation in space is tied to survival and sanity. To be disoriented in space is to be psychotic." See Edward T. Hall and Mildred Reed Hall, "The Sounds of Silence," in James P. Spradley and David W. McCurdy (eds), *Conformity and Conflict: Readings in Cultural Anthropology* (Boston: Little, Brown, 1987).

10. The exhibition was part of Festival Internacional de la Raza '92. The artworks were produced in the Silkscreen Studios of Self Help Graphics, Los Angeles, and in the studios of Strike Editions in Austin, Texas. Self Help Graphics and the Galería Sin Fronteras, Austin, Texas, organized the exhibitions.

11. Among the alternative galleries and art centers that combat assimilation are the Guadalupe Cultural Arts Center in San Antonio, Mexic-Arte Museum and Sin Fronteras Gallery in Austin, Texas, and the Mission Cultural Center in San Francisco.

12. For a discussion of Chicano posters, almanacs, calendars, and cartoons that join "images and texts to depict community issues as well as historical and cultural themes," and that metaphorically link Chicano struggles for self-determination with the Mexican Revolution, and establish "a cultural and visual continuum across borders," see Tomás Ybarra-Fausto's "Gráfica/Urban Iconography" in *Chicano Expressions: A New View in American Art, April 14–July 31, 1986* (New York: INTAR Latin American Gallery, 1986), pp. 21–4.

READING, REREADING, AND ANALYSIS

1. What terms and ideas seem to be *most* important to Anzaldúa? Are they the same as the ones you identified in her title?

2. Choose two definitions or examples that help you to explain what Anzaldúa means by *"nepantla"* or "borderlands," and take some notes explaining each term. In a group, share your findings and list all the meanings that Anzaldúa associates with both words.

3. Individually or in a group, make a list of the positive and productive possibilities of being a border artist. Then make a list of the threats, dangers, and obstacles faced by border artists. On the basis of your analysis, would you advise someone to become a border artist?

4. Select two or three passages from the essay in which Anzaldua "mixes" Spanish and English. What effect does this mixing have on you as a reader? What effects do you think Anzaldúa might be trying to produce using this approach?

5. What does Anzaldúa mean on page 60 when she says that "metaphors are gods"? Make a list of the places where Anzaldúa uses metaphors in her essay. Rewrite one of the passages without using metaphor. What do these metaphors enable Anzaldúa to accomplish?

6. What is the tone of Anzaldúa's piece? What emotions do you think she expresses? Make a short list of places in the text where you think her language is especially revealing.

RESPONDING THROUGH WRITING: BUILDING AN INTERPRETATION

7. Find at least two passages in which Anzaldúa comments on her feelings and thoughts as she views the exhibits in the Denver museum. How does she make sense of her participation as a visitor to the museum? Is her experience unique? In a brief essay (one or two pages), compare her experience with the expectations you had formed before reading the essay.

8. Using the lists you produced for question 3, write an essay examining the positive and negative aspects of being a border artist. Which of these aspects would be the same for any artist? Which are specific to border artists?

9. Summarize Anzaldúa's article using only English words and phrases and without using metaphors. Write a paper in which you present your summary and compare it with Anzaldúa's essay. How do Anzaldúa's rhetorical strategies of mixing languages and using metaphor affect the content of her essay? Were you able to achieve the same affects without using those strategies? Would someone reading your summary be surprised by Anzaldúa's essay?

10. Using your ideas from question 5, write a short paper exploring the effects of Anzaldúa's authorial voice. How does she use emotion and strong (even, perhaps, bitter) language to make her point? Does her essay ask for more than just an intellectual response?

GOING FURTHER: LEARNING
FROM OTHER SOURCES

11. Search a map of the North American continent to identify the geographical "borderland" that Anzaldúa is talking about in this essay. List some other potential "borderlands" that you see on the map.

12. Search the Internet using "borderlands" as your keyword. From a brief sampling of the websites you find, list some of the meanings and issues associated with this concept. Try the same search term in a reference database that includes sources from scholarly journals, such as Academic Search Elite, and list some of the meanings and issues involving "borderlands" that appear in the articles you find. In a group, discuss the differences between the two lists.

APPLYING WHAT YOU'VE LEARNED

13. Ralph Ellison, in "The Little Man at Chehaw Station" (p. 151), is, like Gloria Anzaldúa, describing what it means to be "American." Would these two writers agree with each other on this issue? How might Ellison's "little man" respond to one of Anzaldúa's examples of border art?

14. Like Anzaldúa, Haunani-Kay Trask is interested in the role of language in building culture and identity. How might Anzaldúa respond to Trask's critique of non-Hawaiian historians and her insistence on "authenticity" in "From a Native Daughter" (p. 539)? Write a paper in which you discuss the role of language in the experiences of marginality that Anzaldúa and Trask describe.

15. In "I Stand Here Writing" (p. 455), Nancy Sommers writes of her difficulty in trying to find a way to write that is true to her life. Can the resulting essay be considered a "border text"? How well does Anzaldúa's term fit in this case?

SVEN BIRKERTS

Sven Birkerts (b. 1951) is a critic and book reviewer who writes frequently for the *New York Times Book Review*, the *Atlantic Monthly*, and the *New Republic*. Although he has taught creative writing and composition at Harvard University, Bennington College, and Emerson College, Birkerts holds no advanced degrees. His love of books came not from formal training in criticism but from years of working as a bookstore clerk who read during his lunch hour. Birkerts is the author of six books of criticism, including *The Gutenberg Elegies,* from which "The Owl Has Flown" was taken. Birkerts is currently a lecturer at Mount Holyoke College, a member of the Bennington Writing Seminars, and the editor of AGNI, a literary magazine.

> Visit the AGNI website to read more about Birkerts's ideas. Read his latest "rant," "The Decline of the West and Other Animadversions," at <http://www.bu.edu/agni/essays-reviews/online/2004/birkerts-nytbr.html>.

WHAT DO YOU KNOW? WHAT DO YOU EXPECT TO DISCOVER?

Before reading the essay, take a moment to consider the following questions.

1. As you go through an ordinary day, take note of all the written language you see (books, signs, newspapers, advertisements, logos, product packaging, e-mail, Internet sites, and so on). Write a paragraph explaining how you decide which written texts to attend to in your everyday life. How much of the language do you notice, and how much do you ignore? Are these texts meant for you? How do you know? Do you feel that the world around you produces too many texts, too few, the right amount?

2. In the essay that follows, Birkerts discusses the concept of wisdom; he argues that we may be losing touch with the quality of wisdom and suggests possible ways to regain it. Brainstorm on your own or with others and list all the words and images you associate with wisdom. Recall and take notes on two situations in which you have connected to the quality of wisdom in some form. What are its key attributes? How would you define the term?

3. Birkerts argues that, because of our reading habits, our memory has "all but atrophied from lack of use" (p. 73). Without refreshing your memory, write down the longest quote you can remember from a written or spoken source. After that, write down the longest poem or song lyric you can remember. How does your

memory rate? Can you explain why you have remembered what you have?

❧

The Owl Has Flown

Reading has a history. It was not always and everywhere the same. We may think of it as a straightforward process of lifting information from a page; but if we considered it further, we would agree that information must be sifted, sorted, and interpreted. Interpretive schemes belong to cultural configurations, which have varied enormously over time. As our ancestors lived in different mental worlds, they must have read differently, and the history of reading could be as complex as the history of thinking.

—ROBERT DARNTON, *The Kiss of Lamourette*

Reading and thinking are kindred operations, if only because both are actually and historically invisible. Of the two, reading has the stronger claim to invisibility, for thought at least finds a home from time to time in the written sign, whereas the *reception* of the written sign leaves no trace unless in written accounts after the fact. How do people experience the written word, and how have those experiencings, each necessarily unique, changed in larger collective ways down the centuries? The few indications we have only whet the speculative impulse.

We know from historians, for example, that before the seventh century there were few who read silently (writing some centuries before, Saint Augustine professed astonishment that Saint Ambrose read without moving his lips); that in Europe in the late Middle Ages and after, designated readers often entertained or edified groups at social or work-related gatherings. Then there is the fascinating study of Menocchio, the sixteenth-century miller. Historian Carlo Ginzburg anatomizes his intellectual universe by triangulating between Menocchio's few books and the depositions taken at his trial for heresy. In *The Cheese and the Worms*, Ginzburg combines scholarly excavation with shrewd surmise to suggest how this lettered worker assembled a cosmology—one compounded in part from the rich reserves of the dominantly oral culture, and in part from his intense and methodical, if also fanciful, readings of the few texts he owned.

After Menocchio's day, with the proliferation of mechanically produced books and the general democratization of education, reading not only spread rapidly, but changed its basic nature. As Robert Darnton writes in his essay, "The First Steps Toward a History of Reading," summarizing the conclusions of his fellow historian Rolf Engelsing:

> From the Middle Ages until sometime after 1750, according to Engelsing, men read "intensively." They had only a few books—the Bible, an almanac, a devotional work or two—and they read them over and over again, usually aloud and in groups, so that a narrow range of traditional literature became deeply impressed on their consciousness. By 1800 men were reading "extensively." They read all kinds of material, especially periodicals and newspapers, and read it only once, and then raced on to the next item.

That centrifugal tendency has of course escalated right into our present, prompted as much by the expansion of higher education and the demands of social and professional commerce as by the astronomical increase in the quantity of available print. Newspapers, magazines, brochures, advertisements, and labels surround us everywhere—surround us, indeed, to the point of having turned our waking environment into a palimpsest of texts to be read, glanced at, or ignored. It is startling to recall the anecdote about the philosopher Erasmus pausing on a muddy thoroughfare to study a rare scrap of printed paper flickering at his feet.

As we now find ourselves at a cultural watershed—as the fundamental process of transmitting information is shifting from mechanical to circuit-driven, from page to screen—it may be time to ask how modifications in our way of reading may impinge upon our mental life. For how we receive information bears vitally on the ways we experience and interpret reality.

What is most conspicuous as we survey the general trajectory of reading across the centuries is what I think of as the gradual displacement of the vertical by the horizontal—the sacrifice of depth to lateral range, or, in Darnton's terms above, a shift from intensive to extensive reading. When books are rare, hard to obtain, and expensive, the reader must compensate through intensified focus, must like Menocchio read the same passages over and over, memorizing, inscribing the words deeply on the slate of the attention, subjecting them to an interpretive pressure not unlike what students of scripture practice upon their texts. This is ferocious reading—prison or "desert island" reading—and where it does not assume depth, it creates it.

In our culture, access is not a problem, but proliferation is. And the reading act is necessarily different than it was in its earliest days. Awed and intimidated by the availability of texts, faced with the all but impossible task of discriminating among them, the reader tends to move across surfaces, skimming, hastening from one site to the next without allowing the words to resonate inwardly. The inscription is light but it covers vast territories: quantity is elevated over quality. The possibility of maximum focus is undercut by the awareness of the un-read texts that await. The result is that we know countless more "bits" of information, both important and trivial, than our ancestors. We know them without a stable sense of context, for where the field is that vast all schemes must be seen as provisional. We depend far less on memory; that faculty has all but atrophied from lack of use.

Interestingly, this shift from vertical to horizontal parallels the overall societal shift from bounded lifetimes spent in single locales to lives lived in geographical dispersal amid streams of data. What one loses by forsaking the village and the magnification resulting from the repetition of the familiar, one may recoup by gaining a more inclusive perspective, a sense of the world picture.

This larger access was once regarded as worldliness—one trav-elled, knew the life of cities, the ways of diverse people . . . It has now become the birthright of anyone who owns a television set. The mod-ern viewer is a cosmopolitan at one remove, at least potentially. He has a window on the whole world, is positioned, no matter how poor or well-to-do, to receive virtually the same infinite stream of data as every other viewer. There is almost nothing in common between the villager conning his book of scriptures by lantern-light and the con-temporary apartment dweller riffling the pages of a newspaper while attending to live televised reports from Bosnia.

How is one to assess the relative benefits and liabilities of these intrinsically different situations? How do we square the pluses and minuses of horizontal and vertical awareness? The villager, who knows every scrap of lore about his environs, is blessedly unaware of cataclysms in distant lands. News of the Lisbon earthquake of 1755 took months to travel across Europe. The media-besotted urbanite, by contrast, never loses his awareness of the tremors in different parts of the world.

We may ask, clumsily, which person is happier, or has a more vital grip on experience? The villager may have possessed his world more pungently, more sensuously; he may have found more sense in things owing both to the limited scope of his concern and the depth of his in-formation—not to mention his basic spiritual assumptions. But I also take seriously Marx's quip about the "idiocy of rural life." Circum-scribed conditions and habit suggest greater immersion in circum-stance, but also dullness and limitation. The lack of a larger perspective hobbles the mind, leads to suspiciousness and wary conservativism; the clichés about peasants are probably not without foundation. But by the same token, the constant availability of data and macroperspectives has its own diminishing returns. After a while the sense of scale is at-tenuated and a relativism resembling cognitive and moral paralysis may result. When everything is permitted, Nietzsche said, we have ni-hilism; likewise, when everything is happening everywhere, it gets harder to care about anything. How do we assign value? Where do we find the fixed context that allows us to create a narrative of sense about our lives? Ideally, I suppose, one would have the best of both worlds— the purposeful fixity of the local, fertilized by the availability of en- hancing vistas. A natural ecology of information and context.

We are experiencing in our times a loss of depth—a loss, that is, of the very paradigm of depth. A sense of the deep and natural con- nectedness of things is a function of vertical consciousness. Its apoth- eosis is what was once called wisdom. Wisdom: the knowing not of facts but of truths about human nature and the processes of life. But swamped by data, and in thrall to the technologies that manipulate it, we no longer think in these larger and necessarily more imprecise terms. In our lateral age, living in the bureaucracies of information, we don't venture a claim to that kind of understanding. Indeed, we tend to act embarrassed around those once-freighted terms—*truth, meaning, soul, destiny* . . . We suspect the people who use such words of being soft and nostalgic. We prefer the deflating one-liner that re- assures us that nothing need be taken that seriously; we inhale the at- mospheres of irony.

Except, of course, when our systems break down and we hurry to the therapist's office. Then, trying to construct significant narratives that include and explain us, we reach back into that older lexicon. "'My life doesn't seem to make sense—things don't seem to mean very much." But the therapist's office is a contained place, a paren- thetic enclosure away from the general bustle. Very little of what tran- spires there is put into social circulation. Few people would risk exposing their vulnerable recognitions to the public glare.

The depth awareness, where it exists, is guarded as a secret. If we have truly wise people among us, they avoid the spotlights—it is part of their wisdom to do so. For the fact is that there is no public space available to individuals who profess the vertical awareness. At best there are pop pulpits, public television slots that can accommodate a Joseph Campbell, Betty Friedan, or Rabbi Kushner.

Wisdom, an ideal that originated in the oral epochs—Solomon and Socrates represent wisdom incarnate, and Athena or Minerva were wisdom deified—is predicated on the assumption that one per- son can somehow grasp a total picture of life and its laws, compre- hending the whole and the relation of parts. To *comprehend*: to "hold together." We once presumed that those parts added up, that there was some purpose or explanation to our being here below. If that pur- pose could not be fully fathomed, if it rested with God or Providence, it could at least be addressed and questioned.

The explosion of data—along with general societal secularization and the collapse of what the theorists call the "master narratives" (Christian, Marxist, Freudian, humanist . . .)—has all but destroyed the premise of understandability. Inundated by perspectives, by lateral vistas of information that stretch endlessly in every direction, we no longer accept the possibility of assembling a complete picture. Instead of carrying on the ancient project of philosophy—attempting to discover the "truth" of things—we direct our energies to managing information. The computer, our high-speed, accessing, storing, and sorting tool, appears as a godsend. It increasingly determines what kind of information we are willing to traffic in; if something cannot be written in code and transmitted, it cannot be important.

The old growth forests of philosophy have been logged and the owl of Minerva has fled. Wisdom can only survive as a cultural ideal where there is a possibility of vertical consciousness. Wisdom has nothing to do with the gathering or organizing of facts—this is basic. Wisdom is a seeing *through* facts, a penetration to the underlying laws and patterns. It relates the immediate to something larger—a context, yes, but also to a big picture that refers to human endeavor *sub specie aeternitatis,* under the aspect of eternity. To see through data, one must have something to see through *to.* One must believe in the possibility of a comprehensible whole. In philosophy this is called the "hermeneutic circle"—one needs the ends to know which means to use, and the means to know which ends are possible. And this assumption of ends is what we have lost. It is one thing to absorb a fact, to situate it alongside other facts in a configuration, and quite another to contemplate that fact at leisure, allowing it to declare its connection with other facts, its thematic destiny, its resonance.

Resonance—there is no wisdom without it. Resonance is a natural phenomenon, the shadow of import alongside the body of fact, and it cannot flourish except in deep time. Where time has been commodified, flattened, turned into yet another thing measured, there is no chance that any piece of information can unfold its potential significance. We are destroying this deep time. Not by design, perhaps, but inadvertently. Where the electronic impulse rules, and where the psyche is conditioned to work with data, the experience of deep time is impossible. No deep time, no resonance; no resonance, no wisdom. The only remaining oases are churches (for those who still worship) and the offices of therapists. There, paying dearly for fifty minutes, the client gropes for a sense of coherence and mattering. The therapist listens, not so much explaining as simply fostering the possibility of resonance. She allows the long pauses and silences—a bold subversion of societal expectations—because only where silence is possible can the vertical engagement take place.

There is one other place of sanctuary. Not a physical place—not church or office—but a metaphysical one. Depth survives, condensed and enfolded, in authentic works of art. In anything that can grant us true aesthetic experience. For this experience is vertical; it transpires in deep time and, in a sense, secures that time for us. Immersed in a ballet performance, planted in front of a painting, we shatter the horizontal plane. Not without some expense of energy, however. The more we live according to the lateral orientation, the greater a blow is required, and the more disorienting is the effect. A rather unfortunate vicious cycle can result, for the harder it is to do the work, the less inclined we are to do it. Paradoxically, the harder the work, the more we need to do it. We cannot be put off by the prospect of fatigue or any incentive-withering sense of obligation.

What is true of art is true of serious reading as well. Fewer and fewer people, it seems, have the leisure or the inclination to undertake it. And true reading is hard. Unless we are practiced, we do not just crack the covers and slip into an alternate world. We do not get swept up as readily as we might be by the big-screen excitements of film. But if we do read perseveringly we make available to ourselves, in a most portable form, an ulterior existence. We hold in our hands a way to cut against the momentum of the times. We can resist the skimming tendency and delve; we can restore, if only for a time, the vanishing assumption of coherence. The beauty of the vertical engagement is that it does not have to argue for itself. It is self-contained, a fulfillment.

1994

READING, REREADING, AND ANALYSIS

1. Working individually or in a group, list the qualities that Birkerts associates with his key terms "depth," "wisdom," and "resonance." Choose one of those terms and create a definition for it using examples from Birkerts and from your own knowledge and experience. How does the term you have chosen to define differ from the other two?

2. Birkerts uses a series of oppositions such as intensive/extensive, vertical/horizontal, and quantity/quality. How do such oppositions help him organize ideas for his readers? How do such oppositions help him make sense of reading practices over time? Do you see your own reading practices as being either intensive or extensive, either vertical or horizontal?

3. Find two passages or examples from Birkerts's text that help you to explain what he means by "deep time." Take notes explaining as much as you can about each definition or example (and noting the page numbers on which they occur). Add one or two examples from your own knowledge and experience. Bring your notes and citations to class.

4. On your own or in a group, come up with some additional evidence in support of Birkerts's argument and some counterevidence (examples that help to challenge, refute, or show the limits of Birkerts's argument). Prepare to debate the strengths and weaknesses of Birkerts's claims using the evidence you have assembled.

RESPONDING THROUGH WRITING: BUILDING AN INTERPRETATION

5. What does Birkerts see as the difference between discovering "truth" and "managing information." Are these two complementary, mutually exclusive, or two sides of the same coin? Write a paper in which you explore these ideas and apply them to your own reading practices.

6. Write an essay in which you use Birkerts's ideas to analyze your Internet experience (in question 9). Your response should consider some of the following questions: To what extent did your reading on the Web demonstrate the "loss of depth," or "lateral" reading, that Birkerts talks about? To what extent did it create a different kind of reading? To what extent did it involve "wisdom" and "resonance" as he defines them? Is it possible to experience "deep time" on the Internet?

7. Using ideas and examples from Birkerts and the material generated in response to question 4, write a paper in which you either support and extend Birkerts's views or take a position that opposes his or offers alternative insights. No matter which side you take, include at least one piece of counterevidence to your own position, acknowledge the potential validity of that counterevidence, and find a way to refute it.

GOING FURTHER: LEARNING FROM OTHER SOURCES

8. Look up the myth of Minerva in an encyclopedia or on the Internet. Why does Birkerts choose the myth of Minerva and the owl as a metaphor? What does Birkerts's use of the myth tell you about his sense of purpose and audience?

9. Spend thirty minutes surfing the Internet with a pen next to your keyboard. Take notes on the kinds of reading you do as you surf. Afterward, write a one-page paper telling the detailed story of your surfing experiences: where you went, what you read, how you read, what you saw, and what you skipped over.

APPLYING WHAT YOU'VE LEARNED

10. In "The Triumph of Tinkering," Sherry Turkle argues that how we use technology—and how we teach others to use it—determines its value as a positive or negative force in culture. Use Birkerts's concepts of "deep time" and "loss of depth" to analyze the

different experiences of the students described in Turkle's essay. Would his analysis differ from Turkle's? Why or why not?

11. Use Birkerts's discussion of vertical and horizontal consciousness to help you analyze Gloria Anzaldúa's "reading" of the Aztec exhibition in the Denver Museum of Natural History. In what ways are Birkerts's discussions of reading and wisdom similar to or different from Anzaldúa's experience of attending the exhibition? Why might Anzaldúa object to your use of Birkerts's terminology as a framework to interpret her argument?

12. Birkerts argues that, amid our world of surfaces, "depth survives, condensed and enfolded, in authentic works of art" (p. 75). Compare Birkerts's brief comment with Jeanette Winterson's more complete statement about the value of art in "Imagination and Reality" to Dorothy Allison's discussion of the function of art in "This is Our World," or to both. What does art *do* that makes it so important to these writers?

13. Using the work you did in question 1 to define Birkerts's key terms "depth," "wisdom," and "resonance," apply these concepts to two other essays in this collection. Compare the extent to which reading each of those two essays led you to an experience of depth, resonance, or wisdom and where each failed. What qualities in each essay tended to provoke a "deep" or "intensive" experience, and what qualities tended to keep you on a shallow, horizontal level?

Julie Charlip

Julie Charlip (b. 1954) is Associate Professor of History at Whitman College, where she specializes in Latin American Studies. In a profile written for the college magazine by an admiring student, Charlip is quoted as saying, "I want students to have a sense of what the hard issues are in terms of continuity and changes in society. I want students to go home at Thanksgiving and have fights." Charlip's most recent book, *Cultivating Coffee,* examines the role of agriculture and landholding policy in the lives of Nicaraguan farmers from 1880 to 1930.

> To learn more about working-class culture in the United States, visit the Center for Working Class Studies at <http://www.as.ysu.edu/~cwcs/>.

WHAT DO YOU KNOW? WHAT DO YOU EXPECT TO DISCOVER?

Before reading the essay, take a moment to consider the following questions.

1. How do we identify a person's class status? Are class distinctions based primarily on how much money people have, their level of education, their ways of speaking or dressing, where they live, the kinds of houses or cars they own, their sense of entitlement, how they behave in various settings? Come up with specific examples of factors that have led you to guess a person's class status or that have led others to characterize your class status.

2. Charlip's title mentions the "Classless Society." Write a short paragraph giving an example of a real or fictional "classless society." What does that term suggest to you?

3. According to the "American Dream," our society provides opportunities for people to move between class boundaries, to become upwardly mobile. Given your own knowledge and experiences, do you think those opportunities are still available? Does it seem easy, difficult, or impossible to move from one class to another?

4. Compared with other factors, such as race, gender, and religion, how important is class in determining a person's identity?

⚉

A Real Class Act

Searching for Identity in the Classless Society

Marx and Engels wrote, "Society as a whole is more and more splitting up into two great hostile camps, into two great classes directly facing each other—bourgeoisie and proletariat" (10). If only that were true, things might be more simple. But in late twentieth-century America, it seems that society is splitting more and more into a plethora of class factions—the working class, the working poor, lower-middle class, upper-middle class, lower uppers, and upper uppers. I find myself not knowing what class I'm from.

In my days as a newspaper reporter, I once asked a sociology professor what he thought about the reported shrinking of the middle class. Oh, it's not the middle class that's disappearing, he said, but the working class. His definition: if you earn thirty thousand dollars a year working in an assembly plant, come home from work, open a beer and watch the game, you are working class; if you earn twenty thousand dollars a year as a school teacher, come home from work to a glass of white wine and PBS, you are middle class.

How do we define class? Is it a matter of values, lifestyles, taste? Is it the kind of work you do, your relationship to the means of production? Is it a matter of how much money you earn? Are we allowed to choose? In this land of supposed classlessness, where we don't have the tradition of English society to keep us in our places, how do we know where we really belong? The average American will tell you he or she is "middle class." I'm sure that's what my father would tell you. But I always felt that we were in some no man's land, suspended between the classes, sharing similarities with some and recognizing sharp, exclusionary differences from others. What class do I come from? What class am I in now? As an historian, I seek the answers to these questions in the specificity of my past.

A Family Heritage

All of us are the products not just of our immediate upbringing but also of the past that our parents and grandparents transmit. This is why class is never a matter of money alone. (Just ask the people with old money about the nouveau riche.)

My mother was the daughter of Russian Jewish immigrants who came to Lawrence, Massachusetts, in the early 1900s, before the revolution and during the pogroms. Her father died of pneumonia when she was a little girl, leaving her mother to raise five children during the Depression. Her mother ran a corner grocery, and she was too kind-hearted to deny her neighbors credit. The result was little for her own family, and my mother grew up in poverty. She was loath to talk about it, but when pressed she converted what must have been a nightmarish existence into the stuff of a warm-hearted B movie. "Oh, we were poor but happy," she would say. She finally revealed more when a high school history teacher assigned me to interview my parents about the Great Depression. My mother had two strong memories: the sight of families with all their belongings on the street, evicted from repossessed homes, and her sisters chasing the ragman to sell old cloth to get money for food. (It was a lasting legacy. Years later, when she died, I found an entire drawer filled with scraps of fabric cut from clothes she had hemmed.)

Mom's older brother moved to Trenton, New Jersey, and it was there that she met my father. Dad's grandparents had emigrated from Poland and Russia, settling in New York. His father moved to Trenton to seek his fortune, and he found it. They say every family has a story of a fortune made and lost; in mine, it's the story of Grandpa the bootlegger. Grandpa was one of the wealthiest men in Trenton. He had the Trenton police force and high-ranking officials on his payroll. Dad grew up knowing he didn't have to worry about money, yet his father, fearful of the federal authorities, was reluctant to display wealth. He bought old cars, and the family lived in apartments over the stores that were a front for his business. Dad tells colorful stories about working for his father, soaking corks to put in the bottles of "alky," putting liquor labels on bottles. But the only real comforts the wealth provided were the sumptuous meals that Grandpa hosted as patriarch. "He always set a good table," Dad recalled, a legacy Dad continued, along with his love for opera. Eventually, an angry cohort reported Grandpa to the feds, and he lost everything.

While Grandpa's wealth gave Dad a sense of financial security, he knew these ill-gotten gains did not provide him entry into the upper classes. In a touching memoir, Dad recalls that by error he was allowed to attend a junior high school in a rich neighborhood and how he hoped some of the "class" from the other students, the ones from the other side of the tracks, would rub off on him.

The Small Business Blues

Grandpa's talent for illegal business didn't carry over into legitimate enterprises, and when he died Harry's Supply Co. was nearly bankrupt, but Grandma begged Dad to take it over. Harry's Supply was a bar, restaurant, and party supply store located in an old downtown building: a long, narrow, high-ceilinged rowhouse that I remember as dusty and grimy, very different from the modern glass-and-chrome stores in the suburbs. The building itself was rented, a fact that puzzled me as a child; just what, I wondered, did my father own?

The staff consisted of Dad, Grandma, the part-time bookkeeper, the truck driver, and the warehouse kid. And, of course, my sister and me—a family business that was quite literally a *family* business.

Dad worked at the store from nine to five, Monday through Saturday. After dinner and a brief rest, he'd head down to his basement workshop. Dad had hit on the idea of imprinting matches, napkins, and ribbons as novelty items for parties and weddings. The printing process, hot stamping, combined enormous pressure and heat to impress loose type or lines of type through colored foil. I have a chilling childhood memory of Dad crushing his finger in the machine. For him, there was no employer to sue, no workmen's compensation or union benefits; there wasn't even much time to recuperate.

Dad would print until late at night, then get up to face another day at the store. Sunday, his "day off," would be spent mostly printing in that workshop. As a kid, I never really understood the supposed freedom of "being your own boss." It seemed to me that Dad was the prisoner, not the warden, of Harry's Supply. Because Dad couldn't leave the store unattended, there were no vacations. Instead, we went to New York for dinner and a Broadway show twice a year. We really couldn't afford vacations, anyway. As Dad put it, first you paid the employees and the bills; then if there was something left, it was yours. As a result, our resources varied drastically from week to week. Years later, after Dad lost the store to tax problems, he became manager for a former competitor. For the first time, he said, he looked forward to payday.

In Marxian terms, Dad's position as shopkeeper made him petit bourgeois, but what does that mean in actuality? Did that role make him an exploiter profiting from the work of his employees, a conservative force in society? That hardly seems accurate. He worked alongside his employees, for far longer hours and frequently for less money, while championing the liberal causes of change. Simultaneously, in Marxian terms, Dad was an artisan who owned his own tools. But again, what does this mean? That he was a skilled craftsman, an owner of small capital but threatened by the competition of big capital and mass production? In popular stereotypes, the petit bourgeois should have rising prosperity, a comfortable lifestyle imitating the upper classes and disdaining the lower. The artisan should be a worker with greasy hands, more skilled than the assembly-line worker but not in the same league as the middle class. But both Marxian and popular concepts seem simplistic when compared with reality.

Whether in Marxian or popular terms, my own role was clear: I was Dad's employee, owning only my labor power. This was no middle-class set of household chores, make-work designed to teach a sense of responsibility. I didn't receive an allowance; I earned wages. This was my job, a serious and essential part of Dad's business. When I grew up, he had to hire someone else.

I don't remember how old I was when I started work. Before I could count, I sorted matchbooks and paper napkins by color. Later, I packed the printed matches, cut imprinted ribbons, glued ribbons into glasses as novelty items, made car decorations for weddings, and printed on a small machine. I was paid for my work at less than the legal wage. Still, by the time I was twelve I earned enough to buy my own clothes. I also had hand-me-downs from my sister, Lindsey, and my parents would buy the more expensive items, such as winter coats, boots, or a fancy dress for a wedding, but essentially I was on my own. If there were no orders for me to work on, then I couldn't earn money.

Dad paid by the unit for the work I did at home and by the hour during summers when I worked in the store and punched the time clock. At times, Lindsey and I felt exploited. I was probably eight and Lindsey twelve when she convened the first labor negotiations. We sat Dad down and she declared that he either upped our wages or we'd go on strike. He laughed, amused at our youthful savvy. And he gave in. After all, Lindsey was right: if we quit, he'd have to hire "real" employees and pay at least the minimum wage.

Working for a parent, however, is not like working for any other employer; no other boss can forge such bonds of obligation. While the typical employer-employee relationship is impersonal, the family business relationship is patriarchal in the most literal and theoretical sense. Dad and I clashed as I grew up and wanted a social life. I insisted that Dad give me at least forty-eight hours' notice on orders for my work, as he usually did with his own work and that of his non-family suppliers. But on more than one Friday night he arrived home with orders due the next day. Already dressed for a party or a dance, waiting for my ride, I would complain bitterly of his unfairness, initially refusing to do the work. With a mixture of Jewish guilt and theater, Dad would blame the late order on my grandmother, whom I could not challenge. He would muse that he would have to do my work after finishing his own at midnight, and finally he would pledge to take me to the dance or party as soon as I finished. I always gave in, and Dad always saw that I made it, however belatedly, to parties and dances. But the responsibility of the work was always there; I could negotiate, but I couldn't quit.

Life in the 'Burbs

Harry's Supply was in Trenton, but my parents moved to a suburb, Hamilton Township, in 1955. This, however, was no case of white flight or upward mobility to the more affluent suburbs. Unlike the more prosperous communities that ringed Trenton—Ewing Township, Lawrence Township—Hamilton was a largely undeveloped, and therefore inexpensive, area. My father's first choice was to stay in Trenton, but he couldn't afford the housing prices. Instead he bought a small split-level tract home in a brand-new suburb designed for the veterans using their GI loan benefits.

Lindsey and I shared a bedroom and a bed. The small third bedroom was converted into a study for the two of us. A friend of Dad's built unvarnished shelves with a stand for the huge dictionary; two hinged panels pulled down to become our desks. The room was lined with books, mostly Book-of-the-Month Club selections and *Reader's Digest* condensed books, a few classics but no encyclopedias. The book collection was evidence to me that Dad must have been an avid reader in his youth, but I never saw him read a book. He devoured the local newspapers and an assortment of news magazines, but work left no time for leisure reading.

I read ravenously and uncritically; my parents were happy to see me reading but provided no guidance on my choices. I never knew whether they were allowing me my freedom—Dad wasn't allowed to have comic books as a child—or whether they were unprepared to judge. As a result, I still wince when people mention childhood classics that were not a part of my reading, and I have a deep aversion to the trashy novels that some of my colleagues delight in as respite from the serious, grad-student load.

In my childhood neighborhood, the fathers' occupations—most mothers stayed home—ranged from policeman to pharmacist, from working class to rising middle class. My best friend's father owned a pharmacy. Carol had music lessons, which I envied, and each summer visited her grandmother's beach house in tony Medford Lakes. When I went to the beach with Mom's family, eight aunts, uncles, and cousins piled into a rented apartment or bungalow.

Carol's family moved away to Princeton, following the expected pattern for neighborhoods like ours. These were supposed to be starter homes, where the middle class starts families and careers. Theoretically, there would be promotions and raises, or businesses would succeed and families would move to bigger and better homes. My father would still be in our little split-level had it not been for Interstate 295 cutting a swath directly through our house. After a protracted battle led by my father, we accepted a paltry settlement and moved to a new home in 1969. The new house cost more than the government settlement, and of course interest rates were higher and Dad was older, meaning a twenty-year instead of a thirty-year mortgage. What little savings the family had were wiped out.

The new house was bigger (at fifteen I finally had my own room), a three-bedroom ranch in another planned neighborhood with every house one of three models. Outside, it looked like the American Dream. But inside, the front room was virtually empty—there was one chair and my grandmother's cast-off table—and the den in the back was furnished with two rather shabby couches. We finally got a couch for the front room when my uncle gave us his old one.

Ends never met, the furniture was well worn, new clothes were limited, and yet my parents spent enormous amounts of money on food. They bought steak, veal, lamb—the legacy, I'm sure, of Mom's chasing the ragman and Grandpa's admonition always to set a good table. I found these contradictions confusing and viewed them as a middle-class façade pasted over a working-class income, not realizing that working-class incomes often were higher than ours. Nowhere was this contradiction sharper than at the restaurants. Because of Dad's business, we spent many Sundays dining out, patronizing the businesses that patronized Harry's Supply. The meal was a business expense, and Dad usually came away with an order for merchandise. Many of the restaurants were casual, but others were ones we could never have afforded if not for the business connection. My favorite was Princeton's elegant Lahiere's. We dressed in our best clothes and learned to casually order escargots. But Lindsey and I marveled at the other patrons, whose wealth gave them a graceful ease while we carefully, nervously watched our manners.

On the other hand, I once went out to dinner with a group of friends, among them the daughters of a chiropractor. They seemed comfortably middle class to me. They had an above-ground pool, the kids didn't have to work, and their dad didn't work on weekends. But with five children, the family rarely went out to eat. I remember my friends freezing at the array of silverware. I couldn't understand how they could have more money than my family yet not know the social graces. I began to see that there was a complex interconnection between money and lifestyle, between social skills and acceptance. I didn't see then, however, that the obsession with manners is a middle-class phenomenon, as Paul Fussell notes in his book *Class*. The uppers feel entitled to do as they please—just think of the photo by Weegee of the gowned and jeweled dowager with her leg hiked unceremoniously on the table. And for whom did Lahiere's keep loaner ties at the front desk? Certainly not for those who wouldn't dare show up at such a restaurant without one.

I saw more contradictions with a new set of friends across town. We lived in a largely gentile area, and my parents, concerned about my social life, joined the Jewish Community Center and enrolled me in the youth group, B'nai B'rith Girls, which had a brother chapter of "nice Jewish boys," Aleph Zadik Aleph. I had always been amused by the stereotype of rich Jews, so foreign to my life. But at the community center, I thought I was the anomaly among these solidly middle- and upper-middle-class kids. Only three of my friends lived in Hamilton Township; the rest lived in Ewing or Lawrence, the high-income suburbs, or in the one "good" neighborhood left in Trenton. The Trenton girls, of course, did not attend Trenton High School. They were usually enrolled in Villa Victoria Academy, an excellent private Catholic girls' school with so many Jewish students that it closed for the High Holy Days.

Through the community center I became close friends with the daughter of Dad's attorney, a local judge. Her well-appointed home always had a quiet formality about it. In my home the TV was usually on, and we had a tendency to yell across the house. My friend's family was in another league: they had a cleaning woman, they had a boat, and they had enough money for private schools.

The Educational Divide

Eileen and I started out attending the same high school, but her parents quickly transferred her to the Hun School in Princeton. She read authors that I was not exposed to until college, and the curriculum included a class for girls called "How to Be a Gracious Member of Society," focusing on such important points as the care and storage of your furs and hosting a dinner party.

I, of course, continued at the local high school, Hamilton High West. The school was declared to be in a "depressed area" because of the adjacent African American neighborhood. There were at least thirty-five students to a class, and sometimes there were not enough books to go around. New college graduates taught there because the federal government reduced their college loans for each year of work in a "depressed area." Certainly no one ever thought of teaching us to be gracious; teachers routinely referred to the students as "animals" and called our parents ignorant. Some of our graduates were college bound, others functionally illiterate.

It was determined from an early age that I would go to college. A teacher at Kisthardt Elementary School, where two grades routinely shared a room and a teacher, told my parents that I was "college material." I was lucky that this was decided in my earliest school years, because students were tracked by perceived ability, and those who were not seen as college material didn't have access to preparatory classes. Many a bright but economically disadvantaged student whose home life was not conducive to studying could be passed over by the tests.

As we entered junior high school, college-bound students were separated from those in business or commercial curricula. I confounded the administration, however, when I insisted on a mix: algebra, junior business training, Spanish, and typing. I had been raised to be practical, and I wanted some tangible skills.

My career goals were vague; all I was sure of was that I loved to write. The only junior high teacher to take an interest in me was an

English teacher who encouraged my writing. It was during a typing class in high school that I made my decision. If I spent the rest of my life behind a typewriter, it would be to record *my* words, not someone else's. I decided on journalism largely because I was influenced by my father, who had been founder and editor of his base paper in the Navy and who had longed to be a journalist, but he put those dreams aside to take over the family business. My decision was also a practical one, though. How else could I possibly support myself as a writer?

My family was intent on my attending college, but we understood none of the complexities of preparing for and choosing a school. I relied on my high school guidance counselor, a woman of great enthusiasm but little competence. I dreamed of going away to school and she encouraged me, guiding me to apply to Bates and Colby Colleges in Maine, Wesleyan University in Connecticut, and Ithaca College in New York. I had never heard of them, but I didn't want to go to the local schools, Trenton State College or Rider College. I never even daydreamed about schools like Princeton University, fifteen miles and fifteen light years away. Such schools were for other people, those who came out of the college preparatory academies.

I assumed, however, that I would be accepted and given financial aid at the schools we selected because everyone told me that I was smart enough to do it. I didn't understand that it was a rare student from my high school who could make it beyond Trenton State College because our training was so inadequate. And my grades were erratic. While I excelled in English, history, Spanish, anything that captured my interest and involved writing, I failed miserably at math and science. School administrators informed me that if I could excel in the social sciences and humanities, then I must be struggling in math and the physical sciences out of pure perversity. My parents tried to help, but they had never studied algebra, geometry, chemistry. There were no tutors, and the teachers facing crowded classrooms didn't worry about those of us who fell behind. I was lost and there were no guides. I gave up and huddled in the back of the room with author-philosopher Ayn Rand's *The Fountainhead* hidden inside my algebra book. Further, I tended to neglect my studies in favor of editing an award-winning newspaper for B'nai B'rith Girls and editing the high school newspaper before quitting in a censorship battle.

I also consulted a cousin with a doctorate in psychology, the only person in my family to have an advanced degree and whom I'd met only once. (Although many of my cousins started college, most dropped out.) His advice was to visit every campus for a personal interview to impress them with my enthusiasm and interest. I vividly remember visiting Bates with my mother. It was winter, and it was cold in Maine. She wore her good wool coat, the one to which she had sewn a small mink collar, the one she had had all my life. The dean of students greeted us in his plush office and looked my mother up and down with a sniff of disdain. Clearly he thought we were so far beneath him that he didn't need to mask his scorn. I felt small and inadequate and terribly sorry for Mom.

I was, as expected, rejected by Bates and by Wesleyan, wait-listed by Colby, which meant no financial aid, and accepted to Ithaca with no funding. I was stunned, but I had also learned by then that nothing comes easy. Mom and Dad raised me on a steady diet of such clichés as "Money doesn't grow on trees" and "Nothing comes without hard work." I dreaded what seemed to be my only option, Mercer County Community College, little more than an extension of high school. My sister and her husband lived in Bucks County, Pennsylvania, and he studied at Bucks County Community College, a much better school. High school quality depends on the local tax base, and because Bucks County was affluent, it had a higher caliber of students at the community college and attracted better faculty. I decided to use their address and go to Bucks.

I remember going into the cellar where Dad was working to tell him my plans: go to Bucks, transfer later to another school, and work my way through college. For the first time in my life, I saw my father cry. "It wasn't supposed to be like this," he said. "I've let you down; I was supposed to pay for your education." I was touched but also stunned; I had been raised to make my own way. I didn't feel let down in the least.

The Newspaper Game

I landed a newspaper job the same week that I started college and worked twenty-five to thirty hours a week during the semester, full time summers. I earned high grades, and I still dreamed of going away to a big-name, four-year college, but my co-workers dissuaded me. After all, they said, you want to be a journalist and you've already got a job. Go to school in Trenton and keep working here. So I transferred to Rider College, the only local campus offering journalism. It was the easy way out: journalism classes were a snap after two years in the business. I felt that I had my career launched; college meant merely that piece of paper.

Rider was known mostly as a business school, and its journalism department was small. It wasn't until I left for a job in Kansas that I heard about the big journalism programs at midwestern universities. And when I moved on to California, I met reporters who majored in "serious" subjects—political science, economics—and brought that knowledge to journalism. It seemed that I'd learned a trade rather than received an education.

That feeling had been forged at *The Trentonian*. Journalism today may earn some respect, but when I started in 1972, Watergate was just developing and journalism was very suspect. Our old-fashioned tabloid newsroom, where we squashed our cigarette butts on the floor, was more akin to *The Front Page* than *All the President's Men.* Most reporters didn't have college degrees; they joked that journalism graduates had to be retaught everything. Starting there at eighteen, I grew up in a rough-and-tumble newsroom where reporters were skilled workers, perhaps, but certainly not professionals. We had a union, we bargained collectively, we threatened strikes.

As I moved on to other newspapers and journalism became more popular, I saw a trend toward better-educated reporters, self-identified professionals. While the scrappy self-trained reporters could still go far, the ones who ended up covering Washington, working as foreign correspondents, or writing books were often children of the elite. I filled my gaps with avid reading and lots of attitude. (A woman in journalism in the 1970s needed a lot of brass.) I was tough and smart, and since journalism takes you from the gutter to mansions, I learned to function in vastly different situations.

But my attitude, formed in Trenton, was fundamentally working class, and I brought that to Kansas, where I helped organize a union and ended up unofficially blacklisted. When I finally found a job—a union one—in Fresno, California, I jumped at the chance. But in a few years, I was dissatisfied with journalism. It wasn't just Trenton or Wichita or Fresno, I discovered. Partly I was disillusioned, a watchdog for justice fighting with editors who were ambitious climbers and publishers just out to make money. And despite journalism's seemingly endless variety, I began to find that the names changed while the stories remained the same. So I took a leave of absence and went to Central America to find myself.

From Managua to Los Angeles

I had first become interested in Central America when I wrote about a Latin America solidarity group in Fresno. They showed films and sponsored lectures, and their information clashed dramatically with the news stories that came across the wires. I decided to see for myself, satisfying my curiosity and my restlessness. I intended to travel throughout Central America, starting in Nicaragua at a school that would help me brush up my Spanish, place me in a private home, and give me guided tours. I fell in love with the country and stayed till my money ran out.

Nicaragua impressed me because the 1979 revolution had brought rapid change, seeming to compress the usual slow movement of history. Coming from a country where most people believe that voting makes no difference and "you can't fight city hall," I found Nicaragua refreshing. Despite dire poverty and US-waged aggression, Nicaraguans believed they held their future in their hands, and they were involved and excited by the prospects.

At thirty years old, twelve years after I began in journalism, I walked into a research institute in Nicaragua and asked how one got a job there. They admired my interest, my writing and editing experience, but wondered what I knew about Latin America and Third World problems. I decided on the spot; I was going back to school.

This time, I had a little more savvy than in my high school days. Deciding to get a master's degree in Latin American studies, I researched the schools and applied to the best, UCLA and the University of Texas at Austin. When I was accepted and UCLA recruited me with a fellowship, I was amazed. Would I really be able to fulfill my dream of attending a major university?

My parents, however, were shocked. Dad couldn't understand why I would leave an award-winning career. The idea of changing careers was alien to him; where I grew up, people kept their jobs for life. In Trenton, the ultimate job was to work for the state, with civil-service security. My mother couldn't understand what I'd do with a master's degree. "Now you're a journalist," she'd say. "When you get this degree, what will you be?"

I thought *they* were naïve until I got to UCLA. When I told an adviser that I wanted to use my M.A. to do research, she laughed at me. She said that I would need a Ph.D. and I would have to choose another field because I couldn't get a Ph.D. in Latin American studies. This, I thought, was my big chance. A high-ranking student at UCLA could be accepted at Princeton, Harvard, Yale—a working-class kid from Trenton in the Ivy League! Then my naïveté became clearer. Dr. E. Bradford Burns explained to me that I should consider not just universities but specific departments, indeed, specific fields within departments. The Ivy League schools offered at best one or two historians specializing in Latin America compared to UCLA's four, who included leaders in the field. The important thing, he said, was to find a professor who wanted to work with me; he encouraged me to stay at UCLA, which I didn't even realize has one of the country's top ten history departments. I had never imagined that I would study for a Ph.D., much less that a renowned professor would want to work with me.

I don't think Dr. Burns, who became my chair and mentor, ever realized just how uninformed I was about the machinations of academe. All those years as a journalist had made me adept at soliciting information in a way that sometimes masked my limited knowledge, a skill that prepared me well for graduate school and the often brutal games played by graduate students in seminars.

I needed that ability to pose when I arrived at UCLA because I was terrified. I remember one of my first classes, "The Political Economy of Latin America," taught by the brilliant Dr. Jeffry Frieden. During the first week, a student in the class casually asked a question about the Porfiriato, the period when Porfirio Diaz ruled Mexico. I had never heard the term, and I thought in dismay that I was clearly in over my head. Everyone seemed to know more than I did, to have better educations, to have read works that were never part of my curriculum. By the end of the quarter, however, the other student had dropped out, and I was still there, being encouraged to go on for a Ph.D. That support was crucial. Without mentors to reassure me, answer my questions, help guide me through the system, I would have been lost.

The master's degree confused my parents, but the Ph.D. is something else. They are very proud of their daughter the doctor, the future professor, and so am I. Students who come from privileged backgrounds, and there are many at UCLA, can never understand what it means to me. Graduates of fine colleges, they affect a jaded pose, a grad-school chic, about UCLA. I find UCLA to be a wonderland of knowledge and resources. They have no idea what it is like to go to unknown, inferior schools with limited resources. They are mostly children of the upper class, and they have a sense of entitlement that I will never know and that I will always envy. They have always known they belong at UCLA. I feel grateful that I was allowed in. Despite my accomplishments—awards, fellowships, teaching assistantships—I still have the sneaking suspicion that someone will shout "Fraud!" and send me away. A part of me doesn't believe that I can really know as much as they do or that I will ever fit in. Surely, this is all a mistake, and they will find me out someday. That's why they can take time out to read a bodice ripper while I feel I must read Dostoyevsky. After all, Dostoyevsky has nothing to do with Latin American history but everything to do with a well-read background; the problem isn't knowing the material in class but knowing the references made over cappuccino.

Those graduate students who are to the manor born have been groomed; everything in their backgrounds has prepared them for this life. To me, they are the diners at Lahiere's with their easy grace. They studied Russian in high school, read the classics as undergraduates, traveled extensively. And while I have bested many of them with ease, I will always feel that I have to work harder simply because my background has not entitled me.

Perhaps that is the greatest tragedy of a working-class background, if that is what mine is. The nagging feeling of inferiority intimidates many of us, sometimes to such an extent that fine minds never turn to academe. Some start and don't finish because the environment is so alien and because they can no longer tolerate worrying that they are frauds as they compete with those who are entitled. Graduate school is about more than what you know; it is an elite system designed to maintain the status quo. Social training and attitude matter here. Graduate students are expected to adapt to a system that is arcane and virtually medieval in its form. This is no stretch for the students who dined in eating clubs on the gothic Princeton campus. Ah, but the distance for the student who was just down the road at Rider College!

Where Do I Belong?

What class am I from? How do you reconcile the definition of the bourgeois who owns his own business with the reality of the small businessman and his pile of debts? An employer's outlook with my Dad's labor-leaning, staunchly Democratic views? The opera buff who loves Broadway shows with the supposedly uncultured artisan working with his hands in the cellar? Even Marx and Engels, who defined the dual-class system, recognized the complexities. In part three of *Capital*, Marx notes that even in classically industrialized England, "intermediate and transitional strata obscure the class boundaries" (Bottomore 75). But Marx saw those strata as transitional, disappearing with the march of capitalism and its dualistic structure.

The great Flo Kennedy, the attorney who represented Black Panthers and the prostitutes' organization COYOTE, maintains that there are only those who work and those who don't. If you have to work for a living, Kennedy says, no matter how much money you make you are working class. On some level, she is right. The belief that we are different obscures the socioeconomic truth that a tiny percentage of the elite in this country owns the real wealth and the rest of us are dependent on them. In Kennedy's purely theoretical terms, there is no difference between a blue-collar union worker, my father the small businessman, and a corporate executive making a hundred thousand dollars a year. However, we all know that money does matter. The difference in income buys the wealthier among us opportunities for education, travel, upward mobility, entrance into groups with their own private signs and signals of inclusion and exclusion. It is possible, perhaps, for all of these groups to reach the same political conclusions. But there are differences in our psyches, in our expectations, our sense of entitlement, and the ways we move through the world. Those differences are rarely addressed by political theorists, but they are important.

The reality of class in America is more complex than dualistic models allow. On the surface, my father's small business and our home in the suburbs are the visage of the petit bourgeoisie, the middle class, the American Dream. Beyond that facile categorization is the reality of hard work, little money, limited opportunities, and far more insecurity than that of the blue-collar worker who has a steady paycheck and job benefits.

In *Class,* Paul Fussell notes that even our definition of the term is conditioned by our class standing: "At the bottom, people tend to believe that class is defined by the amount of money you have. In the middle, people grant that money has something to do with it, but think education and the kind of work you do almost equally important. Nearer the top, people perceive that taste, values, ideas, style and behavior are indispensable criteria of class, regardless of money or occupation or education" (3). Fussell comes up with nine classes— top out-of-sight, upper, upper middle, middle, high proletarian, mid-proletarian, low proletarian, destitute, and bottom out-of-sight. It's a tricky business, and I guess my background falls somewhere in the high proletarian to middle range. The middle class, according to Fussell, suffers from psychic insecurity, is concerned about manners and appearances, and includes salesmen and managers; the high proles are the former lower-middle class, skilled workers and craftsmen, who pride themselves on independence.

To what class do I belong now, as I head from grad-school poverty to the rather ill-paid life of the mind? Marx and Engels placed intellectuals somewhat outside the class dialectic, perhaps rising from one of the classes but choosing to ally with one class or the other, the conservatives protecting the interests of the state and the progressives siding with the working class. Similarly, Fussell would call us "category X," not members of a class at all. Formerly called "bohemians," Fussell writes: "You are not born an X person, as you are born and reared a prole or a middle. You become an X person, or, to put it more bluntly, you earn X-personhood by a strenuous effort of discovery in which curiosity and originality are indispensable. And in discovering that you can become an X person, you find the only escape from class" (212–13).

On the latter, of course, Fussell is dead wrong. Scratch an X-person's bohemian, even eccentric, façade, and you'll find attitudes and a sense of self molded by membership in a particular class. I can never escape from my class background, and there's nothing quite like the hallowed, upper-class halls of academe to remind me of it. As a journalist, I was a professional outsider, observing and criticizing. As an academic, however, I must now be an insider, functioning within a system designed by and for the elite. I know all too well the system's effect on me; the question is whether I can affect the system.

Works Cited

Bottomore, Tom, ed. *A Dictionary of Marxist Thought.* Oxford: Basil Blackwell, 1985.

Fussell, Paul. *Class.* New York: Ballantine, 1983.

Marx, Karl, and Friedrich Engels. *The Communist Manifesto.* Ed. Samuel H. Beer. New York: Meredith Corp., 1955.

READING, REREADING, AND ANALYSIS

1. Why does Charlip have a hard time identifying her social class? Find two examples in the essay wherein the factors that normally define a person's class become confusing or misleading.

2. To what extent is Charlip's family story a positive case study of the American Dream of opportunity and upward mobility? In a group, find three examples in the essay supporting the case that this is a success story and three examples that argue against that claim.

3. On page 92 Charlip says, "The difference in income buys the wealthier among us opportunities for education, travel, upward mobility, entrance into groups with their own private signs and signals of inclusion and exclusion. . . . But there are differences in our psyches, in our expectations, our sense of entitlement, and the ways we move through the world." Unpack the details of this passage, consider how it relates to the surrounding context, and use an example from somewhere else in the essay to help explain what she means by this statement. In a group, compare the examples you have chosen and discuss the extent to which you agree or disagree with Charlip's claim here.

4. Working from Charlip's essay, come up with a survey of ten or more questions that would help to identify a person's class status. What would you need to know about a person's background, experiences, and attitudes to characterize his or her class?

RESPONDING THROUGH WRITING: BUILDING AN INTERPRETATION

5. Building on the work you did for question 2, write an essay exploring both the extent to which the American Dream of opportunity and upward mobility is alive, well, and functioning today and the extent to which it has failed. Use concrete examples from Charlip and from your own knowledge and experience to examine both sides of this debate.

6. Using Charlip's essay as an example and the data gathered in question 8, write your own class narrative in which you describe all the factors and circumstances that tend to place your family within or beyond the boundaries of a particular class.

7. Write a short essay in which you use examples from Charlip's essay to make a case for the key factors that most clearly determine a person's class status. Does class status depend primarily on

money, on education, on language, behavior or attitude, on family background? Which factors seem most important in Charlip's experience and why? Are there factors beyond the issue of class that seem crucial in Charlip's case?

GOING FURTHER: LEARNING
FROM OTHER SOURCES

8. Using the survey you developed in question 4, interview an older family member to gather a history of your family's class background. In what ways does it seem similar to or different from Charlip's family background?

9. Charlip builds on the ideas of Karl Marx and Paul Fussell in this essay. Using a scholarly database such as Academic Search Elite, look up one of these two writers and find out as much as you can about his theory of class. Compare the information you find with the way in which Charlip introduces and discusses that writer. What kinds of background information did she choose to leave out?

10. Find the dictionary definition of "class" that seems to best explain Charlip's key term and is most relevant in the context of her essay. Test that definition against the different examples Charlip includes in her essay. What factors does Charlip include in the essay that contradict or go beyond the dictionary definition of class?

APPLYING WHAT YOU'VE LEARNED

11. Using Charlip's essay, Dorothy Allison's "This Is Our World," and bell hooks's "keeping close to home," compare the ways in which class status seems to shape people's identities. In each case, what are the key factors—region, race, family background, educational experiences, values, and so on—that most affect the writer's class identity? Based on these three essays, to what extent does it seem possible for a person to change her class status?

12. To what extent can people choose and shape their own identities, or is identity determined primarily by factors outside an individual's control? Test the extent to which individuals seem to have control or seem to lack control over the way their identities develop using examples from Charlip and from one of the following: Gloria Anzaldúa's "Chicana Artists," Richard Rodriguez's "Blaxicans," Barbara Mellix's "From Outside, In," or Erin McGraw's "Bad Eyes."

13. In "keeping close to home," bell hooks discusses the problems
    that can occur when education separates people from their
    working-class families and backgrounds. Use hooks's ideas to
    consider the relationship between family and education in Char-
    lip, hooks, and Barbara Mellix's "From Outside, In."

SCOTT DEVEAUX

Scott DeVeaux (b. 1954) is Associate Professor of Music at the University of Virginia, where he specializes in the study of jazz. DeVeaux has written numerous reviews and articles, and has edited essay collections on George Gershwin, Thelonious Monk, Miles Davis, Lester Young, and The Grateful Dead. His book, *The Birth of Bebop: A Social and Musical History*, won the American Book Award in 1997. DeVeaux presents jazz as both a product of the social forces of race and class in America and an aesthetic development of modernism and popular music. "Progress and the Bean" is a chapter in *The Birth of Bebop*. DeVeaux is also a jazz composer.

> To learn more about Coleman Hawkins and jazz before 1930, see the Red Hot Jazz archive at <http://www.redhotjazz.com>.

WHAT DO YOU KNOW? WHAT DO YOU EXPECT TO DISCOVER?

Before reading the essay, take a moment to consider the following questions.

1. When artistic or musical styles change, can that change be described as "progress"? Are the newer styles improvements on the older styles, or are they simply different?

2. Think of a musician or a singer who was once quite popular but who has since become less popular (or even unpopular). What accounts for this shift in popularity? Are the songs that once were loved still worth listening to? Why or why not?

3. Are you familiar with the word "paradigm" or the phrase "paradigm shift"? What do these terms mean? Give an example of a paradigm shift if you can think of one.

Progress and the Bean

In spite of all that is written, said and done, this great, big, incontrovertible fact stands out,—the Negro is progressing, and that disproves all the arguments in the world that he is incapable of progress.

JAMES WELDON JOHNSON

There's no such thing as bop music, but there's such a thing as progress.

COLEMAN HAWKINS

Alto saxophonist Cannonball Adderley remembered it later as a childhood moment that set the direction for his life. His father took him to see the Fletcher Henderson band at the City Auditorium in Tampa, Florida. Featured in the band was the imposing tenor saxophonist Coleman Hawkins. "Man, it was a great day for me," said Adderley. "I think he was the most interesting looking jazz musician I've ever seen in my life. He just looked so authoritative. I kept looking at him. I never did look at Fletcher. I said, 'Well, that's what I want to do when I grow up.' "

Adderley was neither the first nor the last musician to be impressed by Coleman Hawkins. In a field in which charismatic figures were no rarity, Hawkins had a special quality. Hawk, or Bean—as he was affectionately nicknamed—was not a particularly striking or flamboyant man. And yet his quiet dignity and utter confidence in his abilities commanded respect, even awe—at least from musicians, who were in the best position to judge Hawkins's artistic achievement. In a familiar anecdote, a younger musician encountering Hawkins for the first time in the 1960s reportedly told Adderley that the older saxophonist made him nervous: "Man, I told him Hawkins was *supposed* to make him nervous. Hawkins has been making other Sax players nervous for forty years."

Hawkins's place as one of the founders of jazz is secure. He was among the earliest generation of jazz musicians, the men and women who unselfconsciously created a new art form. He is often called the father of the tenor saxophone, the first to discover the expressive potential of an instrument previously thought to have a limited emotional range, and therefore the patriarch of a lineage that extends through John Coltrane, Sonny Rollins, and other moderns to the present.

In the sweep of jazz history, Hawkins is usually classified as a swing musician. This label not only narrows the focus to a particular phase of

Figure 8 Coleman Hawkins and Duke Ellington. Photograph. (Down Beat Magazine Archives.)

his career, but also suggests that the artistic attitudes and techniques he acquired during that time served as his compass for the remainder of his life. It also strongly implies that his moment of significance was limited to a specific historical moment: the Swing Era, when his distinctive approach to improvisation was widely accepted as the model for all saxophonists and the standard against which they were measured.

"Body and Soul," recorded in 1939, shortly after his return from a self-imposed five-year exile in Europe, remains Hawkins's best-known record and a landmark in the history of jazz recording, not least for the fact that it was simultaneously a commercial success and admired and studied by musicians. But Hawkins is represented by hundreds of other recordings, from his pre-1934 solos with Fletcher Henderson to the flood of records for various independent labels in the early 1940s. Each combines a confident and assertive manner with a bracing, complex harmonic language that anticipated many of the innovations later associated with bebop, including the so-called flatted fifths. With each recording, his reputation as an innovator grew. "Coleman Hawkins was *the* saxophonist then," remembers pianist Billy Taylor. "Hawk was most highly respected," agrees bassist Milt Hinton. "He seemed to be the most creative man of the era. Everybody just thought he was the top man."

This stature, however, did not long outlive bebop. After 1945 Hawkins's influence declined, and his standing in jazz history automatically became problematic. Even in his last years, as he matched himself against John Coltrane, Thelonious Monk, and Sonny Rollins, he was considered less a full participant in contemporary musical life than an icon—a living legend—of the art.

Hawkins's decline in status is not unexpected. A history of style usually boils down to a history of innovation: novel techniques that stand out against the background of common practice and can be shown, after the fact, to point to the future. Only stylistic "advances" give shape and momentum to such a historical narrative. It follows that the cutting edge must be kept sharp. With jazz, the pace of change has been particularly brisk. Major artists are routinely and unsentimentally shunted from the vanguard to obsolescence before they reach middle age, their later work marginalized or forgotten, their historical role diminished.

Such seems to have been the fate of Coleman Hawkins. In 1944, as he approached his fortieth birthday, his prestige and influence were at their peak. This moment of glory was overshadowed, however, by the onslaught of bebop, and with it, his reputation as innovator vanished. He is now remembered as making only a brief appearance on the periphery of the bop revolution, despite having been very much on the scene. Even the comforting role of paterfamilias to the younger generation has been denied him. The swing tenor saxophonist universally acknowledged to have served as source and inspiration for the emergent idiom is not Hawkins, but Lester Young.

The frequent rhetorical pairing of Coleman Hawkins and Lester Young has the air of a cautionary tale, with Young's rise coming at the expense of Hawkins's decline. The issue is rhythm: specifically, the "logical rhythmic change" that Martin Williams saw as the mainspring of stylistic evolution in jazz. If evolution in jazz is about rhythm, then the "cool" rhythmic language pioneered by Young is a touchstone. As "the most gifted and original improviser between Louis Armstrong and Charlie Parker" (in Williams's reading), Lester Young is the conduit between the path-breaking innovations of early jazz and the revolution of the 1940s. His improvised solos, full of ironic understatement and witty, unpredictable manipulation of phrase lengths and rhythmic motives, contrasted starkly with the earnest effusions of Hawkins's playing. Young's rhythmic approach anticipated the future, as Hawkins's more ponderous idiom did not. As tenor saxophonist Dexter Gordon, who came of age in the mid-1940s, put it: "Hawk was the master of the horn, a musician who did everything possible with it, the right way. But when Pres [Lester Young] appeared, we all started listening to him alone. Pres had an entirely new sound, one that we seemed to be waiting for."

Some musicians date the passing of the mantle even earlier, to an incident in 1933 in which Hawkins, still a soloist with the Fletcher Henderson band, found himself locked in a marathon after-hours jam session at the Cherry Blossom in Kansas City with Ben Webster, Herschel Evans, and Lester Young. Mary Lou Williams was rousted from her sleep at four in the morning to relieve the exhausted piano players: "Get up, pussycat, Hawkins has got his shirt off and is still blowing." The event, now a staple of jazz folklore, found Hawkins struggling for hours to shake off the competition until finally giving up, tearing off in his Cadillac to make the next job in St. Louis. Mary Lou Williams, herself a historian (she devoted much of her later life to jazz education) had no trouble drawing the moral from this ritual combat: "Yes, Hawkins was king until he met those crazy Kansas City tenor men."

As the critic Jed Rasula has noted, jazz historians are fond of such "primal torch-passing scenes": colorful anecdotes that seem to embody the abstract workings of history. In this case, the story is all the more compelling for being somewhat in advance of events. Hawkins, after all, remained king for a good while longer, his reputation hardly damaged by this obscure encounter in the provinces. But the handful of participant-observers at the Cherry Blossom had seen the future. Through the telling and retelling of the story, later generations have joined them as privileged insiders, better attuned to the true workings of history than the majority of those who lived through it. Hawkins's day had passed almost before it had begun.

Thus, Hawkins's encounters with the bebop revolution have been reduced to mere historical curiosity. Dizzy Gillespie has put it more generously than most: "Hawkins had the great taste in music to understand my generation and to come with us." But the image is still oddly skewed—deliberately so, perhaps, given Gillespie's penchant for self-mocking humor: the young unknowns as the leaders, the forty-year-old "most creative man of the era" as the follower. In early 1944, when Hawkins became increasingly involved with the bop generation, the word *bebop* did not yet exist. Over the course of the year, Hawkins systematically employed musicians from the emerging underground. A recording session under Hawkins's leadership in February of that year featured Gillespie and Max Roach, while his working bands for 1944 included such well-known bebop pioneers as Thelonious Monk, Kenny Clarke, and Oscar Pettiford, as well as others now more obscure: Howard McGhee, "Little Benny" Harris, Vic Coulsen.

For his early encouragement of bebop musicians, Hawkins has been given his due. Unlike others of his generation, whose attitude toward bop ranged from hostility to resentment to bemused indifference, Hawkins championed the music, earning him a degree of loyalty (Thelonious Monk remained a lifelong friend) and respect. The title of a tune from a 1946 recording session, which included J. J. Johnson, Milt Jackson, Fats Navarro, and Max Roach, pays tribute to the relationship between the older saxophonist and his young protégés: "Bean and the Boys."

To make sense of this relationship, one must move beyond the compelling simplifications that dominate jazz history. Music cannot be reduced to a narrative of stylistic development, just as the complexity of a life lived in music cannot be flattened into a set of musical characteristics. This dictum is especially true for bebop, a movement that reflected the totality of the artist's consciousness.

For the bop musicians, Hawkins had a special relevance. As keen-eared aspiring artists, they paid close attention to Hawkins's musical legacy, appropriating some elements while rejecting others. But they also understood these details of craftsmanship as part of a broader picture, inseparable from the qualities of personality and intellect that informed the achievements of an extraordinary elite: black jazz musicians in midcentury America.

Hawkins shared many traits with the Dukes and Counts of that elite: the unshakable confidence of the successfully self-taught man, a tireless professional ambition, and a sense of dignity, tending toward inner reserve, under even the most trying of circumstances. Still, even among his peers, Hawkins stood out. The quality that arrested the attention of the youthful Cannonball Adderley was Hawkins's sense of *purpose*. This quality found its most obvious manifestation in his restless exploration of technical resources, but it cannot be reduced to them. It was both social and musical. The peculiar combination of personal traits and musical abilities that marked Hawkins—steely ambition, a strong intellect, and virtuosity—characterized the bebop revolution as well. He was, as Sonny Rollins has recently put it, one of its most prominent "role models": the prototypical progressive jazz musician.

Jazz and Progress

The word *progressive* makes many people in the late twentieth century uncomfortable. It calls to mind an ideology of continuous and irreversible betterment, one singularly out of sync with contemporary thought and experience.

In particular, it is grating to find notions of progress applied to the arts. To claim progress in the fields of science and technology is one thing. Some may argue whether such "advances" actually improve life, but few disagree that new solutions to old problems have rendered previous efforts obsolete. Old technologies are discarded without a second thought: the slide rule and the typewriter may have equipped one generation, but to the next, they become puzzling curiosities. In the arts, however, such wholesale dismissal of the past seems unthinkable. As museums attest, the old retains its power and actively shapes the sensibilities of the present.

Within the arts, music is a special case. Compared with the tangible objects of the visual arts, music is an inherently evanescent art, more process than product. Music notation, of course, was invented

centuries ago as a corrective. Written music embodies musical structure independent of any given performance and makes the category
of a "work" possible. But it took time for the reification of music as
composition to take effect. The museum-like quality of the "classical" European repertory dates back no earlier than the nineteenth
century. Only in the past hundred years has the music of the past, the
canon of "timeless" masterpieces, come to dominate the present and
undermine any notion of music's evanescence. Before this time, music was created primarily for current value: to be used and discarded.
No one gave much thought to what generations beyond the reach of
memory might have done, or to what future generations might think.

For jazz, the more modern technology of recording served a function parallel to that of notation. Jazz was a music created, like any
other, for immediate consumption. Through recording, particular performances of music were transmuted into durable artifacts capable of
outlasting the particular circumstances of their creation. Recordings
were not necessarily treated with reverence: like other products of
mass-market capitalism, they were meant to be used up. But some
survived, in attics and junk shops, to be picked over in later years by
eager record collectors.

Jazz history itself grew out of discography, a rational system of
classification devised to help collectors sort the "classic" jazz recordings from the ephemera of popular culture. This process led to the
wholesale rescue of jazz recordings from planned obsolescence and
gradually to the jazz consumers' consciousness of the music as an art
form. Today recordings are seen as jazz's museum, housing works of
lasting value. It follows that new additions to the museum do not displace the old. The innovations of subsequent decades, whether by
Charlie Parker or Ornette Coleman, do not diminish the value placed
on contributions by King Oliver or Duke Ellington, but rather furnish
another wing in the museum. The process is value neutral: growth,
not progress.

It would be a mistake, however, to read this ideology back into the
circumstances of the musicians who created the recordings. At the outset of Hawkins's career, jazz was not art music, but dance music. While
record collectors shivered in private ecstasy listening to their favorite
treasures, others gathered in large public spaces to enjoy dancing to the
finest music they could find. Dance music is by nature ephemeral—
which does not mean that it is unimportant or inartistic, but simply
that it tends not to survive its time. In popular music, continual change
is essential, as in sartorial fashion. It is a marker of generational identity, and every generation has the privilege of mocking its predecessor
as hopelessly outdated and unhip. For those growing up in the first half
of the century, surrounded by the ongoing triumphs of technology, it
was virtually irresistible to associate change with progress.

Hawkins broke into the music business in the early 1920s as a
callow teenager in rumpled, ill-kept clothes that earned him the

nickname "Greasy," but quickly evolved into a dapper sophisticate, keenly sensitive to the imperatives of fashion. To his horror, his involvement with the dance music of the Jazz Age, captured on dozens of recordings with the Henderson band, later became the fetish of jazz collectors and critics. They delighted in playing these recordings in his presence, and the mortified Hawkins acted as if he had just been shown faded photographs of his youthful self in clownishly outmoded attire. The mature Hawkins thought of himself as perpetually young, perpetually in step, and hated admitting to a past. Confronted with evidence of it, he immediately countered with the notion of progress.

That Hawkins was not alone in this regard is evident in the French critic André Hodeir's complaint, from the mid-1950s, that musicians of the swing generation "naively believed their music better than that of their predecessors, just as they would have judged a 1938 automobile faster and more comfortable than a 1925 model." Hawkins, who insisted on owning the latest-model Cadillac, would have appreciated the analogy, but would probably have objected to being characterized as naive. His sense of progress in music was grounded not simply in a chauvinism of the up-to-date, but in an awareness of undeniable improvements in things that could be objectively measured. Musicians played faster, extended the ranges of their instruments, had better control over intonation and timbre (which is not to say that they conformed to European standards, but that any deviations from those standards were *intentional*). They had, on the whole, a sounder grasp of the intellectual components of music: the ability to translate musical notation into sounds and sounds into musical notation, a working knowledge of the syntax of tonal harmony, and a carefully calculated rhythmic assurance that made the dance music of the 1920s seem comparatively awkward and stiff. All of these skills had become the minimum professional equipment for musicians in the 1930s and 1940s, and counted as progress—real, hard-won achievement.

Jazz critics continually held up earlier jazz for admiration, but Hawkins was pained at the thought. "It's like a man thinking back to when he couldn't walk, he had to crawl," he complained after rehearing one of his solos twenty years later. That art, out of all areas of human endeavor, should be singled out and denied the possibility of systematic improvement made him indignant: "That's amazing to me, that so many people in music won't accept progress. It's the only field where advancement meets so much opposition. You take doctors— look what medicine and science have accomplished in the last twenty or thirty years. That's the way it should be in music—that's the way it has to be."

The analogy between science and art that Hawkins suggests seems improbable, but as generations of scholars have discovered, the work of science historian Thomas Kuhn offers some intriguing points of comparison. In science, entire fields are occasionally transformed, or brought into being, by new organizing principles: the discovery of antibiotics in medicine, plate tectonics in geology, quantum mechanics in physics. In *The Structure of Scientific Revolutions,* Kuhn identified such breakthroughs as new "paradigms" and saw in them the basis for understanding revolutionary change in science. Similar breakthroughs have characterized the arts; indeed, the animating purpose of Kuhn's study was to adapt concepts of revolution already widespread in the humanities for use in the sciences. What have come to be known as paradigm shifts in both the humanities and the sciences are the disjunctures dramatized in the telling of history—the sudden irruption of a new sensibility, a fresh way of seeing things, embodied in a particular set of techniques and procedures that becomes the model for all to follow.

Still, as Kuhn emphasizes, the dramatic, paradigm-shattering breakthrough is not characteristic of scientific activity as a whole. What he calls "normal science" is the unglamorous but necessary work that uses the prevailing paradigm to pose problems, and systematically solve them. Progress—the incremental accumulation of knowledge—is made possible only by such unremitting labor. Scientists do not seek revolutionary insights for their own sake (although the achievements of a handful of radical innovators are properly lionized). Most simply extend the existing framework further and assume, for want of any evidence to the contrary, that it will go on indefinitely.

The analogy with jazz seems straightforward and helps in part to explain Coleman Hawkins's preoccupation with progress. One of the most influential truisms of recent historical writing is that jazz was given something like an initial paradigm by "the first great soloist," Louis Armstrong. According to Martin Williams, "jazz musicians spent the late twenties and early thirties absorbing Armstrong's rhythmic ideas, the basis of his swing." Armstrong's performances, especially his recordings from the 1920s, defined the exacting discipline of the improvised solo and provided concrete examples of the rhythmic principle of swing.

For the next two decades, hundreds of musicians applied themselves to the task of absorbing and extending Armstrong's example. The "problems" they sought to "solve" (both words crop up frequently in the secondary literature) differed from a scientist's experiments in that their ultimate goals were aesthetic. But, like a scientist, these musicians systematically applied principles inherent in the original paradigm to novel contexts. Specifically, they learned from Armstrong's example how to construct a solo and how to swing, and they learned to do this within their own musical personalities, on their own instruments, and in the context of changing fashions in dance music. The process can be viewed as intuitive and holistic (learning how to "tell a story"), or intellectual and reducible to such technical problems as range, speed, and articulation. Responsibility for achievement was individual: personal improvement. But, as Coleman Hawkins proudly saw, the net result for the discipline was progress.

Bebop, to continue the analogy, figures as a major paradigm shift. Through the transformative example of Charlie Parker and Dizzy Gillespie, jazz in the 1940s experienced a "reconstitution of the field from new fundamentals." All the familiar symptoms of revolution, the world turned upside down, are there: the youth of the revolutionaries; the startling, unexpected nature of the new insight; the specter of an older generation clinging to the old paradigm, even as hordes of new practitioners rush to embrace the new; and finally, the triumph of the new paradigm and the recasting of the field in its image.

But what is the relationship of the new order to the old? How and why do such revolutions arise? As Kuhn emphasizes, a paradigm is not lightly set aside. It is the foundation of a field, and those who run counter to it risk no longer being recognized as members of the discipline. New paradigms emerge only in moments of great crisis, when the usual ways of doing things prove wholly inadequate. At such times, practitioners are forced, almost against their deepest instincts, to devise radical new ways of constructing their professional world. It is not enough for historians to admire the originality and brilliance of the new paradigm, as if originality and brilliance were sufficient explanation. They must also understand the extraordinary pressures that turned dedicated practitioners into revolutionaries and pushed them to the reckless step of abandoning the old paradigm.

What, then, was the crisis that provoked the bebop revolution? As we have seen, something like a "crisis theory" is already in place in the bebop story. It suggests that by the beginning of the 1940s, jazz musicians found themselves frustrated by the prevailing paradigm. The encouragingly brisk pace of development that had characterized jazz to this point slowed, as if something were impeding musicians from progressing further. Some have imputed the difficulty to musical style per se. "I do not think that one can hear the impeccable swing of a player like Lionel Hampton," wrote Martin Williams, "without sensing that some sort of future crisis was at hand in the music, that . . . a kind of jazz as melodically dull as a set of tone drums might well be in the offing." But this is not a comfortable argument, since it suggests that the musical language itself is somehow at fault. The more usual approach, as I have already noted, is to deflect the blame for the crisis away from the music toward external forces (such as commercialism). Bebop thus emerges as a musical solution to a social problem—or more precisely, a reassertion of the autonomy of music-making in the face of social pressures.

I would frame the argument differently. At the risk of overextending the analogy between art and science, one further aspect of Kuhn's analysis deserves to be mentioned. The revolutions he describes happen not to science in the abstract, but to communities of professional scientists. Insofar as the concept of paradigm "stands for the entire constellation of beliefs, values, techniques, and so on shared by the members of a given community," it is sociological: a "disciplinary matrix" that grounds the putatively autonomous pursuit of science in social realities. To understand fundamental change in science, one must account for its social dimension—not just its institutions (degree programs, journals, scholarly associations), but the cultural values that underlie informal behavior: how information is disseminated, reputations made, and conflicts between competing paradigms resolved.

I would argue that fundamental change in music must similarly be understood as social and cultural as well as musical. The proper analogy for a paradigm in jazz is not musical style, but something like Kuhn's "disciplinary matrix": the sum total of practices, values, and commitments that define jazz as a profession. The romantic myth of the artist working in isolation from (or even in opposition to) the outside world may seem congenial or convenient to jazz critics. But myth it is. All activity in the arts takes place within what the sociologist Howard Becker has called an "art world": "the network of people whose cooperative activity, organized by their joint knowledge of conventional means of doing things, produces the kind of art works that [the] art world is noted for." Only within this context can the decisions of individual jazz musicians to effect dramatic changes not only in musical style, but also in their social role as professional musicians, be properly interpreted.

1997

READING, REREADING, AND ANALYSIS

1. Find three to five places in this essay where DeVeaux uses, defines, or expands on the idea of "progress." Jot down the page number and take notes on the way he talks about the concept of "progress" in each example. Bring your notes to class.

2. DeVeaux makes a distinction between "growth" and "progress." Reread that section in the essay (pp. 102–04) and find an example in the essay that helps you to explain, in your own words, the difference he is exploring.

3. Consider the following claim by DeVeaux in light of his discussion of Thomas Kuhn and paradigm shifts later in the essay: "Music cannot be reduced to a narrative of stylistic development, just as the complexity of a life lived in music cannot be flattened into a set of music characteristics. This dictum is especially true for bebop, a movement that reflected the totality of the artist's consciousness" (p. 101). Take some time to analyze what that means. Which words or phrases seem the most significant to you? Write a brief

explanation of the quotation by using and defining one or two of those key words or phrases.

4. In a group, explain what DeVeaux is trying to show with the specific example of Coleman Hawkins. What does DeVeaux see as the larger implications of Hawkins's achievement?

RESPONDING THROUGH WRITING: BUILDING AN INTERPRETATION

5. Write an essay exploring the idea of "progress" using DeVeaux and your own experiences and observations. You might begin by sketching out some preliminary ideas in response to the following questions: How is "progress" defined in this essay? Why do some people argue that there is no "progress" in the field of music, whereas others, including Hawkins, argue the opposite? What do you think? Use your answers to these questions to help you develop your thesis.

6. Write a short essay interpreting the relationships you see between art and progress, on the one hand, and technology and progress, on the other hand. What does DeVeaux's essay illustrate about the relationship between art and technology? Remember that musicians like Hawkins depend on technological advances such as modern recording equipment and radio.

GOING FURTHER: LEARNING FROM OTHER SOURCES

7. Use the Internet to find some of the music of the swing and bebop musicians that DeVeaux mentions in the essay: Louis Armstrong, Coleman Hawkins, Charlie Parker, and Dizzy Gillespie. (Hint: Use a search engine such as Google, HotBot, or AltaVista, and look for audio selections.) Describe this music by comparing what you hear with a contemporary piece of music that you like. What are some of the differences between this older music and the music of today? What are some of the things that seem to have changed over time? Is the word "progress" appropriate in describing those changes? Write a paragraph outlining your discoveries.

8. Using the combined search terms "progress and paradigm," search a reference database such as Academic Search Elite, that includes a range of sources from scholarly journals. Skim your findings and print out the titles and abstracts of several articles that seem interesting in relation to DeVeaux.

Seeing

When I was six or seven years old, growing up in Pittsburgh, I used to take a precious penny of my own and hide it for someone else to find. It was a curious compulsion; sadly, I've never been seized by it since. For some reason I always "hid" the penny along the same stretch of sidewalk up the street. I would cradle it at the roots of a sycamore, say, or in a hole left by a chipped-off piece of sidewalk. Then I would take a piece of chalk, and, starting at either end of the block, draw huge arrows leading up to the penny from both directions. After I learned to write I labeled the arrows: SURPRISE AHEAD or MONEY THIS WAY. I was greatly excited, during all this arrow-drawing, at the thought of the first lucky passer-by who would receive in this way, regardless of merit, a free gift from the universe. But I never lurked about. I would go straight home and not give the matter another thought, until, some months later, I would be gripped again by the impulse to hide another penny.

It is still the first week in January, and I've got great plans. I've been thinking about seeing. There are lots of things to see, unwrapped gifts and free surprises. The world is fairly studded and strewn with pennies cast broadside from a generous hand. But—and this is the point—who gets excited by a mere penny? If you follow one arrow, if you crouch motionless on a bank to watch a tremulous ripple thrill on the water and are rewarded by the sight of a muskrat kit paddling from its den, will you count that sight a chip of copper only, and go your rueful way? It is dire poverty indeed when a man is so malnourished and fatigued that he won't stoop to pick up a penny. But if you cultivate a healthy poverty and simplicity, so that finding a penny will literally make your day, then, since the world is in fact planted in pennies, you have with your poverty bought a lifetime of days. It is that simple. What you see is what you get.

I used to be able to see flying insects in the air. I'd look ahead and see, not the row of hemlocks across the road, but the air in front of it. My eyes would focus along that column of air, picking out flying insects. But I lost interest, I guess, for I dropped the habit. Now I can see birds. Probably some people can look at the grass at their feet and discover all the crawling creatures. I would like to know grasses and sedges—and care. Then my least journey into the world would be a field trip, a series of happy recognitions. Thoreau, in an expansive mood, exulted, "What a rich book might be made about buds, including, perhaps, sprouts!" It would be nice to think so. I cherish mental images I have of three perfectly happy people. One collects stones. Another—an Englishman, say—watches clouds. The third lives on a coast and collects drops of seawater which he examines microscopically and mounts. But I don't see what the specialist sees, and so I cut myself off, not only from the total picture, but from the various forms of happiness.

Unfortunately, nature is very much a now-you-see-it, now-you-don't affair. A fish flashes, then dissolves in the water before my eyes like so much salt. Deer apparently ascend bodily into heaven; the brightest oriole fades into leaves. These disappearances stun me into stillness and concentration; they say of nature that it conceals with a grand nonchalance, and they say of vision that it is a deliberate gift, the revelation of a dancer who for my eyes only flings away her seven veils. For nature does reveal as well as conceal: now-you-don't-see-it, now-you-do. For a week last September migrating red-winged blackbirds were feeding heavily down by the creek at the back of the house. One day I went out to investigate the racket; I walked up to a tree, an Osage orange, and a hundred birds flew away. They simply materialized out of the tree. I saw a tree, then a whisk of color, then a tree again. I walked closer and another hundred blackbirds took flight. Not a branch, not a twig budged: the birds were apparently weightless as well as invisible. Or, it was as if the leaves of the Osage orange had been freed from a spell in the form of red-winged blackbirds; they flew from the tree, caught my eye in the sky, and vanished. When I looked again at the tree the leaves had reassembled as if nothing had happened. Finally I walked directly to the trunk of the tree and a final hundred, the real diehards, appeared, spread, and vanished. How could so many hide in the tree without my seeing them? The Osage orange, unruffled, looked just as it had looked from the house, when three hundred redwinged blackbirds cried from its crown. I looked downstream where they flew, and they were gone. Searching, I couldn't spot one. I wandered downstream to force them to play their hand, but they'd crossed the creek and scattered. One show to a customer. These appearances catch at my throat; they are the free gifts, the bright coppers at the roots of trees.

It's all a matter of keeping my eyes open. Nature is like one of those line drawings of a tree that are puzzles for children: Can you find hidden in the leaves a duck, a house, a boy, a bucket, a zebra, and a boot? Specialists can find the most incredibly well-hidden things. A book I read when I was young recommended an easy way to find caterpillars to rear: you simply find some fresh caterpillar droppings, look up, and there's your caterpillar. More recently an author advised me to set my mind at ease about those piles of cut stems on the ground in grassy fields. Field mice make them; they cut the grass down by degrees to reach the seeds at the head. It seems that when the grass is tightly

FIGURE 9 Ansel Adams, *Roots. Foster Gardens, Honolulu, Hawaii*, 1948. 7½ ×
6 ³⁄₁₆ in. Collection of Marjorie and Leonard Vernon, Los Angeles. (© Ansel
Adams Publishing Rights Trust/CORBIS.)

packed, as in a field of ripe grain, the blade won't topple at a single cut
through the stem; instead, the cut stem simply drops vertically, held in
the crush of grain. The mouse severs the bottom again and again, the
stem keeps dropping an inch at a time, and finally the head is low
enough for the mouse to reach the seeds. Meanwhile, the mouse is positively littering the field with its little piles of cut stems into which, presumably, the author of the book is constantly stumbling.

If I can't see these minutiae, I still try to keep my eyes open. I'm always on the lookout for antlion traps in sandy soil, monarch pupae

near milkweed, skipper larvae in locust leaves. These things are utterly common, and I've not seen one. I bang on hollow trees near water, but so far no flying squirrels have appeared. In flat country I watch every sunset in hopes of seeing the green ray. The green ray is a seldom-seen streak of light that rises from the sun like a spurting fountain at the moment of sunset; it throbs into the sky for two seconds and disappears. One more reason to keep my eyes open. A photography professor at the University of Florida just happened to see a bird die in midflight; it jerked, died, dropped, and smashed on the ground. I squint at the wind because I read Steward Edward White: "I have always maintained that if you looked closely enough you could *see* the wind—the dim, hardly-made-out, fine debris fleeing high in the air." White was an excellent observer, and devoted an entire chapter of *The Mountains* to the subject of seeing deer: "As soon as you can forget the naturally obvious and construct an artificial obvious, then you too will see deer."

But the artificial obvious is hard to see. My eyes account for less than one percent of the weight of my head; I'm bony and dense; I see what I expect. I once spent a full three minutes looking at a bullfrog that was so unexpectedly large I couldn't see it even though a dozen enthusiastic campers were shouting directions. Finally I asked, "What color am I looking for?" and a fellow said, "Green." When at last I picked out the frog, I saw what painters are up against: the thing wasn't green at all, but the color of wet hickory bark.

The lover can see, and the knowledgeable. I visited an aunt and uncle at a quarter-horse ranch in Cody, Wyoming. I couldn't do much of anything useful, but I could, I thought, draw. So, as we all sat around the kitchen table after supper, I produced a sheet of paper and drew a horse. "That's one lame horse," my aunt volunteered. The rest of the family joined in: "Only place to saddle that one is his neck"; "Looks like we better shoot the poor thing, on account of those terrible growths." Meekly, I slid the pencil and paper down the table. Everyone in that family, including my three young cousins, could draw a horse. Beautifully. When the paper came back it looked as though five shining, real quarter horses had been corraled by mistake with a papier-mâché moose; the real horses seemed to gaze at the monster with a steady, puzzled air. I stay away from horses now, but I can do a creditable goldfish. The point is that I just don't know what the lover knows; I just can't see the artificial obvious that those in the know construct. The herpetologist asks the native, "Are there snakes in that ravine?" "Nosir." And the herpetologist comes home with, yessir, three bags full. Are there butterflies on that mountain? Are the bluets in bloom, are there arrowheads here, or fossil shells in the shale?

Peeping through my keyhole I see within the range of only about thirty percent of the light that comes from the sun; the rest is infrared and some little ultraviolet, perfectly apparent to many animals, but invisible to me. A nightmare network of ganglia, charged and firing without my knowledge, cuts and splices what I do see, editing it for my brain. Donald E. Carr points out that the sense impressions of one-celled animals are not edited for the brain: "This is philosophically interesting in a rather mournful way, since it means that only the simplest animals perceive the universe as it is."

A fog that won't burn away drifts and flows across my field of vision. When you see fog move against a backdrop of deep pines, you don't see the fog itself, but streaks of clearness floating across the air in dark shreds. So I see only tatters of clearness through a pervading obscurity. I can't distinguish the fog from the overcast sky; I can't be sure if the light is direct or reflected. Everywhere darkness and the presence of the unseen appalls. We estimate now that only one atom dances alone in every cubic meter of intergalactic space. I blink and squint. What planet or power yanks Halley's Comet out of orbit? We haven't seen that force yet; it's a question of distance, density, and the pallor of reflected light. We rock, cradled in the swaddling band of darkness. Even the simple darkness of night whispers suggestions to the mind. Last summer, in August, I stayed at the creek too late.

Where Tinker Creek flows under the sycamore log bridge to the tear-shaped island, it is slow and shallow, fringed thinly in cattail marsh. At this spot an astonishing bloom of life supports vast breeding populations of insects, fish, reptiles, birds, and mammals. On windless summer evenings I stalk along the creek bank or straddle the sycamore log in absolute stillness, watching for muskrats. The night I stayed too late I was hunched on the log staring spellbound at spreading, reflected stains of lilac on the water. A cloud in the sky suddenly lighted as if turned on by a switch; its reflection just as suddenly materialized on the water upstream, flat and floating, so that I couldn't see the creek bottom, or life in the water under the cloud. Downstream, away from the cloud on the water, water turtles smooth as beans were gliding down with the current in a series of easy, weightless push-offs, as men bound on the moon. I didn't know whether to trace the progress of one turtle I was sure of, risking sticking my face in one of the bridge's spider webs made invisible by the gathering dark, or take a chance on seeing the carp, or scan the mudbank in hope of seeing a muskrat, or follow the last of the swallows who caught at my heart and trailed it after them like streamers as they appeared from directly below, under the log, flying upstream with their tails forked, so fast.

But shadows spread, and deepened, and stayed. After thousands of years we're still strangers to darkness, fearful aliens in an enemy camp with our arms crossed over our chests. I stirred. A land turtle on the bank, startled, hissed the air from its lungs and withdrew into its shell. An uneasy pink here, an unfathomable blue there, gave great suggestion of lurking beings. Things were going on. I couldn't see whether that sere rustle I heard was a distant rattlesnake, slit-eyed, or a nearby sparrow kicking in the dry flood debris slung at the foot of a willow. Tremendous action roiled the water everywhere I looked, big action, inexplicable. A tremor welled up beside a gaping muskrat burrow in the bank and I caught my breath, but no muskrat appeared. The ripples continued to fan upstream with a steady, powerful thrust. Night was knitting over my face an eyeless mask, and I still sat transfixed. A distant airplane, a delta wing out of nightmare, made a gliding shadow on the creek's bottom that looked like a stingray cruising upstream. At once a black fin slit the pink cloud on the water, shearing it in two. The two halves merged together and seemed to dissolve before my eyes. Darkness pooled in the cleft of the creek and rose, as water collects in a well. Untamed, dreaming lights flickered over the sky. I saw hints of hulking underwater shadows, two pale splashes out of the water, and round ripples rolling close together from a blackened center.

At last I stared upstream where only the deepest violet remained of the cloud, a cloud so high its underbelly still glowed feeble color reflected from a hidden sky lighted in turn by a sun halfway to China. And out of that violet, a sudden enormous black body arced over the water. I saw only a cylindrical sleekness. Head and tail, if there was a head and tail, were both submerged in cloud. I saw only one ebony fling, a headlong dive to darkness; then the waters closed, and the lights went out.

I walked home in a shivering daze, up hill and down. Later I lay openmouthed in bed, my arms flung wide at my sides to steady the whirling darkness. At this latitude I'm spinning 836 miles an hour round the earth's axis; I often fancy I feel my sweeping fall as a breakneck arc like the dive of dolphins, and the hollow rushing of wind raises hair on my neck and the side of my face. In orbit around the sun I'm moving 64,800 miles an hour. The solar system as a whole, like a merry-go-round unhinged, spins, bobs, and blinks at the speed of 43,200 miles an hour along a course set east of Hercules. Someone has piped, and we are dancing a tarantella until the sweat pours. I open my eyes and I see dark, muscled forms curl out of water, with flapping gills and flattened eyes. I close my eyes and I see stars, deep stars giving way to deeper stars, deeper stars bowing to deepest stars at the crown of an infinite cone.

"Still," wrote van Gogh in a letter, "a great deal of light falls on everything." If we are blinded by darkness, we are also blinded by light. When too much light falls on everything, a special terror results. Peter Freuchen describes the notorious kayak sickness to which Greenland Eskimos are prone. "The Greenland fjords are peculiar for the spells of completely quiet weather, when there is not enough wind to blow out a match and the water is like a sheet of glass. The kayak hunter must sit in his boat without stirring a finger so as not to scare the shy seals away. . . . The sun, low in the sky, sends a glare into his eyes, and the landscape around moves into the realm of the unreal. The reflex from the mirror-like water hypnotizes him, he seems to be unable to move, and all of a sudden it is as if he were floating in a bottomless void, sinking, sinking, and sinking. . . . Horror-stricken, he tries to stir, to cry out, but he cannot, he is completely paralyzed, he just falls and falls." Some hunters are especially cursed with this panic, and bring ruin and sometimes starvation to their families.

Sometimes here in Virginia at sunset low clouds on the southern or northern horizon are completely invisible in the lighted sky. I only know one is there because I can see its reflection in still water. The first time I discovered this mystery I looked from cloud to no-cloud in bewilderment, checking my bearings over and over, thinking maybe the ark of the covenant was just passing by south of Dead Man Mountain. Only much later did I read the explanation: polarized light from the sky is very much weakened by reflection, but the light in clouds isn't polarized. So invisible clouds pass among visible clouds, till all slide over the mountains; so a greater light extinguishes a lesser as though it didn't exist.

In the great meteor shower of August, the Perseid, I wail all day for the shooting stars I miss. They're out there showering down, committing hara-kiri in a flame of fatal attraction, and hissing perhaps at last into the ocean. But at dawn what looks like a blue dome clamps down over me like a lid on a pot. The stars and planets could smash and I'd never know. Only a piece of ashen moon occasionally climbs up or down the inside of the dome, and our local star without surcease explodes on our heads. We have really only that one light, one source for all power, and yet we must turn away from it by universal decree. Nobody here on the planet seems aware of this strange, powerful taboo, that we all walk about carefully averting our faces, this way and that, lest our eyes be blasted forever.

Darkness appalls and light dazzles; the scrap of visible light that doesn't hurt my eyes hurts my brain. What I see sets me swaying. Size and distance and the sudden swelling of meanings confuse me, bowl me over. I straddle the sycamore log bridge over Tinker Creek in the summer. I look at the lighted creek bottom: snail tracks tunnel the mud in quavering curves. A crayfish jerks, but by the time I absorb what has happened, he's gone in a billowing smokescreen of silt. I look at the water: minnows and shiners. If I'm thinking minnows, a carp will fill my brain till I scream. I look at the water's surface: skaters, bubbles, and leaves sliding down. Suddenly, my own face, reflected, startles me witless. Those snails have been tracking my face! Finally, with a shuddering wrench of the will, I see clouds, cirrus clouds. I'm dizzy, I fall in. This looking business is risky.

Once I stood on a humped rock on nearby Purgatory Mountain, watching through binoculars the great autumn hawk migration below, until I discovered that I was in danger of joining the hawks on a vertical migration of my own. I was used to binoculars, but not, apparently, to balancing on humped rocks while looking through them. I staggered. Everything advanced and receded by turns; the world was full of unexplained foreshortenings and depths. A distant huge tan object, a hawk the size of an elephant, turned out to be the browned bough of a nearby loblolly pine. I followed a sharp-shinned hawk against a featureless sky, rotating my head unawares as it flew, and when I lowered the glass a glimpse of my own looming shoulder sent me staggering. What prevents the men on Palomar from falling, voiceless and blinded, from their tiny, vaulted chairs?

I reel in confusion; I don't understand what I see. With the naked eye I can see two million light-years to the Andromeda galaxy. Often I slop some creek water in a jar and when I get home I dump it in a white china bowl. After the silt settles I return and see tracings of minute snails on the bottom, a planarian or two winding round the rim of water, roundworms shimmying frantically, and finally, when my eyes have adjusted to these dimensions, amoebae. At first the amoebae look like muscae volitantes, those curled moving spots you seem to see in your eyes when you stare at a distant wall. Then I see the amoebae as drops of water congealed, bluish, translucent, like chips of sky in the bowl. At length I choose one individual and give myself over to its idea of an evening. I see it dribble a grainy foot before it on its wet, unfathomable way. Do its unedited sense impressions include the fierce focus of my eyes? Shall I take it outside and show it Andromeda, and blow its little endoplasm? I stir the water with a finger, in case it's running out of oxygen. Maybe I should get a tropical aquarium with motorized bubblers and lights, and keep this one for a pet. Yes, it would tell its fissioned descendants, the universe is two feet by five, and if you listen closely you can hear the buzzing music of the spheres.

Oh, it's mysterious lamplit evenings, here in the galaxy, one after the other. It's one of those nights when I wander from window to window, looking for a sign. But I can't see. Terror and a beauty insoluble are a ribband of blue woven into the fringes of garments of things both great and small. No culture explains, no bivouac offers real haven or rest. But it could be that we are not seeing something. Galileo thought comets were an optical illusion. This is fertile ground: since we are certain that they're not, we can look at what our scientists have been saying with fresh hope. What if there are *really* gleaming, castellated cities hung upside-down over the desert sand? What limpid lakes and cool date palms have our caravans always passed untried? Until, one by one, by the blindest of leaps, we light on the road to these places, we must stumble in darkness and hunger. I turn from the window. I'm blind as a bat, sensing only from every direction the echo of my own thin cries.

I chanced on a wonderful book by Marius von Senden, called *Space and Sight*. When Western surgeons discovered how to perform safe cataract operations, they ranged across Europe and America operating on dozens of men and women of all ages who had been blinded by cataracts since birth. Von Senden collected accounts of such cases; the histories are fascinating. Many doctors had tested their patients' sense perceptions and ideas of space both before and after the operations. The vast majority of patients, of both sexes and all ages, had, in von Senden's opinion, no idea of space whatsoever. Form, distance, and size were so many meaningless syllables. A patient "had no idea of depth, confusing it with roundness." Before the operation a doctor would give a blind patient a cube and a sphere; the patient would tongue it or feel it with his hands, and name it correctly. After the operation the doctor would show the same objects to the patient without letting him touch them; now he had no clue whatsoever what he was seeing. One patient called lemonade "square" because it pricked on his tongue as a square shape pricked on the touch of his hands. Of another postoperative patient, the doctor writes, "I have found in her no notion of size, for example, not even within the narrow limits which she might have encompassed with the aid of touch. Thus when I asked her to show me how big her mother was, she did not stretch out her hands, but set her two index-fingers a few inches apart." Other doctors reported their patients' own statements to similar effect. "The room he was in . . . he knew to be but part of the house, yet he could not conceive that the whole house could look bigger"; "Those who are blind from birth . . . have no real conception of height or distance. A house that is a mile away is thought of as nearby, but requiring the taking of a lot of steps. . . . The elevator that whizzes him up and down gives no more sense of vertical distance than does the train of horizontal."

For the newly sighted, vision is pure sensation unencumbered by meaning: "The girl went through the experience that we all go through and forget, the moment we are born. She saw, but it did not mean anything but a lot of different kinds of brightness." Again, "I asked the patient what he could see; he answered that he saw an extensive field of light, in which everything appeared dull, confused, and in motion. He could not distinguish objects." Another patient saw "nothing but a confusion of forms and colours." When a newly sighted girl saw photographs and paintings, she asked, " 'Why do they put those dark marks all over them?' 'Those aren't dark marks,' her mother explained, 'those are shadows. That is one of the ways the eye knows that things have shape. If it were not for shadows many things would look flat.' 'Well, that's how things do look,' Joan answered. 'Everything looks flat with dark patches.' "

But it is the patients' concepts of space that are most revealing. One patient, according to his doctor, "practiced his vision in a strange fashion; thus he takes off one of his boots, throws it some way off in front of him, and then attempts to gauge the distance at which it lies;

he takes a few steps towards the boot and tries to grasp it; on failing to reach it, he moves on a step or two and gropes for the boot until he finally gets hold of it." "But even at this stage, after three weeks' experience of seeing," von Senden goes on, " 'space,' as he conceives it, ends with visual space, i.e., with colour-patches that happen to bound his view. He does not yet have the notion that a larger object (a chair) can mask a smaller one (a dog), or that the latter can still be present even though it is not directly seen."

In general the newly sighted see the world as a dazzle of color-patches. They are pleased by the sensation of color, and learn quickly to name the colors, but the rest of seeing is tormentingly difficult. Soon after his operation a patient "generally bumps into one of these colour-patches and observes them to be substantial, since they resist him as tactual objects do. In walking about it also strikes him—or can if he pays attention—that he is continually passing in between the colours he sees, that he can go past a visual object, that a part of it then steadily disappears from view; and that in spite of this, however he twists and turns—whether entering the room from the door, for example, or returning back to it—he always has a visual space in front of him. Thus he gradually comes to realize that there is also a space behind him, which he does not see."

The mental effort involved in these reasonings proves overwhelming for many patients. It oppresses them to realize, if they ever do at all, the tremendous size of the world, which they had previously conceived of as something touchingly manageable. It oppresses them to realize that they have been visible to people all along, perhaps unattractively so, without their knowledge or consent. A disheartening number of them refuse to use their new vision, continuing to go over objects with their tongues, and lapsing into apathy and despair. "The child can see, but will not make use of his sight. Only when pressed can he with difficulty be brought to look at objects in his neighbourhood; but more than a foot away it is impossible to bestir him to the necessary effort." Of a twenty-one-year-old girl, the doctor relates, "Her unfortunate father, who had hoped for so much from this operation, wrote that his daughter carefully shuts her eyes whenever she wishes to go about the house, especially when she comes to a staircase, and that she is never happier or more at ease than when, by closing her eyelids, she relapses into her former state of total blindness." A fifteen-year-old boy, who was also in love with a girl at the asylum for the blind, finally blurted out, "No, really, I can't stand it any more; I want to be sent back to the asylum again. If things aren't altered, I'll tear my eyes out."

Some do learn to see, especially the young ones. But it changes their lives. One doctor comments on "the rapid and complete loss of that striking and wonderful serenity which is characteristic only of those who have never yet seen." A blind man who learns to see is ashamed of his old habits. He dresses up, grooms himself, and tries to make a good impression. While he was blind he was indifferent to objects unless they were edible; now, "a sifting of values sets in . . . his thoughts and wishes are mightily stirred and some few of the patients are thereby led into dissimulation, envy, theft and fraud."

On the other hand, many newly sighted people speak well of the world, and teach us how dull is our own vision. To one patient, a human hand, unrecognized, is "something bright and then holes." Shown a bunch of grapes, a boy calls out, "It is dark, blue and shiny. . . . It isn't smooth, it has bumps and hollows." A little girl visits a garden. "She is greatly astonished, and can scarcely be persuaded to answer, stands speechless in front of the tree, which she only names on taking hold of it, and then as 'the tree with the lights in it.' " Some delight in their sight and give themselves over to the visual world. Of a patient just after her bandages were removed, her doctor writes, "The first things to attract her attention were her own hands; she looked at them very closely, moved them repeatedly to and fro, bent and stretched the fingers, and seemed greatly astonished at the sight." One girl was eager to tell her blind friend that "men do not really look like trees at all," and astounded to discover that her every visitor had an utterly different face. Finally, a twenty-two-year-old girl was dazzled by the world's brightness and kept her eyes shut for two weeks. When at the end of that time she opened her eyes again, she did not recognize any objects, but, "the more she now directed her gaze upon everything about her, the more it could be seen how an expression of gratification and astonishment overspread her features; she repeatedly exclaimed: 'Oh God! How beautiful!'"

I saw color-patches for weeks after I read this wonderful book. It was summer; the peaches were ripe in the valley orchards. When I woke in the morning, color-patches wrapped round my eyes, intricately, leaving not one unfilled spot. All day long I walked among shifting color-patches that parted before me like the Red Sea and closed again in silence, transfigured, whenever I looked back. Some patches swelled and loomed, while others vanished utterly, and dark marks flitted at random over the whole dazzling sweep. But I couldn't sustain the illusion of flatness. I've been around for too long. Form is condemned to an eternal danse macabre with meaning: I couldn't unpeach the peaches. Nor can I remember ever having seen without understanding; the color-patches of infancy are lost. My brain then must have been smooth as any balloon. I'm told I reached for the moon; many babies do. But the color-patches of infancy swelled as meaning filled them; they arrayed themselves in solemn ranks down distances which unrolled and stretched before me like a plain. The moon rocketed away. I live now in a world of shadows that shape and distance color, a world where space makes a kind of terrible sense. What gnosticism is this, and what physics? The fluttering patch I saw in my nursery window— silver and green and shape-shifting blue—is gone; a row of Lombardy poplars takes its place, mute, across the distant lawn. That humming oblong creature pale as light that stole along the walls of my room at night, stretching exhilaratingly around the corners, is gone, too, gone the night I ate of the bittersweet fruit, put two and two together and puckered forever my brain. Martin Buber tells this tale: "Rabbi Mendel once boasted to his teacher Rabbi Elimelekh that evenings he saw the angel who rolls away the light before the darkness, and mornings the angel who rolls away the darkness before the light. 'Yes,' said Rabbi Elimelekh, 'in my youth I saw that too. Later on you don't see these things any more.' "

Why didn't someone hand those newly sighted people paints and brushes from the start, when they still didn't know what anything was? Then maybe we all could see color-patches too, the world unraveled from reason, Eden before Adam gave names. The scales would drop from my eyes; I'd see trees like men walking; I'd run down the road against all orders, hallooing and leaping.

Seeing is of course very much a matter of verbalization. Unless I call my attention to what passes before my eyes I simply won't see it. It is, as Ruskin says, "not merely unnoticed, but in the full, clear sense of the word, unseen." My eyes alone can't solve analogy tests using figures, the ones which show, with increasing elaborations, a big square, then a small square in a big square, then a big triangle, and expect me to find a small triangle in a big triangle. I have to say the words, describe what I'm seeing. If Tinker Mountain erupted, I'd be likely to notice. But if I want to notice the lesser cataclysms of valley life, I have to maintain in my head a running description of the present. It's not that I'm observant; it's just that I talk too much. Otherwise, especially in a strange place, I'll never know what's happening. Like a blind man at the ball game, I need a radio.

When I see this way I analyze and pry. I hurl over logs and roll away stones; I study the bank a square foot at a time, probing and tilting my head. Some days when a mist covers the mountains, when the muskrats won't show and the microscope's mirror shatters, I want to climb up the blank blue dome as a man would storm the inside of a circus tent, wildly, dangling, and with a steel knife claw a rent in the top, peep, and, if I must, fall.

But there is another kind of seeing that involves a letting go. When I see this way I sway transfixed and emptied. The difference between the two ways of seeing is the difference between walking with and without a camera. When I walk with a camera, I walk from shot to shot, reading the light on a calibrated meter. When I walk without a camera, my own shutter opens, and the moment's light prints on my own silver gut. When I see this second way I am above all an unscrupulous observer.

It was sunny one evening last summer at Tinker Creek; the sun was low in the sky, upstream. I was sitting on the sycamore log bridge with the sunset at my back, watching the shiners the size of minnows who were feeding over the muddy sand in skittery schools. Again and again, one fish, then another turned for a split second across the current and flash! the sun shot out from its silver side. I couldn't watch for it. It was always just happening somewhere else, and it drew my vision just as it disappeared: flash, like a sudden dazzle of the thinnest blade, a sparking over a dun and olive ground at chance intervals from every direction. Then I noticed white specks, some sort of pale petals, small, floating from under my feet on the creek's surface, very slow and steady. So I blurred my eyes and gazed towards the brim of my hat and saw a new world. I saw the pale white circles roll up, roll up, like the world's turning, mute and perfect, and I saw the linear flashes, gleaming silver, like stars being born at random down a rolling scroll of time. Something broke and something opened. I filled up like a new wineskin. I breathed an air like light; I saw a light like water. I was the lip of a fountain the creek filled forever; I was ether, the leaf in the zephyr; I was flesh-flake, feather, bone.

When I see this way I see truly. As Thoreau says, I return to my senses. I am the man who watches the baseball game in silence in an empty stadium. I see the game purely; I'm abstracted and dazed. When it's all over and the white-suited players lope off the green field to their shadowed dugouts, I leap to my feet; I cheer and cheer.

But I can't go out and try to see this way. I'll fail, I'll go mad. All I can do is try to gag the commentator, to hush the noise of useless interior babble that keeps me from seeing just as surely as a newspaper dangled before my eyes. The effort is really a discipline requiring a lifetime of dedicated struggle; it marks the literature of saints and monks of every order East and West, under every rule and no rule, discalced and shod. The world's spiritual geniuses seem to discover universally that the mind's muddy river, this ceaseless flow of trivia and trash, cannot be dammed, and that trying to dam it is a waste of effort that might lead to madness. Instead you must allow the muddy river to flow unheeded in the dim channels of consciousness; you raise your sights; you look along it, mildly, acknowledging its presence without interest and gazing beyond it into the realm of the real where subjects and objects act and rest purely, without utterance. "Launch into the deep," says Jacques Ellul, "and you shall see."

The secret of seeing is, then, the pearl of great price. If I thought he could teach me to find it and keep it forever I would stagger barefoot across a hundred deserts after any lunatic at all. But although the pearl may be found, it may not be sought. The literature of illumination reveals this above all: although it comes to those who wait for it, it is always, even to the most practiced and adept, a gift and a total

FIGURE 10 Todd Walker, *A photograph of a leaf is not the leaf. It may not even be a photograph.* 1971. Photo-silkscreen, 22⅜ × 15½ in. Collection of the artist. (© Todd Walker. Courtesy of the Todd Walker Foundation.)

surprise. I return from one walk knowing where the killdeer nests in the field by the creek and the hour the laurel blooms. I return from the same walk a day later scarcely knowing my own name. Litanies hum in my ears; my tongue flaps in my mouth Ailinon, alleluia! I cannot cause light; the most I can do is try to put myself in the path of its beam. It is possible, in deep space, to sail on solar wind. Light, be it particle or wave, has force: you rig a giant sail and go. The secret of seeing is to sail on solar wind. Hone and spread your spirit till you yourself are a sail, whetted, translucent, broadside to the merest puff.

When her doctor took her bandages off and led her into the garden, the girl who was no longer blind saw "the tree with the lights in it." It was for this tree I searched through the peach orchards of summer, in the forests of fall and down winter and spring for years. Then one day I was walking along Tinker Creek thinking of nothing at all and I saw the tree with the lights in it. I saw the backyard cedar where the mourning doves roost charged and transfigured, each cell buzzing with flame. I stood on the grass with the lights in it, grass that was wholly fire, utterly focused and utterly dreamed. It was less like seeing than like being for the first time seen, knocked breathless by a powerful glance. The flood of fire abated, but I'm still spending the power. Gradually the lights went out in the cedar, the colors died, the cells unflamed and disappeared. I was still ringing. I had been my whole life a bell, and never knew it until at that moment I was lifted and struck. I have since only very rarely seen the tree with the lights in it. The vision comes and goes, mostly goes, but I live for it, for the moment when the mountains open and a new light roars in spate through the crack, and the mountains slam.

1974

READING, REREADING, AND ANALYSIS

1. Find examples in Dillard's essay that help you explain the difference between seeing as "analyzing and prying" and seeing as "letting go." Share your findings in a group and then list all the examples in the essay that would fit primarily into the first category and all those that would fit primarily into the second category.

2. Practice some of the observational techniques that Dillard models in this essay. Write a paragraph in which you mimic or even parody her techniques for focusing the reader's attention on a particular object or phenomenon.

3. Analyze one place in which Dillard quotes another writer. What does her interpretation of the quotation teach you about that writer? What does Dillard seem to learn from that writer? What point is she trying to make in using that quotation?

4. What does Dillard mean by the term "artificial obvious" on page 114? In a group, find some examples from this essay and some examples from your own knowledge and experience that help you to define and explain the term.

RESPONDING THROUGH WRITING: BUILDING AN INTERPRETATION

5. Return to the notes you took for "What Do You Know?" question 2. Return to the patch of ground you observed to see if Dillard's essay has given you a fresh perspective, allows you to see some additional aspects of that place. Write a short paper in which you use those notes to tell the story of your various observational encounters with that place.

6. Write a short paper in which you use examples from Dillard and from your own observation and experience to explain some of the different ways of seeing that she discusses in this essay: seeing by constructing an "artificial obvious," seeing as "a matter of verbalization," seeing as "analyzing and prying," and seeing as "letting go." Does Dillard seem to find some of those ways of seeing more valuable than others? Does she believe that some are riskier than others? Which do you find most valuable or most risky?

7. Write a short account of something you have seen, using some of Dillard's stylistic techniques to lend drama and significance to your description. Feel free to exaggerate or parody some of her techniques to make your account sound like Dillard's.

8. Summarize the first two and last two paragraphs of this essay. Then write a paragraph or two explaining why Dillard chose to begin and end her essay in those ways. Why did she choose those two particular stories? What larger theme, thesis, or argument is she conveying? What are some of the differences in the way she presents that thesis at the end of the essay as compared with the beginning? What does she learn or what ideas does she develop in between?

GOING FURTHER: LEARNING FROM OTHER SOURCES

9. Using a reference database such as Academic Search Elite, which includes sources from scholarly journals, and MAS Full Text Ultra, which includes general-interest and current-events magazines, try search terms such as "nature writing" or "seeing and nature" to find examples of other writers observing the natural world. What differences do you notice between Dillard's tone, word choice, and descriptions and those of the other writers you find? Identify several differences and bring examples to class.

10. Observe a particular natural specimen—a plant, a tree, an animal, or something of the kind—and note every detail you can

see. Then, do an Internet search to find more information about that natural specimen: place of origin, habitat, growing cycle, reproductive traits, and so on. Return to your observation with this fresh information; are you able to notice details that you had previously overlooked?

APPLYING WHAT YOU'VE LEARNED

11. Although Dillard is talking about seeing and Erin McGraw is talking about the loss of sight, are there points of connection between these two essays? For example, does Dillard's distinction between seeing as "analyzing and prying" and seeing as "letting go" apply to McGraw's examples as well? Write an essay in which you compare their ways of seeing in relation to your own experiences with sight.

12. Write an essay in which you use terms from Walker Percy's "The Loss of the Creature" to analyze Dillard's examples. Does she help to dispel the "symbolic packaging" that might prevent us from experiencing the natural world, or does she contribute to that packaging? Does she aid in the "loss of the creature" or in its recovery? Use specific examples from Dillard to explore the connection.

13. Use Dillard's terms to analyze Jane Tompkins's way of seeing in "At the Buffalo Bill Museum, June, 1988." In what places is Tompkins "analyzing and prying," and in what places is she "letting go"? What approach would she value the most? Is Tompkins's relationship to her subject matter analogous to Dillard's relationship to nature? What are some of the similarities and differences?

Julie English Early

Julie English Early (b. 1945) is a Professor of English at the University of Alabama, Huntsville. "The Spectacle of Science and Self: Mary Kingsley" was taken from *Natural Eloquence: Women Reinscribe Science* (1997), a collection of essays edited by Barbara T. Gates and Ann B. Shteir that explores the often overlooked scientific contributions of women in the nineteenth and twentieth centuries. In this essay, Early concentrates on the idiosyncratic style of British writer Mary Kingsley, showing how Kingsley's rhetoric sheds light on the received ideas of scientific presentation in the late nineteenth century.

> For more information on Mary Kingsley and a map of her travels in Africa, see <http://www.loe.org/series/discovery_women/kingsley.php>.

WHAT DO YOU KNOW? WHAT DO YOU EXPECT TO DISCOVER?

Before reading the essay, take a moment to consider the following questions.

1. Make a list of all the women scientists you can think of. What is the greatest scientific achievement accomplished by a women? Why have there been so few well-known women in science?

2. When an explorer or a traveler writes about the places she has visited, should she emphasize objective and factual information, or should she write of her reactions and her feelings? What is the difference between those two styles, and what are the consequences of choosing one or the other?

3. Early's essay is an analysis of the life and writings of Mary Kingsley, a naturalist and ethnographer who published her major books at the end of the nineteenth century. Just going on what you know of women in the nineteenth century (and perhaps a quick glimpse at the photo of Kingsley on page 129), what might you expect her personality or her demeanor to be?

⅞

The Spectacle of Science and Self
Mary Kingsley

Mary Kingsley somewhat regularly skirmished with her publisher, Macmillan, during the preparation *of Travels in West Africa* (1897). Macmillan was confused by its narrative voice, and unsure of its serious or comedic intent; he thought readers would even be uncertain of its author's gender. Kingsley protested, "It does not matter to the General Public what I am as long as I tell them the truth" (Macmillan Letters, 18 December 1894). Kingsley's optimism about the General Public, what she knowingly called the G.P., was realized: a little more than a year later, her book "took the world by storm" (Smith and Ward 349). Yet the confidence she expressed was also disingenuous; the generosity of the G.P. would have to be cultivated.

In the year before publishing *Travels in West Africa,* Kingsley consciously produced and managed a public presence on the lecture platform and in the periodical press that established her not only as a naturalist, an ethnographer, and an observer of West African affairs, but as a distinctly unusual one. Long before her book appeared, Mary Kingsley was an event: a vastly entertaining, sometimes puzzling, and often controversial self-performer—who also laid claim to serious science. This incongruous and compelling public presence guaranteed that *TWA* would be reviewed in publications across the broadest spectrum: from *Punch* to the Royal Geographical Society's *Geographical Journal,* from the *Illustrated London News* to the *Edinburgh Review.* But if Kingsley's unusual public presence guaranteed attention to her work, it also foregrounded her pointed disorientation of conventional expectations in which the image of the proper scientist stood for the value of the science presented. In her person and in her work, Kingsley stood for reconfigurations that could potentially forestall calcification of disciplines mistakenly confident that their "inherent" objectivity and remote, respectable demeanor were signs of substance. Her methodological and textual self-consciousness pointed to theoretical and political concerns that anthropology would only slowly come to address.

In creating her public presence, Kingsley was astute about herself, her material, and the politics of the sciences at the end of the century. Wisely understanding opportunities for the unconventional contributor to the still loosely formed disciplines of the human sciences, she brought her anthropological fieldwork rather than the work of the naturalist directly to the public. Kingsley limited discussion of collect-

FIGURE 11 Mary Henrietta Kingsley (1862–1900). Studio Portrait c. 1897 by A. E. Hull, London. (By courtesy of the National Portrait Gallery, London.)

ing and classifying natural specimens to direct exchanges with the British Museum, which, however, provided her with approval in an adjacent discipline. *TWA*, for example, includes plates of the "new" fishes named for her, and, as two of the text's five appendices, the museum reports on her finds. When she received them, she wrote Macmillan with details of the value of her collection, adding, "these things ought to shed a sort of glow of respectability over me" (16 February 1896).

Credentialed only by an impressive intellect, extensive independent study, and firsthand experience, Kingsley lacked an institutional imprimatur and recognized the value of that "sort of glow." The museum's approval secured her a place in the respectable world of species and genera, but as a borrowed glow, also gave her a position from which to challenge a tradition of gentlemanly good science. A clearly defined model of achievement in which the clubbish worth of the individual was collapsed with the value of "his" work shaped, for example, the Royal Geographical Society—a capacious institutional umbrella for all travel-related study. At mid-century, when RGS president Sir Roderick Murchison added public lectures by notable non-members, some found the measure too liberally enthusiastic: "[his] popular methods in the reception of the lion of the hour . . . were distasteful to some of the great men of science. . . . There was some uneasiness even amongst his friends" (Mill 80).

At the end of the century, even with pressures on professional societies to adjust their perspectives,[1] Kingsley had good reason to use whatever informal certification she could obtain.[2] Her disadvantages in the face of the gentleman's respectable model were nearly all-encompassing. She was a woman; she had not been formally educated; and, despite the Kingsley name, she did not fully embrace the preferred demeanor of class and/or the professions. As she wrote Macmillan, "I am afraid you have taken up with a complicated criminal" (16 February 1896). Excluded from formal channels of learning, Kingsley, like many women, was a gifted autodidact who educated herself from her father's library, a quixotic collection that may have reflected the individuality of its owner but could prove a treacherous guide for his self-tutored daughter. She recounted that as a young woman

> I happened on a gentleman who knew modern chemistry and tried my information on him. He said he had not heard anything so ridiculous for years, and recommended I should be placed in a museum as a compendium for exploded chemical theories, which hurt my feelings very much and I cried bitterly at not being taught things.[3]

Nonetheless, Kingsley had greater experience of her father's library than she had of her father, who existed principally in entertaining letters sent sporadically from his travels around the world. Kingsley's daily influences were not the famous Kingsley relatives, but her mother, a cockney cook whom George Kingsley had married four days before Mary's birth, and the Baileys, her mother's working-class family. At home, Kingsley gained a vocabulary and a cadence to her speech that stood her in good stead with Liverpool's West African traders; but when she moved in other circles, she would choose to control (or not to control) certain tendencies. One newspaper review of a lecture complained of her fashionable gesture of dropping *g*'s, a criticism that amused her "when I am trying so hard to hold on to the 'h's'" (unidentified letter quoted in Frank 24). Her conversational informality was equally an issue. During the preparation of *TWA*, Macmillan's editorial consultant, Henry Guillemard, had consistently attempted to "professionalize" her language and to cut her stories short. She had just as consistently resisted. In the preface, Kingsley parodies the style she has refused, demonstrates her own agility in moving among styles, and takes full responsibility for her choice: "It is I who have declined to ascend to a higher level of lucidity and correctness of diction than I am fitted for" (viii).

In the flux of social and professional redefinitions of the '90s, Kingsley did not attempt to disguise her disadvantages, but instead plainly saw their potential for disturbing existing hierarchies. She wrote to her friend Lady Macdonald:

> I am really beginning to think that . . . the person who writes a book and gets his FRGS [Fellow of the Royal Geographical Society] etc, is a peculiar sort of animal only capable of seeing a certain set of things and always seeing them the same way, and you and me are not of this species somehow. What are we to call ourselves? (undated letter quoted in Gwynn 131)

Kingsley, another "species" who neither would see only "'a certain set of things," nor always "[see] them the same way," built upon the traditional collapse of the person and the work to redefine its implications and possibilities. Whether the "lion of the hour" or, as she put it, "the sea-monster of the season," Kingsley called attention to herself as much as to her material, even multiplying and exaggerating the marginalities she could represent to elude a too swift classification in any one of them.[4]

Just as she would caution against the arrogance of too readily reading the cultures of West Africa, so did she subvert any easy readability of Mary Kingsley. A rather slight figure in her mid-thirties, she appeared on the lecture platform in somber black silks several decades out of fashion. Introducing herself at one gathering, she suggested, "I expect I remind you of your maiden aunt—long since deceased."[5] The archaic chapter headings to TWA, too, speak in the voice of another age: Chapter IV, "Which the general reader may omit as the voyager gives herein no details of Old Calabar or of other things of general interest, but discourses diffusely on the local geography and the story of the man who wasted coal" (73). Parodic, pointedly anachronistic, even dandyish, the device recalls a time when the dandy was the "natural" province of the leisured aristocrat, but is now one of the many modes that the woman and her text may, at will, dress up in. Any presuppositions suggested by her "quaint but modest appearance" (*Advertiser and Exchange Gazette* (Hull), 13 November 1897, quoted in Frank 246) and archaic respectability were confounded by her "unladylike" views: Kingsley, for example, supported the liquor traffic, deplored the activities of missionaries, preferred the company of the "palm-oil ruffians," the West Coast traders, and named as her favorite West African tribe, the cannibal Fan. With grim flippancy, Kingsley portrayed herself as an anachronism—a survivor of West Africa, the White Man's Grave; a woman with experiences in pursuit of scientific study as thrilling as those of Mungo Park and Richard Burton in pursuit of geographic knowledge and conquest; and a woman, seeming oddly out of time and place, with the riveting drama, wit, and timing of a masterful (and generally masculine) raconteur.

Kingsley's hyperbolic and flippant humor served as the readiest characteristic for her critics to fasten onto, offering them the opportunity for what appeared even willful misunderstanding. She wrote Macmillan following a lecture early in her public appearances: "The Scotch seem to have on the whole understood me perfectly, not so some distinguished English friends who are now attacking me for speaking flippantly on cannibalism" (16 February 1896). Kingsley's discursive storytelling was, in fact, tightly controlled, relying on impeccable timing, making its points by indirection, surprise, exaggeration, and often irony—a narrative style that fully controls its persona, its material, and its audience. At the beginning of their correspondence, Kingsley wrote Professor and Mrs. E. B. Tylor: "I very humbly beg to plead that statements I make seemingly light-heartedly have really had put into them weeks, sometimes months, of very hard work. . . . It is my apology and I know many things I am going to publish require an apology" (1 October 1896).[6] Her style on the platform and later in her books—what reviewers frequently called "racy"[7]—brought thousands to her dramatic lantern slide lectures; audiences of 1,800 to 2,000 were not unusual.[8] Audiences of the 1890s with a culturally induced appetite for spectacle were little concerned with what to make of her, but instead found her gratifyingly informative and entertaining.

Unlike the General Public, scientific and professional observers were troubled by their inability to explain a woman who cavalierly ruptured the connection between sober science and the demeanor of the scientist. Even Tylor's obituary memoir, while it praises her work, betrays his faint puzzlement over how to account for it:

> Some of Mary Kingsley's readers may have been led astray by her light chaffy style into calling her superficial. . . . During the few years I had the privilege of her friendship, I came to appreciate her power of getting to the back of the negro mind. In her own peculiar way she will hardly be replaced. (Green 7)[9]

Incongruent not only with the demeanor of the proper scientist, Kingsley's self-presentation, "her own peculiar way," prompted an array of defensive memoirs that sought to construct a "normative" woman behind the screen of her talent for farce, disconcertingly deadpan tales, and uncomfortably pointed wit. Alice Green, for example, stressed domestic skills: "She was a skilled nurse, a good cook, a fine needlewoman, an accomplished housewife" (3). Dennis Kemp's memoir for the *London Quarterly Review* stressed devotion to her younger brother, Charley ("a most beautiful love-story might be told"

[143–44]); their relations were, in fact, strained. As she had asked, "What are we to call ourselves?"

Decidedly captivating and decidedly odd, Kingsley was clearly adept at performing herself, but also at performing science. Kingsley's critics perhaps registered only imperfectly that the self-performance that brought her a popular audience was intrinsic to her critique of disciplinarity. On the lecture platform and in the narrative voice of her writing, the dual texts of self and science are virtually inseparable. Above all, Kingsley's work reflects a belief not only in the fundamental narrativity of science, but in its constructed nature and voice.[10] Demanding that her audiences attend to the person in the work, Kingsley entangles the stories of self and science to draw attention to a process of learning rather than remote pronouncements of science's definitive conclusions. Focusing on the all too human elements of the human sciences, she effectively avoids a charge of watered-down science in which oversimplifications are offered to satisfy an untutored audience, and instead represents the greater complexities of the practices of science. Through her presence, "her own peculiar way," Kingsley insisted that central to that practice, for good or ill, is its practitioner, a truth too often obscured in Olympian male discourse.

Kingsley's practice suggested that one could not begin to see the ways in which the observer is implicated until the European self, too, could be an object of scrutiny, itself destabilized and denaturalized. Her self-performance refuses the potentially possessive, all-comprehending eye of her audience just as her representations of West Africa disturb the possessive and certain gaze of imperial male narratives—either those of conquest or those indirectly serving conquest through science.[11] She closes the preface to *TWA* with a rather startling warning— and charge—to her readers: "Your superior culture-instincts may militate against your enjoying West Africa" (ix), she told them. Kingsley literally made a spectacle of herself in order to intervene in assumptions of her discipline. In self-performance, she denaturalized the proper woman and the proper scientist to focus on barriers to interpretation formed by an observer's too well-defined self with "superior-culture instincts"—an emphasis that had led Tylor to speculate that the quality of her work may have been enabled by a mysterious "genius and sympathy with the barbarian mind" (Green 7).

In this, Tylor, of course, reflects racial developmental theories grounding nineteenth-century ethnography and anthropology. Entwined with a self-justifying imperialist mission, disciplines concerned with cultural difference placed multifaceted difference on a linear scale ascending to Western European social organization and values. Kingsley too would announce herself "a Darwinian to the core," while also subscribing to a polygenist view of racial and sexual differences as one of kind not evolutionary degree.[12] While she would publicly rank different orders (the white man, the white woman, then all

Africans), paradoxically the racism of essential difference also enabled her to insist on taking the West African on his or her own terms, and to rationalize her preference for a culture deemed savage. Tylor's view of her affinity with "the barbarian mind" reiterated her self-characterization in a letter of introduction to the Tylors: "I seem to have a mind so nearly akin to that of the savage that I can enter into his thoughts and fathom them" (1 October 1896). In this identification Kingsley appropriated, not possessive racial superiority, but nineteenth-century developmental theories that placed women and children closer than the white male to what was deemed the (particularly) black savage state.[13] The identification effectively "naturalized" the congeniality that West African social and spiritual systems held for her, and that Tylor had identified as "sympathy" and a "power of getting to the back of the negro mind." Tylor, however, also saw, incongruous to this schema, Kingsley's "genius," an unsettling acknowledgment producing the uncomfortable wonder threading through his praise of her work. Kingsley's work was certainly framed by a racist superstructure; once inside the frame, however, her interest focused on discerning the coherence and integrity of a cultural system. Kingsley defined her work, the study of fetish, rather simply as "the governing but underlying ideas of a man's [*sic*] life" (*TWA* 68). Her large view, theoretically as applicable to British "truths" as to any other culture's, became enacted in the spectacle of herself as British Woman, a produced cultural construction, no more natural than any other. Even more unsettling to careful readers such as Tylor, West African fetish ultimately appeared to Kingsley in many ways more coherent and congenial than Victorian Britain's fetish.[14]

On the lecture platform, Kingsley made both the observer and the observed "artifacts" worthy of study, and through her discursive tales foregrounded the interaction between them. Her work, particularly on the lecture circuit, would answer the question posed in an 1895 address by the retiring president of the American Association for the Advancement of Science, "The Aims of Anthropology": "But you will naturally ask, To what end this accumulating and collecting, this filling of museums with the art products of savages and the ghastly contents of charnel houses? Why write down their stupid stories and make notes of their obscene rites?" (Brinton 63). Certainly, paramount for Kingsley was the effort to disorient prevailing notions of "savage" and "ghastly," "stupid" and "obscene," and to question the methodological structure implied by "accumulating and collecting." Kingsley offered, not a catalog neatly labeled, but a multivoiced narrative of mutual misperceptions and perceptions, alternate scales of value, and, always, a sense of the provisional and partial nature of any "truths." She reoriented her audience to different angles of vision by including countless anecdotal sidesteps that center on exchanges between West Africans who are exceedingly smart about the

Europeans they deal with and Europeans who remain remarkably stupid about their relations with West Africans.[15] In pointed contrast to theorists who assumed "the native" could not understand the origin or significance of customs and practices, Kingsley suggested a more realistic (and amusingly deflating) alternative: when seeking explanations, "[t]he usual answer is, 'It was the custom of our fathers,' but that always and only means, 'We don't intend to tell'" (*TWA* 477). In a practical application, Kingsley suggests challenges to a hierarchy of power in terms her audience can understand. England, "that nation of shopkeepers," for example, will find West Africans formidable in the Victorians' own terms: "[In Africa], young and old, men and women, regard trade as the great affair of life, [and] take to it as soon as they can toddle" (*TWA* 56). In Kingsley's view, on the matter of trade West Africans can hold their own, and it is up to the Englishman to prove that he is "an intelligent trader who knows the price of things" ("Lecture on West Africa" 267).

The European not only fails to see the West African apart from preconceptions, but also fails to see himself in the transaction. The two closely connected failures are brought together in Kingsley's insistence on learning to see the unfamiliar and on learning to see the familiar as unfamiliar—whether this is seeing "a racy maiden aunt" as scientist on the lecture platform, or seeing the presence of both the narrator and West Africans in her texts. Without remade vision, the scientist could be (or the audience could be gulled by) someone like "a German gentleman once who evolved a camel out of his inner consciousness. It was a wonderful thing; still, you know, it was not a good camel, only a thing which people personally unacquainted with camels could believe in" (*TWA* 10). Kingsley contrasts the vision produced by an "inner consciousness" with the gradual and receptive process of learning to see the forest: "As you get used to it, what seemed at first an inextricable tangle ceases to be so. . . . a whole world grows up out of the gloom before your eyes" (*TWA* 101); "The proudest day in my life was the day on which an old Fan hunter said to me—'Ah! you see'" (102). In Kingsley's lexicon, only relearned vision can ground, morally or intellectually, comprehension of the practices of West Africans: "At first you see nothing but a confused stupidity and crime; but when you get to see—well! . . . you see things worth seeing" (103). Kingsley, herself "a complicated criminal," as she had told Macmillan, and the West African, thought to embody "stupidity and crime," are indeed not what they seem, "but when you get to see—well!"

Kingsley's awareness of the complexities of vision and comprehension that must precede scientific interpretation strikes at the heart of the claim for mastery over another culture that was underwritten by professional suppositions of uninflected objectivity. Not surprisingly, reviews of her work during her lifetime are less interested than the obituary memoirs in puzzling over apparent incongruities between the style of the woman and the quality of her work and are more concerned with damping a disruptive, even alarming presence. Her most judicious critics find themselves unable to dismiss her work as unsound, but have instead to rely on distinguishing the higher and lower values of theory and praxis. One of *TWA*'s most significant reviews, Alfred Lyall's *Edinburgh Review* essay, places Kingsley in relation to F. B. Jevons and F. Max Müller. As a collector of materials, she is distinct from (and inferior to) the "philosophic savant" (Jevons and Müller) who "remains at home to receive what is brought to him . . . to classify, collate, and form his scientific inductions" (213). Kingsley was nonetheless pleased that the *Edinburgh Review* found her a force to contend with and was equanimous about Lyall's condescending (and gender-based) distinction, for much of her work, as the reviewer for *Folk-Lore* recognized, was a critique of armchair theorists:

> Miss Kingsley's repeated cautions to the anthropological student as to the reception and interpretation of evidence, the patience, the ingenuity, the tenacity of purpose, the open-mindedness required, and her warnings, none too emphatic, that no master-key will open all locks, are of a kind that ingenious theorists too often forget. ("Travels in West Africa" 163)

Kingsley, in fact, was an able—and cautious—theoretician who readily targeted the weaknesses of Frazer's "master-key," *The Golden Bough,* in her correspondence with Tylor,[16] and she well knew, as a later review of *West African Studies* pointed out, that in *TWA* "her observations [on the relation of witchcraft to religion] . . . have brought her athwart the theory of Sir Alfred Lyall and Professor Jevons" (Hartland 448).

Lyall uses both Kingsley's style and her method of organization to disqualify her work from the realm of higher science, hazarding that "she may peradventure have become unconsciously possessed by a jocose and humoristic fiend, whom in this Christian land she would do well to cast out" (214–15).[17] In his attempt to undo the threat of Kingsley's eclectic self-performance, Lyall reconstructs her as domestic worker, a scrubwoman to science, and makes the markers to a hierarchy of value clear: "From this curious and valuable description of primitive beliefs and customs in their natural state of entangled confusion we turn to the philosophic and well-ordered survey of their origin, interconnexion, and underlying psychology that is presented to us by Mr. Jevons" (224). Her work is both "curious and valuable," but Lyall cannot acknowledge the valuable disciplinary implications of its curiosity. In preferring an adaptation of the orderly classifications of natural science, he reflects an unwillingness to recognize, first, that one culture has indeed encountered rather than simply studied another, and second, that the encounter inevitably will be complex and untidy. On the lecture platform, Kingsley had the resources of her own physicality, her animated mannerisms, her incongruent appearance, and her discursive asides in the voice of the "'jocose and humoristic fiend" to disorient the linking of authority and appropriateness. In person, Kingsley could use these resources to complicate schematic classifications as she liked. By framing her first book as a travel narrative, she established continuity between public performance and text through a genre that seemed most accommodating to her performative practice. Yet, in negotiations with Macmillan's editor, she found she would have to fight to include in her books the wealth of information that Lyall mistook for a "natural state of entangled confusion." As her letters indicate, her narrative "confusion" was carefully considered, and reflected a virtue in African storytelling: "Very few African stories bear on one subject alone, and they hardly ever stick to a point" (*TWA* 436). Kingsley contrasted her own work and writing with science's traditional, male model:

> These white men who make a theory first and then go hunting travellers' tales for facts to support the same may say what they please of the pleasure of the process. Give me the pleasure of getting a mass of facts and watching them. It is just like seeing a crystal build itself up. But it *is* slower I own. (To Alice Stopford Green, 27 March 1897, quoted in Birkett 173)

Her later book, *West African Studies,* includes a central portion of analysis reflecting her theorizing, the crystal that had grown, but she also insisted on retaining narrativity to show the crystal growing. She wrote Macmillan,

> The new book, though it will seem flippant enough and to spare when it is done, is heavy work for me. I am holding onto the main idea, round which it is written, by the scruff of its neck— but the selection of the facts that will bring that idea clearly out to the minds of people who do not know is hard work. (4 October 1897)

She reported one reader's response when she was preparing its opening section:

> She always tells me . . . that I *ought not* to go on like that. Take myself seriously, etc. I really *am* always serious and 'duller than a great thaw' compared with the things I speak of, and I feel you really cannot understand W.A. unless you understand the steamboat. . . . this laughable stuff is in the thing—just as much as fetish is, etc.; and when Lyall and Mrs. G. and Guillemard and Strong and so on come along and expect me to stand on my head, all my innate vulgarity breaks out. (undated letter quoted in Gwynn 55)

Indiscriminate inclusiveness is here marked as a sign of class difference that separates her from the "white men who make a theory first and then go hunting . . . facts." Further, Kingsley's insistence that the steamboat "is in the thing" registers her acuity about adaptations of indigenous cultures to British imperialism. An outsider by class and gender, Kingsley uses her "innate vulgarity" to invert the delicacy of the "practices too disgusting to mention" school of ethnography. In this version the sense of delicacy or indelicacy shifts from the observed to the observer, and from science to the politicized self embedded in the science.[18]

Kingsley's agentless construction of a self in which "vulgarity breaks out" is a consistent and characteristic mode often borrowed by critics who see her as unable to control the "naturally" unconventional and her career as the fortuitous, if surprising, effect of that inability. Yet her success was clearly anything but natural. Kingsley carefully managed her career even before her December 1895 arrival from her second major trip to West Africa. She had proposed a book to Macmillan a full year before her return; a notation on her 18 December 1894 letter indicates "Miss Kingsley accepts 1/2 profits on her book of travels. Dec. 1894." In Liverpool, a Reuters news service reporter interviewed her: his story, a somewhat sensational summary of her "exploits" in pursuit of fish and fetish with a sprinkling of her highly quotable remarks, appeared as a news/feature in important British and American dailies. Subsequently, the *Spectator* took issue with some of those remarks, then printed her rejoinder, other readers' responses, and so on.[19] This initial "conversation" in the periodical press is an early measure of the ways in which she will be misunderstood: Townsend, the *Spectator* writer, errs in taking her comments to support his racist views, while in another *Spectator* piece responding to her corrections, she is chastised for appearing to defend cannibalism ("Negro Capacity"). The first month of her presence in the press established the ways in which she would stay in the public eye as she engendered and managed controversy. In the following weeks, she continued to elaborate and defend her views, thus adding the voice of the judicious (if controversial) interpreter of important scientific information to her status as a public event.[20]

Against her editor's advice, Kingsley's initial editorial column debates quickly gave way to consistent publishing in journals for an informed readership (she published twenty-seven articles in less than five years) and an exhausting lecture schedule. Guillemard was concerned that overexposure would cause the public to tire of her and that her unconventionality would damage her claims to serious science. She wrote Macmillan: "Dr. Guillemard has gone for me like a tiger for publishing articles. I am sorry if you similarly object to my having done so but my commercial instinct tells me that if I had not done so I should by now be forgotten by the fickle public" (6 July 1896). With her articles in periodicals like the *Liverpool Geographical Society* and the *Scottish Geographical Magazine,* "the fickle public" included the scientific community as well as the informed readership of *Cornhill* and the *National Review.* Kingsley saw no incompatibility of her "commercial instinct" with scholarly substance. At the same time that she was courting the G.P., she was writing Macmillan to urge *TWA*'s presentation as a scholarly work. "Personally I should like the book to be about the size and general get up of your Westermarck on Human Marriage" (1 May 1896).

Macmillan acquiesced in the book's "get up"; Guillemard's concerns about controlling Kingsley's public presence appeared, according to his lights, coherent with the stature of the work she intended. Indeed, the size and format of the published work were somewhat forbidding; its 743 pages, including five appendices and an index, belied its pose as a travel narrative, and its uncut pages—and stiff price of 21s.—announced a serious work. Nonetheless, the range of publications that reviewed *TWA* indicated that, after a year of Kingsley's omnipresence in periodicals and on the lecture circuit, its audience had become nearly everyone; published on 21 January 1897, it was in its fifth edition by June, and an abridged version appeared by the end of the year (Frank 230). *Punch* complained of its length, and other reviewers remarked on the onerous task of cutting so many pages; but, even if the book were more reviewed and talked about than read, the breadth of response validated Kingsley's commercial instincts. By the time that St. Loe Strachey reviewed her second book, *West African Studies,* for the *Spectator,* he could preface a passage from it with the unlikelihood, "In case anybody does not know how Miss Kingsley writes . . ." (169).[21] In many wholly respectable quarters, Kingsley had successfully forced a reconsideration of the appropriate demeanor of science and the scientist. That this was an issue—and an issue that she won—is reflected in the numbers of reviews that felt compelled to authenticate her: "Miss Kingsley is a true scientist," the *Church Quarterly* avowed ("West African Problems"); the *Folk-Lore* reviewer insisted she showed "the true scientific spirit" (Hartland); *Nature* found "much material of the greatest scientific importance" ("West African Fetish"); the *Dial* identified "a thoroughly scientific temper" (Stanley); and even the RGS's *Geographical Journal* grudgingly deemed her work "to possess permanent value" (Heawood).

Understandably, Kingsley found nothing threatening in the notion of popularizing science, if that meant bringing its processes under scrutiny, for she understood popularization as communicating the joys of process and the complex, provisional nature of discovery. Just as important, she represented the necessary but often serendipitous violations of methodology that conveyed the capacious vision and open mind required for good science. The qualities needed to practice science were also the qualities that Kingsley demanded of an audience that would watch a woman work. Kingsley's own experience could model an audience's response: "One by one I took my old ideas derived from books and thoughts based on imperfect knowledge and weighed them against the real life around me, and found them either worthless or wanting" (*TWA* 6). As a self-educated scholar, Kingsley applied a discerning critical judgment and demanded that audiences similarly evaluate authority independent of institutional credentials and "professional" demeanor. Despite her respect for the work of E. B. Tylor, "this greatest of Ethnologists" (*TWA* 435), Kingsley read and evaluated his work with great care. After hearing a paper that he had presented, she wrote to ask for a copy: "I want to read it and reread it for I am not smart on my intellectual legs, and like Mark Twain's horse frequently desire to lean up against a wall and think" (25 May 1898).

Kingsley's concern with reaching both the general and the scientific public reflected her understanding that science offered opportunities to challenge not only the demeanor of authority, but the methodology of authority; that those opportunities were themselves market-driven; and that they were not limited to the practice of science. In Kingsley's view, the General Public was an entity that could be named, marshaled, and empowered to resist an increasingly arcane and remote posture of professionalization across a broad spectrum.[22] Kingsley used herself as a prime "artifact" to communicate a conviction that the human sciences could be a space of meeting for marginalized voices, and that the empowered marginal voice could have significance extending considerably beyond a critique of the practice of science. Her debates on cultural and religious practices in West Africa, and on British economic, political, and administrative policies, argued for interconnections of knowledge forming a larger project of reconfiguring cultural and gendered commitments. Kingsley's practice openly challenged the pure and isolate construction of scientific inquiry, and the imperial politics those constructions supported. Regrettably, the breadth of her interests has retrospectively been parceled out—largely to historical studies, area studies, genre studies, and feminist studies often focusing on Englishwomen in relation to the nineteenth-century British racism of empire. Splintering her interests, isolating what appear to be clear statements (yet necessarily choosing them from among disarmingly contradictory pieces of text) to bring together a satisfactorily coherent "whole," has not made Kingsley any less elusive today than she was to her contemporaries. "I foresee a liability to become diffuse," she said as the anecdotes in *TWA* multiplied. Readings of Kingsley's work that ignore that diffusion miss the destabilizing metadiscursive critique that her career embodies.

Kingsley was always concerned to make her information matter: by reconfiguring the processes of science, by revising the common view of West Africa, and by showing the fundamental importance of scientific understanding to the practical workings of the British Empire. As a "conscience of imperialism"[23] Kingsley repeatedly argued in her lectures and in fiery periodical exchanges that scientific understanding of the coherence of West African practices and beliefs must be brought to bear on devising political and economic policies that would impose the least institutional apparatus and that would least interfere with West Africans. Correcting the missionaries' moralistic perception of one practice, she explained its practical significance, commenting to Tylor, "What a charming world that black world is—always so proper and so reasonable away down inside" (16 April 1898). Kingsley refused the categorization and hierarchical charting of practices that would override contextualization and instead pointed to a plurality of culture with insistence particularly upon the coherence of cultures of often disarming difference. Intelligent and respectful policy acknowledging in difference—and beyond difference—a world "so proper and so reasonable away down inside" would come about only under pressure from an informed public, a public with the tools for critically resisting the certainties of the authoritative voice.

Kingsley's management of her career—her impulse to take it to the public—owed much to her partisanship for free trade in West Africa, and to her hopes about the place of science within the common purview. However, just as her economic policies for West Africa swam against the tide of increased governmental administration, so too did her desire to make specialized knowledge accessible swim against the tide of increasingly determined institutional professionalization. Her career was overwhelmingly productive and successful, but, diminishing its potential to make a significant difference, unfortunately brief. Kingsley was in the public eye only a little over four years. She died in South Africa in June of 1900. Entering a discipline at a time when its methodologies were not yet "closed," Kingsley made substantial demands on its self-consciousness by forcing attention to the narrativity of science, and to the positioning of its narrator. With only a few short years of her public presence, however, the self-consciousness of the human sciences that she insisted upon was regrettably tabled for some time to come.

1997

Mary H. Kingsley (1862–1900): Major Works:

Travels in West Africa, Congo Français, Corisco and Cameroons (1897)

West African Studies (1899)

Life in West Africa (1899)

The Story of West Africa (1900)

Notes on Sport and Travel (1900) [By George Henry Kingsley, with a memoir by his daughter Mary H. Kingsley]

Notes

My thanks to Sheila Sullivan for comments on drafts of this essay, to Martha Vicinus for guiding my thinking about the 1890s, to the University of Chicago and the NEH for financial support of research, and to the University of Alabama in Huntsville's Humanities Center for supporting travel to conferences.

1. In 1892–93, the RGS Council selected twenty-two "well-qualified ladies" for membership. The intensely debated policy was overturned; women were not again elected until 1913. Lord Curzon wrote to "contest *in toto* the general capability of women to contribute to scientific geographical knowledge" (*Times*, 31 May 1893). Gender also introduced class issues with "derogatory references to school teachers and governesses," (Birkett 219). See Middleton 11–16; Birkett 211–30.

2. Kingsley asked E. B. Tylor to sponsor her in the anthropological institute ("I am for a West Coaster fairly respectable & will not steal the other members' umbrellas or hats if I am allowed to join and pay my fee" [25 May 1898]). For the most part, Kingsley objected to women in professional societies, and found informal networks preferable. She wrote Alice Green: "Set yourself to gain personal power. . . . [T]he reins of power . . . are lying on the horse's neck; quietly get them into your hands and drive" (14 March 1900, quoted in Birkett 233).

3. Kingsley included this incident in an autobiographical essay ("In the Days of My Youth"). Other personal detail appears in her two-hundred-page preface to her father's *Notes on Sport and Travel* (1900). Both pieces stress the Kingsley connection, but Katherine Frank gives a more candid view of an unhappy childhood of isolation and social exclusion by the Kingsleys.

4. Kingsley first appeared in print (5 December 1895) angrily to rebut the *Daily Telegraph*'s New Woman label in their story of her arrival at Liverpool (3 December 1895).

5. A member of the audience recalled her appearance as "a bit of stagecraft designed to heighten her achievements" (E. Muriel Joy to Dorothy Middleton, 22 June 1966, quoted in Frank 258).

6. Highly regarding his work, Kingsley called Tylor her "great ju-ju" and initiated correspondence on returning to England.

7. The *Nation* termed it "racy . . . unconventional" ("Travels in West Africa"), although later cautioned that "the author . . . [falls] into colloquy, even into vulgarity, and almost profanity" ("West African Studies"); the *Bookman* noted "racy . . . even slangy English" (Dods); *The Illustrated London News* identified "a romping style" ("Notes on Books"); *Punch* saw "humour that bubbles over in all places" ("Our Booking-Office").

8. Frank summarizes some of her engagements (214–22, 234–40, 245–47, 252-58). Within eight weeks of her return to England, she wrote Macmillan detailing a punishing schedule: "I am going to Scotland for the reading of my paper at the RSGS then onto Glasgow . . . on the 12th I am to be in Liverpool for their Geographical and the Chamber of Commerce here have asked me for a paper. Professor Mahaffey . . . has also asked me to Dublin" (31 January 1896). By 1897 she had hired an agent (Frank 215).

9. The first article of the first issue of the African Society's journal (the society was founded in Kingsley's memory) was a tribute with reminiscences from friends and colleagues.

10. For foundational work, see Geertz; Clifford and Marcus. The latter considers the textuality of ethnography, but excludes a feminist perspective

because, Clifford explains, "[feminist ethnography] has not produced either unconventional forms of writing or a developed reflection on ethnographic textuality as such" (21). In *Imperial Eyes* (1992), Mary Louise Pratt considers gendered positioning of narratives in relation to imperialist ideology. For specific discussion of gender and disciplinarity, see Moore.

11. The possessive, masculine view that feminizes the landscape has been widely commented on, e.g., Kolodny; Griffin. Ungendered cultural views appear in Said; Sternberger. Pratt's *Imperial Eyes* specifically considers the "eye" of scientific travel writing.

12. See Stocking's superb intellectual history for detailed analysis of currents of thought and their competing positions in the nineteenth-century development of the discipline.

13. In their survey of nineteenth-century intellectual currents concerning women, Helsinger et al. conclude, "[t]his equation of woman and black is one of the most important features of the Woman Question" (2:91). For detail of the anthropological debate on woman's place in the hierarchy, see Stocking 187–237.

14. Examining fully the complexities of Kingsley's work in relation to race exceeds the scope of this essay. Kingsley publicly committed to political and scientific agendas of imperialism and the hierarchies of social Darwinism that embed racism. Readers who have found such precise lines inadequate to the representations and strategies of her texts have, however, tended to shape defensive arguments. In light of Kingsley's decentering strategies, approaches to her work that categorize it as racist, nonracist, or the apologetic "not-so-racist" may close down valuable inquiry into the incoherencies of acquiescence and resistance in the conflicted position of British women enabled by imperialism. This essay elaborates Kingsley's self-performance as one aspect of that incoherence: the specific nature of her gendered intervention in the professional discourse "denaturalized" the hierarchies underwriting nineteenth-century ethnography and imperialism at the same time that she committed to both.

15. In this essay, I use the broad term "West Africans" to discuss Kingsley's general perspective. Her books carefully specify indigenous peoples and cultures of the region.

16. Kingsley prefaced a ten-page letter to Tylor detailing Frazer's errors on animism and totemism, "My cap frills are vibrating with vexation" (9 April 1898). In *TWA*, she is dismissive: "I was particularly confident that from Mr. Frazer's book, *The Golden Bough*, I had got a semi-universal key to the underlying idea of native custom and belief. But I soon found this was very far from being the case" (435).

17. Virtually all reviewers commented on style before considering her positions. Many delighted in it, but others shared Lyall's distaste, expressing it with less avuncular preciosity. *Nature*'s angry reviewer felt that "hyperbole is frequently carried too far. . . . Serious students who, when they ask for facts, do not care to be offered a cryptic joke" ("Miss Kingsley's Travels"). The reviewer for *Science* allowed that "an easy flippancy of manner . . . carries you on, . . . [although] the writer is 'on very thin ice'. . . . The off-hand way in which some rather serious problems are treated is hardly fair" (Libbey).

18. Kingsley "vulgarized" herself in text by foregrounding breaches of conventional delicacy and an exaggerated horror of them. These incidents frequently involve mishaps with sex- and gender-marked clothing when she is with Europeans. Readings of these episodes as signs of a self-effacing and anxiety-ridden gender conservatism seem to miss the point.

19. Slightly different versions appear in the *Daily Telegraph* (3 Dec. 1895), the *New York Times* (2 December 1895), and the London *Times* ("Miss Kingsley's Travels," 2 December 1895). Her comments on "the nature of the West African" quickly elicited a *Spectator* article that misunderstood her (Townsend, 7 December 1895); she responded in the letters column (28 December 1895); the same issue ran an article responding to her letter ("Negro Capacity"). The *New York Times* then commented on the entire exchange ("African Character Studied," 10 January 1896). The *Illustrated London News* ("Lady Traveler," 4 January 1896) profiled this new public figure (with photographs that she supplied). The RGS's *Geographical Journal* introduced her material: "Miss Kingsley has kindly sent, at short notice, the following notes on her recent journeys in West Africa" ("Miss Kingsley's Travels").

20. Less than three weeks after her return, Guillemard wrote, "I am quite a distinguished person here because I am a friend of Miss Kingsley. I enliven the dinner table with anecdotes about you. . . . Your book should run—I estimate—to about the 68th thousand, like Mrs. Henry Wood's *East Lynne* or Zola's *The Debacle*" (Macmillan Letters, 20 December 1895).

21. In the first week, 1,200 copies of *West African Studies* were sold (Frank 261).

22. Kingsley was acutely aware of ironies in distinguishing the professional from general public: "These literary and scientific institutions amuse me much. They . . . inform you they don't want science. . . . [but] 'something bright and amusing and magic lantern slides'" (to E. Sidney Harland, 25 March 1897, quoted in Birkett 203). Adapting to audiences from Oxbridge societies to Boys' Institutes in city slums, she profited from question-and-answer sessions to craft in text an implied dialogue considerably removed from the magisterial pronouncements that Lyall favored.

23. Kingsley's political activity was substantial. Historian Kenneth Dike Nworah argues that the self-named "Third Party" opposed the racist school that "advertised the inferiority and incapacity" of the West African, and the damaging philanthropic and missionary interests that would denationalize West Africa by eroding its traditional systems. The "Liverpool Sect" "was mainly apotheosized in the ideals of Mary Kingsley, John Holt, and E. D. Morel." In Nworah's view, the "small but perceptible sect . . . identified itself with the development of a true colonial conscience in Britain" (349–50). Although earlier free trade had meant the slave trade, Kingsley had faith in the process of knowledge (to which she contributed). Her advocacy reflected a utopian view of trade in which the skills of West Africans would ground an equality of interest with Europe and obviate the need for any "benevolent" control that would imbalance relations.

Works Cited

"African Character Studied." *New York Times,* 10 January 1896, 2.

Birkett, Dea. *Spinsters Abroad; Victorian Lady Explorers.* Oxford and New York: Basil Blackwell, 1989.

Brantlinger, Patrick. *Rule of Darkness; British Literature and Imperialism, 1830–1914.* Ithaca: Cornell UP, 1988.

Brinton, Daniel G. "The Aims of Anthropology." *Popular Science Monthly* 48 (November 1895): 59–72.

Bullen, Frank T. "Some Memories of Mary Kingsley." *Mainly about People,* 16 June 1900, 570.

Clifford, James, and George E. Marcus, eds. *Writing Culture: The Poetics and Politics of Ethnography.* Berkeley: U of California P, 1986.

Dods, Marcus. "West African Studies." *Bookman* 15 (March 1899): 179–80.

Fling, J. E. "Mary Kingsley—A Reassessment." *Journal of African History* 4, no.1 (1963): 105–26.

Frank, Katherine. *A Voyager Out: The Life of Mary Kingsley.* Boston: Houghton Mifflin, 1986.

Geertz, Clifford. *Works and Lives: The Anthropologist as Author.* Stanford: Stanford UP, 1988.

Green, Alice Stopford. "Mary Kingsley." *Journal of the African Society* 1 (1901): 1–16.

Griffin, Susan. *Woman and Nature.* New York: Harper & Row, 1978.

Gwynn, Stephen. *The Life of Mary Kingsley.* London: Macmillan, 1932.

Harland, E. Sidney. "West African Studies." *Folk-Lore* 10 (1899): 447–50.

Heawood, Edward. "Some New Books on Africa." *Geographical Journal* 13 (April 1899): 412–22.

Helsinger, Elizabeth K., Robin Lauterbach Sheets, and William Veeder. *The Woman Question: Society and Literature in Britain and America, 1837–1883.* 3 vols. New York: Garland, 1983.

Kemp, Dennis. "The Late Miss M.H. Kingsley." *London Quarterly Review* 94 (1900): 137–52.

Kingsley, George. *Notes on Sport and Travel, with a Memoir by His Daughter, Mary H. Kingsley.* London: Macmillan, 1900.

Kingsley, Mary H. "In the Days of My Youth; Chapter of Autobiography." *Mainly about People,* 20 May 1899, 468–69.

Kingsley, Mary H. "A Lecture on West Africa." *Cheltenham Ladies' College Magazine* 38 (Autumn 1898): 264–80.

Kingsley, Mary H. Letters to George Macmillan. Macmillan Papers. Correspondence. Manuscript Collection. British Library, London.

Kingsley, Mary H. Letters to Professor and Mrs. E. B. Tylor. Photocopies from originals in the possession of D. J. Holt. Manuscript Collection. Rhodes House Library, Oxford.

Kingsley, Mary H. "The Negro Future." *Spectator* 75 (28 December 1895): 930–31.

Kingsley, Mary H. *Travels in West Africa, Congo Français, Corisco and Cameroons.* London: Macmillan, 1897.

Kingsley, Mary H. *West African Studies.* London: Macmillan, 1899.

Kolodny, Annette. *The Lay of the Land: Metaphor as Experience and History in American Life and Letters.* Chapel Hill: U of North Carolina P, 1975.

"Lady Traveller in West Africa, A." *Illustrated London News* 108 (4 January 1896): 19.

Libbey, William. "Scientific Literature: Travels in West Africa." *Science*, n.s. 6, no. 139 (27 August 1897): 325–26.

Lyall, Alfred. "Origins and Interpretations of Primitive Religions." *Edinburgh Review* 186 (July 1897): 213–44.

Markham, Clements R. *The Fifty Years' Work of the Royal Geographical Society.* London: John Murray, 1881.

Middleton, Dorothy. *Victorian Lady Travellers.* Chicago: Academy Chicago, 1982.

Mill, Hugh Robert. *The Record of the Royal Geographical Society, 1830–1930.* London: Royal Geographical Society, 1930.

Mills, Sara. *Discourses of Difference: An Analysis of Women's Travel Writing and Colonialism.* London: Routledge, 1991.

"Miss Kingsley's Travels." *Times,* 2 December 1895, 6.

"Miss Kingsley's Travels in West Africa." *Geographical Journal* 7 (1896): 95–96.

"Miss Kingsley's Travels in West Africa." *Nature* 55 (4 March 1897): 416–17.

"Miss Mary Kingsley." *Times,* 6 June 1900, 8.

Moore, Henrietta L. *Feminism and Anthropology.* Minneapolis: U of Minnesota P, 1988.

"Negro Capacity—A Suggestion." *Spectator* 75 (28 December 1895): 927–28.

"Notes on Books." *Illustrated London News* 110 (6 February 1897): 185.

Nworah, Kenneth Dike. "The Liverpool 'Sect' and British West African Policy, 1895–1915." *Journal of the Society of African Affairs* 70 (July 1971): 222–35.

"Our Booking-Office." *Punch* 112 (20 February 1897): 88.

Pakenham, Thomas. *The Scramble for Africa: White Man's Conquest of the Dark Continent from 1876 to 1912.* New York: Avon Books, 1991.

Pratt, Mary Louise. *Imperial Eyes: Travel Writing and Transculturation.* London and New York: Routledge, 1992.

Robinson, Ronald, and John Gallagher with Alice Denny. *Africa and the Victorians.* New York: St. Martin's, 1961.

Said, Edward W. *Orientalism.* New York: Vintage Books, 1979.

Showalter, Elaine. *Sexual Anarchy: Gender and Culture at the Fin-de-Siècle.* New York: Viking Penguin, 1990.

Smith, Lucy Toulmin, and Mrs. Humphrey [sic] Ward. *Folk-Lore* 11 (1900):348–50.

Stanley, Hiram M. "An English Woman in West Africa." *Dial* 22 (16 March 1897): 183–84.

Sternberger, Dolf. *Panorama of the Nineteenth Century.* Translated by Joachim Neugroschel, with an introduction by Erich Heller. New York: Urizen Books, 1977.

Stevenson, Catherine. "Female Anger and African Politics: The Case of Two Victorian 'Lady Travellers.'" *Turn-of-the-Century Women* 2 (Summer 1985): 7–17.

Stevenson, Catherine. *Victorian Women Travel Writers in Africa.* Boston: G. K. Hall, 1982.

Stocking, George W., Jr. *Victorian Anthropology*. New York: Free P, 1987.

Strachey, J. St. Loe. "Miss Mary Kingsley." *Spectator* 84 (16 June 1900): 836.

Strachey, J. St. Loe. "West African Studies." *Spectator* 82 (4 February 1899): 169–71.

Townsend, Meredith. "The Negro Future." *Spectator* 75 (7 December 1895): 815–17.

"Travels in West Africa." *Folk-Lore* 8 (1897): 162–65.

"Travels in West Africa." *Nation* 64 (1 April 1897): 249.

Walker, Bruce. "Travels in West Africa." *Athenaeum*, no. 3615 (6 February 1897): 173–76.

"West African Fetish." *Nature* 60 (13 July 1899): 243–44.

"West African Problems." *Church Quarterly* 49 (October 1899): 98–115.

"West African Studies." *Nation* 68 (23 March 1899): 228–29.

READING, REREADING, AND ANALYSIS

1. Choose an example from the essay that shows how Mary Kingsley challenged the accepted images of "the scientist" of her day. Write a paragraph summarizing the example you have chosen, identifying what people's expectations of scientists at the time were, and discussing how Kingsley differed from, challenged, or opposed them.

2. As a group or individual project, divide a sheet into two columns. Make a list in one column of all the potential disadvantages that Mary Kingsley had to overcome to be accepted by the general public as a "scientist." In the other column, list what she did to overcome each disadvantage or even to turn it into an advantage. What does the list tell you about how and why Kingsley went against the accepted expectations and practices of scientific protocols? What are the advantages of resisting "respectability" as she did?

RESPONDING THROUGH WRITING: BUILDING AN INTERPRETATION

3. Write a short paper analyzing the strategies that Mary Kingsley used in the effort to present herself as a "scientist" to the general public. To what extent did she seem to be deliberately challenging contemporary expectations of scientists? To what extent was she just seeking acceptance for herself and her methods? Use specific quotations and examples from the essay to help you support and explain your response.

4. Write a "travel narrative" of a recent trip you took. (The "trip" can be anything from a simple drive to the grocery store to a vaca-

tion in Europe.) Direct your narrative to an imaginary (or real) pen pal or friend who is unfamiliar with the culture, place, and people you are describing. Use as many of Mary Kingsley's techniques as possible to engage your reader's interest: Mix personal narrative with anthropological or "scientific" details; show your own perspective interacting with the perspective of the "people" you are studying; or use your gender, class, appearance, or interests to your best advantage in presenting yourself as a "scientist" of human life.

5. What do you suppose Early means when she writes that "Kingsley was clearly adept at performing herself, but also at performing science" (p. 134)? Why does Kingsley's self or her science need to be "performed"? What is Early arguing about the connection between Kingsley's work and the "spectacle" in the title of the essay?

GOING FURTHER: LEARNING FROM OTHER SOURCES

6. Use a reference database, such as Health Source Plus, that includes scientific publications, and try a keyword search using "fish," "beetle," or some other topic that would have interested Mary Kingsley. From your list of results choose one article that seems to be intended for the general public and one that seems intended for a more specialized scientific community. What are some of the clues that help you make that distinction? Bring your two articles and your notes on the differences to class.

7. See what you can find out about Mary Kingsley through an Internet search search using Google or Yahoo. Has her credibility or influence increased or grown in any way? Is she still of interest to people? Are there accounts of her that differ in any significant ways from Early's? Look closely into at least one website that mentions Early. How do the authors write about her?

APPLYING WHAT YOU'VE LEARNED

8. Write an essay comparing Kingsley's methods of "popularizing science" with those of Michio Kaku or Sherry Turkle. To what extent does Kaku or Turkle seem to adopt Kingsley's use of "racy" topics, her mixing of personal narrative with scientific data, or her interest in seeing "things worth seeing"? Does Kaku or Turkle ever seem to "make a theory first and then go hunting traveller's tales for facts to support the same" (p. 138)? Your essay should explore the relationship between science and writing. How can writing serve the goals of science?

9. Maya Lin is the young sculptor who designed the Vietnam Veterans Memorial in Washington D.C. Consider Lin's case, as Marita Sturken tells it, through the "lens" that Early has set up in describing Kingsley's travails. How does Kingsley's experience as an unexpected and, by some, unwanted success provide a model for Lin's experience? In both cases, how much of the controversy had to do with gender? Why might these women accept (and even in important ways encourage) that controversy?

10. Write an essay using Annie Dillard's ideas about "seeing" to analyze Mary Kingsley's methods as described by Early. Does Kingsley approach seeing primarily as "analyzing and prying" or as "letting go (Dillard, p. 122)? What would Dillard think about Kingsley's "insistence on learning to see the unfamiliar and on learning to see the familiar as unfamiliar" (p. 136)? Feel free to draw on your own knowledge and experience of "learning to see the unfamiliar" in writing this essay, but work with specific quotations and examples from Dillard and Kingsley to make your points as well.

RALPH ELLISON

Ralph Ellison (1914–1994) was a novelist and critic who began his career in 1938 as a writer and researcher for the Federal Writers' Project in New York City. His experiences as a young black man from Oklahoma encountering the politics and prejudices of the supposedly "free" North were the foundation for his best-known work, the 1952 novel *Invisible Man.* Similarly, Ellison's study of music at the Tuskegee Institute in Alabama informs "The Little Man at Chehaw Station," the first essay in his collection *Going to the Territory* (1986).

> **To learn more about Ralph Ellison, surf his webliography at <http://www. centerx. gseis.ucla.edu/weblio/ellison.html>.**

WHAT DO YOU KNOW? WHAT DO YOU EXPECT TO DISCOVER?

Before reading the essay, take a moment to consider the following questions.

1. What topics does Ellison's biography suggest he is interested in? What do you know about those topics? Knowledge can come from personal experience, stories you've heard, other classes you've taken, or other reading you've done.

2. Use an Internet search engine such as Google to find more information about Ellison and to learn about the location of Chehaw Station.

3. In his essay, Ellison talks about American identity. One metaphor he discusses is the image of America as a "melting pot." What does the metaphor mean to you, and what alternative metaphors for American cultural identity come to mind and why?

❧

The Little Man at Chehaw Station

It was at Tuskegee Institute during the mid-1930s that I was made aware of the little man behind the stove. At the time I was a trumpeter majoring in music, and had aspirations of becoming a classical composer. As such, shortly before the little man came to my attention, I had outraged the faculty members who judged my monthly student's recital by substituting a certain skill of lips and fingers for the intelligent and artistic structuring of emotion that was demanded in performing the music assigned to me. Afterward, still dressed in my hired tuxedo, my ears burning from the harsh negatives of their criticism, I had sought solace in the basement studio of Hazel Harrison, a highly respected concert pianist and teacher. Miss Harrison had been one of Ferruccio Busoni's prize pupils, had lived (until the rise of Hitler had driven her back to a U.S.A. that was not yet ready to recognize her talents) in Busoni's home in Berlin, and was a friend of such masters as Egon Petri, Percy Grainger and Sergei Prokofiev. It was not the first time that I had appealed to Miss Harrison's generosity of spirit, but today her reaction to my rather adolescent complaint was less than sympathetic.

"But, baby," she said, "in this country you must always prepare yourself to play your very best wherever you are, and on all occasions."

"But everybody tells you that," I said.

"Yes," she said, "but there's more to it than you're usually told. Of course you've always been taught to *do* your best, *look* your best, *be* your best. You've been told such things all your life. But now you're becoming a musician, an artist, and when it comes to performing the classics in this country, there's something more involved." Watching me closely, she paused. "Are you ready to listen?"

"Yes, ma'am."

"All right," she said, you must *always* play your best, even if it's only in the waiting room at Chehaw Station, because in this country there'll always be a little man hidden behind the stove."

"A *what?*"

She nodded. "That's right," she said. "There'll always be the little man whom you don't expect, and he'll know the *music,* and the *tradition,* and the standards of *musicianship* required for whatever you set out to perform!"

Speechless, I stared at her. After the working-over I'd just received from the faculty, I was in no mood for joking. But no, Miss Harrison's face was quite serious. So what did she mean? Chehaw Station was a lonely whistle-stop where swift north- or southbound trains paused with haughty impatience to drop off or take on passengers; the point where, on homecoming weekends, special coaches crowded with festive visitors were cut loose, coupled to a waiting switch engine, and hauled to Tuskegee's railroad siding. I knew it well, and as I stood beside Miss Harrison's piano, visualizing the station, I told myself, *She has got to be kidding!*

For in my view, the atmosphere of Chehaw's claustrophobic little waiting room was enough to discourage even a blind street musician from picking out blues on his guitar, no matter how tedious his wait for a train. Biased toward disaster by bruised feelings, my imagination pictured the vibrations set in motion by the winding of a trumpet within that drab, utilitarian structure: first shattering, then bringing its walls "a-tumbling down"—like Jericho's at the sounding of Joshua's priest-blown ram horns.

True, Tuskegee possessed a rich musical tradition, both classical and folk, and many music lovers and musicians lived or moved through its environs, but—and my regard for Miss Harrison notwithstanding—Chehaw Station was the last place in the area where I would expect to encounter a connoisseur lying in wait to pounce upon some rash, unsuspecting musician. Sure, a connoisseur might hear the haunting, blues-echoing, train-whistle rhapsodies blared by fast express trains as they thundered past, but the classics? Not a chance!

So as Miss Harrison watched to see the effect of her words, I said with a shrug, "Yes, ma'am."

She smiled, her prominent eyes a-twinkle. "I hope so," she said. "But if you don't just now, you will by the time you become an artist. So remember the little man behind the stove."

With that, seating herself at her piano, she began thumbing through a sheaf of scores, a signal that our discussion was ended.

So, I thought, *you ask for sympathy and you get a riddle.* I would have felt better if she had said, "Sorry, baby, I know how you feel, but after all, I was *there,* I *heard* you, and you treated your audience as though you were some kind of confidence man with a horn. So forget it, because I will not violate my own standards by condoning sterile musicianship." Some such reply, by reaffirming the "sacred principles" of art to which we were both committed, would have done much to supply the emotional catharsis for which I was appealing. By refusing, she forced me to accept full responsibility and thus learn from my offense. The condition of artistic communication is, as the saying goes, hard but fair.

But although disappointed and puzzled by Miss Harrison's sibylline response, I respected her artistry and experience too highly to dismiss it. Besides, something about her warning of a cultivated taste that asserted its authority out of obscurity sounded faintly familiar. Hadn't I once worked for an eccentric millionaire who prowled the halls and ballrooms of his fine hotel looking like a derelict who had wandered in off the street? Yes! And woe unto the busboy or waiter, hallman or maid—or anyone else—caught debasing the standards of that old man's house. For then, lashing out with the abruptness of reality shattering the contrived façade of a practical joke, the apparent beggar revealed himself as an extremely irate and exacting host of taste.

Thus, as I leaned into the curve of Miss Harrison's Steinway and listened to an interpretation of a Liszt rhapsody (during which she carried on an enthusiastic, stylistic analysis of passages that Busoni himself had marked for expressional subtlety), the little man of Chehaw Station fixed himself in my memory. And so vividly that

today he not only continues to engage my mind, but often material-
izes when I least expect him.

As, for instance, when I'm brooding over some problem of literary criticism—like, say, the rhetoric of American fiction. Indeed, the
little stove warmer has come to symbolize nothing less than the
enigma of aesthetic communication in American democracy. I especially associate him with the metamorphic character of the general
American audience, and with the unrecognized and unassimilated elements of its taste. For me he represents that unknown quality which
renders the American audience far more than a receptive instrument
that may be dominated through a skillful exercise of the sheerly
"rhetorical" elements—the flash and filigree—of the artist's craft.
While that audience is eager to be transported, astounded, thrilled, it
counters the artist's manipulation of forms with an attitude of antagonistic cooperation, acting, for better or worse, as both collaborator
and judge. Like a strange orchestra upon which a guest conductor
would impose his artistic vision, it must be exhorted, persuaded, even
wooed, as the price of its applause. It must be appealed to on the basis of what it assumes to be truth as a means of inducting it into new
dimensions of artistic truth. By playing artfully upon the audience's
sense of experience and form, the artist seeks to shape its emotions
and perceptions to his vision, while it, in turn, simultaneously coop-
erates and resists, says yes and says no in an it-takes-two-to-tango
binary response to his effort. As representative of the American audience writ small, the little man draws upon the uncodified *Americanness* of his experience, whether of life or of art, as he engages in a
silent dialogue with the artist's exposition of forms, offering or rejecting the work of art on the basis of what he feels to be its affirmation
or distortion of American experience.

Perhaps if they were fully aware of his incongruous existence, the
little man's neighbors would reject him as a source of confusion, a
threat to social order, and a reminder of the unfinished details of this
powerful nation. But out of a stubborn individualism born of his democratic origins, he insists upon the cultural necessity of his role, and
argues that if he didn't exist, he would have to be invented. If he were
not already manifest in the flesh, he would still exist and function as
an idea and ideal because—like such character traits as individualism,
restlessness, self-reliance, love of the new, and so on—he is a linguistic product of the American scene and language, and a manifestation
of the idealistic action of the American word as it goads its users toward a perfection of our revolutionary ideals.

For the artist, a lightning rod attracting unexpected insights and
a warning against stale preconceptions, the man behind Chehaw's
stove also serves as a metaphor for those individuals we sometimes
meet whose refinement of sensibility is inadequately explained by
family background, formal education or social status. These individu-

als seem to have been sensitized by some obscure force that issues undetected from the chromatic scale of American social hierarchy: a force that throws off strange, ultrasonic ultrasemi-semitones that create within those attuned to its vibrations a mysterious enrichment of personality. In this, heredity doubtless plays an important role, but whatever that role may be, it would appear that culturally and environmentally such individuals are products of errant but sympathetic vibrations set up by the tension between America's social mobility, its universal education, and its relative freedom of cultural information. Characterized by a much broader "random accessibility" than class and economic restrictions would appear to allow, this cultural information includes many of the finest products of the arts and intellect— products that are so abundantly available in the form of books, graphics, recordings, and pictorial reproductions as to escape sustained attempts at critical evaluation. Just how these characteristics operate in concert involves the mysterious interaction between environment and personality, instinct and culture. But the frequency and wide dispersal of individuals who reveal the effects of this mysterious configuration of forces endows each American audience, whether of musician, poet, or plastic artist, with a special mystery of its own.

I say "mystery," but perhaps the phenomenon is simply a product of our neglect of serious cultural introspection, our failure to conceive of our fractured, vernacular-weighted culture as an intricate whole. And since there is no reliable sociology of the dispersal of ideas, styles, or tastes in this turbulent American society, it is possible that, personal origins aside, the cultural circumstances here described offer the intellectually adventurous individual what might be termed a broad "social mobility of intellect and taste"—plus an incalculable scale of possibilities for self-creation. While the force that seems to have sensitized those who share the little man of Chehaw Station's unaccountable knowingness—call it a climate of free-floating sensibility—appears to be a random effect generated by a society in which certain assertions of personality, formerly the prerogative of high social rank, have become the privilege of the anonymous and the lowly.

If this be true, the matter of the artist's ability to identify the mixed background and general character of his audience can be more problematical than might be assumed. In the field of literature it presents a problem of rhetoric, a question of how to fashion strategies of communication that will bridge the many divisions of background and taste which any representative American audience embodies. To the extent that American literature is both an art of discovery and an artistic agency for creating a consciousness of cultural identity, it is of such crucial importance as to demand of the artist not only an eclectic resourcefulness of skill, but an act of democratic faith. In this light, the American artist will do his best not only because of his dedication to his form and craft, but because he realizes that despite an inevitable unevenness of composition, the chances are that any American audience will conceal at least *one* individual whose knowledge and taste will complement or surpass his own. This (to paraphrase Miss Harrison) is because even the most homogeneous audiences are culturally mixed and embody, in their relative anonymity, the mystery of American cultural identity.

This identity—tentative, controversial, constantly changing—is confusing to artist and audience alike. To the audience, because it is itself of mixed background, and seldom fully conscious of the cultural (or even political) implications of its own wide democratic range. To the artist, because in the broadest thrust of his effort he directs his finest effects to an abstract (and thus ideal) refinement of sensibility which, because it is not the exclusive property of a highly visible elite, is difficult to pinpoint. As one who operates within the historical frame of his given art, the artist may direct himself to those who are conscious of the most advanced state of his art: his artistic peers. But if his work has social impact, which is one gauge of its success as symbolic communication, it will reach into unpredictable areas. Many of us, by the way, read our first Hemingway, Fitzgerald, Mann in barbershops, and heard our first opera on phonographs. Thus, the ideal level of sensibility to which the American artist would address himself tends to transcend the lines of class, religion, region, and race—floating, as it were, free in the crowd. There, like the memory registers of certain computer systems, it is simultaneously accessible at any point in American society. Such are the circumstances that render the little man at Chehaw Station not only possible but inevitable.

But who, then, *is* this little man of Miss Harrison's riddle? From behind what unlikely mask does he render his judgments? And by what magic of art can his most receptive attention, his grudging admiration, be excited? No idle questions these; like Shakespeare's Hamlet, the little man has his pride and complexity. He values his personal uniqueness, cherishes his privacy, and clings to that tricky democratic anonymity which makes locating him an unending challenge. Hamlet masked himself with madness; the little man plays mute. Drawn to the brightness of bright lights, he cloaks himself in invisibility—perhaps because in the shadow of his anonymity he can be both the vernacular cat who looks at (and listens to) the tradition-bound or fad-struck king *and* the little boy who sees clearly the artist-emperor's pretentious nakedness. García Lorca writes of a singer who presented an audience of *cante hondo* lovers with a voice and restraint of passion better suited to a recital of *bel canto*. "Hurray," responded a deadpan Spanish cousin of the ghost of Chehaw Station, "for the school of Paris!"

Which is to say that having been randomly exposed to diverse artistic conventions, the little man has learned to detect the true transcendent ambience created by successful art from chic shinola. "Form should fit function," says he, "and style theme. Just as punishment should fit crime—which it seldom does nowadays—or as a well-made shoe the foot." Something of an autodidact, he has his own hierarchal ranking of human values, both native American and universal. And along with these, his own range of pieties—filial, sacred, racial—which constitute, in effect, the rhetorical "stops" through which his sensibilities are made responsive to artistic structurings of symbolic form.

Connoisseur, critic, trickster, the little man is also a day-coach, cabin-class traveler, but the timing of his arrivals and departures is uncertain. Sometimes he's there, sometimes he's here. Being quintessentially American, he enjoys the joke, the confounding of hierarchal expectations fostered by his mask: that cultural incongruity through which he, like Brer Rabbit, is able to convert even the most decorous of audiences into his own brier patch and temper the chilliest of classics to his own vernacular taste. Hence, as a practitioner of art, a form of symbolic communication that depends upon a calculated refinement of statement and affect, the American artist must also know the special qualities of that second instrument: his native audience; an audience upon which—arousing, frustrating, and fulfilling its expectations to the conventionalized contours of symbolic action—he is called upon to play as a pianist upon a piano. But here a special, most American problem arises. Thanks to the presence of the little man, this second instrument can be most unstable in its tuning, and downright ornery in its responses. In approaching it, the artist may, if he will, play fast and loose with modes and traditions, techniques and styles, but only at his peril does he treat an American audience as though it were as easily manipulated as a jukebox.

Reject the little man in the name of purity or as one who aspires beyond his social station or cultural capacity—fine! But it is worth remembering that one of the implicitly creative functions of art in the U.S.A. (and certainly of narrative art) is the defining and correlating of diverse American experiences by bringing previously unknown patterns, details and emotions into view along with those that are generally recognized. Here one of the highest awards of art is the achievement of that electrifying and creative collaboration between the work of art and its audience that occurs when, through the unifying force of its vision and its power to give meaningful focus to apparently unrelated emotions and experiences, art becomes simultaneously definitive of specific and universal truths.

In this country, the artist is free to choose, but cannot limit, his audience. He may ignore the unknown or unplaced sector of the public, but the mystifications of snobbery are of no avail against the little man's art hunger. Having arrived at his interest in art through familiar but uncharted channels, he disdains its use either as a form of so-

cial climbing or of social exclusion. Democratically innocent of hierarchal striving, he takes his classics as he takes his tall tales or jazz:
without frills. But while self-effacing, he is nevertheless given to a democratic touchiness, and is suspicious of all easy assumptions of superiority based upon appearances. When fretted by an obtuse artistic
hand, he can be quite irritable, and what frets him utterly is any attitude that offends his quite human pieties by ignorance or disregard
for his existence.

And yet the little man feels no urge to impose censorship upon the
artist. Possessing an American-vernacular receptivity to change, a
healthy delight in creative attempts at formalizing irreverence, and a
Yankee trader's respect for the experimental, he is repelled by works of
art that would strip human experience, especially American experience,
of its wonder and stubborn complexity. Not that he demands that his
own shadowy image be dragged into each and every artistic effort; that
would make a shambles of art's necessary illusion by violating the social reality in which he finds his being. It is enough that the artist
(above all, the novelist, dramatist, poet) forge images of American experience that resonate symbolically with his own ubiquitous presence.
In *The Great Gatsby*, Nick Carraway tells us, by way of outlining his
background's influence upon his moral judgments, that his family fortune was started by an Irish uncle who immigrated during the Civil
War, paid a substitute to fight in his stead, and went on to become
wealthy from war profiteering. Enough said! This takes hardly a paragraph, but the themes of history, wealth and immigration are struck
like so many notes on a chime. Assuming his Afro-American identity,
costume and mask, the little man behind the stove would make the subtle symbolic connections among Gatsby's ill-fated social climbing, the
wealthy wastrels whose manners and morals are the focus of the action,
the tragic ironies echoing so faintly from the Civil War (that seedbed of
so many Northern fortunes), and his own social condition; among the
principles of democracy that form the ground upon which the novel's
drama of manners and social hierarchy is enacted, and the cost to
Gatsby of confusing the promises of democracy with the terms governing their attainment. In so doing, the little underground-outsider would
incorporate the inside-outsider Gatz-Gatsby's experience into his own,
and his own into Gatsby's—a transposition that Gatsby would probably have abhorred but one that might have saved his life.

Or again, the little man, by imposing collaboratively his own vision of American experience upon that of the author, would extend
the novel's truth to levels below the threshold of that frustrating and
illusory social mobility which forms the core of Gatsby's anguish. Responding out of a knowledge of the manner in which the mystique of
wealth is intertwined with the American mysteries of class and color,
he would aid the author in achieving the more complex vision of
American experience that was implicit in his material. As a citizen,

the little man endures with a certain grace the social restrictions that limit his own social mobility, but *as a reader* he demands that the relationship between his own condition and that of those more highly placed be recognized. He senses that American experience is of a whole, and he wants the interconnections revealed. This not out of a penchant for protest, nor out of petulant vanity, but because he sees his own condition as an inseparable part of a larger truth in which the high and the lowly, the known and the unrecognized, the comic and the tragic are woven into the American skein. Having been attuned at Chehaw Station to the clangor of diverse bell sounds, he asks not for *whom* the bell tolls, only that it be struck artfully and with that fullness of resonance which warns all men of man's fate. At his best he does not ask for scapegoats, but for the hero as witness. How ironic it was that in the world of *The Great Gatsby* the witness who could have identified the driver of the death car that led to Gatsby's murder was a black man whose ability to communicate (and communication implies moral judgment) was of no more consequence to the action than that of an ox that might have observed Icarus's sad plunge into the sea. (This, by the way, is not intended as a criticism of Fitzgerald, but only to suggest some of the problems and possibilities of artistic communication in the U.S.A.) In this light, the little man is a cautionary figure who challenges the artist to reach out for new heights of expressiveness. If we ignore his possible presence, violence might well be done to that ideal of cultivated democratic sensibility which was the goal of the likes of Emerson and Whitman, and for which the man at Chehaw Station is a metaphor. Respect his presence and even the most avant-garde art may become an agency for raising the general level of artistic taste. The work of art is, after all, an act of faith in our ability to communicate symbolically.

But why would Hazel Harrison associate her humble metaphor for the diffusion of democratic sensibility with a mere whistle-stop? Today I would guess that it was because Chehaw Station functioned as a point of arrival and departure for people representing a wide diversity of tastes and styles of living. Philanthropists, businessmen, sharecroppers, students and artistic types passed through its doors. But the same, in a more exalted fashion, is true of Carnegie Hall and the Metropolitan Museum; all three structures are meeting places for motley mixtures of people. So while it might require a Melvillean imagination to reduce American society to the dimensions of either concert hall or railroad station, their common feature as gathering places, as juncture points for random assemblies of sensibilities, reminds us again that in this particular country even the most homogeneous gatherings of people are mixed and pluralistic. Perhaps the mystery of American cultural identity contained in such motley mixtures arises out of our persistent attempts to reduce our cultural diversity to an easily recognizable unity.

On the other hand, Americans tend to focus on the diverse parts of their culture (with which they can more easily identify), rather than on its complex and pluralistic wholeness. But perhaps they identify with the parts because the whole is greater, if not of a different quality, than its parts. This difference, that new and problematic quality—call it our "Americanness"—creates out of its incongruity an uneasiness within us, because it is a constant reminder that American democracy is not only a political collectivity of individuals, but culturally a collectivity of styles, tastes and traditions.

In this lies the source of many of our problems, especially those centering upon American identity. In relationship to the cultural whole, we are, all of us—white or black, native-born or immigrant—members of minority groups. Beset by feelings of isolation because of the fluid, pluralistic turbulence of the democratic process, we cling desperately to our own familiar fragment of the democratic rock, and from such fragments we confront our fellow Americans in that combat of civility, piety and tradition which is the drama of American social hierarchy. Holding desperately to our familiar turf, we engage in that ceaseless contention whose uneasily accepted but unrejectable purpose is the projection of an ever more encompassing and acceptable definition of our corporate identity as Americans. Usually this contest (our improvised moral equivalent for armed warfare) proceeds as a war of words, a clash of styles, or as rites of symbolic sacrifice in which cabalistic code words are used to designate victims consumed with an Aztec voracity for scapegoats. Indeed, so frequently does this conflict erupt into physical violence that one sometimes wonders if there is any other viable possibility for co-existing in so abstract and futuristic a nation as this.

The rock, the terrain upon which we struggle, is itself abstract, a terrain of ideas that, although man-made, exerts the compelling force of the ideal, of the sublime: ideas that draw their power from the Declaration of Independence, the Constitution, and the Bill of Rights. We stand, as we say, united in the name of these sacred principles. But indeed it is in the name of these same principles that we ceaselessly contend, affirming our ideals even as we do them violence.

For while we are but human and thus given to the fears and temptations of the flesh, we are dedicated to principles that are abstract, ideal, spiritual: principles that were conceived linguistically and committed to paper during that contention over political ideals and economic interests which was released and given focus during the period of our revolutionary break with traditional forms of society, principles that were enshrined—again linguistically—in the documents of state upon which this nation was founded. Actuated by passionate feats of revolutionary will which released that dynamic power for moralizing both man and nature, instinct and society, which is a property of linguistic forms of symbolic action, these principles—democracy, equality, individual freedom and universal justice—now move us as articles of faith. Holding them sacred, we act (or *fail* to act) in their names. And in the freewheeling fashion of words that are summoned up to name the ideal, they prod us ceaselessly toward the refinement and perfection of those formulations of policy and configurations of social forms of which they are the signs and symbols. As we strive to conduct social action in accordance with the ideals they evoke, they in turn insist upon being made flesh. Inspiriting our minds and bodies, they dance around in our bones, spurring us to make them ever more manifest in the structures and processes of ourselves and our society. As a nation, we exist in the communication of our principles, and we argue over their application and interpretation as over the rights of property or the exercise and sharing of authority. As elsewhere, they influence our expositions in the area of artistic form and are involved in our search for a system of aesthetics capable of projecting our corporate, pluralistic identity. They interrogate us endlessly as to who and what we are; they demand that we keep the democratic faith.

Words that evoke our principles are, according to Kenneth Burke, charismatic terms for transcendent order, for perfection. Being forms of symbolic action, they tend, through their nature as language, to sweep us in tow as they move by a process of linguistic negation toward the ideal. As a form of *symbolic* action, they operate by negating nature as a given and amoral condition, creating endless series of man-made or man-imagined positives. By so doing, they nudge us toward that state of human rectitude for which, ideally, we strive. In this way, Burke contends, man uses language to moralize both nature and himself. Thus, in this nation the word democracy possesses the aura of what Burke calls a "god-term," and all that we are and do exists in the magnitude of its intricate symbolism. It is the rock upon which we toil, and we thrive or wane in the communication of those symbols and processes set in motion in its name.

In our national beginnings, all redolent with Edenic promises, was the word *democratic,* and since we vowed in a war rite of blood and sacrifice to keep its commandments, we act in the name of a word made sacred. Yes, but since we are, as Burke holds, language-using, language-misusing animals—beings who are by nature vulnerable to both the negative *and* the positive promptings of language as symbolic action—we Americans are given to eating, regurgitating, and, alas, reeating even our most sacred words. It is as though they contain a substance that is crucial to our national existence but that, except in minute and infrequently ingested doses, we find extremely indigestible. Some would call this national habit of word-eating an exercise in the art of the impossible; others attribute it to the limitations imposed by the human condition. Still others would describe it as springing from the pathology of social hierarchy, a reaction to certain built-in conditions of our democracy that are capable of amelioration but impossible to cure. Whatever the case may be, it would seem that for many our cultural diversity is as indigestible as the concept of democracy in which it is grounded. For one thing, principles in action are enactments of ideals grounded in a vision of perfection that transcends the limitations of death and dying. By arousing in the believer a sense of the disrelation between the ideal and the actual, between the perfect word and the errant flesh, they partake of mystery. Here the most agonizing mystery sponsored by the democratic ideal is that of our unity-in-diversity, our oneness-in-manyness. Pragmatically we cooperate and communicate across this mystery, but the problem of identity that it poses often goads us to symbolic acts of disaffiliation. So we seek psychic security from within our inherited divisions of the corporate American culture while gazing out upon our fellows with a mixed attitude of fear, suspicion and yearning. We repress an underlying anxiety aroused by the awareness that we are representative not only of one but of several overlapping and constantly shifting social categories, and we stress our affiliation with that segment of the corporate culture which has emerged out of our parents' past—racial, cultural, religious—and which we assume, on the basis of such magical talismans as our mother's milk or father's beard, that we "know." Grounding our sense of identity in such primary and affect-charged symbols, we seek to avoid the mysteries and pathologies of the democratic process. But that process was designed to overcome the dominance of tradition by promoting an open society in which the individual could achieve his potential unhindered by his ties to the past. Here, theoretically, social categories are open, and the individual is not only considered capable of transforming himself, but is encouraged to do so. However, in undertaking such transformations he opts for that psychic uncertainty which is a condition of his achieving his potential, a state he yearns to avoid. So despite any self-assurance he might achieve in dealing with his familiars, he is nevertheless (and by the nature of his indefinite relationship to the fluid social hierarchy) a lonely individual who must find his own way within a crowd of other lonely individuals. Here the security offered by his familiar symbols of identity is equivocal. And an overdependence upon them as points of orientation leads him to become bemused, gazing backward at a swiftly receding—if not quasi-mythical—past, while stumbling headlong into a predescribed but unknown future.

So perhaps we shy from confronting our cultural wholeness because it offers no easily recognizable points of rest, no facile certainties as to who, what or where (culturally or historically) we are. Instead, the whole is always in cacophonic motion. Constantly changing its mode, it appears as a vortex of discordant ways of living and tastes, values and traditions, a whirlpool of odds and ends in which the past courses in uneasy juxtaposition with those bright, futuristic principles and promises to which we, as a nation, are politically committed. In our vaguely perceived here and now, even the sounds and symbols spun off by the clashing of group against group appear not only alarmingly off-key, but threatening to our inherited eyes, ears, and appetites. Thus in our intergroup familiarity there is a brooding strangeness, and in our underlying sense of alienation a poignant, although distrusted, sense of fraternity. Deep down, the American condition is a state of unease.

During the nineteenth century an attempt was made to impose a loose conceptual order upon the chaos of American society by viewing it as a melting pot. Today that metaphor is noisily rejected, vehemently disavowed. In fact, it has come under attack in the name of the newly fashionable code word "ethnicity," reminding us that in this country code words are linguistic agencies for the designation of sacrificial victims, and are circulated to sanction the abandonment of policies and the degrading of ideas. So today, before the glaring inequities, unfulfilled promises and rich possibilities of democracy, we hear heady evocations of European, African and Asian backgrounds accompanied by chants proclaiming the inviolability of ancestral blood. Today blood magic and blood thinking, never really dormant in American society, are rampant among us, often leading to brutal racial assaults in areas where these seldom occurred before. And while this goes on, the challenge of arriving at an adequate definition of American cultural identity goes unanswered. (What, by the way, is one to make of a white youngster who, with a transistor radio screaming a Stevie Wonder tune glued to his ear, shouts racial epithets at black youngsters trying to swim at a public beach—and this in the name of the ethnic sanctity of what has been declared a neighborhood turf?)

The proponents of ethnicity—ill concealing an underlying anxiety and given a bizarre bebopish stridency by the obviously American vernacular inspiration of the costumes and rituals ragged out to dramatize their claims to ethnic (and genetic) insularity—have helped give our streets and campuses a rowdy, All Fool's Day carnival atmosphere. In many ways, then, the call for a new social order based upon the glorification of ancestral blood and ethnic background acts as a call to cultural and aesthetic chaos. Yet while this latest farcical phase in the drama of American social hierarchy unfolds, the irrepressible movement of American culture toward the integration of its diverse elements continues, confounding the circumlocutions of its staunchest opponents.

In this regard I am reminded of a light-skinned, blue-eyed, Afro-American-featured individual who could have been taken for anything from a sun-tinged white Anglo-Saxon, an Egyptian, or a mixed-breed American Indian to a strayed member of certain tribes of Jews. This young man appeared one sunny Sunday afternoon on New York's Riverside Drive near 151st Street, where he disrupted the visual peace of the promenading throng by racing up in a shiny new blue Volkswagen Beetle decked out with a gleaming Rolls Royce radiator. As the flow of strollers came to an abrupt halt, this man of parts emerged from his carriage with something of that magical cornucopian combustion by which a dozen circus clowns are exploded from an even more miniaturized automobile. Looming as tall as a professional basketball center, he unfolded himself and stretched to his full imposing height.

Clad in handsome black riding boots and fawn-colored riding breeches of English tailoring, he took the curb wielding, with an ultra-pukka-sahib haughtiness, a leather riding crop. A dashy dashiki (as bright and as many-colored as the coat that initiated poor Joseph's troubles in biblical times) flowed from his broad shoulders down to the arrogant, military flare of his breeches-tops, while six feet six inches or so above his heels, a black homburg hat tilted at a jaunty angle floated majestically on the crest of his huge Afro-coiffed head.

As though all this were not enough to amaze, delight, or discombobulate his observers—or precipitate an international incident involving charges of a crass invasion of stylistic boundaries—this apparition proceeded to unlimber an expensive Japanese single-lens reflex camera, position it atop the ornamental masonry balustrade which girds Riverside Park in that area, and activate its self-timer. Then, with a ballet leap across the walk, he assumed a position beside his car. There he rested his elbow upon its top, smiled, and gave himself sharp movie director's commands as to desired poses, then began taking a series of self-portraits. This done, he placed the camera upon the hood of his Volkswagen and took another series of self-shots in which, manipulating a lengthy ebony cigarette holder, he posed himself in various fanciful attitudes against the not-too-distant background of the George Washington Bridge. All in all, he made a scene to haunt one's midnight dreams and one's noon repose.

Now, I can only speculate about what was going on in the elegant gentleman's mind, who he was, or what visual statement he intended to communicate. I only know that his carefully stylized movements (especially his "pimp-limp" walk) marked him as a native of the U.S.A., a home-boy bent upon projecting and recording with native verve something of his complex sense of cultural identity. Clearly he had his own style, but if—as has been repeatedly argued—the style is the man, who on earth was this fellow? Viewed from a rigid ethnocultural perspective, neither his features nor his car nor his dress was of a whole. Yet he conducted himself with an obvious pride of person and of property, inviting all and sundry to admire and wonder in response to himself as his own sign and symbol, his own work of art. He had gotten himself, as the Harlem saying goes, "together," and whatever sheerly ethnic identity was communicated by his costume depended upon the observer's ability to see order in an apparent cultural chaos. The man himself was hidden somewhere within, his complex identity concealed by his aesthetic gesturing. And his essence lay not in the somewhat comic clashing of styles, but in the mixture, the improvised form, the willful juxtaposition of modes.

Perhaps to the jaundiced eyes of an adversary of the melting-pot concept, the man would have appeared to be a militant black nationalist bent upon dramatizing his feelings of alienation—and he may have been. But most surely he was not an African or an Englishman. His Volks-Rolls-Royce might well have been loaded with Marxist tracts and Molotov cocktails, but his clashing of styles nevertheless sounded an integrative, vernacular note, an American compulsion to improvise upon the given. His garments were, literally and figuratively, of many colors and cultures, his racial identity interwoven of many strands. Whatever his politics, sources of income, hierarchal status and such, he revealed his essential "Americanness" in his free-wheeling assault upon traditional forms of the Western aesthetic. Whatever the identity he presumed to project, he was exercising an American freedom and was a product of the melting pot and the conscious or unconscious comedy it brews. Culturally he was an American joker. If his Afro and dashiki symbolized protest, his boots, camera, Volkswagen and homburg imposed certain qualifications upon that protest. In doing so, they played irreverently upon the symbolism of status, property and authority, and suggested new possibilities of perfection. More than expressing protest, these symbols ask the old, abiding American questions: Who am I? What about me?

Still, ignoring such questions (as they would ignore the little man of Chehaw Station), the opponents of the melting-pot concept utter their disavowals with an old-fashioned, camp-meeting fervor—solemnly, and with an air of divine revelation. Most amazingly, these attacks upon the melting pot are led by the descendants of peasants or slaves or inhabitants of European ghettos, people whose status as spokesmen is a product of that very melting of hierarchal barriers they now deny. With such an attitude, it is fortunate that they, too, are caught up in the society's built-in, democracy-prodded movement toward a perfection of self-definition. Hence such disavowals, despite their negative posture, have their positive content. And to the extent that they are negatives uttered in an attempt to create certain attitudes and conditions that their exponents conceive as positives, these disavowals are, in part, affirmations of the diverse and unique pasts out of which have emerged the many groups that this nation comprises. As such they might well contribute to a clarification of our pluralistic cultural identity, and are thus a step in the direction of creating a much-needed cultural introspection.

As of now, however, I see the denial of that goal of cultural integration for which the melting pot was an accented metaphor as the current form of an abiding American self-distrust. I see it as an effort to dismiss the mystery of American identity (our unity-within-diversity) with a gesture of democracy-weary resignation, as an attempt to dispel by sociological word-magic the turbulence of the present, and as a self-satisfied vote against that hope which is so crucial to our cultural and political fulfillment. For if such disavowals be viable, what about the little man behind the stove?

Ironically, the attacks on the melting-pot idea issue from those who have "made it." Having been reborn into a higher hierarchal status, they now view those who have *not* made it as threats to their newly achieved status, and therefore would change both the rules and the game plan. Thus they demonstrate anew the built-in opportunism of their characteristically American shortness of memory. But lest we ourselves forget, the melting-pot concept was never so simplistic or abstract as current arguments would have it. Americans of an earlier day, despite their booster extravagances, recognized the difference between the ideal and the practical, even as they clung desperately to, and sought to default upon, the responsibilities that went with achieving their democratic ideal. Their outlook was pragmatic, their way with culture vernacular, an eclectic mixing of modes. Having rejected the hierarchal ordering of traditional societies, they improvised their culture as they did their politics and institutions—touch and go, by ear and by eye—fitting new form to new function, new function to old form. Deep down they sensed that in the process of nation-building their *culture,* like their institutions, was always more "American" (that futuristic concept) than they could perceive—or even fully accept—it to be. Even the slaves, although thrust below the threshold of social hierarchy, were given a prominent place in our national iconography; their music, poetic imagery and choreography were grudgingly recognized as seminal sources of American art. In the process of creating (and re-creating or diverting) themselves, the melting-pot Americans brazenly violated their ideals. They kept slaves or battened on the products of slave labor. They exploited and abused those who arrived later than themselves, kinsmen and aliens alike. While paying lip service to their vaunted forms of justice, they betrayed, brutalized and scapegoated one another in the name of the Constitution, the Bill of Rights, and the Ten Commandments. But because of their fidelity to their parents' customs and their respect for the pieties of their traditions, if not for those of their fellows, none of the groups that made up the total culture ever really desired to lose its sense of its unique past, not even when that past lay clouded in slavery.

Instead, they wished to use the techniques, ways of life, and values developed within their respective backgrounds as sources of morale in that continuing process of antagonistic cooperation, and of adjusting the past to the present in the interest of the future, which was so necessary in building what they imagined as a more humane society. Indeed, during their most candid, self-accepting moments they saw themselves as living embodiments of the ancestral past, people who had seized the democracy-sponsored opportunity to have a second chance. As such, they saw themselves as the best guarantee that whatever was most desirable and salvageable from that past would be retained and brought to flower, free of hierarchal hindrances. The little man behind the stove would know from his own condition that the melting-pot concept was a conceit, but his forced awareness of American cultural pluralism would assure him that it was by no means the product of a con game contrived by the powerful. Here not even the powerful were so perceptive.

So our current disavowals are not only misdirected; they are productive of more social disorder, more crises of cultural and personal identity than they could possibly resolve. It is here, on the level of culture, that the diverse elements of our various backgrounds, our heterogeneous pasts, have indeed come together, "melted" and undergone metamorphosis. It is here, if we would but recognize it, that elements of the many available tastes, traditions, ways of life, and values that make up the total culture have been ceaselessly appropriated and made their own—consciously, unselfconsciously, or imperialistically—by groups and individuals to whose own backgrounds and traditions they are historically alien. Indeed, it was through this process of cultural appropriation (and misappropriation) that Englishmen, Europeans, Africans, and Asians *became* Americans.

The Pilgrims began by appropriating the agricultural, military, and meteorological lore of the Indians, including much of their terminology. The Africans, thrown together from numerous ravaged tribes, took up the English language and the biblical legends of the ancient Hebrews and were "Americanizing" themselves long before the American Revolution. They also had imposed upon them a goodly portion of European chromosomes, and thereby "inherited" both an immunity to certain European diseases and a complexity of bloodlines and physical characteristics that have much to do with the white American's reluctance to differentiate between race and culture, African and American, and are a major source of our general confusion over American identity. One of the many questions posed by the man on Riverside Drive is how one so "white" could be simply "black" without being impossibly simpleminded. Especially when his skin and facial bone structure ask, "Where went the blood of yesteryear?" There is no point in answering the question as did Villon, because the man's face was as Anglo and his hairstyle as Afro as his car's radiator and body were English and German.

Everyone played the appropriation game. The whites took over any elements of Afro-American culture that seemed useful: the imagery of folklore, ways of speaking, endurance of what appeared to be hopeless hardship, and singing and dancing—including the combination of Afro-American art forms that produced the first musical theater of national appeal: the minstrel show. And in improvising their rather tawdry and opportunistic version of a national mythology, the moviemakers—Christian and Jewish, Northerners and Southerners—ransacked and distorted for their own purposes the backgrounds and images of everyone, including the American Indians.

So, melting-pot disclaimers notwithstanding, Americans seem to have sensed intuitively that the possibility of enriching the individual self by such pragmatic and opportunitistic appropriations has constituted one of the most precious of their many freedoms. Having opted for the new, and being unable to create it out of thin air or from words inscribed on documents of state, they did what came naturally: they pressured the elements of the past and present into new amalgams. In lieu of a usable cultural tradition, there were always the cultural improvisations of the Afro-Americans, the immigrants, or design-gifted religious groups like the Shakers—all so close to eye and ear, hand and imagination. Considering that the newness achieved by Americans has often been a matter of adapting to function and a matter of naming, of designation, we are reminded of how greatly the "Americanness" of American culture has been a matter of Adamic wordplay—of trying, in the interest of a futuristic dream, to impose unity upon an experience that changes too rapidly for linguistic or political exactitude. In this effort we are often less interested in what we are than in projecting what we will be. But in our freewheeling appropriations of culture we appear to act on the assumption that as members of a "nation of nations," we are, by definition and by the processes of democratic cultural integration, the inheritors, creators and creations of a culture of cultures.

So perhaps the complex actuality of our cultural pluralism is perplexing because the diverse interacting elements that surround us, traditional and vernacular, not only elude accepted formulations, but take on a character that is something other than their various parts. Our old familiar pasts become, in juxtaposition with elements appropriated from other backgrounds, incongruously transformed, exerting an energy (or synergy) of a different order than that generated by their separate parts—and this with incalculable results. Nor should we forget the role played by objects and technology in the integration of our cultural styles, and in the regional and political unification of the nation. If we put the blues, bluegrass music, English folk songs, et cetera, together with Afro-American rhythms and gospel shouts, we have, God help us, first rock and now "funk," that most odoriferous of musical(?) styles. Still, such mixtures of cultural elements are capable of igniting exciting transformations of culture. Even more mysteriously (and here, perhaps, we have a further source of the little man of Chehaw Station's rich sensibility), they provide for exciting and most unexpected metamorphoses within the self-creating personality.

Frankly, many of the foregoing speculations have been arrived at over the years since I left Tuskegee. If I had been more mature or perceptive back when I first heard of the little man behind the stove, an object that lay atop Miss Harrison's piano would have been most enlightening. It was a signed Prokofiev manuscript that had been presented to her by the composer. Except for the signature, it looked like countless other manuscripts. Yet I suspect that to anyone who possessed a conventional notion of cultural and hierarchal order, its presence in such a setting would have been as incongruous as a Gutenberg Bible on the altar of a black sharecropper's church or a dashiki worn with a homburg hat. Still, there it was, an artifact of contemporary music, a folio whose signs and symbols resonated in that setting with the intricate harmonies of friendship, admiration and shared ideals through which it had found its way from Berlin to Tuskegee. Once there, and the arrangement of society beyond the campus notwithstanding, it spoke eloquently of the unstructured possibilities of culture in this pluralistic democracy. Yet despite its meticulous artistic form, in certain conventional minds its presence could arouse intimations of the irrational—of cultural, if not social, chaos.

Given the logic of a society ordered along racial lines, Miss Harrison's studio (or even the library) was simply off limits for such an artifact, certainly in its original form. But there it was, lying in wait to play havoc with conventional ideas of order, lending a wry reality to Malraux's observation that art is an assault upon logic. Through its presence, the manuscript had become an agency of cultural transformation and synthesis. By charging Miss Harrison's basement studio with the spirit of living personages, ideals and purposes from afar, it had transformed that modest room from a mere spot on a segregated Negro campus into an advanced outpost on the frontiers of contemporary music, thus adding an unexpected, if undetected, dimension to Alabama's cultural atmosphere. In my innocence I viewed the manuscript as a property of Miss Harrison's, a sign of her connection with gifted artists across the ocean. It spoke to me of possibility. But that it also endowed the scene—place, studio, campus—with a complex cultural ambiguity escaped my conscious mind. Though aware of certain details of the total scene, I was unattuned to the context in which they sounded, the cultural unity-within-diversity that the combination of details made manifest. Perhaps we are able to see only that which we are prepared to see, and in our culture the cost of insight is an uncertainty that threatens our already unstable sense of order and requires a constant questioning of accepted assumptions.

Had I questioned Miss Harrison as to how the racial identity of her little Chehaw man squared with the culture she credited to him, she might well have replied:

"Look, baby, the society beyond this campus is constantly trying to confuse you about the relationship between culture and race. Well, if you ask me, artistic talent might have something to do with race, but you do *not* inherit culture and artistic skill through your genes. No, sir. These come as a result of personal conquest, of the individual's applying himself to that art, that music—whether jazz, classical, or folk—which helps him to realize and complete himself. And that's true *wherever* the music or art of his choice originates."

Or in the words of André Malraux (whom I was to discover a year or two later), she might have told me that music is important as an artistic form of symbolic action "because its function is to let men escape from their human condition, not by means of an evasion, but through a possession, [for] art is a way of possessing destiny." And that therefore, even at racially segregated Tuskegee (as witnessed by, among countless other details, the library and Miss Harrison's Prokofiev manuscript), one's "cultural heritage is the totality, not of works that men must respect [or that are used to enhance the mystifications that support an elite], but those that can help them live." Entering into a dialogue with Malraux, she might have added on a more specifically American note: "Yes, and most important, you must remember that in this country things are always all shook up, so that people are constantly moving around and rubbing off on one another culturally. Nor should you forget that here all things—institutions, individuals and roles—offer more than the function assigned them, because beyond their intended function they provide forms of education and criticism. They challenge, they ask questions, they offer suggestive answers to those who would pause and probe their mystery. Most of all, remember that it is not only the images of art or the sound of music that pass through walls to give pleasure and inspiration; it is in the very *spirit* of art to be defiant of categories and obstacles. They are, as transcendent forms of symbolic expression, agencies of human freedom."

Three years later, having abandoned my hope of becoming a musician, I had just about forgotten Miss Harrison's mythical little man behind the stove. Then, in faraway New York, concrete evidence of his actual existence arose and blasted me like the heat from an internally combusted ton of coal.

As a member of the Federal Writers' Project, I was spending a clammy late-fall afternoon of freedom circulating a petition in support of some now long-forgotten social issue that I regarded as indispensable to the public good. I found myself inside a tenement building in San Juan Hill, a Negro district that disappeared with the coming of Lincoln Center. Starting on the top floor of the building, I had collected an acceptable number of signatures, and having descended from the ground floor to the basement level, was moving along the dimly lit hallway toward a door through which I could hear loud voices. They were male Afro-American voices, raised in violent argument. The language was profane, the style of speech a Southern idiomatic vernacular such as was spoken by formally uneducated Afro-American workingmen. Reaching the door, I paused, sounding out the lay of the land before knocking to present my petition.

But my delay led to indecision. Not, however, because of the loud, unmistakable anger sounding within; being myself a slum dweller, I knew that voices in slums are often raised in anger, but that the *rhetoric* of anger, itself cathartic, is not necessarily a prelude to physical violence. Rather, it is frequently a form of symbolic action, a verbal equivalent of fisticuffs. No, I hesitated because I realized that behind the door a mystery was unfolding. A mystery so incongruous, outrageous, and surreal that it struck me as a threat to my sense of rational order. It was as though a bizarre practical joke had been staged and its perpetrators were waiting for me, its designated but unknowing scapegoat, to arrive: a joke designed to assault my knowledge of American culture and its hierarchal dispersal. At the very least, it appeared that my pride in my knowledge of my own people was under attack.

For the angry voices behind the door were proclaiming an intimate familiarity with a subject of which, by all the logic of their linguistically projected social status, they should have been oblivious. The subject of their contention confounded all my assumptions regarding the correlation between educational levels, class, race and the possession of conscious culture. Impossible as it seemed, these foul-mouthed black workingmen were locked in verbal combat over which of two celebrated Metropolitan Opera divas was the superior soprano!

I myself attended the opera only when I could raise the funds, and I knew full well that opera-going was far from the usual cultural pursuit of men identified with the linguistic style of such voices. Yet, confounding such facile logic, they were voicing (and loudly) a familiarity with the Met far greater than my own. In their graphic, irreverent, and vehement criticism they were describing not only the two sopranos' acting abilities, but were ridiculing the gestures with which each gave animation to her roles, and they shouted strong opinions as to the ranges of the divas' vocal equipment. Thus, with such a distortion of perspective being imposed upon me, I was challenged either to solve the mystery of their knowledge by entering into their midst or to leave the building with my sense of logic reduced forever to a level of college-trained absurdity.

So challenged, I knocked. I knocked out of curiosity, I knocked out of outrage. I knocked in fear and trembling. I knocked in anticipation of whatever insights—malicious or transcendent, I no longer cared which—I would discover beyond the door.

For a moment there was an abrupt and portentous silence; then came the sound of chair legs thumping dully upon the floor, followed by further silence. I knocked again, loudly, with an authority fired by an impatient and anxious urgency.

Again silence, until a gravel voice boomed an annoyed "Come in!"

Opening the door with an unsteady hand, I looked inside, and was even less prepared for the scene that met my eyes than for the content of their loudmouthed contention.

In a small, rank-smelling, lamp-lit room, four huge black men sat sprawled around a circular dining-room table, looking toward me with undisguised hostility. The sooty-chimneyed lamp glowed in the center of the bare oak table, casting its yellow light upon four water tumblers and a half-empty pint of whiskey. As the men straightened in their chairs I became aware of a fireplace with a coal fire glowing in its grate, and leaning against the ornate marble facing of its mantelpiece, I saw four enormous coal scoops.

"All right," one of the men said, rising to his feet. "What the hell can we do for *you?*"

"And we ain't buying nothing, buddy," one of the seated men added, his palm slapping the table.

Closing the door, I moved forward, holding my petition like a flag of truce before me, noting that the men wore faded blue overalls and jumper jackets, and becoming aware that while all were of dark complexion, their blackness was accentuated in the dim lamplight by the dust and grime of their profession.

"Come on, man, speak up," the man who had arisen said. "We ain't got all day."

"I'm sorry to interrupt," I said, "but I thought you might be interested in supporting my petition," and began hurriedly to explain.

"Say," one of the men said, "you look like one of them relief investigators. You're not out to jive us, are you?"

"Oh, no, sir," I said. "I happen to work on the Writers' Project . . ."

The standing man leaned toward me. "You on the Writers' Project?" he said, looking me up and down.

"That's right," I said. "I'm a writer."

"Now is that right?" he said. "How long you been writing?"

I hesitated. "About a year," I said.

He grinned, looking at the others. "Y'all hear that? Ol' Homeboy here has done up and jumped on the *gravy* train! Now that's pretty good. Pretty damn good! So what did you do before that?" he said.

"I studied music," I said, "at Tuskegee."

"Hey, now!" the standing man said. "They got a damn good choir down there. Y'all remember back when they opened Radio City? They had that fellow William L. Dawson for a director. Son, let's see that paper."

Relieved, I handed him the petition, watching him stretch it between his hardened hands. After a moment of soundlessly mouthing the words of its appeal, he gave me a skeptical look and turned to the others.

"What the hell," he said, "signing this piece of paper won't do no good, but since Home here's a musician, it won't do us no harm to help him out. Let's go along with him."

Fishing a blunt-pointed pencil from the bib of his overalls, he wrote his name and passed the petition to his friends, who followed suit.

This took some time, and as I watched the petition move from hand to hand, I could barely contain myself or control my need to unravel the mystery that had now become far more important than just getting their signatures on my petition.

"There you go," the last one said, extending the petition toward me. "Having our names on there don't mean a thing, but you got em."

"Thank you," I said. "Thank you very much."

They watched me with amused eyes, expecting me to leave, but, clearing my throat nervously, I stood in my tracks, too intrigued to leave and suddenly too embarrassed to ask my question.

"So what are you waiting for?" one of them said. "You got what you came for. What else do you want?"

And then I blurted it out. "I'd like to ask you just one question," I said.

"Like what?" the standing one said.

"Like where on earth did you gentlemen learn so much about grand opera?"

For a moment he stared at me with parted lips; then, pounding the mantelpiece with his palm, he collapsed with a roar of laughter. As the laughter of the others erupted like a string of giant firecrackers, I looked on with growing feelings of embarrassment and insult, trying to grasp the handle of what appeared to be an unfriendly joke. Finally, wiping coal-dust-stained tears from his cheeks, he interrupted his laughter long enough to initiate me into the mystery.

"Hell, son," he laughed, "we learn it down at the Met, that's where . . ."

"You learned it *where?*"

"At the Metropolitan Opera, just like I told you. Strip us fellows down and give us some costumes and we make about the finest damn bunch of Egyptians you ever seen. Hell, we been down there wearing leopard skins and carrying spears or waving things like palm leafs and ostrich-tail fans for *years!*"

Now, purged by the revelation, and with Hazel Harrison's voice echoing in my ears, it was my turn to roar with laughter. With a shock of recognition I joined them in appreciation of the hilarious American joke that centered on the incongruities of race, economic status and culture. My sense of order restored, my appreciation of the arcane ways of American cultural possibility was vastly extended. The men were products of both past *and* present; were both coal heavers *and* Met extras; were both workingmen *and* opera buffs. Seen in the clear, pluralistic, melting-pot light of American cultural possibility, there was no contradiction. The joke, the apparent contradiction, sprang from my attempting to see them by the light of social concepts that cast less illumination than an inert lump of coal. I was delighted, because during a moment when I least expected to encounter the little man behind the stove (Miss Harrison's vernacular music critic, as it were), I had stumbled upon four such men. Not behind the stove, it is true, but even more wondrously, they had materialized at an even more unexpected location: at the depth of the American social hierarchy and, of all possible hiding places, behind a coal pile. Where there's a melting pot there's smoke, and where there's smoke it is not simply optimistic to expect fire, it's imperative to watch for the phoenix's vernacular, but transcendent, rising.

1986

READING, REREADING, AND ANALYSIS

1. Who is the "little man at Chehaw Station"? Write a paragraph describing him and discussing his significance.

2. In a group, find two examples that show Ellison's attitude toward the "melting pot" concept of democracy. Prepare a presentation for the class in which you explain the "melting pot" concept and describe Ellison's attitude toward it using the evidence you have found.

3. Who is Ellison's audience? What is he trying to tell his audience about the rhetorical concept of audience? As a member of Ellison's audience, are you a version of the "little man"?

4. As a group, examine the anecdote about the VW and consider how that example relates to Ellison's larger argument in this essay. Compare the point Ellison is making in this example with the anecdotes he uses to begin and end the essay. Present your findings to the class.

5. What does Ellison mean on page 157 when he writes,

   Connoisseur, critic, trickster, the little man is also a day-coach, cabin-class traveler, but the timing of his arrivals and departures is uncertain. Sometimes he's there, sometimes he's here. Being quintessentially American, he enjoys the joke, the confounding of hierarchical expectations fostered by his mask: that cultural incongruity through which he, like Brer Rabbit, is able to convert even the most decorous of audiences into his own brier patch and temper the chilliest of classics to his own vernacular taste."

Individually or in a group, make a list of examples of the "little man" in Ellison's essay. Review your list, and then come up with your own example of the "little man." Where might one find him today and why? Might one find the "little woman" as well?

RESPONDING THROUGH WRITING: BUILDING AN INTERPRETATION

6. Examine Ellison's use of the "melting pot" metaphor. What are the problems with this metaphor? What are its strengths? Write a paper in which you analyze this metaphor and its ability to describe the American population. You might also consider including a discussion of another metaphor you have read about or heard of that you think provides a more accurate description, or consider inventing a metaphor of your own.

7. Write a short paper describing your own version of the "little man at Chehaw station." What metaphor or story best conveys your ideas about audience or your vision of the American audience? How do your ideas compare with Ellison's?

8. In four or five sentences, summarize what you take to be Ellison's thesis or main argument. Next, reflect on what steps you had to take to create your summary. (What was hard and what was easy?) Then explain in writing (one or two pages) your summarizing process—what you did to write your four- or five-sentence summary, and why.

9. Write a two- or three-page paper in which you discuss Ellison's concluding sentence: "Where there's a melting pot there's smoke, and where there is smoke it is not simply optimistic to expect fire, it's imperative to watch for the phoenix's vernacular, but transcendent, rising." What is significant about this sentence? How does it relate to the essay as a whole? How does it relate to your own experience?

GOING FURTHER: LEARNING FROM OTHER SOURCES

10. Use the Internet or your library's reference section to learn more about Prokofiev (Ellison, p. 152). What does Ellison's use of this example tell us about how he imagines his audience? How much does he expect us to know? What impression do you get of Ellison from this and other examples in the essay?

11. Using Academic Search Elite or a similar reference database that includes a range of scholarly journal articles, try several searches using "melting pot," "American culture," and "multicultural" as search terms. Scan your results list to find differing attitudes toward the "melting pot" concept and to find metaphors other than "melting pot" that people use to describe American culture. Print out your best findings and bring them to class.

APPLYING WHAT YOU'VE LEARNED

12. Compare Ellison's ideas about ethnicity and democracy with those of Richard Rodriguez in "'Blaxicans' and Other Reinvented Americans," or those of Julie Charlip in "A Real Class Act: Searching for Identity in the Classless Society," or those of bell hooks in "keeping close to home: class and education," or those of Christopher Lasch in "The Lost Art of Argument." Would Rodriguez or Charlip or hooks or Lasch share Ellison's reaction to the "melting pot" metaphor? To what extent would they understand "the little man" and why?

13. Write a paper using ideas and examples from Dorothy Allison's "This Is Our World" to further explain and to evaluate Ellison's discussion of American identity. To what extent would Allison support or find problems with Ellison's analysis? Would Ellison likely agree or disagree with the following claim by Allison: "We are not the same. We are a nation of nations. Regions, social classes, economic circumstances, ethical systems, and political convictions—all separate us even as we pretend they do not" (p. 49)?

14. According to Ellison, "Perhaps we are able to see only that which we are prepared to see, and in our culture the cost of insight is an uncertainty that threatens our already unstable sense of order and requires a constant questioning of accepted assumptions" (p. 169). Reflect on Ellison's claim: Does it ring true for you? If yes, why? If not, why not? Use the most significant ideas that arise from your reflection on the quotation to help you write an essay that examines seeing and understanding as presented in Annie Dillard's "Seeing," Thomas Kuhn's "The Historical Structure of Scientific Discovery," and Walker Percy's "The Loss of the Creature."

STUART EWEN

Stuart Ewen (b. 1945) is Distinguished Professor in the Department of Film and Media Studies and Director of the MFA Program in Integrated Media Arts at Hunter College. He is also a professor in the Ph.D. Programs in History, Sociology and American Studies at the City University of New York Graduate Center. Ewen is the author of *All Consuming Images: The Politics of Style in Contemporary Culture* and *PR!: The Social History of Spin,* among other works. "The Marriage Between Art and Commerce" is a chapter in *All Consuming Images,* which served as the source for an award-winning Public Television Series, "The Public Mind." In addition to lecturing on art and design at museums and universities around the country, Ewen has taken his social and political criticism to the street. Using the name Archie Bishop, Ewen has produced political protest art and street installations for the past thirty years.

> For a glimpse at how style continues to influence our style today, see the PBS website for "The Merchants of Cool" at <http://www.pbs.org/wgbh/pages/frontline/shows/cool/>.

WHAT DO YOU KNOW? WHAT DO YOU EXPECT TO DISCOVER?

Before reading the essay, take a moment to consider the following questions.

1. What topics does Ewen's biography suggest he is interested in? What do you know about those topics? Knowledge can come from personal experience, stories you've heard, other classes you've taken, or other reading you've done.

2. What relationships do you see between "Art" and "Commerce"? Ewen's use of the metaphor "Marriage" suggests a union between art and commerce, yet these two terms have often also been discussed as being at odds. Why and how might art and commerce also be an odd couple?

3. In the essay that follows, Ewen discusses how businesses began to emphasize style and advertising. What are some products or services that are memorable to you because they have stylish marketing or stylish appearance? What gives or creates the impression of style?

☟

The Marriage Between Art and Commerce

Integrated Visions

In the United States, and throughout much of industrialized Europe, the years between 1890 and the 1920s saw qualitative changes in the organization of industries and in methods of production. Industrial corporations grew into giant enterprises, implementing an increasingly mechanized system of mass production.

In the midst of these changes, culture itself was undergoing a fateful transition. If *culture* can be understood as the accumulated stock of understandings and practices by which a given people live and maintain themselves in a given society, the industrialization of daily life may be said to have, in large measure, displaced the customary fabric of culture. Increasingly, resources of survival were being produced by modern systems of mass manufacture. As this mode of production demanded broadened national or international markets, corporations made expanded use of advertising, among other merchandising techniques. Advertising not only sought to inform people about the availability and appeal of industrially produced goods, it also contributed to a restructured perception of the resources and alternatives that were available to people in their everyday lives.

Partly as a response to unprecedented marketing needs; partly to establish a uniform and easily recognizable corporate identity; partly in response to avant-garde tendencies in the arts, giant industrial corporations began to develop multipurpose styling divisions in the first decades of the twentieth century. A pioneer in this development was Walter Rathenau, head of Allgemeine Elektricitäts-Gesellschaft (AEG), the huge German electric company that had been founded (as Deutsche Edison Gesellschaft) by his father, Emil, in 1883.

By 1907 AEG had become one of Europe's great industrial corporations. It "had a capital value exceeding 100 million marks and employed some 70,000 people. Its sales catalogs listed hundreds of different products."[1] Rathenau, according to his friend Franz Blei, was a man possessed and disturbed by the chaotic social world that had emerged alongside the apparatus of corporate industrialism. Rathenau held the passionate conviction that spiritual content and form could be given to the chaotic and inert body of trade and industry.[2]

For Rathenau, it was necessary to invent a new definition and application of style, one not rooted in the past, but derived from "the techniques of mass production and . . . the widespread dissemination of industrial products." What made Rathenau unique was his implementation of this idea within the bureaucratic structure of a modern corporation. Believing that a new style, all industrial aesthetic, could be a "means of alleviating the devastation that industrialization had wrought on such basic areas as labor, production, housing, and human relations," Rathenau commissioned Peter Behrens, an architect and designer, to create a uniform corporate *look* for the AEG. Behrens's assignment was "to redesign the company's buildings, products, and publicity material," from a huge "turbine hall down to tiny publicity seals."[3] Between 1907 and 1914, Behrens created what he called an "artistic context," designed to encompass all elements of the corporation. This was the beginning of the consciously promulgated "corporate image," a uniform reminder that in a world of the ephemeral, the corporation is a constant.

In the nineteenth century, an indiscriminate reverence for the grandiosities of the past had given rise to a shoddy imagistic chaos. By the early twentieth century, the industrial exigencies of coordination, standardization, and control were beginning to find aesthetic expression, part of a move toward more coherent corporate design strategies. Behrens's work at AEG created the prototype for industrial design departments to come. He understood that design could not be limited to a particular building or commodity. In order for design to project a new "spiritual content," it was necessary to erect an imagistic panorama: a new symbolic totality, constituted by an interconnected, cross-referenced, visible world.

This integrated vision was remarkably inclusive in its application. Behrens designed lamps, table fans, humidifiers, motors, dental drills, light switches, clocks, electric kettles, electric heaters, and numerous other products. His designs also shaped the factories in which these products were manufactured, the exhibition pavilions in which they were displayed, and the advertisements by which they were promoted. In each case, Behrens's designs were infused with the look of the "modern." Clean lines and a strictly regulated geometry replaced the encrusted ornamentation that had marked many industrial products to that time. Where ornament did appear, it was spare and understated, its links with the past for the most part severed.

Consumer Engineering

In the United States, during the years that Behrens worked at AEG, the instrumental use of style as a business device was also gaining adherents and practitioners. Speaking to the Chicago Commercial Club in 1907, Daniel H. Burnham, the architect and chief designer of the Columbian Exposition, asserted an intimate and important link between style and profitability. "Beauty," he advised his audience, "has always paid better than any other commodity, and always will."[4] By

1915, the marriage between business planning and aesthetics had already shaped the visible aspect of commerce.

One of the most ubiquitous examples of this development was advertising. Writing in 1914, Walter Lippmann commented upon the flowering of advertising as a sign that businessmen were attempting to "take charge of consumption as well as production." Inextricably linked to the development of consciously styled products, advertising projected images of these products, and of the "happy" consumers who purchased them, across the horizons of everyday life. A seductive, imagistic panorama had been installed above the American landscape:

> The eastern sky [is] ablaze with chewing gum, the northern with toothbrushes and underwear, the western with whiskey, and the southern with petticoats, the whole heavens . . . [are] brilliant with monstrously flirtatious women, . . . When you glance at magazines . . . [a] rivulet of text trickles through the meadows of automobiles, baking powders, corsets and kodaks.[5]

Business was coming to embrace advertising as the "ignition system of the economy, the dynamo of mass dissatisfaction and the creator of illusions in a most materialistic world."[6] Advertising was becoming established as what C. Wright Mills once called "the prime means of acclaim."[7]

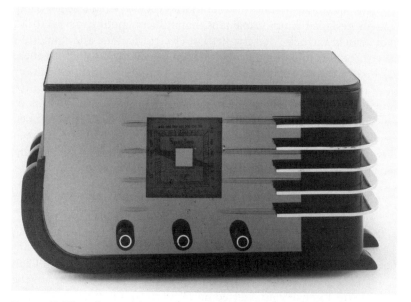

FIGURE 12 The influence of consumer engineering can be seen in this 1936 radio, designed by Walter Dorwin Teague. (The Minneapolis Institute of Arts.)

From the 1920s onward, advertising agencies broadened their field of action, organizing multifaceted merchandising campaigns for clients. A central figure in the development of this coordinated image-management was Earnest Elmo Calkins, of the Calkins & Holden advertising agency. Calkins intuited that the success of merchandising depended on the ability to construct an unbroken, imagistic corridor between the product being sold and the consciousness (and unconsciousness) of the consumer. Following this logic, Calkins created an agency that linked a diverse but interrelated range of "creative services," including product design, packaging, aesthetic counseling, and, of course, advertising. Calkins assembled an extraordinarily talented and innovative staff, including Egmont Arens, a leading product and package designer, and Walter Dorwin Teague, who, along with a few others, would become one of the most influential industrial designers from the 1930s on. While at Calkins & Holden, between 1929 and 1933, Arens coined the phrase "consumer engineering" to describe what was entailed in a complex, coordinated merchandising effort.

Central to consumer engineering was the notion that style, or, as Calkins called it, "beauty," was the "new business tool," whose intelligent use could generate sales and profits. Following in a path laid by Walter Rathenau and Peter Behrens at AEG, Calkins delineated many of his ideas in "Beauty The New Business Tool," published in *The Atlantic Monthly* in 1927. In the article, Calkins offered a historical account of the systematic integration of business and aesthetics. In the early days of industrialism, he noted, the use of beauty was piecemeal, or disregarded as an economic factor. Where goods were decorative they lacked "integrity"; they celebrated the values of another time, while ignoring the signals of the machine age. Calkins himself was enamored with modern art—"the new art," he called it—and he believed that even more than realism, this art contained enormous powers of "suggestion." Advertising artists, influenced by these modern artistic developments, pioneered in the transformation and aestheticization of business. The youthful advertising industry, Calkins argued, "seized upon the power of the artist to say things which could not be said in words, and thus a large group of men trained in artistic standards was brought to work in close conjunction with factories producing goods." This mixture left its mark across the wide tableau of American commercial life.

> This first step toward making the advertising attractive was to make the goods attractive. It was frequently necessary to introduce the article sold into the advertisement, or at least its package, and most products and packages were so ugly or so commonplace *they spoiled the picture; and thus began that steady, unremitting pressure on the manufacturer to make his*

goods or packages worthy of being placed in an artistic setting.
Bales and boxes and cans and wrappers and labels and trade-marks were revised and redesigned.[8]

The first merchandise to be affected by these make-overs were fashion goods and cosmetics. Then, General Motors (GM) began to implement general design strategies in the production of automobiles, leading to the development of the GM "Styling Section," under the directorship of Harley Earl. General Electric coordinated the design of their image and products as well. Phonographs and radios, two important fixtures in the new way of life that was emerging, were also seductively styled. Moving beyond product design and labeling, advertising now entered the realm of retail environments:

> These better designed goods and packages demanded a better environment in which to be sold, and thus we have a revolution in the furnishing of shops and stores. The old-fashioned store was a stereotype—a long, narrow room with two windows and a door in front and in back, counters down the full length on both sides. . . . Today, the store has given way to the shop* . . . The shop front, the tinting of the walls, the furniture, the arrangement of goods—everything has been transformed. . . . Everything is done to create a setting for the new style of goods. You see this in every industry.[9]

Continuing his rhapsody on a totally administered environment, Calkins discussed the innovative uses of color and light in the creation of a sensuous commercial atmosphere. Behind all of these stylistic metamorphoses lay the bottom line: *sales.* "Beauty is introduced into material objects," he explained, "to enhance them in the eyes of the purchaser. The appeal of efficiency alone is nearly ended. Beauty is the natural and logical next step. It is in the air."[10]

Ultimately, Calkins's approach was not one of combining efficiency and aesthetics. A product's efficiency, its durability, was, for Calkins, a stumbling block to sales. Beauty, according to Calkins, would allow for the undermining of the efficiency factor, stimulating compulsive consumption. He wrote that "this new influence on articles of barter and sale is largely used to make people dissatisfied with what they have of the old order, still good and useful and efficient, but lacking in the newest touch. In the expressive slang of the day . . . [these goods] 'date.'"[11]

By the end of the 1920s, the stylization of the marketplace was in full swing. It had influenced goods, packages, retail establishments,

---

*The term *store* connotes a place where goods are simply stored; the arrival of the term *shop* implies an increased focus on the act of consumption.

advertisements. It had also affected the orientation of the popular mass media. Previously, style had been a concern in publications geared toward a primarily wealthy audience; the 1920s witnessed the flowering of style in magazines aimed at a mass market. Robert S. Lynd, the sociologist, noted that the "increased emphasis on style was encouraged by advertising and editorial content in periodicals and newspapers" of the 1920s. He continued,

> The *Ladies' Home Journal,* for example, after devoting but 16% of its non-fiction editorial content to fashion in 1918 and 1920, raised this to 28% in 1921 and to 30 in 1922–23, while popular magazines have increasingly taken over high style artists formerly used only by exclusive style journals such as *Vogue* and *Harper's Bazaar.*[12]

The play of surfaces was becoming a deliberate and decisive component of consumer merchandising, and a more general obsession of the consumer culture. Seventy years before Calkins's "Beauty The New Business Tool" appeared in *The Atlantic,* Oliver Wendell Holmes had predicted that the ephemeral surface would soon overwhelm the objective world in the pages of the same magazine. Holmes's vision had been prophetic. Vast new industries were now engaged in the process and business of generating evanescent meanings. This turn of events was not unnoticed by Egon Friedell, writing in Vienna in 1931. "There are no realities anymore," he lamented. "There is only apparatus. . . . *Neither are there goods any more, but only advertisements:* the most valuable article is the one most effectively lauded, the one that the most capital has gone to advertise. We call all this," he added, "Americanism."[13]

Image and Desire

In service of the emerging apparatus of representation, many corporations simultaneously employed a social scientific apparatus; for monitoring and analyzing mass psychology; for studying—among other things—the impact of images on the mind of the consumer. "Understanding the consumer's mind," wrote ad man Harry Dexter Kitson in 1923, comes down to the question of appealing to and enhancing desire. To do this, he proposed, it is necessary to create a context in which "pictures are painted before the consumer's imagination representing the pleasurable aspects of possession of the commodity."[14]

Such strategic thinking, however, went beyond making rational appeals to the consumer's desire for pleasure. Styling, it was increasingly argued, must speak to the unconscious, to those primal urges and sensations that are repressed in the everyday confines of civilization. Like art, psychoanalysis was being evaluated as a "new business

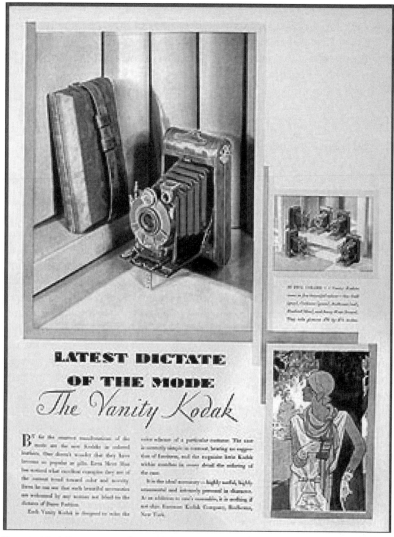

FIGURE 13 Advertisement for Kodak. (Found at http://historyproject.ucdavis.edu/
imageapp.php?Major=AD&Minor=AS&slideNum=50.00.)

tool." Roy Sheldon, who along with Egmont Arens wrote the definitive guide *Consumer Engineering* (1932), spoke of the "astonishing
fruits" being borne by the work of Freud, Jung, Alfred Adler, Pavlov,
and others. These pioneers in the areas of psychoanalysis and behav-
ioral psychology, they asserted, were providing business with tools
that could be used to its "active advantage."

    An example of this approach is seen in Sheldon and Arens's in-
strumental discussion of the *sense of touch* which, along with smell,
was the least acknowledged and most repressed of the senses in mod-

ern Western civilization. Taking cues from Freud's ruminations on "civilization and its discontents," they outlined a technique for product merchandising:

> If it is true that the exigencies of civilization have driven it [the sense of touch] below the surface, it persists in the unconscious mind as a powerful motivating force. Every day the average person makes hundreds of judgements in which the sense of touch casts the deciding vote, whether or not it rises into the consciousness. . . . undercover decisions [are] made by this sense. Such simple judgements as the acceptance or rejection of a towel, washrag, hairbrush, underwear, stockings, hinge upon how these things feel in the hands; their acceptance or rejection is motivated by the unconscious.[15]

Given this reality, they maintained, the study of human sensory systems and the integration of this study with merchandising practice was essential. Designs should be executed with an appeal to tactile senses. On some level, Sheldon and Arens saw style as a symbolic return of the repressed, offering consumers a subliminal promise of polymorphous gratification. Rather than verbal appeals in advertising, they were proposing a depth-psychological strategy, one that would promote "the exploitation of the 'sublimated sense' in the field of product design":

> Manufacturing an object that delights this [tactile] sense is something that you do but don't talk about. Almost everything which is bought is handled. After the eye, the hand is the first censor to pass on acceptance, and if the hand's judgement is unfavorable, the most attractive object will not gain the popularity it deserves. On the other hand, merchandise designed to be pleasing to the hand wins an approval that may never register in the mind, but which will determine additional purchases. . . . *Make it snuggle in the palm.*[16]

By the 1930s, such approaches to emotion, desire, and the unconscious had become part of the jargon of the style industries. Harold Van Doren, a major industrial designer of the period, noted that "design is fundamentally the art of using lines, forms, tones, colors and textures to arouse an emotional reaction in the beholder."[17] The very meaning of aesthetics was changing. Once the study of beauty and its universal appeal, it was becoming, within the style industries, a study of art insofar as it could provoke and promote consumer response. At a time when the idea of "art for art's sake" was taking hold as a dominant faith among art critics, *art for control's sake* was becoming the dominant practice in the marketplace.

Jean Abel, of the Pasadena Architects School of Arts, wrote of the ideas of "simplification and control" as the paramount concepts governing "modern design." To Abel, designs should be accessible to as many people as possible and should be executed—deliberately—with specific responses in mind. To do this, designers needed to understand that design "speaks a scientific language, with universal laws and principles, governing elements." An effective use of this semiological "language," Abel insisted, could help artists and their employers achieve the "conscious control of ideas":

> The design of today is dynamic. In diagonal lines it moves with the speed and precision of the airplane. In geometric forms, it presents the cold calculating power of the adding machine. In color, it suffocates, chills, shocks or soothes through choices and combinations of hues, values and intensities. It invents strange realms, insane with distortion; or creates new worlds, ideal with release into new spaces, *hence the need of control.*[18]

Not all designers employed such a scientific (psychological or semiotic) approach; many worked more intuitively. From the 1930s onward, however, major figures in industrial design had internalized such instrumental thinking into their work. For Harold Van Doren, the role of the industrial designer was "to interpret the function of useful things in terms of appeal to the eye; to endow them with beauty of form and color; above all to create in the consumer the desire to possess."[19] For J. Gordon Lippincott, another designer, "the appearance of a product" had become "an integral feature in its success or failure" as "the industrial designer . . . seeks to imbue the consumer with the desire of ownership."[20] Raymond Loewy put it more concisely. Industrial design was "the shaping of everyday life with the marketplace in mind."[21]

In the commercial world of style, the fundamental assumption underlying the "shaping of everyday life" is that life must visibly change, every day. Roland Barthes called this phenomenon *neomania,* a madness for perpetual novelty where "the new" has become defined strictly as a "purchased value," something to buy.[22] What will appear next is not always predictable. That *something new* will appear is entirely predictable. "Style obsolescence," reported a major industrial design firm in 1960, "is the *sine qua non* of product success."[23]

In the 1930s, with the consumer economy in serious straits, styling and "style obsolescence" came to the forefront as methods designed to stimulate markets, and to keep them stimulated. Roy Sheldon and Egmont Arens counseled that "styles wear out faster than gears," and encouraged industry to utilize style to motivate purchases.[24] Earnest Calkins concurred, and suggested that even durable goods must be reconceptualized and sold as if they were nondurables:

> Goods fall into two classes, those we use, such as motor-cars or safety razors, and those we use *up,* such as toothpaste or soda biscuit. Consumer engineering must see to it that we use *up* the

kind of goods we now merely use. Would any change in the goods or habits of people speed up their consumption? Can they be displaced by newer models: Can artificial obsolescence be created? Consumer engineering does not end until we can consume all we can make.[25]

Such thinking was catalyzed by the collapse of markets during the Depression, and it has persevered as the basic logic of consumer capitalism ever since. Though the long-term ecological implications of this trajectory may be disastrous, from a strictly merchandising point of view, it is *the air we breathe*. Style and changes in style, once part of a privileged competition among merchant princes, have become routine ingredients in almost everybody's lives, from the clothes we wear to our daily gruel. With the institutionalization of "style obsolescence," the perpetual challenge to offer *something new* became a cornerstone of business planning. While corporations, and political institutions, and people of wealth and power employ and project images of stability for themselves, daily life—for most other Americans—carries a visual message of unpredictability and impermanence.

Another of Oliver Wendell Holmes's predictions has come to pass. In 1859 Holmes had written that "every conceivable object" would soon "scale off its surface for us." Like animals in a trophy hunt, all manners of "Nature and Art" would be hunted down "for their skins," with the carcasses left to rot. To a large extent, this describes the practices of the style industries today. In their continual search for ever-evolving novelty, all manners of human expression and creativity are mined for their surfaces: their *look*, their *touch*, their *sound,* their *scent.* This booty is then attached to the logic of the marketplace: mass produced and merchandised. Visions of a preindustrial, more "natural" form of life are appropriated by the corporate food industry. Graffiti artists from the Bronx provide "the look" for Macy's new fall line. The "anti-style" of the punk subculture inspires the layout for a Warner Communications annual report. All faces are seen; few are heard from.

Whatever the "skin," or its vernacular origin, its meaning is most often compromised or lost once it enters the style market. The meaning that *will* remain constant, that *will* be expressed across the shifting tableau of style—regardless of the skins it appropriates—is the continual message of consumption. Art historians speak of *styles*—Gothic, Romanesque, neoclassical, and so on—as coherent embodiments of the epochs that produced them. The facades of style in contemporary culture, however, are ever-changing, often incoherent. It is this volatility that embodies the period we inhabit. Style is something to be *used up*. Part of its significance is that it will lose significance.

1988

Notes

1. Tilmann Buddensieg and Henning Rogge, *Industriekultur: Peter Behrens and the AEG,* trans. I. B. White (1984), p. x.
2. Ibid., p. 2.
3. Ibid., pp. x, 2.
4. Paul S. Boyer, *Urban Masses and Moral Order in America, 1820–1920* (1978), p. 264.
5. Walter Lippmann, *Drift and Mastery* (1914), pp. 52–53.
6. George Mowry, ed., *The Twenties: Fords, Flappers and Fantasies* (1963), p. 15. See also Stuart Ewen, *Captains of Consciousness* (1976), for a fuller discussion of the rise of modern advertising.
7. C. Wright Mills, *The Power Elite* (1956), p. 84.
8. Earnest Elmo Calkins, "Beauty The New Business Tool," *The Atlantic Monthly* 140 (August 1927), pp. 147–48, emphasis added.
9. Ibid., p. 149.
10. Ibid., p. 151.
11. Ibid., p. 152.
12. Robert S. Lynd, "The People as Consumers," in Report of the President's Research Committee on Social Trends, *Recent Social Trends in the United States* (1933), p. 878.
13. Egon Friedell, *A Cultural History of the Modern Age: The Crisis of the European Soul from the Black Death to the World War,* 3 vols. (1954), 3: 475–76.
14. Harry Dexter Kitson, "Understanding the Consumer's Mind," *The Annals* 110 (November 1923), pp. 131–38.
15. Roy Sheldon and Egmont Arens, *Consumer Engineering* (1932), p. 97.
16. Ibid., pp. 100–101, emphasis added.
17. Harold Van Doren, *Industrial Design* (1940), pp. 121–22.
18. Jean Abel, "An Explanation of Modern Art," *California Arts and Architecture* 37 (June 1930), pp. 34–35.
19. Van Doren, *Industrial Design,* p. xviii.
20. J. Gordon Lippincott, *Design for Business* (1947), p. 19.
21. Raymond Loewy, *Industrial Design* (1979), p. 8.
22. Roland Barthes, *The Fashion System* (1983), p. 300.
23. J. Gordon Lippincott and Walter Margulies, "We Couldn't Have Done It in Wichita," *Industrial Design* 7 (October 1960), p. 103.
24. Sheldon and Arens, *Consumer Engineering,* pp. 61, 63.
25. Ibid., pp. 13–14.

READING, REREADING, AND ANALYSIS

1. How does Ewen define culture? Make a list with page numbers to indicate places in the essay where Ewen defines or talks about culture. Then make a list of your own ideas about what culture is. Bring both lists to class.

2. What does it mean to say that someone has "style"? In a group, share your associations with the term. Then find an example in

which Ewen discusses issues of style and compare his use of the term with yours. Present your findings to the class.

3. Bring an advertisement to class. In a group, discuss the different ways in which the advertiser is relying on our expectations and understandings of "style."

4. What does Ewen mean by the phrase "the play of surfaces" (p. 183), and what is its relationship to the phenomenon of "neomania," a term Ewen attributes to Roland Barthes?

5. What does Ewen mean on page 185 when he writes,

> The very meaning of aesthetics was changing. Once the study of beauty and its universal appeal, it was becoming, within the style industries, a study of art insofar as it could provoke and promote consumer response. At a time when the idea of "art for art's sake" was taking hold as a dominant faith among art critics, *art for control's sake* was becoming the dominant practice in the marketplace.

6. Ewen describes how folks in business and industry came to embrace beauty as a means of "stimulating compulsive consumption" (p. 182). What is "compulsive consumption"? Make a list of examples of it. Examine your list for relationships between beauty and consumption.

RESPONDING THROUGH WRITING: BUILDING AN INTERPRETATION

7. Ewen quotes Egon Friedell who, in 1931, wrote: "There are no realities anymore. . . . There is only apparatus. . . . Neither are there goods any more, but only advertisements: the most valuable article is the one most effectively lauded, the one that the most capital has gone to advertise. We call this . . . Americanism." Write a journal entry that examines what Friedell and Ewen mean by "Americanism." Write a second journal entry that applies the quotation to another aspect of American life, such as politics, education, or family life. Is it true, for instance, that the "most valuable" politician is the one who has the most money to spend on advertising?

8. Write a paper in which you use Ewen's ideas about style to analyze an advertisement. What qualities does the ad want you to associate with the product? How does the paradox of style—that "part of its significance is that it will lose significance"—apply?

9. In four or five sentences, summarize Ewen's main argument in "The Marriage Between Art and Commerce." Next, list two examples of products Ewen mentions, and then add two examples that he might have used but didn't.

10. Write a short paper (three pages) in which you meditate on relationships you see between style and desire. Think about what Ewen says about both terms, but also think about and discuss possible relationships between style, desire, and writing.

GOING FURTHER: LEARNING FROM OTHER SOURCES

11. Use an Internet directory such as Yahoo or About to examine a corporate website that includes advertising. What is the company's corporate image? Is the website selling you a product, a service, or the company itself? Who is likely to visit the website and why?

12. According to Ewen, who is Peter Behrens and why is he important? For the next class, find out what you can about Behrens on the Internet, and then write a journal entry that discusses relationships you see between Ewen's interest in Behrens's work and Ewen's concern with modern ideas about product advertising and obsolescence.

APPLYING WHAT YOU'VE LEARNED

13. Write a paper using terms and ideas from Zita Ingham's "Landscape, Drama, and Dissensus" to test Ewen's claims about the function of advertising. Find a print advertisement that interests you, and use Zita Ingham's terms—emotional appeal, logical appeal, and ethical appeal (p. 250)—to analyze the rhetoric of the ad. How does your analysis connect to Ewen's argument? What is the particular style of the ad? What associations do the advertisers want you to have with the product or service? Beyond the literal product being sold, what other concepts or messages is the ad selling?

14. Compare Ewen's account of the history and development of the advertising industry with Susan Sontag's account of the history and development of photography in her essay, "In Plato's Cave." What are some of the effects of these two developments on the way we think about the world? Are there ways in which Sontag's vision of photography's effect on our culture challenges or points to the limitations of Ewen's vision?

15. In "From the Frying Pan into the Fire," Arlie Russell Hochschild, like Ewen, discusses aspects of "the industrialization of daily life" (p. 215). Also like Ewen, Hochschild emphasizes advertising. Indeed, she begins her essay with a close reading of a Quaker

Instant Oatmeal advertisement. Use Ewen's discussion of advertising and style to examine Hochschild's close reading of the Oatmeal ad and its relation to her larger argument about the "industrialization of daily life." Does her analysis emphasize the ad's style? What seems to be the driving force of the ad, according to Hochschild? How does the ad promote compulsive consumption, desire, and consumer control—ideas Ewen discusses? What does Hochschild's close reading of the ad tell you about art, commerce, and daily life?

The Measure of Progress

The progress of the past, as well as that of the future, is measured by criticism—for criticism exists only where there is faith in ability to improve.

We do not criticise an ox cart or condemn the tallow dip, for the simple reason that they are obsolete. During the reconstruction period through which our country is now passing, if the public does not criticise any public utility or other form of service, it is because there seems little hope for improvement.

The intricate mechanism of telephone service is, under the most favorable conditions, subject to criticism, for the reason that it is the most intimate of all personal services.

The accomplishment of the telephone in the past fixed the quality of service demanded today; a greater accomplishment in quality and scope of service will set new standards for the future.

AMERICAN TELEPHONE AND TELEGRAPH COMPANY
AND ASSOCIATED COMPANIES

One Policy   *One System*   *Universal Service*

"Mention The Geographic—It identifies you"

FIGURE 14 Advertisement for AT&T. (Found at <http://myinsulators.com/commokid/telephones/1920s_telephone_ads.htm>.)

FIGURE 15 Advertisement by the Cleanliness Institute. (Found at <http://history-project.ucdavis.edu/imageapp.php?Major=AD&Minor=P&SlideNum=56.00>.)

RICHARD FLORIDA

Richard Florida (b. 1957) is Heinz Professor of Regional Economic Development at Carnegie Mellon University, where he teaches public policy and urban planning. He is the author of seven books, including *The Rise of the Creative Class: And How It's Transforming Work, Leisure, Community and Everyday Life* (2002), for which he is best known. Florida argues that recent changes in the way people live and work are a result of the emergence of creativity as an economic force. For its controversial ideas, *Creative Class* won the Annual *Washington Monthly* Political Book Award for 2002 and earned a place on the *Harvard Business Review*'s List of Breakthrough Ideas for 2004.

> For more information, see <http://www.creativeclass.org> or <http://www.heinz.cmu.edu/~florida>.

WHAT DO YOU KNOW? WHAT DO YOU EXPECT TO DISCOVER?

Before reading this essay, take a moment to consider the following questions.

1. What topics does Florida's biography suggest he is interested in? What do you know about those topics? Knowledge can come from personal experience, stories you've heard, other classes you've taken, or other reading you've done.

2. What does the title lead you to expect from this essay? Make a list of the key events or actions of your "everyday life." What kinds of everyday-life transformations have you undergone? If you haven't undergone any such transformations, then what accounts for the continuity in your everyday life?

3. Florida analyzes how significant aspects of life in the United States have been changing dramatically since the 1950s. In particular, he focuses on the role of creativity in cultural and social transformations. What impact does creativity have on your everyday life? What acts or intellectual abilities best indicate your creativity? Why?

⌀

The Transformation of Everyday Life

Something's happening here but you don't know what it is, do you, Mr. Jones?

—Bob Dylan

Here's a thought experiment. Take a typical man on the street from the year 1900 and drop him into the 1950s. Then take someone from the 1950s and move him Austin Powers–style into the present day. Who would experience the greater change?

At first glance the answer seems obvious. Thrust forward into the 1950s, a person from the turn of the twentieth century would be awestruck by a world filled with baffling technological wonders. In place of horse-drawn carriages, he would see streets and highways jammed with cars, trucks and buses. In the cities, immense skyscrapers would line the horizon, and mammoth bridges would span rivers and inlets where once only ferries could cross. Flying machines would soar overhead, carrying people across the continent or the oceans in a matter of hours rather than days. At home, our 1900-to-1950s time-traveler would grope his way through a strange new environment filled with appliances powered by electricity: radios and televisions emanating musical sounds and even human images, refrigerators to keep things cold, washing machines to clean his clothes automatically, and much more. A massive new super market would replace daily trips to the market with an array of technologically enhanced foods, such as instant coffee or frozen vegetables to put into the refrigerator. Life itself would be dramatically extended. Many once-fatal ailments could be prevented with an injection or cured with a pill. The newness of this time-traveler's physical surroundings—the speed and power of everyday machines—would be profoundly disorienting.

On the other hand, someone from the 1950s would have little trouble navigating the physical landscape of today. Although we like to think ours is the age of boundless technological wonders, our second time-traveler would find himself in a world not all that different from the one he left. He would still drive a car to work. If he took the train, it would likely be on the same line leaving from the same station. He could probably board an airplane at the same airport. He might still live in a suburban house, though a bigger one. Television would have more channels, but it would basically be the same, and he could still catch some of his favorite 1950s shows on reruns. He would know how, or quickly learn how, to operate most household appliances—even the personal computer, with its familiar QWERTY keyboard. In fact with just a few exceptions, such as the PC, the Internet, CD and DVD players, the cash machine and a wireless phone he could carry with him, he would be familiar with almost all current-day technology. Perhaps disappointed by the pace of progress, he might ask: "Why haven't we conquered outer space?" or "Where are all the robots?"

On the basis of big, obvious technological changes alone, surely the 1900-to-1950s traveler would experience the greater shift, while the other might easily conclude that we'd spent the second half of the twentieth century doing little more than tweaking the great waves of the first half.[1]

But the longer they stayed in their new homes, the more each time-traveler would become aware of subtler dimensions of change. Once the glare of technology had dimmed, each would begin to notice their respective society's changed norms and values, and the ways in which everyday people live and work. And here the tables would be turned. In terms of adjusting to the social structures and the rhythms and patterns of daily life, our second time-traveler would be much more disoriented.

Someone from the early 1900s would find the social world of the 1950s remarkably similar to his own. If he worked in a factory, he might find much the same divisions of labor, the same hierarchical systems of control. If he worked in an office, he would be immersed in the same bureaucracy, the same climb up the corporate ladder. He would come to work at 8 or 9 each morning and leave promptly at 5, his life neatly segmented into compartments of home and work. He would wear a suit and tie. Most of his business associates would be white and male. Their values and office politics would hardly have changed. He would seldom see women in the workplace, except as secretaries, and almost never interact professionally with someone of another race. He would marry young, have children quickly thereafter, stay married to the same person and probably work for the same company for the rest of his life. In his leisure time, he'd find that movies and TV had largely superseded live stage shows, but otherwise his recreational activities would be much the same as they were in 1900; taking in a baseball game or a boxing match, maybe playing a round of golf. He would join the clubs and civic groups befitting his socioeconomic class, observe the same social distinctions, and fully expect his children to do likewise. The tempo of his life would be structured by the values and norms of organizations. He would find himself living the life of the "company man" so aptly chronicled by writers from Sinclair Lewis and John Kenneth Galbraith to William Whyte and C. Wright Mills.[2]

Our second time-traveler, however, would be quite unnerved by the dizzying social and cultural changes that had accumulated between the 1950s and today. At work he would find a new dress code, a new schedule, and new rules. He would see office workers dressed like folks relaxing on the weekend, in jeans and open-necked shirts, and be shocked to learn they occupy positions of authority. People at the office would seemingly come and go as they pleased. The younger ones might sport bizarre piercings and tattoos. Women and even non-whites would be managers. Individuality and self-expression would be valued over conformity to organizational norms—and yet these people would seem strangely puritanical to this time-traveler. His ethnic jokes would fall embarrassingly flat. His smoking would get him banished to the parking lot, and his two-martini lunches would raise genuine concern. Attitudes and expressions he had never thought about would cause repeated offense. He would continually suffer the painful feeling of not knowing how to behave.

Out on the street, this time-traveler would see different ethnic groups in greater numbers than he ever could have imagined—Asian-, Indian-, and Latin-Americans and others—all mingling in ways he found strange and perhaps inappropriate. There would be mixed-race couples, and same-sex couples carrying the upbeat-sounding moniker "gay." While some of these people would be acting in familiar ways—a woman shopping while pushing a stroller, an office worker having lunch at a counter—others, such as grown men clad in form-fitting gear whizzing by on high-tech bicycles, or women on strange new roller skates with their torsos covered only by "brassieres"—would appear to be engaged in alien activities.

People would seem to be always working and yet never working when they were supposed to. They would strike him as lazy and yet obsessed with exercise. They would seem career-conscious yet fickle—doesn't anybody stay with the company more than three years?—and caring yet antisocial: What happened to the ladies' clubs, Moose Lodges and bowling leagues? While the physical surroundings would be relatively familiar, the *feel* of the place would be bewilderingly different.

Thus, although the first time-traveler had to adjust to some drastic technological changes, it is the second who experiences the deeper, more pervasive transformation. It is the second who has been thrust into a time when lifestyles and worldviews are most assuredly changing—a time when the old order has broken down, when flux and uncertainty themselves seem to be part of the everyday norm.

The Force Behind the Shift

What caused this transformation? What happened between the 1950s and today that did not happen in the earlier period? Scholars and pundits have floated many theories, along with a range of opinions on whether the changes are good or bad. Some bemoan the passing of traditional social and cultural forms, while others point to a rosy future based largely on new technology. Yet on one point most of them agree. Most tend to see the transformation as something that's being done to us unwittingly. Some complain that certain factions of society have imposed their values on the rest of us; others say that our own inventions are turning around to reshape us. They're wrong.

Society is changing in large measure because we want it to. Moreover it is changing neither in random chaotic ways nor in some mysterious collective-unconscious way, but in ways that are perfectly sensible and rational. The logic behind the transformation has been unclear to this point because the transformation is still in progress. But lately a number of diverse and seemingly unconnected threads are starting to come together. The deeper pattern, the force behind the shift, can now be discerned.

That driving force is the rise of human creativity as the key factor in our economy and society. Both at work and in other spheres of our lives, we value creativity more highly than ever, and cultivate it more intensely. The creative impulse—the attribute that distinguishes us, as humans, from other species—is now being let loose on an unprecedented scale. The purpose of this book is to examine how and why this is so, and to trace its effects as they ripple through our world.

Consider first the realm of economics. Many say that we now live in an "information" economy or a "knowledge" economy. But what's more fundamentally true is that we now have an economy powered by human creativity. Creativity—"the ability to create meaningful new forms," as Webster's dictionary puts it—is now the *decisive* source of competitive advantage. In virtually every industry, from automobiles to fashion, food products, and information technology itself, the winners in the long run are those who can create and keep creating. This has always been true, from the days of the Agricultural Revolution to the Industrial Revolution. But in the past few decades we've come to recognize it clearly and act upon it systematically.

Creativity is multidimensional and comes in many mutually reinforcing forms. It is a mistake to think, as many do, that creativity can be reduced to the creation of new blockbuster inventions, new products and new firms. In today's economy creativity is pervasive and ongoing: We constantly revise and enhance every product, process and activity imaginable, and fit them together in new ways. Moreover, technological and economic creativity are nurtured by and interact with artistic and cultural creativity. This kind of interplay is evident in the rise of whole new industries from computer graphics to digital music and animation. Creativity also requires a social and economic environment that can nurture its many forms. Max Weber said long ago that the Protestant ethic provided the underlying spirit of thrift, hard work and efficiency that motivated the rise of early capitalism. In similar fashion, the shared commitment to the creative spirit in its many, varied manifestations underpins the new creative ethos that powers our age.

Thus creativity has come to be the most highly prized commodity in our economy—and yet it is not a "commodity." Creativity comes from people. And while people can be hired and fired, their creative capacity cannot be bought and sold, or turned on and off at will. This is why, for instance, we see the emergence of a new order in the workplace. Hiring for diversity, once a matter of legal compliance, has become a matter of economic survival because creativity comes in all colors, genders and personal preferences. Schedules, rules and dress codes have become more flexible to cater to how the creative process works. Creativity must be motivated and nurtured in a multitude of ways, by employers, by people themselves and by the communities where they locate. Small wonder that we find the creative ethos bleeding out from the sphere of work to infuse every corner of our lives.

At the same time, entirely new forms of economic infrastructure, such as systematic spending on research and development, the high-tech startup company and an extensive system of venture finance, have evolved to support creativity and mobilize creative people around promising ideas and products. Capitalism has also expanded its reach to capture the talents of heretofore excluded groups of eccentrics and nonconformists. In doing so, it has pulled off yet another astonishing mutation: taking people who would once have been viewed as bizarre mavericks operating at the bohemian fringe and setting them at the very heart of the process of innovation and economic growth. These changes in the economy and in the workplace have in turn helped to propagate and legitimize similar changes in society at large. The creative individual is no longer viewed as an iconoclast. He—or she—is the new mainstream.

In tracing economic shifts, I often say that our economy is moving from an older corporate-centered system defined by large companies to a more people-driven one. This view should not be confused with the unfounded and silly notion that big companies are dying off. Nor do I buy the fantasy of an economy organized around small enterprises and independent "free agents."[3] Companies, including very big ones, obviously still exist, are still influential and probably always will be. I simply mean to stress that as the fundamental source of creativity, people are the critical resource of the new age. This has far-reaching effects—for instance, on our economic and social geography and the nature of our communities.

It's often been said that in this age of high technology, "geography is dead" and place doesn't matter any more.[4] Nothing could be further from the truth: Witness how high-tech firms themselves concentrate in specific places like the San Francisco Bay Area or Austin or Seattle. Place has become the central organizing unit of our time, taking on many of the functions that used to be played by firms and other organizations. Corporations have historically played a key economic role in matching people to jobs, particularly given the long-term employment system of the post–World War II era. But today corporations are far less committed to their employees and people change jobs frequently, making the employment contract more contingent. In this environment, it is geographic place rather than the corporation that provides the organizational matrix for matching people and jobs. Access to talented and creative people is to modern business what access to coal and iron ore was to steelmaking. It determines where companies will choose to locate and grow, and this in turn changes the ways cities must compete. As Hewlett-Packard CEO Carley Fiorina once told this nation's governors: "Keep your tax incentives and highway interchanges; we will go where the highly skilled people are."[5]

Creative people, in turn, don't just cluster where the jobs are. They cluster in places that are centers of creativity and also where they like to live. From classical Athens and Rome, to the Florence of the Medici and Elizabethan London, to Greenwich Village and the San Francisco Bay Area, creativity has always gravitated to specific locations. As the great urbanist Jane Jacobs pointed out long ago, successful places are multidimensional and diverse—they don't just cater to a single industry or a single demographic group; they are full of stimulation and creativity interplay.[6] In my consulting work, I often tell business and political leaders that places need a people climate— or a creativity climate—as well as a business climate. Cities like Seattle, Austin, Toronto and Dublin recognize the multidimensional nature of this transformation and are striving to become broadly creative communities, not just centers of technological innovation and high-tech industry. If places like Buffalo, Grand Rapids, Memphis and Louisville do not follow suit, they will be hard-pressed to survive.

Our fundamental social forms are shifting as well, driven by forces traceable to the creative ethos. In virtually every aspect of life, weak ties have replaced the stronger bonds that once gave structure to society. Rather than live in one town for decades, we now move about. Instead of communities defined by close associations and deep commitments to family, friends and organizations, we seek places where we can make friends and acquaintances easily and live quasi-anonymous lives. The decline in the strength of our ties to people and institutions is a product of the increasing number of ties we have. As a retired industrialist who was the head of a technology transfer center in Ottawa, Canada, told me: "My father grew up in a small town and worked for the same company. He knew the same fourteen people in his entire life. I meet more people than that in any given day."[7] Modern life is increasingly defined by contingent commitments. We progress from job to job with amazingly little concern or effort. Where people once found themselves bound together by social institutions and formed their identities in groups, a fundamental characteristic of life today is that we strive to create our own identities.[8] It is this creation and re-creation of the self, often in ways that reflect our creativity, that is a key feature of the creative ethos.

In this new world, it is no longer the organizations we work for, churches, neighborhoods or even family ties that define us. Instead, we do this ourselves, defining our identities along the varied dimensions of our creativity. Other aspects of our lives—what we consume, new forms of leisure and recreation, efforts at community-building—then organize themselves around this process of identity creation.

Furthermore, when we think about group identity in this new world, we must rethink our notions of class. We often tend to classify people on the basis of their consumption habits or lifestyle choices, or, more crudely, by their income level. For instance, we often equate middle income with middle class. Though I view these things as significant markers of class, they are not its primary determinants. A *class* is a cluster of people who have common interests and tend to think, feel and behave similarly, but these similarities are fundamentally determined by economic function—by the kind of work they do for a living. All the other distinctions follow from that. And a key fact of our age is that more of us than ever are doing creative work for a living.

The New Class

The economic need for creativity has registered itself in the rise of a new class, which I call the Creative Class. Some *38 million* Americans, 30 percent of all employed people, belong to this new class. I define the core of the Creative Class to include people in science and engineering, architecture and design, education, arts, music and entertainment, whose economic function is to create new ideas, new technology and/or new creative content. Around the core, the Creative Class also includes a broader group of *creative professionals* in business and finance, law, health care and related fields. These people engage in complex problem solving that involves a great deal of independent judgment and requires high levels of education or human capital. In addition, all members of the Creative Class—whether they are artists or engineers, musicians or computer scientists, writers or entrepreneurs—share a common creative ethos that values creativity, individuality, difference and merit. For the members of the Creative Class, every aspect and every manifestation of creativity—technological, cultural and economic—is interlinked and inseparable.

The key difference between the Creative Class and other classes lies in what they are primarily paid to do. Those in the Working Class and the Service Class are primarily paid to execute according to plan, while those in the Creative Class are primarily paid to create and have considerably more autonomy and flexibility than the other two classes to do so. There are gray areas and boundary issues in my scheme of things, to be sure. And while some may quibble with my definition of the Creative Class and the numerical estimates that are based on it, I believe it has a good deal more precision than existing, more amorphous definitions of knowledge workers, symbolic analysts or professional and technical workers.

The class structure of the United States and other advanced nations has been the subject of great debate for well over a century. For a host of writers in the 1800s and 1900s, the big story was the rise, and then the decline, of the Working Class.[9] For writers like Daniel Bell and others in the middle to later 1900s, a second big story was the rise of a postindustrial society in which many of us shifted from making goods to delivering services.[10] The big story unfolding now— one that has been unfolding for some time—is the rise of the Creative Class, the great emerging class of our time.

The reason modern society feels so different to our time-traveler is the staggering growth of this class. Over the twentieth century, the Creative Class grew from roughly 3 million workers to its current size, a tenfold-plus increase; since 1980 alone it has more than doubled. Roughly 15 million Americans, more than 12 percent of the workforce, compose the Super-Creative Core of this new class. The Creative Class in the United States today is larger than the traditional Working Class—for instance those who work in manufacturing, construction and transportation industries.

The long sweep of the twentieth century has seen the rise and fall of the Working Class, which peaked at roughly 40 percent of the U.S. workforce between 1920 and 1950 before beginning its long slide to roughly a quarter of the workforce today. The Service Class, which includes fields such as personal care, food service and clerical work, has grown steadily over the same period, doubling from roughly 16 to 30 percent of the workforce between 1900 and 1950 before climbing to more than 45 percent by 1980. With some 55 million members today it is the largest class in terms of sheer numbers.

Although the Creative Class remains somewhat smaller than the Service Class, its crucial economic role makes it the most influential. The Creative Class is also considerably larger than the class of "organization men" described in William Whyte's 1956 book. Like Whyte's managerial class, which "set the American temper" in the 1950s, the Creative Class is the norm-setting class of our time. But its norms are very different: Individuality, self-expression and openness to difference are favored over the homogeneity, conformity and "fitting in" that defined the organizational age. Furthermore, the Creative Class is dominant in terms of wealth and income, with its members earning nearly twice as much on average as members of the other two classes.

But the sacrifices we will make for money are very different from those once made by Whyte's organization men. Very few of us work for the same large company or organization for life, and we are far less likely to pin our identity or sense of self-worth on whom we work for. We balance financial considerations against the ability to be ourselves, set our own schedules, do challenging work and live in communities that reflect our values and priorities. According to one large-scale survey of people who work in information technology fields—a relatively conservative subgroup of the Creative Class—challenge and responsibility, the ability to work a flexible schedule and a secure and stable work environment all rank ahead of money as the key elements of what people value in their jobs. The upheaval in our private lives is epitomized by one well-publicized statistic: Fewer than one-quarter of all Americans (23.5 percent) accounted for by the 2000 Census lived in a "conventional" nuclear family, down from 45 percent in 1960.[11] These profound changes are not, as commonly portrayed, signs of the reckless self-indulgence of a spoiled people. They are undergirded by a simple economic rationality. We live by our creativity, so we try to take care of it and seek environments that allow it to flourish—much as the blacksmith once cared for his forge, and farmers took care of the oxen that drove their plows.

Creativity in the world of work is not limited to members of the Creative Class. Factory workers and even the lowest-end service workers always have been creative in certain valuable ways. Also, the creative content of many working-class and service-class jobs is growing—a prime example being the continuous-improvement programs on many factory floors, which call on line workers to contribute ideas as well as their physical labor. On the basis of these trends, I expect that the Creative Class, which is still emergent, will continue to grow in coming decades, as more traditional economic functions are transformed into Creative Class occupations. . . . I strongly believe that the key to improving the lot of underpaid, underemployed and disadvantaged people lies not in social welfare programs or low-end make-work jobs—nor in somehow bringing back the factory jobs of the past—but rather in tapping the creativity of these people, paying them appropriately for it and integrating them fully into the Creative Economy.

Not all is rosy in this emerging mainstream of the Creative Age. With no big company to provide security, we bear much more risk than the corporate and working classes of the organizational age did. We experience and often create high levels of mental and emotional stress, at work and at home. We crave flexibility but have less time to pursue the things we truly desire. The technologies that were supposed to liberate us from work have invaded our lives. And though the Creative Class does not have a monopoly on creativity, it certainly has cornered the lion's share of the market for it—while segmenting both the labor market and society in new ways. Significant fault lines are appearing as the values, attitudes and aspirations of the Creative Class inexorably clash with those of the other established classes. Our society may well be splitting into two or three separate types of economies, cultures and communities, with deepening divides of education, occupation and geographic location.

The nation's geographic center of gravity has shifted away from traditional industrial regions toward new axes of creativity and innovation. The Creative Class is strongly oriented to large cities and regions that offer a variety of economic opportunities, a stimulating environment and amenities for every possible lifestyle. The nation's leading creative centers include major East Coast regions like Washington, D.C., Boston and the greater New York region, and leading high-tech centers like the San Francisco Bay Area, Seattle and Austin. These places offer something for everyone—vibrant urban districts, abundant natural amenities and comfortable suburban "nerdistans" for techies so inclined.[12] But large regions do not have an exclusive hold on the members of this new class. Smaller places like Boulder, Colorado and Santa Fe, New Mexico boast significant concentrations of the Creative Class, as do less obvious places like Gainesville, Florida; Provo, Utah; and Huntsville, Alabama.

This remaking of our economic geography is intimately tied to class identity. Today's professionals see themselves as members of a broad creative force, not as corporate officers or organization men. Thus they gravitate to stimulating creative environments—to places that offer not only opportunities and amenities, but openness to diversity, where they feel they can express themselves and validate their identities. They are fleeing older working-class strongholds and in many cases avoiding newer but conservative Sunbelt cities—increasingly opting out of places where tradition is more valued and where the social norms of the organizational age still prevail. In fact, many of these places are being almost entirely abandoned by the Creative Class.

One of the most significant fault lines of our age is the growing geographic segregation of the Creative Class and the other classes. The geographic trends I will describe in this book do *not* favor the tightly knit old-style communities that are so often celebrated in our songs, stories and sentimental TV commercials. Moreover, a number of serious social commentators in recent years have urged us to recultivate and rebuild the old forms of "social capital" found in these communities. Such efforts are fruitless, since they fly in the face of today's economic realities. A central task ahead is developing new forms of social cohesion appropriate to the Creative Age.

The Transformation of Everyday Life

Economic shifts are thus altering the structure of everyday life. The rise and decline of the New Economy did not cause these changes, though it did help push them to the surface and make them more noticeable. In a deeper and more pervasive way, the September 11,

2001, tragedy and subsequent terrorist threats have caused Americans, particularly those in the Creative Class, to ask sobering questions about what really matters in our lives. What we are witnessing in America and across the world extends far beyond high-tech industry or any so-called New Economy: It is the emergence of a new society and a new culture—indeed a whole new way of life. It is these shifts that will prove to be the most enduring developments of our time. And they thrust hard questions upon us. For now that forces have been unleashed that allow us to pursue our desires, the question for each of us becomes: What do we really want?

I have spent the past several years conducting research on the changing attitudes and desires of the Creative Class and the other classes, as well as the key factors that have brought new attitudes to the fore. I have interviewed and conducted focus groups with people across the United States and elsewhere. I have visited companies and communities of all kinds in my attempts to determine what is going on. And with teams of colleagues and graduate students, I delved deeply into statistical correlations to develop more substantial evidence of the fundamental trends and patterns. Based on my research, I would describe several dimensions of the transformation that I see, corresponding to several basic categories of human existence: work, lifestyle, time and community. In each case, the changes reflect a society in which the creative ethos is on the rise.

The No-Collar Workplace

Artists, musicians, professors and scientists have always set their own hours, dressed in relaxed and casual clothes and worked in stimulating environments. They could never be forced to work, yet they were never truly not at work. With the rise of the Creative Class, this way of working has moved from the margins to the economic mainstream. While the no-collar workplace certainly appears more casual than the old, it replaces traditional hierarchical systems of control with new forms of self-management, peer recognition and pressure and intrinsic forms of motivation, which I call *soft control*. In this setting, we strive to work more independently and find it much harder to cope with incompetent managers and bullying bosses. We trade job security for autonomy. In addition to being fairly compensated for the work we do and the skills we bring, we want the ability to learn and grow, shape the content of our work, control our own schedules and express our identities through work. And companies of all types, including large established ones, are adapting to this change by striving to create new workplaces that are more amenable to creative work. In this, they have no choice: Either they will create these kinds of environments or they will wither and die.

The Experiential Lifestyle

Because we identify ourselves as creative people, we increasingly demand a lifestyle built around creative experiences. We are impatient with the strict separations that previously demarcated work, home and leisure. Whereas the lifestyle of the previous organizational age emphasized conformity, the new lifestyle favors individuality, self-statement, acceptance of difference and the desire for rich multidimensional experiences. David Brooks has argued in his clever book *Bobos in Paradise* that the new culture represents a blending of bourgeois and bohemian values.[13] But we have done more than blend these two categories; we have transcended them completely so that they no longer even apply. Spurred on by the creative ethos, we blend work and lifestyle to construct our identities as creative people. In the past, people often literally "identified" themselves through several basic social categories: occupation, employer and family status (husband, wife, father, mother). Today, the people in my interviews identify themselves through a tangle of connections to myriad creative activities. One person may be simultaneously a writer, researcher, consultant, cyclist, rock climber, electronic/world music/acid jazz lover, amateur gourmet cook, wine enthusiast or micro-brewer. The people in my interviews report that they have little trouble integrating such multiple interests and personae. This kind of synthesis is integral to establishing a unique creative identity. It's almost impossible to be a nonconformist today because conformity is no longer an issue. But at the same time, this more open attitude toward lifestyle forms a deep and growing division between the Creative Class and the more traditional classes.

The Time Warp

Creative people always have experienced and even cultivated a blurring of time. Writers, artists, musicians, scientists and inventors often have erratic and irregular schedules, working from home and seemingly playing at work. Now more of us do as well. How we organize and use time is changing in ways that go far beyond simplistic notions of the "overworked American" or the 24/7 workday. The core issue is not when we work or the number of hours we put in, but that our use of time has intensified. We pack every second—whether at work or at leisure—full of creative stimuli and experiences. And as we do so, our conception of time has completely morphed. The old boundaries that told us when we should do certain things have faded into oblivion. We in fact work at times when we are supposed to be off and play when we are supposed to be working. This is because creativity cannot be switched on and off at predetermined times, and is itself an odd mixture of work and play. Writing a book, producing a work of art or developing new software requires long periods of intense concentration, punctuated by the need to relax, incubate ideas and recharge. So too does designing a new marketing campaign or investment strategy.

A whole new social construction of time is thus emerging—and not only in how we use our time from day to day, but in how we use it over the course of a life. Careers, for instance, now tend to be front-loaded. Rather than climb the corporate ladder as they grow older, people now often pack their most intense and productive creative work into their younger years, when their potential for advancement and sheer physical energy are at a peak. Meanwhile the time-consuming obligations of marriage and children are deferred: The average age of women at childbearing in the United States recently topped thirty for the first time in history. Not only have the midlife crisis and midlife career change become more prevalent, they are being augmented by the "quarter-life" and "three-quarter-life" changes as people of all ages continue to seek new outlets for their creative capacities.

The Creative Community

Creative people have always gravitated to certain kinds of communities, such as the Left Bank in Paris or New York's Greenwich Village. Such communities provide the stimulation, diversity and a richness of experiences that are the wellsprings of creativity. Now more of us are looking for the same thing. Even if the community we choose isn't quite the kind of place where Gertrude Stein would live, it tends to meet a lot of the same basic criteria: a place that enables us to reflect and reinforce our identities as creative people, pursuing the kind of work we choose and having ready access to a wide range of lifestyle amenities. In place of the tightly knit urban neighborhoods of the past or alienated and generic suburbs, we prefer communities that have a distinctive character. These communities are defined by the impermanent relationships and loose ties that let us live the quasi-anonymous lives we want rather than those that are imposed on us.

The key to understanding all of these shifts lies in seeing them as part of a more global change—as thickly interwoven strands of a single underlying transformation that is affecting every dimension of our lives. This transformation is the shift to an economic and social system based on human creativity. Most people would never suppose that changes in our tastes for work, lifestyle and community might be driven by such basic economic changes. I argue that they are.

Romanticizing the Future, Glorifying the Past

After reading scores of books and countless articles on today's social changes. I have come to the conclusion that much of the time we are locked in a misleading and fruitless debate. The two sides in this debate amount to little more than flip sides of the same coin, opposing mythologies steeped in outdated ideologies, equally short-sighted and misleading.

On one side is an eclectic group of commentators with a utopian faith in the power of technology to cure virtually all social and economic ills. According to techno-futurists like George Gilder and Kevin Kelly, the combination of new technology and unfettered market forces promises to deliver us from the mundanities of everyday work and life and lead us toward an ever more prosperous and liberated future.[14] Greater numbers of people are able to manage their careers as virtual "free agents," to use Dan Pink's phrase, moving from job to job or project to project at will, free from bureaucratic incompetence and the inanities of everyday office life.[15] More and more people will live "virtual" lives, coming together in on-line communities of like-minded individuals. There will be less and less need to shop or go to the movies when anything we desire can be delivered to our homes from a giant on-line mall. We can escape the constraints of geography; escape harsh, dirty and congested cities; and give up long commutes in favor of working from wherever we happen to be.[16]

Juxtaposed to this view are those who believe technology and unbridled market forces are making us work harder and faster, leaving us less time to enjoy each other and our interests, destroying human connections and damaging our neighborhoods and communities. If the techno-utopians romanticize the future, these techno-pessimists glorify the past. Unfettered hypercapitalism is leading to the end of work and the demise of high-paying, secure jobs, according to social critics like Jeremy Rifkin.[17] Worse yet, the elimination of such jobs destroys an important source of social stability, argues Richard Sennett, casting people adrift, corroding our collective character and damaging the very fiber of society.[18] The workplace is evolving into an increasingly stressful and dehumanizing "white-collar sweatshop" in Jill Fraser's view, beset by long hours and chronic overwork.[19] In the eyes of the cultural critic Tom Frank, business has become an all-powerful and hegemonic cultural force, as entities like MTV and The Gap turn alternative-culture symbols into moneymaking devices.[20] Neighborhoods, cities and society as a whole are losing the strong sense of community and civic-minded spirit that were the source of our prosperity, argues Robert Putnam.[21] In his nostalgia for a bygone era of VFW halls, bowling leagues, Cub Scout troops and Little League, Putnam contends that the demise of these repositories of "social capital" is the source of virtually all of our woes.

Despite their obvious ideological differences, all of these viewpoints suggest that forces beyond our control are exogenously reshaping our work, communities and lives. All, as a result, underestimate the extent and power of the ongoing social changes at work today. By insisting that these social changes are somehow imposed on us, all of these commentators avoid the real question of our age: Why are we *choosing* to live and work like this? Why do we want this life, or think that we do?

In an insightful essay, the economic historian Paul David points to the limits of this kind of thinking.[22] It is not technology per se that powers long-run economic growth. Technology is certainly important, but the sources of growth are more complicated and messy. Long-run growth requires a series of gradually accumulating changes in the organizational and institutional fabric of society, taking place over perhaps half a century. These changes are not dictated by technology; rather they are the result of incremental shifts in human behavior and social organization. We have been going through such a process of social adaptation, organizational readjustment and changing personal expectations. At first glance, these recent changes seem centered on new forms of information and biotechnology, much as the Industrial Revolution seemed to be powered by new machines and new forms of energy. But upon closer examination, the current transformation, like its predecessor, turns out to be broader.

The deep and enduring changes of our age are not technological but social and cultural. They are thus harder to see, for they result from the gradual accumulation of small, incremental changes in our day-to-day lives. These changes have been building for decades and are only now coming to the fore.

Notes

1. For a careful empirical comparison of technological change at the turn of the twentieth century versus modern times, see Robert Gordon, "Does the New Economy Measure Up to the Great Inventions of the Past?" Cambridge, Mass.: National Bureau of Economic Research, Working Paper No. 7833, August 2000. His answer is a resounding no. The great majority of the technological inventions in the National Academy of Engineering's "Greatest Engineering Accomplishments of the 20th Century" occurred prior to 1950. Only two of the top ten occurred after World War II (semiconductor electronics, no. 5, and computers, no. 8), while the Internet, the subject of so much New Economy hype, ranks thirteenth. See www.greatachievements.org.

2. Among the most popular, indeed classic works in this vein, see Sinclair Lewis, *Main Street*. New York: Harcourt, Brace and Company, 1920; and *Babbitt*. New York: Harcourt, Brace and World, 1922; William H. Whyte, Jr., *The Organization Man*. New York: Simon and Schuster, 1956; David Riesman, *The Lonely Crowd: A Study of the Changing American Character*. New Haven: Yale University Press, 1950; C. Wright Mills, *White Collar: The American Middle Classes*. New York: Oxford University Press, 1951; John Kenneth Galbraith, *The New Industrial State*. New York: Houghton-Mifflin, 1967. Also see Anthony Sampson, *Company Man: The Rise and Fall of Corporate Life*. New York: Times Books, 1995.

3. There are many statements of the free agent view, but the most notable is Daniel Pink, *Free Agent Nation: How America's New Independent Workers Are Transforming the Way We Live*. New York: Warner Books, 2001.

4. Again there are many statements of this view, but for a contemporary one see Kevin Kelly, *New Rules for the New Economy: 10 Radical Strategies for a Connected World*. New York: Viking, 1998.

5. Fiorina preceded me in speaking to the Annual Meeting of the National Governors Association in Washington, D.C., in winter 2000, where she made these remarks.

6. Jacobs's work is the classic statement of these themes. See Jane Jacobs, *The Death and Life of Great American Cities*. New York: Random House, 1961; *The Economy of Cities*. New York: Random House, 1969; *Cities and the Wealth of Nations*. New York: Random House, 1984.

7. Personal interview by author, Ottawa, Canada, September 2001.

8. On this point see Manuel Castells, *The Power of Identity: The Information Age: Economy, Society, and Culture, Volume I*. Oxford: Blackwell Publishers Ltd., 1997.

9. The classic statement here is that of Karl Marx in both *Capital* and *The Communist Manifesto* among his many other works.

10. Daniel Bell, *The Coming of Post-Industrial Society*. New York: Basic Books, 1973.

11. "The Changing American Family." *New York Times*, May 15, 2001.

12. The concept of the "nerdistan" is Joel Kotkin's, see *The New Geography: How the Digital Revolution is Reshaping the American Landscape*. New York: Random House, 2000.

13. David Brooks, *Bobos in Paradise: The New Upper Class and How They Got There*. New York: Simon and Schuster, 2001.

14. Kelly, *New Rules for the New Economy*; George Gilder, *Telecosm: How Infinite Bandwidth Will Revolutionize Our World*. New York: The Free Press, 2000; *Microcosm: The Quantum Revolution in Economics and Technology*. New York: Simon and Schuster, 1989. Also see William J. Mitchell, *City of Bits: Space, Place and the Infobahn*. Cambridge: MIT Press, 1995.

15. Pink, *Free Agent Nation*.

16. The number of books touting the advantages of the virtual world is astounding; see, for example, Don Tapscott, *The Digital Economy: Promise and Peril in the Age of Networked Intelligence*. New York: McGraw Hill, 1996; and Diane Coyle, *The Weightless World: Strategies for Managing in a Digital Economy*. Cambridge: MIT Press, 1997.

17. Jeremy Rifkin, *The End of Work: The Decline of the Global Labor Force and the Dawn of the Post-Market Era*. New York: Putnam, 1995.

18. Richard Sennett, *The Corrosion of Character: The Personal Consequences of Work in the New Capitalism*. New York: W.W. Norton, 1998.

19. Jill Andresky Fraser, *White-Collar Sweatshop: The Deterioration of Work and Its Rewards in Corporate America*. New York: W.W. Norton, 2001. Of course the classic statement of the overwork thesis is Juliet Schor, *The Overworked American*. New York: Basic Books, 1991.

20. Tom Frank, *One Market Under God: Extreme Capitalism, Market Populism, and the End of Economic Development*. New York: Doubleday, 2001; and *The Conquest of Cool: Business Culture, Counterculture, and*

the Rise of Hip Consumerism. Chicago: University of Chicago Press, 1997.

21. Robert Putnam, *Bowling Alone: The Collapse and Revival of American Community.* New York: Simon and Schuster, 2000.

22. See Paul David, "Understanding Digital Technology's Evolution and the Path of Measured Productivity Growth: Present and Future in the Mirror of the Past," in Eric Brynolfsson and Brian Kahin (eds.), *Understanding the Digital Economy.* Cambridge: MIT Press, 2001.

READING, REREADING, AND ANALYSIS

1. What changes in society have you personally experienced in the last ten years? What changes have you only read or heard about? How might Florida's man from the 1950s experience the changes you have listed?

2. What ideas and values seem most important to the people Florida identifies as members of the Creative Class? Do you share similar values? Why or why not?

3. Bring an advertisement to class that either shows the symbolic power of creativity (speaks to the culture of time as Florida asserts) or emphasizes the Working Class or the Service Class as Florida identifies those two alternatives to the new Creative Class. In a group, compare and discuss the advertisements in the terms of Florida's essay.

4. Individually or in a group, make a list of positive qualities Florida associates with the Creative Class. Next, make a list of the possible criticisms of the Creative Class and of Florida's praise of the class. Which criticisms seem the strongest? How might Florida respond to and counter or try to offset the criticisms the group raises?

5. What does Florida mean on page 201 when he says,

   In this new world, it is no longer the organizations we work for, churches, neighborhoods or even family ties that define us. Instead, we do this ourselves, defining our own identities along the varied dimensions of our creativity. Other aspects of our lives—what we consume, new forms of leisure and recreation, efforts at community-building—then organize themselves around this process of identity creation.

6. In a group, discuss the contrast Florida draws between an outlook that emphasizes determinism—there are "forces beyond our control," which transform "our work, communities and lives"—and an outlook that emphasizes personal control, one that asks, "Why are we *choosing* to live and work like this?" (p. 209). Members of

the group should compare their own outlook with the two Florida distinguishes.

RESPONDING THROUGH WRITING: BUILDING AN INTERPRETATION

7. In four or five sentences, summarize the key features Florida attributes to what he calls the Creative Class.

8. Using the ad you brought in for question 3, write an essay that discusses how the ad might be said to illustrate some of Florida's key claims about the Creative Class, or write about how the ad might be said to work against some of Florida's key claims.

9. Do your academic and social experiences in college so far relate to Florida's claim of a transformation of everyday life? Write an essay in which you reflect on relationships between creativity, learning in college, and your goals beyond college. In your essay, you might explore some of the following questions: What role does creativity play in your learning? How does our learning in college relate to the drive to create our own identities? Does any of your learning in college work against one or more of Florida's main claims in his essay?

10. Write a short paper in which you reflect on Florida's claim that "significant fault lines are appearing as the values, attitudes and aspirations of the Creative Class inexorably clash with those of the other established classes. Our society may well be splitting into two or three separate types of economies, cultures and communities, with deepening divides of education, occupation and geographic location" (p. 203–04).

GOING FURTHER: LEARNING FROM OTHER SOURCES

11. Use a reference database such as EBSCO or InfoTrac to find more information about George Gilder and Kevin Kelly, people Florida calls "techno-futurists" (p. 208). After doing your research, compare your take on Gilder and Kelly with Florida's description of their views. In addition to Florida's take on Gilder and Kelly, what other criticisms do you find in your research about their views?

12. Use a search engine such as Google or AltaVista to make the following search: "capitalism and creativity." Of the sources you find, which ones interest you the most? Why? Make a list of the most common connections you find in the sources you read (ex-

amine at least six sources). In a group, compare your findings with those of your peers.

APPLYING WHAT YOU'VE LEARNED

13. In "From the Frying Pan into the Fire," Arlie Russell Hochschild describes and evaluates how workplace efficiency standards transform key aspects of our home life. After reading Hochschild's essay, do you see her sharing Florida's perspective on transformations of everyday life? Write a paper that compares Hochschild's and Florida's orientations toward work, time, and cultural changes. Be sure to quote and discuss specific key passages from the essays, such as the following statement by Florida:

> The core issue is not when we work or the number of hours we put in, but that our use of time has intensified. We pack every second—whether at work or at leisure—full of creative stimuli and experiences. And as we do so, our conception of time has completely morphed. The old boundaries that told us when we should do certain things has faded into oblivion. We in fact work at times when we are supposed to be off and play when we are supposed to be working. This is because creativity cannot be switched on and off at predetermined times, and is itself an odd mixture of work and play (p. 206).

    If you see differences in their views, then which makes more sense to you, or what other view might you offer as a more sensible view than their perspectives?

14. Like Florida, Michio Kaku in "Second Thought: The Genetics of a Brave New World?" and Lawrence Lessig in "Introduction to Free Culture" discuss major technological innovations transforming life in the United States. Write an essay in which you reflect on the most significant arguments or lessons you see in the writers' texts in relation to your desires and life goals. Do any of your views about the arguments the writers present change as a result of reading and reflecting on their positions? Have any of the views you held before reading the essays changed as a result of thinking and writing about these three texts?

15. After reading Julie Charlip's "A Real Class Act: Searching for Identity in the Classless Society," write an essay that explores whether or not Charlip is a member of Florida's Creative Class. Do you think Charlip would interpret capitalism as Florida does and talk about class from the same perspective as Florida? Why or why not? What lessons about class are we to take from Charlip and Florida, and which seem to be the most significant from your perspective? Why?

ARLIE RUSSELL HOCHSCHILD

Arlie Russell Hochschild (b. 1940) is Professor of Sociology at the University of California, Berkeley. Her interest in the impact of contemporary capitalism on everyday life is reflected in the titles of her most recent books: *The Commercialization of Intimate Life: Notes from Home and Work* (in which the essay below appears), *The Time Bind: When Work Becomes Home and Home Becomes Work*, and *The Second Shift: Working Parents and the Revolution at Home*. Her ability to communicate with both general and scholarly audiences has been recognized by the American Sociological Association with its Award for Public Understanding of Sociology.

> For more information on Hochschild and her work, see
> <http://sociology.berkeley.edu/faculty/hochschild>.

WHAT DO YOU KNOW? WHAT DO YOU EXPECT TO DISCOVER?

Before reading the essay, take a moment to consider the following questions.

1. What topics does Hochschild's biography suggest that she is interested in? What do you know about those topics? Knowledge can come from personal experience, stories you've heard, other classes you've taken, or other reading you've done.

2. What does her title lead you to expect from this essay? What might the "Frying Pan" signify as a metaphor? Likewise, what might the "Fire" signify as a metaphor? Looking up and comparing the definitions of these words can help you make connections.

3. Hochschild analyzes how aspects of our jobs have reshaped aspects of our lives at home. If you have a job or have had one, think about how the job may structure one or more aspects of your life away from work. Aside from the making of money, how might one's job revise or reshape one's life at home?

⚡

From the Frying Pan into the Fire

An advertisement for Quaker Oats cereal in an issue of *Working Mother* magazine provides a small window on the interplay between consumption and the application of the idea of efficiency to private time in modern America.[1] In the ad, a mother, dressed in a business suit, affectionately hugs her smiling son. Beneath the image, we read: "Instant Quaker Oatmeal, for moms who have a lot of love but not a lot of time." The ad continues with a short story: "Nicky is a very picky eater. With Instant Quaker Oatmeal, I can give him a terrific hot breakfast in just 90 seconds. And I don't have to spend any time coaxing him to eat it!"

The ad then presents "facts" about mother and child: "Sherry Greenberg, with Nicky, age four and a half, Hometown: New York City, New York, Occupation: Music teacher, Favorite Flavor: Apples and Cinnamon." The designers of this ad, we could imagine, want us to feel we've been let in on an ordinary moment in a middle-class American morning. In this ordinary moment, Sherry Greenberg is living according to a closely scheduled, rapidly paced "adult" time, while Nicky is living according to a more dawdling, slowly paced "child" time. So the mother faces a dilemma. To meet her work deadline, she must get Nicky on "adult" time. But to be a good mother it is desirable to give her child a hot breakfast—"hot" being associated with devotion and love. To cook the hot breakfast, though, Sherry needs *time*. The ad suggests that it is the cereal itself that solves the problem. It conveys love because it is hot, but it permits efficiency because it's quickly made. The cereal would seem to reconcile an image of American motherhood of the 1950s with the female work role of 2000 and beyond.

The cereal also allows Sherry to avoid the unpleasant task of struggling with her child over scarce time. In the ad, Nicky's slow pace is implicitly attributed to his character ("Nicky is a very picky eater") and not to the fact that he is being harnessed to an accelerating pace of adult work time or protesting an adult speed-up by staging a "slowdown." By permitting the mother to avoid a fight with her son over time, the ad brilliantly evokes a common problem and proposes a commodity as a solution.

Attached to the culture of time shown in the ad is a key but hidden social logic. This modern working mother is portrayed as resembling Frederick Taylor, the famed efficiency expert of modern industry. The principle of efficiency is not located, here, at work in the person of the owner, the foreman, or the worker. It is located in the worker-as-mother. We do not see a boss pressing the worker for more efficiency at the office. Instead, we see a mother pressing her son to eat more efficiently at home. This efficiency-seeking is transferred from man to woman, from workplace to home, and from adult to child. Nicky becomes his own task master, quickly gobbling his breakfast himself because it is so delicious. Frederick Taylor has leapt the fence from factory to home, adult to child, and jumped, it seems, into the cereal box itself. Frederick Taylor has become a commodity. *It* provides efficiency. Thus, the market reinforces the idea of efficiency twice—once at a locus of production, where the worker is pressed to work efficiently, and again, as a supplier of consumer goods, where it promises to deliver the very efficiency it also demands.

Quaker Oats cereal may be a paradigm for a growing variety of goods and services—frozen dinners, computer shopping services, cell phones,[2] and the like—that claim to save time for busy working parents. They often save time at home. But the ethic of "saving time" raises the question of what we want to save time for.[3] In the case above, the photo of the happy mother and child suggests that the mother is rushing her son through breakfast, not to race out to an all-absorbing job at a dot-com company, but to teach a few piano lessons. The picture doesn't challenge our idea of the primacy, even sacredness, of Nicky's home. So we don't much notice the sly insinuation of Frederick Taylor into the scene.

Conventional Versus Unconventional Wisdom

If, through modern Western eyes, the Greenbergs of this ad were a normal family, we could imagine them feeling that family life superseded all other aspects of life. That is, according to modern conventional wisdom, a happy family life is an end in itself. Earning and spending money are the means for achieving this end. Home and community are primary; workplace and mall are secondary. When we go out to work, it's to put bread on the table for the family. When we shop at the mall, it's often to buy a Christmas, birthday, or house present "for the family." Put in other terms, we often see the home and the community as sacred, and the workplace and the mall as profane. We are who we are at home and in our communities. We do what we do at work and buy what we buy at the mall.

To be sure, we make exceptions for the odd workaholic here or shopaholic there, but, as the terms imply, an overconcern with the profane realms of work and mall are, given this way of seeing things, off moral limits. Sherry Greenberg fits right in. She is in her kitchen feeding her son. She has what one imagines to be a manageable job. It's just that she's wanting to hurry things along a bit.

Implicit in this conventional view of family life is the idea that our use of time is like a language. We speak through it. By either what we say we want to spend time doing or what we actually spend time doing, we say what it is we hold sacred. Maybe we don't think of it just this way, but we assume that each "spending time" or each statement of feeling about time ("I wish I could spend time") is a bow from the waist to what we hold dear. It is a form of worship. Again, Sherry Greenberg is symbolizing the importance of family. It's just that she's slightly on the edge of that conventional picture because she's in a hurry to get out of it. The Quaker Oats ad both appeals to this family-comes-first picture of life and subtly challenges it, by taking sides with her desire to feed Nicky "efficiently."

The subtle challenge of the ad points, I believe, to a larger contradiction underlying stories like that of the Greenbergs. Reflecting on my research on the Fortune 500 company I call Amerco, I'll try to explore it. Increasingly, our belief that family comes first conflicts with the emotional draw of both workplace and mall. Indeed, I would argue that a constellation of pressures is pushing men and women further into the world of workplace and mall. And television—a pipeline, after all, to the mall—is keeping them there. Family and community life have meanwhile become less central as places to talk and relate, and less the object of collective rituals.

Many of us respond to these twin trends, however, not by turning away from family and community, but by actually elevating them in moral importance. Family and community are not a realm in decline, as David Popenoe argues about the family and Robert Putnam argues for the community. To many people, both have become even more important morally. We encapsulate the idea of the cherished family.[4] We separate ideal from practice. We separate the idea of "spending time with X" from the idea of "believing in the importance of X." We don't link what we think with what we do. Or as one Amerco employee put it, using company language, "I don't walk the talk at home." This encapsulation of our family ideal allows us to accommodate to what is both a pragmatic necessity and a competing source of meaning—the religion of capitalism. I say pragmatic necessity, because most Americans, men and women alike, have to work for food and rent.

At the same time, a new cultural story is unfolding. It is not that capitalism is an unambiguous object of worship. After all, American capitalism is, in reality, a highly complex, internally diverse economic system for making, advertising, and selling things. But, without overstating the case, it seems true that capitalism is a cultural as well as an economic system and that the symbols and rituals of this cultural system compete with, however much they seem to serve, the symbols and rituals of community and family. This means that working long hours and spending a lot of money—instead of spending time together—have increasingly become *how* we say "I love you" at home. As Juliet Schor argues in *The Overspent American,* over the last twenty years, Americans have raised the bar on what feels like enough money to get along. In 1975, according to a Roper poll, 10 percent of people mentioned a second color TV as part of "the good life," and 28 percent did in 1991. A 1995 Merck Family Fund poll showed that 27 percent of people who earned $100,000 or more agreed with the statement, "I cannot afford to buy everything I really need." At the same time, between 1975 and 1991, the role of family in people's idea of "the good life" declined while the importance of having money increased. The importance of having a happy marriage to "the good life" declined from 84 percent in 1975 to 77 percent in 1991. Meanwhile having "a lot of money" went from 38 percent in 1975 to 55 percent in 1991.[5]

How much of a stretch is it, I wonder, to go from the trends Schor points out to Harvey Cox's daring thesis: that capitalism has become a religion? As Cox puts it:

> Just as a truly global market has emerged for the first time in human history, that market is functioning without moral guideposts and restraints, and it has become the most powerful institution of our age. Even nation-states can often do little to restrain or regulate it. More and more, the idea of "the market" is construed, not as a creation of culture ("made by human hands," as the Bible says about idols), but as the "natural" way things happen. For this reason, the "religion" the market generates often escapes criticism and evaluation or even notice. It becomes as invisible to those who live by it as was the religion of the preliterate Australians whom Durkheim studied, who described it as just "the way things are."[6]

Capitalism has, Cox suggests, its myth of origin, its legends of the fall, its doctrine of sin and redemption, its notion of sacrifice (state belt-tightening), and its hope of salvation through the free market system. Indeed, if in the Middle Ages the church provided people with a basic orientation to life, the multinational corporation's workplace, with its "mission statements," its urgent deadlines, its demands for peak performance and total quality, does so today. Paradoxically, what would seem like the most secular of systems (capitalism), organized around the most profane of activities (making a living, shopping), provides a sense of the sacred. So what began as a *means* to an end—capitalism the means, a good living as the end—has become an *end* itself. It's a case of mission drift writ large. The cathedrals of capitalism dominate our cities. Its ideology dominates our airwaves. It calls for sacrifice, through long hours of work, and offers its blessings, through commodities. When the terrorists struck the twin towers on 9/11, they were, perhaps, aiming at what they conceived of as a more powerful rival temple, another religion. Heartless as they were, they were correct to see capitalism, and the twin towers as its symbol, as a serious rival religion.

Like older religions, capitalism partly creates the anxieties to which it poses itself as a necessary answer. Like the fire-and-brimstone sermon that begins with "Man, the lowly sinner," and ends with "Only this church can redeem you," so the market ethos defines the poor or unemployed as "unworthy slackers" and offers work and a higher standard of living as a form of salvation. Capitalism is not, then, simply a system in the *service of* family and community; it *competes* with the family. When we separate our fantasy of family life, our ideas of being a "good mother and father" from our daily expressions of parenthood, our ideals live timelessly on while we worship at the biggest altar in town, with ten-hour days and long trips to the mall.

A constellation of forces seems to be pressing in the direction of the religion of capitalism. And while no one wants to go back to the "frying pan" of patriarchy, we need to look sharp about the fire of market individualism under capitalism. It is in the spirit of looking at that fire that we can examine several conditions that exacerbate the tendency to apply the principle of efficiency to private life.

The first factor is the inevitable—and on the whole I think beneficial—movement of women into the paid workforce.[7] Exacerbating this squeeze on time is the overall absence of government or workplace policies that foster the use of parental leave or shorter, more flexible hours. Over the last twenty years, workers have also been squeezed by a lengthening workweek. According to a recent International Labor Organization report on working hours, Americans are putting in longer hours than workers of any other industrialized nation. We now work two weeks longer each year than our counterparts in Japan, the vaunted long-work-hour capital of the world.[8] American married couples and single-parent families are also putting in more hours in the day and more weeks in the year than they did thirty years ago. Counting overtime and commuting time, a 1992 national sample of men averaged 48.8 hours of work, and women, 41.7.[9] Work patterns vary by social class, ethnicity, race, and the number and ages of children, of course. But, overall, between 1969 and 1996 the increase in American mothers' paid work combined with a shift toward single-parent families has led to an average decrease of 22 hours a week of parental time available (outside of paid work) to spend with children.[10] And the emotional draw of a work culture is sometimes strong enough to outcompete a weaker family culture.

The Other Side of the Market Religion: Not Walking the Talk at Home

If capitalism began as a means but became an end in itself, then families and local communities must daily face a competing urgency system and a rival conception of time. Company deadlines compete with school plays. Holiday sales at the mall vie with hanging out at home.

The company's schedule and rules have come, for workers, to define those of families. For the managers and production workers at Amerco, the company I studied for the *Time Bind*, the debut of a certain kind of product and its "product life cycle" came to prevail over personal anniversaries and school holidays. When family events did take precedence, they did so on company terms. As one woman explained, "My mother died and I went back to arrange for the funeral and all. I went for four days. The company gives us that for bereavement, and so that's the time I spent." In the early industrial period in Europe, whole workforces disappeared at festival time, or workers put an iron bar in the machinery, stopped the assembly line, and took a break. Company time did not always rule.

In response to the challenge of this competing urgency system, I've argued, many families separate their ideal of themselves as "a close family" from a life that in reality is more hurried, fragmented, crowded, and individualized than they would like. They develop the idea of a hypothetical family, the family they would be if only they had time. And then they deal with life in a contrary fashion.

Many Amerco employees came home from a long workday to fit many necessary activities into a limited amount of time. Although there were important exceptions, many workers tried to go through domestic chores rapidly if for no other reason than to clear some space in which to go slowly. They used many strategies to save time—they planned, delegated, did several things simultaneously. They packed one activity close up against the next, eliminating the framing around each event, periods of looking forward to or back upon an event, which might have heightened its emotional impact. A 2:00 to 2:45 play date, 2:45 to 3:15 shopping trip, 3:15 to 4:45 visit to Grandma, and so on. As one mother, a sales manager, said with satisfaction, "What makes me a good employee at work is what makes me able to do all I do at home; I'm a multitasker, but [with a laugh] at work I get paid for it."

With all these activities, family time could be called "hurried" or "crowded." But in fact many working parents took a sporting "have fun" attitude toward their hurried lives: "Let's see how fast we can do this! Come on, kids, let's go!" They brought their image of the family closer to the reality of it by saying, in effect, "We like it this way." They saw hassle as challenge. In other families, parents seemed to encourage children to develop schedules parallel to and as hectic as their own. For example, the average annual vacation time both at Amerco—and in the United States as a whole—is twelve days, while schoolchildren typically have summer holidays of three months. So one Amerco mother placed her eight-year-old son in a nearby summer program and explained to him, in a you're-going-to-love-this way, "You have your job to go to, too." She talked about her schedule as she might have talked about a strenuous hike. She was having fun roughing it with multitasking and chopped-up time.

Another way of resolving the contradiction between ideal and reality was to critique the fun ethic and say, in effect, "Family life isn't supposed to be fun. It's supposed to be a hassle, but we're in the hassle together, and why isn't that okay?" This often carried families over long stretches of time, but it prevented family members from giving full attention to each other. Time was hurried (not enough time allotted for an activity—15-minute baths, 20-minute dinners, for example). Or time was crowded (one or more people were doing more than one thing at a time). Or it was uncoordinated. Only two out of four people could make it to dinner, the ball game, the reunion. If there was not some chronic avoidance of a deep tension, families usually also took another approach. They *deferred* having a good time. Instead of saying, "This hassle is fun," they said, in effect, "This hassle isn't fun. But we'll have fun *later*." They waited for the weekend, for their vacation, for "quality time."

But the more a family deferred the chance for relaxed communication, the more anxious they sometimes became about it. One man told me: "My wife and I hadn't had time together for a long time, so we decided to take some 'marital quality time' by going out to a restaurant to eat dinner together. We had a nice dinner and afterwards went for a walk. We passed a toy store and my wife wanted to shop for a toy for our child. But I told her, 'No, you have a different quality time with our child. This is *our* quality time.' So we spent the rest of the evening arguing about whose quality time it was we were spending."

Another long-hours Amerco executive seemed to take this strategy of deferral to an extreme. When I asked him whether he wished he'd spent more time with his three daughters when they were growing up, he answered, "Put it this way, I'm pleased with how they turned out." This father loved his daughters, but he loved them as results. Or rather, his feeling was "I want my wife to enjoy the process of raising them. I'll enjoy that vicariously. What I will enjoy directly is the result, the young adults." So he didn't think family life should or shouldn't be fun while the kids were small and adolescent. That was his wife's specialty. He was deferring his real enjoyment until his daughters had grown up. Even Amerco parents who spent far more time with their children occasionally justified this time in terms of future results. They were pleased at how "old for their age" their children were, how "ahead," given a limited expenditure of parental time. Perhaps, most parents held a double perspective on their children—they cared about the child as he or she was growing up and about the child as he or she emerged in adulthood. Most oriented toward the family as a source of intrinsic pleasure were women and workers in the middle or lower ranks of the company; least oriented in this way were upper management or professional men—the congregation and the priests.

From the top to the bottom of the Amerco workforce, workers were forced to answer the challenge of capitalism—not simply as a system that gave them jobs, money, and stuff, but as a system that offered them a sense of purpose and guidance in a confusing time. They had to deal with the religion of capitalism, its grip on honor and sense of worth, its subtraction from—or absorption of—family and community life. We've emerged from an era in which most women had little or no paid work to a era in which most do. Are women jumping from the frying pan of patriarchy into the fire of capitalism? Just as the early industrial workforces took off at festival time, because they were not yet "disciplined" to capitalism, maybe postindustrial ones will work out their own way of living a balanced life. There could be a balance not just between the role of piano teacher, say, and mother, but between the unpaid *world* of home and community and the money *world* of work and mall. That may be the deeper issue underlying the ad for Quaker Oats cereal. For, our cultural soil is surreptitiously prepared for ads, like that for Quaker Oats cereal, that make you spend time buying one more thing that promises to save time—which increasingly we spend earning and buying.

Notes

This essay, which has been substantially revised, takes as its starting point "Globalization, Time, and the Family," first published in German by the Institut für die Wissenschaften von Menchen, Vienna, 1998, and included in *Am Ende des Millenniums,* edited by Kraysztof Michalski (Stuttgart: Klett-Cotta, 2000), pp. 180–203.

1. See Hochschild 1997a. *The Time Bind: When Work Becomes Home and Home Becomes Work.* New York: Metropolitan Books. Revised edition, with new introduction, New York: Holt, 2000.

2. Cell phones, home fax machines, car dictating machines, and similar gadgets are marketed, purchased, and used on the premise that these machines, like the cereal, will "save time"—so that the consumer can then enjoy more leisure. In practice, though, such technology often becomes a delivery system for pressure to do more paid work. Along with new technology come new norms. Electronic mail, for example, once hailed as a way of "saving time" has escalated expectations shortening the period of time one has before one is considered rude or inattentive not to reply.

3. Among affluent Americans, time-saving goods and services also force parents to define parenthood less in terms of production and more in terms of consumption. For example, a "good mother" in the American middle class is often seen as one who prepares her child's birthday, bakes the cake, blows up the balloons, invites her child's friends to a party. Increasingly, the busy working mother is tempted to buy the cake; in addition, new birthday services are available in American cities to help organize the party, send out the invitations, buy the gifts, blow up the balloons, and set up the food. The definition of a "good mother" moves from production to

consumption. The "good mother" is now one who enjoys the party with the child. The gift is one of derationalized time.

4. See Gillis, John R. 1994. "What's behind the Debate on Family Values?" Plenary Session, Section on Sociology of Family, American Sociological Association, Chicago, August; also Popenoe, David, 1989. *Disturbing the Nest: Family Change and Decline in Modern Societies.* Aldine De Gruyter; and Putnam, Robert D. 2000. *Bowling Alone: The Collapse and Revival of American Community.* New York: Simon and Schuster.

5. Schol, Juliet. 1998, *The Overspent American: Upscaling, Downshifting, and the New Consumer.* New York: Basic Books. pp. 16–17.

6. Cox, Harvey. 2001, "Mammon and the Culture of the Market: A Socio-Theological Critique." In Richard Madsen, William M. Sullivan, Ann Swidler, and Steven M. Tipton, eds., *Meaning and Modernity: Religion, Polity and Self.* Berkeley: University of California Press. pp. 124–35.

7. Some commentators blame women's movement into paid work for the strains experienced at home—including the high divorce rate. But I would argue that it is not women's paid work per se, but work in the absence of the necessary social adjustments in the structure of care—male sharing of care at home, family-friendly workplace policies, and social honor associated with care—that make the difference.

8. Doohan, John. 1999. "Working Long, Working Better?" *World of Work: The Magazine of the International Labour Organization,* no 31, September/October. The 600-page ILO report compared hours of work in 240 countries. In "Welcome to the New Company Town" (*Fortune,* January 10, 2000: 62–70), Jerry Useem cites 751 time-management titles listed on Amazon.com, including *Eating on the Run* and *Please Hold: 102 Things to Do While You Wait on the Phone.*

9. Galinsky, Ellen, James Bond and Dana Friedman 1993, *The Changing Workforce: Highlights of the National Study.* New York: Families and Work Institute. p. 9.

10. "Families and the Labor Market, 1969–1999: Analyzing the Time Crunch," May 1999, Report by the Council of Economic Advisors, Washington, D.C. Also a 2000 report found that 46 percent of workers work 41 hours or longer, 18 percent of them 51 hours or longer (see Center for Survey Research and Analysis, University of Connecticut, "2000 Report on U.S. Working Time"). Another recent study found that elementary school teachers—those in what is often thought to be a "woman's" job—reported working ten-hour days (see Drago, Robert, et al. 1999 "New Estimates of Working Time for Teachers." *Monthly Labor Review* 122 (April): 31–41) Less time away from work means less time for children. Nationwide, half of children wish they could see their fathers more, and a third wish they could see their mothers more Coolsen, Peter, Michelle Seligson, and James Garbino. 1985. *When School's Out and Nobody's Home.* Chicago: National Committee for the Prevention of Child Abuse; Hewlett, Sylvia Ann. 1991. *When the Bough Breaks: The Cost of Neglecting Our Children.* New York: Basic Books, p. 105. A growing number of commentators draw links, often carelessly, between this decline in family time and a host of problems, including school failure and alcohol and drug abuse (Hewlett 1991).

READING, REREADING, AND ANALYSIS

1. How do you "save time" in your life? What do you save it for?

2. What terms or ideas seem most important to Hochschild? What, for instance, is Taylorization? And what does Hochschild mean by "the religion of capitalism" (p. 217)?

3. Bring an advertisement to class that either shows the symbolic power of efficiency (speaks to the culture of time) or shows how capitalism serves as a religion.

4. Individually or in a group, make a list of positive qualities associated with the Instant Quaker Oatmeal advertisement Hochschild discusses. Also make a list of the criticisms of the advertisement that Hochschild suggests. Is her discussion of the ad an effective way to begin her essay? Why or why not? Is she reading "too much" into the ad? What are your favorite parts of her analysis of the ad and what questions might you like to ask her about her analysis of the ad?

5. What does Hochschild mean on page 217 when she says,

   > It is not that capitalism is an unambiguous object of worship. After all, American capitalism is, in reality, a highly complex, internally diverse economic system for making, advertising, and selling things. But, without overstating the case, it seems true that capitalism is a cultural as well as an economic system and that the symbols and rituals of this cultural system compete with, however much they seem to serve, the symbols and rituals of community and family.

6. In a group, discuss Hochschild's contrast between the "'frying pan' of patriarchy" and the "fire of market individualism under capitalism" (p. 219). Compare your findings with each group member's initial response to Hochschild's title. How did your expectations square with your reading of the essay?

RESPONDING THROUGH WRITING: BUILDING AN INTERPRETATION

7. In four or five sentences, summarize Hochschild's analysis of the "movement of women into the paid workforce." Next, in a short essay (one or two pages), discuss connections you see between your summary and Hochschild's analysis of "Sherry Greenberg" in the Instant Quaker Oats ad.

8. Using the ad you brought in for question 3, write an analysis of the ad that models or parallels Hochschild's approach in her analysis of the Instant Quaker Oats ad. Next, write an analysis of your ad that does not mirror Hochschild's approach. Finally, write a short essay (two or three pages) in which you compare your first analysis with your second. What are the key differences of emphasis and of approach?

9. How does the drive for efficiency affect your home or dorm life? Similarly, how does it affect your approaches to your university studies? Write an essay in which you reflect on relationships between efficiency and learning in college. In your essay, you might explore some of the following questions: Is your learning efficient? Is it supposed to be efficient? Might there be an argument that models of efficiency could be counterproductive to learning?

10. Write a short paper in which you test one of Hochschild's premises: that increasingly the local shopping mall provides for many people a "a sense of the sacred" as a site of "symbols and rituals."

GOING FURTHER: LEARNING FROM OTHER SOURCES

11. Use an encyclopedia or search a reference database to find out more about Frederick Taylor. How or why is Taylor celebrated, and how or why is he criticized? Do you see any connections between Taylor's theories of efficiency and writing instruction? If so, what are the connections? If not, do you think it would be a good idea to emphasize efficiency in your composition classes? Why or why not?

12. Use a search engine such as Google or AltaVista to make the following search: "capitalism and religion." Of the sources you find, which ones interest you the most and why? Make a list of the most common connections you find in the sources you read (examine at least six sources). In a group, compare your findings with those of your peers.

APPLYING WHAT YOU'VE LEARNED

13. In "The Lost Art of Argument," Christopher Lasch says we are publicly unaware of so many issues not because schools are failing to teach students but because we have forsaken public debate and left important public decisions to be settled efficiently by so-called experts. Use Hochschild's discussion of efficiency to help

you analyze Lasch's analysis of the redefining of democracy in the early twentieth century by advocates of professionalism such as Walter Lippmann.

14. Compare Hochschild's analysis of advertising—for example, how a commodity such as Instant Quaker Oats can be marketed as a "solution" to a "common problem"—with Stuart Ewen's discussion of advertising, particularly of product novelty versus style obsolescence, in "The Marriage Between Art and Commerce." Think about how perspectives on the issue of desire appear in both Hochschild's and Ewen's analyses. How is the topic of desire central to Hochschild's as well as to Ewen's argument, and what differences do you see in their analyses of desire?

15. Use Sven Birkerts's discussion of "vertical" versus "horizontal" engagement with texts to help you analyze Hochschild's discussion of efficiency and the refiguration of the sacred, home and community, on the one hand, and of the profane, work and shopping, on the other hand. In your analysis, you might also consider the following questions: What is the wisdom of efficiency? How does Birkerts's discussion of "resonance" relate or not relate to Hochschild's discussion of the "religion of capitalism"?

BELL HOOKS

bell hooks, (b. 1952) is the pen name of Gloria Jean Watkins, the daughter of a custodian and a domestic worker in Hopkinsville, Kentucky. In the introduction to her book *talking back: thinking feminist, thinking black* (in which this essay appears), hooks explains that pressure in her rural community to keep private things private, to not "talk back" to figures in authority, was a major obstacle to her becoming a writer and an independent thinker: "One of the many reasons I chose to write using the pseudonym bell hooks [. . .], was to construct a writer-identity that would challenge and subdue all impulses leading me away from speech into silence." As bell hooks, Watkins has been anything but silent. She has written over thirty books, taught at five universities and lectured at many more. She is a self-described "black woman intellectual, revolutionary activist," who is currently a Distinguished Professor of English at City College in New York.

> **For more information on bell hooks, see <http://www.allaboutbell.com/>.**

WHAT DO YOU KNOW? WHAT DO YOU EXPECT TO DISCOVER?

Before reading the essay, take a moment to consider the following questions.

1. What does "keeping close to home" mean to you? What do you do to maintain your relationships with the members of your family even as you make decisions about your life that take you away from your childhood home life?

2. bell hooks asks us to think about social class and how it is informed by education. What role do you think education has in constituting and maintaining a community?

3. hooks compares her way of expressing herself at home with the way she expresses herself at school. Why might someone act or speak (or write) differently in those two places? What differences do you see between your "home" self and your "academic" self?

⌁

keeping close to home:
class and education

We are both awake in the almost dark of 5 a.m. Everyone else is sound asleep. Mama asks the usual questions. Telling me to look around, make sure I have everything, scolding me because I am uncertain about the actual time the bus arrives. By 5:30 we are waiting outside the closed station. Alone together, we have a chance to really talk. Mama begins. Angry with her children, especially the ones who whisper behind her back, she says bitterly, "Your childhood could not have been that bad. You were fed and clothed. You did not have to do without—that's more than a lot of folks have and I just can't stand the way y'all go on." The hurt in her voice saddens me. I have always wanted to protect mama from hurt, to ease her burdens. Now I am part of what troubles. Confronting me, she says accusingly, "It's not just the other children. You talk too much about the past. You don't just listen." And I do talk. Worse, I write about it.

Mama has always come to each of her children seeking different responses. With me she expresses the disappointment, hurt, and anger of betrayal: anger that her children are so critical, that we can't even have the sense to like the presents she sends. She says, "From now on there will be no presents. I'll just stick some money in a little envelope the way the rest of you do. Nobody wants criticism. Everybody can criticize me but I am supposed to say nothing." When I try to talk, my voice sounds like a twelve year old. When I try to talk, she speaks louder, interrupting me, even though she has said repeatedly, "Explain it to me, this talk about the past." I struggle to return to my thirty-five year old self so that she will know by the sound of my voice that we are two women talking together. It is only when I state firmly in my very adult voice, "Mama, you are not listening," that she becomes quiet. She waits. Now that I have her attention, I fear that my explanations will be lame, inadequate. "Mama," I begin, "people usually go to therapy because they feel hurt inside, because they have pain that will not stop, like a wound that continually breaks open, that does not heal. And often these hurts, that pain has to do with things that have happened in the past, sometimes in childhood, often in childhood, or things that we believe happened." She wants to know, "What hurts, what hurts are you talking about?" "Mom, I can't answer that. I can't speak for all of us, the hurts are different for everybody. But the point is you try to make the hurt better, to heal it, by understanding how it came to be. And I know you feel mad when we say something happened or hurt that you don't remember being that way, but the past isn't like that, we don't have the same memory of it. We remember things differently. You know that. And sometimes folk feel hurt about stuff and you just don't know or didn't realize it, and they need to talk about it. Surely you understand the need to talk about it."

Our conversation is interrupted by the sight of my uncle walking across the park toward us. We stop to watch him. He is on his way to work dressed in a familiar blue suit. They look alike, these two who rarely discuss the past. This interruption makes me think about life in a small town. You always see someone you know. Interruptions, intrusions are part of daily life. Privacy is difficult to maintain. We leave our private space in the car to greet him. After the hug and kiss he has given me every year since I was born, they talk about the day's funerals. In the distance the bus approaches. He walks away knowing that they will see each other later. Just before I board the bus I turn, staring into my mother's face. I am momentarily back in time, seeing myself eighteen years ago, at this same bus stop, staring into my mother's face, continually turning back, waving farewell as I returned to college—that experience which first took me away from our town, from family. Departing was as painful then as it is now. Each movement away makes return harder. Each separation intensifies distance, both physical and emotional.

To a southern black girl from a working-class background who had never been on a city bus, who had never stepped on an escalator, who had never travelled by plane, leaving the comfortable confines of a small town Kentucky life to attend Stanford University was not just frightening; it was utterly painful. My parents had not been delighted that I had been accepted and adamantly opposed my going so far from home. At the time, I did not see their opposition as an expression of their fear that they would lose me forever. Like many working-class folks, they feared what college education might do to their children's minds even as they unenthusiastically acknowledged its importance. They did not understand why I could not attend a college nearby, an all-black college. To them, any college would do. I would graduate, become a school teacher, make a decent living and a good marriage. And even though they reluctantly and skeptically supported my educational endeavors, they also subjected them to constant harsh and bitter critique. It is difficult for me to talk about my parents and their impact on me because they have always felt wary, ambivalent, mistrusting of my intellectual aspirations even as they have been caring and supportive. I want to speak about these contradictions because sorting through them, seeking resolution and reconciliation has been important to me both as it affects my development as a writer, my effort to be fully self-realized, and my longing to remain close to the family and community that provided the groundwork for much of my thinking, writing, and being.

Studying at Stanford, I began to think seriously about class differences. To be materially underprivileged at a university where most folks (with the exception of workers) are materially privileged provokes such thought. Class differences were boundaries no one wanted to face or talk about. It was easier to downplay them, to act as though we were all from privileged backgrounds, to work around them, to confront them privately in the solitude of one's room, or to pretend that just being chosen to study at such an institution meant that those of us who did not come from privilege were already in transition toward privilege. To not long for such transition marked one as rebellious, as unlikely to succeed. It was a kind of treason not to believe that it was better to be identified with the world of material privilege than with the world of the working class, the poor. No wonder our working-class parents from poor backgrounds feared our entry into such a world, intuiting perhaps that we might learn to be ashamed of where we had come from, that we might never return home, or come back only to lord it over them.

Though I hung with students who were supposedly radical and chic, we did not discuss class. I talked to no one about the sources of my shame, how it hurt me to witness the contempt shown the brown-skinned Filipina maids who cleaned our rooms, or later my concern about the $100 a month I paid for a room off-campus which was more than half of what my parents paid for rent. I talked to no one about my efforts to save money, to send a little something home. Yet these class realities separated me from fellow students. We were moving in different directions. I did not intend to forget my class background or alter my class allegiance. And even though I received an education designed to provide me with a bourgeois sensibility, passive acquiescence was not my only option. I knew that I could resist. I could rebel. I could shape the direction and focus of the various forms of knowledge available to me. Even though I sometimes envied and longed for greater material advantages (particularly at vacation times when I would be one of few if any students remaining in the dormitory because there was no money for travel), I did not share the sensibility and values of my peers. That was important—class was not just about money; it was about values which showed and determined behavior. While I often needed more money, I never needed a new set of beliefs and values. For example, I was profoundly shocked and disturbed when peers would talk about their parents without respect, or would even say that they hated their parents. This was especially troubling to me when it seemed that these parents were caring and concerned. It was often explained to me that such hatred was "healthy and normal." To my white, middle-class California roommate, I explained the way we were taught to value our parents and their care, to understand that they were not obligated to give us care. She would always shake her head, laughing all the while, and say, "Missy, you will learn that it's different here, that we think differently." She was right. Soon, I lived alone, like the one Mormon student who kept to himself as he made a concentrated effort to remain true to his religious beliefs and values. Later in graduate school I found that classmates believed "lower class" people had no beliefs and values. I was silent in such discussions, disgusted by their ignorance.

Carol Stack's anthropological study, *All Our Kin,* was one of the first books I read which confirmed my experiential understanding that within black culture (especially among the working class and poor, particularly in southern states), a value system emerged that was counter-hegemonic, that challenged notions of individualism and private property so important to the maintenance of white-supremacist, capitalist patriarchy. Black folk created in marginal spaces a world of community and collectivity where resources were shared. In the preface to *Feminist Theory: from margin to center,* I talked about how the point of difference, this marginality can be the space for the formation of an oppositional world view. That world view must be articulated, named if it is to provide a sustained blueprint for change. Unfortunately, there has existed no consistent framework for such naming. Consequently both the experience of this difference and documentation of it (when it occurs) gradually loses presence and meaning.

Much of what Stack documented about the "culture of poverty," for example, would not describe interactions among most black poor today irrespective of geographical setting. Since the black people she described did not acknowledge (if they recognized it in theoretical terms) the oppositional value of their world view, apparently seeing it more as a survival strategy determined less by conscious efforts to oppose oppressive race and class biases than by circumstance, they did not attempt to establish a framework to transmit their beliefs and values from generation to generation. When circumstances changed, values altered. Efforts to assimilate the values and beliefs of privileged white people, presented through media like television, undermine and destroy potential structures of opposition.

Increasingly, young black people are encouraged by the dominant culture (and by those black people who internalize the values of this hegemony) to believe that assimilation is the only possible way to survive, to succeed. Without the framework of an organized civil rights or black resistance struggle, individual and collective efforts at black liberation that focus on the primacy of self-definition and self-determination often go unrecognized. It is crucial that those among us who resist and rebel, who survive and succeed, speak openly and honestly about our lives and the nature of our personal struggles, the means by which we resolve and reconcile contradictions. This is no easy task. Within the educational institutions where we learn to develop and strengthen our writing and analytical skills, we also learn to think, write, and talk in a manner that shifts attention away from personal experience. Yet if we are to reach our people and all people, if we are to remain connected (especially those of us whose familial backgrounds are poor and working-class), we must understand that the telling of one's personal story provides a meaningful example, a way for folks to identify and connect.

Combining personal with critical analysis and theoretical perspectives can engage listeners who might other wise feel estranged, alienated. To speak simply with language that is accessible to as many folks as possible is also important. Speaking about one's personal experience or speaking with simple language is often considered by academics and/or intellectuals (irrespective of their political inclinations) to be a sign of intellectual weakness or even anti-intellectualism. Lately, when I speak, I do not stand in place—reading my paper, making little or no eye contact with audiences—but instead make eye contact, talk extemporaneously, digress, and address the audience directly. I have been told that people assume I am not prepared, that I am anti-intellectual, unprofessional (a concept that has everything to do with class as it determines actions and behavior), or that I am reinforcing the stereotype of black people as non-theoretical and gutsy.

Such criticism was raised recently by fellow feminist scholars after a talk I gave at Northwestern University at a conference on "Gender, Culture, Politics" to an audience that was mainly students and academics. I deliberately chose to speak in a very basic way, thinking especially about the few community folks who had come to hear me. Weeks later, Kum-Kum Sangari, a fellow participant who shared with me what was said when I was no longer present, and I engaged in quite rigorous critical dialogue about the way my presentation had been perceived primarily by privileged white female academics. She was concerned that I not mask my knowledge of theory, that I not appear anti-intellectual. Her critique compelled me to articulate concerns that I am often silent about with colleagues. I spoke about class allegiance and revolutionary commitments, explaining that it was disturbing to me that intellectual radicals who speak about transforming society, ending the domination of race, sex, class, cannot break with behavior patterns that reinforce and perpetuate domination, or continue to use as their sole reference point how we might be or are perceived by those who dominate, whether or not we gain their acceptance and approval.

This is a primary contradiction which raises the issue of whether or not the academic setting is a place where one can be truly radical or subversive. Concurrently, the use of a language and style of presentation that alienates most folks who are not also academically trained reinforces the notion that the academic world is separate from real life, that everyday world where we constantly adjust our language and behavior to meet diverse needs. The academic setting is separate only when we work to make it so. It is a false dichotomy which suggests that academics and/or intellectuals can only speak to one another, that we cannot hope to speak with the masses. What is true is that we make choices, that we choose our audiences, that we choose voices to hear and voices to silence. If I do not speak in a language that can be understood, then there is little chance for dialogue. This issue of language and behavior is a central contradiction all radical intellectuals, particularly those who are members of oppressed groups, must continually confront and work to resolve. One of the clear and present dangers that exists when we move outside our class of origin, our collective ethnic experience, and enter hierarchical institutions which daily reinforce domination by race, sex, and class, is that we gradually assume a mind-set similar to those who dominate and oppress, that we lose critical consciousness because it is not reinforced or affirmed by the environment. We must be ever vigilant. It is important that we know who we are speaking to, who we most want to hear us, who we most long to move, motivate, and touch with our words.

When I first came to New Haven to teach at Yale, I was truly surprised by the marked class divisions between black folks—students and professors—who identify with Yale and those black folks who work at Yale or in surrounding communities. Style of dress and self-presentation are most often the central markers of one's position. I soon learned that the black folks who spoke on the street were likely to be part of the black community and those who carefully shifted their glance were likely to be associated with Yale. Walking with a black female colleague one day, I spoke to practically every black person in sight (a gesture which reflects my upbringing), an action which disturbed my companion. Since I addressed black folk who were clearly not associated with Yale, she wanted to know whether or not I knew them. That was funny to me. "Of course not," I answered. Yet when I thought about it seriously, I realized that in a deep way, I knew them for they, and not my companion or most of my colleagues at Yale, resemble my family. Later that year, in a black women's support group I started for undergraduates, students from poor backgrounds spoke about the shame they sometimes feel when faced with the reality of their connection to working-class and poor black people. One student confessed that her father is a street person, addicted to drugs, someone who begs from passersby. She, like other Yale students, turns away from street people often, sometimes showing anger or contempt; she hasn't wanted anyone to know that she was related to this kind of person. She struggles with this, wanting to find a way to acknowledge and affirm this reality, to claim this connection. The group asked me and one another what we do to remain connected, to honor the bonds we have with working-class and poor people even as our class experience alters.

Maintaining connections with family and community across class boundaries demands more than just summary recall of where one's roots are, where one comes from. It requires knowing, naming, and being ever-mindful of those aspects of one's past that have enabled and do enable one's self-development in the present, that sustain and support, that enrich. One must also honestly confront barriers that do exist, aspects of that past that do diminish. My parent's ambivalence about my love for reading led to intense conflict. They (especially my mother) would work to ensure that I had access to books, but would threaten to burn the books or throw them away if I did not conform to other expectations. Or they would insist that reading too much would drive me insane. Their ambivalence nurtured in me a like uncertainty about the value and significance of intellectual endeavor which took years for me to unlearn. While this aspect of our class reality was one that wounded and diminished, their vigilant insistence that being smart did not make me a "better" or "superior" person (which often got on my nerves because I think I wanted to have that sense that it did indeed set me apart, make me better) made a profound impression. From them I learned to value and respect various skills and talents folk might have, not just to value people who read books and talk about ideas. They and my grandparents might say about somebody, "Now he don't read nor write a lick, but he can tell a story," or as my grandmother would say, "call out the hell in words."

Empty romanticization of poor or working-class backgrounds undermines the possibility of true connection. Such connection is based on understanding difference in experience and perspective and working to mediate and negotiate these terrains. Language is a crucial issue for folk whose movement outside the boundaries of poor and working-class backgrounds changes the nature and direction of their speech. Coming to Stanford with my own version of a Kentucky accent, which I think of always as a strong sound quite different from Tennessee or Georgia speech, I learned to speak differently while maintaining the speech of my region, the sound of my family and community. This was of course much easier to keep up when I returned home to stay often. In recent years, I have endeavored to use various speaking styles in the classroom as a teacher and find it disconcerts those who feel that the use of a particular patois excludes them as listeners, even if there is translation into the usual, acceptable mode of speech. Learning to listen to different voices, hearing different speech challenges the notion that we must all assimilate—share a single, similar talk—in educational institutions. Language reflects the culture from which we emerge. To deny ourselves daily use of speech patterns that are common and familiar, that embody the unique and distinctive aspect of our self is one of the ways we become estranged and alienated from our past. It is important for us to have as many languages on hand as we can know or learn. It is important for those of us who are black, who speak in particular patois as well as standard English to express ourselves in both ways.

Often I tell students from poor and working-class backgrounds that if you believe what you have learned and are learning in schools and universities separates you from your past, this is precisely what will happen. It is important to stand firm in the conviction that nothing can truly separate us from our pasts when we nurture and cherish that connection. An important strategy for maintaining contact is ongoing acknowledgement of the primacy of one's past, of one's background, affirming the reality that such bonds are not severed automatically solely because one enters a new environment or moves toward a different class experience.

Again, I do not wish to romanticize this effort, to dismiss the reality of conflict and contradiction. During my time at Stanford, I did go through a period of more than a year when I did not return home. That period was one where I felt that it was simply too difficult to mesh my profoundly disparate realities. Critical reflection about the choice I was making, particularly about why I felt a choice had to be made, pulled me through this difficult time. Luckily I recognized that the insistence on choosing between the world of family and community and the new world of privileged white people and privileged ways of knowing was imposed upon me by the outside. It is as though a mythical contract had been signed somewhere which demanded of us black folks that once we entered these spheres we would immediately give up all vestiges of our underprivileged past. It was my responsibility to formulate a way of being that would allow me to participate fully in my new environment while integrating and maintaining aspects of the old.

One of the most tragic manifestations of the pressure black people feel to assimilate is expressed in the internalization of racist perspectives. I was shocked and saddened when I first heard black professors at Stanford downgrade and express contempt for black students, expecting us to do poorly, refusing to establish nurturing bonds. At every university I have attended as a student or worked at as a teacher, I have heard similar attitudes expressed with little or no understanding of factors that might prevent brilliant black students from performing to their full capability. Within universities, there are few educational and social spaces where students who wish to affirm positive ties to ethnicity—to blackness, to working-class backgrounds—can receive affirmation and support. Ideologically, the message is clear—assimilation is the way to gain acceptance and approval from those in power.

Many white people enthusiastically supported Richard Rodriguez's vehement contention in his autobiography, *Hunger of*

Memory, that attempts to maintain ties with his Chicano background impeded his progress, that he had to sever ties with community and kin to succeed at Stanford and in the larger world, that family language, in his case Spanish, had to be made secondary or discarded. If the terms of success as defined by the standards of ruling groups within white-supremacist, capitalist patriarchy are the only standards that exist, then assimilation is indeed necessary. But they are not. Even in the face of powerful structures of domination, it remains possible for each of us, especially those of us who are members of oppressed and/or exploited groups as well as those radical visionaries who may have race, class, and sex privilege, to define and determine alternative standards, to decide on the nature and extent of compromise. Standards by which one's success is measured, whether student or professor, are quite different for those of us who wish to resist reinforcing the domination of race, sex, and class, who work to maintain and strengthen our ties with the oppressed, with those who lack material privilege, with our families who are poor and working-class.

When I wrote my first book, *Ain't I A Woman: black women and feminism,* the issue of class and its relationship to who one's reading audience might be came up for me around my decision not to use footnotes, for which I have been sharply criticized. I told people that my concern was that footnotes set class boundaries for readers, determining who a book is for. I was shocked that many academic folks scoffed at this idea. I shared that I went into working-class black communities as well as talked with family and friends to survey whether or not they ever read books with footnotes and found that they did not. A few did not know what they were, but most folks saw them as indicating that a book was for college-educated people. These responses influenced my decision. When some of my more radical, college-educated friends freaked out about the absence of footnotes, I seriously questioned how we could ever imagine revolutionary transformation of society if such a small shift in direction could be viewed as threatening. Of course, many folks warned that the absence of footnotes would make the work less credible in academic circles. This information also highlighted the way in which class informs our choices. Certainly I did feel that choosing to use simple language, absence of footnotes, etc. would mean I was jeopardizing the possibility of being taken seriously in academic circles but then this was a political matter and a political decision. It utterly delights me that this has proven not to be the case and that the book is read by many academics as well as by people who are not college-educated.

Always our first response when we are motivated to conform or compromise within structures that reinforce domination must be to engage in critical reflection. Only by challenging ourselves to push against oppressive boundaries do we make the radical alternative possible, expanding the realm and scope of critical inquiry. Unless we share radical strategies, ways of rethinking and revisioning with students, with kin and community, with a larger audience, we risk perpetuating the stereotype that we succeed because we are the exception, different from the rest of our people. Since I left home and entered college, I am often asked, usually by white people, if my sisters and brothers are also high achievers. At the root of this question is the longing for reinforcement of the belief in "the exception" which enables race, sex, and class biases to remain intact. I am careful to separate what it means to be exceptional from a notion of "the exception."

Frequently I hear smart black folks, from poor and working-class backgrounds, stressing their frustration that at times family and community do not recognize that they are exceptional. Absence of positive affirmation clearly diminishes the longing to excel in academic endeavors. Yet it is important to distinguish between the absence of basic positive affirmation and the longing for continued reinforcement that we are special. Usually liberal white folks will willingly offer continual reinforcement of us as exceptions—as special. This can be both patronizing and very seductive. Since we often work in situations where we are isolated from other black folks, we can easily begin to feel that encouragement from white people is the primary or only source of support and recognition. Given the internalization of racism, it is easy to view this support as more validating and legitimizing than similar support from black people. Still, nothing takes the place of being valued and appreciated by one's own, by one's family and community. We share a mutual and reciprocal responsibility for affirming one another's successes. Sometimes we have to talk to our folks about the fact that we need their ongoing support and affirmation, that it is unique and special to us. In some cases we may never receive desired recognition and acknowledgement of specific achievements from kin. Rather than seeing this as a basis for estrangement, for severing connection, it is useful to explore other sources of nourishment and support.

I do not know that my mother's mother ever acknowledged my college education except to ask me once, "How can you live so far away from your people?" Yet she gave me sources of affirmation and nourishment, sharing the legacy of her quilt-making, of family history, of her incredible way with words. Recently, when our father retired after more than thirty years of work as a janitor, I wanted to pay tribute to this experience, to identify links between his work and my own as writer and teacher. Reflecting on our family past, I recalled ways he had been an impressive example of diligence and hard work, approaching tasks with a seriousness of concentration I work to mirror and develop, with a discipline I struggle to maintain. Sharing these thoughts with him keeps us connected, nurtures our respect for each other, maintaining a space, however large or small, where we can talk.

Open, honest communication is the most important way we maintain relationships with kin and community as our class experience and backgrounds change. It is as vital as the sharing of resources. Often financial assistance is given in circumstances where there is no meaningful contact. However helpful, this can also be an expression of estrangement and alienation. Communication between black folks from various experiences of material privilege was much easier when we were all in segregated communities sharing common experiences in relation to social institutions. Without this grounding, we must work to maintain ties, connection. We must assume greater responsibility for making and maintaining contact, connections that can shape our intellectual visions and inform our radical commitments.

The most powerful resource any of us can have as we study and teach in university settings is full understanding and appreciation of the richness, beauty, and primacy of our familial and community backgrounds. Maintaining awareness of class differences, nurturing ties with the poor and working-class people who are our most intimate kin, our comrades in struggle, transforms and enriches our intellectual experience. Education as the practice of freedom becomes not a force which fragments or separates, but one that brings us closer, expanding our definitions of home and community.

READING, REREADING, AND ANALYSIS

1. Why do you think that bell hooks begins her essay with a narrative, a story of her conversation with her "Mama"? What does the story add to our understanding of her points about class and education?

2. How does hooks define class? Is it just about how much money you make? What else is involved?

3. Who do you think hooks's audience is? What do you think her purpose is in writing this essay?

4. Why does hooks pursue an academic career if it hurts her relationship with her family? What does she tell us about her education that makes it seem worth the emotional cost?

5. hooks asks us to consider the consequences of "assimilation." How is she using this term? Is she in favor of assimilation, or against it?

6. Do you think that hooks sees herself as a role model? Does she "solve" the contradictions she points out?

7. In her essay, hooks champions what she calls "open, honest communication" (p. 238). Do you think she is completely open and honest here? Why does she think these terms are important,

and how does she demonstrate her commitment to openness, to honesty?

RESPONDING THROUGH WRITING:
BUILDING AN INTERPRETATION

8. hooks offers suggestions about and strategies for approaching our education. On page 236, she tells us that "always our first response when we are motivated to conform or compromise within structures that reinforce domination must be to engage in critical reflection." What do you suppose she means by "critical reflection"? Drawing on an example from your own experience at school, describe how "critical reflection" might have improved that experience.

9. Drawing on bell hooks's essay and your own knowledge and experience, develop an essay that takes as its subject either "class and education" or, more broadly, "transformation." How has learning transformed or shaped your identity and your sense of self? What parts of you has it *not* affected?

10. In a couple of places, hooks mentions that some people wish to "romanticize" the struggles of poor or working-class people. How is she using this word and what is her attitude toward romanticized accounts? In an essay of two pages, discuss the importance of representing struggle without editing out what hooks calls the "conflict and contradiction." What can such accounts teach us or show us?

GOING FURTHER: LEARNING
FROM OTHER SOURCES

11. Search the Web for information on bell hooks. What do you find that surprises you? How do other people speak of her? Does she appear to be pursuing the goals and objectives she describes in this essay?

12. In an academic database, look up the concept of "social class" and its relation to education. What issues do you find? How are other writers defining class? What other terms seem to come up often?

APPLYING WHAT YOU'VE LEARNED

13. Like Sherry Turkle in "The Triumph of Tinkering" and Dorothy Allison in "This Is Our World," bell hooks begins with a

personal narrative and moves toward a more recognizable analytic voice with a thesis and a more formal vocabulary. hooks, however, speaks much more directly about *why* she makes that shift: "Combining personal with critical analysis and theoretical perspectives can engage listeners who might otherwise feel estranged, alienated" (p. 232). Using hooks's essay as a resource, analyze either Turkle's or Allison's essay as an attempt to "engage listeners." How does the personal material contribute to the impact of the primary thesis?

14. In "Chicana Artists: Exploring *Nepantla, el Lugar de la Frontera*," Gloria Anzaldúa defines "*nepantla*" as the Nahuatl word for "an in-between state, that uncertain terrain one crosses when moving from one place to another, when changing from one class, race, or gender position to another, when traveling from the present identity into a new identity" (p. 61). In "keeping close to home: class and education," bell hooks writes about the ways that her transition from her home community in Kentucky to college at Stanford has influenced her as a writer, scholar, and teacher. How does Anzaldúa's idea of "*nepantla*" and her presentation of a *mestizaje* position apply to hooks's narrative and her thoughts about it? How would you apply Anzaldúa's "*nepantla*" to your own experience entering college? In the process of writing your essay, consider the implications of language, culture, and class as you think about the potential connections between these two pieces of writing and your own experience.

15. Richard Rodriguez humorously argues in "'Blaxicans' and Other Reinvented Americans" that "assimilation happens." He says he is neither for nor against assimilation, and uses the paradoxical statement—"I am Chinese"—to make the point that the categories used to describe different immigrant communities have become obsolete or misleading. Why does bell hooks's similar ambivalence about assimilation lead her to such different conclusions?

ZITA INGHAM

Zita Ingham, (b. 1952) is Professor of English at Southwestern Oregon Community College. She received her doctorate in Rhetoric and Composition from the University of Arizona and her bachelor's degree in Bacteriology from the University of California, Berkeley. "Landscape, Drama, and Dissensus: The Rhetorical Education of Red Lodge, Montana" is excerpted from the essay collection edited by Carl G. Herndl and Stuart C. Brown, *Green Culture: Environmental Rhetoric in Contemporary America* (1996).

To learn more about Red Lodge, visit <http://www.redlodge.com>.

WHAT DO YOU KNOW? WHAT DO YOU EXPECT TO DISCOVER?

Before reading the essay, take a moment to consider the following questions.

1. What topics does Ingham's biography suggest she is interested in? What do you know about those topics? Knowledge can come from personal experience, stories you've heard, other classes you've taken, or other reading you've done.

2. Before reading Ingham's essay, freewrite for five minutes on what you imagine Red Lodge, Montana, to be like. After freewriting, do a Google search of Red Lodge, Montana, and compare what you find on the Internet with your freewriting.

3. Make a list of images or characters from the Wild West that you are familiar with. You might think particularly about how the Wild West is portrayed in films and on television. After compiling your list, read Ingham's essay and compare your list with her discussion of Wild West issues past and present.

※

Landscape, Drama, and Dissensus
The Rhetorical Education of Red Lodge, Montana

Some Better Way to Live

On the night of Friday, 19 June 1992, more than 120 people milled around in the main hall of the Roberts Senior Citizens Center in Red Lodge, Montana. An old Western drama was about to be enacted, with all the usual players: ranchers, townspeople, miners. The central player in the Western drama has always been the land—the land as water, timber, ore, grazing rights, creatures—and the subject of this drama is, as always, land use. Who has, and who will have, the right to do what with the land in and around Red Lodge? The conflict persists, down through the decades—"who runs this town?"—although more sophisticated ways of asking that question have evolved. If indeed the town will build an airport, what part of the landscape would become the runway, the parking area, the flyway? Who owns Rock Creek, the stream that runs through town? Who has the right to walk along it? Who controls—who determines and who benefits from—the zoning and taxing of the supremely developable ranch land surrounding the town? Who decides what constitutes "ownership" and "control" of the land and its resources?

The boundaries between the western dramas of novels and films, and the historical dramas of the West—range wars, Indian wars, all the larger and smaller conflicts over land use—have long been blurred; the qualities of each illuminate the other. In writing about the Western drama, as seen in movies such as *Shane* and *High Noon,* Jane Tompkins and, earlier, Peter Homans investigate this "moral dynamic." For Tompkins, as she argues in *West of Everything: The Inner Life of Westerns,* this dynamic culminates in a "moment of moral ecstasy. The hero is *so right* (that is, so wronged) that he can kill with impunity. . . . The feeling of supreme righteousness in this instant is delicious and hardly to be distinguished from murderousness" (229). She argues that what's most important about this moment—the shoot-out as the moment of righteous violence on which the mythic stories of the West turn—is our ability to reflect on it. This "moment of righteous ecstasy, . . . the moment of murderousness. . . . [is] a moment when there's still time to stop, there's still time to reflect, there's still time to recall what happened in *High Noon,* there's still time to say, 'I don't care who's right or who's wrong. There has to be some better way for people to live' " (233). For Homans, "the key to the Western" is "[t]his process whereby desire is at once indulged and veiled. . . . What is required is that temptation be indulged while providing the appearance of having been resisted" (89). As the transparency of this dynamic of Western films and novels becomes more popularly evident, some communities in the West have begun attempts at living some better way.

This better way, at least for the community of Red Lodge, begins as a traditional Western, as what Homans describes as a "puritan morality tale in which the savior-hero redeems the community from the temptations of the devil" (89). In Red Lodge a group of concerned residents formed the Beartooth Front Community Forum and invited Luther Propst to conduct a series of community dialogue workshops. Propst is executive director of the Sonoran Institute, a nonprofit conservation organization based in Tucson, Arizona, that promotes the Successful Communities Dialogue program as a way to help resolve community disputes. The stage was set: a limited and unstable economic base made land use a charged issue, tensions arose from increasing population and impending development, and polarized factions in the community verbally fought each other. Enter the redemptive stranger, come to put things right and then vanish, leaving behind a more peaceful and productive, not to mention grateful, community.

But this is not the old West. Discussion, argument, legal actions, and decrees replace shoot-outs. Finding a better way to live and to manage environmental issues such as land use rests on language, on the use of language to discover, initiate, persuade, understand, anger, conciliate: on rhetoric. In June 1992, citizens in Red Lodge met to begin a process that has changed the economic, environmental, and sociocultural identity of the town and will continue to do so. Crucial to those changes has been the rhetorical education of many of its residents. Through public forums, workshops, committee meetings, committee reports to the communities, and news stories, residents of Red Lodge began to discuss and argue in public. Where once, for instance, townspeople grumbled about what the owners of large ranches might do when the financial rewards of development exceeded those of ranching, they now meet to develop plans. There is broad-based citizen participation in zoning and environmental impact studies and in grant writing to foster local economic development.

Because these situations—all rhetorical, all dependent on how people are persuaded by the use of language—now exist, residents are learning to articulate what they believe about the community, its past, present, and future, and their actions depend on what they articulate. The Beartooth Front forum meeting on that Friday night and the next day in June 1992 initiated a rhetorical education of active citizens—training and practice in how and what to argue with each other. This essay describes some features of the initial steps of this rhetorical education.

The Rhetoric of Community

Whether we adopt Aristotle's definition of rhetoric as the discovery of "the available means of persuasion" (24), or J. Frederick Crews's notion of rhetoric as "the placement of ideas" (6), or the definition of rhetoric as the possibilities of language to deform as well as formulate the truth of events, places, people, ideas, rhetoric is situated and can be analyzed only in the context of literal and figurative location. A speaker or writer—a rhetor—always occupies a particular ideological, cultural, geographical place from which to speak or write. The rhetor's rhetorical stance, as delineated by Wayne Booth, depends on the contexts of "the available arguments about the subject itself, the interests and peculiarities of the audience, and the voice, the implied character of the speaker" (141). Members of audiences, in turn, listen, read, and respond from their own places. As the messages fly back and forth in communities like Red Lodge, or even as they hang in the air without visible, immediate responses, communication changes the speakers and listeners, the writers and readers themselves, and this exchange can transform both the community and its environment. As M. Jimmie Killingsworth notes, "In addition to changing language and changing minds, the enterprise of rhetoric suggests that speakers and writers have the power to transform the site of discourse, the community itself" (110). In the case of Red Lodge, as in many other locations of environmental disputes, the rhetorical enterprise alters not only the rhetorical landscape, but the physical landscape as well.

The Scene

Red Lodge, Montana (population 2,000), lies at the foot of the Beartooth mountain range, northeast of Yellowstone National Park, and like other Montana towns in the Yellowstone area, Red Lodge is changing rapidly. The area encompassed by the Greater Yellowstone ecosystem—which includes parts of Montana, Idaho, and Wyoming and all of the communities in and around Yellowstone and Grand Teton National Parks and the surrounding national forests—faces particular pressure to resolve issues associated with rapid population growth. The 1990 census shows that if the twenty adjacent counties in this area were considered as one state, it would be the fastest-growing state in the country. Between 1991 and 1992, subdivision activity in Carbon County, where Red Lodge is located, increased 44 percent, most occurring along the Beartooth Front. This figure does not include parcels twenty acres or larger, which are currently exempt from evaluation. Carbon County ranks first in Montana Greater Yellowstone ecosystem counties in land development on a per capita basis ("Successful Communities" 5).

Because of economic and demographic pressures, Red Lodge and towns like it are forced to resolve issues (even if by ignoring them) that will determine qualities of the population and of the environment in the future. To do that, and to insure that the resolutions consider the well-being of as many residents as possible, the citizens of Red Lodge need to learn how to argue better, how to speak and write to each other and to others about these issues. The first requirement for the "rhetorical health" of a community is that opportunities exist for all voices to be heard. Seeking consensus, in the context of a community beginning to grapple with issues of growth, is not perhaps as useful as the thorough exploration of "dissensus." Rhetorical theorist John Trimbur suggests that the goal of consensus in a community may not be as useful as was once thought. Depending on its political context, dissensus can replace consensus as "a powerful instrument . . . to generate differences, . . . and to transform the relations of power that determine who may speak and what counts as a meaningful statement" ("Consensus and Difference" 602). Before communities can approach the resolution of issues, Trimbur suggests,

> we will need to rehabilitate the notion of consensus by redefining it in relation to a rhetoric of dissensus. We will need, that is, to look at collaborative learning not merely as a process of consensus-making but, more importantly, as a process of identifying differences and locating these differences in relation to each other. (610)

Trimbur is speaking about the "community" of a writing classroom, but his insight into consensus and dissensus applies to other, larger communities; as we all know, consensus is notoriously difficult in environmental disputes. In order to resolve their disputes and protect their environment, communities like Red Lodge need to engage in the collaborative learning that characterizes Trimbur's rhetorical education. A community of residents who hold differing opinions about, for instance, whether or not to build an airport for their town must learn to articulate their differences and to explore their different values and how these would shape their environment.

The danger of beginning to talk to each other is always the same: the pressure for consensus, the ultimate requirement of consent, is always uncomfortable. If the nature of events or the community demands consensus, the situation can, paradoxically, dissolve, the rhetorical enterprise break down, and the various factions withdraw, taking with them the chance to resolve the issue. Everyone is aware of this risk; it often constitutes the basis of factional power. Everyone in Red Lodge knows, for example, that drawing larger businesses requires an airport, that airports destroy huge amounts of wildlife habitat, and that, eventually, some residents will have to concede something. That kind of anticipation of concessions inhibits the rhetorical process from the beginning. For Trimbur, as for the organizers of the Beartooth Front Community Forum, "The revised notion of consensus I am proposing here depends paradoxically on its deferral, not its realization" ("Consensus and Difference" 614). This essay describes the way this community and the Sonoran Institute use the strategy of deferred consensus.

The Script

The process of planning a future for Red Lodge was deliberate and initiated by local citizens but catalyzed by outsiders. The rhetorical education of Red Lodge began with the activism of an ad hoc group of citizens, but was guided by a Successful Communities Dialogue workshop developed by the Sonoran Institute. The Sonoran Institute, a nonprofit conservation organization based in Tucson, Arizona, was created in 1990 with technical and financial assistance from the World Wildlife Fund. The institute's mission is to work "nationwide to preserve the integrity of protected natural areas and adjacent communities by cooperatively resolving potential conflicts between conservation and meeting the needs and aspirations of adjacent communities and landowners. The Institute also works to insure that development occurring adjacent to protected areas adheres to the highest level of environmental compatibility and sensitivity" (*Annual Report 1991–1992* i). The institute first began with projects to protect Saguaro National Monument outside Tucson, but now has extended its work throughout the West and into Mexico. The institute is guided by a board of directors that includes conservation and business leaders, and "works with diverse groups (including natural resource managers, landowners, conservation leaders, and local officials) to create and implement tangible projects which link sustainable development and protection of natural resources" (*Annual Report 1991–1992* i). One such project, with the goal of initiating activities at the local level, is the Successful Communities Dialogue workshops. Such workshops (which began in 1988 as a pilot program of the Conservation Foundation, now incorporated in the World Wildlife Fund) have been held in various communities throughout the Greater Yellowstone area. These workshops use something like Killingsworth's idea of the enterprise of rhetoric to resolve environmental disputes and, ultimately, preserve natural resources. The emphasis on deferred consensus is key to the initial stages of community dialogue.

Propst and the Beartooth Front Community Forum organizers argue that community members must develop a consciousness of rhetorical stance, of how citizens stand in relation to each other, given their view points. Community members must become more conscious and more deliberate in their uses of language so that they can know what they want to argue for in relation to Red Lodge and how to go about manifesting and settling those arguments. Increasingly, serious environmental disputes are resolved by outside mediators through a process that leaves existing community relations mostly untouched. In contrast, the rhetorical education promoted in Red Lodge helps communities develop and articulate working relationships themselves. Outside mediators help parties reach agreement relative to a specific conflict, with a process and outcome that may be voluntary or may be legally determined. But in the case of community dialogue, building and remaining a community is the goal, rather than more or less specific consensus. In the literature of environmental mediation, where building community is more likely to be seen as the "socialization of opponents" (Lake 62), leaving antagonisms and misunderstandings intact, less than ideal valuations of "community" are evident. In his investigation of the dynamics of mediation, Scott Mernitz uses social and psychological research into the nature of community conflict to argue for the positive social effects of mediation:

> conflict tends to act in group-binding and group-preserving capacity. Conflict maintains, rather than disrupts, the well-balanced society by facilitating communication and defining relationships and group structures, so as to clarify for a participant his position and status relative to others. . . . conflict and the ensuing settlement establish and maintain the balance of power, so that a legitimate distribution of resources is achieved. Parties perceive themselves *in equilibrium*—a condition that is the desired end of most conflict situations. (51)

In this view, mediation—the search for a resolution of conflict that has escalated into litigation—seems successful when a balance of power is reached. In contrast, community dialogue has as its goal not equilibrium, but connection.

A crucial difference between the approach of community dialogue and that of mediation is in the timing of intervention in the community's history and in assumptions about the rhetorical effectiveness of community members and factions. The Sonoran Institute tries to intervene early in the process because it believes individuals can develop the rhetorical skills and set up the rhetorical situations that prevent litigious conflicts. Mediators, on the other hand, generally intervene only at the eleventh hour and use their knowledge of rhetorical skills and situations to facilitate agreements, not to facilitate the education of community members in ways to reach agreements on their own. Thus, the Sonoran Institute's idea of rhetorical dialogue about the environment ties the health of the environment to the rhetorical health of the community. If environmental health can be defined as the flourishing of diverse species, then rhetorical health denotes the flourishing of diverse voices.

The rhetorical education of Red Lodge began with this workshop in June 1992. The objectives of the two-day forum, conducted by Luther Propst, were "(1) to bring together diverse citizens, organizations, and government agencies to identify local values and assets, develop a vision for the future of the community and identify practical and tangible steps for realizing this vision; and (2) to provide a forum and process for informed communications and consensus-building that transcend the limits of single-value advocacy and special interest politics" ("Successful Communities" 3). These objectives are fundamentally rhetorical in nature: bringing members of the community into dialogue with each other, articulating a vision of the community's future and steps toward the manifestation of that vision (which only exists in language), and providing outlets and strategies for "informed communication." In essence, the workshop was a place, a situation, to display the value of skill in rhetoric, and to argue that changes in the community and its natural environment depend first on the kinds of rhetorical choices citizens make.

Advance Notice

The crucial step in this process of rhetorical education was to provide a forum for discussion. The rhetoric surrounding the invitation to discuss the town's future is an example of how rhetorical education begins with the demonstration and modeling of strategies, attitudes, rhetorical stances. In studying events at Red Lodge, Kenneth Burke's rhetorical concept of "identification" is useful, because the impetus for the entire process of planning the community's future depends on the reinforcement of Red Lodge *as* a community. The crucial strategy is an attitude of social cohesion: the adoption, by individuals, of a common identity from which to act together. In Burke's words,

> "Identification" at its simplest is also a deliberative device, as when the politician seeks to identify himself with his audience. . . . But identification can also be an end, as when people earnestly yearn to identify themselves with some group or other. Here they are not necessarily being acted upon by a conscious external agent, but may be acting upon themselves to this end. ("Rhetoric—Old and New" 203)

The persuasive aim of the forum was to enable residents to envision themselves as a community—"acting upon themselves" by identifying with each other, by establishing stances in relationship to each other. In the context of the discussion at Red Lodge, the "external agent," the Sonoran Institute, uses the desire to facilitate identification between individuals within the community as a persuasive strategy—as a way of increasing its credibility in the community and as a way of demonstrating the power of such a strategy, such an attitude. All of the forum activities—the presentations by community members and by outside "experts," the recounting of regional and individual histories, the small and large group discussions—are strategies to increase group identification among community members.

Identification began with flyers posted around town in early June announcing that the Beartooth Front Community Forum (the group "dedicated to forging cooperative solutions to the challenges of tomorrow," as noted on the flyer) would be sponsoring a community dialogue, a Friday evening and all-day Saturday event to which "You're Invited! Share your thoughts about growth and economic development, preservation, and other important matters affecting you and your family." The sponsoring group, although anonymous, makes an appeal to its audience based on its credibility as constructed on the flyer: the group is "dedicated," earnest in recognizing and valiant in meeting the "challenges of tomorrow," and fair, not elitest but "cooperative." The flyer's authors also display the virtuous aim of including as many residents as possible in the invitation; the forum was advertised as "FREE," and "Lunch will be provided on Saturday. Babysitting is available if needed." Citizens were not only invited to lunch, but also to "Please lend a hand!" to participate in "forging cooperative solutions to the challenges of tomorrow." The initial anonymity of the group prevented its being dismissed because of objections to certain members, and no doubt such an appeal would draw the skeptical—those wondering who these people were and what they were planning—as well as those who wished to become proponents for change. Anonymity also prevented the forum from being perceived as a closed group. Cooperation and inclusion are further emphasized by the question posed in the largest type on the flyer, "WHAT KIND OF FUTURE WOULD YOU CHOOSE FOR RED LODGE AND THE BEARTOOTH FRONT?" The flyer invites identification with the community at large by suggesting that every community member can have a voice in planning. Over 120 residents attended the opening session of the workshop, more than 5 percent of the population of the town.

The Lights Dim: Opening Shots

The Friday evening session of the workshop began with an invocation by Kent Young, a Red Lodge attorney, to remember that these meetings were not about "what we *don't* want the community to be, but what we *want* the community to be." The question at the core of the long-standing Western dilemma—"who runs this town?"—is revised, cast positively, if a bit more vaguely: "What do you want Red Lodge to be?" The answer being formulated here assumes that individuals who make up the community will have the opportunity and ability to decide and to act on achieving those goals. For the moment—for as long as possible—the naiveté of these assumptions is suspended, as the organizers and other residents tacitly agree to participate.

The program begins with a visually rich, unabashedly emotional appeal to an idealistic sense of community in general, and an ideal sense of Red Lodge in particular. The audience watches a slide montage, by local photographer Merv Coleman, entitled "Red Lodge, A Place for All Seasons": fields of flowers, quaint downtown views, rodeo scenes, children playing in the snow, dancers at the town festival, all set to John Denver's sentimental and familiar "Season Suite" ("Oh, I love the life around me"). The audience oohs and aahs at the scenes, whispering to each other the names of particular places and people as they appear. Afterward, the moderator acknowledges the show as "meant to bring a tear to your eye." The strength of persuasion that rests on just such an arousal of the audience's emotions was articulated by Aristotle, who argued the importance of this appeal of *pathos*:

> Particularly in political oratory . . . it adds much to an orator's influence that his own character should look right and that he should be thought to entertain the right feelings towards his hearers; and also that his hearers themselves should be in just the right frame of mind. . . . The Emotions are all those feelings that so change men as to affect their judgements. (91)

A sentimental view of Red Lodge appeals emotionally, but the program organizers cannot allow the audience to feel it is being manipulated, because that would undercut the program's *ethos,* its credibility. *Ethos* rests on the appeal of a speaker's character who "should be thought to entertain the right feelings towards his hearers." The argument for community connections rests on the perceptions that the program organizers have moral authority, that they are committed to what's best for the community but not domineering in their methods.

The *pathos*, the emotional appeal of the arguments, is established, as is the *ethos*—the credibility, good will, and intelligence—of the program organizers. The work that remains is to get down to the subject at hand: Red Lodge, as it exists now and as it is envisioned. The program completes the triumvirate of Aristotle's modes of persuasion by moving on to *logos*, rational appeals. The appeals to logic—the most basic being the various reasons why Red Lodge, as an entire community, needs to plan for its future—begin with a series of speakers, of whom Luther Propst will be the last. The speakers are public figures and experts, specialists in the issues that affect the community. The rhetorical intention of this part of the program is to ground the discussions in evidence from authorities, to encourage participation, and to set the context—one of reasoned discussion—for tomorrow's workshop. The desired rhetorical effect is a commitment to action.

John Prinkki, a Carbon County commissioner, notes fundamental changes in the area: growth in Red Lodge and the paradoxical decline in the tax base. Because of the lack of oil revenue in recent years, the tax base has dropped from $30 million to $17 million. He asserts the county's commitment to working with businesses, and reiterates what residents often say: "We are looking for better than service industry jobs; we need a diverse business community." He ends by citing two instances of lack of city/county planning that have created problems: the inability of the county to maintain existing roads while building new, outlying roads, and a development, the Country Club Estates, that continues to draw heavily on tax money because of a lack of controls on the developer. Prinkki aligns himself with his listeners by asserting that their concerns are his. He argues that Red Lodge has severe economic problems, some of which could be averted by better planning and by controls on development.

Other speakers include Barbara Campbell, head of a private community development consulting firm and author of the 1989 Carbon County Economic Development Plan, who speaks on the three greatest needs of the area: adequate infrastructure (roads, sewage), affordable housing, and jobs. The most polemical, and also the most knowledgeable, of the speakers, she warns that "big developers *will* come, and they can easily take away any chance you have for self-direction."

The participation of speakers such as Prinkki and Campbell, who are the most knowledgeable about the economic issues of the county, insures that the dialogue proceeds from a foundation of authority, of facts. Both authorities argue for planning, but implicit in these arguments is the notion that the environment is at risk because of economic development. It is assumed, by the speakers, the program organizers, and the audience, that challenges to the environmental health of the community will result from the growth of its economy. Whether or not this assumption is valid, it underlies the entire workshop. Campbell's final remark, that developers are set to pounce on Red Lodge, is especially motivating, because anyone in the audience can reel off the names of small western communities that did not muster the resources and vision to remain "livable" as they grew. What these speakers most strongly argue for, based on the logic of their knowledge and experience, is immediate action.

The Hero: Where's the Shoot-out?

Luther Propst begins his presentation by establishing his own ethical appeal: as a former Washington lawyer, who worked there for the World Wildlife Fund, he tells a self-denigrating and actually funny lawyer joke, about the obsolescence of lab rats, who are being replaced by Washington lawyers because these occur in greater numbers and because "there are some things even rats won't do." In beginning his logical appeal, he cites demographic trends in particular counties in the Greater Yellowstone area, thereby assuring the audience that he's an expert, even though he's an outsider—perhaps an expert in ways only an outsider can be. He has a slide show of his own, displaying results of lack of planning for conservation from around the country. The scenes are familiar to anyone who has traveled even a little: conversion of farmland to suburbs, loss of regional architectural character and degradation of historical features because of commercial development, obliteration of landscape features, human conflict with wildlife. He contrasts these with views of instances of effective planning: clustered housing, retention of local architecture in commercial development, protection of views and wildlife habitat. He emphasizes the goal of these workshops: that residents of Red Lodge can set an agenda for action, whatever that agenda and action may be, but only if they act quickly and as a community. The urgency to act has been established by Prinkki and Campbell as well; Propst underscores it, and takes the further steps of suggesting concrete possibilities.

Propst argues that the real power to effect conservation and preservation is always at the local level. He briefly delineates factors that "successful communities" have drawn on to best enact this power, including special physical aspects of the community, shared community vision, and proactive policies. Most important to successful communities is the willingness to look beyond ecological and economic factors to the quality of the lives of all community members and to work beyond laying down regulations, which, in Propst's words, "are too blunt a tool with which to fashion a livable community." Propst cites the need for "hometown heroes"—local individuals who can channel energy into constructive rather than divisive agendas, who cultivate responsible, local developers, and who remain active to ensure plans are implemented and developments monitored.

In describing the factors of such communities, Propst constructs an ideal that Red Lodge can aspire to, while maintaining that this ideal has been successfully approximated in other places. To return to Burke's concept of identification, which "includes the realm of transcendence" ("Rhetoric—Old and New" 203), "The machinery of language is so made that things are necessarily placed in terms of a range broader than the terms for those things themselves" (*Language as Symbolic Action* 200). At the heart of the strategies used by Propst and the organizers of the forum are those that draw on transcending the view of Red Lodge as it is today, on Richard Weaver's ideal function of rhetoric, which, "at its truest seeks to perfect men by showing them better versions of themselves" (16). And better versions of their communities.

Propst ends with a series of rhetorical devices. He enhances his ethos, the credibility of his character, and disarms anticonservation arguments by citing research that shows that the economic vitality of a community is intimately connected to the quality of life of all inhabitants—that scenery does indeed provide jobs. He underscores his authority by elaborating on problems in nearby communities, such as those faced in relation to the proposed Targhee Ski Resort expansion in Driggs, Idaho, where, Propst suggests, residents have not yet identified common interests and goals. He casts the workshop experience itself positively, differentiating it from contentious public hearing processes, and suggests that nearby communities that face seemingly insurmountable problems have attempted too late the process the forum demonstrates, providing further motivation for the residents of Red Lodge to begin work now.

These presentations have moved from community members and to authoritative outsiders, from emotional appeals to appeals based on the credibility and authority of the speakers. The local presenters rely more on identification with the audience based on devotion to their hometown and its inhabitants, while the outside authorities use quantifiable information about the economic situation, or about cases of similar situations and outcomes in other communities. The combined rhetorical thrust, the major argument for action, rests on the premise that Red Lodge suffers from a variety of economic woes that will increase as environmental degradation increases, given present economic and demographic trends. The desired rhetorical outcome is the motivation of citizens to discuss and reach consensus on an agenda for action, although not yet to reach consensus on particular actions.

By forestalling consensus on particular decisions and actions the community should take, forum organizers hoped to solidify individual commitments to the community and to action on its behalf. Propst argues that the community can begin to create its agenda when it begins to identify where there is consensus, where there is not, and where there are degrees of consensus. To return to Trimbur's critique of "community" in the literature of rhetoric and social theory, "the ideal of community participates in . . . a metaphysics that denies difference" ("Ideal of the Community" 1). Although, as Trimbur believes, "the desire for mutual understanding and reciprocity underlying the ideal of community is similar to the desire for identification that underlies racial and ethnic chauvinism"—a community is defined by what it excludes—Propst aims for a wider definition of community in Red Lodge. Propst suggests that residence and action, not degree of conformation to viewpoints, determine membership in the community, and that the idea of community in Red Lodge admits differences, and in fact those differences are to be studied. The danger for the community is not lack of consensus on an issue, but divisiveness that prevents any possibility of action. While the Sonoran Institute is a proponent of environmental conservation and historical preservation, not interested in mediating neutral solutions, in this forum Propst's purposes are to increase awareness of options for resolving issues, not to push particular resolutions.

Audience as Actors

Saturday's forum begins with stories. Two residents speak; a local rancher in his sixties gives a brief history of ranching in Carbon County, and a young housewife and nurse recounts her personal history in Red Lodge. Both cover the changes in the area, recent and not so recent, and cite shared histories in support of the communal effort required today and in the future. Albert Ellis tells of one Montana pioneer who, when asked on his ninetieth birthday if he'd seen a lot of changes in his lifetime, answered, "You bet I have, sonny, and I voted against every one of them." In recounting the changes that have affected ranching, Ellis reminds us that, however stubborn Montanans are, change will come, and citizens need to direct it. Kim Shelley relies on a personal, emotional appeal to make her point: how her family were forced for economic reasons to move away for part of her childhood, and now she's grateful to be back. She reminds the audience of the biggest snowstorm last winter, and how cars parked in the streets were buried: "We all wondered, why do we live here? But that's why—because of nature." She shares her worries about having to leave again, forever, if the hospital, presently in a financially precarious position, should have to close, and reminds us that despite what she loves about living in a small town, a higher population would mean saving the hospital. She ends with a plea for concerted effort: "I know I just can't not try to give something back to this town." The audience, most of whom are at least acquainted with Ellis and Shelley, identify with the historical and personal narratives that range across time, gender, age, and profession and which constitute an acknowledgment of the foundation of the community (or an idealized view of that foundation): hard times, the identity of the region based on the difficulties encountered here, that identity in opposition to what lies beyond it, changes past, changes to come. Taken together, the two narratives set a rhetorical stage, a context in which discussion of community values will take place in a different light. Ellis and Shelley have modeled their stories, their rhetorical stances as community members, and now the other residents take up this same task in smaller groups.

All the other narratives come spilling out as audience members introduce themselves to each other in these smaller, randomly formed groups of nine or ten. For example, one group is facilitated by Keith Zimmer, owner of a T-shirt business on Red Lodge's main street, and includes a rancher's wife, housewives, a teacher, a city roads worker, the owner of a secretarial business, a ski resort worker. Their talk about positive aspects of living in Red Lodge provides common ground for the rest of the discussion. This common ground elicits

Burkean identification and demonstrates the usefulness of story *as* argument, as Walter R. Fisher points out in *Human Communication as Narration:* "The world as we know it is a set of stories that must be chosen among in order for us to live life in a process of continual re-creation" (5). What these stories argue for, explicitly and implicitly, is action to preserve qualities of Red Lodge. In this group, Nancy Krekeler's story, for instance, is about how she left a lucrative job in Washington, D.C. years ago to join the working class of Red Lodge: "Tourists thought we all were twins, when they'd see us in the morning helping them onto the skilift and in the evening waiting on them at dinner. . . . Everyone gives up something to be here, whether you've always lived here or you're from somewhere else." Bob Holm, a city roads worker, recounts how he used to make his living working construction in other parts of the country, how his kids were really raised by his wife alone. These stories, and indeed all the stories and conversation that day, argue for particular visions of Red Lodge, past and future.

Even in the first round of discussion, the group is tempted to jump ahead to the town's problems, past defining "what we love about Red Lodge." Within five minutes, Bob Holm is wondering aloud if the town could ever pass a resort tax to pay for infrastructure development; Ruth Uebar says she thinks some development is good, that the golf course fits in with the atmosphere of the town, and then Mike Beye complains that the streets leading out of the golf course development look like "7-11 territory; is a strip mail next?" Zimmer calls them back to the task at hand, and the group devises a list of the town's positive attributes: its western flavor, natural environment, physical safety, political diversity, spirit of giving and openness, and its access to wilderness, health care, and skiing. People in the group state that what they like most is always meeting friends all over town, at the post office and stores, and "being able to hold a conversation with a 'wrong number' on the phone." Members of the group all agree that they don't want outside developers "to be able to do *anything.*" After an hour, the small groups break up to form the large group (about ninety people in all), and the facilitators of each group report their group members' lists of attributes. The next two rounds of discussion proceed similarly.

In this way every participant at the meeting is guaranteed a voice, and at this point no hierarchy of problems or solutions is established, so all concerns can be expressed. In these discussions, individuals express concern over degradation of the environment as easily as concern over lack of economic opportunity, and these concerns are not seen as conflicting. Participants are tempted to voice their personal concerns and solutions, but because each group must report its results for the question being put to it, discussion irrelevant to the task is held in check.

In the third round of dialogue, the groups identify specific steps to meet threats and achieve goals. The group agrees on the needs to organize, to use the public forums—the newspaper, meetings like this, town government meetings—to insure better communication among the townspeople, to gather information about property restrictions and zoning, to establish committees to research and initiate action on particular issues. Imagining the individuals likely to be on these committees, the group begins to wonder, what's to stop committee members from acting out of special interests or not acting at all? Propst joins the group and points out that the first objective is to establish committees that will continue the dialogue, not solve problems or take positions on issues yet, and that diversity of committee membership is crucial to success. The priorities are community dialogue and recognition of dissensus. The rhetorical processes that may eventually facilitate consensus on particular issues—the processes, strategies, attitudes that individuals and committees use to persuade other people to align themselves with particular views and actions—depend on both the sense of community (the feeling that the people of the town are connected to each other in ways that benefit them) and the sense of diversity (that both individuals and the larger group will accommodate "other" viewpoints and actions).

Intermission: Implications

That a "rhetorical education" of Red Lodge began with this forum is seen by the continued dialogue in the public discourse of the town; the success of this education is seen in the activities and achievements of citizen groups originating at the June 1992 forum. In the months following the first forum, criticism of the workshop and meetings circulated, and response to rumors provided a forum for organizers and participants to further their work. In August 1992, these comments from the organizers appeared in a letter to the editor of the *Montana Free Press:*

> We'd also like to take this opportunity to state again that the Beartooth Front Community Forum is a non-political community-based organization. We have no agenda and are not supported by any interest groups. While we hope to inspire people to express their opinions, the Forum as a body does not take stands. Our sole goal is to involve as many people as possible in discussions about planning for our community's future. (Beartooth Front Community Forum Steering Committee 3)

In November, the contradictory rumors that the Beartooth Front Community Forum is a front for developers and that its purpose is to halt all development were countered in another letter from the steering committee, appearing in the same newspaper, explaining that

> The Community Forum is not an "it"—a political organization with positions or an agenda. The Community Forum is a process, a *vehicle,* through which any and all residents of the area can try to have a voice in the future of their home. ("Thanks From the Forum Front" 4).

In the March 1993 "Beartooth Front Community Forum Progress Report," the authors conclude with an emotional appeal that valorizes the sense of a community made up of individuals who hold different viewpoints:

> Those involved in the Forum (as well as those on the sidelines) have been impressed with the scope and energy of their fellow volunteers. Many expected the community would not find such consensus; others expected that projects would not get off the ground so quickly; still others that enthusiasm would wane. Those expectations have been dashed magnificently. . . . the journey—the process—has been as exciting as its results. We have come together, in our disparate beliefs and needs and ambitions, to affirm our love for this area. We have come together to dream about its future, and share those dreams. We have seen how similar the dreams are, how within the realm of possibility. And in that process we have come together as that wondrous and often elusive entity, a community. (Beartooth Front Community Forum 7)

The forum participants tie the ideal of community to the ideal of every voice being heard, replacing, momentarily, the typical view of consensus, in which all community members agree to viewpoints and courses of action. They see consensus, as Trimbur does, as not necessarily "an acculturative practice that reproduces business as usual" but "as an oppositional one that challenges the prevailing conditions of production" ("Consensus and Difference" 614).

These kinds of sophisticated rhetorical moves continue: more letters to the editor, two more well-attended public forums with significant numbers of new participants, increased interest in local government as measured by attendance at town meetings. Committees formed at the end of the first forum, on 23 June 1992, have, by the persuasive strategies in their grant writing, received grants totaling over $300,000 to initiate a planning process for the town and its surrounding one-mile area, to establish water quality testing of the town's creek, to study the creation of a local development corporation, and to construct a site near the town for viewing local elk herds. The community of Red Lodge, through effective rhetorical work that realizes an agenda driven by both economic and environmental health, is forging some better way to live.

Red Lodge, 1995: The Sequel

Lest this movie seem saddled with an unrealistically happy ending, the results visible three years after the first Successful Communities Dialogue workshop continue to point to tangible successes. A specific, broad-based planning process has been established, led by the Beartooth Front Alliance, which enjoys the support of a wide range of citizens, including the chamber of commerce, a group of quilters who raise funds, and a group of ranchers. The Alliance is currently completing a planning initiative—funded by $20,000 from the city council—that has developed from several meetings, each attended by about a hundred people, over the last six months. Smaller but very important projects have developed as well: volunteer water quality monitors continue to gather data on the Rock Creek drainage, and the town now has a Boys and Girls Club that serves two hundred children, with an average of sixty children participating every weekday afternoon.

The Alliance has narrowed its focus to the town of Red Lodge for the present, although they continue to solicit rural participants especially, sometimes by inviting ranchers and cowboys to speak at the meetings. While the town has not implemented all the ideas that came out of the first meetings, successful planning efforts and other projects contribute to a heightened sense of shared community and viable opportunities in the town. These would not have developed without the community's deliberate and inclusive rhetorical activities, facilitated by the Beartooth Front Alliance and the Successful Communities workshops.

1996

Works Cited

Aristotle. *The Rhetoric and the Poetics of Aristotle.* Trans. W. Rhys Roberts and Ingram Bywater. New York: Modern Library, 1984.

Beartooth Front Community Forum. "Progress Report." March 1992.

Beartooth Front Community Forum Steering Committee. Letter to the editor. *Montana Free Press,* August 1992, 3.

Beartooth Front Community Forum Steering Committee. "Thanks from the Forum Front." *Montana Free Press,* November 1992.

Booth, Wayne C. "The Rhetorical Stance." *College Composition and Communication* 14 (1963): 139–145.

Burke, Kenneth. *Language as Symbolic Action: Essays on Life, Literature, and Method.* Berkeley: U of California P, 1966.

Burke, Kenneth. "Rhetoric—Old and New." *Journal of General Education* 5 (April 1951): 203.

Crews, Frederick, and Ann Jesse Van Sant. *The Random House Handbook.* 4th ed. New York: Random House, 1984.

Ferguson, Gary. "Guest Opinion: Beartooth Front Forum Advocates Public Involvement in Planning Issues." *Montana Free Press,* November 1992, 6.

Fisher, Walter. *Human Communication as Narration: Toward a Philosophy of Reason, Value, and Action.* Columbia: U of South Carolina P, 1987.

Homans, Peter. "The Western: The Legend and the Cardboard Hero." *Look,* 13 March 1962, 82–89.

Killingsworth, M. Jimmie. "Discourse Communities—Local and Global." *Rhetoric Review* 11 (1992): 110–122.

Lake, Laura. " Characterizing Environmental Mediation." *Environmental Mediation: The Search for Consensus.* Boulder, CO: Westview P, 1980.

Mernitz, Scott. *Mediation of Environmental Disputes: A Sourcebook.* New York: Praeger, 1980.

Propst, Luther, and Trudy Halvorson. "Successful Communities in Greater Yellowstone; Revised Draft, May 13, 1993." Tucson: Sonoran Institute, 1993.

"The Sonoran Institute Annual Report, 1991–1992." Tucson: Sonoran Institute, 1992.

"Successful Communities Dialogue." Tucson: Sonoran Institute, 1992.

Tompkins, Jane. *West of Everything: The Inner Life of Westerns.* New York: Oxford UP, 1992.

Trimbur, John. "Consensus and Difference in Collaborative Learning." *College English* 51 (1989): 601–616.

Trimbur, John. "The Ideal of the Community and the Politics of Difference." *Social Theory and Practice* 12 (Spring 1986): 110–121.

Weaver, Richard. *Ethics of Rhetoric.* Chicago: Henry W. Regnery, 1953.

READING, REREADING, AND ANALYSIS

1. As a group, discuss the genre of the Western and list its elements. (You might refer to the list you created for prereading question 3, which precedes the essay. What are some recent examples of Westerns? Next, discuss what Ingham sees as specifically "western" about Red Lodge's problems and their proposed "solutions." Use a particular example or examples from Ingham's essay to help explain your interpretation.

2. In your journal, discuss what Ingham means by "rhetorical education." Look up the word "rhetoric" in your dictionary. How does the definition compare with your sense of what Ingham means by the term? How does "rhetoric" contribute to solving the problems of Red Lodge?

3. Individually or in a group, list the features of "mediation" and of "community dialogue." What do they have in common? What distinguishes them?

4. In a group, find two passages in Ingham's essay where she discusses the concepts of "consensus" and "dissensus" and discuss them so that your group can explain to the rest of your classmates what Ingham means by the terms. Your explanation should include positive and negative aspects of each.

5. Ingham discusses the rhetorical concepts of pathos, ethos, and logos. Put these three terms into your own words, and think of an example for each term.

6. Ingham quotes a statement by John Trimbur: "The revised notion of consensus I am proposing here depends paradoxically on its deferral, not its realization." What does Trimbur mean, and why does Ingham refer to Trimbur in her essay? What does he help her do?

RESPONDING THROUGH WRITING:
BUILDING AN INTERPRETATION

7. Write a short paper comparing the "give and take" methods used by the different constituencies in Red Lodge with a situation you have witnessed or know about in which a community or a group had to reach a potentially contentious decision. What rhetorical methods were used in each case and what was learned from those methods: What level of "rhetorical education" took place in each case?

8. Write a letter to a local editor, governmental representative, or community group on behalf of a cause you care about, and be sure to use at least two of the three rhetorical terms—pathos, ethos, and logos—you paraphrased in question 5. In a group, analyze the letters to decide which forms of appeal are being implemented by each writer, which approaches seem the most convincing, and why.

9. Bring in flyers for campus or local events or direct mail from charities, editorials, articles, or ads from local or national political campaigns. Analyze the rhetoric. How do the examples you have brought to class construct their audience? What are they "selling"? What types of appeals (ethos, logos, pathos) are they manipulating? Write a paper discussing your findings. Be sure to attach a copy of the flyer, letter, or other document that your paper refers to.

10. The meetings in Red Lodge are motivated by recognition of the dangers of "environmental degradation." Think about other possible examples of environmental deterioration—perhaps on campus, in town, in your state, or in some part of your country.

Use some of Ingham's ideas to help you write a paper that pro-poses a plan to address potential "environmental degradation" by motivating citizens to "liv[e] some better way" (p. 253). What difficulties do you anticipate or imagine, and what strategies might work best to help produce "a sense of shared community and viable opportunities" for folks?

GOING FURTHER: LEARNING FROM OTHER SOURCES

11. In a database that includes a range of scholarly sources, such as Academic Search Elite, use the search terms "environment and ar-gument" or "environment and debate" to find another example of an environmental issue that has created dissension in a community. Think of the movie genre you might use to describe the community debate around this issue: action movie, horror movie, science fic-tion movie? Bring the article and your notes to class.

12. Use an academic search engine to help you research the Sonoran Institute. What kinds of projects does the institute currently work on? Also, use the search engine to help research recent develop-ment in Red Lodge, Montana. What kind of growth has occurred since 1995?

APPLYING WHAT YOU'VE LEARNED

13. Write an essay in which you build a definition of "rhetoric" us-ing quotations and examples from Ingham's essay and use it to identify problems involving rhetoric in Witold Rybczynski's "Designs for Escape" (p. 427), in Haunani-Kay Trask's "From a Native Daughter" (p. 539), or Richard Rodriguez's "'Blaxicans' and Other Reinvented Americans" (p.420). In each case, what are the problems involving language, and what solutions might a "rhetorical education" provide?

14. Ingham puts a great deal of faith in the powers of rhetoric tactics such as John Trimbur's "strategy of deferred consensus" (p. 246). Think about whether or not such a rhetorical strategy would be useful in dealing with the kinds of problems Michio Kaku dis-cusses in his essay, "Second Thoughts: The Genetics of a Brave New World?" Write a paper in which you discuss the pros and cons of applying some of Ingham's rhetorical emphases to Kaku's concerns. What do you think Ingham would make of Kaku's call for "an educated citizenry" to help make decisions about cutting-edge technology and science such as the biomolecular revolution

(p. 265)? In what way is Kaku also concerned with attempts at living some better way?

15. Write a five-page paper in which you present and support an argument that you have developed from thinking about the significances you see in Ingham's essay and Christopher Lasch's "The Lost Art of Argument." This assignment is not asking for a simple compare/contrast approach. Instead, you need to reflect on Ingham's and Lasch's main argument to create and develop your own argument in response to their theses.

MICHIO KAKU

Michio Kaku (b. 1947) is Henry Semat Professor of Theoretical Physics at the City College and the Graduate Center of the City University of New York. In addition to teaching and lecturing at universities around the world, Kaku hosts a weekly hour-long radio program on science. He has also appeared on television news shows and in several documentaries. Of his nine books, the last two, *Hyperspace: A Scientific Odyssey Through Parallel Universes, Time Warps, and the Tenth Dimension* (1995) and *Visions: How Science Will Revolutionize the Twenty-first Century* (1997), were written for popular audiences and became international bestsellers. "Second Thoughts: The Genetics of a Brave New World?" is a chapter from *Visions*.

> **To learn more about Michio Kaku or to ask him a question, go to <http://www.mkaku.org/>.**

WHAT DO YOU KNOW? WHAT DO YOU EXPECT TO DISCOVER?

Before reading the essay, take a moment to consider the following questions.

1. What topics does Kaku's biography suggest he is interested in? What do you know about those topics? Knowledge can come from personal experience, stories you've heard, other classes you've taken, or other reading you've done.

2. Make a list of ideas you have about, and associations you have with, the word "genetics." Given the use of the word "genetics" in the title, what are you expecting to find when you read Kaku's essay?

3. If you have read Aldous Huxley's novel *Brave New World*, then make a list of the plot features and characters that stand out in your memory. If you have not read Huxley's novel, then use a popular Internet search engine such as Google to find some information on the novel.

⚂

Second Thoughts

The Genetics of a Brave New World?

There are some things about which we must simply say you can't do.

—James Watson

Any attempt to shape the world and modify human personality in order to create a self-chosen pattern of life involves many unknown consequences. Human destiny is bound to remain a gamble, because at some unpredictable time and in some unforeseeable manner nature will strike back.

—René Dubos, *Mirage of Health*, 1959

The very reductionism to the molecular level that is fueling the medical revolution also poses the greatest moral challenge we face. We need to decide to what extent we want to design our descendants.

—Arthur Caplan, University of Pennsylvania Center for Bioethics

THE DNA REVOLUTION gives us at least two startling divergent visions of the future. One vision, promoted by the biotech industry, is that of health and prosperity: gene therapy will eliminate hereditary diseases and possibly cure cancer, bioengineering will create new drugs to vanquish infectious diseases, and gene splicing will create new animals and plants which will feed the world's exploding population.

However, a much darker vision of the future was painted by Aldous Huxley in his unsettling yet prophetic book *Brave New World*, written in 1932, with the world still reeling from the unremitting savagery unleashed by World War I and from the grinding poverty of the Great Depression.

The novel is set six hundred years in the future, when a similar series of disastrous wars have convinced the world's leaders to impose a radical new order. Recoiling from the chaos of the past, they decide to impose a Utopia based on happiness and stability, rather than concepts that have proven to be inherently unstable and messy, such as democracy, freedom, and justice. To be unhappy is against the law of the land. And the key to this state-mandated paradise is biotechnology.

Babies are mass-produced in huge embryo factories and are cloned to produce a caste system of Alpha, Beta, Gamma, Delta, and Epsilon human beings. By restricting the oxygen given to the embryos, scientists can cause selective brain damage and clone an army of obedient workers. The most brain-damaged are the Epsilon morons, subhumans who are carefully brainwashed into happily doing all the menial labor in society. The highest caste are the Alphas, who are, by contrast, carefully groomed and educated to become the ruling elite. Happiness is guaranteed by incessant, numbing brainwashing and unlimited access to mind-dulling drugs and sex.

The world was scandalized by Huxley's outrageous novel, and many attempts were made to censor it. Ironically, events have outpaced even Huxley's fertile imagination. In the 1950s he wrote: "I projected it six hundred years into the future. Today, it seems quite possible that the horror may be upon us within a single century."[1] But even a century may seem too long; already, many of his technological predictions are within grasp.

Huxley's predictions were certainly prophetic. He wrote in a time when the laws of embryonic development were largely unknown. Less than forty years later, however, Louise Brown, the first "test tube baby," was born. By the 1980s, parents had a wide selection of commercially available birthing options: embryos can be frozen and then thawed out years later, infertile couples could employ surrogate mothers to bear their children, and even grandmothers could give birth to their own grandchildren (by having the fertilized egg taken from their grown daughter implanted into their uterus). And with the coming of the biomolecular revolution, many of his other predictions may also be within reach—human cloning, selective breeding, and so on.

Therefore the question must be asked: which future will we choose?

In this chapter, I will look at how the biomolecular revolution will impact on society, for better or for worse. Few will dispute the tremendous accomplishments and potential of the biomolecular revolution. However, even the creators of the revolution have expressed reservations about the moral and ethical direction of this revolution if its excesses are not checked. In a democracy, only informed debate by an educated citizenry can make the mature decisions about a technology so powerful that we can dream of controlling life itself.

Nuclear Energy vs. Genetic Revolution

The awesome scientific knowledge that will be unveiled early in the next century must be tempered by the enormous ethical, social, and political questions that it raises. One framework in which to discuss the implications of the biomolecular revolution is to compare it with the nuclear revolution.

Biomolecular scientists are determined to avoid the kind of blunders committed in atomic energy research, which was originally conducted in total secrecy under the cloak of "national security." Because there was little democratic discussion of the implications of atomic energy, the

United States is now faced with seventeen leaking nuclear weapons dumps, which may cost upward of $500 billion to clean up. The human price is incalculable; unethical radiation experiments were conducted on 20,000 unsuspecting human subjects since the 1940s, including injecting plutonium into the veins of innocent patients, releasing radioactive materials over populated areas, and exposing pregnant women.

Mindful of this parallel, the originators of the Human Genome Project set aside 3 percent of the budget for what they called the Ethical, Legal, and Social Implications Branch (ELSI) of the Human Genome Project. It is the first time in history that a crash government project has ever devoted even a fraction of its resources to larger societal questions.

One danger that both supporters and critics of the technology fear is the equivalent of a Three Mile Island—i.e., a catastrophic accident due largely to human error, design flaws, or inadequate testing that could endanger the lives of millions and give the entire industry a black eye.

But there is an important difference between the atomic and biomolecular revolutions. It is possible, to some degree, to control the proliferation of nuclear weapons because of the tens of billions of dollars in resources necessary to develop a large nuclear infrastructure, complete with enrichment facilities, reactors, and top nuclear scientists. One cannot simply start up a nuclear program in one's basement. For example, the flow of enriched uranium and plutonium is restricted via stringent security measures, which has been one of the principal reasons only a handful of nations possess nuclear weapons today.[2] The genie cannot be put back into the bottle, but we can limit the number of genies set loose on the world.

The nature of bioengineering is radically different. With only a modest $10,000 investment, one can conduct biotech experiments in one's living room and begin to manipulate the genome of plants and animals. With a few million, one can create a fledgling biotech industry. The low initial investment, high return, and potential for feeding its people are some reasons why a poor nation such as Cuba has decided to jump into biotechnology.

But this also means that biotechnology is impossible to contain. One cannot restrict the flow of DNA; it's everywhere. Because the technology can never be entirely banned, it is important to discuss and decide which of the various technologies should be allowed to flourish and which ones should be restricted, either via governmental fiat or by social and political pressure.

You Can't Recall a Crop

Jane Rissler of the Union of Concerned Scientists worries that the lack of proper oversight may release a seemingly harmless gene into our food supply which may cause life-threatening allergies to the unwary

customer. (Banana genes, for example, have been inserted into tomatoes; such tomatoes could be unwittingly eaten by children with severe
allergies to bananas.) Rebecca Goldburg, senior scientist at the Environmental Defense Fund, points out that there are 5 million people
with food allergies ranging from mild to life-threatening. Goldburg recounts the recent case of a soybean that was engineered to contain a
gene from the Brazil nut. Subsequent testing by the company showed
that it was allergenic and could have caused life-threatening shock if
the product had been prematurely released to the public.[3]

Critics also worry that the FDA is approving new foods for the
supermarket without adequate testing, while the Department of Agriculture allows companies to do field testing without permits. "I think
they've taken a good idea and taken it too far," concludes Rebecca
Goldburg.[4]

Under pressure from powerful agribusiness interests to cut red
tape, the Department of Agriculture streamlined the process of field
testing these plants. From 1987 to 1995, 500 field test permits covering forty new species were granted by the Agriculture Department (including barley, carrots, chicory, soybeans, peanuts, broccoli, cranberry,
various berries, and watermelons) with minimal oversight.[5]

What worries Goldburg is that the same corporations that are
pushing pesticides are now pushing genetically altered plants that are
more resistant to pesticides. This, she thinks, smacks of self-interest.
The net result will be that farmers buy more pesticides, thinking that
their crops can handle the increased load, which means more pesticides in our foods, and potentially the creation of a new generation of
pesticide-resistant bugs. This could spark a new "arms race" between
insects and bioengineered products, creating a host of "super-bugs"
that are resistant to potent levels of pesticides and also leaving more
pesticides in our food.

But the primary fear is that entirely new plants never seen before
in nature may escape into the wild once the floodgates are opened,
where they may displace native plants and take over whole ecosys-
tems, with unforeseen results.

"If the plants are raised outdoors and the new genes get into the
wild gene pool, it could have a potentially destabilizing effect on the
ecological system," says Jeremy Rifkin of the Foundation for Economic Trends, one of the leading critics of the biotech revolution.

The worry over transgenic crops is summarized by the phrase:
"bioengineered crops can't be recalled." Many critics point out the
unforeseen consequences of alien species being introduced, deliberately or accidentally, into new environments, as has happened with
zebra mussels, Dutch elm disease, kudzu, and chestnut blight.[6] The
delicate ecological balance can be severely affected by a new species.

A case in point is the African bee (*Apis mellifera adansonii
scrutellata*, sometimes referred to as the "killer bee" by the press),
which was deliberately imported into Brazil in 1957 to replace the

European honeybee (*Apis mellifera*), which did not adjust well to the daylight cycle of the country's equatorial climate.[7] When scores of queen bees escaped, this highly aggressive species spread out of control and wreaked havoc with the bee industry. Unlike the gentler European bee, the African bee is easily aroused and attacks and swarms by the thousands. It has already killed 1,000 people and caused millions of dollars in losses.

Today, the African bee is the dominant bee species over 20 million square kilometers of the Western Hemisphere, including all of South and Central America. The bees reached Texas in 1990, Arizona in 1993, and are expected to colonize most of the American Southwest until they are stopped by the colder climate of the North around the year 2000.

This is a telling example of how humans have upset a natural ecosystem by unwittingly introducing a new life form which is aggressive enough to displace the milder, domestic one.

Instead of pesticides, Rissler advocates an alternative vision of the future, something called "sustainable agriculture," which involves using natural enemies of certain insects to control their population, which can be done without pesticides. By balancing the ecology of insects in a field, one may be able to keep certain insect populations within limits by importing its natural enemies.

"Who Owns the Genome?"

Critics point out that the secret of life is being unraveled by companies with the freewheeling morality which prevailed in the Wild West. *Science* even devoted its cover to the issue with the title "Who Owns the Genome?"

Daniel Cohen, of the Center for the Study of Human Polymorphisms in Paris, has compared the patenting process to "trying to patent the stars. . . . By patenting something without knowing the use of it, you inhibit industry. That could be a catastrophe."[8]

In 1996, Jeremy Rifkin led a coalition to protest the patenting of the tumor suppressor breast cancer gene *BRCA1*. Myriad Genetics of Salt Lake City, whose scientists isolated the gene in 1994, patented it and began marketing commercially available genetic tests. The coalition argued that patenting the gene would jeopardize women's privacy, especially if the information wound up in the hands of insurance companies. It also argued that patenting genes constricts scientific competition, drives up prices, and allows private industry to reap profits from publicly funded research.[9]

But Collins believes that this thorny problem will gradually disappear with time. "When the Human Genome Project is done, all the sequences are going to be publicly available; no one is going to be able to patent the sequence anymore. At that point, the patenting (if there is patenting, and I think there will be) will be on uses of the sequence, showing that this particular region can be used to make a product that benefits people. And that will probably be for the best."[10]

Genes and Privacy

"Should you have a legal right to demand someone accused of rape to give a DNA sample?" asks James Watson. "Should you, if you're running for President, have to say what your DNA constitution is?"[11] What might have happened if J. Edgar Hoover, the pugnacious and ruthless director of the FBI, had the genetic profiles of politicians in his drawer? Watson wonders. For many decades, J. Edgar Hoover bullied politicians because he had their sexual peccadilloes and drinking habits on file. How much more pressure might he have applied if he knew the complete genetic history of Washington's sometimes wayward politicians?

What is to prevent someone from swiping strands of hair from a presidential candidate and having them genetically analyzed? John Kennedy, for example, may never have been elected President had it been known that he had a serious medical problem with his adrenal glands, which became known only after his death. Recent studies of preserved DNA samples taken in 1967 from former Vice President Hubert Humphrey showed they possessed a cancerous p-53 mutation associated with bladder cancer (Humphrey died of cancer in 1976). With modern techniques, he could have been diagnosed as being predisposed to cancer before the 1968 presidential elections, possibly eliminating him from the race. David Sidransky of Johns Hopkins, who led this study, says, it "could have changed the course of political history."[12]

A related question concerns mandatory testing. Already, DNA data banks in this country are being formed by testing prisoners. But should the government be allowed to force people to be tested against their will? Arthur Caplan of the Center for Bioethics believes that thirty years from now, health costs in the United States will be so exorbitant that some in the government may be tempted to call for mandatory testing for genetic diseases and simply refuse to pay the health costs for a baby whose genetic disease was preventable if it had been tested.[13]

Caplan believes that within fifteen years the debate over whether or not to have your future baby genetically tested will become even more raucous than the abortion debate today. Are you irresponsible if you have children without genetic testing? And if so, should the government pay for such genetic irresponsibility? Eventually, he believes, people who have children without genetic testing may be treated as pariahs.

Next, what happens if our genome is leaked out publicly, to our employers, our insurance company, our fiancé, especially for those who harbor potentially deleterious genes? Since time immemorial, societies have committed some form of genetic discrimination. People with obvious deformities or diseases were taunted, labeled witches (as in Huntington's disease), systematically isolated from society, or even killed. What is new, however, is that today it will be possible to screen individuals for a genetic disease even if the disease never appears. Someone who may never suffer from a particular genetic disease may be denied insurance or a job if the person has a high probability of developing a genetic disease.

Nancy Wexler, head of the Ethical, Legal, and Social Implications Branch (ELSI) of the Human Genome Project, says, "Genetic information itself is not going to hurt the public. What could hurt the public is existing social structures, policies, and prejudices against which information can ricochet. We need genetic information right now in order to make better choices so we can live better lives. We need the improved treatments that will eventually be developed using genetic information. So I think the answer is certainly not to slow down the advancing science, but to try, somehow, to make the social system more accommodating to the new knowledge."

According to the now defunct Office of Technology Assessment, the former investigative arm of the U.S. Congress, 164,000 applications for medical insurance are being turned down for medical reasons. The OTA report stated: "Applicants for insurance plans are already being asked to provide information to prospective insurers related to genetic conditions like sickle cell anemia. Some experts fear that individual policies will become increasingly difficult to acquire as more genetic screening tests become available."[14]

A recent study done by Harvard and Stanford universities identified 200 cases in which people were denied insurance, fired from their jobs, or prevented from adopting children because of their genes.

Four bills have been introduced in Congress and twenty bills in various state legislatures to prohibit genetic discrimination. Fourteen states have so far passed laws against it. President Clinton in 1996 signed a bill that prohibits insurance companies from discriminating on the basis of a "preexisting condition."

Genetic discrimination could also affect your marriage prospects. Since everyone has some genetic disease in their genome, this could play havoc with dating rituals. Already, there are dating services exclusively for singles who have tested negative for AIDS. In the future, there may be dating services for people who have tested negative for potentially fatal diseases, like cancer.

But Collins thinks some of these fears of "genetic wallflowers" are exaggerated. "Those concerns are somewhat lessened when you realize that we are all walking around with four or five genes that are pretty badly screwed up, and maybe another twenty or thirty that are moderately defective. So if you're going to wait around for the perfect genetic specimen to walk in, to be your mate, you're going to be single for the rest of your life. It's not going to happen. And you're not going to be able to offer them a perfect genetic specimen either. So we are all flawed. That's the way it is."[15]

Are Genes Us?

One area that could cause considerable misunderstanding is the link between genes and human behavior. Although human behavior is influenced by genes in complex ways, to say that we have a gene for this or that behavior goes too far. Caplan thinks that for the next thirty to forty years this link between genes and behavior will be a "ticking time bomb." While he believes that math ability, personality types, mental illness (depression and schizophrenia), homosexuality, alcoholism, and obesity all have genetic roots, he cautions, "It would be silly to just equate our behavior with genes. It's obvious that even in the same family twins don't turn out to have precisely the same behavior."[16] Genes are only one ingredient in the mix.

Christopher Wills of the University of California at San Diego says, "Simply determining the sequence of all this DNA will not mean we have learned everything there is to know about human beings, any more than looking up the sequence of notes in a Beethoven sonata gives us the capacity to play it. In the future, the true virtuosos of the genome will be those who can put this information to work, and who can appreciate the subtle interactions of genes with each other and with the environment."[17]

Mistakes have already been made. In 1996, the announcement that the gene *D4DR* controls "novelty seeking" in humans made the front page of the *New York Times*. But an exhaustive study of 331 people failed to show any such link.[18]

A more controversial claim which has not held up under scrutiny is the genetic link to violence. The initial controversy was sparked in 1965 by a study which reportedly found that out of 197 patients in a high-security mental hospital in Scotland, 3.5 percent had an unusual XYY chromosome. XYY males were widely stereotyped as being violent and subnormal.[19] The press dubbed the Y chromosome the "criminal chromosome."[20] (Actually, later studies showed that males with XYY chromosomes are known to be more widespread than previously thought, and 96 percent of them lead perfectly normal lives. The most common traits among XYY males seem to be tallness, higher IQ than normal, and slight slurring of speech.)

There is a lesson for the future. By 2020, when personalized DNA sequencing is widely available, there will be many claims to have isolated the "violence gene." By then, it will be a simple matter to correlate prison populations with any number of genes. Genes will certainly be discovered which will, superficially at least, appear to be associated with violent individuals. For example, genes will be found which influence the production of male hormones like testosterone, which some believe may increase aggression under certain circumstances. However, to claim that the "violence gene" has been discovered might be a gross error. Although these genes may in fact be found in a tiny fraction of violent individuals, the vast majority of violent individuals may be linked to totally unrelated factors (e.g., poverty or racism).

This controversy erupted again in 1992, when preparations were made for a major government-funded conference on violence and genetics. African-American critics charged that the conference was unbalanced, giving the impression that genetics was a driving feature of violence, rather than one among a host of contributing factors. Said psychiatrist Peter Breggin, "If you think back, the genetic policy argument used to be that blacks were docile—in one generation they are now genetically violent. This is not science. This is the use of psychiatry and science in the interest of racist social policy."[21]

One controversy about the genetic roots of behavior which will continue for many decades into the future concerns one of the touchiest issues in modern society, race and IQ. In general, most molecular biologists avoid simplistic comments about genes being the sole source of human behavior. However, there is a tendency of others, especially those with a hidden political agenda, to use the results of genetic research to support their often exaggerated claims.

The whole question of DNA, genetics, and race burst upon the national scene in 1995 with the publication of *The Bell Curve* by Richard Hernstein and Charles Murray. It soon ignited a national controversy and opened deep wounds.

Some facts are indisputable. African-Americans consistently score about 10 percent lower than white Americans on the IQ exam. And Asian-Americans consistently score a bit higher than Caucasians. But does that mean that Asian-Americans are a bit smarter than Caucasians, who are in turn 10 percent smarter than African-Americans?

From an evolutionary point of view, it seems unlikely that race and intelligence are strongly linked. The various races of the earth began to diverge about 100,000 years ago in waves of migration from Africa, long after humans had evolved their large brains, which took millions of years of evolution. So the races of the world are a relatively new phenomenon, whereas human intelligence is much more ancient. (DNA analysis, furthermore, clearly shows that the greatest genetic variations exist not between races, but within the races. So the genetic distance between Richard Hernstein and Nelson Mandela, for example, may be much smaller in principle, than the genetic difference between Hernstein and Murray.)

Caplan, echoing the comments of many other scientists, believes that intelligence is actually multidimensional, involving many facets that are totally neglected by IQ exams. He concludes: *"The Bell*

Curve was pretty dopey. Psychiatrists and geneticists know that intelligence is a very complex trait made up of many different things. We all know people who can compute well but can't interact socially with anyone, or people who are very good at finding their way around a neighborhood and others who cannot seem to locate the door in their house. Many different things contribute to intelligence. *The Bell Curve* didn't reflect any of this."[22]

One lesson for the future is this: Commentators have noted that the issue of race and IQ usually surfaces during times of economic hardship. Inevitably, because of the business cycle, there will be many periods in the twenty-first century when the economy descends into recession. Demagogues looking for scapegoats will find a receptive ear among the millions who are thrown out of work. In American history, racial theories of intelligence usually receive widespread publicity during times of economic crisis, when people feel threatened by new waves of immigrants. In 1923, for example, Carl Brigham published *A Study of American Intelligence,* using IQ tests to prove that Alpine and Mediterranean "races" were inferior to the Nordic "race" and that Africans were inferior to both. This fueled the movement to exclude people from Southern and Eastern Europe, especially Italians and Jews. One congressman said, "The primary reason for the restriction of the alien stream . . . is the necessity for purifying and keeping pure the blood of America."[23] President Calvin Coolidge, who signed the Immigration Act enforcing quotas on certain nationalities, was on record as stating, "Biological laws show . . . that Nordics deteriorate when mixed with other races."[24]

After 2020: Manipulating Our Germ Line?

Beyond 2020 new ethical questions are likely to be raised. Gene therapy . . . relies on manipulating the genes of somatic cells. Thus the new genes cannot be passed on to succeeding generations. The new genes die when the patient eventually dies. But germ-line therapy would change the genome of our sex cells, so the new gene can be passed on permanently to our offspring. As with transgenic mice, using microinjection of human embryos to permanently change the genetic heritage of the patient could, for example, eliminate cystic fibrosis from a family forever.

Although the idea of eliminating genetic diseases from one's germ line is appealing, there is also enormous potential to misuse germ-line therapy. By and large, the scientific community is against the idea of germ-line therapy. In 1988, the European Research Council stated flatly, "Germ-line gene therapy should not be contemplated."[25] There are, however, some disagreements among scientists.[26]

Would parents opt for germ-line gene therapy, if it were available, to choose the height, sex, strength, eye, and hair color of their children?

"Are you kidding? Yes!" claims Arthur Caplan.[27] There is ample evidence that some families, given the chance, would readily pay to have this done. Parents already try to shape their children in hundreds of ways, such as giving them lessons in piano, languages, sports, etc. "I think there is no doubt that many parents will want to use genetic information to design their kids," Caplan says.[28]

But is this a good thing? The question is: what should be the role of doctors? Are they servants who are expected to simply carry out the wishes of the consumer? Or do we want them to be ministers and guardians of morality, deciding what forms of treatment are unethical? Caplan predicts that it's going to be "one whopping moral debate."[29]

Yet banning such therapy could create a thriving black market in germ-line therapy, especially in Third World countries. Even a simple test such as determining the sex of the unborn infant is causing a major demographic earthquake.

"The use of this technology for sex selection insults the reasons I went into genetics in the first place. Sex is not a disease but a trait!" declares Francis Collins.[30]

Will parents, for example, primarily ask for children who are male, tall, strong, and handsome? The answer, unfortunately, in many countries and in many families, is yes. The laws of evolution dictate that animals will try to give every possible genetic advantage to their unborn children. And humans are no different. Consciously or unconsciously, we want our children to have a head start on life.

To poor families in the Third World, the idea of tinkering with their unborn children seems one way out of poverty. Even before gene modification becomes a reality in the next century, the introduction of a simple device like the sonogram is creating a major demographic shift in China and India, with grave implications for the next generation.

In large portions of the developing world, peasant families place an inordinate emphasis on male children. Not only do male children carry on the name and enjoy numerous feudal privileges, but families with females are required to prepare an expensive dowry at the time of marriage, which is a drain on a poverty-stricken family's finances. According to Monica Das Gupta of Harvard University, from 1981 to 1991 a million girls in India were lost to selective abortions when sonograms were introduced. Four million other girls simply "disappeared" during their first four to six years of life. In other words, 3.6 percent of the female population for that age bracket disappeared.[31]

China's one-child-per-family policy, which has finally brought its population explosion under control, had the unintended side effect of fostering female infanticide. Informal estimates of the young female population in rural areas have shown that up to 10 million female children are "missing." On the southern coast of China, the normal sex ratio, which is 100 females to every 103 male babies born, became skewed in 1995 to 100 females for every 115.4 males. [32]

If the introduction of the simple sonogram could unleash this demographic nightmare, think of the social upheaval that could result from the ability to genetically control our progeny. To give a mild example, in the case of the genetically engineered human growth hormone (HGH)—which only children who suffer from HGH deficiency or chronic kidney failure can qualify for—a recent study found that 60 percent of the children receiving HGH did not qualify. Apparently, anxious parents, concerned about the height of their children, have been pressuring doctors to administer HGH, even at costs of up to $16,000 a year for treatments.[33]

Inevitably, science in the twenty-first century will require the passing of certain laws to prohibit rampant meddling with the human genome, and certainly the human germ line. Some argue that pernicious genetic defects which have caused excruciating pain and suffering for generations should be eliminated from our germ line forever. Others argue the Law of Unintended Side Effects—that by playing God we will inadvertently cause even more suffering later. The question that will dominate ethical battles in the next century is precisely where this fine line should be drawn. Many scientists believe genetic manipulation of our germ line for strictly cosmetic reasons should be banned, as this is a frivolous (and potentially dangerous) application of a powerful technology. However, if it can be proven that grotesque diseases like Huntington's serve no practical purpose, then an equally powerful case can be made to eliminate them forever from one's germ line.

There may be no definitive answer to where to draw the line, as public perceptions and scientific advances change over the decades. However, since random chemical errors, cosmic rays, chemical pollution, poor diet, and other environmental insults continually create new mutations in our genome, it is a question that will be with us for centuries to come.

To Clone a Human

Some predictions from Huxley's *Brave New World* remain firmly in the distant future. At present, it is impossible to bring a fertilized egg to full term in a test tube. Thus, Huxley's prediction that birthing might be replaced by huge embryo factories is far beyond today's technology. Reproducing the delicate, complex chemical environment found in a womb necessary to nurture a human fetus for nine months will probably remain technically out of reach for several decades.

The cloning of humans, however, is now distinctly within the realm of possibility. The astonishing announcement by Ian Wilmut of the successful cloning of an adult sheep has opened up enormous ethical and social questions. Many biologists now believe that only technical and legal barriers prevent the cloning of humans.

The ramifications of human cloning are considerable, ranging from the silly and the humane to the fantastic:

- Prominent athletes from different sports and even different decades may be cloned to create a lucrative "dream team."
- Wealthy individuals and aging monarchs without children might bequeath their fortunes and thrones to their clones.
- Parents might want to clone a child who died from a fatal disease or accident.
- Cells may be stolen from famous or glamorous figures and then sold to people who want these individuals for children.
- Graves of famous people may be raided to obtain DNA samples capable of being cloned.
- Dictators may create armies of cloned soldiers or slaves with great physical strength but limited mental capacity, or human hybrids resembling the nightmares from *The Island of Dr. Moreau.*

Other possibilities, such as cloning individuals to perform the undesirable menial tasks necessary for society, as in *Brave New World,* are not such farfetched concepts, given the fact that industrialized societies already import cheap immigrant labor to perform these duties.

Some have even speculated about a mythical society based entirely on clones, in which males would be superfluous. Parthenogenesis, whereby a female produces offspring without a male, could become the dominant mode of human reproduction. (In the long term, such a society would probably be unstable, since one of the evolutionary purposes of sex is to ensure genetic diversity, which is essential to survival in a constantly changing environment.)

There will certainly be a demand for this technology, legal or not. If some parents yearn for a "chip off the old block," then why settle for anything less than an exact copy? Some see clones as fulfilling a deep-seated wish for immortality. After all, the search for immortality probably led the Pharaohs of Egypt to build the pyramids and dying kings to build opulent tombs. Cloning offers a kind of immortality that would be infinitely cheaper.

Cloning also raises a host of other unresolved questions. Theologians have debated whether a human clone has a "soul." If humans can be cloned without limit, then what determines their individuality and essence? Ethicists have asked whether it is morally right to force our own genetic desires onto our offspring, who have no say in the matter. Moralists have been disturbed at the thought of the hundreds of embryos that may be sacrificed in order to produce a single successful clone. Lawyers have asked what are the legal rights of clones—can they assume the legal rights, privileges, and debts of their predecessor? If clones are produced in order to "harvest" their organs, what happens if they refuse to be sacrificed?

Certain things are clear. There is no guarantee that cloning well-known figures will produce equally great offspring. In the movie *The Boys from Brazil,* for example, neo-Nazis cloned young versions of Hitler to resurrect the Third Reich. However, many historians have argued that it was the economic collapse of the German middle classes in the 1930s that set the stage for fascism and gave rise to Hitler. A social or political movement is rarely created by one man alone. Cloning Hitler may do no more than produce a second-rate artist. Similarly, cloning an Einstein does not guarantee that a great physicist will be born, since Einstein lived in a time when physics was in deep crisis; many of the great problems in physics today have already been solved. Great individuals are probably as much the product of great turmoil and opportunity as the product of favorable genes.

It may be that human cloning will be banned in most countries. Even before Wilmut's announcement, the United Kingdom passed the Human Embryo Act prohibiting experimentation on human embryos. President Bill Clinton previously restricted federal funding for human embryo research. In 1997, a federal panel appointed by President Clinton recommended legislation to restrict both public and private research for at least three years.

Ironically, barring some unforeseen technical problem, it is likely that human cloning will soon become a fact of life. Laws banning cloning will simply push cloning research into private, foreign, and underground laboratories, which will be able to continue this line of research because start-up costs are so low and the economic incentives so attractive.

Because of the laws of the marketplace, some predict a small but bustling underground economy based on cloning. "I don't see how you can stop these things. We are at the mercy of these technological developments. Once they're here, it's hard to turn back," says bioethicist Daniel Callahan of the Hastings Center in Briarcliff Manor.[34]

In the future, it is likely that a small fraction of society will, in fact, be clones, given the demand for cloning. For the most part, society may eventually learn to accept the presence of small numbers of clones, in the same way that society has already accepted the presence of test tube babies from surrogate mothers and other unorthodox birthing options.

For all the controversy generated by cloning, the ultimate social impact from these clones could ultimately be negligible. People will learn that the few clones that exist will probably not pose a threat to society. After all, we already live in a world with twins; the more insidious possibility is that cloning may revive the eugenics movement.

The Eugenics Movement

We sometimes forget that the eugenics movement in the United States has a long and unsavory history with deep roots in our culture.

The movement's founder and chief propagandist was Francis Galton, a cousin of Charles Darwin. Inspired by Darwin's work, Galton spent several decades studying the ancestral trees of eminent writers, scientists, philosophers, artists, and statesmen and became convinced that their great abilities were passed down from generation to generation. (Coming from a wealthy family, Galton was apparently blind to environmental influences. He could not admit that perhaps poor people rarely produced great statesmen because they spent most of their time trying to survive.)

Galton concluded that it would be desirable "to produce a highly gifted race of men by judicious marriages during several consecutive generations." In 1883, he coined the word "eugenics" from the Greek to mean "endowed by heredity with noble qualities."[35] Attempts were even made to breed the perfect race. In 1886, Elizabeth Nietzsche, the sister of the philosopher, selected a group of pure-blooded individuals and set sail for Paraguay to create Nueva Germania (New Germany). According to geneticist Steve Jones: "'Today the people of Nueva Germania are poor, inbred, and diseased. Their Utopia has failed."[36]

One of Galton's disciples was Charles Davenport, a professor at the University of Chicago. He used his influence to launch a major institution at Cold Spring Harbor on Long Island to collect a massive database on family hereditary histories. His popular book *Heredity in Relation to Eugenics* helped to inspire the eugenics movement in the United States. In the book, not only did he call for selective breeding to enhance the intellectual qualities found among artists, musicians, scientists, etc., but he also said it may be necessary to use forcible methods to eliminate undesirables with unwanted characteristics. "Society must protect itself," he wrote. "As it claims the right to deprive the murderer of his life so also may it annihilate the hideous serpent of hopelessly vicious protoplasm."[37]

In 1927, this was given legal stature when the U.S. Supreme Court upheld the constitutionality of sterilization in the case of *Buck v. Bell,* involving a Virginia sterilization statute. Justice Oliver Wendell Holmes wrote: "It is better for all the world, if instead of waiting to execute degenerate offspring for crime, or to let them starve for their imbecility, society can prevent those who are manifestly unfit for continuing their kind. The principle that sustains compulsory vaccination is broad enough to cover cutting the Fallopian tubes."[38]

By 1930, twenty-four states had passed laws allowing for the sterilization of a wide variety of "undesirables," which included criminals, epileptics, the insane, and the retarded. By 1941, 36,000 people were sterilized in the United States.

The Nazis openly expressed a deep gratitude to the eugenics movement in the United States, which provided an inspiration for their own ideas. Eugenics was incorporated as an integral part of the Nazi ideology, based on breeding the Aryan "master race." Eventually, millions would he rounded up, thrown into camps, or gassed, victims of the abstract, theoretical ideas proposed by the eugenicists.

Many of these ideas still percolate in the United States. In the 1980s, Nobel Prize-winning physicist William Shockley, co-inventor of the transistor, called for Nobel Laureates to contribute to a sperm bank. Any eligible female could then perform her duty to humanity and improve the human race by being inseminated from this sperm bank of "geniuses."

One long-term danger for the far future is that those who are the wealthiest will be able to afford to improve their germ line, while others will not, leaving the rest of society behind, eventually creating a new biological caste system. Gregory Kavka, a philosopher at the University of California at Irvine, says, "Any such move toward genetic enhancement has the potential of reestablishing social inequality, though along new lines. Old aristocracies of birth, color, or gender may dissipate, only to be replaced by a new genetic aristocracy, or 'genetocracy.' "[39]

The deep fracture lines of society could become chasms if only the wealthy have access to choosing their germ line (eventually creating a nightmarish, two-tiered society like the one portrayed by H. G. Wells in *The Time Machine*, when the Morlocks toiled with their machines in underground caverns while the childlike Eloi pranced and frollicked aboveground).[40]

In the future, society must be wary of those who would use the benefits of the genetics revolution to further their own social agenda.

Biological Warfare

But perhaps the greatest fear concerning biotechnology is the deliberate misuse of this technology, especially for warfare.

Unfortunately, biological warfare has a long and ugly history. When conquest or national survival is at stake, nations often resort to the most destructive weapons at their disposal, including biological ones.

One of the earliest recorded uses of biological warfare was in 600 B.C., when Solon from Athens contaminated the water supply of the city of Kirrah with the poisonous hellebore plant. During the fourteenth century the Tartars catapulted the bodies of dead plague victims over the walls of the Crimean town of Kaffa in order to ignite an epidemic. And in the eighteenth century both British soldiers and U.S. government agents traded smallpox-infected blankets to Native Americans, which accelerated their extermination.[41]

During World War I, 100,000 tons of poison gases (chlorine, phosgene, and mustard gas) were used to kill 100,000 soldiers and incapacitate 1.3 million more.[42]

During World War II, the Nazis gassed millions of Jews, Russians, Gypsies, and other "undesirables," and Japanese conducted hideous germ warfare experiments on prisoners of war (even Britain and the United States had plans, never put into effect, to use anthrax as a weapon, either stored in 200-kilogram bombs or employed as a poison to infect enemy livestock).[43]

In March 1995, a fanatical Buddhist cult in Japan unleashed the nerve gas sarin in the Tokyo subway system, killing twelve and injuring 5,500. The only thing that prevented tens of thousands from dying was the fact that the mixture was impure. (Like other nerve agents, sarin, developed by the Germans in the 1930s, blocks the chemical acetylcholinesterase, which is necessary for the transmission of nerve impulses.) There is evidence that this same cult actively tried to obtain samples of the Ebola virus as well.

But perhaps the greatest fear is that an accidental release of an incurable virus from one of the biological warfare centers (such as Fort Detrick outside Washington, D.C.) may threaten the very existence of the human race. A mutated, airborne Ebola or HIV virus could infect most of the planet within a matter of weeks or months.

Some scientists' greatest fears were voiced by Karl Johnson of the CDC when he said, "I worry about all this research on virulence. It's only a matter of months—years, at most—before people nail down the genes for virulence and airborne transmission in influenza, Ebola, Lassa, you name it. And then any crackpot with a few thousand dollars' worth of equipment and a college biology education under his belt could manufacture bugs that would make Ebola look like a walk around the park."[44]

Such a doomsday scenario cannot be ignored. D. A. Henderson, who helped to lead the campaign against smallpox, has observed: "Where would we be today if HIV were to become an airborne pathogen? And what is there to say that a comparable infection might not do so in the future?"[45]

A warring nation could also use biotechnology to create a disease to destroy an enemy's crops, thereby unleashing famine. "It can easily be done. This is not science fiction," says A. N. Mukhopadyay, dean of agriculture for the G. S. Pant University in India.[46]

Barbara Rosenberg of the Federation of American Scientists, comments: "None of the equipment is so high-tech that it could not be homemade by any nation intent on developing BW [biological warfare] capacity. No nation is immune to the dangers."[47]

At the annual meeting of the American Society of Tropical Medicine and Hygiene in Honolulu in 1989, scientists staged an extraordinary but purely hypothetical war games exercise involving germ warfare. In that exercise, a civil war and mass chaos erupts in central Africa. An airborne Ebola virus suddenly emerges out of the squalor of a refugee camp. Within days, it begins to spread outside the camp, eventually reaching the airports and spreading to Europe and America. Within ten days, it reaches Washington, D.C., New York,

Honolulu, Geneva, Frankfurt, Manila, Bangkok. Within a month, a global pandemic is unleashed, triggering worldwide panic.[48]

Recalling that chilling exercise, Karl Johnson said, "You may say 'ridiculous,' but I don't think we can disregard that possibility. It was, and still is, a potential," he says.[49]

Perhaps one of the most frightening forms of germ warfare to contemplate is what are called "ethnic weapons"—i.e., genetically altered germs which attack specific ethnic groups or races. Ethnic weapons were first proposed publicly in 1970 in *Military Review* magazine, which noted that certain Asian people cannot digest milk.[50] The article used this example to demonstrate that certain races are vulnerable to certain chemicals.

Recently declassified documents reveal that back in 1951 the U.S. Navy conducted top secret tests to determine how vulnerable it was to an enemy attack which selectively affected primarily African-American defense workers by using *Coccidioides immitis,* which causes San Joaquin Valley fever, which kills ten times more African-Americans than Caucasians.[51]

Charles Piller, author of *Gene Wars,* notes that San Joaquin Valley fever, a systemic fungal disease, was developed by the United States as a potential biological weapon back in the 1940s. Military planners once considered mutating the organism so that it would attack one specific ethnic group.[52]

Legislating the Genome

Francis Collins says, "I am not such a Pollyanna as to imagine that information this powerful cannot in some future instance be used in the wrong way. . . . If you believe that one of the strongest mandates of humankind is to pursue ways to alleviate human suffering, you really can't be against this research. But it's knowledge. It's not good or evil. It's just knowledge."[53]

But knowledge is power, and power is inherently a political and social question. To help clarify the essential issues at stake with the genetics of the future, the ELSI has come out with simple guidelines for dealing with some of these thorny ethical issues. What they advocate is this:

Fairness for all—no genetic discrimination

The right to privacy—prevent disclosure

The delivery of health care—services made available to all

The need for education—raising public consciousness

These guidelines identify some of the essential issues and give cogent responses to them. However, how to implement these guidelines is still in question. Ultimately, many of these ethical questions may be solved by a combination of social pressure, legislation, and treaties between nations.

There is no viable way to completely stop the progress of science—but we must find a way to carefully control the excesses of technology. Certain aspects of genetics research may need to be banned entirely. But the best overall policy is to air the risks and potentials of genetics research in public, and democratically pass laws which will shape the direction of the technology toward alleviating sickness and pain.

Caplan thinks that some of the simpler questions can be resolved by peer pressure. For example, today many women in their late thirties or older voluntarily ask that an amniocentesis be performed, which can determine if the fetus is suffering from Down's syndrome. In the future, as testing for more genetic diseases is perfected, women may voluntarily agree to be tested during their pregnancy.

Other issues, however, will require outright legislation. Already, for example, several bills in Congress are being considered to ban insurance companies from discriminating on the basis of one's genetic makeup.

Similarly, society may have to pass legislation to decide which germ-line therapies will be banned. For example, is being short a disease? Many scientists working on gene therapy are horrified that the fruits of their work may be used for purely cosmetic reasons. They argue persuasively that germ-line therapy for cosmetic reasons should be banned, but germ-line therapy might be allowed for certain classes of debilitating genetic diseases.

Ultimately, the question of germ warfare will have to be decided by treaty. The Biological Weapons Convention of 1972, signed by the United States, the former Soviet Union, and scores of other countries, was a milestone in trying to ban or restrict germ warfare. Unfortunately, it was signed before the coming of recombinant DNA technology; hence there are many potential flaws. First, it banned the use of biological weapons for "hostile purposes or armed conflict." However, in the age of recombinant DNA, there is precious little difference between the offensive and defensive use of deadly germs. Second, it outlawed the "development" of germ weapons, but allowed for "research" on them. Unfortunately, this means that it is legal to do "research" on large quantities of deadly germs with the intent to use them in a future war. In the biotech business, there is no great distinction between researching a biological weapon and developing it.

Given that there is no easy dividing line between defensive and offensive uses of germ warfare, ultimately the entire field of biological weapons might have to be banned. In 1995, in a report by the Office of Technology Assessment, seventeen countries were said to be working on biological weapons.[54]

Ultimately there must be tight international restrictions on this kind of weapons technology, including on-site inspections, dismantling known biological weapons facilities, monitoring the flow of certain chemicals and life forms, etc. It will not be easy, but such guarantees are necessary to prevent dangerous life forms from emerging from renegade laboratories.

Banning these weapons of war may be generally accepted once nations realize that biological weapons are unstable, unpredictable, and unreliable in actual warfare.

Ultimately, society must make democratic decisions on whether or not to restrict certain kinds of technology. Unlike nuclear technology, the debate about the risks and benefits of biotechnology is in its early stages, giving society time in which to decide which forms of the technology should be allowed to flourish and which ones should be restricted. In a democracy, what is decisive is informed debate by an enlightened electorate.

1997

Notes

1. Aldous Huxley, *Brave New World,* Harper, New York, 1946, p. xvii.
2. The avowed nuclear powers are the United States, Great Britain, France, Russia, and China, although the nuclear status of the various parts of the former Soviet Union are still being negotiated. The South African government admitted to creating seven atomic bombs, which it has since dismantled. Israel is reputed to have about two hundred atomic bombs. India exploded an atomic bomb in the 1970s. Pakistan is believed to have nuclear weapons. The status of North Korea is not clear.
3. Interview with Rebecca Goldburg.
4. *New York Times,* Aug. 27, 1995, p. 30.
5. Interview with Rebecca Goldburg.
6. Ibid.
7. Ibid.
8. Thomas F. Lee, *Gene Future,* Plenum Press, New York, 1993, p. 301.
9. *Discover,* Jan. 1997, p. 78.
10. Interview with Francis Collins.
11. Lois Wingerson, *Mapping Our Genes,* Penguin Books, New York, 1990, p. 297.
12. *Newsweek,* Dec. 23, 1996, p. 47.
13. Interview with Arthur Caplan.
14. Jeff Lyon and Peter Gorner, *Altered Fates,* W. W. Norton, New York, 1995, p. 484.
15. Interview with Francis Collins.
16. Interview with Arthur Caplan, July 21, 1996.
17. Christopher Wills, *Exons, Introns, and Talking Genes,* Basic Books, New York, 1991, p. 10.
18. *Washington Post,* Nov. 4, 1996, p. A2.
19. Usually, males have XY, and females have XX chromosomes.
20. Wingerson, *Mapping Our Genes,* p. 95.

21. *Washington Post,* Jan. 29, 1995, p. C4.
22. Interview with Arthur Caplan.
23. Enzo Russo and David Cove, *Genetic Engineering,* W. H. Freeman, New York, 1991, p. 170.
24. Thomas F. Lee, *The Human Genome Project,* Plenum Press, New York, 1991, p. 276.
25. Lee, *Gene Future,* p. 160.
26. At the Council for International Organizations of Medical Sciences, meeting in Japan in 1990, the participants took a different position: "Although germ-cell gene therapy is not contemplated at present, continued discussion of germ-cell gene therapy is nonetheless important. The option of germ-cell therapy must not be prematurely foreclosed. It may someday offer clinical benefits attainable in no other way." (Ibid., p. 161.)
27. Interview with Arthur Caplan
28. Ibid.
29. Ibid.
30. Interview with Francis Collins.
31. *Washington Post,* May 11, 1996, p. A1.
32. *New York Times,* June 7, 1996, p. A11.
33. *Science News,* Sept. 7, 1996, p. 154.
34. *Time,* March 10, 1997, p. 72.
35. Lee, *The Human Genome Project,* p. 275.
36. Steve Jones, *The Language of Genes,* Anchor Books, New York, 1993, p. 224.
37. Ibid., p. 224.
38. Ibid., p. 150.
39. Cranor, *Are Genes Us?,* p. 170.
40. The irony in all of this is that the Morlocks have their ultimate revenge. They eat the Eloi.
41. Suzuki, *Genetics,* p. 197.
42. Ibid.
43. Ibid.
44. Ibid.
45. Ibid.
46. Ibid.
47. Ibid.
48. Ibid., pp. 93–94.
49. Ibid.
50. Charles Piller and Keith R. Yamamoto, *Gene Wars,* William Morrow, New York, 1988, p. 99.
51. These secret tests were conducted at the military's Mechanicsburg, Pennsylvania, supply depot. The document says, "Within this system there are employed large numbers of laborers, including many Negroes, whose incapacitation would seriously affect the operation of the supply system. Since Negroes are more susceptible to *Coccidioides* than are whites, this fungus was simulated by using *Asperfillus fumigatus.*" (Ibid.)
52. Interview with Charles Piller; Piller and Yamamoto, *Gene Wars,* p. 100.
53. Interview with Francis Collins.
54. *Scientific American,* Dec. 1996, p. 62.

READING, REREADING, AND ANALYSIS

1. In the first section of the essay, Kaku offers two visions of the future that scientific and technological changes might create, one positive and one negative. As you read, create two columns in which you list the main examples of each vision. In groups, compare the examples in each column and add positive or negative predictions you have heard, imagined, read, or seen depicted on television or in movies. Which column tends to have more extreme fictional examples? What are some of your group's reactions to each column (for example, amusement, anxiety, disbelief)?

2. Choose one issue that Kaku discusses in the essay: bioengineered foods, mandatory DNA or genetic testing, links between genes and behavior, manipulating germ lines, cloning, eugenics, or biological warfare. Summarize the important aspects of the issue. What does an "enlightened electorate" need to know about this issue? What point is Kaku making by discussing this issue?

3. Make a list of possible dangers from genetic engineering that you had never heard of or imagined until you read Kaku's essay. Which possible dangers seem the most threatening and why?

4. According to Kaku's essay, what are some possibilities, good and bad, that might result from "germ-line therapy"?

5. Think about movies you have seen or books you have read that present wonders and potential horrors of science. How was science represented? In society in general, how is science understood in relation to ideas of progress and why?

6. When discussing the possibility of "designer children," Kaku writes the following:

> But is this a good thing? The question is: what should be the role of doctors? Are they servants who are expected to simply carry out the wishes of the consumer? Or do we want them to be ministers and guardians of morality, deciding what forms of treatment are unethical? (p. 274).

What are your responses to the questions Kaku raises and why? What have you learned from reading his essay, and has reading his essay caused you to rethink your position on an issue?

RESPONDING THROUGH WRITING: BUILDING AN INTERPRETATION

7. Near the beginning of his essay, Kaku states his faith in the workings of democracy: "In a democracy, only informed debate by an educated citizenry can make the mature decisions about a

technology so powerful that we can dream of controlling life itself" (p. 265). Write a paper in which you use one or two specific examples from Kaku to test this claim. Who controls the debate on this issue? Who has access to the pertinent information? Can an "informed . . . and educated" citizen have an impact on this issue? What hope does Kaku offer us that democracy has the power to handle these issues?

8. Write your own science fiction account of a future in which one major technological change mentioned by Kaku has come to pass. Use your fictional narrative to show some of the imagined implications of that change on people's lives.

9. Kaku calls upon us to have a national debate on the issues he raises. As a way of starting such a debate, choose one of the potential issues in biotechnology that he identifies. Write an argument in favor of and an argument against some potential use of that technology (approximately one page each). Which is more persuasive and why?

10. In four or five sentences, summarize Kaku's discussion of the use of sonograms to determine the sex of a fetus.

GOING FURTHER: LEARNING FROM OTHER SOURCES

11. Use Lexis/Nexis, Newspaper Source, or a similar database that includes newspaper articles to find out what has happened with the Human Genome Project since Kaku published this chapter. In a group, pool your findings and list the major developments. What has been accomplished to date, and what impact does that news have on the point Kaku is trying to make with this example?

12. Using a popular search engine, such as Google, try the keyword "doomsday" and sample several of the resulting websites. Try another search on Google using the keywords "science and technology and future" and do a comparative sampling. Choose one representative sample website from each search and list the similarities and differences in the way the two websites portray the future. In a group, compare your findings and note the places where the websites from either search seem to overlap with Kaku's vision of technology's role in our future.

APPLYING WHAT YOU'VE LEARNED

13. Kaku's ideas about democratic debate remain rather undefined. Use ideas from Christopher Lasch's "The Lost Art of Argument"

or from Zita Ingham's "Landscape, Drama, and Dissensus: The Rhetorical Education of Red Lodge, Montana" to imagine a possible, effective means for encouraging the kind of debate that Kaku thinks we need. Write a short paper using ideas from Lasch or Ingham to explore the possibility of a democratic debate around one of the issues Kaku discusses. (You may choose to write this paper as an editorial encouraging your readers to enter into such a debate.)

14. Construct an essay in which you examine the debate in two or three sections of Kaku's text in the framework of "sovereignty" and "symbolic package," key terms from Walker Percy's "The Loss of the Creature." Reflect on what Percy's terminology helps you see or better understand in the debate Kaku presents and discuss what you have learned.

15. According to Kaku, "Knowledge is power, and power is inherently a political and social question" (p. 281). In a variety of ways, the essays in *Making Sense* are about perspectives on knowledge. Choose two of them, and use Kaku's statement to help you analyze the political and social dynamics of power in the two essays. Here are some possible choices if you are uncertain about which two essays to write about: Julie Charlip's "A Real Class Act: Searching for Identity in the Classless Society," Sven Birkerts's "The Owl has Flown," Nancy Sommers's "I Stand Here Writing," Julie English Early's "The Spectacle of Science and Self: Mary Kingsley," Barbara Mellix's "From Outside, In," Susan Sontag's "In Plato's Cave,' Jane Tompkins's "At the Buffalo Bill Museum, June 1988," Haunani-Kay Trask's "From a Native Daughter," or Jeanette Winterson's "Imagination and Reality."

THOMAS KUHN

Thomas Kuhn (1922–1996) was a Professor of Philosophy and the History of Science at the Massachusetts Institute of Technology from 1979 to 1991. Kuhn wrote "The Historical Structure of Scientific Discovery" while a graduate student in theoretical physics at Harvard University. Soon after receiving his doctorate in physics, Kuhn left the laboratory to pursue his interest in the structure of change in scientific thought. Kuhn is considered one of the founders of the history of science, and his concept of the paradigm shift is considered one of the most influential ideas in twentieth-century intellectual history.

> To learn more about Thomas Kuhn, and the paradigm, see <http://www.cs.ucr.edu/~khanhvo/paradigm.html>.

WHAT DO YOU KNOW? WHAT DO YOU EXPECT TO DISCOVER?

Before reading the essay, take a moment to consider the following questions.

1. What topics does Kuhn's biography suggest he is interested in? What do you know about those topics? Knowledge can come from personal experience, stories you've heard, other classes you've taken, or other reading you've done.

2. When you see or hear the word "discovery," what comes to mind? Make a list of ten discoveries you feel are most significant to your life.

3. When you think about science, which discoveries come to mind? Which scientists can you link with particular discoveries? How do you think a scientist goes about making a discovery?

⌀

The Historical Structure of
Scientific Discovery

My object in this article is to isolate and illuminate one small part of what I take to be a continuing historiographic revolution in the study of science. The structure of scientific discovery is my particular topic, and I can best approach it by pointing out that the subject itself may well seem extraordinarily odd. Both scientists and, until quite recently, historians have ordinarily viewed discovery as the sort of event which, though it may have preconditions and surely has consequences, is itself without internal structure. Rather than being seen as a complex development extended both in space and time, discovering something has usually seemed to be a unitary event, one which, like seeing something, happens to an individual at a specific time and place.

This view of the nature of discovery has, I suspect, deep roots in the nature of the scientific community. One of the few historical elements recurrent in the textbooks from which the prospective scientist learns his field is the attribution of particular natural phenomena to the historical personages who first discovered them. As a result of this and other aspects of their training, discovery becomes for many scientists an important goal. To make a discovery is to achieve one of the closest approximations to a property right that the scientific career affords. Professional prestige is often closely associated with these acquisitions.[1] Small wonder, then, that acrimonious disputes about priority and independence in discovery have often marred the normally placid tenor of scientific communication. Even less wonder that many historians of science have seen the individual discovery as an appropriate unit with which to measure scientific progress and have devoted much time and skill to determining what man made which discovery at what point in time. If the study of discovery has a surprise to offer, it is only that, despite the immense energy and ingenuity expended upon it, neither polemic nor painstaking scholarship has often succeeded in pinpointing the time and place at which a given discovery could properly be said to have "been made."

That failure, both of argument and of research, suggests the thesis that I now wish to develop. Many scientific discoveries, particularly the most interesting and important, are not the sort of event about which the questions "Where?" and, more particularly, "When?" can appropriately be asked. Even if all conceivable data were at hand, those questions would not regularly possess answers. That we are persistently driven to ask them nonetheless is symptomatic of a fundamental inappropriateness in our image of discovery. That inappropriateness is here my main concern, but I approach it by considering first the historical problem presented by the attempt to date and to place a major class of fundamental discoveries.

The troublesome class consists of those discoveries—including oxygen, the electric current, X rays, and the electron—which could not be predicted from accepted theory in advance and which therefore caught the assembled profession by surprise. That kind of discovery will shortly be my exclusive concern, but it will help first to note that there is another sort and one which presents very few of the same problems. Into this second class of discoveries fall the neutrino, radio waves, and the elements which filled empty places in the periodic table. The existence of all these objects had been predicted from theory before they were discovered, and the men who made the discoveries therefore knew from the start what to look for. That foreknowledge did not make their task less demanding or less interesting, but it did provide criteria which told them when their goal had been reached.[2] As a result, there have been few priority debates over discoveries of this second sort, and only a paucity of data can prevent the historian from ascribing them to a particular time and place. Those facts help to isolate the difficulties we encounter as we return to the troublesome discoveries of the first class. In the cases that most concern us here there are no benchmarks to inform either the scientist or the historian when the job of discovery has been done.

As an illustration of this fundamental problem and its consequences, consider first the discovery of oxygen. Because it has repeatedly been studied, often with exemplary care and skill, that discovery is unlikely to offer any purely factual surprises. Therefore it is particularly well suited to clarify points of principle.[3] At least three scientists—Carl Scheele, Joseph Priestley, and Antoine Lavoisier—have a legitimate claim to this discovery, and polemicists have occasionally entered the same claim for Pierre Bayen.[4] Scheele's work, though it was almost certainly completed before the relevant researches of Priestley and Lavoisier, was not made public until their work was well known.[5] Therefore it had no apparent causal role, and I shall simplify my story by omitting it.[6] Instead, I pick up the main route to the discovery of oxygen with the work of Bayen, who, sometime before March 1774, discovered that red precipitate of mercury (HgO) could, by heating, be made to yield a gas. That aeriform product Bayen identified as fixed air (CO_2), a substance made familiar to most pneumatic chemists by the earlier work of Joseph Black.[7] A variety of other substances were known to yield the same gas.

At the beginning of August 1774, a few months after Bayen's work had appeared, Joseph Priestley, repeated the experiment, though probably independently. Priestley, however, observed that the gaseous product would support combustion and therefore changed the identification. For him the gas obtained on heating red precipitate was nitrous air (N_2O), a substance that he had himself discovered more than two years before.[8] Later in the same month Priestley made a trip to Paris and there informed Lavoisier of the new reaction. The latter repeated the experiment once more, both in November 1775 and in February 1774. But, because he used tests somewhat more elaborate than Priestley's, Lavoisier again changed the identification. For him, as of May 1775, the gas released by red precipitate was neither fixed air nor nitrous air. Instead, it was "[atmospheric] air itself entire without alteration . . . even to the point that . . . it comes out more pure."[9] Meanwhile, however, Priestley had also been at work, and, before the beginning of March 1775, he, too, had concluded that the gas must be "common air." Until this point all of the men who had produced a gas from red precipitate of mercury had identified it with some previously known species.[10]

The remainder of this story of discovery is briefly told. During March 1775 Priestley discovered that his gas was in several respects very much "better" than common air, and he therefore reidentified the gas once more, this time calling it "dephlogisticated air," that is, atmospheric air deprived of its normal complement of phlogiston.° This conclusion Priestley published in the *Philosophical Transactions,* and it was apparently that publication which led Lavoisier to reexamine his own results.[11] The reexamination began during February 1776 and within a year had led Lavoisier to the conclusion that the gas was actually a separable component of the atmospheric air which both he and Priestley had previously thought of as homogeneous. With this point reached, with the gas recognized as an irreducibly distinct species, we may conclude that the discovery of oxygen had been completed.

But to return to my initial question, when shall we say that oxygen was discovered and what criteria shall we use in answering that question? If discovering oxygen is simply holding an impure sample in one's hands, then the gas had been "discovered" in antiquity by the first man who ever bottled atmospheric air. Undoubtedly, for an experimental criterion, we must at least require a relatively pure sample like that obtained by Priestley in August 1774. But during 1774 Priestley was unaware that he had discovered anything except a new way to produce a relatively familiar species. Throughout that year his "discovery" is scarcely distinguishable from the one made earlier by

---

° **Phlogiston** Was once believed to be the element that caused combustion and that was given off by anything burning.

Bayen, and neither case is quite distinct from that of the Reverend Stephen Hales, who had obtained the same gas more than forty years before.[12] Apparently to discover something one must also be aware of the discovery and know as well what it is that one has discovered.

But, that being the case, how much must one know? Had Priestley come close enough when he identified the gas as nitrous air? If not, was either he or Lavoisier significantly closer when he changed the identification to common air? And what are we to say about Priestley's next identification, the one made in March 1775? Dephlogisticated air is still not oxygen or even, for the phlogistic chemist, a quite unexpected sort of gas. Rather it is a particularly pure atmospheric air. Presumably, then, we wait for Lavoisier's work in 1776 and 1777, work which led him not merely to isolate the gas but to see what it was. Yet even that decision can be questioned, for in 1777 and to the end of his life Lavoisier insisted that oxygen was an atomic "principle of acidity" and that oxygen *gas* was formed only when that "principle" united with caloric, the matter of heat.[13] Shall we therefore say that oxygen had not yet been discovered in 1777? Some may be tempted to do so. But the principle of acidity was not banished from chemistry until after 1810 and caloric lingered on until the 1860s. Oxygen had, however, become a standard chemical substance long before either of those dates. Furthermore, what is perhaps the key point, it would probably have gained that status on the basis of Priestley's work alone without benefit of Lavoisier's still partial reinterpretation.

I conclude that we need a new vocabulary and new concepts for analyzing events like the discovery of oxygen. Though undoubtedly correct, the sentence "Oxygen was discovered" misleads by suggesting that discovering something is a single simple act unequivocally attributable, if only we knew enough, to an individual and an instant in time. When the discovery is unexpected, however, the latter attribution is always impossible and the former often is as well. Ignoring Scheele, we can, for example, safely say that oxygen had not been discovered before 1774; probably we would also insist that it had been discovered by 1777 or shortly thereafter. But within those limits any attempt to date the discovery or to attribute it to an individual must inevitably be arbitrary. Furthermore, it must be arbitrary just because discovering a new sort of phenomenon is necessarily a complex process which involves recognizing both *that* something is and *what* it is. Observation and conceptualization, fact and the assimilation of fact to theory, are inseparably linked in the discovery of scientific novelty. Inevitably, that process extends over time and may often involve a number of people. Only for discoveries in my second category—those whose nature is known in advance—can discovering *that* and discovering *what* occur together and in an instant.

Two last, simpler, and far briefer examples will simultaneously show how typical the case of oxygen is and also prepare the way for a somewhat more precise conclusion. On the night of 13 March 1781, the astronomer William Herschel made the following entry in his journal: "In the quartile near Zeta Tauri . . . is a curious either nebulous star or perhaps a comet."[14] That entry is generally said to record the discovery of the planet Uranus, but it cannot quite have done that. Between 1690 and Herschel's observation in 1781 the same object had been seen and recorded at least seventeen times by men who took it to be a star. Herschel differed from them only in supposing that, because in his telescope it appeared especially large, it might actually be a *comet*! Two additional observations on 17 and 19 March confirmed that suspicion by showing that the object he had observed moved among the stars. As a result, astronomers throughout Europe were informed of the discovery, and the mathematicians among them began to compute the new comet's orbit. Only several months later, after all those attempts had repeatedly failed to square with observation, did the astronomer Lexell suggest that the object observed by Herschel might be a planet. And only when additional computations, using a planet's rather than a comet's orbit, proved reconcilable with observation was that suggestion generally accepted. At what point during 1781 do we want to say that the planet Uranus was discovered? And are we entirely and unequivocally clear that it was Herschel rather than Lexell who discovered it?

Or consider still more briefly the story of the discovery of X rays, a story which opens on the day in 1895 when the physicist Roentgen interrupted a well-precedented investigation of cathode rays because he noticed that a barium platinocyanide screen far from his shielded apparatus glowed when the discharge was in process.[15] Additional investigations—they required seven hectic weeks during which Roentgen rarely left the laboratory—indicated that the cause of the glow traveled in straight lines from the cathode ray tube, that the radiation cast shadows, that it could not be deflected by a magnet, and much else besides. Before announcing his discovery Roentgen had convinced himself that his effect was not due to cathode rays themselves but to a new form of radiation with at least some similarity to light. Once again the question suggests itself: When shall we say that X rays were actually discovered? Not, in any case, at the first instant, when all that had been noted was a glowing screen. At least one other investigator had seen that glow and, to his subsequent chagrin, discovered nothing at all. Nor, it is almost as clear, can the moment of discovery be pushed back to a point during the last week of investigation. By that time Roentgen was exploring the properties of the new radiation he had *already* discovered. We may have to settle for the remark that X rays emerged in Würzburg between 8 November and 28 December 1895.

The characteristics shared by these examples are, I think, common to all the episodes by which unanticipated novelties become subjects for scientific attention. I therefore conclude these brief remarks by discussing three such common characteristics, one which may help to provide a framework for the further study of the extended episodes we customarily call "discoveries."

In the first place, notice that all three of our discoveries—oxygen, Uranus, and X rays—began with the experimental or observational isolation of an anomaly, that is, with nature's failure to conform entirely to expectation. Notice, further, that the process by which that anomaly was educed displays simultaneously the apparently incompatible characteristics of the inevitable and the accidental. In the case of X rays, the anomalous glow which provided Roentgen's first clue was clearly the result of an accidental disposition of his apparatus. But by 1895 cathode rays were a normal subject for research all over Europe; that research quite regularly juxtaposed cathode-rays tubes with sensitive screens and films; as a result, Roentgen's accident was almost certain to occur elsewhere, as in fact it had. Those remarks, however, should make Roentgen's case look very much like those of Herschel and Priestley. Herschel first observed his oversized and thus anomalous star in the course of a prolonged survey of the northern heavens. That survey was, except for the magnification provided by Herschel's instruments, precisely of the sort that had repeatedly been carried through before and that had occasionally resulted in prior observations of Uranus. And Priestley, too—when he isolated the gas that behaved almost but not quite like nitrous air and then almost but not quite like common air—was seeing something unintended and wrong in the outcome of a sort of experiment for which there was much European precedent and which had more than once before led to the production of the new gas.

These features suggest the existence of two normal requisites for the beginning of an episode of discovery. The first, which throughout this paper I have largely taken for granted, is the individual skill, wit, or genius to recognize that something has gone wrong in ways that may prove consequential. Not any and every scientist would have noted that no unrecorded star should be so large, that the screen ought not to have glowed, that nitrous air should not have supported life. But that requisite presupposes another which is less frequently taken for granted. Whatever the level of genius available to observe them, anomalies do not emerge from the normal course of scientific research until both instruments and concepts have developed sufficiently to make their emergence likely and to make the anomaly which results recognizable as a violation of expectation.[16] To say that an unexpected discovery begins only when something goes wrong is to say that it begins only when scientists know well both how their instruments and how nature should behave. What distinguished Priestley, who saw an anomaly, from Hales, who did not, is largely the considerable articulation of pneumatic techniques and expectations that had come into being during the four decades which separate their two isolations of oxygen.[17] The very number of claimants indicates that after 1770 the discovery could not have been postponed for long.

The role of anomaly is the first of the characteristics shared by our three examples. A second can be considered more briefly, for it has provided the main theme for the body of my text. Though awareness of anomaly marks the beginning of a discovery, it marks only the beginning. What necessarily follows, if anything at all is to be discovered, is a more or less extended period during which the individual and often many members of his group struggle to make the anomaly lawlike. Invariably that period demands additional observation or experimentation as well as repeated cogitation. While it continues, scientists repeatedly revise their expectations, usually their instrumental standards, and sometimes their most fundamental theories as well. In this sense discoveries have a proper internal history as well as prehistory and a posthistory. Furthermore, within the rather vaguely delimited interval of internal history, there is no single moment or day which the historian, however complete his data, can identify as the point at which the discovery was made. Often, when several individuals are involved, it is even impossible unequivocally to identify any one of them as the discoverer.

Finally, turning to the third of these selected common characteristics, note briefly what happens as the period of discovery draws to a close. A full discussion of that question would require additional evidence and a separate paper, for I have had little to say about the aftermath of discovery in the body of my text. Nevertheless, the topic must not be entirely neglected, for it is in part a corollary of what has already been said.

Discoveries are often described as mere additions or increments to the growing stockpile of scientific knowledge, and that description has helped make the unit discovery seem a significant measure of progress. I suggest, however, that it is fully appropriate only to those discoveries which, like the elements that filled missing places in the periodic table, were anticipated and sought in advance and which therefore demanded no adjustment, adaptation, and assimilation from the profession. Though the sorts of discoveries we have here been examining are undoubtedly additions to scientific knowledge, they are also something more. In a sense that I can now develop only in part, they also react back upon what has previously been known, providing a new view of some previously familiar objects and simultaneously changing the way in which even some traditional parts of science are practiced. Those in whose area of special competence the new phenomenon falls often see both the world and their work differently as they emerge from the extended struggle with anomaly which constitutes the discovery of that phenomenon.

William Herschel, for example, when he increased by one the time-honored number of planetary bodies, taught astronomers to see new things when they looked at the familiar heavens even with instruments more traditional than his own. That change in the vision of astronomers must be a principal reason why, in the half century after the discovery of Uranus, twenty additional circumsolar bodies were added to the traditional seven.[18] A similar transformation is even clearer in the aftermath of Roentgen's work. In the first place, established techniques for cathode-ray research had to be changed, for scientists found they had failed to control a relevant variable. Those changes included both the redesign of old apparatus and revised ways of asking old questions. In addition, those scientists most concerned experienced the same transformation of vision that we have just noted in the aftermath of the discovery of Uranus. X rays were the first new sort of radiation discovered since infrared and ultraviolet at the beginning of the century. But within less than a decade after Roentgen's work, four more were disclosed by the new scientific sensitivity (for example, to fogged photographic plates) and by some of the new instrumental techniques that had resulted from Roentgen's work and its assimilation.[19]

Very often these transformations in the established techniques of scientific practice prove even more important than the incremental knowledge provided by the discovery itself. That could at least be argued in the cases of Uranus and of X rays; in the case of my third example, oxygen, it is categorically clear. Like the work of Herschel and Roentgen, that of Priestley and Lavoisier taught scientists to view old situations in new ways. Therefore, as we might anticipate, oxygen was not the only new chemical species to be identified in the aftermath of their work. But, in the case of oxygen, the readjustments demanded by assimilation were so profound that they played an integral and essential role—though they were not by themselves the cause—in the gigantic upheaval of chemical theory and practice which has since been known as the chemical revolution. I do not suggest that every unanticipated discovery has consequences for science so deep and so far-reaching as those which followed the discovery of oxygen. But I do suggest that every such discovery demands, from those most concerned, the sorts of readjustment that, when they are more obvious, we equate with scientific revolution. It is, I believe, just because they demand readjustments like these that the process of discovery is necessarily and inevitably one that shows structure and that therefore extends in time.

1962

Notes

1. For a brilliant discussion of these points, see R. K. Merton, "Priorities in Scientific Discovery: A Chapter in the Sociology of Science," *American Sociological Review* 22 (1957): 635. Also very relevant, though it did not appear until this article had been prepared, is F. Reif, "The Competitive World of the Pure Scientist," *Science* 134 (1961): 1957.

2. Not all discoveries fall so neatly as the preceding into one or the other of my two classes. For example, Anderson's work on the positron was done in complete ignorance of Dirac's theory from which the new particle's existence had already been very nearly predicted. On the other hand, the immediately succeeding work by Blackett and Occhialini made full use of Dirac's theory and therefore exploited experiment more fully and constructed a more forceful case for the positron's existence than Anderson had been able to do. On this subject see N. R. Hanson, "Discovering the Positron," *British Journal for the Philosophy of Science* 12 (1961): 194; 12 (1962): 299. Hanson suggests several of the points developed here. I am much indebted to Professor Hanson for a preprint of this material.

3. I have adapted a less familiar example from the same viewpoint in "The Caloric Theory of Adiabatic Compression," *Isis* 49 (1958): 132. A closely similar analysis of the emergence of a new theory is included in the early pages of my essay "Energy Conservation as an Example of Simultaneous Discovery," in *Critical Problems in the History of Science*, ed. M. Clagett (Madison: University of Wisconsin Press, 1959), pp. 321–56. . . . Reference to these papers may add depth and detail to the following discussion.

4. The still classic discussion of the discovery of oxygen is A. N. Meldrum, *The Eighteenth Century Revolution in Science: The First Phase* (Calcutta, 1930), chap. 5. A more convenient and generally quite reliable discussion is included in J. B. Conant, *The Overthrow of the Phlogiston Theory: The Chemical Revolution of 1775–1789,* Harvard Case Histories in Experimental Science, case 2 (Cambridge: Harvard University Press, 1950). A recent and indispensable review which includes an account of the development of the priority controversy, is M. Daumas, *Lavoisier, théoricien et expérimentateur* (Paris, 1955), chaps. 2 and 3. H. Guerlac has added much significant detail to our knowledge of the early relations between Priestley and Lavoisier in his "Joseph Priestley's First Papers on Gases and Their Reception in France," *Journal of the History of Medicine* 12 (1957): 1 and in his very recent monograph, *Lavoisier: The Crucial Year* (Ithaca: Cornell University Press, 1961). For Scheele see J. R. Partington, A *Short History of Chemistry,* 2d ed. (London, 1951), pp. 104–109.

5. For the dating of Scheele's work, see A. E. Nordenskjöld, *Carl Wilhelm Scheele, Nachgelassene Briefe und Aufzeichnungen* (Stockholm, 1892).

6. U. Bocklund ("A Lost Letter from Scheele to Lavoisier," *Lychnos,* 1957–58, pp. 39–62) argues that Scheele communicated his discovery of oxygen to Lavoisier in a letter of 30 Sept. 1774. Certainly the letter is important, and it clearly demonstrates that Scheele was ahead of both Priestley and Lavoisier at the time it was written. But I think the letter is not quite so candid as Bocklund supposes, and I fail to see how Lavoisier could have drawn the discovery of oxygen from it. Scheele describes a procedure for reconstituting common air, not for producing a new gas, and

that, as we shall see, is almost the same information that Lavoisier received
from Priestley at about the same time. In any case, there is no evidence that
Lavoisier performed the sort of experiment that Scheele suggested.

7. P. Bayen, "Essai d'expériences chymiques, faites sur quelques précipités
de mercure, dans la vue de découvrir leur nature, Seconde partie," *Observations sur la physique* 3 (1774): 280–295, particularly pp. 289–291.

8. J. B. Conant, *The Overthrow of the Phlogiston Theory,* pp. 34–40.

9. Ibid., p. 23. A useful translation of the full text is available in Conant.

10. For simplicity I use the term *red precipitate* throughout. Actually, Bayen
used the precipitate; Priestley used both the precipitate and the oxide
produced by direct calcination of mercury; and Lavoisier used only the
latter. The difference is not without importance, for it was not unequivocally clear to chemists that the two substances were identical.

11. There has been some doubt about Priestley's having influenced Lavoisier's
thinking at this point, but, when the latter returned to experimenting
with the gas in February 1776, he recorded in his notebooks that he had
obtained "l'air dephlogistique de M. Priestley" (M. Daumas, *Lavoisier,*
p. 36).

12. J. R. Partington, *A Short History of Chemistry,* p. 91.

13. For the traditional elements in Lavoisier's interpretations of chemical
reactions, see H. Metzger, *La philosophie de la matière chez Lavoisier*
(Paris, 1935), and Daumas, *Lavoisier,* chap. 7.

14. P. Doig, *A Concise History of Astronomy* (London: Chapman, 1950),
pp. 115–116.

15. L. W. Taylor, *Physics, the Pioneer Science* (Boston: Houghton Mifflin
Co., 1941), p. 790.

16. Though the point cannot be argued here, the conditions which make the
emergence of anomaly likely and those which make anomaly recognizable
are to a very great extent the same. That fact may help us understand the
extraordinarily large amount of simultaneous discovery in the sciences.

17. A useful sketch of the development of pneumatic chemistry is included in
Partington, *A Short History of Chemistry,* chap. 6.

18. R. Wolf, *Geschichte der Astronomie* (Munich, 1877), pp. 513–515,
683–693. The prephotographic discoveries of the asteroids is often seen as
an effect of the invention of Bode's law. But that law cannot be the full explanation and may not even have played a large part. Piazzi's discovery of
Ceres, in 1801, was made in ignorance of the current speculation about a
missing planet in the "hole" between Mars and Jupiter. Instead, like Herschel, Piazzi was engaged on a star survey. More important, Bode's law
was old by 1800 (ibid., p. 683), but only one man before that date seems
to have thought it worthwhile to look for another planet. Finally, Bode's
law, by itself, could only suggest the utility of looking for additional planets; it did not tell astronomers where to look. Clearly, however, the drive
to look for additional planets dates from Herschel's work on Uranus.

19. For α-, β-, and γ-radiation, discovery of which dates from 1896, see
Taylor, *Physics,* pp. 800–804. For the fourth new form of radiation, N
rays, see D. J. S. Price, *Science Since Babylon,* (New Haven: Yale University Press, 1961), pp. 84–89. That N rays were ultimately the source of a
scientific scandal does not make them less revealing of the scientific community's state of mind.

READING, REREADING, AND ANALYSIS

1. As a group, discuss what Kuhn means by "anomaly" and its relationship to the three-stage discovery process Kuhn describes: prehistory, internal history, and posthistory.

2. What does Kuhn mean when he says that scientists "struggle to make the anomaly lawlike" (p. 295)? Find an example in Kuhn that helps you to explain the quotation, and write a paragraph summarizing your findings.

3. In a group, track the organization of Kuhn's essay by looking at the first sentence of each of his paragraphs. List the main organizational moves he makes. What kinds of transitional words and phrases, such as "As an illustration of this" or "I conclude that," does he use to help you follow his train of thought?

4. Choose one of the examples of discovery that Kuhn uses—X ray, the planet Uranus, or oxygen—and take some notes on how that example connects to Kuhn's larger argument or thesis about discovery and scientific progress.

5. In a group, compare your notes from question 4 and decide which examples are most helpful in explaining Kuhn's main thesis and why. As a group, choose a quotation that helps identify Kuhn's main thesis; present the quotation and the group's findings to the class.

6. Look at how many footnotes Kuhn uses and study a few of them. What purposes do the footnotes serve in Kuhn's essay? Why might they be helpful for many readers?

RESPONDING THROUGH WRITING: BUILDING AN INTERPRETATION

7. Write a short paper using one or more examples from Kuhn to explore his ideas about scientific discovery. Why does Kuhn believe that it is so hard to pinpoint the moment of scientific discovery? What do the examples you have chosen show about the difficulties of attributing a who or a when to a given situation?

8. Reread Kuhn's first paragraph and then write a short paper (two or three pages) in which you discuss the significance of the first paragraph. What is its purpose? What does it help Kuhn accomplish? What is its relation to the body of the text that follows?

9. Write a four- or five-page paper in which you test Kuhn's key ideas about discovery on an event such as Columbus's so-called

discovery of the New World or on Copernicus's discovery and its aftermath.

10. Near the end of his essay, Kuhn writes, "Though the sorts of discoveries we have here been examining are undoubtedly additions to scientific knowledge, they are also something more. . . . They also react back upon what has previously been known, providing a new view of some previously familiar objects and simultaneously changing the way in which even some traditional parts of science are practiced" (p. 295). In a short paper, reflect on what it may mean to "provid[e] a new view of some previously familiar objects." If possible, think of an example or two that Kuhn does not discuss, and use the example or examples to help you describe how and why one might get a new view of the familiar. How does such a process help us learn?

GOING FURTHER: LEARNING FROM OTHER SOURCES

11. Find information about the discovery of the planet Uranus (including pictures) on the Internet or in an encyclopedia. How does your research compare with Kuhn's explanation of its discovery? Next, find information about Neptune. What does your research reveal about Neptune's discovery? How is the process like or unlike the process that Kuhn describes?

12. Using a reference database that includes a range of scholarly sources, such as Academic Search Elite, try combining the search term "paradigm" with a general scientific topic, such as oxygen: "paradigm and oxygen." Then try a search in the same database using "paradigm" with a general nonscientific topic, such as education, crime, or justice: "paradigm and education," for example. Take notes from several of the articles you find showing how the term "paradigm" is used in these differing contexts.

APPLYING WHAT YOU'VE LEARNED

13. Write a paper using Kuhn's ideas about scientific discovery to analyze one or more examples from Michio Kaku's "Second Thoughts: The Genetics of a Brave New World?" In what ways do the "discoveries" Kaku describes present "who" and "when" problems similar to those discussed by Kuhn? To what extent can they be described as "anomalies"? Do Kaku's examples offer an understanding of scientific discovery that is different from Kuhn's?

14. Write a paper using Kuhn's essay and Scott DeVeaux's "Progress and the Bean" to discuss the idea of progress. In what ways does DeVeaux's argument seem to benefit from Kuhn's ideas about progress and discovery? To what extent do these ideas about progress from Kuhn's scientific world seem useful in DeVeaux's field of music? To what extent are they applicable to other fields as well?

15. In the essay "Imagination and Reality," Jeanette Winterson describes the way artists use imagination to "see outside of a dead vision" (p. 604). Write an essay comparing that process with the process of scientific discovery described by Kuhn. What are some of the overlaps and differences in the roles of the artist and the scientist?

CHRISTOPHER LASCH

Christopher Lasch (1932–1994) was professor of history at the University of Rochester. He was also a cultural critic well known for his biting social and political commentary. In particular, he protested against consumer capitalism's effects on American culture and against the growing power of bureaucratic elites. "The Lost Art of Argument" is taken from *The Revolt of the Elites and the Betrayal of Democracy* (1995), a book completed just prior to his death.

> To learn more about Lasch and others who share his political ideas, see the home page of The Preservation Institute, an organization "dedicated to developing a new politics that recognizes the limits of technology," at <http://www.preservenet.com/>.

WHAT DO YOU KNOW? WHAT DO YOU EXPECT TO DISCOVER?

Before reading the essay, take a moment to consider the following questions.

1. How do you decide what you think about the ideas and issues in the world around you? Do you read, watch, or listen to news sources? How do you decide which sources to trust and which will influence your opinion?

2. How many definitions can you come up with for the word "argument"? Who *has* arguments? Who *makes* arguments? What is the difference between the two?

3. What role do experts play in a democracy? Should people who have more experience or more knowledge about a subject have more power to make decisions about the public policies that affect this subject? Or does everyone deserve an equal chance to voice her or his opinions?

⅋

The Lost Art of Argument

For many years now we have been regaled with the promise of the information age. The social effects of the communications revolution, we are told, will include an insatiable demand for trained personnel, an upgrading of the skills required for employment, and an enlightened public capable of following the issues of the day and of making informed judgments about civic affairs. Instead we find college graduates working at jobs for which they are vastly overqualified. The demand for menial labor outstrips the demand for skilled specialists. The postindustrial economy, it appears, promotes an interchangeability of personnel, a rapid movement from one type of work to another, and a growing concentration of the labor force in technically backward, labor-intensive, nonunion sectors of the economy. Recent experience does not bear out the expectation that technological innovations, improvements in communications in particular, will create an abundance of skilled jobs, eliminate disagreeable jobs, and make life easy for everyone. Their most important effect, on the contrary, is to widen the gap between the knowledge class and the rest of the population, between those who find themselves at home in the new global economy and who "relish the thought that the information flows to them can become bigger" all the time (in the words of Arno Penzias of AT&T Bell Laboratories) and those who, having little use for cellular phones, fax machines, or on-line information services, still live in what Penzias contemptuously refers to as the Age of Paper Work.

As for the claim that the information revolution would raise the level of public intelligence, it is no secret that the public knows less about public affairs than it used to know. Millions of Americans cannot begin to tell you what is in the Bill of Rights, what Congress does, what the Constitution says about the powers of the presidency, how the party system emerged or how it operates. A sizable majority, according to a recent survey, believe that Israel is an Arab nation. Instead of blaming the schools for this disheartening ignorance of public affairs, as is the custom, we should look elsewhere for a fuller explanation, bearing in mind that people readily acquire such knowledge as they can put to good use. Since the public no longer participates in debates on national issues, it has no reason to inform itself about civic affairs. It is the decay of public debate, not the school system (bad as it is), that makes the public ill informed, notwithstanding the wonders of the age of information. When debate becomes a lost art, information, even though it may be readily available, makes no impression.

What democracy requires is vigorous public debate, not information. Of course, it needs information too, but the kind of information it needs can be generated only by debate. We do not know what we need to know until we ask the right questions, and we can identify the right questions only by subjecting our own ideas about the world to the test of public controversy. Information, usually seen as the precondition of debate, is better understood as its by-product. When we get into arguments that focus and fully engage our attention, we become avid seekers of relevant information. Otherwise we take in information passively—if we take it in at all.

Political debate began to decline around the turn of the century, curiously enough at a time when the press was becoming more "responsible," more professional, more conscious of its civic obligations. In the early nineteenth century the press was fiercely partisan. Until the middle of the century papers were often financed by political parties. Even when they became more independent of parties, they did not embrace the ideal of objectivity or neutrality. In 1841 Horace Greeley launched his *New York Tribune* with the announcement that it would be a "journal removed alike from servile partisanship on the one hand and from gagged, mincing neutrality on the other." Strong-minded editors like Greeley, James Gordon Bennett, E. L. Godkin, and Samuel Bowles objected to the way in which the demands of party loyalty infringed upon editorial independence, making the editor merely a mouthpiece for a party or faction, but they did not attempt to conceal their own views or to impose a strict separation of news and editorial content. Their papers were journals of opinion in which the reader expected to find a definite point of view, together with unrelenting criticism of opposing points of view.

It is no accident that journalism of this kind flourished during the period from 1830 to 1900, when popular participation in politics was at its height. Of the eligible voters, 80 percent typically went to the polls in presidential elections. After 1900 the percentage declined sharply (to 65 percent in 1904 and 59 percent in 1912), and it has continued to decline more or less steadily throughout the twentieth century. Torchlight parades, mass rallies, and gladiatorial contents of oratory made nineteenth-century politics an object of consuming popular interest, in which journalism served as an extension of the town meeting. The nineteenth-century press created a public forum in which issues were hotly debated. Newspapers not only reported political controversies but participated in them, drawing in their readers as well. Print culture rested on the remnants of an oral tradition. Print was not yet the exclusive medium of communication, nor had it severed its connection with spoken language. The printed language was still shaped by the rhythms and requirements of the spoken word, in particular by the conventions of verbal argumentation. Print served to create a larger forum for the spoken word, not yet to displace or reshape it.

The Lincoln-Douglas debates exemplified the oral tradition at its best. By current standards, Lincoln and Douglas broke every rule of political discourse. They subjected their audiences (which were as large as fifteen thousand on one occasion) to a painstaking analysis of complex issues. They spoke with considerably more candor, in a pungent, colloquial, sometimes racy style, than politicians think prudent today. They took clear positions from which it was difficult to retreat. They conducted themselves as if political leadership carried with it an obligation to clarify issues instead of merely getting elected.

The contrast between these justly famous debates and present-day presidential debates, in which the media define the issues and draw up the ground rules, is unmistakable and highly unflattering to ourselves. Journalistic interrogation of political candidates—which is what debate has come to—tends to magnify the importance of journalists and to diminish that of the candidates. Journalists ask questions—prosaic, predictable questions for the most part—and press the candidates for prompt, specific answers, reserving the right to interrupt and to cut the candidates short whenever they appear to stray from the prescribed topic. To prepare for this ordeal, candidates rely on their advisers to stuff them full of facts and figures, quotable slogans, and anything else that will convey the impression of wide-ranging, unflappable competence. Faced not only with a battery of journalists ready to pounce on the slightest misstep but with the cold, relentless scrutiny of the camera, politicians know that everything depends on the management of visual impressions. They must radiate confidence and decisiveness and never appear to be at a loss for words. The nature of the occasion requires them to exaggerate the reach and effectiveness of public policy, to give the impression that the right programs and the right leadership can meet every challenge.

The format requires all candidates to look the same: confident, untroubled, and therefore unreal. But, it also imposes on them the obligation to explain what makes them different from the others. Once the question has to be asked, it answers itself. Indeed, the question is inherently belittling and degrading, a good example of TV's effect of lowering the object of estimation, of looking through every disguise, deflating every pretension. Bluntly stated with the necessary undertone of all-pervasive skepticism that is inescapably part of the language of TV, the question turns out to be highly rhetorical. What makes *you* so special? Nothing.

This is the quintessential question raised by TV, because it is in the medium's nature to teach us, with relentless insistence, that no one is special, contrary claims notwithstanding. At this point in our history the best qualification for high office may well be a refusal to cooperate with the media's program of self-aggrandizement. A candidate with the courage to abstain from "debates" organized by the media would automatically distinguish himself from the others and command a good deal of public respect. Candidates should insist on directly debating each other instead of responding to questions put to them by commentators and pundits. Their passivity and subservience lower them in the eyes of the voters. They need to recover their self-respect by challenging the media's status as arbiters of public discussion. A refusal to play by the media's rules would make people aware of the vast, illegitimate influence the mass media have come to exercise in American politics. It would also provide the one index of character that voters could recognize and applaud.

What happened to the tradition exemplified by the Lincoln-Douglas debates? The scandals of the Gilded Age gave party politics a bad name. They confirm the misgivings entertained by the "best men" ever since the rise of Jacksonian democracy. By the 1870s and 1880s a bad opinion of politics had come to be widely shared by the educated classes. Genteel reformers—"mugwumps" to their enemies—demanded a professionalization of politics, designed to free the civil service from party control and to replace political appointees with trained experts. Even those who rejected the invitation to declare their independence from the party system, like Theodore Roosevelt (whose refusal to desert the Republican party infuriated the "independents"), shared the enthusiasm for civil service reform. The "best men" ought to challenge the spoilsmen on their own turf, according to Roosevelt, instead of retreating to the sidelines of political life.

The drive to clean up politics gained momentum in the progressive era. Under the leadership of Roosevelt, Woodrow Wilson, Robert La Follette, and William Jennings Bryan, the progressives preached "efficiency," "good government," "bipartisanship," and the "scientific management" of public affairs and declared war on "bossism." They attacked the seniority system in Congress, limited the powers of the Speaker of the House, replaced mayors with city managers, and delegated important governmental functions to appointive commissions staffed with trained administrators. Recognizing that political machines were welfare agencies of a rudimentary type, which dispensed jobs and other benefits to their constituents and thereby won their loyalty, the progressives set out to create a welfare state as a way of competing with the machines. They launched comprehensive investigations of crime, vice, poverty, and other "social problems." They took the position that government was a science, not an art. They forged links between government and the university so as to assure a steady supply of experts and expert knowledge. But they had little use for public debate. Most political questions were too complex, in their view, to be submitted to popular judgment. They liked to contrast the scientific expert with the orator, the latter a useless windbag whose rantings only confused the public mind.

Professionalism in politics meant professionalism in journalism. The connection between them was spelled out by Walter Lippmann in a notable series of books: *Liberty and the News* (1920), *Public Opinion* (1922), and *The Phantom Public* (1925). These provided a founding charter for modern journalism, the most elaborate rationale for a journalism guided by the new ideal of professional objectivity. Lippmann held up standards by which the press is still judged—usually with the result that it is found wanting.

What concerns us here, however, is not whether the press has lived up to Lippmann's standards but how he arrived at those standards in the first place. In 1920 Lippmann and Charles Merz published a long essay in the *New Republic* examining press coverage of the Russian Revolution. This study, now forgotten, showed that American papers gave their readers an account of the Revolution distorted by anti-Bolshevik prejudices, wishful thinking, and sheer ignorance. *Liberty and the News* was also prompted by the collapse of journalistic objectivity during the war, when the newspapers had appointed themselves "defenders of the faith." The result, according to Lippmann, was a "breakdown of the means of public knowledge." The difficulty went beyond war or revolution, the "supreme destroyers of realistic thinking." The traffic in sex, violence, and "human interest"—staples of modern mass journalism—raised grave questions about the future of democracy. "All that the sharpest critics of democracy have alleged is true if there is no steady supply of trustworthy and relevant news."

In *Public Opinion* and *The Phantom Public*, Lippmann answered the critics, in effect, by redefining democracy. Democracy did not require that the people literally govern themselves. The public's stake in government was strictly procedural. The public interest did not extend to the substance of decision making: "The public is interested in law, not in the laws; in the method of law, not in the substance." Questions of substance should be decided by knowledgeable administrators whose access to reliable information immunized them against the emotional "symbols" and "stereotypes" that dominated public debate. The public was incompetent to govern itself and did not even care to do so, in Lippmann's view. But as long as rules of fair play were enforced, the public would be content to leave government to experts—provided, of course, that the experts delivered the goods, the ever-increasing abundance of comforts and conveniences so closely identified with the American way of life.

Lippmann acknowledged the conflict between his recommendations and the received theory of democracy, according to which citizens ought to participate in discussions of public policy and to have a hand, if only indirectly, in decision making. Democratic theory, he argued, had roots in social conditions that no longer obtained. It presupposed an "omnicompetent citizen," a "jack of all trades" who could be found only in a "simple self-contained community." In the "wide and unpredictable environment" of the modern world, the old ideal of citizenship was obsolete. A complex industrial society required a government carried on by officials who would necessarily be guided—since any form of direct democracy was now impossible—either by public opinion or by expert knowledge. Public opinion was unreliable because it could be united only by an appeal to slogans and "symbolic pictures." Lippmann's distrust of public opinion rested on the epistemological distinction between truth and mere opinion. Truth, as he conceived it, grew out of disinterested scientific inquiry; everything else was ideology. The scope of public debate accordingly had to be severely restricted. At best public debate was a disagreeable necessity—not the very essence of democracy but its "primary defect," which arose only because "exact knowledge," unfortunately, was in limited supply. Ideally public debate would not take place at all; decisions would be based on scientific "standards of measurement" alone. Science cut through "entangling stereotypes and slogans," the "threads of memory and emotion" that kept the "respon-sible administrator" tied up in knots.

The role of the press, as Lippmann saw it, was to circulate information, not to encourage argument. The relationship between information and argument was antagonistic, not complementary. He did not take the position that reliable information was a necessary precondition of argument; on the contrary, his point was that information precluded argument, made argument unnecessary. Arguments were what took place in the absence of reliable information. Lippmann had forgotten what he learned (or should have learned) from William James and John Dewey: that our search for reliable information is itself guided by the questions that arise during arguments about a given course of action. It is only by subjecting our preferences and projects to the test of debate that we come to understand what we know and what we still need to learn. Until we have to defend our opinions in public, they remain opinions in Lippmann's pejorative sense—half-formed convictions based on random impressions and unexamined assumptions. It is the act of articulating and defending our views that lifts them out of the category of "opinions," gives them shape and definition, and makes it possible for others to recognize them as a description of their own experience as well. In short, we come to know our own minds only by explaining ourselves to others.

The attempt to bring others around to our own point of view carries the risk, of course, that we may adopt their point of view instead. We have to enter imaginatively into our opponents' arguments, if only for the purpose of refuting them, and we may end up being persuaded by those we sought to persuade. Argument is risky and unpredictable, therefore educational. Most of us tend to think of it (as Lippmann thought of it) as a clash of rival dogmas, a shouting match in which neither side gives any ground. But arguments are not won by shouting down opponents. They are won by changing opponents' minds—something that can happen only if we give opposing arguments a respectful hearing and still persuade their advocates that there is something wrong with those arguments. In the course of this activity we may well decide that there is something wrong with our own.

If we insist on argument as the essence of education, we will defend democracy not as the most efficient but as the most educational form of government, one that extends the circle of debate as widely as possible and thus forces all citizens to articulate their views, to put their views at risk, and to cultivate the virtues of eloquence, clarity of thought and expression, and sound judgment. As Lippmann noted, small communities are the classic locus of democracy—not because they are "self-contained," however, but simply because they allow everyone to take part in public debates. Instead of dismissing direct democracy as irrelevant to modern conditions, we need to re-create it on a large scale. From this point of view the press serves as the equivalent of the town meeting.

This is what Dewey argued, in effect—though not, unfortunately, very clearly—in *The Public and Its Problems* (1927), a book written in reply to Lippmann's disparaging studies of public opinion. Lippmann's distinction between truth and information rested on a "spectator theory of knowledge," as James W. Carey explains in his *Communication as Culture*. As Lippmann understood these matters, knowledge is what we get when an observer, preferably a scientifically trained observer, provides us with a copy of reality that we can all recognize. Dewey, on the other hand, knew that even scientists argue among themselves. "Systematic inquiry," he contended, was only the beginning of knowledge, not its final form. The knowledge needed by any community—whether it was a community of scientific inquirers or a political community—emerged only from "dialogue" and "direct give and take."

It is significant, as Carey points out, that Dewey's analysis of communication stressed the ear rather than the eye. "Conversation," Dewey wrote, "has a vital import lacking in the fixed and frozen words of written speech. . . . The connections of the ear with vital and outgoing thought and emotion are immensely closer and more varied than those of the eye. Vision is a spectator; hearing is a participator."

The press extends the scope of debate by supplementing the spoken word with the written word. If the press needs to apologize for anything, it is not that the written word is a poor substitute for the pure language of mathematics. What matters, in this connection, is that the written word is a poor substitute for the spoken word. It is an acceptable substitute, however, as long as written speech takes spoken speech and not mathematics as its model. According to Lippmann, the press was unreliable because it could never give us accurate representations of reality, only "symbolic pictures" and stereotypes. Dewey's analysis implied a more penetrating line of criticism. As Carey puts it, "The press, by seeing its role as that of informing the public, abandons its role as an agency for carrying on the conversation of our culture." Having embraced Lippmann's ideal of objectivity, the press no longer serves to cultivate "certain vital habits" in the community: "the ability to follow an argument, grasp the point of view of another, expand the boundaries of understanding, debate the alternative purposes that might be pursued."

The rise of the advertising and public relations industries, side by side, helps to explain why the press abdicated its most important function—enlarging the public forum—at the same time that it became more "responsible." A responsible press, as opposed to a partisan or opinionated one, attracted the kind of readers advertisers were eager to reach: well-heeled readers, most of whom probably thought of themselves as independent voters. These readers wanted to be assured that they were reading all the news that was fit to print, not an editor's idiosyncratic and no doubt biased view of things. Responsibility came to be equated with the avoidance of controversy because advertisers were willing to pay for it. Some advertisers were also willing to pay for sensationalism, though on the whole they preferred a respectable readership to sheer numbers. What they clearly did not prefer was "opinion"—not because they were impressed with Lippmann's philosophical arguments but because opinionated reporting did not guarantee the right audience. No doubt they also hoped that an aura of objectivity, the hallmark of responsible journalism, would also rub off on the advertisements that surrounded increasingly slender columns of print.

In a curious historical twist, advertising, publicity, and other forms of commercial persuasion themselves came to be disguised as information. Advertising and publicity substituted for open debate. "Hidden persuaders" (as Vance Packard called them) replaced the old-time editors, essayists, and orators who made no secret of their partisanship. Information and publicity became increasingly indistinguishable. Most of the "news" in our newspapers—40 percent, according to the conservative estimate of Professor Scott Cutlip of the University of Georgia—consists of items churned out by press agencies and public relations bureaus and then regurgitated intact by the "objective" organs of journalism. We have grown accustomed to the idea that most of the space in newspapers, so called, is devoted to advertising—at least two-thirds in most newspapers. But if we consider public relations as another form of advertising, which is hardly far-fetched since private, commercially inspired enterprises fuel both, we now have to get used to the idea that much of the "news" consists of advertising too.

The decline of the partisan press and the rise of a new type of journalism professing rigorous standards of objectivity do not assure a steady supply of usable information. Unless information is generated by sustained public debate, most of it will be irrelevant at best, misleading and manipulative at worst. Increasingly information is generated by those who wish to promote something or someone—a product, a cause, a political candidate or office-holder—without arguing their case on its merits or explicitly advertising it as self-interested material either. Much of the press, in its eagerness to inform the public, has become a conduit for the equivalent of junk mail. Like the post office—another institution that once served to extend the sphere of face-to-face discussion and to create "committees of correspondence"—it now delivers an abundance of useless, indigestible information that nobody wants, most of which ends up as unread waste. The most important effect of this obsession with information, aside from the destruction of trees for paper and the mounting burden of "waste management," is to undermine the authority of the word. When words are used merely as instruments of publicity or propaganda, they lose their power to persuade. Soon they cease to mean anything at all. People lose the capacity to use language precisely and expressively or even to distinguish one word from another. The spoken word models itself on the written word instead of the other way around, and ordinary speech begins to sound like the clotted jargon we see in print. Ordinary speech begins to sound like "information"—a disaster from which the English language may never recover.

1995

READING, REREADING, AND ANALYSIS

1. As you read, develop a definition of what Lasch means when he talks about the "decay in public debate." What does the phrase suggest? What does Lasch believe are some of the consequences of that decay? What historical reasons does he give for that decay?

2. Summarize Lasch's discussion of the history of print journalism's relationship to public debate. Work in groups to create a chronology showing the role of the press in the nineteenth century and how it changed in subsequent periods.

3. Various ideas of "democracy" are presented throughout this essay, not only by Lasch himself, but also by Walter Lippmann, John Dewey, and others. List as many different uses of the concept of "democracy" as you can find in Lasch's essay, share them in groups, and discuss the differences that emerge.

4. Analyze an argument from a front-page newspaper story or a network news story. Do Lasch's descriptions of modern-day journalism seem justified? Why or why not? To what extent are you simply presented with objective information and to what extent are you presented with a debate?

RESPONDING THROUGH WRITING

5. Lasch seems critical of the "aura of objectivity" that became part of the professionalization of the modern press. How can he argue that public debate actually declined with the rise of an "objective," "neutral," and more professional press? Use examples from his essay, as well as from newspapers, the Internet, and television sources, to write a paper that explains and tests his claims. From your research and observation, are Lasch's arguments about the modern-day press accurate? Do professionalization and the goal of neutrality damage public debate? Do you see any echoes in today's press of the nineteenth-century role of journalism that Lasch praises?

6. Lasch argues that there has been a decline in the kind of public debate that is the key to a working democracy. Test Lasch's argument by considering the press coverage of a current political issue. Choose a newspaper article as the basis for your analysis. Does the article have an "aura of objectivity," does it present information, or does it openly argue an opinion? Does it present a "painstaking analysis of complex issues" (p. 304)? Does it show more than one side to the issue or help you to understand the controversy? Does it offer evidence of a public debate or a way in which public debate might reshape this political issue? Which of the historical factors that Lasch brings up would best explain the way the article is written? Even if you end up disagreeing with Lasch, you must demonstrate an understanding of his examples and his point of view.

GOING FURTHER: LEARNING
FROM OTHER SOURCES

7. Lasch does not mention the newest information medium—the Internet. Choose a recent news issue and find an account of it published in a well-known newspaper. Then, using an Internet directory such as About or Yahoo find two websites that relate to that same issue. Finally, look for that issue (or a similar one) being addressed on a television or radio talk show. What are the differences in the way the information is presented? How much information is given? How reliable does the information seem? How objective does the source seem? What degree of public debate is indicated (does the source present quotes from people with contradictory views on the subject, for example)?

8. Using your library's reference collection or a database such as JStor that includes historical journals, look up the Lincoln-Douglas debates discussed by Lasch (p. 304). Take some notes

comparing their methods of debate with those of a current political debate or of a set of current campaign advertisements or brochures. Bring your notes to class.

APPLYING WHAT YOU'VE LEARNED

9. Compare Lasch's and Sven Birkerts's views on how our reading practices create and define the world we live in. How might different practices of reading (and public debate) lead to (positive or negative) changes? Discuss to what extent these two authors seem to be merely resistant to advances in information technology and to what extent you find their cautions justifiable. Use examples from the essays and from your own knowledge and experiences to answer these questions.

10. Use Lasch's ideas about argument and the role of public debate to analyze examples from Gloria Anzaldúa's "Chicana Artists: Exploring *Nepantla, el Lugar de la Frontera*" or Zita Ingham's "Landscape, Drama, Dissensus: The Rhetorical Education of Red Lodge, Montana." Could any of the rhetorical strategies used by Anzaldúa or by the Red Lodge community be used productively in larger American political debates, or is their use limited to small communities? Explain why.

11. How might Lasch's conception of the role of debate and discussion in a healthy democracy help to explain Dorothy Allison's idea of art in her essay, "This Is Our World"? Is Allison's confrontational, individualistic art a version of "democracy" through art? What might be the consequences of a culture designed to promote that kind of art? As you write, be sure to take note of any key differences you see between Lasch and Allison.

Lawrence Lessig

Lawrence Lessig (b. 1961) has a varied academic background, earning bachelor's degrees in economics and management from the University of Pennsylvania, a master's in philosophy from Cambridge, and a law degree from Yale. He is currently a Professor of Law at Stanford University, a monthly columnist for *Wired Magazine*, and an advocate of a common-sense approach to copyright policy and the Internet. In addition to teaching at the country's major law schools, arguing cases before the Supreme Court, and serving as an expert witness in *Department of Justice v. Microsoft*, Lessig has written three books, including *Free Culture*, from which this introduction was taken.

> **For more information on *Free Culture* and Professor Lessig,** see <http://www.free-culture.cc/>.

WHAT DO YOU KNOW? WHAT DO YOU EXPECT TO DISCOVER?

Before reading the essay, take a moment to consider the following questions.

1. Have you ever downloaded music or video from the Web without paying for it? Is that "stealing"? Is it "sharing"? What's the difference?

2. Think of writing as a creative act. Can you own words? Or can anyone use them? What about sentences or ideas?

3. Lessig argues that the development of the Internet has revealed some giant flaws in how we think about property. What do you think, for example, about record companies who sue people who download music? How has the Internet changed our ideas of property?

≪

"Introduction" to *Free Culture*

On December 17, 1903, on a windy North Carolina beach for just shy of one hundred seconds, the Wright brothers demonstrated that a heavier-than-air, self-propelled vehicle could fly. The moment was electric and its importance widely understood. Almost immediately, there was an explosion of interest in this newfound technology of manned flight, and a gaggle of innovators began to build upon it.

At the time the Wright brothers invented the airplane, American law held that a property owner presumptively owned not just the surface of his land, but all the land below, down to the center of the earth, and all the space above, to "an indefinite extent, upwards."[1] For many years, scholars had puzzled about how best to interpret the idea that rights in land ran to the heavens. Did that mean that you owned the stars? Could you prosecute geese for their willful and regular trespass?

Then came airplanes, and for the first time, this principle of American law—deep within the foundations of our tradition, and acknowledged by the most important legal thinkers of our past—mattered. If my land reaches to the heavens, what happens when United flies over my field? Do I have the right to banish it from my property? Am I allowed to enter into an exclusive license with Delta Airlines? Could we set up an auction to decide how much these rights are worth?

In 1945, these questions became a federal case. When North Carolina farmers Thomas Lee and Tinie Causby started losing chickens because of low-flying military aircraft (the terrified chickens apparently flew into the barn walls and died), the Causbys filed a lawsuit saying that the government was trespassing on their land. The airplanes, of course, never touched the surface of the Causby's land. But if, as Blackstone, Kent, and Coke had said, their land reached to "an indefinite extent, upwards," then the government was trespassing on their property, and the Causbys wanted it to stop.

The Supreme Court agreed to hear the Causby's case. Congress had declared the airways public, but if one's property really extended to the heavens, then Congress's declaration could well have been an unconstitutional "taking" of property without compensation. The Court acknowledged that "it is ancient doctrine that common law ownership of the land extended to the periphery of the universe." But Justice Douglas had no patience for ancient doctrine. In a single paragraph, hundreds of years of property law were erased. As he wrote for the Court,

> [The] doctrine has no place in the modern world. The air is a public highway, as Congress has declared. Were that not true,

every transcontinental flight would subject the operator to countless trespass suits. Common sense revolts at the idea. To recognize such private claims to the airspace would clog these highways, seriously interfere with their control and development in the public interest, and transfer into private ownership that to which only the public has a just claim.[2]

"Common sense revolts at the idea."

This is how the law usually works. Not often this abruptly or impatiently, but eventually, this is how it works. It was Douglas's style not to dither. Other justices would have blathered on for pages to reach the conclusion that Douglas holds in a single line: "Common sense revolts at the idea." But whether it takes pages or a few words, it is the special genius of a common law system, as ours is, that the law adjusts to the technologies of the time. And as it adjusts, it changes. Ideas that were as solid as rock in one age crumble in another.

Or at least, this is how things happen when there's no one powerful on the other side of the change. The Causbys were just farmers. And though there were no doubt many like them who were upset by the growing traffic in the air (though one hopes not many chickens flew themselves into walls), the Causbys of the world would find it very hard to unite and stop the idea, and the technology, that the Wright brothers had birthed. The Wright brothers spat airplanes into the technological meme pool; the idea then spread like a virus in a chicken coop; farmers like the Causbys found themselves surrounded by "what seemed reasonable" given the technology that the Wrights had produced. They could stand on their farms, dead chickens in hand, and shake their fists at these newfangled technologies all they wanted. They could call their representatives or even file a lawsuit. But in the end, the force of what seems "obvious" to everyone else— the power of "common sense"—would prevail. Their "private interest" would not be allowed to defeat an obvious public gain.

Edwin Howard Armstrong is one of America's forgotten inventor geniuses. He came to the great American inventor scene just after the titans Thomas Edison and Alexander Graham Bell. But his work in the area of radio technology was perhaps the most important of any single inventor in the first fifty years of radio. He was better educated than Michael Faraday, who as a bookbinder's apprentice had discovered electric induction in 1831. But he had the same intuition about how the world of radio worked, and on at least three occasions, Armstrong invented profoundly important technologies that advanced our understanding of radio.

On the day after Christmas, 1933, four patents were issued to Armstrong for his most significant invention—FM radio. Until then, consumer radio had been amplitude-modulated (AM) radio. The theorists of the day had said that frequency-modulated (FM) radio could never work. They were right about FM radio in a narrow band of spectrum. But Armstrong discovered that frequency-modulated radio in a wide band of spectrum would deliver an astonishing fidelity of sound, with much less transmitter power and static.

On November 5, 1935, he demonstrated the technology at a meeting of the Institute of Radio Engineers at the Empire State Building in New York City. He tuned his radio dial across a range of AM stations, until the radio locked on a broadcast that he had arranged from seventeen miles away. The radio fell totally silent, as if dead, and then with a clarity no one else in that room had ever heard from an electrical device, it produced the sound of an announcer's voice: "This is amateur station W2AG at Yonkers, New York, operating on frequency modulation at two and a half meters."

The audience was hearing something no one had thought possible:

> A glass of water was poured before the microphone in Yonkers; it sounded like a glass of water being poured. . . . A paper was crumpled and torn; it sounded like paper and not like a crackling forest fire. . . . Sousa marches were played from records and a piano solo and guitar number were performed. . . . The music was projected with a live-ness rarely if ever heard before from a radio "music box."[3]

As our own common sense tells us, Armstrong had discovered a vastly superior radio technology. But at the time of his invention, Armstrong was working for RCA. RCA was the dominant player in the then dominant AM radio market. By 1935, there were a thousand radio stations across the United States, but the stations in large cities were all owned by a handful of networks.

RCA's president, David Sarnoff, a friend of Armstrong's, was eager that Armstrong discover a way to remove static from AM radio. So Sarnoff was quite excited when Armstrong told him he had a device that removed static from "radio." But when Armstrong demonstrated his invention, Sarnoff was not pleased.

> I thought Armstrong would invent some kind of a filter to remove static from our AM radio. I didn't think he'd start a revolution— start up a whole damn new industry to compete with RCA.[4]

Armstrong's invention threatened RCA's AM empire, so the company launched a campaign to smother FM radio. While FM may have been a superior technology, Sarnoff was a superior tactician. As one author described,

> The forces for FM, largely engineering, could not overcome the weight of strategy devised by the sales, patent, and legal offices to subdue this threat to corporate position. For FM, if allowed to develop unrestrained, posed . . . a complete reordering of

radio power . . . and the eventual overthrow of the carefully restricted AM system on which RCA had grown to power.[5]

RCA at first kept the technology in house, insisting that further
tests were needed. When, after two years of testing, Armstrong grew
impatient, RCA began to use its power with the government to stall
FM radio's deployment generally. In 1936, RCA hired the former head
of the FCC and assigned him the task of assuring that the FCC assign
spectrum in a way that would castrate FM—principally by moving
FM radio to a different band of spectrum. At first, these efforts failed.
But when Armstrong and the nation were distracted by World War II,
RCA's work began to be more successful. Soon after the war ended,
the FCC announced a set of policies that would have one clear effect:
FM radio would be crippled. As Lawrence Lessing described it,

> The series of body blows that FM radio received right after the
> war, in a series of rulings manipulated through the FCC by the
> big radio interests, were almost incredible in their force and de-
> viousness.[6]

To make room in the spectrum for RCA's latest gamble, television, FM radio users were to be moved to a totally new spectrum
band. The power of FM radio stations was also cut, meaning FM
could no longer be used to beam programs from one part of the country to another. (This change was strongly supported by AT&T, because the loss of FM relaying stations would mean radio stations
would have to buy wired links from AT&T.) The spread of FM radio
was thus choked, at least temporarily.

Armstrong resisted RCA's efforts. In response, RCA resisted Armstrong's patents. After incorporating FM technology into the emerging standard for television, RCA declared the patents invalid—
baselessly, and almost fifteen years after they were issued. It thus
refused to pay him royalties. For six years, Armstrong fought an
expensive war of litigation to defend the patents. Finally, just as the
patents expired, RCA offered a settlement so low that it would not
even cover Armstrong's lawyers' fees. Defeated, broken, and now
broke, in 1954 Armstrong wrote a short note to his wife and then
stepped out of a thirteenth-story window to his death.

This is how the law sometimes works. Not often this tragically,
and rarely with heroic drama, but sometimes, this is how it works.
From the beginning, government and government agencies have been
subject to capture. They are more likely captured when a powerful interest is threatened by either a legal or technical change. That powerful interest too often exerts its influence within the government to get
the government to protect it. The rhetoric of this protection is of
course always public spirited; the reality is something different. Ideas
that were as solid as rock in one age, but that, left to themselves,

would crumble in another, are sustained through this subtle corruption of our political process. RCA had what the Causbys did not: the power to stifle the effect of technological change.

There's no single inventor of the Internet. Nor is there any good date upon which to mark its birth. Yet in a very short time, the Internet has become part of ordinary American life. According to the Pew Internet and American Life Project, 58 percent of Americans had access to the Internet in 2002, up from 49 percent two years before.[7] That number could well exceed two thirds of the nation by the end of 2004.

As the Internet has been integrated into ordinary life, it has changed things. Some of these changes are technical—the Internet has made communication faster, it has lowered the cost of gathering data, and so on. These technical changes are not the focus of this book. They are important. They are not well understood. But they are the sort of thing that would simply go away if we all just switched the Internet off. They don't affect people who don't use the Internet, or at least they don't affect them directly. They are the proper subject of a book about the Internet. But this is not a book about the Internet.

Instead, this book is about an effect of the Internet beyond the Internet itself: an effect upon how culture is made. My claim is that the Internet has induced an important and unrecognized change in that process. That change will radically transform a tradition that is as old as the Republic itself. Most, if they recognized this change, would reject it. Yet most don't even see the change that the Internet has introduced.

We can glimpse a sense of this change by distinguishing between commercial and noncommercial culture, and by mapping the law's regulation of each. By "commercial culture" I mean that part of our culture that is produced and sold or produced to be sold. By "noncommercial culture" I mean all the rest. When old men sat around parks or on street corners telling stories that kids and others consumed, that was noncommercial culture. When Noah Webster published his "Reader," or Joel Barlow his poetry, that was commercial culture.

At the beginning of our history, and for just about the whole of our tradition, noncommercial culture was essentially unregulated. Of course, if your stories were lewd, or if your song disturbed the peace, then the law might intervene. But the law was never directly concerned with the creation or spread of this form of culture, and it left this culture "free." The ordinary ways in which ordinary individuals shared and transformed their culture—telling stories, reenacting scenes from plays or TV, participating in fan clubs, sharing music, making tapes—were left alone by the law.

The focus of the law was on commercial creativity. At first slightly, then quite extensively, the law protected the incentives of creators by granting them exclusive rights to their creative work, so that they could sell those exclusive rights in a commercial market-plce.[8] This is also, of course, an important part of creativity and culture, and it has become an increasingly important part in America. But in no sense was it dominant within our tradition. It was instead just one part, a controlled part, balanced with the free.

This rough divide between the free and the controlled has now been erased.[9] The Internet has set the stage for this erasure and, pushed by big media, the law has now affected it. For the first time in our tradition, the ordinary ways in which individuals create and share culture fall within the reach of the regulation of the law, which has expanded to draw within its control a vast amount of culture and creativity that it never reached before. The technology that preserved the balance of our history—between uses of our culture that were free and uses of our culture that were only upon permission—has been undone. The consequence is that we are less and less a free culture, more and more a permission culture.

This change gets justified as necessary to protect commercial creativity. And indeed, protectionism is precisely its motivation. But the protectionism that justifies the changes that I will describe below is not the limited and balanced sort that has defined the law in the past. This is not a protectionism to protect artists. It is instead a protectionism to protect certain forms of business. Corporations threatened by the potential of the Internet to change the way both commercial and noncommercial culture are made and shared have united to induce lawmakers to use the law to protect them. It is the story of RCA and Armstrong; it is the dream of the Causbys.

For the Internet has unleashed an extraordinary possibility for many to participate in the process of building and cultivating a culture that reaches far beyond local boundaries. That power has changed the marketplace for making and cultivating culture generally, and that change in turn threatens established content industries. The Internet is thus to the industries that built and distributed content in the twentieth century what FM radio was to AM radio, or what the truck was to the railroad industry of the nineteenth century: the beginning of the end, or at least a substantial transformation. Digital technologies, tied to the Internet, could produce a vastly more competitive and vibrant market for building and cultivating culture; that market could include a much wider and more diverse range of creators; those creators could produce and distribute a much more vibrant range of creativity; and depending upon a few important factors, those creators could earn more on average from this system than creators do today—all so long as the RCAs of our day don't use the law to protect themselves against this competition.

Yet, as I argue in the pages that follow, that is precisely what is happening in our culture today. These modern-day equivalents of the early twentieth-century radio or nineteenth-century railroads are using their power to get the law to protect them against this new, more efficient, more vibrant technology for building culture. They are succeeding in their plan to remake the Internet before the Internet remakes them.

It doesn't seem this way to many. The battles over copyright and the Internet seem remote to most. To the few who follow them, they seem mainly about a much simpler brace of questions—whether "piracy" will be permitted, and whether "property" will be protected. The "war" that has been waged against the technologies of the Internet—what Motion Picture Association of America (MPAA) president Jack Valenti calls his "own terrorist war"[10]—has been framed as a battle about the rule of law and respect for property. To know which side to take in this war, most think that we need only decide whether we're for property or against it.

If those really were the choices, then I would be with Jack Valenti and the content industry. I, too, am a believer in property, and especially in the importance of what Mr. Valenti nicely calls "creative property." I believe that "piracy" is wrong, and that the law, properly tuned, should punish "piracy," whether on or off the Internet.

But those simple beliefs mask a much more fundamental question and a much more dramatic change. My fear is that unless we come to see this change, the war to rid the world of Internet "pirates" will also rid our culture of values that have been integral to our tradition from the start.

These values built a tradition that, for at least the first 180 years of our Republic, guaranteed creators the right to build freely upon their past, and protected creators and innovators from either state or private control. The First Amendment protected creators against state control. And as Professor Neil Netanel powerfully argues,[11] copyright law, properly balanced, protected creators against private control. Our tradition was thus neither Soviet nor the tradition of patrons. It instead carved out a wide berth within which creators could cultivate and extend our culture.

Yet the law's response to the Internet, when tied to changes in the technology of the Internet itself, has massively increased the effective regulation of creativity in America. To build upon or critique the culture around us one must ask, Oliver Twist–like, for permission first. Permission is, of course, often granted—but it is not often granted to the critical or the independent. We have built a kind of cultural nobility; those within the noble class live easily; those outside it don't. But it is nobility of any form that is alien to our tradition.

The story that follows is about this war. Is it not about the "centrality of technology" to ordinary life. I don't believe in gods, digital or otherwise. Nor is it an effort to demonize any individual or group, for neither do I believe in a devil, corporate or otherwise. It is not a morality tale. Nor is it a call to jihad against an industry.

It is instead an effort to understand a hopelessly destructive war inspired by the technologies of the Internet but reaching far beyond its code. And by understanding this battle, it is an effort to map peace. There is no good reason for the current struggle around Internet technologies to continue. There will be great harm to our tradition and culture if it is allowed to continue unchecked. We must come to understand the source of this war. We must resolve it soon.

Like the Causbys' battle, this war is, in part, about "property." The property of this war is not as tangible as the Causbys', and no innocent chicken has yet to lose its life. Yet the ideas surrounding this "property" are as obvious to most as the Causbys' claim about the sacredness of their farm was to them. We are the Causbys. Most of us take for granted the extraordinarily powerful claims that the owners of "intellectual property" now assert. Most of us, like the Causbys, treat these claims as obvious. And hence we, like the Causbys, object when a new technology interferes with this property. It is as plain to us as it was to them that the new technologies of the Internet are "trespassing" upon legitimate claims of "property." It is as plain to us as it was to them that the law should intervene to stop this trespass.

And thus, when geeks and technologists defend their Armstrong or Wright brothers technology, most of us are simply unsympathetic. Common sense does not revolt. Unlike in the case of the unlucky Causbys, common sense is on the side of the property owners in this war. Unlike the lucky Wright brothers, the Internet has not inspired a revolution on its side.

My hope is to push this common sense along. I have become increasingly amazed by the power of this idea of intellectual property and, more importantly, its power to disable critical thought by policy makers and citizens. There has never been a time in our history when more of our "culture" was as "owned" as it is now. And yet there has never been a time when the concentration of power to control the *uses* of culture has been as unquestioningly accepted as it is now.

The puzzle is, Why?

Is it because we have come to understand a truth about the value and importance of absolute property over ideas and culture? Is it because we have discovered that our tradition of rejecting such an absolute claim was wrong?

Or is it because the idea of absolute property over ideas and culture benefits the RCAs of our time and fits our own unreflective intuitions?

Is the radical shift away from our tradition of free culture an instance of America correcting a mistake from its past, as we did after a bloody war with slavery, and as we are slowly doing with inequality? Or is the radical shift away from our tradition of free culture yet another example of a political system captured by a few powerful special interests?

Does common sense lead to the extremes on this question because common sense actually believes in these extremes? Or does common sense stand silent in the face of these extremes because, as with Armstrong versus RCA, the more powerful side has ensured that it has the more powerful view?

I don't mean to be mysterious. My own views are resolved. I believe it was right for common sense to revolt against the extremism of the Causbys. I believe it would be right for common sense to revolt against the extreme claims made today on behalf of "intellectual property." What the law demands today is increasingly as silly as a sheriff arresting an airplane for trespass. But the consequences of this silliness will be much more profound.

Notes

Throughout this text, there are references to links on the World Wide Web. As anyone who has tried to use the Web knows, these links can be highly unstable. I have tried to remedy the instability by redirecting readers to the original source through the Web site associated with this book. For each link below, you can go to <http://free-culture.cc/notes> and locate the original source by clicking on the number after the # sign. If the original link remains alive, you will be redirected to that link. If the original link has disappeared, you will be redirected to an appropriate reference for the material.

1. St. George Tucker, *Blackstone's Commentaries* 3 (South Hackensack, N.J.: Rothman Reprints, 1969), 18.
2. United States v. Causby, U.S. 328 (1946): 256, 261. The Court did find that there could be a "taking" if the government's use of its land effectively destroyed the value of the Causbys' land. This example was suggested to me by Keith Aoki's wonderful piece, "(Intellectual) Property and Sovereignty: Notes Toward a Cultural Geography of Authorship," *Standford Law Review* 48 (1996): 1293, 1333. See also Paul Goldstein, *Real Property* (Mineola, N.Y.: Foundation Press, 1984), 1112–13.
3. Lawrence Lessing, *Man of High Fidelity: Edwin Howard Armstrong* (Philadelphia: J. B. Lippincott Company, 1956), 209.
4. See "Saints: The Heroes and Geniuses of the Electronic Era," First Electronic Church of America, at www.webstationone.com/fecha, available at link #1.
5. Lessing, 226.
6. Lessing, 256.
7. Amanda Lenhart, "The Ever-Shifting Internet Population: A New Look at Internet Access and the Digital Divide," Pew Internet and American Life Project, 15 April 2003: 6, available at link #2.
8. This is not the only purpose of copyright, though it is the overwhelmingly primary purpose of the copyright established in the federal constitution. State copyright law historically protected not just the commercial interest in publication, but also a privacy interest. By granting authors the exclusive right to first publication, state copyright law gave authors the power to control the spread of facts about them. See Samuel D. Warren and Louis D. Brandeis, "The Right to Privacy," *Harvard Law Review* 4 (1890): 193, 198–200.

9. See Jessica Litman, *Digital Copyright* (New York: Prometheus Books, 2001), ch. 13.

10. Amy Harmon, "Black Hawk Download: Moving Beyond Music, Pirates Use New Tools to Turn the Net into an Illicit Video Club," *New York Times,* 17 January 2002.

11. Neil W. Netanel, "Copyright and a Democratic Civil Society," *Yale Law Journal* 106 (1996): 283.

READING, REREADING, AND ANALYSIS

1. Where, in your own experience, have you seen instances of the conflict Lessig describes? Do you have strong feelings about your "cultural freedom"?

2. What terms or ideas seem most important to Lessig? What, for instance, does Lessig mean when he says, "we are less and less a free culture, more and more a permission culture" (p. 320)?

3. Lessig introduces his topic with two historical examples. What do the stories of the Causbys and Edwin Armstrong contribute to his argument?

4. Lessig shows us how legal arguments sometimes invoke "common sense" over legal precedent. How is common sense determined? Explain Lessig's comment that "ideas that were as solid as rock in one age crumble in another" (pp. 318–319).

5. What is the relationship between creativity and ownership? Look at your answers to question 2 in the "What do you know?" section, and reconsider them as you think through Lessig's article. Does a person wholly own what he or she creates?

RESPONDING THROUGH WRITING: BUILDING AN INTERPRETATION

6. Why does Lessig make a distinction between commercial and noncommercial culture? Give fresh examples of each, and write a brief paper considering the implications of Lessig's argument on your examples.

7. Examine Lessig's claim that "we have built a kind of cultural nobility" (p. 321). What evidence does he give to support this claim? Help him out with an example of your own. Write an essay that explores the consequences of setting up our culture in this way.

8. Using your answers from question 3 and looking closely at Lessig's transition from one example (the Causbys) to another (Edwin Armstrong), write one or two paragraphs that explain the re-

lationship between the two anecdotes. Why does Lessig put them together here? Why not use only one? Use your paragraphs as the basis for a paper that analyzes the RCA example Lessig provides. What, specifically, does Lessig want us to think about what RCA chooses to do?

9. What does Lessig overlook or oversimplify? Are there good reasons why the law often supports corporate culture? Look closely at one or two of Lessig's boldest claims and write a three-page paper exploring the counterarguments. What are the benefits of the property laws as they have evolved?

GOING FURTHER: LEARNING FROM OTHER SOURCES

10. Use an encyclopedia or searh a reference database to find more information about FM radio. Is Edwin Armstrong mentioned? Who gets the credit for advancing that technology? Is there any mention of the problems Lessig tells us about? Why or why not?

11. Go to Lessig's own website, <http://www.lessig.org>, and look critically at how he presents himself and his project. What values or organizations does he consciously identify himself with? What do you suppose his motivations are? How does he earn his living? Does his selling of his books on "freedom" contradict his views in any way?

MAKING CONNECTIONS: APPLYING WHAT YOU'VE LEARNED

12. Consider writing as a form of cultural property. In her essay "I Stand Here Writing," Nancy Sommers weaves together an array of stories and insights documenting her fluid thoughts about writing and identity. She does not, however, address the legal boundaries of thoughts or writing. Using Lessig's essay as your support, examine Sommers's ideas with respect to creativity and ownership. When is an idea "new," and when is it simply recycled (or stolen)?

13. Sherry Turkle thinks of computers as technological "instruments," enabling a "playful exploration" that fosters creativity and progress. She seems to share Lessig's belief in the revolutionary impact of technological innovation. But she, too, sees plenty of obstacles to that creativity. Are her obstacles the same as Lessig's? In an essay of at least four complete pages, develop an argument about the barriers to what Lessig calls "free

culture" and the consequences of these barriers. Be sure to consider Turkle's examples and her focus on education as a site for discussion.

14. Scott McCloud's comics essay, "Setting the Record Straight," samples from a number of familiar images from our culture (see especially the large globe on page 349). Does he owe these sources a royalty for "borrowing" their creative property? Should he? In an essay that points to at least one of McCloud's examples, explore the implications of Lessig's argument about "free culture." Should we be free to use anything we like in our own creative work?

EMILY MARTIN, BJORN CLAESON, WENDY RICHARDSON, MONICA SCHOCH-SPANA, AND KAREN-SUE TAUSSIG

Emily Martin (b. 1944) is a Professor of Anthropology at Princeton University. Martin's research focuses on science and medicine as forms of knowledge about the body and the world. Her teaching includes courses on the anthropology of health, the practice of ethnography, and the study of U.S. society and culture. She is the author of four books, including her most recent, *Flexible Bodies: Tracking Immunity in American Culture from the Days of Polio to the Age of AIDS* (1994). Martin was previously a professor at Johns Hopkins University where her coauthors were among her graduate students. "Scientific Literacy, What It Is, Why It's Important, and Why Scientists Think We Don't Have It" is from *Naked Science: Anthropological Inquiry into Boundaries, Power, and Knowledge,* a collection of essays edited by Laura Nader.

> To learn more about the state of scientific literacy in this country and around the globe, visit the website of the National Center for Science Literacy, Education and Technology at <http://www.amnh.org/nationalcenter/>.

WHAT DO YOU KNOW? WHAT DO YOU EXPECT TO DISCOVER?

Before reading the essay, take a moment to consider the following questions.

1. Examine the title of this essay and the names of the authors who have written it. Who are the authors? Who appears to be their intended audience? What does "scientific literacy" mean to you? What does the title lead you to expect from the article?

2. Write a few sentences using an image or a metaphor to explain how you think about AIDS in relation to your body's immune system. Compare your response to those of other members of your group.

3. The following essay explores how people gain and make sense of scientific knowledge. Make a quick list of any scientific subjects about which you feel you have some knowledge. Try to recall the last time you encountered new science-related information and how you responded.

⍥

Scientific Literacy,
What It Is, Why It's Important,
and Why Scientists Think We Don't Have It
The Case of Immunology and the Immune System

"Science matters," we have been told in a recent spate of publications. In *Science Matters: Achieving Scientific Literacy,* "science literacy" is defined as "the knowledge you need to understand public issues . . . to put new [scientific] advances into a context that will allow you to take part in the national debate about them" (1991a:xii). Unproblematic as this definition might seem at first glance, the authors contend that by any measure, "Americans as a whole simply have not been exposed to science sufficiently or in a way that communicates the knowledge they need to have to cope with the life they will have to lead in the twenty-first century" (xv). This dire (and, we would like to argue, unfair) diagnosis becomes more understandable when one confronts the extremely narrow and technocratic content of the knowledge contained in *Science Matters* and most other books about science literacy. For example, in media publications spun off from *Science Matters,* readers are given a "pop quiz" that tests scientific literacy, a quiz that the great majority of Americans at all educational levels would fail (Hazen and Trefil 1991b). One question from the quiz is:

The blueprint for every form of life is contained in

a. The National Institutes of Health near Washington, D.C.

b. DNA molecules

c. Proteins and carbohydrates

d. Viruses

For Hazen and Trefil, the correct answer, measuring a person's ability to understand public issues and function responsibly as citizens, is *b.* But in a broader, and more socially and culturally informed, definition of science literacy, one might wish people to debate the postulated role of DNA as the blueprint for every form of life. Following the lead of Ruth Hubbard and Eliza Wald in *Exploding the Gene Myth,* for example, one might hope that people would appreciate how little about every life form is actually determined by the gene.

Following the lead of Bruno Latour, one might want people to understand how much the establishment of science "facts" owe[s] to the funds and credibility given particular researches by institutions like the one mentioned in answer *a*, the National Institutes of Health near Washington, DC (Latour 1987).

Even though some publications on science literacy contain reference to social and cultural issues, these issues are usually posed as afterthoughts, or at least as reflections to ponder after the real science is mastered. For example, in *Benchmarks for Science Literacy*, the summary section on "health technology" for high-school students lists six paragraphs of facts about the genetics, immunology, and epidemiology of health. Not until the seventh paragraph do we read that "biotechnology has contributed to health improvement in many ways, but its cost and application have led to a variety of controversial social and ethical issues" (American Association for the Advancement of Science 1993:207).

In our social anthropological research we are uncovering another picture of what science literacy might consist of by asking nonscientists, at all educational levels and from a variety of ethnic and socioeconomic settings, to tell us in their own terms what they know about health and their bodies, in particular about immunity and the immune system.[1] In this paper we will introduce some examples of this knowledge and argue that the definition of scientific "literacy" needs to be broadened to include the existential, metaphysical, moral, political, and social knowledge that is already embedded in people's talk about the immune system and the actions they take to protect it. Below we introduce four stories we were told about the immune system by people in four quite different contexts. We will argue that the people in these stories are engaged in producing what Clifford Geertz has called "local knowledge"; that is, "the artisan task of seeing broad principles in parochial facts" (1983:168) and "stories about events cast in imagery about principles" (215).

Story 1.   Professor Keller, a scientist and a professor of microbiology at a large northeastern university, is teaching an undergraduate class on the biology of cancer and AIDS. He seeks to alleviate his students' sense of helplessness in the face of both social expectations and health-endangering illnesses by encouraging students to look within themselves to guide their lives and to find the resources to maintain their health.[2] The class, which he teaches every semester to about five hundred people, is known by students as "the best class on campus."

Professor Keller brings to the class a critical awareness of the limits of Western medical science. In particular, he stresses its lack of understanding of the powers inherent in the human body. He raises questions about the causes of cancer and other illnesses and suggests the possibility that Western medicine cannot answer these questions. He tells stories about miraculous recoveries from illnesses and invites to the class ordinary men and women who have performed feats of self-healing deemed impossible by the medical establishment, thus suggesting everything we do not know about healing. And he criticizes the medical establishment for being "completely interested in keeping all alternatives off the books."

The purpose of the class, then, is to teach students "other ways of thinking" about the body, self, health, illness, and death and to "empower" students by giving them a sense of their internal capacity for control over their lives, a capacity that is ignored or denied by medical science. To this end he uses "biology as . . . a common language"; he "talks the language that [the students] are ready to hear" and "interweaves it with stuff that they are not ready to hear, but that they will accept because it is interwoven."

The description of the immune system is part of this common language. As students scribble furiously in their notebooks, Professor Keller tells them about the amazing world within their own bodies: the "dumb" macrophages who "eat foreign objects, stick them out of their own body," and "present" them to "smarter" cells; the "advanced" T-helper cells, "the quarterbacks of the immune system," who "send signals from one part of the immune system to another"; the B cells "who can recognize any foreign shape"; and the suppressor T cells "who are in charge of keeping the immune system within bounds."

Professor Keller stretches students' imaginations by using this depiction of the world of the immune system as a "metaphor for the real power we have" inside us. He tells students that they are powerful, "so much more powerful than [they] even imagine." According to Professor Keller:

> If you believe you've got this, then . . . you start believing you're powerful. . . . I tell this group, "you have this stuff. Your B lymphocytes are incredible. . . . And it's us, and we're really strong." I think they're saying, "Oh." And you almost stand up a little taller and you walk around and say "I'm powerful." . . . It's almost like the scientific version of thinking about an angel or a protector or something that they probably did in the middle ages.

The amazing world of the immune system is not separated from us; rather, "it is us." To know about it gives us a sense of a powerful self.

Mike took Professor Keller's class two years ago. Now, in his final year of college, he ponders the possibilities that lie ahead. According to Mike:

> I think a lot of people, at that age [their twenties], they want to do something with social justice and they really want to get involved. I think it bothers a lot of people, just with the environment, education, and health care, everything. And they don't know if they should go into being a social worker. . . . [There's]

kind of a pull between that end of the spectrum and the other end of living a realistic, not a realistic life, but I mean you have to make a lot of sacrifices . . . if you go that route.

Professor Keller's class "gave you the feeling," he says, that "you're in control" of your life:

> Even before this class, I promised never to do something I really didn't want to do, and if I didn't want to do it, I'd go on to something else. And so in taking this class I think it just reinforced that, to really go with a gut feeling, go with what you're happy with, go with what you feel good about.

The class empowered Mike to "go into" and believe in himself.

But Mike believes Professor Keller's presentation of the immune system had little impact on him. Mike could see no connection between himself and an immune system that seemed to be existing independently inside his body. As he says:

> [They] show how the immune system fights off disease. I think they make it sound as if it's only the immune system. The immune system and the disease . . . this happens here, and then this, this, then this happens, then this step, and this type of cell invades here, the virus attacks the white cells. . . . I couldn't relate to that, I felt that that couldn't help me, so I didn't take anything from it. I didn't care about it.

The microprocesses of the immune system may be "amazing [and] overwhelming," but, to him, they are distant, and not empowering.

In contrast to Mike, Elizabeth came to Professor Keller's class with a conception of the world as a series of separate, but interconnected layers. According to her:

> Everything's all connected. . . . Inside me is like a whole other universe. . . . I have like micro cells within me, and then I'll go up to the bones and the organs, put together, and then just after that just my automatic systems, just like my breathing and stuff like that, and then comes my self. . . . And like this building that I'm living in is like a monster and I'm part of . . . that person, and then this building is part of this town, which is like another person. . . .

Her immune system may be a "separate community in there," like her other organs, but she is nevertheless able to relate to it and interact with it.

This sense of connection with her immune system creates the possibility for her empowerment. For Elizabeth, the immune system is more than a mechanism of use only in emergencies to "fight diseases." She interacts with it on a "day-to-day" basis. During their twenty years together, she says, she and her immune system have gotten used to each other:

> It's gotten used to my way of living. My lack of sleep, and my bad eating habits, it's sort of grown to accept it, because I'm not sick the entire school year, but I hardly sleep the entire school year, and I don't eat right. If I were to get a new immune system, then I would be sick the entire school year until I had it trained that this is me and this is how I function, so help me out a little bit.

Rather than changing her life to meet the needs of her immune system, she has been able to "train" it to accommodate her life. In the context of her conception of the interconnectedness of the world, and her day-to-day interaction with her immune system, scientific knowledge of the immune system becomes empowering. For her, the immune system is, indeed, the "scientific version of . . . an angel or a protector."

Story 2.   Two of our informants, George and Phillip, are a gay white male couple in their early twenties. Coming of age sexually in the first decade of the AIDS epidemic, these two men have known gay circles as places in which conversations about the immune system are commonplace. Interest in a possible lover readily becomes an interest in whether or not he has been tested for HIV and whether or not he will wear a condom. Concern over a friend or acquaintance with AIDS easily becomes worry over his falling T-cell count. While Keller's students may gain a sense of empowerment from his lectures on the immune system, Phillip and George, who have witnessed the loss of a generation of gay men to AIDS and who have heeded the safe-sex campaign among gays, speak more of vulnerability. In their descriptions of the immune system and AIDS, they draw heavily upon an idiom of boundaries. Their talk of boundaries, safety, and risk, used in depicting the body and the threat of HIV, is consonant with their descriptions of danger on a different scale, danger that threatens the neighborhood through crime.

Phillip laments that AIDS and a preoccupation with protecting oneself, that is, wearing a condom, is at odds with love, which is an act of letting down one's barriers. He explains:

> a lot of time, and this happens with straight and gay people . . . the issue of love enters the scenario and sometimes . . . when you love someone [you] don't feel that . . . you should have to protect yourself, and I think that not using protection is a result of that, because [you] feel that you love this person, that this persons loves [you] and because you love each other, you shouldn't have to hide or protect anything about yourself from this person.

The biology of sex and of HIV mandates a barrier, the condom, between two bodies, while the sociality of lovemaking mandates openness between two people.

Others share the concerns of Phillip and George about crime in the neighborhood. They also hold similar cognitive maps of dangerous and safe zones in the area. Residents and business owners, for instance, have organized a citizens' patrol of the neighborhood streets at night to supplement the surveillance provided by the police department. A fatal shotgun blast to the face of a young gay man who was leaving an after-hours nightclub in late spring of 1990 was the event instigating the patrols. In this murder, people saw a number of dangers that the neighborhood unfortunately hosts. Some gays and lesbians considered it another example of the increasing violence directed toward the homosexual community during a time marked by a fear of AIDS. A few considered it the plight of a neighborhood not cohesive enough to exclude such "outsiders" as criminals.

Crucial to the initial stages of the organization of this citizens' group were debates over what area of the neighborhood the patrol would cover. The limited number of participants to schedule for patrols constrained the size of the beat, as did the decision not to place patrols on the "questionable" streets, those being the most peripheral. Patrols were not to walk east of Lake Avenue or west of Central Street. To go beyond these limits was to put oneself in considerable danger, particularly if on foot. Within the perimeter, however, patrols would monitor the streets for crime, calling in the police to investigate and remove, if necessary, suspicious characters from the neighborhood.

Concern over bad areas spilling into good ones and criminal elements circulating within the neighborhood prompted residents to be keenly watchful of activities in their area. Phillip and George are similarly vigilant against the threats that may lie outside their "little, cozy square." Apprehension about the breach of boundaries, however, also marks their appraisal of the threat that HIV poses to the body. Mindful of their safety on the streets and cautious about any contact with "bodily" fluids that may contain HIV, Phillip and George elaborate the social significance of boundaries.

Story 3.   Another informant, Bill, also made references to boundaries in his discussion of the immune system, relating "borders" of the body to those of nation-states. Bill is a white man in his thirties. He lives with his wife, originally from Argentina, in a small row house. Theirs was one of the first racially integrated neighborhoods in Baltimore. The residents are both renters and owners and many live openly as gay couples. When asked why he and his wife chose this area of Baltimore, Bill explained,

> I think affordability is part of it, although I think probably mostly sort of progressive community type stuff.... Affordability, community, yeah not only views of people but also the fact that people did stuff here, they were active. We wanted to live somewhere where there was a community association we could get involved in stuff if we wanted to, that sort of thing.

Bill's concern with individual rights and autonomy were evident throughout our interview. Significantly, his interest in decentralization was reflected in the way he described his work and also became apparent when he began to talk about the immune system. Bill has a degree in architecture but found that office-oriented work did not appeal to him. In graduate school he took a course on creating low-income housing in developing countries. He found this approach more satisfying. This is how Bill described his interest. "In a developing country context, housing is, is all user. I mean the best [that] the public realm, the government and stuff, can do is maybe push a few laws aside or give somebody a scrap of land, but other than that it's whatever, whatever the user or the squatter or whatever can do for themselves." His research took him to Sri Lanka and Chile.

Working on a housing project for the city of Boston, Bill felt involving the community in decisions was, as he put it, a "more progressive way to deal with this notion of developing houses." He now works as a development consultant for nonprofit organizations, including the family center in his neighborhood. Bill's fascination with questions of local autonomy and centralized power were also plain when we asked what he knew about the immune system. At first he was reserved and responded, "I don't think I think much about the immune system per se. . . . I mean the immune system is all these little white blood cells running around eating up all the bad shit in your body right? That's my understanding of the immune system technically speaking."

As Bill oriented his thoughts around a metaphor of organized systems of authority, however, he became excited and the immune system took on a larger significance. He went on to say,

> I mean there's a natural policing thing that happens in the body right? And, I mean it's an incredible policing thing, when you think about it, or at least it's incredible in my mind, because it's a system-wide authority that works. I don't know of any system-wide authorities that work in our culture, so this is amazing right?

Having compared the immune system to a social system, Bill has given it a culture that can be compared to our own. If the metaphor of the police state makes the immune system comprehensible to Bill, at the same time it also becomes a commentary on political organization. It allows him to relate different states of the body to different political systems. As he exclaimed, "I'm sure there are diseases [in which] the immune system ends up destroying the body. . . . It's more like an Argentina or a Bulgaria kind of immune system."

Through his use of a body-country metaphor Bill reveals his conceptions of both bodies and nations as bounded and independent. When asked how he would describe to a child how the body repairs, or takes care of itself, he answered:

> It would [be] an explanation that would involve having to explain that the body is a self-contained system, that it has its own

discipline. . . . I suppose one would want to use a metaphor, you know. . . . Obviously using Argentina or Bulgaria would be an ineffective metaphor. You would have to think of something in the child's world that was a comfortable notion of a closed, self-nurturing system.

As a closed system, the body must protect its boundaries. The body when sick, like a nation at war, is threatened by what Bill describes as, "a foreign organism . . . that is competing for the body's resources in some way or another." Having described the body as a social system, Bill also encountered the moral dilemmas of the social world. What about the individual's rights? What about cultural relativism? In reference to a *Time* magazine cartoon drawing of a virus and a white blood cell fighting, Bill said:

> I was thinking about this notion of good guy versus bad guy. It's really pretty silly because, I mean the virus is just trying to make a living right? It's trying to bring up its family just like the white blood cells are, so there's not really . . . a clear good and bad in it, unless you take somebody's point of view of the larger . . . organism, then you have a point of view. . . . It depends on where you position yourself, where you sit.

By using a social metaphor to describe the body, it becomes a system with logic, an aggregate of players with motivations and intentions. Earlier in the interview Bill explained, "It's easy to talk about policing systems and white blood cells being the good guys and all this kind of good stuff, and then making metaphors around countries, these political things are easy things to talk about and understand for me."

The nation-body metaphors that Bill uses not only enable him to understand the immune system. As Bill suggested earlier, his descriptions of the body also become a commentary on the social world. The words he uses to describe the world of the body also orient his understanding of social interaction and global politics. The role of the politician can move from the global politics of the cold war to the global politics described in the immune system. Looking at a micrograph of bacteria being showered with enzymes, Bill exclaims:

> Oh that's neat! This is great. I mean this is like star wars and I don't mean Reagan's version. This is like a battle, an action shot, right? This thing blowing the other one away. That's great. See, if the people that are so good at making those kind of stupid political arguments, like Reagan, so good at actually convincing people about things like star wars? If he would concentrate that level of creative fabrication [on these] kind of issues, I think this would be a better world to live in.

Later in the interview, discussing the effectiveness of prevention in the control of AIDS, Bill returned to the issue of star wars. We asked, "How effective do you think prevention would be?" Bill responded,

> From what I understand of the disease, again which isn't much, but the way in which it is spread, it sounds like it could probably be very effective. . . . People don't talk much about prevention, I don't even know what something like that might look like. It's interesting though actually. . . . Earlier I was . . . [speaking about] Reagan with his star wars thing. That was a preventative piece and people really sought that out, right? 'Cause it was the notion of things going up and intercepting . . . right? And that actually, I mean that's, those are like, that's like a giant condom network, right, in a sense. So that's actually interesting. So maybe there is some hope, maybe there is a political angle on prevention that is every bit as sellable as curing. I don't know.

In order to communicate his understanding of the immune system and orient his thoughts, Bill has chosen the image of the nation-state. To Bill the topic of the immune system is versatile and allows him to move the discussion from health and illness to issues of global politics and the rights of the individual. Discussion of the immune system becomes a forum to think not only about our bodies and scientific "facts," but about political structures and what positions we must take to understand the rights of others. But these are not just arbitrary subjects held together by a central metaphor, they are also interconnected queries of great relevance to Bill. By speaking about the immune system, Bill was able to convey his views on the interrelations of preventative health, national priorities, and individual rights.

Story 4.   Unlike Bill, for whom AIDS is one of many questions about individual rights and national structures, for Mara, AIDS and the problems of immunity are of primary concern. Mara is a thirty-one-year-old white woman who works as a technical writer for an engineering firm, volunteers by writing grant applications for a local performing arts group, and lives with her husband in a quiet Baltimore neighborhood. All four of Mara's college roommates have died from AIDS. In 1989 Mara became the primary care giver for another close friend who was sick with AIDS. She was with him when he died in a hospice the day after her thirtieth birthday. He was over six feet tall and weighed seventy pounds when he died. Mara is an AIDS activist. In describing her experience with AIDS she said that "a lot of gay people are very angry, a lot of straight people too. And especially those of us involved in the arts—to watch our world crumble, and nobody even look at us . . . nobody even give a shit . . . and we're fighting for little bones that they throw us." She told us that AIDS, the body, and health are things that she thinks about every single day of her life.

Mara is, by anybody's standards, scientifically literate. During our interview we showed her an unlabeled micrograph of a white blood cell surrounding an asbestos fiber and asked her what she thinks of when she sees such pictures. Her instant and stunning response was, "Oh, that's an asbestos fiber in a white blood cell."

Mara's familiarity with the language of science seems to come from her experience with AIDS. She is extremely well informed about the disease, how it is transmitted, and different possibilities for treatment. She is able to clearly articulate her understanding of what she thinks happens inside the body of someone with AIDS. She told us that what she imagines happens inside the body of someone with AIDS has "changed" with the course of the disease. She said, "I used to feel like it was a total loss of control, and like it was Sisyphus, that you would push it up the hill just two feet and then it will roll back down over you. I used to feel like it was only chaos. Now I feel like it's still chaos but that we have a handle on it. . . . I know that it is war, absolutely, it's war inside the body." She goes on to tell us:

> I've never seen anything like this . . . seen twenty-six-year-old men not able to make it up the stairs. I have never seen diarrhea so bad that, that, you put a mouth full of water in your mouth and swallow it and you, you are having explosive diarrhea. . . . This is the weirdest and the most bizarre thing I can . . . imagine. I mean, every nightmare that I ever would have had of what could happen to the human body has come true, and we're right in it every day.

Mara's concern is about the effects of the disease on society. She believes that AIDS is something society may not be able to withstand. She told us that she feels "like we all have AIDS . . . whether we have the virus or not." When asked to elaborate on her suggestion that everybody has AIDS, Mara said, "I really believe that we all have AIDS. I mean, I don't believe that I carry the virus in my body, and I've proven that to myself by getting tested, but my life has been changed forever by AIDS, and I feel that by the time the crisis is over, if it's ever over, and that I'm not sure about, everyone will be touched by it, directly affected by it."

Mara's answer to a question regarding her view of what the course of the disease will be in the United States and the world also reflects her concern for society. She told us:

> I think we're really in for it. . . . I don't have any hope at all. I used to, but I don't. I think that it's, it's here . . . widespread throughout the general population. . . . We're already seeing it moving heavily into the IV-drug-using populations of color in our urban areas. I think that the next really big hit is going to be

teenagers and people in their early twenties. Where you first saw it was in a population that, in general, had access to medical care, had access to knowledge and information about their bodies, and in general works, so the course of their illness is a little different. . . . I think that in the inner cities we're seeing a holocaust, and I don't . . . have any idea how, how it can be slowed down or stopped at this point, unless the government took on a real heavy campaign.

While Mara sees the effects of AIDS moving easily through society, she doesn't think that the virus is very contagious. She describes the disease as "just a virus." She said:

That's one of the things I say . . . like when people give value judgments about people with AIDS, I mean it's just a virus, the virus . . . happens to be transmitted by people having sex with each other, it's blood borne, so it's . . . specific in its transmission route. But that's all it is . . . just a virus. . . . I think it's very difficult to get it. . . . I mean I think it's impossible to get it unless you engage in unprotected sex, or share needles. . . . I worked with bare hands on bodies of people that were sick. . . . I've been splashed with vomit, I've been splashed with feces, I've been splashed with . . . saliva, tears, sweat, the whole bit, and if anybody was going to get AIDS from having contact, I would have it.

Mara sees her role as an activist as "something that is every day, all day. . . . I feel like I do it every day. But you know, that's what an activist does." She describes her role, telling us:

I don't talk in a prejudiced way about people with AIDS. Some of it is hands-on, direct care where I'm needed. . . . I also . . . have kind of a special challenge, being a heterosexual female, voices like mine aren't often heard. . . . I can go to a Baptist church and say I'm a married, heterosexual female, I'm thirty-one years old, and here's what I've been through. And they will let me in.

She also sees her role on what she calls a "microlevel" and describes her boss who "told AIDS jokes and made comments" when she first started working with him and now she describes him as "real sensitized to [AIDS], and real supportive and . . . share[s] with me . . . issues of his own, having to do with a brother who died of cancer at twenty." In spite of the horror she finds in the reality of AIDS, she also expresses hope about possibilities for new kinds of collective awareness.

Mara discusses her experiences with death by talking about caring for her friend and being with him when he died. Significantly, although she sees the effects of AIDS as "every nightmare that . . . could happen to the human body" and as a "holocaust," she describes her friend's death as "really an amazing and positive experience." She describes his death, telling us that:

> He could sort of talk. And then he died, but when he died it was really wild because our eyes were really glued to each other. It was like his eyes died. That was it. His heart kept beating for a while, but it was great. It was like catching the baby. . . . I felt different the next day. . . . I have felt different ever since. . . . He was such a strong, intelligent person. . . . He died in a really, in sort of a strong way, strange to say but really true. And so there are times, when that strength and that endurance and that ability, it doesn't seem like it's all gone, and some of it, I felt like I got a big hit of that power from him.

For Mara, death is not only about dying. Her concept of death is imbued with a concept of transcendence and involves ideas about strength and birth.

Logically following from her ideas about death, Mara does not see the body as a boundary. Mara's discussion of her relationships with her friends who have died illustrates her ideas about metaphysical relationships. One of Mara's concerns is about keeping the memory of her friends alive. She feels their presence in her life and makes a point of talking about them. In her discussion of her friend's death she told us that:

> You know . . . I try to keep him, he's the person that I knew the best that died of AIDS, but . . . there are other people too that I . . . try to remember as they go through all . . . this process I always do talk to them . . . those people won't be around to be uncles to my kids. . . . There's a huge crowd of people with whom I hung around in college, and that was real important . . . the whole intellectual development. . . . Everything else was leading up to that time. Those people were very important to me. But they're not there, and I can't pick up the phone and call "Scott" and tell him about the book I just read and I can't pick up the phone and call "Gary" and, you know, ask him a question about my hairstyle. I mean, you know, I can't, I can't do that, and so I feel like we have a responsibility—those of us who have been with these people, in their lives but also through their illness—not only to carry on the stories about them and . . . facts about their [lives]. They don't have children, or people sitting around the fire talking about them. But also the way they died was so unnecessary, and sometimes I really feel like their spirits are really noisy in my ear.

These stories illustrate that science literacy is much more than merely knowing some basic "facts" and simple concepts (Hazen and

Trefil 1991a:xix). Individuals use "facts" in very different ways and often make them work with their particular local circumstances as well as express their most overarching views of the world. Bill uses "facts" he has learned about the immune system to construct broader visions about the nature of social and political forms that relate to his political views and actions. Mara weaves "facts" she has learned about the immune system into profoundly moral and metaphysical views of the meaning of life and death. These views enable her to maintain both important relationships in her life and hope of a better society.

Both Bill and Mara relate disease to a state of war, a metaphor that is not uncommon in scientific texts, the popular media, or conversations with our informants. To Mara the horror of war expresses her shock over the effects of AIDS. For Bill, a metaphorical national system of authority in a defended nation-state provides a way to understand immunity as a system.

Using metaphor to conceptualize the body may affect our conceptualization of social situations. Some theorists emphasize the interactive nature of the elements paired in a metaphor, so that when Dante says "Hell is a lake of ice," the hearer extends the association of "hell" to a "lake of ice," thus transforming both elements of the metaphor (Hesse 1961; Black 1962:37). Through the use of a body/war metaphor we may not only be thinking of the body as naturally warlike, but we may also be thinking of the state of war as natural.

While Bill and Mara both make use of a metaphor that associates war with an immutable part of our biological nature (the immune system), at the same time they also suggest that AIDS is not only a biological but a social condition. Bill expressed his belief that a change in national priorities from the arms race to health would make prevention effective in the control of AIDS. To Mara the body/war metaphor not only speaks of a war within the body but of a social war being waged upon bodies. Within the contexts of their larger commentaries, Bill's and Mara's uses of the war/body metaphor signify much more than just ways to understand science.

In these stories people use scientific "facts" to create knowledge about a whole range of topics. For George and Phillip, to talk about the immune system is to talk above all about boundaries. Talk of boundaries appeared in another area of our research, participant-observation in a laboratory pursuing immunological research. In this research setting, the central tenet of contemporary immunology is the ability of the immune system to distinguish self from nonself. As our examples have just shown, when nonscientists talk about the immune system they also talk above all about boundaries. Those between the self and others—spatial, racial, gendered, class, and relational—and how these various boundaries can clash or be superimposed in complex ways. The concept of the boundary between self and nonself is a touchstone for broader social meanings. Since we find such concepts so commonly in interviews, it raises the question of whether the central role of boundaries in current research immunology is not culturally based in its inception.[3]

This position is explicit in Keller's view of his course. He intends much more than "facts" to be conveyed by his scientific account of the immune system. The students respond in kind. Certainly Mike did not take away "facts" about the immune system from his biology course, but rather the idea that in life one should "go into" and believe in one's self.

One might ask if implicit and local knowledge might be integrated into all areas of science, including those covered in overviews such as *Science Matters*. Suppose that the "facts" of science entail a whole worldview that is often left implicit. If it were made explicit, the way would be opened to begin a dialogue with people who might be living with different worldviews. Certainly such a dialogue would fit with Mara's vision of a better society. Quizzes from the experts which we, the public, fail, could give way to conversations about matters in which we are all experts in our own way.

Recognizing that worldviews are inscribed in scientific images would allow scientists to examine the implicit cultural assumptions that are used to explain scientific "facts." What else is being communicated when scientists describe the immune system as a national defense force or a T-cell as a quarterback?

The "facts" of science, important as they are, can never be more than tiny pieces of the maps that people devise to guide them in life. Even if we could all magically be made to "know" the answers to the science pop quiz, the process of our coming to know those "facts" would entail our embedding them in the diverse social, political, moral, and metaphysical meanings with which we construct our daily lives.

We began by asking how scientific literacy might be defined. We have shown that the people we interviewed are highly literate in the enormously complex social, political, moral, and metaphysical aspects of such matters as health or illness. If we were to turn now to a detailed look at Hazen and Trefil's notion of what it would take to be literate about these issues, we might be struck by the narrowly technocratic nature of the knowledge they regard as relevant. We might wonder whether that knowledge would really be sufficient to enable meaningful public discussion of AIDS, for example. This raises the question of whether it is actually scientists, rather than members of the public, that suffer from illiteracy on the range of considerations that need to be brought to bear on these complex human issues.

1996

Notes

This title is a slightly modified version of the title of the introductory chapter of Robert M. Hazen and James Trefil's *Science Matters: Achieving Scientific Literacy* (1991a).

1. An extended account of the fieldwork is contained in Martin (1994). All quotations are from observed situations or interviews.
2. We have used pseudonyms for the names of the people we interviewed as well as street names.
3. See G. E. R. Lloyd's *Revolutions of Wisdom* (1987) for how concepts from daily life were taken up into early science.

READING, REREADING, AND ANALYSIS

1. Throughout this essay, the people interviewed come up with various metaphors to describe their understanding of and attitude toward AIDS. List as many of those metaphors as you can find, noting page numbers as you go. What are some of the differences between the metaphors and what do those differences suggest about each person's attitude and perspective? What do the authors of this essay seem to mean by the term "metaphor"? Why are they so interested in the metaphors that various people use?

2. In the fourth paragraph, the authors attribute the term "local knowledge" to Clifford Geertz. Define "local knowledge" in your own words. How do the authors use it to challenge or complicate the idea that "scientific literacy" is "merely knowing some basic facts and simple concepts" (p. 341)? Working in groups, characterize elements in each of the four stories that could be called "local knowledge."

3. Choose one of the four stories as an example of different kinds of scientific literacy. How is one of the people in that story thinking about the immune system? What metaphors does that person use to help himself understand how the immune system works? How do the details of that person's life affect how he understands the immune system?

RESPONDING THROUGH WRITING: BUILDING AN INTERPRETATION

4. Write an essay in which you describe your own view of the immune system and compare it with the four views presented here. Which metaphors help you to make sense of the immune system and which would you disagree with? In what ways do the four case studies in the article help you to frame your own ideas? How has reading this article affected your way of thinking about the immune system?

5. How might a scientist respond to the authors' conclusion that scientists and not the public might "suffer from illiteracy on the range of considerations that need to be brought to bear on these complex human issues" (p. 343)? Write a paper in which you explore the relationship between scientific facts and local knowledge. What does it mean to "know" something? Is knowledge the same for everyone?

GOING FURTHER: LEARNING FROM OTHER SOURCES

6. Find a website or a book or magazine that discusses HIV/AIDS in some detail. (Hint: On the Internet, try "The Megasite Project: A Megasite Comparing Health Information Megasites and Search Engines," <http://henry.ugl.lib.umich.edu/megasite/toc.html>, for evaluations and links to the best health sites.) Take note of all the metaphorical language you see. (Keep in mind that words such as "defenses," "attack," and "shield" are all examples of metaphorical language.) What kinds of stories about the disease does the language suggest? Compare your examples with one of the four stories in this essay.

APPLYING WHAT YOU'VE LEARNED

7. Examine the descriptions of how scientists work in Thomas Kuhn's "The Historical Structure of Scientific Discovery" (p. 289). How might Kuhn define "scientific literacy"? Write a paper in which you explore how Kuhn might respond to the argument presented by Martin and her coauthors.

8. Write an essay analyzing how Martin's interviewees make sense of scientific information in comparison with the various responses to the Vietnam Veterans Memorial described by Marita Sturken in "The Wall, The Screen and the Image." What role does "local knowledge" play in each case? How important are metaphors in shaping people's attitudes?

9. In "The Triumph of Tinkering," Sherry Turkle describes a comparable situation in which people's individual ways of understanding and attitudes affect how they make sense of scientific material. What might Turkle learn from Martin and her coauthors and vice versa? Write a paper in which you test the extent to which the lessons from one essay could be usefully applied to the other. To what extent have computer programmers used local knowledge to reimagine and reshape their field, for example? In what ways might Turkle's bricolage method be applied to the problem of scientific literacy raised by Martin?

Scott McCloud

Scott McCloud (b. 1960) is a comic book writer and artist who now runs <http://www. scottmccloud.com>, a website that serves as the launchpad for his online comics experiments. "Setting the Record Straight" is the first chapter of his book *Understanding Comics* (1993). He has now published a second book, *Reinventing Comics* (2000).

> You can read more about Scott McCloud and other contemporary comic book artists at <http://www.scottmccloud.com/links/links. html>.

WHAT DO YOU KNOW? WHAT DO YOU EXPECT TO DISCOVER?

Before reading the essay, take a moment to consider the following questions.

1. List any comics you remember reading or that you still read. Note what kinds of things you have learned from reading comics.

2. Generate a quick list of all the qualities you associate with art such as painting and literature. Create a second list of all the qualities you associate with comics.

Setting the Record Straight

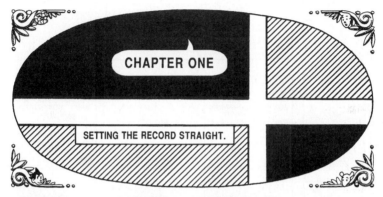

THE ARTFORM--THE *MEDIUM*--KNOWN AS COMICS IS A *VESSEL* WHICH CAN HOLD ANY *NUMBER* OF *IDEAS* AND *IMAGES*.

COMICS
Writers
ARTISTS
Trends
GENRES
STYLES
Subject matter
THEMES

THE *"CONTENT"* OF THOSE IMAGES AND IDEAS IS, OF COURSE, UP TO *CREATORS*, AND WE ALL HAVE DIFFERENT *TASTES*.

GLUG
GLUG

PTUI!!!

GAAK
WHEEEEZ
KAF! KAF!
GLUGH-GGH...

ahem

THE *TRICK* IS TO NEVER MISTAKE THE *MESSAGE*--

--FOR THE *MESSENGER*.

COMICS

AT ONE TIME OR ANOTHER VIRTUALLY *ALL* THE GREAT MEDIA HAVE RECEIVED *CRITICAL EXAMINATION*, IN AND OF *THEMSELVES*.

WRITTEN WORD
MUSIC
VIDEO
THEATRE
VISUAL ART
FILM

BUT FOR *COMICS*, THIS ATTENTION HAS BEEN *RARE*. *

LET'S SEE IF WE CAN HELP *RECTIFY* THE SITUATION.

*EISNER'S OWN *COMICS AND SEQUENTIAL ART* BEING A HAPPY EXCEPTION.

*JUXTAPOSED= ADJACENT, SIDE-BY-SIDE.
GREAT ART SCHOOL WORD.

* OR "OCELOT'S CLAW" DEPENDING ON WHOSE BOOK YOU READ.
THIS SEQUENCE IS BASED ON A READING BY MEXICAN HISTORIAN
AND ARCHAEOLOGIST ALFONSO CASO.

FIRST, WE SEPARATE WORDS FROM *PICTURES*.

8-DEER "TIGER'S CLAW"

(A NAME)

11 HOUSE 12 MONKEY
(A DATE)

GOD XIPE'S BUNDLE

(GLYPH FOR PLACE WHOSE NAME WE DON'T KNOW.)

THEN *REVERSE* IT AND STRAIGHTEN IT OUT (THE ORIGINAL READ RIGHT-TO-LEFT AND *ZIGZAGGED*.) AND *BEGIN*:

THE YEAR: *1049 AD*
THE DATE: *MAY 3* *
THE PLACE: *HERE!*

OUR HERO, *8-DEER "TIGER'S CLAW,"* CONQUERS THE PLACE AND CAPTURES THE *9-YEAR-OLD PRINCE, 4-WIND "SERPENT OF FIRE."*

8-DEER ALSO CAPTURES THE PRINCE'S OLDER BROTHERS, *10-DOG "EAGLE COPAL BURNING"* AND *6-HOUSE "ROW OF FLINT KNIVES"* AND PUTS 'EM ON ICE.

(I'M TAKING THE TRANSLATOR'S WORD ON THIS ONE.)

THE FOLLOWING YEAR, *8-DEER* AND (PROBABLY) HIS BROTHER, DISGUISED AS *TIGERS*, ENGAGE IN *SACRIFICIAL GLADITORIAL COMBAT* WITH THE PRINCE, *10-DOG*, AND ANOTHER WARRIOR DISGUISED AS *DEATH*.

8-DEER KILLS THE OTHER PRINCE, *6-HOUSE "ROW OF FLINT KNIVES"* EIGHT DAYS LATER.

*WE KNOW THE YEAR; I'M JUST *GUESSING* AT THE DATE REPRESENTED BY "12 MONKEY"

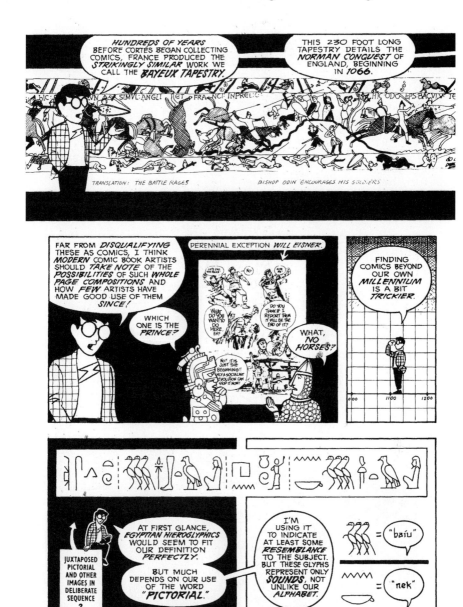

READING *LEFT TO RIGHT* WE SEE THE *EVENTS* OF THE CONQUEST, IN *DELIBERATE CHRONOLOGICAL ORDER* UNFOLD BEFORE OUR VERY *EYES*.

AS WITH THE *MEXICAN CODEX*, THERE ARE NO *PANEL BORDERS* PER SE, BUT THERE ARE CLEAR DIVISIONS OF SCENE BY *SUBJECT MATTER*.

DUKE WILLIAM REMOVES HIS HELMET TO RALLY HIS SOLDIERS   HAROLD'S ARMY IS CUT TO PIECES

THUS, THEIR *REAL* DESCENDENT IS *THE WRITTEN WORD* AND NOT COMICS.

"ses tu baíu abta, hennu-nek baíu amenta"

"FOLLOW THEE, THE SOULS OF THE EAST. PRAISE THEE, THE SOULS OF THE WEST."

EGYPTIAN *PAINTING* IS *ANOTHER MATTER*. SOME, LIKE THIS, MAY *SEEM* TO BE CONCERNED WITH SEQUENCE, BUT ARE ACTUALLY SHOWING TWO DIFFERENT LOCATIONS, EVENTS AND CASTS, GROUPED ONLY BY *SUBJECT*.

I HAD BEEN TRYING TO FIND *SEQUENCE* IN EGYPTIAN PAINTINGS FOR *YEARS* WHEN I BEGAN THIS BOOK AND WAS READY TO CALL IT QUITS--

--UNTIL I DISCOVERED THAT THE BOOKS I HAD BEEN USING AS REFERENCE--

--HAD ONLY BEEN SHOWING ME *PART* OF THE PICTURE!

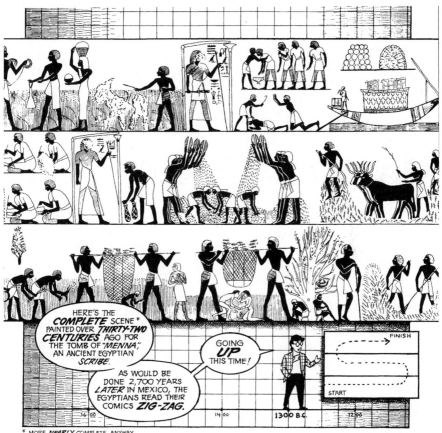

HERE'S THE **COMPLETE** SCENE * PAINTED OVER **THIRTY-TWO CENTURIES** AGO FOR THE TOMB OF *"MENNA,"* AN ANCIENT EGYPTIAN *SCRIBE.*

AS WOULD BE DONE 2,700 YEARS *LATER* IN MEXICO, THE EGYPTIANS READ THEIR COMICS **ZIG-ZAG.**

GOING **UP** THIS TIME!

FINISH
START

16 00   14 00   13 00 B.C.   12 00

* MORE *NEARLY* COMPLETE, ANYWAY.

STARTING AT THE **LOWER LEFT,** WE SEE THREE WORKERS REAPING WHEAT WITH THEIR SICKLES--

PAINTING TRACED FOR BLACK AND WHITE REPRODUCTION.

-- THEN CARRYING IT IN **BASKETS** TO A **THRESHING** LOCATION. (IN THE BACKGROUND TWO GIRLS FIGHT OVER BITS OF WHEAT LEFT BEHIND, AS TWO WORKERS SIT UNDER A TREE, ONE SLEEPING, ONE PLAYING THE *FLUTE!*)

THE SHEAVES ARE THEN *RAKED OUT* INTO A *THICK CARPET OF WHEAT.*

THEN OXEN TREAD *KERNELS* OUT OF THE HUSKS.

NEXT, PEASANTS SEPARATE THE WHEAT FROM THE CHAFF.

OLD MENNA HIMSELF LOOKS ON-- *

--AS LOYAL SCRIBES RECORD THE YIELD ON THEIR TABLETS.

NOW AN OFFICIAL USES A MEASURING ROPE TO *SURVEY THE LAND* AND DECIDE HOW MUCH WHEAT IS OWED IN *TAXES.*

AND AS MENNA WATCHES, FARMERS *LATE* IN PAYING THEIR TAXES ARE *BEATEN.*

I'LL *GLADLY ADMIT* THAT I HAVE *NO IDEA* WHERE OR *WHEN* COMICS ORIGINATED. LET *OTHERS* WRESTLE WITH *THAT* ONE.

? B.C.   ? A.D.

I'VE ONLY SCRATCHED THE *SURFACE* IN THIS CHAPTER... *TRAJAN'S COLUMN, GREEK PAINTING, JAPANESE SCROLLS...* ALL THESE HAVE BEEN SUGGESTED AND ALL SHOULD BE EXPLORED.

BUT THERE IS *ONE* EVENT WHICH LOOMS AS LARGE IN *COMICS* HISTORY AS IT DOES IN THE HISTORY OF THE *WRITTEN WORD.*

THE INVENTION OF PRINTING.

* FACE GOUGED OUT BY FUTURE GENERATIONS OF LEADERS

ART RESTORED FOR CLARITY -- OTHERWISE UNCHANGED.

WITH THE INVENTION OF PRINTING,* THE ART-FORM WHICH HAD BEEN A DIVERSION OF THE *RICH* AND *POWERFUL* NOW COULD BE ENJOYED BY *EVERYONE!*

POPULAR TASTES HAVEN'T *CHANGED* MUCH IN *FIVE CENTURIES.* CHECK OUT *"THE TORTURES OF SAINT ERASMUS,"* CIRCA 1460. WORD HAS IT THIS GUY WAS A VERY POPULAR CHARACTER.

THE SOPHISTICATION OF THE PICTURE-STORY DID *GROW,* HOWEVER, REACHING GREAT HEIGHTS IN THE NIMBLE HANDS OF *WILLIAM HOGARTH.*

HERE IS A TINY PIECE (ABOUT *ONE TWENTIETH*) OF THE SECOND PLATE FROM HOGARTH'S SIX-PLATE PICTURE-STORY *"A HARLOT'S PROGRESS,"* PUBLISHED IN 1731.

DESPITE THE LOW *"PANEL-COUNT,"* THESE LUSH, RENDERED PICTURES TELL A STORY RICH IN DETAIL AND MOTIVATED BY STRONG SOCIAL CONCERNS.

* MAYBE I SHOULDN'T SAY "INVENT". EUROPEANS WERE A BIT LATE IN DISCOVERING PRINTING.

HOGARTH'S STORIES WERE FIRST EXHIBITED AS A SERIES OF *PAINTINGS* AND LATER SOLD AS A PORTFOLIO OF *ENGRAVINGS.*

BOTH THE PAINTINGS AND ENGRAVINGS WERE DESIGNED TO BE VIEWED *SIDE-BY-SIDE --IN SEQUENCE!*

"A HARLOT'S PROGRESS" AND ITS SEQUEL *"A RAKE'S PROGRESS"* PROVED SO POPULAR, NEW *COPYRIGHT LAWS* WERE CREATED TO PROTECT THIS NEW FORM.

GRRR!!

THE FATHER OF THE *MODERN* COMIC IN MANY WAYS IS *RODOLPHE TÖPFFER*, WHOSE LIGHT SATIRIC PICTURE STORIES, STARTING IN THE MID-1800's, EMPLOYED *CARTOONING* AND *PANEL BORDERS*, AND FEATURED THE FIRST INTERDEPENDENT COMBINATION OF *WORDS* AND *PICTURES* SEEN IN EUROPE.

[TRANSLATION BY E. WIESE.]

UNFORTUNATELY, TÖPFFER HIMSELF FAILED TO GRASP AT FIRST THE FULL POTENTIAL OF HIS INVENTION, SEEING IT AS A MERE *DIVERSION,* A SIMPLE *HOBBY...*

"IF FOR THE FUTURE, HE [TÖPFFER] WOULD CHOOSE A LESS FRIVOLOUS SUBJECT AND RESTRICT HIMSELF A LITTLE, HE WOULD PRODUCE THINGS BEYOND ALL CONCEPTION."
-Goethe

EVEN SO, TÖPFFER'S CONTRIBUTION TO THE *UNDERSTANDING* OF COMICS IS CONSIDERABLE, IF ONLY FOR HIS REALIZATION THAT HE WHO WAS NEITHER ARTIST NOR WRITER--

-- HAD CREATED AND MASTERED A FORM WHICH WAS AT ONCE *BOTH* AND *NEITHER.*

A LANGUAGE ALL ITS OWN.

BRITISH CARICATURE MAGAZINES KEPT THE TRADITIONS ALIVE AND AS THE *20TH* CENTURY DREW NEAR, THE COMICS WE *CALL* COMICS BEGAN TO APPEAR AND EVENTUALLY TO *THRIVE* IN A STEADY STREAM OF WAKING DREAMS THAT HAS YET TO ABATE.

| 1870 | 1880 | 1890 | 1900 | 1910 | 1920 | 1930 | 1940 |

BUT EVEN IN *THIS* CENTURY, OUR DEFINITION CAN HELP TO ILLUMINATE THE WORKS OF SOME UNSUNG HEROES.

JUXTAPOSED PICTORIAL AND OTHER IMAGES IN DELIBERATE SEQUENCE

SOME OF THE MOST *INSPIRED* AND *INNOVATIVE* COMICS OF OUR CENTURY HAVE NEVER RECEIVED RECOGNITION *AS* COMICS, NOT SO MUCH *IN SPITE* OF THEIR SUPERIOR QUALITIES AS *BECAUSE* OF THEM.

FOR MUCH OF THIS CENTURY, THE WORD "COMICS" HAS HAD SUCH *NEGATIVE CONNOTATIONS* THAT MANY OF COMICS' MOST *DEVOTED PRACTITIONERS* HAVE PREFERRED TO BE KNOWN AS *"ILLUSTRATORS," "COMMERCIAL ARTISTS"* OR, AT BEST, *"CARTOONISTS"!*

TANTRUM

Jules Feiffer

Shel Silverstein

The Snowman

RAYMOND BRIGGS

MILT GROSS

HEART OF

AND SO, COMICS' LOW SELF-ESTEEM IS *SELF-PERPETUATING!* THE HISTORICAL PERSPECTIVE NECESSARY TO *COUNTERACT* COMICS' NEGATIVE IMAGE IS OBSCURED *BY* THAT NEGATIVITY.

WOODCUT ARTIST *LYND WARD* IS ONE SUCH *MISSING LINK.* WARD'S SILENT *"WOODCUT NOVELS"* ARE POWERFUL MODERN FABLES, NOW *PRAISED* BY COMICS ARTISTS, BUT SELDOM RECOGNIZED *AS* COMICS.

FROM WARD'S *GOD'S MAN,* 1929

ARTISTS LIKE WARD AND BELGIAN *FRANS MASEREEL* SAID MUCH THROUGH THEIR WOODCUTS ABOUT THE POTENTIAL OF COMICS, BUT FEW IN THE COMICS COMMUNITY OF THE DAY COULD *GET THE MESSAGE.*

THEIR *DEFINITION* OF COMICS, *THEN AS NOW,* WAS SIMPLY TOO *NARROW* TO INCLUDE SUCH WORK.

FROM FRANK MASEREEL'S *PASSIONATE JOURNEY,* 1919.

QUITE A *DIFFERENT* CASE IS MAX ERNST'S SURREAL *"COLLAGE NOVEL," A WEEK OF KINDNESS.*

THIS 182 PLATE SEQUENCE OF COLLAGES IS WIDELY CONSIDERED A *MASTERPIECE* OF *20TH CENTURY ART,* BUT NO ART HISTORY TEACHER WOULD *DREAM* OF CALLING IT *"COMICS"!*

YET, DESPITE THE LACK OF A *CONVENTIONAL STORY,* THERE IS NO MISTAKING THE CENTRAL ROLE WHICH *SEQUENCE* PLAYS IN THE WORK. ERNST DOESN'T WANT YOU TO *BROWSE* THE THING, HE WANTS YOU TO *READ* IT!

IF WE DON'T EXCLUDE *PHOTOGRAPHY* FROM OUR DEFINITION, THEN HALF OF *AMERICA* HAS BEEN IN COMICS AT ONE TIME OR ANOTHER.

IN *SOME* COUNTRIES, PHOTO-COMICS ARE, IN FACT, QUITE *POPULAR.*

MEANWHILE, *PICTURES IN SEQUENCE* ARE FINALLY BEING RECOGNIZED AS THE EXCELLENT *COMMUNICATION TOOL* THAT THEY ARE, BUT *STILL* NOBODY REFERS TO THEM AS *COMICS!* *"DIAGRAMS"* SOUNDS MORE *DIGNIFIED,* I SUPPOSE.

1 **2** **3** **4**

FROM *STAINED GLASS WINDOWS* SHOWING BIBLICAL SCENES IN ORDER TO *MONET'S SERIES PAINTINGS,* TO YOUR *CAR OWNER'S MANUAL,* COMICS TURN UP *ALL OVER* WHEN *SEQUENTIAL ART* IS EMPLOYED AS A DEFINITION.

THANKS TO MATT FEAZELL FOR THE SUGGESTIONS.

com·ics (kom'iks)**n.** plural in form, used with a singular verb. **1.** Juxtaposed pictorial and other images in deliberate sequence, intended to convey information and/or to produce an aesthetic response in the viewer.

FOR ALL THE DOORS THAT OUR DEFINITION *OPENS,* THERE IS ONE WHICH IT *CLOSES.*

SINGLE PANELS LIKE *THIS* ONE ARE OFTEN *LUMPED IN* WITH COMICS, YET THERE'S NO SUCH THING AS A SEQUENCE OF *ONE!*

"Mommy, why ain't I Juxtaposed?"

SUCH SINGLE PANELS MIGHT BE CLASSIFIED AS *"COMIC ART"* IN THE SENSE THAT THEY DERIVE PART OF THEIR *VISUAL VOCABULARY* FROM COMICS--

BUT I SAY THEY'RE NO MORE *COMICS* THAN THIS STILL OF *HUMPHREY BOGART* IS *FILM!*

HI, BOGEY.

THEY ARE *CARTOONS*, AS AM *I*, AND THERE IS A *LONG-STANDING RELATIONSHIP* BETWEEN COMICS AND CARTOONS.

-- BUT THEY ARE NOT THE SAME THING! ONE IS AN APPROACH TO *PICTURE-MAKING* -- A *STYLE*, IF YOU LIKE -- WHILE THE OTHER IS A *MEDIUM* WHICH OFTEN *EMPLOYS* THAT APPROACH.

HEY!

MORE ON THIS *LATER*.

THIS SAME *SINGLE PANEL* MIGHT ALSO BE LABELLED COMICS FOR ITS JUXTAPOSITION OF *WORDS* AND PICTURES.

"Mommy, why ain't Juxtaposed?!"

A GREAT MAJORITY OF MODERN COMICS *DO* FEATURE WORDS AND PICTURES IN COMBINATION AND IT'S A SUBJECT WORTHY OF STUDY, BUT WHEN USED AS A *DEFINITION* FOR COMICS, I'VE FOUND IT TO BE A LITTLE TOO *RESTRICTIVE* FOR MY TASTE.

OF COURSE, IF ANYONE WANTS TO WRITE A BOOK TAKING THE *OPPOSITE* VIEW, YOU CAN BET I'LL BE THE FIRST IN LINE TO *BUY* A COPY!

IF COMICS' SPECTACULARLY VARIED *PAST* IS ANY INDICATION, COMICS' *FUTURE* WILL BE VIRTUALLY *IMPOSSIBLE* TO PREDICT USING THE STANDARDS OF THE *PRESENT*.

BUT OUR DEFINITION CAN OFFER US SOME *CLUES*.

1980   1990   2000   2010   2020   2030   2040

AND *THIS* TIME, THE SECRET IS NOT IN WHAT THE DEFINITION *SAYS* BUT IN WHAT IT *DOESN'T* SAY!

SEQUENTIAL ART

THOSE OF YOU WHO *MAKE* COMICS FOR A LIVING -- OR WOULD *LIKE* TO, SOMEDAY--PROBABLY KNOW THAT KEEPING UP WITH ALL THE *ADVANCES* IN TODAY'S COMICS IS A *FULL-TIME JOB.*

THERE ARE SO MANY COMICS IN PRINT TODAY THAT IT WOULD TAKE AN *ARMY* OF READERS TO STUDY THEM ALL.

HOWEVER MUCH WE MAY TRY TO *UNDERSTAND* THE WORLD OF COMICS AROUND US, A *PART* OF THAT WORLD WILL ALWAYS LIE IN SHADOW-- A *MYSTERY.*

I'LL DO MY *BEST* IN THE FOLLOWING CHAPTERS TO *SHED LIGHT* ON THAT UNSEEN SIDE, BUT AS WE FOCUS ON THE WORLD OF COMICS *AS IT IS,* IT SHOULD BE KEPT IN MIND AT *ALL* TIMES THAT THIS WORLD IS ONLY *ONE--*

--OF MANY *POSSIBLE* WORLDS!

OUR ATTEMPTS TO *DEFINE* COMICS ARE AN *ON-GOING PROCESS* WHICH WON'T END ANYTIME SOON.

A *NEW* GENERATION WILL NO DOUBT *REJECT* WHATEVER THIS ONE FINALLY DECIDES TO ACCEPT AND TRY ONCE MORE TO *RE-INVENT COMICS.*

AND SO THEY SHOULD.

HERE'S TO THE *GREAT DEBATE!*

1993

READING, REREADING, AND ANALYSIS

1. Find several different places where McCloud defines comics. List the different definitions and bring them to class.

2. Write a paragraph analyzing one or more of the frames of this comic strip. What does McCloud do with images that makes this essay different from one that is conventionally written? What are some particular ways in which the images add to his meaning?

3. Bring a "sequence of images" to class that seems to support or challenge traditional ideas about comics. Work in groups to test each person's sequence using McCloud's definition.

4. In a group, create an outline of McCloud's essay in which you list his major points. How does he create transitions from one point to the next? What is the comic book equivalent of a paragraph break?

RESPONDING THROUGH WRITING

5. At the beginning of this essay, McCloud cites the definition of comics as "crude, poorly-drawn, semiliterate, cheap, disposable kiddie fare" (p. 348). Write a two-page paper analyzing the methods he uses to move us beyond that definition. Which of his points do you find persuasive and which do you find unconvincing? Why?

6. Write an essay in which you use McCloud's definition of comics to test a sequence of images that interests you. Is the sequence a comic by his definition? How does the sequence compare with some of the images in McCloud's essay? What future does McCloud predict for comics, and how does that measure up to the future you would predict based on the sequence you have analyzed?

GOING FURTHER: LEARNING FROM OTHER SOURCES

7. In a reference database, such as Academic Search Elite, that includes a range of scholarly sources, do a search using the term "comics." Then do a second search on "comics" using a popular search engine such as Google or Yahoo. What are some of the differences in the results of the two searches? Based on the results of your two searches, what images, terms, and ideas do people seem to associate with comics? Make a list of those associations and bring them to class.

APPLYING WHAT YOU'VE LEARNED

8. Both McCloud and Annie Dillard are trying to illustrate a new way of seeing their subject matter. Write an essay comparing the methods they use to direct our attention to the subject matter in a new way, or to help us understand the process of seeing in a new way. Which methods do you find most successful and why? How would you characterize both writers' purposes overall? What do they most want their essays to accomplish? What arguments are they making?

9. Use ideas and examples from Marita Sturken, Arlie Russell Hochschild, and McCloud to explore how the "artform," the "medium," the ways in which ideas and images are presented—the "messenger"—can affect the content of those ideas and images—the "message" (p. 351). Write an essay in which you examine the impact of the medium or the artform on the message or content that is communicated; use two or more concrete examples.

ERIN McGRAW

Erin McGraw (b. 1957) is Associate Professor of English at Ohio State University, where she teaches creative writing and American fiction. McGraw has won awards for her teaching and for her writing. She is the author of three novels, *The Baby Tree* (2002) *Bodies at Sea* (1989), and *Lies of the Saints* (1996), and has published short stories and essays. McGraw claims to have become a writer to avoid working in the field of financial management. "Bad Eyes" was first published in the *Gettysburg Review.*

> **To learn more about blindness, visit the home page of A Blind Net at <http://www.blind.net/blindind.htm>.**

WHAT DO YOU KNOW? WHAT DO YOU EXPECT TO DISCOVER?

Before reading the essay, take a moment to consider the following questions.

1. What topics does McGraw's biography suggest she is interested in? What do you know about those topics? Knowledge can come from personal experience, stories you've heard, other classes you've taken, or other reading you've done.

2. Think about someone you know with very poor eyesight. How does one function "normally" if one has trouble seeing? What ordinary, everyday tasks that most people take for granted would pose great difficulty for someone with poor vision or, to quote McGraw's title, "bad eyes"?

3. When we read, how and why might we have, metaphorically, "bad eyes"?

✺

Bad Eyes

The subject veers almost uncontrollably toward metaphor, but I mean to take it literally: I have unusually poor vision, minus thirteen hundred diopters and still losing ground, ordinary progressive myopia that never stopped progressing. In me, the process by which light is supposed to focus images at the back of the eye has gone berserk, and the point of focus shifts ever closer to the front, like the projection of a movie falling short of its screen.

My eyeballs aren't round, like marbles or baseballs, but are oblong, like little footballs. This awkward shape puts so much strain on the retinas that a rip has developed in my left one, where the tissue gave out like exhausted cloth. Now my ophthalmologist carefully includes a retina evaluation at annual checks, and I have a list of warning signs that would indicate a significant rupture: sudden, flashing lights; floaters showering into my vision like rain.

Mostly, though, nothing about my vision is so fraught or dramatic. I am shortsighted, is all, mope-eyed, gravel-blind, blind-buck and Davy; a squinter, the sort who taps her companions at plays and baseball games: "What just happened? I missed that." I live in a world where objects collapse into haze. Beyond the narrow realm that my contact lenses permit me to see clearly, I navigate by memory and assumption.

Here are some of the things I can't see, even with my contacts in: a baseball in play, birds in trees, numbers and subtitles on TV, roads at night, constellations, anything by candlelight, street signs, faces of people in cars, faces of people twenty feet away. One of my consistent embarrassments comes from snubbing friends who stood more than a shadow's length from me, friends I didn't even nod to because I couldn't tell who they were. So I've adopted a genial half-smile that I wear when I walk around my neighborhood or down the corridors of the department where I work. I have the reputation of being a very friendly person.

Here are some of the things I can find when I narrow my eyes and look: tiny new weeds in the front garden, fleas scurrying across my dog's belly, gray hairs. My mother, watching me struggle before the bathroom mirror for ten minutes while I spray and brush and bobby-pin to hide the worst of the gray, comments, "I don't know why you bother. You don't have much. No one even sees it."

"I see it every time I look in the mirror."

"Well, you see what you're looking for."

She's told me this all my life. I roll my eyes and keep working the bobby pins.

The glasses I remember best and loved most arrived when I was eight years old. They were my second pair; the first were brown with wings at the corners, the eyeglass equivalent to orthopedic shoes. I was delighted when the doctor announced that they needed to be replaced.

My parents didn't share my delight—only a year had passed since we had gotten that first pair. For six months, unconsciously, I had been moving books closer to my face and inching nearer the TV. Nothing was said about it. I think my parents assumed that I must have been aware of a development so obvious to them, but I was a dreamy, preoccupied child and hadn't noticed that the edges of illustrations in my books were no longer crisp. When I was moved to the front row of my classroom, it never occurred to me to ponder why.

I was pleased to be there, though, and preened in my new glasses. Sleek cat eyes, the white plastic frames featuring jaunty red stripes, they were 1965's cutting edge. I often took them off to admire them. When my correction needed to be stepped up again, I insisted on using the same frames, even though by then I had to keep the glasses on all the time, and could only take pleasure in the candy-cane stripes if I happened to pass a window. In my school pictures for three years running I wore these same glasses. By the third year they were clearly too small for my face, and my eyes practically disappeared behind the thick glass.

Every six months my mother took me to the eye doctor, and nearly every visit meant new, slightly heavier lenses. At first I resented only the hours spent in the waiting room, where I was often the only child, but gradually I began to dread the examination itself, the stinging dilation drops and my frustrating attempts to read the eye chart. While I struggled to focus on letters that seemed to slip and buckle on the far wall, fear bloomed in my stomach.

"T," I would begin rashly, remembering that much from the visit before, but then I strained to make out the next wobbly shape. "U, maybe, or C. It could be O." Not bothering to comment, the doctor tilted back my chair, pulled around one of the clicking, finicky machines, and began the measurements for the next set of lenses. Both he and I ignored my quick, anxious breathing and dry mouth, but when he was finished I burst out of the office as if I were making a jail break.

Back in the world, my panic dropped away, and my worsening vision seemed nothing more than an inconvenience. Perhaps if I had been an outdoorsy kind of child, a girl who noticed leaves or clouds or insect life, I might have grieved the first time I was unable to detect a distant, sly animal. But I wasn't especially fond of the natural world, which was too hot or too cold and full of things that made me itch. The steady loss of detail—my inability first to make out the petals of a flower, and before long to discern the flower at all without glasses to help me—felt unimportant. I jammed on my glasses first thing in the morning, took them off after turning out my light at night, now and then remembered to clean them. Easy enough.

Only occasionally did I get the sense that I was hampered. The sisters at my Catholic school made me take my glasses off before games at recess, a sensible precaution; I was a terrible athlete and could be relied on to stop dead in front of almost any moving object. So I was hit in the face by kickballs, tetherballs, basketballs, and once, memorably, by a softball bat that caught me square on the cheek. The sister blew her whistle and bustled toward me, scolding. Why hadn't I gotten out of the way?

I didn't cry when the bat hit me, although it hurt, but her chiding made my lips start to quiver. I hadn't *seen* it, I protested. All of a sudden something had hit my face; the blow came out of nowhere.

It came out of the batter's box, the sister pointed out. *You shouldn't have been standing so close. You know you can't see well, so you have to be cautious.*

She handed me my glasses and I walked off—sulkily, coddling my sense of injustice—to the nurse's office. The nurse said I'd suffered only a bruise, but I couldn't easily dismiss the incident. Up to that point, no one had told me, *You are at risk, you must take precautions.*

Back at home, I took my glasses off and looked at the house across the street. I recognized its shape and details, but that hardly required vision. I saw the house every day, and could have drawn from memory its long, flat roof and the row of bunkerlike windows.

So I walked up the street, turned onto a cul-de-sac that I didn't know well, and took off my glasses again. Instantly, the turquoise stucco bungalow before me smeared into a vague blue box. I could make out windows, but couldn't tell if the curtains were open or closed; could find the front door but not the mail slot; the wrought-iron handrail but not the steps it accompanied.

A shout erupted and I spun around, shoving my glasses back on to find that the shout had nothing to do with me: a couple of boys were playing catch at the top of the street. Nevertheless, my heart was whapping now, hurting me. I was foolish to stand so publicly, blinking and helpless, right in the middle of the sidewalk. Anyone could have sneaked up, knocked me to the ground, and taken my wallet, if I had had a wallet.

I thought of comic-strip blind beggars on city streets, their canes kicked away, their tin cups stolen. For the first time, my bad eyes took on meaning: they were an invitation to bullies, and the fact that no one had yet taken my glasses and knocked me down was just dumb luck. Pressing my glasses in place, I ran home. This new notion of myself seized my imagination, and I fell asleep for several nights imagining scenarios in which I was unfairly set upon, a lamb before wolves. I saw myself suffering nobly and being remembered reverently.

And then I forgot about my experiment in front of the blue house. I continued to play games without glasses at school, continued to get smacked with kickballs, continued not to be accosted by glasses-snatching bullies. Finally tired of my red-and-white striped glasses, I zipped through half a dozen new pairs, trying out granny glasses in three different shapes, including ones with octagonal lenses that made me look unnervingly like John Lennon.

By the time I was entering junior high, though, I was tired of wearing glasses. More precisely, I was tired of my bespectacled reflection, how glasses made my eyes look tiny and dim, my nose like a tremendous land mass. So I initiated a campaign to get contact lenses, which were just becoming widely available, although not usually for twelve-year-olds. To my astonishment, my cautious, conservative ophthalmologist immediately agreed.

"Contacts help sometimes, with myopia like this," he explained to my skeptical mother. "The theory is that the contact flattens the lens of the eye. It can slow down the disease's progress." I was so elated that I hardly flinched when he called what I had a "disease," a word we usually avoided. And so, a month later, we began a regime that I was in no way ready for.

These were the days when the only contact lenses were made of inflexible plastic, thick by today's standards, hard, immovable foreign bodies that had to be introduced to the protesting eyes at gradual intervals. The first day, the wearer put them in for two hours, then took them out for an hour of recovery, then in again, out, in, out. The second day, three hours.

The optometrist guided my shaking hand, showing me how to slip the lens directly in place. Before I could even look up, I had blinked the contact out; it bounced off the counter beneath us and hit the floor. My mother hissed. The optometrist ordered me not to move; he gently dropped to his knees and patted the linoleum until he found the lens and laboriously cleaned it again.

I blinked the lenses out twice more before he could get them centered on my corneas. Then, tentatively, he stepped back and asked, "How's that?" I was too stunned to answer. For all the talk about wearing schedules and tolerance, no one had told me that contact lenses would *hurt*. Each eye felt as though a hair had been coiled precisely on top of it, and hot, outraged tears poured out. Although the optometrist kept telling me to look up so that he could take measurements, I couldn't keep my eyes from snapping shut. Light was like a blade.

"It always takes a little while," he was telling my mother, "but she'll get used to them. Just take it easy. Don't let her overdo."

No fear of that. I was already frantic to take the lenses back out again, and the remaining hour and forty-five minutes of my first wearing period seemed interminable, an eon of torment. My mother had to lead me back out to the car by the hand; even with the sunglasses the optometrist had given me, I had to close my eyes. Light bouncing off of car windows and storefronts was searing.

For the next month, all I could think about was my eyes. As the optometrist had promised, they began to accommodate to the contacts, but accommodation wasn't comfort. My eyes stung, lightly, all the time. Every blink set the lenses shifting, and that slight movement felt as if it were grinding a ridge into the moist corneal tissue. The irritation made me blink again, shifting the contacts some more.

I spent the summer steeped in resentment. I refused invitations to parties and shopping trips because I had to put my contacts in and take them out, in and out, none of which would have happened if I had had reasonable eyes to begin with. Even after I built up some expertise and didn't have to spend ten minutes tugging the corners of my eyes raw to dislodge the lenses, the contacts kept falling out on their own, vaulting away from my eyes, forcing me to freeze in mid-step. With slow, scared care I would sink to my knees and begin patting first my clothes, then the ground around me, feeling for a tiny, mean-spirited disk.

For the first year I spent a lot of time apologizing about lost lenses, ones I rinsed down the drain or cracked, one that the dog snuffled up, and ones that simply shot out of my eyes and disappeared. My parents were understandably unhappy, and I became familiar with the dread that curled through me as soon as I felt one of the lenses begin to shimmy, the indicator that it would soon try for a getaway.

But that dread, at least, was practical. Cresting through me like high tide was the other dread, the one I had forgotten about and put off for years. With the contacts ejecting themselves at malicious whim, I was constantly aware that my next breath might leave me marooned, half-blind, vulnerable. The fact that no one ever treated me with anything but solicitude—often strangers got down on their hands and knees with me—did nothing to soften my fear. I started to walk more slowly, to avoid shag carpeting, to sit with my head tilted slightly back, hoping gravity would keep the contacts in place. Outside, I lingered by the sides of buildings.

By now the myopia was at a full gallop, and the world I saw without any lenses was no longer blurry; it was pure blur. If, for some reason, I had to walk across a room without glasses or contacts, I shuffled like a blind girl, groping for handholds, batting at the air in case something—a lamp, a shelf, some pot hanging from the ceiling—might be ready to strike. Smudged, bulging shapes crowded against me. I imagined fists or rocks or sudden, steep edges, threats from dreams that seemed probable in this shapeless landscape.

At visits to the ophthalmologist, I strained and fought to see the eye chart, memorizing E F O T Z and F X I O S C before the doctor caught on. I paid closer attention to the toneless way he informed my mother that I needed, again, a stronger correction, and felt my throat clench. My mother said, "I thought the contacts were supposed to slow this down."

"They might be doing that," he said. "There's no way of telling. She might be going downhill even faster without them." He bent over to write notes on my chart, which was half an inch thick by now. My eyes were good enough to see that.

I could see other things, too. I could see the expression on my friend's face when I came to spend the night and unpacked all my cumbersome equipment: cleansing solution, wetting solution, saline solution, and the heat-sterilization unit that had to be plugged in for two hours. I could also see her expression after I emerged from the bathroom wearing my glasses. "Let me try them on," she said. I handed them over to let her giggle and bang into walls, and tried not to betray how anxious I was to get them back.

In biology class, I saw my teacher's impatient look when I told her that I couldn't draw the cells clustered on the microscope's slide. "Just close one eye and draw what you see," she said, and so, hopelessly, I did, even though I knew no cell ever had such peculiar zigzags. When I got my lab book back, the teacher had written, "You obviously have trouble seeing enough. Or correctly."

Maybe it was that prim, striving-for-accuracy last phrase that caught me. Or the clinical tone. Whichever, instead of feeling embarrassed or crushed, I was relieved. In a voice that didn't whine or tremble, her note offered me an interesting new self-definition. I grabbed it.

With relief, I gave up trying to make out faces across a football field and stopped straining to read the face of a bell tower clock, tasks I had been using to gauge my vision's deterioration. By this time I was wearing a new, flexible kind of contact lens made out of silicone, far more comfortable and less apt to fall out, so I was confident enough to stroll across parks and thickly carpeted rooms. I started asking the people around me what words were written on the blackboard, what images were flickering by on the TV screen, and people told me. I was a person who had trouble seeing enough, or correctly, so they filled me in on the nuances I would miss on my own.

At a movie, nodding at the screen, my friend whispered, "She keeps noticing the clock. That clock has something to do with the murder." Or, gesturing at the teacher the next day in class: "She's smiling; she's in a good mood. I'll bet she's started smoking again."

I was being given not only facts, but also interpretations. Those who could see sharply gave me shadow as well as object, context in addition to text. Did I resent all of these explanations and asides, pronounced slowly as if for the dimwitted? Not on your life. Friends and family were making things easy for me, and after years of constant unease, I was happy with that.

I drew other people's opinions over me like a blanket. Sight, it seemed, blended right into insight, and to perceive anything was to make a judgment call. Since the people around me had the first kind of sight, I was willing to grant that they had the second. And then the corollary: since I lacked the one, I surely lacked the other.

Anybody with half an eye can see where this story is going: I got lazy. Knowing that many details were going to be lost to me anyway, I stopped trying to see them. I could get the notion of a landscape, but not the trees it contained; I could recognize a skyline, but not the buildings within it. I was all big picture, untroubled by the little stuff.

During my junior year in college, when I was an exchange student in England, I traveled to public gardens and scenic overlooks and took pictures. Only when the pictures were developed did I find out that candy wrappers had clogged the shrubbery, and that across the top slat of the pretty green park bench somebody had carved BOLLOCKS. These weren't microscopic flaws; they were clear to anybody, even myopic me. I had been fully able to see the candy wrappers, but hadn't bothered to. My photo album from that year is a catalogue of England's trash, none of which I looked at until the pictures came back. Then I felt outraged and—this is the kicker—betrayed.

Somewhere, at a juncture I couldn't pinpoint, I had made a tactical shift in how I used my bad eyes. Not only had I given up trying to see the actual, physical world, but I had begun to let myself see a better world, one cut to my taste and measure, a world that, just for starters, didn't contain flyaway Snickers wrappers. And I believed in that world firmly enough to feel cheated when the wrappers got caught on the thorns of barberry bushes.

My inability to see the physical world had infected my mind: I had learned to deceive myself using my mind's eye, just as my real eyes had been deceiving me for years. When I came home from that year abroad, I saw myself as English and annoyed the daylights out of my friends for months by calling the place we lived in a *flat* (although it was in fact a house), by stowing groceries in the car's *boot,* and by pulling beer out of the refrigerator to let it warm up. Had anyone had a mind's camera in those days, they might have pictured me with highway trash wrapped around my ankles and *BOLLOCKS* scrawled on my forehead.

Permitting someone with so shaky a grasp of reality to enter relationships was just asking for trouble. The catalogue of my romances from those years is unrelievedly dreary—boys taking short vacations from their long-term girlfriends, boys who didn't like girls, boys who needed a place to stay and someone to do the cooking. And then the hurt boys, the ones whose long-term girlfriends had left them, who called their therapists twice a day, who were too depressed to go to class. By this point I hardly need add that I saw nothing inappropriate about any of these choices.

When, at twenty-one, I announced my intention to marry a man I knew only slightly and understood less, dismayed family members and friends ringed around me, trying to make me see how inappropriate the choice was, how poorly we were matched, how little pleasure we took, even then, in each other's company. Their attempts hardened my resolve. I looked into the eyes of my intended and saw a soul misunderstood by the world, whose inability to hold a steady job indicated his need for a supportive wife, whose vague visions of success I could share without quite having to get them into focus.

The marriage lasted seven years—longer than it should have. Even when it finally collapsed, its flimsy walls giving way under disappointment, disillusion, and broken promises on both sides, I still couldn't make sense of the ruin, or understand why it had happened. I couldn't *see,* I wailed to a therapist, week after week.

"If you want to see, you have to look," she told me.

"I do look. But I can't see."

"Then you don't know how to look," she said.

Irritated by the smug shrinkishness of her answer, I said, "Okay. Fine. Tell me how to look."

"This isn't some kind of mystical thing. Just pay attention. Your only problem is that you don't pay attention."

As always when I am handed an accurate piece of information about myself, I was stung. Days had to pass before I calmed down and heard the invitation behind the therapist's words, weeks before I was willing to act on them. Not that I knew how to act. All I knew was that a new world was taking shape at my perceptions' furthest horizons, still distant and faint, but visible just barely.

Five years ago my second husband and I bought a house, the first I had ever owned, and with it came property. The house sits on an ordinary suburban lot; we are not talking about Sissinghurst here. Still, space had to be filled up in gardens and around trees, and I learned, generally by error, about bloom time, soil acidity, shade tolerance, and zone hardiness.

Like most chores, gardening teaches me about myself, and I have learned that I am never going to be a prize-winning gardener whose lilies glisten and whose roses scent the air a block away. But I am a tidy gardener: I make time to stake perennials and deadhead the coreopsis; I struggle to preserve clean edges around the beds.

And I am a heroic weeder, a merciless one, driven. I sometimes come into department stores with dirt under my fingernails from digging out knotweed from planting strips in the parking lot. Many gardening tasks are too heavy for me, or require too delicate a touch, but weeding means the staving off of brute chaos, a task I approach with brio.

A year or so after I started gardening, I visited my mother, who has a garden of her own. Stooping to pluck weeds as we talked, I sought out the infant tufts of Bermuda grass that hadn't yet had a chance to sprawl and colonize. "How can you even *see* those tiny things?" my mother asked, and I was so startled that I paused for a moment, still crouched at plant level.

How *can* I even see those tiny things? I can spot an errant sprig of clover from halfway across the yard, but can't make out the face of a good friend five rows down in an auditorium. I can see my gray hairs as if they were outlined in neon, but can't read a football scoreboard on TV. The college co-ed who didn't notice trash and graffiti has become a woman who scours every scene, vigilant in her pursuit of jarring notes, infelicitous details. She has learned to look, and to pay attention. But she still can't see the picture itself, or the happy accidents it might contain.

Bad eyes pick out the bad—it makes sense. Put like that, the condition sounds dire, requiring corrective lenses for the brain or soul. But my myopia is physical before anything else; I am truly unable to make out the face of my friend in that auditorium, however much I might want to see her. A hinge exists between the literal and the metaphorical reality of my crummy vision. I can bear in mind that my vision is untrustworthy, but I can't change it.

All of which brings me back to my high-school biology teacher, God bless her, who diagnosed me more accurately than anyone else. I am a person who has trouble seeing enough, or correctly. Knowing this, I must go forth with useful caution, avoiding quick turns and snap decisions.

And, truly, I do all right. I haven't yet stepped off a cliff or driven into a pedestrian, and my judgments in recent years seem little worse than anyone else's. I just have to look, then look again. I have to remember that I am seeing only part of the picture. I have to remind myself to allow for my margin of error, and then bear in mind that the world is, always, more populous and bright and bountifully landscaped than it appears.

1998

READING, REREADING, AND ANALYSIS

1. Find several examples in which McGraw demonstrates how her failing eyesight affected her identity, affected how she felt about herself or how she behaved toward others.

2. In a group, track the stages that McGraw goes through in relation to her loss of sight. How does her personality shift in relation to her changing attitudes about not being able to see?

3. Is this essay only valuable as a story about failing eyesight? Find one or two places where McGraw's story seems to have a larger point or significance. Write a paragraph discussing that significance, and exploring what a reader might learn from this account.

4. McGraw starts off with the claim that her "subject veers almost uncontrollably toward metaphor" (p. 371). Working in pairs, see how many metaphors or figures of speech you can find in McGraw's essay. List the ones you see.

5. How and why did McGraw learn "to look, and to pay attention" (p. 380)?

6. What does McGraw mean on page 377 when she writes, " I drew other people's opinions over me like a blanket. Sight, it seemed, blended right into insight, and to perceive anything was to make a judgment call. Since the people around me had the first kind of sight, I was willing to grant that they had the second. And then the corollary: since I lacked the one, I surely lacked the other."

RESPONDING THROUGH WRITING: BUILDING AN INTERPRETATION

7. Why is McGraw able to see some things—"an errant sprig of clover from halfway across the yard"—but not able to see other things from a similar distance, such as the face of a friend "five rows down in an auditorium" (p. 379)? Use examples from her essay and from your own knowledge and experience to explain this seeming contradiction.

8. Using McGraw's essay as a model, choose some other literal process that you have experienced or noticed (for example, learning something new, planting a garden, writing a paper, finding or losing an important object, etc.). Write a paper in which you analyze the process on the literal level but also develop its larger significance, using examples and perhaps some figurative language to help show its broader implications.

9. In four or five sentences, summarize McGraw's main argument in "Bad Eyes." If you can summarize her essay in four or five sentences, then why did McGraw use about nine pages to write her essay? What is the difference in effect between reading a summary and reading the essay?

10. Write an essay (three or four pages) in which you describe and examine a disability or problem you have. Title it "Bad _____" (fill in the blank). Reflect on how McGraw structures her essay and on how she uses metaphors and similes to help her readers see her ideas with greater force and clarity. In your essay, try to use a couple of metaphors or similes that make sense but that avoid being clichés.

GOING FURTHER: LEARNING FROM OTHER SOURCES

11. Search a reference database that includes magazines and journals, such as MAS Full Text Ultra, Newspaper Source, or Lexis/Nexis, for other accounts of nearsightedness or blindness. How common are McGraw's reactions, her sense of fear and potential victimization, for example? What is most unusual about her account

compared with the others you have uncovered? (Hint: Try a variety of search terms, including "blindness," "blindness and story," "nearsighted," and "loss of sight").

12. Use a search engine such as Google to find information on how computer technology may offer help for people with poor vision. Also, look for information on laser eye surgery. If someone with poor eyesight has laser surgery, how much will her or his vision improve, and what are the likely risks or dangers of laser eye surgery?

APPLYING WHAT YOU'VE LEARNED

13. Although Annie Dillard is talking about "seeing" and McGraw is talking about the loss of sight, what points of connection can you find in these two essays? For example, does Dillard's distinction between seeing as "analyz[ing] and pry[ing]" and seeing as "letting go" apply to McGraw's examples as well? Write an essay in which you compare their ways of seeing in relation to your own experiences with sight.

14. In "Scientific Literacy," Emily Martin and her coauthors discuss the process by which different people gain imaginative and scientific insight into the workings of their own bodies and the threat of disease. How does McGraw's account of her nearsightedness compare with the examples that Martin provides? How much "scientific literacy" does McGraw seem to gain? Does she develop her knowledge of the disease in a way that Martin would encourage? Write a paper in which you analyze the degree of "scientific literacy" that McGraw develops in comparison with the other examples that Martin provides.

15. Write a five-page essay in which you make an argument about McGraw's personal essay and another personal essay in *Making Sense,* such as Nancy Sommers's "I Stand Here Writing," Barbara Mellix's "From Outside, In," Julie Charlip's "A Real Class Act: Searching for Identity in the Classless Society," or bell hooks's "keeping close to home: class and education." Think about the purposes of the two essays. Likewise, think about each essay's message, the persona each writer adopts, and the other means of conveying the message. You need to do more than simply say that both writers present a personal style. There must be a larger point that you want to make, and you can arrive at your thesis or larger point by thinking in-depth and asking yourself questions about the two texts in your paper.

BARBARA MELLIX

Barbara Mellix (b. 1945) is the Executive Assistant Dean of the College of Arts and Sciences at the University of Pittsburgh. After completing her undergraduate degree at the University of Pittsburgh, Mellix went on to earn a Masters of Fine Arts degree. In addition to her administrative duties, Mellix teaches writing in the university's English department and writes articles for the alumni magazine. She has won awards for her teaching and writing. "From Outside, In" was originally published in the *Georgia Review.*

> To learn more about the history of black vernacular English, see the article by James Clyde Sellman at The Africana.com website, <http://www.africana.com/research/encarta/tt_262.asp>.

WHAT DO YOU KNOW? WHAT DO YOU EXPECT TO DISCOVER?

Before reading the essay, take a moment to consider the following questions.

1. What topics does Mellix's biography suggest she is interested in? What do you know about those topics? Knowledge can come from personal experience, stories you've heard, other classes you've taken, or other reading you've done.

2. Imagine writing a letter to a professor or to your employer to ask for a favor and then writing a letter to your best friend in which you discuss the letter you wrote to your professor or employer. Would the language in the two letters be the same? How would you present yourself through your language choices in each letter? What language do you use when you want to appear formal, and what kind of language do you use in your ordinary and everyday life?

3. In the essay that follows, Mellix discusses her struggles to learn to write formal standard English and academic discourse for her college classes. Reflect on your own comfort or discomfort with writing. If writing tends to come easy for you, then make a list of reasons why. If writing has posed or still poses problems for you, then make a list of the reasons why. How do you think your composition course will help you strengthen your writing?

⅋

From Outside, In

Two years ago, when I started writing this paper, trying to bring order out of chaos, my ten-year-old daughter was suffering from an acute attack of boredom. She drifted in and out of the room complaining that she had nothing to do, no one to "be with" because none of her friends were at home. Patiently I explained that I was working on something special and needed peace and quiet, and I suggested that she paint, read, or work with her computer. None of these interested her. Finally, she pulled up a chair to my desk and watched me, now and then heaving long, loud sighs. After two or three minutes (nine or ten sighs), I lost my patience. "Looka here, Allie," I said, "you too old for this kinda carryin' on. I done told you this is important. You wronger than dirt to be in here haggin' me like this and you know it. Now git on outta here and leave me off before I put my foot all the way down."

I was at home, alone with my family, and my daughter understood that this way of speaking was appropriate in that <u>context.</u> She knew, as a matter of fact, that it was almost inevitable; when I get angry at home, I speak some of my finest, most cherished black English. Had I been speaking to my daughter in this manner in certain other environments, she would have been shocked and probably worried that I had taken leave of my sense of propriety.

Like my children, I grew up speaking what I considered two distinctly different languages—black English and standard English (or as I thought of them then, the ordinary everyday speech of "country" coloreds and "proper" English)—and in the process of acquiring these languages, I developed an understanding of when, where, and how to use them. But unlike my children, I grew up in a world that was primarily black. My friends, neighbors, minister, teachers—almost everybody I associated with every day—were black. And we spoke to one another in our own special language: *That sho is a pretty dress you got on. If she don' soon leave me off I'm gon tell her head a mess. I was so mad I could'a pissed a blue nail. He all the time trying to low-rate somebody. Ain't that just about the nastiest thing you ever set ears on?*

Then there were the "others," the "proper" blacks, transplanted relatives and one-time friends who came home from the city for weddings, funerals, and vacations. And the whites. To these we spoke standard English. "Ain't?" my mother would yell at me when I used the term in the presence of "others." "You *know* better than that." And I would hang my head in shame and say the "proper" word.

I remember one summer sitting in my grandmother's house in Greeleyville, South Carolina, when it was full of the chatter of city relatives who were home on vacation. My parents sat quietly, only now and then volunteering a comment or answering a question. My mother's face took on a strained expression when she spoke. I could see that she was being careful to say just the right words in just the right way. Her voice sounded thick, muffled. And when she finished speaking, she would lapse into silence, her proper smile on her face. My father was more articulate, more aggressive. He spoke quickly, his words sharp and clear. But he held his proud head higher, a signal that he, too, was uncomfortable. My sisters and brothers and I stared at our aunts, uncles, and cousins, speaking only when prompted. Even then, we hesitated, formed our sentences in our minds, then spoke softly, shyly.

My parents looked small and anxious during those occasions, and I waited impatiently for our leave-taking when we would mock our relatives the moment we were out of their hearing. "Reeely," we would say to one another, flexing our wrists and rolling our eyes, "how dooo you stan' this heat? Chile, it just too hyooo-mid for words." Our relatives had made us feel "country," and this was our way of regaining pride in ourselves while getting a little revenge in the bargain. The words bubbled in our throats and rolled across our tongues, a balming.

As a child I felt this same doubleness in uptown Greeleyville where the whites lived. "Ain't that a pretty dress you're wearing!" Toby, the town policeman, said to me one day when I was fifteen. "Thank you very much," I replied, my voice barely audible in my own ears. The words felt wrong in my mouth, rigid, foreign. It was not that I had never spoken that phrase before—it was common in black English, too—but I was extremely conscious that this was an occasion for proper English. I had taken out my English and put it on as I did my church clothes, and I felt as if I were wearing my Sunday best in the middle of the week. It did not matter that Toby had not spoken grammatically correct English. He was white and could speak as he wished. I had something to prove. Toby did not.

Speaking standard English to whites was our way of demonstrating that we knew their language and could use it. Speaking it to standard-English-speaking blacks was our way of showing them that we, as well as they, could "put on airs." But when we spoke standard English, we acknowledged (to ourselves and to others— but primarily to ourselves) that our customary way of speaking was inferior. We felt foolish, embarrassed, somehow diminished because we were ashamed to be our real selves. We were reserved, shy in the presence of those who owned and/or spoke *the* language.

My parents never set aside time to drill us in standard English. Their forms of instruction were less formal. When my father was feeling particularly expansive, he would regale us with tales of his exploits in the outside world. In almost flawless English, complete with dialogue and flavored with gestures and embellishment, he told us about his attempt to get a haircut at a white barbershop; his refusal to acknowledge one of the town merchants until the man addressed him as "Mister"; the time he refused to step off the sidewalk uptown to let some whites pass; his airplane trip to New York City (to visit a sick relative) during which the stewardesses and porters—recognizing that he was a "gentleman"—addressed him as "Sir." I did not realize then—nor, I think, did my father—that he was teaching us, among other things, standard English and the relationship between language and power.

My mother's approach was different. Often, when one of us said, "I'm gon wash off my feet," she would say, "And what will you walk on if you wash them off?" Everyone would laugh at the victim of my mother's "proper" mood. But it was different when one of us children was in a proper mood. "You think you are so superior," I said to my oldest sister one day when we were arguing and she was winning. "Superior!" my sister mocked. "You mean I'm acting 'biggidy'?" My sisters and brothers sniggered, then joined in teasing me. Finally, my mother said, "Leave your sister alone. There's nothing wrong with using proper English." There was a half-smile on her face. I had gotten "uppity," had "put on airs" for no good reason. I was at home, alone with the family, and I hadn't been prompted by one of my mother's proper moods. But there was also a proud light in my mother's eyes; her children were learning English very well.

Not until years later, as a college student, did I begin to understand our ambivalence toward English, our scorn of it, our need to master it, to own and be owned by it—an ambivalence that extended to the public-school classroom. In our school, where there were no whites, my teachers taught standard English but used black English to do it. When my grammar school teachers wanted us to write, for example, they usually said something like, "I want y'all to write five sentences that make a statement. Anybody git done before the rest can color." It was probably almost those exact words that led me to write these sentences in 1953 when I was in the second grade:

> The white clouds are pretty.
> There are only 15 people in our room.
> We will go to gym.
> We have a new poster.
> We may go out doors.

Second grade came after "Little First" and "Big First," so by then I knew the implied rules that accompanied all writing assignments.

Writing was an occasion for proper English. I was not to write in the way we spoke to one another: The white clouds pretty; There ain't but 15 people in our room; We going to gym; We got a new poster; We can go out in the yard. Rather I was to use the language of "other": clouds *are*, there *are*, we *will*, we *have*, we *may*.

My sentences were short, rigid, perfunctory, like the letters my mother wrote to relatives:

> Dear Papa,
>
> How are you? How is Mattie? Fine I hope. We are fine. We will come to see you Sunday. Cousin Ned will give us a ride.
>
> Love,
> Daughter

The language was not ours. It was something from outside us, something we used for special occasions.

But my coloring on the other side of that second-grade paper is different. I drew three hearts and a sun. The sun has a smiling face that radiates and envelops everything it touches. And although the sun and its world are enclosed in a circle, the colors I used—red, blue, green, purple, orange, yellow, black—indicate that I was less restricted with drawing and coloring than I was with writing standard English. My valentines were not just red. My sun was not just a yellow ball in the sky.

By the time I reached the twelfth grade, speaking and writing standard English had taken on new importance. Each year, about half of the newly graduated seniors of our school moved to large cities—particularly in the North—to live with relatives and find work. Our English teacher constantly corrected our grammar: "Not 'ain't,' but 'isn't.'" We seldom wrote papers, and even those few were usually plot summaries of short stories. When our teacher returned the papers, she usually lectured on the importance of using standard English: "I *am;* you *are;* he, she, or it *is*," she would say, writing on the chalkboard as she spoke. "How you gon git a job talking about 'I is,' or 'I isn't' or 'I ain't'?"

In Pittsburgh, where I moved after graduation, I watched my aunt and uncle—who had always spoken standard English when in Greeleyville—switch from black English to standard English to a mixture of the two, according to where they were or who they were with. At home and with certain close relatives, friends, and neighbors, they spoke black English. With those less close, they spoke a mixture. In public and with strangers, they generally spoke standard English.

In time, I learned to speak standard English with ease and to switch smoothly from black to standard or a mixture, and back again. But no matter where I was, no matter what the situation or occasion, I continued to write as I had in school:

Dear Mommie,

How are you? How is everybody else? Fine I hope. I am fine. So are Aunt and Uncle. Tell everyone I said hello. I will write again soon.

Love,
Barbara

At work, at a health insurance company, I learned to write letters to customers. I studied form letters and letters written by co-workers, memorizing the phrases and the ways in which they were used. I dictated:

Thank you for your letter of January 5. We have made the changes in your coverage you requested. Your new premium will be $150 every three months. We are pleased to have been of service to you.

In a sense, I was proud of the letters I wrote for the company: they were proof of my ability to survive in the city, the outside world—an indication of my growing mastery of English. But they also indicate writing was still mechanical for me, something that didn't require much thought.

Reading also became a more significant part of my life during those early years in Pittsburgh. I had always liked reading, but now I devoted more and more of my spare time to it. I read romances, mysteries, popular novels. Looking back, I realize that the books I liked best were simple, unambiguous: good versus bad and right versus wrong with right rewarded and wrong punished, mysteries unraveled and all set right in the end. It was how I remembered life in Greeleyville.

Of course I was romanticizing. Life in Greeleyville had not been so very uncomplicated. Back there I had been—first as a child, then as a young woman with limited experience in the outside world—living in a relatively closed-in society. But there were implicit and explicit principles that guided our way of life and shaped our relationships with one another and the people outside—principles that a newcomer would find elusive and baffling. In Pittsburgh, I had matured, become more experienced: I had worked at three different jobs, associated with a wider range of people, married, had children. This new environment with different prescripts for living required that I speak standard English much of the time, and slowly, imperceptibly, I had ceased seeing a sharp distinction between myself and "others." Reading romances and mysteries, characterized by dichotomy, was a way of shying away from change, from the person I was becoming.

But that other part of me—that part which took great pride in my ability to hold a job writing business letters—was increasingly drawn to the new developments in my life and the attending possibilities, opportunities for even greater change. If I could write letters for a nationally known business, could I not also do something better, more challenging, more important? Could I not, perhaps, go to college and become a school teacher? For years, afraid and a little embarrassed, I did no more than imagine this different me, this possible me. But sixteen years after coming north, when my youngest daughter entered kindergarten, I found myself unable—or unwilling—to resist the lure of possibility. I enrolled in my first college course: Basic Writing, at the University of Pittsburgh.

For the first time in my life, I was required to write extensively about myself. Using the most formal English at my command, I wrote these sentences near the beginning of the term:

> One of my duties as a homemaker is simply picking up after others. A day seldom passes that I don't search for a mislaid toy, book, or gym shoe, etc. I change the Ty-D-Bol, fight "ring around the collar," and keep our laundry smelling "April fresh." Occasionally, I settle arguments between my children and suggest things to do when they're bored. Taking telephone messages for my oldest daughter is my newest (and sometimes most aggravating) chore. Hanging the toilet paper roll is my most insignificant.

My concern was to use "appropriate" language, to sound as if I belonged in a college classroom. But I felt separate from the language—as if it did not and could not belong to me. I couldn't think and feel genuinely in that language, couldn't make it express what I thought and felt about being a housewife. A part of me resented, among other things, being judged by such things as the appearance of my family's laundry and toilet bowl, but in that language I could only imagine and write about a conventional housewife.

For the most part, the remainder of the term was a period of adjustment, a time of trying to find my bearings as a student in a college composition class, to learn to shut out my black English whenever I composed, and to prevent it from creeping into my formulations; a time for trying to grasp the language of the classroom and reproduce it in my prose; for trying to talk about myself in that language, reach others through it. Each experience of writing was like standing naked and revealing my imperfection, my "otherness." And each new assignment was another chance to make myself over in language, reshape myself, make myself "better" in my rapidly changing image of a student in a college composition class.

But writing became increasingly unmanageable as the term progressed, and by the end of the semester, my sentences sounded like this:

> My excitement was soon dampened, however, by what seemed like a small voice in the back of my head saying that I should be careful with my long awaited opportunity. I felt frustrated and this seemed to make it difficult to concentrate.

There is a poverty of language in these sentences. By this point, I knew that the clichéd language of my Housewife essay was unacceptable, and I generally recognized trite expressions. At the same time, I hadn't yet mastered the language of the classroom, hadn't yet come to see it as belonging to me. Most notable is the lifelessness of the prose, the apparent absence of a person behind the words. I wanted those sentences—and the rest of the essay—to convey the anguish of yearning to, at once, become something more and yet remain the same. I had the sensation of being split in two, part of me going into a future the other part didn't believe possible. As that person, the student writer at that moment, I was essentially mute. I could not—in the process of composing—use the language of the old me, yet I couldn't imagine myself in the language of "others."

I found this particularly discouraging because at midsemester I had been writing in a much different way. Note the language of this introduction to an essay I had written then, near the middle of the term:

> Pain is a constant companion to the people in "Footwork." Their jobs are physically damaging. Employers are insensitive to their feelings and in many cases add to their problems. The general public wounds them further by treating them with disgrace because of what they do for a living. Although the workers are as diverse as they are similar, there is a definite link between them. They suffer a great deal of abuse.

The voice here is stronger, more confident, appropriating terms like "physically damaging," "wounds them further," "insensitive," "diverse"—terms I couldn't have imagined using when writing about my own experience—and shaping them into sentences like, "Although the workers are as diverse as they are similar, there is a definite link between them." And there is the sense of a personality behind the prose, someone who sympathizes with the workers: "The general public wounds them further by treating them with disgrace because of what they do for a living."

What caused these differences? I was, I believed, explaining other people's thoughts and feelings, and I was free to move about in the language of "others" so long as I was speaking *of* others. I was unaware that I was transforming into my best classroom language my own thoughts and feelings about people whose experiences and ways of speaking were in many ways similar to mine.

The following year, unable to turn back or to let go of what had become something of an obsession with language (and hoping to catch and hold the sense of control that had eluded me in Basic Writing), I enrolled in a research writing course. I spent most of the term learning how to prepare for and write a research paper. I chose sex education as my subject and spent hours in libraries, searching for information, reading, taking notes. Then (not without messiness and often-demoralizing frustration) I organized my information into categories, wrote a thesis statement, and composed my paper—a series of paraphrases and quotations spaced between carefully constructed transitions. The process and results felt artificial, but as I would later come to realize I was passing through a necessary stage. My sentences sounded like this:

> This reserve becomes understandable with examination of who the abusers are. In an overwhelming number of cases, they are people the victims know and trust. Family members, relatives, neighbors and close family friends commit seventy-five percent of all reported sex crimes against children, and parents, parent substitutes and relatives are the offenders in thirty to eighty percent of all reported cases.[12] While assault by strangers does occur, it is less common, and is usually a single episode.[13] But abuse by family members, relatives and acquaintances may continue for an extended period of time. In cases of incest, for example, children are abused repeatedly for an average of eight years.[14] In such cases, "the use of physical force is rarely necessary because of the child's trusting, dependent relationship with the offender. The child's cooperation is often facilitated by the adult's position of dominance, an offer of material goods, a threat of physical violence, or a misrepresentation of moral standards."[15]

The completed paper gave me a sense of profound satisfaction, and I read it often after my professor returned it. I know now that what I was pleased with was the language I used and the professional voice it helped me maintain. "Use better words," my teacher had snapped at me one day after reading the notes I'd begun accumulating from my research, and slowly I began taking on the language of my sources. In my next set of notes, I used the word "vacillating"; my professor applauded. And by the time I composed the final draft, I felt at ease with terms like "overwhelming number of cases," "single episode," and "reserve," and I shaped them into sentences similar to those of my "expert" sources.

If I were writing the paper today, I would of course do some things differently. Rather than opening with an anecdote—as my teacher suggested—I would begin simply with a quotation that caught my interest as I was researching my paper (and which I scribbled, without its source, in the margin of my notebook): "Truth does not do so much good in the world as the semblance of truth does evil." The quotation felt right because it captured what was for me the central idea of my essay—an idea that emerged gradually during the making of my paper—and express it in a way I would like to have said it. The anecdote, a hypothetical situation I invented to conform to the information in the paper, felt forced and insincere because it represented—to a great degree—my teacher's understanding of the essay, *her* idea of what in it was most significant. Improving upon my previous experiences with writing, I was beginning to think and feel in the language I used, to find my own voices in it, to sense that how one speaks influences how one means. But I was not yet secure enough, comfortable enough with the language to trust my intuition.

Now that I know that to seek knowledge, freedom, and autonomy means always to be in the concentrated process of becoming—always to be venturing into new territory, feeling one's way at first, then getting one's balance, negotiating, accommodating, discovering one's self in ways that previously defined "others"—I sometimes get tired. And I ask myself why I keep on participating in this highbrow form of violence, this slamming against perplexity. But there is no real futility in the question, no hint of that part of the old me who stood outside standard English, hugging to herself a disabling mistrust of a language she thought could not represent a person with her history and experience. Rather, the question represents a person who feels the consequence of her education, the weight of her possibilities as a teacher and writer and human being, a voice in society. And I would not change that person, would not give back the good burden that accompanies my growing expertise, my increasing power to shape myself in language and share that self with "others."

"To speak," says Frantz Fanon, "means to be in a position to use a certain syntax, to grasp the morphology of this or that language, but it means above all to assume a culture, to support the weight of a civilization."* To write means to do the same, but in a more profound sense. However, Fanon also says that to achieve mastery means to "get" in a position of power, to "grasp," to "assume." This, I have learned—both as a student and subsequently as a teacher—can involve tremendous emotional and psychological conflict for those attempting to master academic discourse. Although as a beginning student writer I had a fairly good grasp of ordinary spoken English and was proficient at what Labov calls "code-switching" (and what John Baugh in *Black Street Speech* terms "style shifting"), when I came face to face with the demands of academic writing, I grew increasingly self-conscious, constantly aware of my status as a black and a speaker of

---

Black Skin, White Masks (1952; rpt. New York: Grove Press, 1967), pp. 17–18.

one of the many black English vernaculars—a traditional outsider. For the first time, I experienced my sense of doubleness as something menacing, a built-in enemy. Whenever I turned inward for salvation, the balm so available during my childhood, I found instead this new fragmentation which spoke to me in many voices. It was the voice of my desire to prosper, but at the same time it spoke of what I had relinquished and could not regain: a safe way of being, a state of powerlessness which exempted me from responsibility for who I was and might be. And it accused me of betrayal, of turning away from blackness. To recover balance, I had to take on the language of the academy, the language of "others." And to do that, I had to learn to imagine myself a part of the culture of that language, and therefore someone free to manage that language, to take liberties with it. Writing and rewriting, practicing, experimenting, I came to comprehend more fully the generative power of language. I discovered—with the help of some especially sensitive teachers—that through writing one can continually bring new selves into being, each with new responsibilities and difficulties, but also with new possibilities. Remarkable power, indeed. I write and continually give birth to myself.

1987

READING, REREADING, AND ANALYSIS

1. Find several examples in the essay that help to explain Mellix's ideas of "doubleness" or "code-switching." Think of some examples from your own knowledge or experience that involve a kind of "code-switching." Bring a list of examples from the essay and from your own experience to class.

2. In a group, create an outline of Mellix's essay, paying particular attention to the transitions she makes from paragraph to paragraph. What are some of the primary changes that she goes through? What are some of the organizational structures or patterns that she uses in this essay?

3. Analyze the way Mellix quotes and interprets Frantz Fanon (pp. 392–393). What is she learning from Fanon? What is she teaching us about Fanon? What point does she want to make using Fanon?

4. Individually or in a group, make a list of examples in Mellix's essay that illustrate "the relationship between language and power" (p. 386).

5. In a group, discuss what Mellix describes as her family's ambivalence toward English, "our scorn of it, our need to master it, to own and be owned by it—an ambivalance that extended to the public-school classroom" (p. 386). Does Mellix's attitude toward

standard English remain ambivalent throughout the essay? Does her attitude change, and if so what evidence can you point to that suggests change?

6. Reflect on the possible meanings of Mellix's essay title, "From Outside, In." Find three key moments or passages in her essay that help you explain Mellix's title.

RESPONDING THROUGH WRITING: BUILDING AN INTERPRETATION

7. Write an essay in which you compare the process by which Mellix became comfortable with academic language and your own experiences in switching from informal to formal languages. What risks are involved in using a new language? What are the rewards and losses?

8. On page 389, Mellix writes: "My concern was to use 'appropriate' language, to sound as if I belonged in a college classroom. But I felt separate from the language—as if it did not and could not belong to me. I couldn't think and feel genuinely in that language, couldn't make it express what I thought and felt about being a housewife." Write a short paper (two or three pages) in which you analyze how Mellix overcomes her writing difficulties.

9. In much of her essay, Mellix describes her uneasiness and self-consciousness when using standard English. In your own experience, what acts or requirements have made you or still make you feel anxious and highly self-conscious? Write some journal entries about your own experiences of uneasiness and self-consciousness and then some journal entries that compare your experiences with Mellix's.

10. In four or five sentences, summarize the speaking and writing lessons presented to Mellix by her father and also by her teachers. In another four or five sentences, summarize what you see as the most important lessons Mellix learns and wants to communicate to her readers.

GOING FURTHER: LEARNING FROM OTHER SOURCES

11. Look up the terms "standard English" and "code-switching" in a scholarly database, such as Academic Search Elite or a similar database recommended by your reference librarian. From the

sources you find, choose five titles and abstracts that seem most deeply or most interestingly related to the issues raised by Mellix, print the list of titles and abstracts, and bring it to class.

12. Use a popular search engine such as Google to find information on Frantz Fanon. Read around in several of the Internet sources you find to learn more about Fanon. Next, use a reference database to find and read a couple of scholarly articles on Fanon. Finally, return to Mellix's discussion of Fanon on page 392. Why is Fanon important for Mellix? What does Mellix gain by discussing and quoting Fanon? In other words, how does Fanon help Mellix support her thesis or main argument?

APPLYING WHAT YOU'VE LEARNED

13. Write an essay analyzing writing advice from Nancy Sommers's "I Stand Here Writing" and from Walter Mosley's "For Authors" in relation to Mellix's account of her evolving relationship to academic language. Would Mellix agree that writing involves "a radical loss of certainty," a key phrase from Sommers's essay? Does Sommers or Mosley experience a kind of "doubleness"? In your essay, be sure to include two or three paragraphs that link your own writing experiences to some of the key ideas and examples you discuss from Mellix, Sommers, and Mosley.

14. Compare ideas and examples from Mellix's essay, Haunani-Kay Trask's "From a Native Daughter," and bell hooks's "keeping close to home: class and education" to write an essay in which you analyze the process of "code-switching" between standard English and other languages. What are some of the risks and losses involved for each of these writers? How do they respond differently to the challenges of communicating between different social groups?

15. Use Gloria Anzaldúa's discussion of "*nepantla*" as a critical lens for analyzing Mellix's transforming sense of self—particularly in relation to her efforts to master standard English, "the language of the classroom" (p. 389). As you move from a rough draft toward a final draft, reflect on how Mellix's experiences also help you better understand Anzaldúa's discussion of "*nepantla*." In other words, in your final draft you will continue to use Anzaldúa's idea of "*nepantla*" to help you examine Mellix's struggles, but you should also discuss how writing about Mellix helps you develop an even better understanding of Anzaldúa than you had before.

WALTER MOSLEY

Walter Mosley (b. 1952) is a writer best known for his hard-boiled detective novels featuring Los Angeles detective Ezekiel "Easy" Rawlins in such books as *Devil in a Blue Dress*. Mosley began his professional life as a computer programmer, but once he started writing, he quit the office and has never looked back. "For Authors, Fragile Ideas Need Loving Every Day" was printed in the "Writers on Writing" column of the *New York Times*.

> **To learn more about Mosley, visit the Walter Mosley page at http://www.twbookmark.com/features/waltermosley/index.html.**

WHAT DO YOU KNOW? WHAT DO YOU EXPECT TO DISCOVER?

Before reading the essay, take a moment to consider the following questions.

1. What topics does Mosley's biography suggest he is interested in? What do you know about those topics? Knowledge can come from personal experience, stories you've heard, other classes you've taken, or other reading you've done.

2. Before reading the essay, freewrite for ten minutes on the title of Mosley's essay. What does it suggest to you and why? What are you expecting from an essay with this title?

3. What other "fragile" things in life "need loving every day"?

✄

For Authors, Fragile Ideas Need Loving Every Day

If you want to be a writer, you have to write every day. The consistency, the monotony, the certainty, all vagaries and passions are covered by this daily reoccurrence.

You don't go to a well once but daily. You don't skip a child's breakfast or forget to wake up in the morning. Sleep comes to you each day, and so does the muse.

She comes softly and quietly, behind your left ear or in a corner of the next room. Her words are whispers, her ideas shifting renditions of possibilities that have not been resolved, though they have occurred and reoccurred a thousand times in your mind. She, or it, is a collection of memories not exactly your own.

These reminiscences surface in dreams or out of abstract notions brought on by tastes and excitations, failures and hopes that you experience continually. These ideas have no physical form. They are smoky concepts liable to disappear at the slightest disturbance. An alarm clock or a ringing telephone will dispel a new character; answering the call will erase a chapter from the world.

Our most precious ability, the knack of creation, is also our most fleeting resource. What might be fades in the world of necessity.

How can I create when I have to go to work, cook my dinner, remember what I did wrong to the people who have stopped calling? And even if I do find a moment here and there—a weekend away in the mountains, say—how can I say everything I need to say before the world comes crashing back with all of its sirens and shouts and television shows?

"I know I have a novel in me," I often hear people say. "But how can I get it out?"

The answer is, always is, every day.

The dream of the writer, of any artist, is a fickle and amorphous thing. One evening you're remembering a homeless man, dressed in clothes that smelled like cheese rinds, who you once stood next to on a street corner in New York. Your memory becomes a reverie, and in this daydream you ask him where he's from. With a thick accent he tells you that he was born in Hungary, that he was a freedom fighter, but that now, here in America, his freedom has deteriorated into the poverty of the streets.

You write down a few sentences in your journal and sigh. This exhalation is not exhaustion but anticipation at the prospect of a wonderful tale exposing a notion that you still only partly understand.

A day goes by. Another passes. At the end of the next week you find yourself in the same chair, at the same hour when you wrote about the homeless man previously. You open the journal to see what you'd written. You remember everything perfectly, but the life has somehow drained out of it. The words have no art to them, you no longer remember the smell. The idea seems weak, it has dissipated, like smoke.

This is the first important lesson that the writer must learn. Writing a novel is gathering smoke. It's an excursion into the ether of ideas. There's no time to waste. You must work with that idea as well as you can, jotting down notes and dialogue.

The first day the dream you gathered will linger, but it won't last long. The next day you have to return to tend to your flimsy vapors. You have to brush them, reshape them, breathe into them and gather more.

It doesn't matter what time of day you work, but you have to work every day because creation, like life, is always slipping away from you. You must write every day, but there's no time limit on how long you have to write.

One day you might read over what you've done and think about it. You pick up the pencil or turn on the computer, but no new words come. That's fine. Sometimes you can't go further. Correct a misspelling, reread a perplexing paragraph, and then let it go. You have re-entered the dream of the work, and that's enough to keep the story alive for another 24 hours.

The next day you might write for hours; there's no way to tell. The goal is not a number of words or hours spent writing. All you need to do is to keep your heart and mind open to the work.

Nothing we create is art at first. It's simply a collection of notions that may never be understood. Returning every day thickens the atmosphere. Images appear. Connections are made. But even these clearer notions will fade if you stay away more than a day.

Reality fights against your dreams, it tries to deny creation and change. The world wants you to be someone known, someone with solid ideas, not blowing smoke. Given a day, reality will begin to scatter your notions; given two days, it will drive them off.

The act of writing is a kind of guerrilla warfare; there is no vacation, no leave, no relief. In actuality there is very little chance of victory. You are, you fear, like that homeless man, likely to be defeated by your fondest dreams.

But then the next day comes, and the words are waiting. You pick up where you left off, in the cool and shifting mists of morning.

2000

READING, REREADING, AND ANALYSIS

1. Identify and summarize one of the lessons that Mosley wants to pass along to others who want to become writers. Although Mosley is talking primarily about fiction writing, to what extent can you apply his advice to the processes involved in college writing?

2. Using Mosley's column as an example, take some notes about advice you might give a group of high school students who want to become proficient college writers. Share your advice in a group and then compile the group's list of advice to present to the class.

3. In a group, make a list of the metaphors and similes Mosley uses in his essay. Which of the figures of speech in the list particularly strikes your fancy or grabs your attention and why?

4. What forces, according to Mosley, threaten a writer's ability to develop in writing promising ideas?

5. Why is writing a novel like "gathering smoke" (p. 397)? Do you think that other types of writing you do in college are also like "gathering smoke"? If so, which type or types of writing and why?

6. On page 398, Mosley writes, "Nothing we create is art at first"? What does he mean by "art"? Do you think his statement applies to your essays for your composition class as well? If yes, why? If not applicable, then why not?

RESPONDING THROUGH WRITING: BUILDING AN INTERPRETATION

7. Try acting on Mosley's advice for one week by keeping a journal in which you write something every day, even if it is only a few sentences about something you observed. At the end of the week, write a short paper, two or three pages, in which you discuss the merits and the drawbacks of Mosley's advice, drawing on quotations from Mosley and from your own journal as evidence for your points.

8. Freewrite for ten minutes about the images and metaphors in the last two paragraphs of Mosley's essay. After you finish, review what you've written. Which of your ideas or sentences stand out to you and why? Write a page about your freewriting, and then write two pages tomorrow about what you wrote today. You might discuss what you have extended and dropped; likewise, you might discuss connections you see between what you are doing and what Mosley describes in his essay.

9. Imagine that one of your high school English teachers has asked you to write a short essay (three pages) to her current class of students about writing in college. Model your essay to your high school teacher on Mosley's column. Describe your writing process and give some advice about the writing process.

10. According to Mosley, "Our most precious ability, the knack of creation, is also our most fleeting resource. What might be fades in the world of necessity" (p. 397). Write a two-page response to Mosley's claim. If you agree with him, explain why in detail. If you disagree with him, explain why in detail.

GOING FURTHER: LEARNING FROM OTHER SOURCES

11. Look up the *New York Times* "Writers on Writing" series using your library's reference services. (Some libraries have online access to the NYT through the Lexis/Nexis database or its equivalent;

others may use reference volumes and microfilm.) Choose one of the other columns in the series and compare the advice given by that writer with Mosley's advice. What are some of the differences in these two writers' approaches to writing? Which column connects best to your own experiences as a writer and why?

12. On the Internet, research what kinds of writing Mosley has had published and how his work has been received by critics and reviewers. (Hint: Searching a reference database such as Academic Search Elite using the author's name will result in a number of reviews.) How do your research findings compare with the answers you would have predicted on the basis of this column only? Bring your findings to class.

APPLYING WHAT YOU'VE LEARNED

13. In "I Stand Here Writing," Nancy Sommers would like to teach her students that "being personal . . . does not mean being autobiographical" (p. 459). Use examples from Sommers and Mosley and from your own knowledge or experience to explain what that might mean. To what extent would Mosley agree with Sommers's other advice to her students, or with the idea that "writing is a radical loss of certainty" (Sommers, p. 454)?

14. In "The Loss of the Creature," Walker Percy describes the way objects, such as the sonnet or the dogfish, can become obscured by "symbolic packages." In his column, is Walter Mosley also creating a "symbolic package" around the process of writing fiction, or does he help to free the process from that symbolic packaging? Use Mosley's piece to explain and to test Percy's definition of "symbolic packages."

15. Write an essay in which you compare Mosley's lessons or rules for writing with Barbara Mellix's discussion of learning to write academic discourse in "From Outside, In." How does Mellix learn to be comfortable with as well as fluent in academic writing? In your paper, be sure to discuss the similarities you see in the lessons Mosley and Mellix discuss, but also discuss any differences you see. What particularly is significant about the difference or differences you identify?

WALKER PERCY

Walker Percy (1916–1990) was a novelist and essayist best known for his depictions of life in the New South. Percy was born in Alabama and raised in Mississippi. He began his professional life as a doctor, practicing pathology at Bellevue Hospital in New York City. Through his work, he contracted tuberculosis. The disease eventually left him too weak either to practice or to teach medicine, and so he began his career as a writer. In his novels and essays, Percy pursued an answer to the modern question, why does scientific progress seem to bring us no closer to understanding how to live? "The Loss of the Creature" has been widely anthologized. It was first published in the essay collection, *The Message in the Bottle: How Queer Man Is, How Queer Language Is, and What One Has to Do with the Other* (1975).

> To learn more about Percy, visit the Walker Percy Project at <http://www.ibiblio.org/wpercy/>.

WHAT DO YOU KNOW? WHAT DO YOU EXPECT TO DISCOVER?

Before reading the essay, take a moment to consider the following questions.

1. Recall factors that caused you to expect certain things from an encounter: a review that created particular expectations about a book, a movie, or a restaurant; descriptions from others that set up expectations about an upcoming vacation; a preset vision of what learning an unfamiliar subject matter, such as a foreign language, physics, or astronomy, would be like. In each case, did those expectations tend to enhance the experience or detract from it? Why?

2. When you travel as a tourist, how important is it for you to get off the beaten path? What are some of the pros and cons of seeking out new experiences? Write a paragraph describing a particular travel experience you have had in order to make a case for or against sticking to preplanned tourist routes.

♯

The Loss of the Creature

Every explorer names his island Formosa, beautiful. To him it is beautiful because, being first, he has access to it and can see it for what it is. But to no one else is it ever as beautiful—except the rare man who manages to recover it, who knows that it has to be recovered.

García López de Cárdenas discovered the Grand Canyon and was amazed at the sight. It can be imagined: One crosses miles of desert, breaks through the mesquite, and there it is at one's feet. Later the government set the place aside as a national park, hoping to pass along to millions the experience of Cárdenas. Does not one see the same sight from the Bright Angel Lodge that Cárdenas saw?

The assumption is that the Grand Canyon is a remarkably interesting and beautiful place and that if it had a certain value P for Cárdenas, the same value P may be transmitted to any number of sightseers—just as Banting's discovery of insulin can be transmitted to any number of diabetics. A counterinfluence is at work, however, and it would be nearer the truth to say that if the place is seen by a million sightseers, a single sightseer does not receive value P but a millionth part of value P.

It is assumed that since the Grand Canyon has the fixed interest value P, tours can be organized for any number of people. A man in Boston decides to spend his vacation at the Grand Canyon. He visits his travel bureau, looks at the folder, signs up for a two-week tour. He and his family take the tour, see the Grand Canyon, and return to Boston. May we say that this man has seen the Grand Canyon? Possibly he has. But it is more likely that what he has done is the one sure way not to see the canyon.

Why is it almost impossible to gaze directly at the Grand Canyon under these circumstances and see it for what it is—as one picks up a strange object from one's back yard and gazes directly at it? It is almost impossible because the Grand Canyon, the thing as it is, has been appropriated by the symbolic complex which has already been formed in the sightseer's mind. Seeing the canyon under approved circumstances is seeing the symbolic complex head on. The thing is no longer the thing as it confronted the Spaniard; it is rather that which has already been formulated—by picture postcard, geography book, tourist folders, and the words *Grand Canyon*. As a result of this preformulation, the source of the sightseer's pleasure undergoes a shift. Where the wonder and delight of the Spaniard arose from his penetration of the thing itself, from a progressive discovery of depths, patterns, colors, shadows, etc., now the sightseer measures his satisfaction *by the degree to which the canyon conforms to the preformed complex*. If it does so, if it looks just like the postcard, he is pleased; he might even say, "Why it is every bit as beautiful as a picture postcard!" He feels he has not been cheated. But if it does not conform, if the colors are somber, he will not be able to see it directly; he will only be conscious of the disparity between what it is and what it is supposed to be. He will say later that he was unlucky in not being there at the right time. The highest point, the term of the sightseer's satisfaction, is not the sovereign discovery of the thing before him; it is rather the measuring up of the thing to the criterion of the preformed symbolic complex.

Seeing the canyon is made even more difficult by what the sightseer does when the moment arrives, when sovereign knower confronts the thing to be known. Instead of looking at it, he photographs it. There is no confrontation at all. At the end of forty years of preformulation and with the Grand Canyon yawning at his feet, what does he do? He waives his right of seeing and knowing and records symbols for the next forty years. For him there is no present; there is only the past of what has been formulated and seen and the future of what has been formulated and not seen. The present is surrendered to the past and the future.

The sightseer may be aware that something is wrong. He may simply be bored; or he may be conscious of the difficulty: that the great thing yawning at his feet somehow eludes him. The harder he looks at it, the less he can see. It eludes everybody. The tourist cannot see it; the bellboy at the Bright Angel Lodge cannot see it: for him it is only one side of the space he lives in, like one wall of a room; to the ranger it is a tissue of everyday signs relevant to his own prospects—the blue haze down there means that he will probably get rained on during the donkey ride.

How can the sightseer recover the Grand Canyon? He can recover it in any number of ways, all sharing in common the stratagem of avoiding the approved confrontation of the tour and the Park Service.

It may be recovered by leaving the beaten track. The tourist leaves the tour, camps in the back country. He arises before dawn and approaches the South Rim through a wild terrain where there are no trails and no railed-in lookout points. In other words, he sees the canyon by avoiding all the facilities for seeing the canyon. If the benevolent Park Service hears about this fellow and thinks he has a good idea and places the following notice in the Bright Angel Lodge: *Consult ranger for information on getting off the beaten track*—the end result will only be the closing of another access to the canyon.

It may be recovered by a dialectical movement which brings one back to the beaten track but at a level above it. For example, after a lifetime of avoiding the beaten track and guided tours, a man may deliberately seek out the most beaten track of all, the most common-place tour imaginable: he may visit the canyon by a Greyhound tour in the company of a party from Terre Haute—just as a man who has lived in New York all his life may visit the Statue of Liberty. (Such dialectical savorings of the familiar as the familiar are, of course, a favorite stratagem of *The New Yorker* magazine.) The thing is recovered from familiarity by means of an exercise in familiarity. Our complex friend stands behind his fellow tourists at the Bright Angel Lodge and sees the canyon through them and their predicament, their picture taking and busy disregard. In a sense, he exploits his fellow tourists; he stands on their shoulders to see the canyon.

Such a man is far more advanced in the dialectic than the sight-seer who is trying to get off the beaten track—getting up at dawn and approaching the canyon through the mesquite. This stratagem is, in fact, for our complex man the weariest, most beaten track of all.

It may be recovered as a consequence of a breakdown of the symbolic machinery by which the experts present the experience to the consumer. A family visits the canyon in the usual way. But shortly after their arrival, the park is closed by an outbreak of typhus in the south. They have the canyon to themselves. What do they mean when they tell the home folks of their good luck: "We had the whole place to ourselves"? How does one see the thing better when the others are absent? Is looking like sucking: the more lookers, the less there is to see? They could hardly answer, but by saying this they testify to a state of affairs which is considerably more complex than the simple statement of the schoolbook about the Spaniard and the millions who followed him. It is a state in which there is a complex distribution of sovereignty, of zoning.

It may be recovered in a time of national disaster. The Bright Angel Lodge is converted into a rest home, a function that has nothing to do with the canyon a few yards away. A wounded man is brought in. He regains consciousness; there outside his window is the canyon.

The most extreme case of access by privilege conferred by disaster is the Huxleyan novel of the adventures of the surviving remnant after the great wars of the twentieth century. An expedition from Australia lands in Southern California and heads east. They stumble across the Bright Angel Lodge, now fallen into ruins. The trails are grown over, the guard rails fallen away, the dime telescope at Battleship Point rusted. But there is the canyon, exposed at last. Exposed by what? By the decay of those facilities which were designed to help the sightseer.

This dialectic of sightseeing cannot be taken into account by planners, for the object of the dialectic is nothing other than the subversion of the efforts of the planners.

The dialectic is not known to objective theorists, psychologists, and the like. Yet it is quite well known in the fantasy-consciousness of the popular arts. The devices by which the museum exhibit, the

Grand Canyon, the ordinary thing, is recovered have long since been stumbled upon. A movie shows a man visiting the Grand Canyon. But the moviemaker knows something the planner does not know. He knows that one cannot take the sight frontally. The canyon must be approached by the stratagems we have mentioned: the Inside Track, the Familiar Revisited, the Accidental Encounter. Who is the stranger at the Bright Angel Lodge? Is he the ordinary tourist from Terre Haute that he makes himself out to be? He is not. He has another objective in mind, to revenge his wronged brother, counterespionage, etc. By virtue of the fact that he has other fish to fry, he may take a stroll along the rim after supper and then we can see the canyon through him. The movie accomplishes its purpose by concealing it. Overtly the characters (the American family marooned by typhus) and we the onlookers experience pity for the sufferers, and the family experience anxiety for themselves; covertly and in truth they are the happiest of people and we are happy through them, for we have the canyon to ourselves. The movie cashes in on the recovery of sovereignty through disaster. Not only is the canyon now accessible to the remnant; the members of the remnant are now accessible to each other; a whole new ensemble of relations becomes possible—friendship, love, hatred, clandestine sexual adventures. In a movie when a man sits next to a woman on a bus, it is necessary either that the bus break down or that the woman lose her memory. (The question occurs to one: Do you imagine there are sightseers who see sights just as they are supposed to? a family who live in Terre Haute, who decide to take the canyon tour, who go there, see it, enjoy it immensely, and go home content? a family who are entirely innocent of all the barriers, zones, losses of sovereignty I have been talking about? Wouldn't most people be sorry if Battleship Point fell into the canyon, carrying all one's fellow passengers to their death, leaving one alone on the South Rim? I cannot answer this. Perhaps there are such people. Certainly a great many American families would swear they had no such problems, that they came, saw, and went away happy. Yet it is just these families who would be happiest if they had gotten the Inside Track and been among the surviving remnant.)

It is now apparent that as between the many measures which may be taken to overcome the opacity, the boredom, of the direct confrontation of the thing or creature in its citadel of symbolic investiture, some are less authentic than others. That is to say, some stratagems obviously serve other purposes than that of providing access to being—for example, various unconscious motivations which it is not necessary to go into here.

Let us take an example in which the recovery of being is ambiguous, where it may under the same circumstances contain both authentic and unauthentic components. An American couple, we will say, drives down into Mexico. They see the usual sights and have a fair time of it. Yet they are never without the sense of missing something.

Although Taxco and Cuernavaca are interesting and picturesque as advertised, they fall short of "it." What do the couple have in mind by "it"? What do they really hope for? What sort of experience could they have in Mexico so that upon their return, they would feel that "it" had happened? We have a clue: Their hope has something to do with their own role as tourists in a foreign country and the way in which they conceive this role. It has something to do with other American tourists. Certainly they feel that they are very far from "it" when, after traveling five thousand miles, they arrive at the plaza in Guanajuato only to find themselves surrounded by a dozen other couples from the Midwest.

Already we may distinguish authentic and unauthentic elements. First, we see the problem the couple faces and we understand their efforts to surmount it. The problem is to find an "unspoiled" place. "Unspoiled" does not mean only that a place is left physically intact; it means also that it is not encrusted by renown and by the familiar (as is Taxco), that it has not been discovered by others. We understand that the couple really want to get at the place and enjoy it. Yet at the same time we wonder if there is not something wrong in their dislike of their compatriots. Does access to the place require the exclusion of others?

Let us see what happens.

The couple decide to drive from Guanajuato to Mexico City. On the way they get lost. After hours on a rocky mountain road, they find themselves in a tiny valley not even marked on the map. There they discover an Indian village. Some sort of religious festival is going on. It is apparently a corn dance in supplication of the rain god.

The couple know at once that this is "it." They are entranced. They spend several days in the village, observing the Indians and being themselves observed with friendly curiosity.

Now may we not say that the sightseers have at last come face to face with an authentic sight, a sight which is charming, quaint, picturesque, unspoiled, and that they see the sight and come away rewarded? Possibly this may occur. Yet it is more likely that what happens is a far cry indeed from an immediate encounter with being, that the experience, while masquerading as such, is in truth a rather desperate impersonation. I use the word *desperate* advisedly to signify an actual loss of hope.

The clue to the spuriousness of their enjoyment of the village and the festival is a certain restiveness in the sightseers themselves. It is given expression by their repeated exclamations that "this is too good to be true," and by their anxiety that it may not prove to be so perfect, and finally by their downright relief at leaving the valley and having the experience in the bag, so to speak—that is, safely embalmed in memory and movie film.

What is the source of their anxiety during the visit? Does it not mean that the couple are looking at the place with a certain standard of performance in mind? Are they like Fabre, who gazed at the world about him with wonder, letting it be what it is; or are they not like the overanxious mother who sees her child as one performing, now doing badly, now doing well? The village is their child and their love for it is an anxious love because they are afraid that at any moment it might fail them.

We have another clue in their subsequent remark to an ethnologist friend. "How we wished you had been there with us! What a perfect goldmine of folkways! Every minute we would say to each other, if only you were here! You must return with us." This surely testifies to a generosity of spirit, a willingness to share their experience with others, not at all like their feelings toward their fellow Iowans on the plaza at Guanajuato!

I am afraid this is not the case at all. It is true that they longed for their ethnologist friend, but it was for an entirely different reason. They wanted him, not to share their experience, but to certify their experience as genuine.

"This is it" and "Now we are really living" do not necessarily refer to the sovereign encounter of the person with the sight that enlivens the mind and gladdens the heart. It means that now at last we are having the acceptable experience. The present experience is always measured by a prototype, the "it" of their dreams. "Now I am really living" means that now I am filling the role of sightseer and the sight is living up to the prototype of sights. This quaint and picturesque village is measured by a Platonic ideal of the Quaint and the Picturesque.

Hence their anxiety during the encounter. For at any minute something could go wrong. A fellow Iowan might emerge from a 'dobe hut; the chief might show them his Sears catalogue. (If the failures are "wrong" enough, as these are, they might still be turned to account as rueful conversation pieces: "There we were expecting the chief to bring us a churinga and he shows up with a Sears catalogue!") They have snatched victory from disaster, but their experience always runs the danger of failure.

They need the ethnologist to certify their experience as genuine. This is borne out by their behavior when the three of them return for the next corn dance. During the dance, the couple do not watch the goings-on; instead they watch the ethnologist! Their highest hope is that their friend should find the dance interesting. And if he should show signs of true absorption, an interest in the goings-on so powerful that he becomes oblivious of his friends—then their cup is full. "Didn't we tell you?" they say at last. What they want from him is not ethnological explanations; all they want is his approval.

What has taken place is a radical loss of sovereignty over that which is as much theirs as it is the ethnologist's. The fault does not lie with the ethnologist. He has no wish to stake a claim to the village; in fact, he desires the opposite: he will bore his friends to death by telling them about the village and the meaning of the folkways. A degree of sovereignty has been surrendered by the couple. It is the nature of the loss, moreover, that they are not aware of the loss, beyond a certain uneasiness. (Even if they read this and admitted it, it would be very difficult for them to bridge the gap in their confrontation of the world. Their consciousness of the corn dance cannot escape their consciousness of their consciousness, so that with the onset of the first direct enjoyment, their higher consciousness pounces and certifies: "Now you are doing it! Now you are really living!" and, in certifying the experience, sets it at nought.)

Their basic placement in the world is such that they recognize a priority of title of the expert over his particular department of being. The whole horizon of being is staked out by "them," the experts. The highest satisfaction of the sightseer (not merely the tourist but any layman seer of sights) is that his sight should be certified as genuine. The worst of this impoverishment is that there is no sense of impoverishment. The surrender of title is so complete that it never even occurs to one to reassert title. A poor man may envy the rich man, but the sightseer does not envy the expert. When a caste system becomes absolute, envy disappears. Yet the caste of layman-expert is not the fault of the expert. It is due altogether to the eager surrender of sovereignty by the layman so that he may take up the role not of the person but of the consumer.

I do not refer only to the special relation of layman to theorist. I refer to the general situation in which sovereignty is surrendered to a class of privileged knowers, whether these be theorists or artists. A reader may surrender sovereignty over that which has been written about, just as a consumer may surrender sovereignty over a thing which has been theorized about. The consumer is content to receive an experience just as it has been presented to him by theorists and planners. The reader may also be content to judge life by whether it has or has not been formulated by those who know and write about life. A young man goes to France. He too has a fair time of it, sees the sights, enjoys the food. On his last day, in fact as he sits in a restaurant in Le Havre waiting for his boat, something happens. A group of French students in the restaurant get into an impassioned argument over a recent play. A riot takes place. Madame la concierge joins in, swinging her mop at the rioters. Our young American is transported. This is "it." And he had almost left France without seeing "it"!

But the young man's delight is ambiguous. On the one hand, it is a pleasure for him to encounter the same Gallic temperament he had heard about from Puccini and Rolland. But on the other hand, the source of his pleasure testifies to a certain alienation. For the young man is actually barred from a direct encounter with anything French excepting only that which has been set forth, authenticated by Puccini and Rolland—those who know. If he had encountered the restaurant scene without reading Hemingway, without knowing that the performance was so typically, charmingly French, he would not have been delighted. He would only have been anxious at seeing things get so out of hand. The source of his delight is the sanction of those who know.

This loss of sovereignty is not a marginal process, as might appear from my example of estranged sightseers. It is a generalized surrender of the horizon to those experts within whose competence a particular segment of the horizon is thought to lie. Kwakiutls are surrendered to Franz Boas; decaying Southern mansions are surrendered to Faulkner and Tennessee Williams. So that, although it is by no means the intention of the expert to expropriate sovereignty—in fact he would not even know what sovereignty meant in this context—the danger of theory and consumption is a seduction and deprivation of the consumer.

In the New Mexican desert, natives occasionally come across strange-looking artifacts which have fallen from the skies and which are stenciled: *Return to U.S. Experimental Project, Alamogordo. Reward.* The finder returns the object and is rewarded. He knows nothing of the nature of the object he has found and does not care to know. The sole role of the native, the highest role he can play, is that of finder and returner of the mysterious equipment.

The same is true of the layman's relation to *natural* objects in a modern technical society. No matter what the object or event is, whether it is a star, a swallow, a Kwakiutl, a "psychological phenomenon," the layman who confronts it does not confront it as a sovereign person, as Crusoe confronts a seashell he finds on the beach. The highest role he can conceive himself as playing is to be able to recognize the title of the object, to return it to the appropriate expert and have it certified as a genuine find. He does not even permit himself to see the thing—as Gerard Hopkins could see a rock or a cloud or a field. If anyone asks him why he doesn't look, he may reply that he didn't take that subject in college (or he hasn't read Faulkner).

This loss of sovereignty extends even to oneself. There is the neurotic who asks nothing more of his doctor than that his symptoms should prove interesting. When all else fails, the poor fellow has nothing to offer but his own neurosis. But even this is sufficient if only the doctor will show interest when he says, "Last night I had a curious sort of dream; perhaps it will be significant to one who knows about such things. It seems I was standing in a sort of alley—" (I have nothing else to offer you but my own unhappiness. Please say that it, at least, measures up, that it is a *proper* sort of unhappiness.)

2

A young Falkland Islander walking along a beach and spying a dead dogfish and going to work on it with his jackknife has, in a fashion wholly unprovided in modern educational theory, a great advantage over the Scarsdale high-school pupil who finds the dogfish on his laboratory desk. Similarly the citizen of Huxley's *Brave New World* who stumbles across a volume of Shakespeare in some vine-grown ruins and squats on a potsherd to read it is in a fairer way of getting at a sonnet than the Harvard sophomore taking English Poetry II.

The educator whose business it is to teach students biology or poetry is unaware of a whole ensemble of relations which exist between the student and the dogfish and between the student and the Shakespeare sonnet. To put it bluntly: A student who has the desire to get at a dogfish or a Shakespeare sonnet may have the greatest difficulty in salvaging the creature itself from the educational package in which it is presented. The great difficulty is that he is not aware that there is a difficulty; surely, he thinks, in such a fine classroom, with such a fine textbook, the sonnet must come across! What's wrong with me?

The sonnet and the dogfish are obscured by two different processes. The sonnet is obscured by the symbolic package which is formulated not by the sonnet itself but by the *media* through which the sonnet is transmitted, the media which the educators believe for some reason to be transparent. The new textbook, the type, the smell of the page, the classroom, the aluminum windows and the winter sky, the personality of Miss Hawkins—these media which are supposed to transmit the sonnet may only succeed in transmitting themselves. It is only the hardiest and cleverest of students who can salvage the sonnet from this many-tissued package. It is only the rarest student who knows that the sonnet must be salvaged from the package. (The educator is well aware that there is something wrong, that there is a fatal gap between the student's learning and the student's life: The student reads the poem, appears to understand it, and gives all the answers. But what does he recall if he should happen to read a Shakespeare sonnet twenty years later? Does he recall the poem or does he recall the smell of the page and the smell of Miss Hawkins?)

One might object, pointing out that Huxley's citizen reading his sonnet in the ruins and the Falkland Islander looking at his dogfish on the beach also receive them in a certain package. Yes, but the difference lies in the fundamental placement of the student in the world, a placement which makes it possible to extract the thing from the package. The pupil at Scarsdale High sees himself placed as a consumer receiving an experience-package; but the Falkland Islander exploring his dogfish is a person exercising the sovereign right of a person in his lordship and mastery of creation. He too could use an instructor and a book and a technique, but he would use them as his subordinates, just as he uses his jackknife. The biology student does not use his scalpel as an instrument; he uses it as a magic wand! Since it is a "scientific instrument," it should do "scientific things."

The dogfish is concealed in the same symbolic package as the sonnet. But the dogfish suffers an additional loss. As a consequence of this double deprivation, the Sarah Lawrence student who scores A in zoology is apt to know very little about a dogfish. She is twice removed from the dogfish, once by the symbolic complex by which the dogfish is concealed, once again by the spoliation of the dogfish by theory which renders it invisible. Through no fault of zoology instructors, it is nevertheless a fact that the zoology laboratory at Sarah Lawrence College is one of the few places in the world where it is all but impossible to see a dogfish.

The dogfish, the tree, the seashell, the American Negro, the dream, are rendered invisible by a shift of reality from concrete thing to theory which Whitehead has called the fallacy of misplaced concreteness. It is the mistaking of an idea, a principle, an abstraction, for the real. As a consequence of the shift, the "specimen" is seen as less real than the theory of the specimen. As Kierkegaard said, once a person is seen as a specimen of race or a species, at that very moment he ceases to be an individual. Then there are no more individuals but only specimens.

To illustrate: A student enters a laboratory which, in the pragmatic view, offers the student the optimum conditions under which an educational experience may be had. In the existential view, however—that view of the student in which he is regarded not as a receptacle of experience but as a knowing being whose peculiar property it is to see himself as being in a certain situation—the modern laboratory could not have been more effectively designed to conceal the dogfish forever.

The student comes to his desk. On it, neatly arranged by his instructor, he finds his laboratory manual, a dissecting board, instruments, and a mimeographed list:

Exercise 22

Materials: 1 dissecting board

                  1 scalpel

                  1 forceps

                  1 probe

                  1 bottle india ink and syringe

                  1 specimen of *Squalus acanthias*

The clue to the situation in which the student finds himself is to be found in the last item: 1 specimen of *Squalus acanthias*.

The phrase *specimen of* expresses in the most succinct way imaginable the radical character of the loss of being which has occurred under his very nose. To refer to the dogfish, the unique concrete existent before him, as a "specimen of *Squalus acanthias*" reveals by its grammar the spoliation of the dogfish by the theoretical method. This phrase, *specimen of,* example of, instance of, indicates the ontological status of the individual creature in the eyes of the theorist. The dogfish itself is seen as a rather shabby expression of an ideal reality, the species *Squalus acanthias*. The result is the radical devaluation of the individual dogfish. (The *reductio ad absurdum* of Whitehead's shift is Toynbee's employment of it in his historical method. If a gram of NaCl is referred to by the chemist as a "sample of" NaCl, one may think of it as such and not much is missed by the oversight of the act of being of this particular pinch of salt, but when the Jews and the Jewish religion are understood as—in Toynbee's favorite phrase—a "classical example of" such and such a kind of *Voelkerwanderung,* we begin to suspect that something is being left out.)

If we look into the ways in which the student can recover the dogfish (or the sonnet), we will see that they have in common the stratagem of avoiding the educator's direct presentation of the object as a lesson to be learned and restoring access to sonnet and dogfish as beings to be known, reasserting the sovereignty of knower over known.

In truth, the biography of scientists and poets is usually the story of the discovery of the indirect approach, the circumvention of the educator's presentation—the young man who was sent to the *Technikum* and on his way fell into the habit of loitering in book stores and reading poetry; or the young man dutifully attending law school who on the way became curious about the comings and goings of ants. One remembers the scene in *The Heart Is a Lonely Hunter* where the girl hides in the bushes to hear the Capehart in the big house play Beethoven. Perhaps she was the lucky one after all. Think of the unhappy souls inside, who see the record, worry about scratches, and most of all worry about whether they are *getting it,* whether they are bona fide music lovers. What is the best way to hear Beethoven: sitting in a proper silence around the Capehart or eavesdropping from an azalea bush?

However it may come about, we notice two traits of the second situation: (1) an openness of the thing before one—instead of being an exercise to be learned according to an approved mode, it is a garden of delights which beckons to one; (2) a sovereignty of the knower—instead of being a consumer of a prepared experience, I am a sovereign wayfarer, a wanderer in the neighborhood of being who stumbles into the garden.

One can think of two sorts of circumstances through which the thing may be restored to the person. (There is always, of course, the direct recovery: A student may simply be strong enough, brave enough, clever enough to take the dogfish and the sonnet by storm, to wrest control of it from the educators and the educational package.) First by ordeal: The Bomb falls; when the young man recovers consciousness in the shambles of the biology laboratory, there not ten inches from his nose lies the dogfish. Now all at once he can see it, directly and without let, just as the exile or the prisoner or the sick man sees the sparrow at his window in all its inexhaustibility; just as the commuter who has had a heart attack sees his own hand for the first time. In these cases, the simulacrum of everydayness and of consumption has been destroyed by disaster; in the case of the bomb, literally destroyed. Secondly, by apprenticeship to a great man: One day a great biologist walks into the laboratory; he stops in front of our student's desk; he leans over, picks up the dogfish, and, ignoring instruments and procedure, probes with a broken fingernail into the little carcass. "Now here is a curious business," he says, ignoring also the proper jargon of the specialty. "Look here how this little duct reverses its direction and drops into the pelvis. Now if you would look into a coelacanth, you would see that it—" And all at once the student can see. The technician and the sophomore who loves his textbook are always offended by the genuine research man because the latter is usually a little vague and always humble before the thing; he doesn't have much use for the equipment or the jargon. Whereas the technician is never vague and never humble before the thing; he holds the thing disposed of by the principle, the formula, the textbook outline; and he thinks a great deal of equipment and jargon.

But since neither of these methods of recovering the dogfish is pedagogically feasible—perhaps the great man even less so than the Bomb—I wish to propose the following educational technique which should prove equally effective for Harvard and Shreveport High School. I propose that English poetry and biology should be taught as usual, but that at irregular intervals, poetry students should find dogfishes on their desks and biology students should find Shakespeare sonnets on their dissecting boards. I am serious in declaring that a Sarah Lawrence English major who began poking about in a dogfish with a bobby pin would learn more in thirty minutes than a biology major in a whole semester; and that the latter upon reading on her dissecting board

> That time of year Thou may'st in me behold
> When yellow leaves, or none, or few, do hang
> Upon those boughs which shake against the cold—
> Bare ruin'd choirs where late the sweet birds sang.

might catch fire at the beauty of it.

The situation of the tourist at the Grand Canyon and the biology student are special cases of a predicament in which everyone finds himself in a modern technical society—a society, that is, in which there is a division between expert and layman, planner and consumer, in which experts and planners take special measures to teach and edify the consumer. The measures taken are measures appropriate to the consumer: The expert and the planner *know* and *plan*, but the consumer *needs* and *experiences*.

There is a double deprivation. First, the thing is lost through its packaging. The very means by which the thing is presented for consumption, the very techniques by which the thing is made available as an item of need-satisfaction, these very means operate to remove the thing from the sovereignty of the knower. A loss of title occurs. The measures which the museum curator takes to present the thing to the public are self-liquidating. The upshot of the curator's efforts are not that everyone can see the exhibit but that no one can see it. The curator protests: Why are they so indifferent? Why do they even deface the exhibits? Don't they know it is theirs? But it is not theirs. It is his, the curator's. By the most exclusive sort of zoning, the museum exhibit, the park oak tree, is part of an ensemble, a package, which is almost impenetrable to them. The archaeologist who puts his find in a museum so that everyone can see it accomplishes the reverse of his expectation. The result of his action is that no one can see it now but the archaeologist. He would have done better to keep it in his pocket and show it now and then to strangers.

The tourist who carves his initials in a public place, which is theoretically "his" in the first place, has good reasons for doing so, reasons which the exhibitor and planner know nothing about. He does so because in his role of consumer of an experience (a "recreational experience" to satisfy a "recreational need") he knows that he is disinherited. He is deprived of his title over being. He knows very well that he is in a very special sort of zone in which his only rights are the rights of a consumer. He moves like a ghost through schoolroom, city streets, trains, parks, movies. He carves his initials as a last desperate measure to escape his ghostly role of consumer. He is saying in effect: I am not a ghost after all; I am a sovereign person. And he establishes title the only way remaining to him, by staking his claim over one square inch of wood or stone.

Does this mean that we should get rid of museums? No, but it means that the sightseer should be prepared to enter into a struggle to recover a sight from a museum.

The second loss is the spoliation of the thing, the tree, the rock, the swallow, by the layman's misunderstanding of scientific theory. He believes that the thing is *disposed of* by theory, that it stands in the Platonic relation of being a *specimen of* such and such an underlying principle. In the transmission of scientific theory from theorist to layman, the expectation of the theorist is reversed. Instead of the marvels of the universe being made available to the public, the universe is disposed of by theory. The loss of sovereignty takes this form: As a result of the science of botany, trees are not made available to every man. On the contrary. The tree loses its proper density and mystery as a concrete existent and, as merely another *specimen of* a species, becomes itself nugatory.

Does this mean that there is no use taking biology at Harvard and Shreveport High? No, but it means that the student should know what a fight he has on his hands to rescue the specimen from the educational package. The educator is only partly to blame. For there is nothing the educator can do to provide for this need of the student. Everything the educator does only succeeds in becoming, for the student, part of the educational package. The highest role of the educator is the maieutic role of Socrates: to help the student come to himself not as a consumer of experience but as a sovereign individual.

The thing is twice lost to the consumer. First, sovereignty is lost: It is theirs, not his. Second, it is radically devalued by theory. This is a loss which has been brought about by science but through no fault of the scientist and through no fault of scientific theory. The loss has come about as a consequence of the seduction of the layman by science. The layman will be seduced as long as he regards beings as consumer items to be experienced rather than prizes to be won, and as long as he waives his sovereign rights as a person and accepts his role of consumer as the highest estate to which the layman can aspire.

As Mounier said, the person is not something one can study and provide for; he is something one struggles for. But unless he also struggles for himself, unless he knows that there is a struggle, he is going to be just what the planners think he is.

1975

READING, REREADING, AND ANALYSIS

1. What is the "creature" that Percy says is lost?

2. What does Percy want us to *do* with his essay? He seems to ask us to discover for ourselves how the world works, and yet he offers his own opinions. Is he just an expert who is guilty of trying to seduce us with his own "preformed" ideas?

3. What would a world full of "sovereign knowers" look like? Is such a place possible? What might be some of the (perhaps unforeseen) consequences of a world in which everybody was trying to seize experience in the ways Percy recommends? Does this thought experiment suggest any problems with Percy's argument?

RESPONDING THROUGH WRITING: BUILDING AN INTERPRETATION

4. What is wrong with trying to get people to see things the way that we do? Doesn't community life depend on shared experiences? Write an essay in which you consider the place of sharing in Percy's argument. If you think he values freedom over connection with others, show where in his text he suggests this. Can one have "sovereignty" and still have relationships with others?

5. Consider Percy's idea of the "sovereign experience" and the examples he uses to explore it. Use one or two of Percy's suggestions to develop your own example of a sovereign experience. Describe the obstacles that arise when one tries to have what Percy refers to as an "authentic" encounter. Are we ever free of the "packaging" that surrounds experience?

GOING FURTHER: LEARNING FROM OTHER SOURCES

6. Find a website for a popular tourist attraction and look for places where it seems to present a "preformed symbolic complex." List several of the ways in which the website tries to predict and even script the experience of tourists, and consider the effects of these gestures. Does the site make any promises or guarantees about the tourist's encounter? What other strategies might it use to entice travelers? Can it avoid offering "preformed" ideas?

APPLYING WHAT YOU'VE LEARNED

7. How is the frustration that Coleman Hawkins exhibits about his fans (in Scott DeVeaux's "Progress and the Bean") emblematic of the packaging that often "encrusts" our experience? What, in Percy's terms, prevents the listener from hearing the "true" Coleman Hawkins?

8. Why might Percy have difficulty having fun at Disney World? Look at Susan Willis's piece through Percy's eyes. Are Willis and Percy arguing the same point? Analyze at least one important difference between the two.

9. Use Percy's ideas about the "symbolic complexes" that can stand between us and real discovery to write a paper analyzing "Scott McCloud's "Setting the Record Straight," Rebecca Solnit's "Aerobic Sisyphus and the Suburbanized Psyche," or Jane Tompkins' "At the Buffalo Bill Museum, June, 1988." To what extent does the essayist's analysis of the comics, walking, or the museum become a "symbolic complex" for you? To what extent do you gain something from that analysis that leads to real discovery or makes up for the loss of the "creature" in some way?

RICHARD RODRIGUEZ

Richard Rodriguez (b. 1944) is a journalist and writer. In addition to his essays for public television's *Lehrer NewsHour,* Rodriguez has written three volumes of his autobiography— *Hunger of Memory: The Education of Richard Rodriguez* (1982), *Days of Obligation: An Argument with My Mexican Father* (1992), and *Brown: The Last Discovery of America* (2002). In this trilogy, Rodriguez uses his own experiences as a Mexican-Amerindian as the basis for an exploration of American attitudes toward race, class, and ethnicity. Rodriguez once told an interviewer, "It takes me a very long time to write. What I try to do when I write is break down the line separating the prosaic world from the poetic word. I try to write about everyday concerns—an educational issue, say, or the problems of the unemployed—but to write about them as powerfully, as richly, as well as I can."

> To read more work by Richard Rodriguez, see <http://www.pbs.org/newshour/essays/richard_rodriguez.html>.

WHAT DO YOU KNOW? WHAT DO YOU EXPECT TO DISCOVER?

Before reading the essay, take a moment to consider the following questions.

1. What topics does Rodriguez's biography suggest he is interested in? What do you know about those topics? Knowledge can come from personal experience, stories you've heard, other classes you've taken, or other reading you've done.

2. What does his title lead you to expect from his essay? Look closely at each word. Circle keywords. Is "Blaxicans" in your dictionary? If not, what might it mean?

3. Rodriguez examines ethnicity and its relation to culture in his essay. Consider your own understanding of the terms "ethnicity" and "culture." Think particularly about how you as well as others might define your own ethnicity. Likewise, think about how your identity is related to culture or cultures. From your own experiences, what do you expect Rodriguez to argue in his essay?

✗

"Blaxicans" and Other Reinvented Americans

There is something unsettling about immigrants because . . . well, because they chatter incomprehensibly, and they get in everyone's way. Immigrants seem to be bent on undoing America. Just when Americans think we know who we are—we are Protestants, culled from Western Europe, are we not?—then new immigrants appear from Southern Europe or from Eastern Europe. We—we who are already here—we don't know exactly what the latest comers will mean to our community. How will they fit in with us? Thus we—we who were here first—we begin to question our own identity.

After a generation or two, the grandchildren or the great-grandchildren of immigrants to the United States and the grandchildren of those who tried to keep immigrants out of the United States will romanticize the immigrant, will begin to see the immigrant as the figure who teaches us most about what it means to be an American. The immigrant, in mythic terms, travels from the outermost rind of America to the very center of American mythology. None of this, of course, can we admit to the Vietnamese immigrant who served us our breakfast at the hotel this morning. In another 40 years, we will be prepared to say to the Vietnamese immigrant that he, with his breakfast tray, with his intuition for travel, with his memory of tragedy, with his recognition of peerless freedoms, he fulfills the meaning of America.

In 1997, Gallup conducted a survey on race relations in America, but the poll was concerned only with white and black Americans. No question was put to the aforementioned Vietnamese man. There was certainly no question for the Chinese grocer, none for the Guatemalan barber, none for the tribe of Mexican Indians who reroofed your neighbor's house.

The American conversation about race has always been a black-and-white conversation, but the conversation has become as bloodless as badminton.

I have listened to the black-and-white conversation for most of my life. I was supposed to attach myself to one side or the other, without asking the obvious questions: What is this perpetual dialectic between Europe and Africa? Why does it admit so little reference to anyone else?

I am speaking to you in American English that was taught me by Irish nuns—immigrant women. I wear an Indian face; I answer to a Spanish surname as well as this California first name, Richard. You might wonder about the complexity of historical factors, the collision of centuries, that creates Richard Rodriguez. My brownness is the illustration of that collision, or the bland memorial of it. I stand before you as an Impure-American, an Ambiguous-American.

In the 19th century, Texans used to say that the reason Mexicans were so easily defeated in battle was because we were so dilute, being neither pure Indian nor pure Spaniard. Yet, at the same time, Mexicans used to say that Mexico, the country of my ancestry, joined two worlds, two competing armies. Jose Vasconcelos, the Mexican educator and philosopher, famously described Mexicans as *la raza cósmica,* the cosmic race. In Mexico what one finds as early as the 18th century is a predominant population of mixed-race people. Also, once the slave had been freed in Mexico, the incidence of marriage between Indian and African people there was greater than in any other country in the Americas and has not been equaled since.

Race mixture has not been a point of pride in America. Americans speak more easily about "diversity" than we do about the fact that I might marry your daughter, you might become we; we might become us. America has so readily adopted the Canadian notion of multiculturalism because it preserves our preference for thinking ourselves separate—our elbows need not touch, thank you. I would prefer *that* table. I can remain Mexican, whatever that means, in the United States of America.

I would propose that instead of adopting the Canadian model of multiculturalism, America might begin to imagine the Mexican alternative—that of a *mestizaje* society.

Because of colonial Mexico, I am mestizo. But I was reinvented by President Richard Nixon. In the early 1970s, Nixon instructed the Office of Management and Budget to identify the major racial and ethnic groups in the United States. OMB came up with five major ethnic or racial groups. The groups are white, black, Asian/Pacific Islander, American Indian/Eskimo, and Hispanic.

It's what I learned to do when I was in college: to call myself a Hispanic. At my university we even had separate cafeteria tables and "theme houses," where the children of Nixon could gather—of a feather. Native Americans united. African-Americans. Casa Hispanic.

The interesting thing about Hispanics is that you will never meet us in Latin America. You may meet Chileans and Peruvians and Mexicans. You will not meet Hispanics. If you inquire in Lima or Bogotá about Hispanics, you will be referred to Dallas. For "Hispanic" is a gringo contrivance, a definition of the world according to European patterns of colonization. Such a definition suggests I have more in common with Argentine-Italians than with American Indians; that there is an ineffable union between the white Cuban and the mulatto Puerto Rican because of Spain. Nixon's conclusion has become the basis for the way we now organize and understand American society.

The Census Bureau foretold that by the year 2003, Hispanics would outnumber blacks to become the largest minority in the United

States. And, indeed, the year 2003 has arrived and the proclamation of Hispanic ascendancy has been published far and wide. While I admit a competition has existed—does exist—in America between Hispanic and black people, I insist that the comparison of Hispanics with blacks will lead, ultimately, to complete nonsense. For there is no such thing as a Hispanic race. In Latin America, one sees every race of the world. One sees white Hispanics, one sees black Hispanics, one sees brown Hispanics who are Indians, many of whom do not speak Spanish because they resist Spain. One sees Asian-Hispanics. To compare blacks and Hispanics, therefore, is to construct a fallacious equation.

Some Hispanics have accepted the fiction. Some Hispanics have too easily accustomed themselves to impersonating a third race, a great new third race in America. But Hispanic is an ethnic term. It is a term denoting culture. So when the Census Bureau says by the year 2060 one-third of all Americans will identify themselves as Hispanic, the Census Bureau is not speculating in pigment or quantifying according to actual historical narratives, but rather is predicting how by the year 2060 one-third of all Americans will identify themselves culturally. For a country that traditionally has taken its understandings of community from blood and color, the new circumstance of so large a group of Americans identifying themselves by virtue of language or fashion or cuisine or literature is an extraordinary change, and a revolutionary one.

People ask me all the time if I envision another Quebec forming in the United States because of the large immigrant movement from the south. Do I see a Quebec forming in the Southwest, for example? No, I don't see that at all. But I do notice the Latin American immigrant population is as much as 10 years younger than the U.S. national population. I notice the Latin American immigrant population is more fertile than the U.S. national population. I see the movement of the immigrants from south to north as a movement of youth—like approaching spring!—into a country that is growing middle-aged. I notice immigrants are the archetypal Americans at a time when we—U.S. citizens—have become post-Americans, most concerned with subsidized medications.

I was at a small Apostolic Assembly in East Palo Alto a few years ago—a mainly Spanish-speaking congregation in an area along the freeway, near the heart of the Silicon Valley. This area used to be black East Palo Alto, but it is quickly becoming an Asian and Hispanic Palo Alto neighborhood. There was a moment in the service when newcomers to the congregation were introduced. Newcomers brought letters of introduction from sister evangelical churches in Latin America. The minister read out the various letters and pronounced the names and places of origin to the community. The congregation applauded. And I thought to myself: It's over. The border is over. These people were not being asked whether they had green cards. They were not being asked whether they arrived here legally or illegally. They were being welcomed within a new community for reasons of culture. There is now a north-south line that is theological, a line that cannot be circumvented by the U.S. Border Patrol.

I was on a British Broadcasting Corporation interview show, and a woman introduced me as being "in favor" of assimilation. I am not in favor of assimilation any more than I am in favor of the Pacific Ocean or clement weather. If I had a bumper sticker on the subject, it might read something like ASSIMILATION HAPPENS. One doesn't get up in the morning, as an immigrant child in America, and think to oneself, "How much of an American shall I become today?" One doesn't walk down the street and decide to be 40 percent Mexican and 60 percent American. Culture is fluid. Culture is smoke. You breathe it. You eat it. You can't help hearing it—Elvis Presley goes in your ear, and you cannot get Elvis Presley out of your mind.

I am in favor of assimilation. I am not in favor of assimilation. I recognize assimilation. A few years ago, I was in Merced, Calif.—a town of about 75,000 people in the Central Valley where the two largest immigrant groups at that time (California is so fluid, I believe this is no longer the case) were Laotian Hmong and Mexicans. Laotians have never in the history of the world, as far as I know, lived next to Mexicans. But there they were in Merced, and living next to Mexicans. They don't like each other. I was talking to the Laotian kids about why they don't like the Mexican kids. They were telling me that the Mexicans do this and the Mexicans don't do that, when I suddenly realized that they were speaking English with a Spanish accent.

On his interview show, Bill Moyers once asked me how I thought of myself. As an American? Or Hispanic? I answered that I am Chinese, and that is because I live in a Chinese city and because I want to be Chinese. Well, why not? Some Chinese-American people in the Richmond and Sunset districts of San Francisco sometimes paint their houses (so many qualifiers!) in colors I would once have described as garish: lime greens, rose reds, pumpkin. But I have lived in a Chinese city for so long that my eye has taken on that palette, has come to prefer lime greens and rose reds and all the inventions of this Chinese Mediterranean. I see photographs in magazines or documentary footage of China, especially rural China, and I see what I recognize as home. Isn't that odd?

I do think distinctions exist. I'm not talking about an America tomorrow in which we're going to find that black and white are no longer the distinguishing marks of separateness. But many young people I meet tell me they feel like Victorians when they identify themselves as black or white. They don't think of themselves in those terms. And they're already moving into a world in which tattoo or ornament or movement or commune or sexuality or drug or rave or electronic bombast are the organizing principles of their identity. The notion that they are white or black simply doesn't occur.

And increasingly, of course, one meets children who really don't know how to say what they are. They simply are too many things. I met a young girl in San Diego at a convention of mixed-race children, among whom the common habit is to define one parent over the other—black over white, for example. But this girl said that her mother was Mexican and her father was African. The girl said "Blaxican." By reinventing language, she is reinventing America.

America does not have a vocabulary like the vocabulary the Spanish empire evolved to describe the multiplicity of racial possibilities in the New World. The conversation, the interior monologue of America cannot rely on the old vocabulary—black, white. We are no longer a black-white nation.

So, what myth do we tell ourselves? The person who got closest to it was Karl Marx. Marx predicted that the discovery of gold in California would be a more central event to the Americas than the discovery of the Americas by Columbus—which was only the meeting of two tribes, essentially, the European and the Indian. But when gold was discovered in California in the 1840s, the entire world met. For the first time in human history, all of the known world gathered. The Malaysian stood in the gold fields alongside the African, alongside the Chinese, alongside the Australian, alongside the Yankee.

That was an event without parallel in world history and the beginning of modern California—why California today provides the mythological structure for understanding how we might talk about the American experience: not as biracial, but as the re-creation of the known world in the New World.

Sometimes truly revolutionary things happen without regard. I mean, we may wake up one morning and there is no black race. There is no white race either. There are mythologies, and—as I am in the business, insofar as I am in any business at all, of demythologizing such identities as black and white—I come to you as a man of many cultures. I come to you as Chinese. Unless you understand that I am Chinese, then you have not understood anything I have said.

READING, REREADING, AND ANALYSIS

1. What terms or ideas seem most important to Rodriguez?

2. Choose two definitions or examples that help you explain what Rodriguez means by the key idea in his title, "Reinvented Americans," and take some notes explaining the idea. In a group, share your findings and list the meanings Rodriguez associates with the idea.

3. Individually or in a group, make a list of the reasons Rodriguez might give for claiming to be Chinese. Then make a list of the positive and productive possibilities of awaking one morning to

find there is neither a white race nor a black race, as Rodriguez imagines in his concluding paragraph. What does he mean by "demythologizing"?

4. What does Rodriguez mean on page 420 when he says, "There is no such thing as a Hispanic race"? If not as a race, then how does Rodriguez define the term "Hispanic"?

5. On page 421, Rodriguez says, "Culture is fluid. Culture is smoke. You breathe it. You eat it." Paraphrase his claim. How does his understanding of culture compare with your own understanding of the idea? Make a list of examples that illustrate Rodriguez's claim and a list that might challenge or not fit neatly into his claim that "culture is fluid."

6. What is the tone of Rodriguez's essay? What emotions do you think he expresses? Make a short list of places in the essay where you think his language is especially revealing.

RESPONDING THROUGH WRITING: BUILDING AN INTERPRETATION

7. In a brief essay (one or two pages), discuss Rodriguez's claim that the "border is over" (p. 420). What does he mean by "border"? Think about more than just one meaning of this term.

8. Using the list you prepared for question 3, write an essay examining the positive and negative aspects of the "demythologizing" Rodriguez discusses in regard to questions of racial distinctions. Who is likely to agree with him and why? Who is likely to disagree with him and why?

9. In three or four sentences, summarize Rodriguez's discussion of the California Gold Rush near the end of his essay. Next, write a brief essay (two or three pages) in which you explain relationships you see between your summary and how Rodriguez begins his essay (think particularly about his first four paragraphs).

10. Using your ideas from question 5, write a short paper exploring the effects of culture in your life. Where it makes sense to do so, make connections between your experiences and Rodriguez's sense of culture.

GOING FURTHER: LEARNING FROM OTHER SOURCES

11. Use a reference database such as Lexis-Nexis to find U.S. Government Census information about immigration. Compare immigration data from the nineteenth century with immigration data

for today and projected numbers for the middle of this century. Compare your findings with Rodriguez's claims about immigration in the United States.

12. Try to search the terms "Blaxican" and "*mestizo*" in a popular search engine such as Google, AltaVista or HotBot. From a brief sampling of the websites you find, list some of the meanings and issues associated with the terms. Try the same search terms in an academic database such as Academic Search Elite, and list some of the meanings and issues involving either or both of the search terms. In a group, note the differences between the two lists.

APPLYING WHAT YOU'VE LEARNED

13. Gloria Anzaldúa, in "Chicana Artists: Exploring *Nepantla, el Lugar de la Frontera*" (p. 54), is, like Rodriguez, describing what it means to be "American." Would these two writers agree with each other on this issue? What is Anzaldúa's attitude toward "border art," and how might Rodriguez respond to it given what you've learned about him from reading and thinking about his essay?

14. Ralph Ellison, in "The Little Man at Chehaw Station" (p. 151), uses the melting-pot metaphor to describe "American" identity. Compare Ellison's use of the metaphor with Rodriguez's arguments about culture and ethnicity. Is Rodriguez an advocate of the melting-pot metaphor or is he advocating an alternative metaphor?

15. Use the ideas of "symbolic packaging" and "sovereignty" from Walker Percy's essay, "The Loss of the Creature" (p. 402), to help you analyze the concepts of culture, ethnicity, and race in Rodriguez's essay. What in Rodriguez's view fosters the repetition of "black-and-white conversation" about race in the United States (p. 418)? Be sure to assess the solution(s) Rodriguez proposes.

WITOLD RYBCZYNSKI

Witold Rybczynski (b. 1943) is the Martin and Margy Meyerson Professor of Urbanism and Director of the Urban Design Program at the University of Pennsylvania and Professor of Real Estate at the Wharton School of Business. Rybczynski is also a practicing architect and the author of eight books, including *Home: A Short History of an Idea* (1986) and *City Life: Urban Expectations in a New World* (1995). "Designs for Escape" was originally published in the *New Yorker.*

> To learn more about Witold Rybczynski, read "Landscape Artist," an interview published in the *Atlantic Monthly* and available online at <http://www.theatlantic.com/unbound/interviews/ba990714.htm>.

WHAT DO YOU KNOW? WHAT DO YOU EXPECT TO DISCOVER?

Before reading the essay, take a moment to consider the following questions.

1. What topics does Rybczynski's biography suggest he is interested in? What do you know about those topics? Knowledge can come from personal experience, stories you've heard, other classes you've taken, or other reading you've done.

2. Before reading the essay, write down as many possible definitions of "escape" as you can think of.

3. In "Designs for Escape," Rybczynski is interested in designs for a dream house. If you could design your own dream house, what would it look like?

✗

Designs for Escape

Last summer, I was in Montreal on a brief visit from Philadelphia, where I now live. I had some small business to conduct there, but the visit was mainly an opportunity to look up old friends. I called Danièle, whom I hadn't seen in a couple of years, and we arranged to have dinner together that evening. She promised to take me to a new bistro, and I looked forward to it: Montreal is no longer the premier city of Canada—that role now belongs to Toronto—and it seemed a bit shabbier than I remembered, but it still has more than its share of exceptional restaurants.

"Shall we meet there?" I asked.

"No," she said, "you must come by the apartment first." She told me excitedly that she wanted to show me the plans of a weekend house that she and Luc were going to build. Danièle is not an architectural neophyte: she had been married to an architect for twenty years. True, the marriage had ended in divorce—Luc, her current beau, is in public relations—and I didn't remember her having expressed strong ideas about architecture in the past. But I knew her ex well; he had been a student of mine. You can't live with someone for twenty years and not be influenced by what that person does. At least, that's what my wife tells me. So I was curious to see what sort of house Danièle had come up with.

She and Luc and I sat around the kitchen table, and they showed me snapshots of the site, which was in the Laurentian Mountains, a popular recreation area north of Montreal. The Laurentians are an old volcanic range, and the worn, rounded mountains recall the Berkshires or the Catskills, but they're wilder, with fewer signs of human habitation. Though I prefer pastoral scenery—rolling fields and gentle hills—to mountains, I had to admit that Danièle and Luc's land was beautiful: a wooded hilltop with long views in several directions.

I sensed that Danièle was a bit nervous about showing me the drawings of the house. That was understandable. She knew that I taught architecture and wrote about domestic design. She and her husband had helped my wife and me when we built our own house in the country. Now it was her turn. Building a house for yourself is exciting, because of the feeling of possibility that a new house carries, and because creating shelter is a basic human urge, whether or not you are an architect. It is the same urge that makes children erect playhouses out of blankets and cardboard boxes, and build sandcastles at the beach. But building a house—a real house—is also scary, and not just because of the money involved or the fear of making mistakes. A new house is revealing. It tells you—and everyone else— "This is how I live. This is what's important to me. This is what I dream about." I think that's why home magazines—from *Ladies' Home Journal* to *Architectural Digest*—have always been popular. It's not just a matter of looking for decorating hints. Rather, houses intrigue us because they tell us so much about their owners.

Danièle spread out the sketches, which had been prepared by a local architect. Siting is always a crucial decision for a country house. I could see that the house would stand almost at the top of the hill, and so would be approached from below, as, ideally, it should be; walking down to a house is always unpleasant. The hilltop had obviously been chosen for the views it offered, but it also meant that the house would be some distance from the road, and would require a short walk through the trees to arrive at the front door.

The floor layout of the house was simple enough. Because of the sloping ground, the lower level, containing two bedrooms and a bathroom, would be dug partly into the ground. The floor above, which could be entered directly from the upper part of the slope, would hold the living areas, and there would be a sleeping loft in a sort of tower. Danièle explained that they wanted to be able to rent a room to skiers during the winter season, which was why the lower level would have its own front door and could be separated from the rest of the house. The exterior would be mainly wood, with several sloping roofs. It was hard to put your finger on the architectural style of the house. It wasn't going to have the curved eaves and dormer windows of the traditional Breton style, which is still popular with many Québécois. Although the functional-looking window frames and rather spare exterior couldn't be called old-fashioned, neither did they seem aggressively modern. I suppose most people would use the term "contemporary."

The three of us got into a long discussion about how best to rearrange one of the bathrooms. I pointed out that if they moved the door to the other side and changed the site of the toilet, they could gain space and improve the circulation in the kitchen area as well. Not very inspirational stuff. I could see that Luc and Danièle expected something more. I had unconsciously fallen into a bad habit of architecture teachers: if you really don't know what to say about a project, focus on some practical improvement, no matter how small. How often had I sat on design juries at the university, taking part in interminable discussions about fire exits or corridor widths, when the real problem was something else entirely.

It wasn't that Danièle and Luc's house looked boring—quite the opposite. "The architect told us that she worked hard to make each side of the house different," Danièle explained. Differences there certainly were, and, I thought, that was part of the problem. The little house was trying too hard to be unusual and interesting. The perimeter was animated by indentations and protrusions—architectural bumps and grinds. Instead of a single sheltering gable, the roof was broken up into several slopes. This is a favorite device of commercial homebuilders and is obviously a crowd pleaser, though the roof has always seemed to me an odd thing to spend your money on. The complexity of the roof was mirrored by the intricacy of the fenestration: there were half a dozen different window shapes and sizes. The modest house was hardly in league with Frank Gehry and Peter Eisenman, but it *was* busy.

I realized that I had to say something more substantive about the house, but I wasn't sure where to start. I think that small, inexpensive houses like Danièle and Luc's should be as simple as possible. This is partly a question of economics; complexity costs money, after all, and

I would rather see a restricted budget devoted to better-quality materials than to architectural bravura. But it is also an aesthetic issue. I like plain farmhouses and straightforward country buildings. They usually look good in the landscape, and they have a kind of directness and honesty that appeals to me. True, they are often really just boxes, but boxes can be given charm through relatively inexpensive details of construction, such as bay windows, trellises, and even shutters.

A simple way to dress up a house is to add a porch. Porches, with their columns, balustrades, and ornamental fretwork, are pleasant to look at, and they are also pleasant places to sit. They are like rooms, but without walls, and they encourage the sort of lazy inactivity that has always seemed to me to be the essence of leisure. I noticed that Danièle's house didn't have any covered outdoor area, and I suggested that they might consider adding a screened porch. This would also be a useful feature, since the Laurentian summers are notorious for their mosquitoes and blackflies.

"No," Luc said, "A porch won't do at all. Porches and balconies are something for a city house. We want our house to look rustic."

That was interesting. I had always associated porches and verandas with country houses. Evidently, for Danièle and Luc they were an urban feature. (Indeed, Montreal row houses traditionally do have verandas.) A little later, they asked me what sort of material I thought should be used to finish the inside walls. I said that I liked plaster wallboard—that it was inexpensive, you could paint it whatever color you wanted, and, furthermore, it was fire-resistant—an important consideration when you're building miles from a fire station. They looked skeptical and said that they had been thinking, rather, of wood. "We want this to be a different sort of place, where we can get away from our city life," Luc said.

A lot of architecture has to do with images—and imaginings. For one person, getting away means a broad porch with a rocking chair and a slowly turning ceiling fan. The image may be the result of a remembered family photograph, or a painting, or even the experience of a real porch somewhere. That particular porch image has haunted me for years—I think I saw it first in a magazine ad for whiskey. And one of the side benefits of watching the film "Out of Africa" is the beautiful porch of Karen Blixen's plantation house in Kenya, with Mozart's Clarinet Concerto playing on a windup gramophone. Alas, for Luc a porch was just a utilitarian appendage. Moreover, the image it conjured up for him was not rural but urban. I also had the impression that he considered porches to be old-fashioned—or maybe just places for old people.

I have always liked farmhouse kitchens—large, comfortable rooms where you can cook and eat and socialize around the kitchen table. (That's probably a remembered image, too.) The plans of Danièle and Luc's house, on the other hand, showed a small efficiency kitchen, with a separate dining area. It was an arrangement that reminded me—but, obviously, not them—of a city apartment. I realized that their idea of getting away from it all was more dynamic than mine: not a cabin in the woods but a striking ski chalet on a hilltop, with different views from each room, beamed ceilings, knotty-pine walls, and a dramatic fireplace. I was starting to understand why the house looked the way it did. It was not a question of money—theirs was hardly an extravagant house. It reflected a different idea of rusticity.

Getting away from it all has a long history; almost as soon as people started living in towns, they felt the need to build country retreats. In ancient times, it was the common practice of wealthy Romans to decamp periodically to country estates. "You should take the first opportunity yourself to leave the din, the futile bustle, and the useless occupations of the city," Pliny the Younger wrote in a letter to a friend. Pliny owned two country retreats, one a large agricultural estate in present-day Umbria, the other his famous seaside villa in Latium, of which he wrote, "There I do most of my writing, and instead of the land I lack, I work to cultivate myself." The sentiment—re-creation—is recognizably modern. Modern-sounding, too, is the Renaissance architect Leon Battista Alberti's advice that "if the villa is not distant, but close by a gate of the city, it will make it easier and more convenient to flit, with wife and children, between town and villa, whenever desirable."

In nineteenth-century America, such flitting usually meant taking a steamboat or a train. Summer houses sprang up along the Hudson River, in New York, and the Schuylkill, in Philadelphia, or in places like Newport, Rhode Island. In Newport you'll find many early examples of the Shingle Style, one of the high accomplishments of American architecture. The Watts Sherman house, designed by the great architect H. H. Richardson in 1874, is irregular in composition, and the granite, the half-timbering, and the wooden shingles on the exterior give it the picturesque appearance that is a trademark of the Shingle Style. Still, it is provided with a drawing room, a dining room, and a library, and so is not really a radical departure from a typical middle-class suburban or urban house of the period.

Although rich New Yorkers commuted to their villas in Newport, these were summer houses, not weekend houses. Indeed, the full weekend—a two-day holiday at the end of the workweek—didn't appear until the twentieth century. It arrived first in Britain, as a one-and-a-half-day holiday, and by the early nineteen-hundreds more and more Americans were also working "short Saturdays." Eventually, the five-day workweek became commonplace, and the combination of the two-day holiday and the automobile produced the vast proliferation of weekend retreats that we know today.

The weekend cottage continues the time-tested tradition of the summer get-away house, but with a crucial difference. Instead of being used for an entire season, it is chiefly a two-day retreat. Hence it is less a place of long and lazy summers than of sometimes frantic spurts of recreation. Perhaps that's why the architecture is often intentionally unusual, with dramatic fireplaces, tall spaces, and cantilevered decks. That was what Luc meant when he said he wanted "a different sort of place." It was probably the late architect Charles Moore who started the trend toward spatial excitement. In the mid-nineteen-sixties he designed a series of weekend houses, chiefly in Northern California, with deceptively simple exteriors and with interiors that were a cross between barns and jungle gyms. Although designed with considerable sophistication, these houses could also be described as the architectural equivalent of the then popular leisure suit. That is, they were intended to put people instantaneously in a different mood and also to tell the world that here the owner was off duty. Moore's approach was influential, and versions of his houses sprang up in vacation spots from Colorado to Vermont.

Like many people, I spend my weekends in a worn pair of shorts and an old polo shirt. Perhaps that's why my ideal of a weekend house is more like a farmhouse—commodious rather than exciting, a place to kick your shoes off and relax, a place that can get scuffed up and still feel comfortable. Sculptural staircases and eye-popping fireplaces are not a priority. Now, I don't want to give the impression that I think weekend houses should be Thoreau-style shacks, without conveniences, or even without luxuries. I would have no objection to a Miele range and a Sub-Zero refrigerator in my country kitchen. After all, that has always been the paradoxical thing about second homes: we want to feel that we're roughing it, but we want our comforts, too. Pliny schlepped around his villa in an old tunic, but he had a proper warmed swimming bath as well as a banqueting hall. When Richardson designed the Watts Sherman house in Newport, he made it look rustic, but he also incorporated a novel amenity. Central heating. Even Thoreau, whose cabin at Walden Pond didn't have a kitchen (in warm weather, he cooked outside over an open fire), regularly walked to nearby Concord to have dinner at friends' houses.

I remember once visiting an Adirondack camp on Lower Saranac Lake. It was one of many in the area that had been built by rich New Yorkers during the Gilded Age. The house itself was typical—a charming, rough-hewn log building with a massive granite fireplace, columns made of peeled and polished tree trunks, and spartan Art-and-Crafts-style furniture. Here was rusticity laid on with a trowel. When this particular camp, Knollwood, was built, in 1899, it consisted of six cottages, a so-called casino (a social gathering place, not a gambling hall), and a boathouse, all designed by William Coulter, the architect of some of the buildings at Sagamore, the Vanderbilts' famous camp. Although the ample cottages contained several bedrooms, there were only small service kitchens. That was because the six families and their guests had their meals prepared and served to them in the casino, which did have a large kitchen. You went boating on the lake and hiking in the forest, but that was no reason you couldn't have a proper dinner, prepared by your New York cook. The Knollwood boathouse contains canoes and handmade Adirondack guide boats but also, on the upper floor, a huge billiard table. I don't think I would require a billiard table in my ideal weekend house, but, on the other hand, I wouldn't do without a compact-disk player. Getting away from it all has always involved compromise as well as a certain degree of make-believe.

It's hard to comment on—let alone judge—other people's fantasies. If Danièle and Luc wanted a house in the country, well, they would have to make their own compromises. I don't think I was really much help to my friends; our ideas of weekend houses were probably just too different. Anyway, we all went out to dinner, the atmosphere in the bistro was convivial, the food was excellent, and everyone had a good time. A week later, when I got home to Philadelphia, I just couldn't resist making some sketches of my own, trying to accommodate all their requirements. I drew a little cottage, twenty feet by thirty feet, clapboard above and with a stone base—for the two bedrooms—below. The house was sheltered by a broad gable roof (to accommodate the sleeping loft). The loft looked down on the main living space, a large family room with a kitchen at one end and a sitting area at the other. In the center of the room, a Franklin stove served for warming cold toes and cold plates. A pair of glazed doors opened onto a large screened porch. It was only a sketch, just to keep my hand in, I told myself. But if I shut my eyes I could almost hear the strains of the Clarinet Concerto in the woods.

1995

READING, REREADING, AND ANALYSIS

1. In your own words, summarize the differences between Luc's ideal house and Rybczynski's ideal.

2. Examine your list from question 2 of the prereading questions and see which of your definitions best describes the type of "escape" that Rybczynski has in mind in his essay.

3. Reread the paragraph that begins "I realized that I had to say something . . ." (p. 427). Put into your own words what Rybczynski means when he says in that paragraph, "It was also an aesthetic issue" (p. 428). You may want to look up the definition of "aesthetic" in your dictionary.

4. In a group, identify the rustic qualities that Rybczynski likes. Compare those qualities with the qualities that Danièle and Luc prefer.

5. What does Rybczynski mean on page 429 when he says, "I was starting to understand why the house looked the way it did. It was not a question of money—theirs was hardly an extravagant house. It reflected a different idea of rusticity."

6. See if you can identify a thesis statement in Rbyczynski's essay. If you do not see an explicit thesis statement in the essay, what would you say is Rbyczynski's implicit thesis?

RESPONDING THROUGH WRITING: BUILDING AN INTERPRETATION

7. Write a paragraph that summarizes the "problem" Rybczynski sees in the design of the house that Danièle and Luc plan to build.

8. Think about why Rybczynski says he prefers a plain style of architecture for a house like the one that Danièle and Luc plan to build. Write a short essay that draws an analogy between the plain style of architecture that Rybczynski prefers and a plain writing style. What are the similarities? How is a "writing style" also an "aesthetic issue" (p. 428)? Is Rybczynski's own writing style plain or fancy?

9. Write an essay that analyzes Rybczynski's diction (his word choice) and his references to architects, movies, and literary figures. In what ways is his writing style not as plain as the "worn pair of shorts and old polo shirt" he likes to wear on weekends" (p. 430)?

10. Write an essay in which you compare your ideal design for escape with Rybczynski's. You will need to summarize his ideal. Be sure to quote from his essay and to discuss the significance of what you quote.

GOING FURTHER: LEARNING FROM OTHER SOURCES

11. Use a popular Internet search engine to find information about three of the architects that Rybczynski mentions in his essay. What kinds of houses or buildings do the architects design? Find photographs or sketches of their work to bring with you to class.

12. Using a reference database that includes general-interest and current-events magazines (such as MAS Full Text Ultra), try several searches using the terms "rustic," and "rustic and life." Scan the results for articles that show some of the differing ways in which people think about that concept.

APPLYING WHAT YOU'VE LEARNED

13. Write an essay that compares Rybczynski's use of "escape" with Tuan's discussion of "escapism" in "Earth: Nature and Culture" (p. 548). Where do their conceptions of "escape" and "escapism" intersect? Where do they diverge? In your essay, you might explore how each writer links art or "aesthetics" to the idea of "escape." What significant relationships do you see between art and escape as a result of reading, thinking, and writing about these two essays?

14. Rybczynski emphasizes leisure, whereas Arlie Russell Hochschild and Rebecca Solnit emphasize work, toil, and hurry. Write a paper in which you use Rybczynski's discussion of escape as it relates to leisure to talk about forces that Hochschild and Solnit criticize for hindering what you might call designs for escape.

15. Write an essay that compares Rybczynski's "aesthetic" ideals with Winterson's ideas about art in "Imagination and Reality." What relationships do you see between the art of architectural design that Rybczynski describes and the powers of art and imagination that Winterson discusses? In your essay, be sure to incorporate key quotations from each text.

REBECCA SOLNIT

Rebecca Solnit (b. 1961) is a writer, art critic, photographer, and antinuclear activist. Her most recent books include *As Eve Said to the Serpent: On Landscape, Gender and Art* and *River of Shadows: Eadweard Muybridge and the Technological Wild West*. She has also curated exhibitions and written catalog essays for museums. "Aerobic Sisyphus and the Suburbanized Psyche" is from *Wanderlust: A History of Walking*.

> For alternative views of walking, see *Walking Magazine* at http:// <www.walkingmag.com/>.

WHAT DO YOU KNOW? WHAT DO YOU EXPECT TO DISCOVER?

Before reading the essay, take a moment to consider the following questions.

1. What topics does Solnit's biography suggest she is interested in? What do you know about those topics? Knowledge can come from personal experience, stories you've heard, other classes you've taken, or other reading you've done.

2. Look up the words "Sisyphus" and "Pschye" in a dictionary or do a Google search for each term on the Internet. What kind of essay do you expect from Solnit given these two terms plus her other keywords in the title, "Aerobic" and "Suburbanized"?

3. Solnit discusses the death of walking in her essay. Most people take walking for granted. What do you suppose that an essay about the death of walking may tell you about your culture and about yourself?

✗

Aerobic Sisyphus and the Suburbanized Psyche

Freedom to walk is not of much use without someplace to go. There is a sort of golden age of walking that began late in the eighteenth century and, I fear, expired some decades ago, a flawed age more golden for some than others, but still impressive for its creation of places in which to walk and its valuation of recreational walking. This age peaked around the turn of the twentieth century, when North Americans and Europeans were as likely to make a date for a walk as for a drink or meal, walking was often a sort of sacrament and a routine recreation, and walking clubs were flourishing. At that time, nineteenth-century urban innovations such as sidewalks and sewers were improving cities not yet menaced by twentieth-century speedups, and rural developments such as national parks and mountaineering were in first bloom. . . . [T]he history of walking is a history of cities and countryside, with a few towns and mountains thrown in for good measure. Perhaps 1970, when the U.S. Census showed that the majority of Americans were—for the first time in the history of any nation—suburban, is a good date for this golden age's tombstone. Suburbs are bereft of the natural glories and civic pleasures of those older spaces, and suburbanization has radically changed the scale and texture of everyday life, usually in ways inimical to getting about on foot. This transformation has happened in the mind as well as on the ground. Ordinary Americans now perceive, value, and use time, space, and their own bodies in radically different ways than they did before. Walking still covers the ground between cars and buildings and the short distances within the latter, but walking as a cultural activity, as a pleasure, as travel, as a way of getting around, is fading, and with it goes an ancient and profound relationship between body, world, and imagination. Perhaps walking is best imagined as an "indicator species," to use an ecologist's term. An indicator species signifies the health of an ecosystem, and its endangerment or diminishment can be an early warning sign of systemic trouble. Walking is an indicator species for various kinds of freedoms and pleasures: free time, free and alluring space, and unhindered bodies.

I. Suburbia

In *Crabgrass Frontier: The Suburbanization of the United States,* Kenneth Jackson outlines what he calls "the walking city" that preceded the development of middle-class suburbs: it was densely populated; it had "a clear distinction between city and country," often by means of walls or some other abrupt periphery; its economic and social functions were intermingled (and "factories were almost nonexistent" because "production took place at the small shops of artisans"); people rarely lived far from work; and the wealthy tended to live in the center of the city. His walking city and my golden age find their end in the suburbs, and the history of suburbia is the history of fragmentation.

Middle-class suburban homes were first built outside London in the late eighteenth century, writes Robert Fishman in another history of suburbs, *Bourgeois Utopias,* so that pious merchants could separate family life from work. Cities themselves were looked upon askance by these upper-middle-class evangelical Christians: cards, balls, theaters, street fairs, pleasure gardens, taverns were all condemned as immoral. At the same time the modern cult of the home as a consecrated space apart from the world began, with the wife-mother as a priestess who was, incidentally, confined to her temple. This first suburban community of wealthy merchant families who shared each other's values sounds, in Fishman's account, paradisiacal and, like most paradises, dull: a place of spacious freestanding houses, with little for their residents to do outside the home and garden. These villas were miniaturized English country estates, and like such estates they aspired to a kind of social self-sufficiency. However, a whole community of farmworkers, gamekeepers, servants, guests, and extended families had inhabited the estate, which usually encompassed working farms and had thus been a place of production, while the suburban home housed little more than the nuclear family and was to become more and more a site only of consumption. Too, the estate was on a scale that permitted walking without leaving the grounds; the suburban home was not, but suburbia would eat up the countryside and diffuse the urban anyway.

It was in Manchester, during the industrial revolution, that the suburb came into its own. The suburb is a product of that revolution, radiating outward from Manchester and the north Midlands, which has so thoroughly fragmented modern life. Work and home had never been very separate until the factory system came of age and the poor became wage-earning employees. Those jobs, of course, fragmented work itself as craftsmanship was broken down into unskilled repetitive gestures in attendance on machines. Early commentators deplored how factory work destroyed family life, taking individuals out of the home and making family members strangers to each other during their prodigiously long workdays. Home for factory workers was little more than a place to recuperate for the next day's work, and the industrial system made them far poorer and unhealthier than they had been as independent artisans. In the 1830s Manchester's manufacturers began to build the first large-scale suburbs to escape the city they had created and to enhance family life for their class. Unlike the London evangelicals, they were fleeing not temptation but ugliness and danger—industrial pollution, the bad air and sanitation of a poorly designed city, and the sight and threat of their miserable workforce.

"The decision to suburbanize had two great consequences," says Fishman. "First the core emptied of residents as the middle class left and workers were pushed out by the conversion of their rooms in the back streets to offices. . . . Visitors were surprised to find an urban core that was totally quiet and empty after business hours. The central business district was born. Meanwhile, the once peripheral factories were now enclosed by a suburban belt, which separated them from the now-distant rural fields. The grounds of the suburban villas were enclosed by walls, and even the tree-lined streets on which they stood were often forbidden except to the residents and their guests. One group of workers attempted to keep open a once-rural footpath that now ran through the grounds of a factory owner's suburban villa. . . . Mr. Jones responded with iron gates and ditches." Fishman's picture shows a world where the fertile mix of urban life in the "walking city" has been separated out into its sterile constituent elements.

The workers responded by fleeing to the fields on Sundays and, eventually, fighting for access to the remaining rural landscape in which to walk, climb, cycle, and breathe. . . . The middle class responded by continuing to develop and dwell in suburbs. Men commuted to work and women to shop by private carriages, then horse-drawn omnibuses (which, in Manchester, were priced too high to accommodate the poor), and eventually trains. In fleeing the poor and the city, they had left behind pedestrian scale. One could walk in the suburbs, but there was seldom anyplace to go on foot in these homogenous expanses of quiet residential streets behind whose walls dwelt families more or less like each other. The twentieth-century American suburb reached a kind of apotheosis of fragmentation when proliferating cars made it possible to place people farther than ever from work, stores, public transit, schools, and social life. The modern suburb as described by Philip Langdon is antithetical to the walking city: "Offices are kept separate from retailing. The housing is frequently divided into mutually exclusive tracts . . . with further subdivision by economic status. Manufacturing, no matter how clean and quiet—today's industries are rarely the noisy, smoke-belching mills of urban memory—is kept away from residential areas or excluded from the community entirely. Street layouts in new developments enforce apartness. To unlock the rigid geographic segregation, an individual needs to obtain a key—which is a motor vehicle. For obvious reasons those keys are not issued to those under sixteen, the very population for whom the suburbs are supposedly most intended. These keys are also denied to some of the elderly who can no longer drive."

Getting a license and a car is a profound rite of passage for modern suburban teenagers; before the car, the child is either stranded at home or dependent upon chauffeuring parents. Jane Holtz Kay, in her book on the impact of cars, *Asphalt Nation,* writes of a study that compared the lives of ten-year-olds in a walkable Vermont small town and an unwalkable southern California suburb. The California children watched four times as much television, because the outdoor world offered them few adventures and destinations. And a recent study of the effects of television on Baltimore adults concluded that the more local news television, with its massive emphasis on sensational crime stories, locals watched, the more fearful they were. Staying home to watch TV discouraged them from going out. That *Los Angeles Times* advertisement for an electronic encyclopedia . . . —"You used to walk across town in the pouring rain to use our encyclopedias. We're pretty confident we can get your kid to click and drag"—may describe the options open to a child who no longer has a library within walking distance and may not be allowed to walk far alone anyway (walking to school, which was for generations the great formative first foray alone into the world, is likewise becoming a less common experience.) Television, telephones, home computers, and the Internet complete the privatization of everyday life that suburbs began and cars enhanced. They make it less necessary to go out into the world and thus accommodate retreat from rather than resistance to the deterioration of public space and social conditions.

These American suburbs are built car-scale, with a diffuseness the unenhanced human body is inadequate to cope with, and just as gardens, sidewalks, arcades, and wilderness trails are a kind of infrastructure for walking, so modern suburbs, highways, and parking lots are an infrastructure for driving. Cars made possible the development of the great Los Angelean sprawls of the American West, those places not exactly suburbs because there is no urbanity to which they are subsidiary. Cities like Albuquerque, Phoenix, Houston, and Denver may or may not have a dense urban core floating somewhere in their bellies like a half-digested snack, but most of their space is too diffuse to be well served by public transit (if it exists) or to be traversed on foot. In these sprawls, people are no longer expected to walk, and they seldom do. There are many reasons why. Suburban sprawls generally make dull places to walk, and a large subdivision can become numbingly repetitious at three miles an hour instead of thirty or sixty. Many suburbs were designed with curving streets and cul-de-sacs that vastly expand distances: Langdon gives an example of an Irvine, California, subdivision where in order to reach a destination a quarter mile away as the crow flies the traveler must walk or drive more than a mile. Too, when walking is not an ordinary activity, a lone walker may feel ill at ease about doing something unexpected and isolated.

Walking can become a sign of powerlessness or low status, and new urban and suburban design disdains walkers. Many places have replaced downtown with shopping malls inaccessible by any means but cars, or by building cities that never had downtowns, buildings meant to be entered through parking garages rather than front doors. In Yucca Valley, the town near Joshua Tree National Park, all the businesses are strung out along several miles of highway, and crosswalks and traffic lights are rare: though, for example, my bank and food store are only a few blocks apart, they are on opposite sides of the highway, and a car is the only safe, direct way to travel between them. Throughout California more than 1,000 crosswalks have been removed in recent years, more than 150 of them in traffic-clogged Silicon Valley, apparently in the spirit of the L.A. planners who proclaimed in the early 1960s, "The pedestrian remains the largest single obstacle to free traffic movement." Many parts of these western sprawl-cities were built without sidewalks altogether, in both rich and poor neighborhoods, further signaling that walking has come to an end by design. Lars Eigner, who during a homeless and largely penniless phase of his life in the 1980s hitchhiked with his dog Lizbeth between Texas and southern California, wrote eloquently about his experiences, and one of the worst came about when a driver dropped him off in the wrong part of town: "South Tucson simply has no sidewalks. I thought at first this was merely in keeping with the general wretchedness of the place, but eventually it seemed to me that the public policy in Tucson is to impede pedestrians as much as possible. In particular, I could find no way to walk to the main part of town in the north except in the traffic lanes of narrow highway ramps. I could not believe this at first, and Lizbeth and I spent several hours wandering on the south bank of the dry gash that divides Tucson as I looked for a walkway."

Even in the best places, pedestrian space is continually eroding: in the winter of 1997–98, New York mayor Rudolph Giuliani decided that pedestrians were interfering with traffic (one could just as well have said, in this city where so many still travel and take care of their business on foot, that cars interfere with traffic). The mayor ordered the police to start citing jaywalkers and fenced in the sidewalks of some of the busiest corners of the city. New Yorkers, to their eternal glory, rebelled by staging demonstrations at the barriers and jaywalking more. In San Francisco, faster and denser traffic, shorter walk lights, and more belligerent drivers intimidate and occasionally mangle pedestrians. Here 41 percent of all traffic fatalities are pedestrians killed by cars, and more than a thousand walkers are injured every year. In Atlanta, the figures are 80 pedestrians killed per year and more than 1,300 injured. In Giuliani's New York, almost twice as many people are killed by cars as are murdered by strangers—285 versus 150 in 1997. Walking the city is not now an attractive prospect for those unequipped to dodge and dash.

Geographer Richard Walker defines urbanity as "that elusive combination of density, public life, cosmopolitan mixing, and free expression." Urbanity and automobiles are antithetical in many ways, for a city of drivers is only a dysfunctional suburb of people shuttling from private interior to private interior. Cars have encouraged the diffusion and privatization of space, as shopping malls replace shopping streets, public buildings become islands in a sea of asphalt, civic design lapses into traffic engineering, and people mingle far less freely and frequently. The street is public space in which First Amendment rights of speech and assembly apply, while the mall is not. The democratic and liberatory possibilities of people gathered together in public don't exist in places where they don't have space in which to gather. Perhaps it was meant that way. As Fishman argues, the suburbs were a refuge—first from the sin and then from the ugliness and anger of the city and its poor. In postwar America "white flight" sent middle-class whites to the suburbs from multiracial cities, and in the new sprawl-cities of the West and suburbs around the country a fear of crime that often seems to be a broader fear of difference is further eliminating public space and pedestrian possibilities. Political engagement may be one of the things suburbs have zoned out.

Early on in the development of the American suburbs, the porch, an important feature for small-town social life, was replaced at the front of the home by the blind maw of the garage (and the sociologist Dean McCannell tells me some new homes have pseudo-porches that make them look sweetly old-fashioned but are actually too shallow to sit on). More recent developments have been more radical in their retreat from communal space: we are in a new era of walls, guards, and security systems, and of architecture, design, and technology intended to eliminate or nullify public space. This withdrawal from shared space seems, like that of the Manchester merchants a century and a half ago, intended to buffer the affluent from the consequences of economic inequity and resentment outside the gates; it is the alternative to social justice. The new architecture and urban design of segregation could be called Calvinist: they reflect a desire to live in a world of predestination rather than chance, to strip the world of its wide-open possibilities and replace them with freedom of choice in the marketplace. "Anyone who has tried to take a stroll at dusk through a neighborhood patrolled by armed security guards and signposted with death threats quickly realizes how merely notional, if not utterly obsolete, is the old idea of 'freedom of the city,'" writes Mike Davis of the nicer suburbs of Los Angeles. And Kierkegaard long ago exclaimed, "It is extremely regrettable and demoralizing that robbers and the elite agree on just one thing—living in hiding."

If there was a golden age of walking, it arose from a desire to travel through the open spaces of the world unarmored by vehicles, unafraid to mingle with different kinds of people. It emerged in a time when cities and countryside grew safer and desire to experience that world was high. Suburbia abandoned the space of the city without returning to the country, and in recent years a second wave of impulse has beefed up this segregation with neighborhoods of high-priced bunkers. But even more importantly, the disappearance of pedestrian space has transformed perception of the relationship between bodies and spaces. Something very odd has happened to the very state of embodiment, of being corporeal, in recent decades.

II. The Disembodiment of Everyday Life

The spaces in which people live have changed dramatically, but so have the ways they imagine and experience that space. I found a strange passage in a 1998 *Life* magazine celebrating momentous events over the past thousand years. Accompanying a picture of a train was this text: "For most of human history, all land transport depended on a single mode of propulsion—feet. Whether the traveler relied on his own extremities or those of another creature, the drawbacks were the same, low cruising speed, vulnerability to weather, the need to stop for food and rest. But on September 15, 1830, foot power began its long slide toward obsolescence. As brass bands played, a million Britons gathered between Liverpool and Manchester to witness the inauguration of the world's first fully steam-driven railway. . . . Despite the death of a member of Parliament who was run down by the train at the opening ceremony, the Liverpool and Manchester inspired a rash of track-laying round the world." The train was, like the factory and the suburb, part of the apparatus of the industrial revolution; just as factories mechanically sped up production, so trains sped up distribution of goods, and then of travelers.

Life magazine's assumptions are interesting; nature as biological and meteorological factors is a drawback rather than an occasional inconvenience; progress consists of the transcendence of time, space, and nature by the train and later the car, airplane, and electronic communications. Eating, resting, moving, experiencing the weather, are primary experiences of being embodied; to view them as negative is to condemn biology and the life of the senses, and the passage does exactly that in its most lurid statement, that "foot power began its long slide toward obsolescence." Perhaps this is why neither *Life* nor the crowd apparently mourned the squashed Parliamentarian. In a way, the train mangled not just that one man's body, but all bodies in the places it transformed, by severing human perception, expectation, and action from the organic world in which our bodies exist. Alienation from nature is usually depicted as estrangement from natural spaces. But the sensing, breathing, living, moving body can be a primary experience of nature too: new technologies and spaces can bring about alienation from both body and space.

In his brilliant *The Railway Journey: The Industrialization of Time and Space in the Nineteenth Century,* Wolfgang Schivelbusch explores the ways trains changed their passengers' perceptions. Early railroad travelers, he writes, characterized this new technology's effects as the elimination of time and space, and to transcend time and space is to begin to transcend the material world altogether—to become disembodied. Disembodiment, however convenient, has side effects. "The speed and mathematical directness with which the railroad proceeds through the terrain destroy the close relationship between the traveler and the traveled space," Schivelbusch writes. "The train was experienced as a projectile, and traveling on it as being shot through the landscape—thus losing control of one's senses. . . . The traveler who sat inside that projectile ceased to be a traveler and became, as noted in a popular metaphor of the century, a parcel." Our own perceptions have sped up since, but trains were then dizzyingly fast. Earlier forms of land travel had intimately engaged travelers with their surroundings, but the railroad moved too fast for nineteenth-century minds to relate visually to the trees, hills, and buildings whipping by. The spatial and sensual engagement with the terrain between here and there began to evaporate. Instead, the two places were separated only by an ever-shortening amount of time. Speed did not make travel more interesting, Schivelbusch writes, but duller; like the suburb, it puts its inhabitants in a kind of spatial limbo. People began to read on the train, to sleep, to knit, to complain of boredom. Cars and airplanes have vastly augmented this transformation, and watching a movie on a jetliner 35,000 feet above the earth may be the ultimate disconnection of space, time, and experience. "From the elimination of the phys-ical effort of walking to the sensorimotor loss induced by the first fast transport, we have finally achieved states bordering on sensory deprivation," writes Paul Virilio. "The loss of the thrills of the old voyage is now compensated for by the showing of a film on a central screen."

The *Life* writers may be right. Bodies are not obsolete by any objective standard, but they increasingly are perceived as too slow, frail, and unreliable for our expectations and desires—as parcels to be transported by mechanical means (though of course many steep, rough, or narrow spaces can only be traversed on foot, and many remote parts of the world can't be reached by any other means; it takes a built environment, with tracks, graded roads, landing strips, and energy sources, to accommodate motor transport). A body regarded as adequate to cross continents, like John Muir's or William Wordsworth's or Peace Pilgrim's, is experienced very differently than a body inadequate to go out for the evening under its own power. In a sense the car has become a prosthetic, and though prosthetics are usually for injured or missing limbs, the auto-prosthetic is for a conceptually impaired body or a body impaired by the creation of a world that is no longer human in scale. In one of the *Alien* movies, the actress Sigourney Weaver lurches along in a sort of mechanized body armor that wraps around her limbs and magnifies her movements. It makes her bigger, fiercer, stronger, able to battle with monsters, and it seems strange and futuristic. But this is only because the relationship between the body and the prosthetic machine is so explicit here, the latter so obviously an extension of the former. In fact, from the first clasped stick and improvised carrier, tools have extended the body's strength, skill, and reach to a remarkable degree. We live in a world where our hands and feet can direct a ton of metal to go faster than the fastest land animal, where we can speak across thousands of miles, blow holes in things with no muscular exertion but the squeeze of a forefinger.

It is the unaugmented body that is rare now, and that body has begun to atrophy as both a muscular and a sensory organism. In the century and a half since the railroad seemed to go too fast to be interesting, perceptions and expectations have sped up, so that many now identify with the speed of the machine and look with frustration or alienation at the speed and ability of the body. The world is no longer on the scale of our bodies, but on that of our machines, and many need—or think they need—the machines to navigate that space quickly enough. Of course, like most "time-saving" technologies, mechanized transit more often produces changed expectations than free time; and modern Americans have significantly less time than they did three decades ago. To put it another way, just as the increased speed of factory production did not decrease working hours, so the increased speed of transportation binds people to more diffuse locales rather than liberating them from travel time (many Californians, for example, now spend three or four hours driving to and from work each day). The decline of walking is about the lack of space in which to walk, but it is also about the lack of time—the disappearance of that musing, unstructured space in which so much thinking, courting, daydreaming, and seeing has transpired. Machines have sped up, and lives have kept pace with them.

The suburbs made walking ineffective transportation within their expanses, but the suburbanization of the American mind has made walking increasingly rare even when it is effective. Walking is no longer, so to speak, how many people think. Even in San Francisco, very much a "walking city" by Jackson's criteria, people have brought this suburbanized consciousness to their local travel, or so my observations seem to indicate. I routinely see people drive and take the bus remarkably short distances, often distances that could be covered more quickly by foot. During one of my city's public transit crises, a commuter declared he could *walk* downtown in the time it took the streetcar, as though walking was some kind of damning comparison—but he had apparently been traveling from a destination so near downtown he could've walked every day in less than half an hour, and walking was one transit option the newspaper coverage never proposed (obvious things could be said about bicycling here, were this not a book about walking). Once I made my friend Maria—a surfer, biker, and world traveler—walk the half mile from her house to the bars on Sixteenth Street, and she was startlingly pleased to realize how close they were, for it had never occurred to her before that they were accessible by foot. Last Christmas season, the parking lot of the hip outdoor equipment store in Berkeley was full of drivers idling their engines and waiting for a parking space, while the streets around were full of such spaces. Shoppers weren't apparently willing to walk two blocks to buy their outdoor gear (and since then I have noticed that nowadays drivers often wait for a close parking spot rather than walk in from the farther reaches of the lot). People have a kind of mental radius of how far they are willing to go on foot that seems to be shrinking; in defining neighborhoods and shopping districts, planners say it is about a quarter mile, the distance that can be walked in five minutes, but sometimes it hardly seems to be fifty yards from car to building.

Of course the people idling their engines at the outdoor equipment store may have been there to buy hiking boots, workout clothes, climbing ropes—equipment for the special circumstances in which people will walk. The body has ceased to be a utilitarian entity for many Americans, but it is still a recreational one, and this means that people have abandoned the everyday spaces—the distance from home to work, stores, friends—but created new recreational sites that are most often reached by car: malls, parks, gyms. Parks, from pleasure gardens to wilderness preserves, have long accommodated bodily recreation, but the gyms that have proliferated wildly in the past couple of decades represent something radically new. If walking is an indicator species, the gym is a kind of wildlife preserve for bodily exertion. A preserve protects species whose habitat is vanishing elsewhere, and the gym (and home gym) accommodates the survival of bodies after the abandonment of the original sites of bodily exertion.

III. The Treadmill

The suburb rationalized and isolated family life as the factory did manufacturing work, and the gym rationalizes and isolates not merely exercise but nowadays even each muscle group, the heart rate, the "burn zone" of most inefficient calorie use. Somehow all this history comes back to the era of the industrial revolution in England. "The Tread-Mill," writes James Hardie in his little book of 1823 on the subject, "was, in the year 1818, invented by Mr. William Cubitt, of Ipswich, and erected in the House of Correction at Brixton, near London." The original treadmill was a large wheel with sprockets that served as steps that several prisoners trod for set periods. It was meant to rationalize prisoners' psyches, but it was already an exercise machine. Their bodily exertion was sometimes used to power grain mills or other machinery, but it was the exertion, not the production, that was the point of the treadmill. "It is its monotonous steadiness and not its severity, which constitutes its terror, and frequently breaks down the obstinate spirit," Hardie wrote of the treadmill's effect in the American prison he oversaw. He added, however, that "the opinions of the medical officers in attendance at the various prisons, concur in declaring that the general health of the prisoners has, in no degree suffered injury, but that, on the contrary, the labor has, in this respect, been productive of considerable benefit." His own prison of Bellevue on New York's East River included 81 male and 101 female vagrants, as well as 109 male and 37 women convicts, and 14 female "maniacs." Vagrancy—wandering without apparent resources or

Figure 16 A typical power-producing treadmill as pictured in *The Operative Mechanic and British Machinist,* 1831. (Image courtesy of Larry Witte. Found at <www.uh.edu/engines/epi374.htm>.)

purpose—was and sometimes still is a crime, and doing time on the treadmill was perfect punishment for it.

Repetitive labor has been punitive since the gods of Greek myth sentenced Sisyphus—who had, Robert Graves tells us, "always lived by robbery and often murdered unsuspecting travelers"—to his famous fate of pushing a boulder uphill. "As soon as he has almost reached the summit, he is forced back by the weight of the shameless stone, which bounces to the very bottom once more; where he wearily retrieves it and must begin all over again, though sweat bathes his limbs." It is hard to say if Sisyphus is the first weight lifter or the first treadmiller, but easy to recognize the ancient attitude to repetitive bodily exertion without practical results. Throughout most of human history and outside the first world nowadays, food has been relatively scarce and physical exertion abundant; only when the status of these two things is reversed does "exercise" make sense. Though physical training was part of ancient Greek citizens' education, it had social and cultural dimensions missing from modern workouts and Sisyphean punishments, and while walking as exercise had long been an aristocratic activity, industrial workers' enthusiasm for hiking, particularly in Britain, Austria, and Germany, suggests that it was far more than a way to make the blood circulate or calories burn. Under the heading "Alienation," Eduardo Galeano wrote a brief essay about fishermen in a remote village of the Dominican Republic puzzling over an advertisement for a rowing machine not very long ago. "Indoors? They use it indoors? Without water? They row without water? And without fish? And without the sun? And without the sky?" they exclaimed, telling the resident alien who has shown them the picture that they like everything about their work *but* the rowing. When he explained that the machine was for exercise, they said "Ah. And exercise—what's that?" Suntans famously became status symbols when most of the poor had moved indoors from the farm to the factory, so that browned skin indicated leisure time rather than work time. That muscles have become status symbols signifies that most jobs no longer call upon bodily strength; like tans, they are an aesthetic of the obsolete.

The gym is the interior space that compensates for the disappearance of outside and a stopgap measure in the erosion of bodies. The gym is a factory for the production of muscles or of fitness, and most of them look like factories: the stark industrial space, the gleam of metal machines, the isolated figures each absorbed in his or her own repetitive task (and like muscles, factory aesthetics may evoke nostalgia). The industrial revolution institutionalized and fragmented labor; the gym is now doing the same thing, often in the same place, for leisure. Some gyms actually are born-again industrial sites. The Chelsea Piers in Manhattan were built in the first decade of this century for ocean liners—for the work of longshoremen, stevedores, and clerks, and for the travel of emigrants and elites. They now house a sports center with indoor track, weight machines, pool, climbing gym, and most peculiarly, a four-story golf driving range, destinations in themselves rather than points of arrival and departure. An elevator takes golfers to their stalls, where all the gestures of golf—walking, carrying, gazing, situating, removing, communicating, retrieving or following the ball—have vanished with the landscape of the golf course. Nothing remains but the single arc of a drive: four tiers of solitary stationary figures making the same gesture, the sharp sound of balls being hit, the dull thud of their landing, and the miniaturized armored-car vehicles that go through the green artificial-grass war zone to scoop up the balls and feed them into the mechanism that automatically pops up another ball as each one is hit. Britain has specialized in the conversion of industrial sites into climbing gyms. Among them are a former electrical substation in London, the Warehouse on Gloucester's Severn River waterfront, the Forge in Sheffield on one side of the Peak District, an early factory in downtown Birmingham, and, according to a surveyor friend, a "six-story former cotton mill near Leeds" I couldn't locate (not to mention a desanctified church in Bristol). It was in some of these buildings that the industrial revolution was born, with the Manchester and Leeds textile mills, Sheffield's iron- and steelworks, the innumerable manufactories of "the workshop of the world" that Birmingham once was. Climbing gyms are likewise established in converted industrial buildings in the United States, or at least in those cities old enough to have once had industrial-revolution architecture. In those buildings abandoned because goods are now made elsewhere and First World work grows ever more cerebral, people now go for recreation, reversing the inclinations of their factory-worker predecessors to go out—to the outskirts of town or at least out-of-doors—in their free time. (In defense of climbing gyms, it should be said they allow people to polish skills and, during foul weather, to stay fit; for some the gym has only augmented the opportunities, not replaced the mountain, though for others the unpredictabilities and splendors of real rock have become dispensible, annoying—or unknown.)

And whereas the industrial revolution's bodies had to adapt to the machines, with terrible consequences of pain, injury, and deformity, exercise machines are adapted to the body. Marx said history happens the first time as tragedy, the second as farce; bodily labor here happens the first time around as productive labor and the second as leisuretime consumption. The deepest sign of transformation is not merely that this activity is no longer productive, that the straining of the arms no longer moves wood or pumps water. It is that the straining of the muscles can require a gym membership, workout gear, special equipment, trainers and instructors, a whole panoply of accompanying expenditures, in this industry of consumption, and the resulting muscles may not be useful or used for any practical purpose. "Efficiency" in exercise means that consumption of calories takes place at the maximum rate, exactly the opposite of what workers aim for, and while exertion for work is about how the body shapes the world, exertion for exercise is about how the body shapes the body. I do not mean to denigrate the users of gyms—I have sometimes been one myself—only to remark on their strangeness. In a world where manual labor has disappeared, the gym is among the most available and efficient compensations. Yet there is something perplexing about this semipublic performance. I used to try to imagine, as I worked out on one or another weight machine, that this motion was rowing, this one pumping water, this one lifting bales or sacks. The everyday acts of the farm had been reprised as empty gestures, for there was no water to pump, no buckets to lift. I am not nostalgic for peasant or farmworker life, but I cannot avoid being struck by how odd it is that we reprise those gestures for other reasons. What exactly is the nature of the transformation in which machines now pump our water but we go to other machines to engage in the act of pumping, not for the sake of water but for the sake of our bodies, bodies theoretically liberated by machine technology? Has something been lost when the relationship between our muscles and our world vanishes, when the water is managed by one machine and the muscles by another in two unconnected processes?

The body that used to have the status of a work animal now has the status of a pet: it does not provide real transport, as a horse might have; instead, the body is exercised as one might walk a dog. Thus the body, a recreational rather than utilitarian entity, doesn't work, but works out. The barbell is only abstracted and quantified materiality to shift around—what used to be a sack of onions or a barrel of beer is now a metal ingot—and the weight machine makes simpler the act of resisting gravity in various directions for the sake of health, beauty, and relaxation. The most perverse of all the devices in the gym is the treadmill (and its steeper cousin, the Stairmaster). Perverse, because I can understand simulating farm labor, since the activities of rural life are not often available—but simulating walking suggests that space itself has disappeared. That is, the weights simulate the objects of work, but the treadmill and Stairmaster simulate the surfaces on which walking takes place. That bodily labor, real or simulated, should be dull and repetitive is one thing; that the multifaceted experience of moving through the world should be made so is another. I remember evenings strolling by Manhattan's many glass-walled second-floor gyms full of rows of treadmillers looking as though they were trying to leap through the glass to their destruction, saved only by the Sisyphean contraption that keeps them from going anywhere at all—though probably they didn't see the plummet before them, only their own reflection in the glass.

I went out the other day, a gloriously sunny winter afternoon, to visit a home-exercise equipment store and en route walked by the University of San Francisco gym, where treadmillers were likewise at work in the plate-glass windows, most of them reading the newspaper (three blocks from Golden Gate Park, where other people were running and cycling, while tourists and Eastern European emigrés were walking). The muscular young man in the store told me that people buy home treadmills because they allow them to exercise after work when it might be too dark for them to go out safely, to exercise in private where the neighbors will not see them sweating, to keep an eye on the kids, and to use their scarce time most efficiently, and because it is a low-impact activity good for people with running injuries. I have a friend who uses a treadmill when it's painfully cold outside in Chicago, and another who uses a no-impact machine whose footpads rise and fall with her steps because she has an injured hamstring (injured by driving cars designed for larger people, not by running). But a third friend's father lives two miles from a very attractive Florida beach, she tells me, full of low-impact sand, but he will not walk there and uses a home treadmill instead.

The treadmill is a corollary to the suburb and the autotropolis: a device with which to go nowhere in places where there is now nowhere to go. Or no desire to go: the treadmill also accommodates the automobilized and suburbanized mind more comfortable in climate-controlled indoor space than outdoors, more comfortable with quantifiable and clearly defined activity than with the seamless engagement of mind, body, and terrain to be found walking out-of-doors. The treadmill seems to be one of many devices that accommodate a retreat from the world, and I fear that such accommodation disinclines people to participate in making that world habitable or to participate in it at all.

It too could be called Calvinist technology, in that it provides accurate numerical assessments of the speed, "distance" covered, and even heart rate, and it eliminates the unpredictable and unforeseeable from the routine—no encounters with acquaintances or strangers, no sudden revelatory sights around a bend. On the treadmill, walking is no longer contemplating, courting, or exploring. Walking is the alternate movement of the lower limbs.

Unlike the prison treadmills, of the 1820s, the modern treadmill does not produce mechanical power but consumes it. The new treadmills have two-horsepower engines. Once, a person might have hitched two horses to a carriage to go out into the world without walking; now she might plug in a two-horsepower motor to walk without going out into the world. Somewhere unseen but wired to the home is a whole electrical infrastructure of power generation and distribution transforming the landscape and ecology of the world—a network of electrical cables, meters, workers, of coal mines or oil wells feeding power plants or of hydropower dams on rivers. Somewhere else is a factory making treadmills, though factory work is a minority experience in the United States nowadays. So the treadmill requires far more economic and ecological interconnection than does taking a walk, but it makes far fewer experiential connections. Most treadmillers read or otherwise distract themselves. *Prevention* magazine recommends watching TV while treadmilling and gives instructions on how treadmill users can adapt their routines to walking about outside when spring comes (with the implication that the treadmill, not the walk, is the primary experience). The *New York Times* reports that people have begun taking treadmill classes, like the stationary bicycling classes that have become so popular, to mitigate the loneliness of the long-distance treadmiller. For like factory labor, treadmill time is dull—it was the monotony that was supposed to reform prisoners. Among the features of the Precor Cardiologic Treadmill, says its glossy brochure, are "5 programmed courses" that "vary in distance, time and incline. . . . The Interactive Weight Loss course maintains your heart rate within your optimum weight loss zone by adjusting workload," while "custom courses allow you to easily create and store personalized programs of up to 8 miles, with variations as small as 1/10th mile increments." It's the custom courses that most amaze me; users can create an itinerary like a walking tour over varied terrain, only the terrain is a revolving rubber belt on a platform about six feet long. Long ago when railroads began to erode the experience of space, journeys began to be spoken of in terms of time rather than distance (and a modern Angeleno will say that Beverly Hills is twenty minutes from Hollywood rather than so many miles). The treadmill completes this transformation by allowing travel to be measured entirely by time, bodily exertion, and mechanical motion. Space—as landscape, terrain, spectacle, experience—has vanished.

2000

READING, REREADING, AND ANALYSIS

1. Do you agree with Solnit that walking is seen today as more of a nuisance than an activity to enjoy?

2. Why does Solnit believe that the "golden age" of walking has disappeared? Why, especially, does she equate the rise of the suburbs with the "golden age's tombstone"?

3. Solnit uses an example of a fisherman puzzling over a rowing machine. What does the example illustrate?

4. What does Solnit mean when she discusses "disembodiment"? Share your answer with classmates in a group. What are the problems Solnit associates with "disembodiment"? Is her perspective valid, or is her argument about "disembodiment" much ado about nothing?

5. Think about commercials you have seen for exercise machines or think about your own use of exercise machines. Is use of exercise equipment a type of punishment, and if so, why do so many people seem to eagerly embrace such punishment?

6. What does Solnit mean on page 447 when she writes:

   > I am not nostalgic for peasant or farmworker life, but I cannot avoid being struck by how odd it is that we reprise those gestures for other reasons. What exactly is the nature of the transformation in which machines now pump our water but we go to other machines to engage in the act of pumping, not for the sake of water but for the sake of our bodies, bodies theoretically liberated by machine technology?

RESPONDING THROUGH WRITING: BUILDING AN INTERPRETATION

7. Solnit has some very strong opinions about the history she describes. Write a short paper analyzing her point of view and looking closely at least two moments in the text where she reveals it. What do you think her goal is in writing this piece? To what extent do you find her argument persuasive?

8. Solnit argues that because of our reliance on trains, cars, and airplanes, we experience a "disembodiment" that greatly changes our sense of space and time. Write a paper in which you explore a part of our lives that is affected by this disembodiment. Develop an example that shows how lives in the twenty-first century have changed, and discuss the consequences of this change. (Note: Do not use either of Solnit's examples, walking or exercise, as your primary example.)

9. In four or five sentences, summarize the main point, as you see it, of Solnit's use of the term "Calvinist" in her essay. What is she trying to convey by using the word "Calvinist"?

10. Write a letter to Solnit in which you discuss your reaction to the following claim in her essay:

> Television, telephones, home computers, and the Internet complete the privatization of everyday life that suburbs began and cars enhanced. They make it less necessary to go out into the world and thus accommodate retreat from rather than resistance to the deteriorization of public space and social conditions (p. 438).

GOING FURTHER: LEARNING FROM OTHER SOURCES

11. Find a website that focuses on the kind of exercise equipment that Solnit describes in her essay. (It could be a gym, fitness, or health website, for example.) Look at the language used to describe what the machines are designed to do. Make a list of the most vivid words, and write a paragraph in which you assess those descriptions in the terms of Solnit's critique. Is there anything odd, funny, or even surprising about the language surrounding exercise?

12. Use an academic search engine to find information about the treadmill as a type of prison punishment. When did prisons stop using treadmills as a form of punishment and why?

APPLYING WHAT YOU'VE LEARNED

13. In "From the Frying Pan into the Fire," Arlie Russell Hochschild discusses how work practices such as the drive for efficiency and how the allure of consumer culture transform life at home for many Americans. Write an essay in which you use Solnit's discussion of relationships between walking and suburbanization to help you discuss Hochschild's analysis. Part of your essay might compare Solnit's claim that "walking is an indicator species for various kinds of freedoms and pleasures: free time, free and alluring space, and unhindered bodies" with Hochschild's discussion of Taylorization.

14. Does the present-day situation that Solnit describes constitute an example of what Walker Percy calls a "radical loss of sovereignty"? Discuss the "Aerobic Sisyphus" in the terms of Percy's essay.

15. Both Solnit and Turkle describe ways in which technology can transform human behavior and habits of mind. Compare the processes of transformation that they describe in order to arrive at your own theory about the gains and drawbacks of a new technology you have experienced.

NANCY SOMMERS

Nancy Sommers (b. 1951) is the Sosland Director of Expository Writing at Harvard University. She is a well-known and often-quoted specialist in the teaching of writing. Sommers coedited *Student Writers at Work, the Bedford Prizes* (1989), *Writing with a Purpose* (1984), *The Harper-Collins Guide to Writing* (1993), and *Fields of Reading* (1986). She has written a number of important articles in the study of composition and rhetoric, including "Responding to Student Writing," "The Language of Coats," and "Revision in the Composing Process." Sommers is currently at work on a study of undergraduate writing at Harvard.

> **To learn more about Sommers's study of Harvard undergraduate writing, go to <http://www.fas.harvard.edu/~expos/>.**

WHAT DO YOU KNOW? WHAT DO YOU EXPECT TO DISCOVER?

Before reading the essay, take a moment to consider the following questions.

1. What topics does Sommers's biography suggest she is interested in? What do you know about those topics? Knowledge can come from personal experience, stories you've heard, other classes you've taken, or other reading you've done.

2. Before reading Sommers's essay, do a Google search for Tillie Olson and her story "I Stand Here Writing." After reading about Olson and her story, what might you expect to find in Sommers's essay, given the similarity of the titles?

3. In her essay, Sommers discusses her family as well as her teaching, blending the personal with the academic. In what ways do your family life and your academic life blend? Do you prefer to keep them separate? Why or why not?

❧

I Stand Here Writing

I stand in my kitchen, wiping the cardamom, coriander, and cayenne off my fingers. My head is abuzz with words, with bits and pieces of conversation. I hear a phrase I have read recently, something about "a radical loss of certainty." But, I wonder, how did the sentence begin? I search the air for the rest of the sentence, can't find it, shake some more cardamom, and a bit of coriander. Then, by some play of mind, I am back home again in Indiana with my family, sitting around the kitchen table. Two people are talking, and there are three opinions; three people are talking, and there are six opinions. Opinions grow exponentially. I fight my way back to that sentence. Writing, that's how it begins: "Writing is a radical loss of certainty." (Or is it uncertainty?) It isn't so great for the chicken when all these voices start showing up, with all these sentences hanging in mid-air, but the voices keep me company. I am a writer, not a cook, and the truth is I don't care much about the chicken. Stories beget stories. Writing emerges from writing.

The truth. Has truth anything to do with the facts? All I know is that no matter how many facts I might clutter my life with, I am as bound to the primordial drama of my family as the earth is to the sun. This year my father, the son of a severe Prussian matriarch, watched me indulge my daughters, and announced to me that he wished I had been his mother. This year, my thirty-ninth, my last year to be thirty-something, my mother—who has a touch of magic, who can walk into the middle of a field of millions of clovers and find the *one* with four leaves—has begun to think I need help. She sends me cards monthly with four-leaf clovers taped inside. Two words neatly printed in capital letters—GOOD LUCK!! I look at these clovers and hear Reynolds Price's words: "Nobody under forty can believe how nearly everything's inherited." I wonder what my mother knows, what she is trying to tell me about the facts of my life.

When I was in high school studying French, laboring to conjugate verbs, the numerous four-leaf clovers my mother had carefully pressed inside her French dictionary made me imagine her in a field of clovers lyrically conjugating verbs of love. This is the only romantic image I have of my mother, a shy and conservative woman whose own mother died when she was five, whose grandparents were killed by the Nazis, who fled Germany at age thirteen with her father and sister. Despite the sheer facts of her life, despite the accumulation of grim knowable data, the truth is my mother is an optimistic person. She has the curious capacity always to be looking for luck, putting her faith in four-leaf clovers, ladybugs, pennies, and other amulets of fortune. She has a vision different from mine, one the facts alone can't explain. I, her daughter, was left, for a long time, seeing only the ironies; they were my defense against the facts of my life.

In this world of my inheritance in which daughters can become their fathers' mothers and mothers know their daughters are entering into a world where only sheer good luck will guide them, I hear from my own daughters that I am not in tune with their worlds, that I am just like a 50s mom, that they are 90s children, and I should stop acting so primitive. My children laugh uproariously at my autograph book, a 1959 artifact they unearthed in the basement of my parents' home. "Never kiss by the garden gate. Love is blind, but the neighbors ain't," wrote one friend. And my best friend, who introduced herself to me on the first day of first grade, looking me straight in the eye—and whispering through her crooked little teeth "the Jews killed Jesus"—wrote in this autograph book: "Mary had a little lamb. Her father shot it dead. Now she carries it to school between two slices of bread."

My ten-year-old daughter, Rachel, writes notes to me in hieroglyphics and tapes signs on the refrigerator in Urdu. "Salaam Namma Man Rachaal Ast" reads one sign. Simply translated it means "Hello, my name is Rachel." Alex, my seven-year-old daughter, writes me lists, new lists each month, visibly reminding me of the many things I need to buy or do for her. This month's list includes a little refrigerator filled with Coke and candy; ears pierced; a new toilet; neon nail polish and *real* adult make-up.

How do I look at these facts? How do I embrace these experiences, these texts of my life, and translate them into ideas? How do I make sense of them and the conversations they engender in my head? I look at Alex's list and wonder what kind of feminist daughter I am raising whose deepest desires include neon nail polish and *real* adult make-up. Looking at her lists a different way, I wonder if this second child of mine is asking me for something larger, something more permanent and real than adult make-up. Maybe I got that sentence wrong. Maybe it is that "Love (as well as writing) involves a radical loss of certainty."

Love is blind, but the neighbors ain't. Mary's father shot her little lamb dead, and now she carries it to school between two slices of bread. I hear these rhymes today, and they don't say to me what they say to my daughters. They don't seem so innocent. I hear them and think about the ways in which my neighbors in Indiana could only see my family as Jews from Germany, exotic strangers who ate tongue, outsiders who didn't celebrate Christmas. I wonder if my daughter Rachel needs to tell me her name in Urdu because she thinks we don't share a common language. These sources change meaning when I ask the questions in a different way. They introduce new ironies, new questions.

I want to understand these living, breathing, primary souces all around me. I want to be, in Henry James's words, "a person upon whom nothing is lost." These sources speak to me of love and loss, of memory and desire, of the ways in which we come to understand something through difference and opposition. Two years ago I heard the word *segue* from one of my students. At first the word seemed peculiar. Segue sounded like something you did only on the Los Angeles freeway. Now I hear that word everywhere, and I have begun using it. I want to know how to segue from one idea to the next, from one thought to the fragment lying beside it. But the connections don't always come with four-leaf clovers and the words GOOD LUCK neatly printed beside them.

My academic need to find connections sends me to the library. There are eleven million books in my University's libraries. Certainly these sanctioned voices, these authorities, these published sources can help me find the connections. Someone, probably some three thousand someones, has studied what it is like to be the child of survivors. Someone has written a manual on how the granddaughter of a severe Prussian matriarch and the daughter of a collector of amulets ought to raise feminist daughters. I want to walk into the fields of writing, into those eleven million books, and find the one book that will explain it all. But I've learned to expect less from such sources. They seldom have the answers. And the answers they do have reveal themselves to me at the most unexpected times. I have been led astray more than once while searching books for the truth.

Once I learned a lesson about borrowing someone else's words and losing my own.

I was fourteen, light years away from thirty-something. High school debate teams across the nation were arguing the pros and cons of the United States Military Aid Policy. It all came back to me as I listened to the news of the Persian Gulf War, as I listened to Stormin' Norman giving his morning briefings, an eerie resonance, all our arguments, the millions of combative words—sorties—fired back and forth. In my first practice debate, not having had enough time to assemble my own sources, I borrowed quote cards from my teammates. I attempted to bolster my position that the U.S. should limit its military aid by reading a quote in my best debate style: "W. W. Rostow says: 'We should not give military aid to India because it will exacerbate endemic rivalries.'"

Under cross-examination, my nemesis, Bobby Rosenfeld, the neighbor kid, who always knew the right answers, began firing a series of questions at me without stopping to let me answer:

"Nancy, can you tell me who W. W. Rostow is? And can you tell my why he might say this? Nancy, can you tell me what 'exacerbate' means? Can you tell me what 'endemic rivalries' are? And exactly what does it mean to exacerbate endemic rivalries'?"

I didn't know. I simply did not know who W. W. Rostow was, why he might have said that, what "exacerbate" meant, or what an "endemic rivalry" was. Millions of four-leaf clovers couldn't have helped me. I might as well have been speaking Urdu. I didn't know who my source was, the context of the source, nor the literal meaning of the words I had read. Borrowing words from authorities had left me without any words of my own.

My debate partner and I went on that year to win the Indiana state championship and to place third in the nationals. Bobby Rosenfeld never cross-examined me again, but for twenty years he has appeared in my dreams. I am not certain why I would dream so frequently about this scrawny kid whom I despised. I think, though, that he became for me what the Sea Dyak tribe of Borneo calls a *ngarong,* a dream guide, someone guiding me to understanding. In this case, Bobby guided me to understand the endemic rivalries within my self. The last time Bobby appeared in a dream he had become a woman.

I learned a more valuable lesson about sources as a college senior. I was the kind of student who loved words, words out of context, words that swirled around inside my mouth, words like *exacerbate, undulating, lugubrious,* and *zeugma.* "She stained her honour or her new brocade," wrote Alexander Pope. I would try to write zeugmas whenever I could, exacerbating my already lugubrious prose. Within the English department, I was known more for my long hair, untamed and untranslatable, and for my long distance bicycle rides than for my scholarship.

For my senior thesis, I picked Emerson's essay "Eloquence." Harrison Hayford, my advisor, suggested that I might just get off my bicycle, get lost in the library, and read all of Emerson's essays, journals, letters. I had picked one of Emerson's least distinguished essays, an essay that the critics mentioned only in passing, and if I were not entirely on my own, I had at least carved out new territory for myself.

I spent weeks in the library reading Emerson's journals, reading newspaper accounts from Rockford and Peoria, Illinois, where he had first delivered "Eloquence" as a speech. Emerson stood at the podium, the wind blowing his papers hither and yon, calmly picking them up, and proceeding to read page 8 followed by page 3, followed by page 6, followed by page 2. No one seemed to know the difference. Emerson's Midwestern audience was overwhelmed by this strange man from Concord, Massachusetts, this eloquent stranger whose unit of expression was the sentence.

As I sat in the library, wearing my QUESTION AUTHORITY T-shirt, I could admire this man who delivered his Divinity School Address in 1838, speaking words so repugnant to the genteel people of Cambridge that it was almost thirty years before Harvard felt safe having him around again. I could understand the Midwestern audience's awe and adulation as they listened but didn't quite comprehend Emerson's stunning oratory. I had joined the debate team not to argue the U.S. Military Aid Policy, but to learn how to be an orator who could stun audiences, to learn a personal eloquence I could never learn at home. Perhaps only children of immigrant parents can understand the embarrassing moments of inarticulateness, the missed connections that come from learning to speak a language from parents who claim a different mother tongue.

As an undergraduate, I wanted to free myself from that mother tongue. Four-leaf clovers and amulets of oppression weighed heavy on my mind, and I could see no connection whatsoever between those facts of my life and the untranslatable side of myself that set me in opposition to authority. And then along came Emerson. Like his Midwest audience, I didn't care about having him whole. I liked the promise and the rhapsodic freedom I found in his sentences, in his invitation to seize life as our dictionary, to believe that "Life was not something to be learned but to be lived." I loved his insistence that "the only thing of value is the active soul." I read that "Books are for the scholar's idle time," and I knew that he had given me permission to explore the world. Going into Emerson was like walking into a revelation; it was the first time I had gone into the texts not looking for a specific answer, and it was the first time the texts gave me the answers I needed. Never mind that I got only part of what Emerson was telling me. I got inspiration, I got insight, and I began to care deeply about my work.

Today I reread the man who set me off on a new road, and I find a different kind of wisdom. Today I reread "The American Scholar," and I don't underline the sentence "Books are for the scholar's idle time." I continue to the next paragraph, underlining the sentence "One must be an inventor to read well." The second sentence doesn't contradict the one I read twenty years ago, but it means more today. I bring more to it, and I know that I can walk into text after text, source after source, and they will give me insight, but not answers. I have learned too that my sources can surprise me. Like my mother, I find myself sometimes surrounded by a field of four-leaf clovers, there for the picking, waiting to see what I can make of them. But I must be an inventor if I am to read those sources well, if I am to imagine the connections.

As I stand in my kitchen, the voices that come to me come by way of a lifetime of reading, they come on the waves of life, and they seem to be helping me translate the untranslatable. They come, not at my bidding, but when I least expect them, when I am receptive enough to listen to their voices. They come when I am open.

If I could teach my students one lesson about writing it would be to see themselves as sources, as places from which ideas originate, to see themselves as Emerson's transparent eyeball, all that they have read and experienced—the dictionaries of their lives—circulating through them. I want them to learn how sources thicken, complicate, enlarge writing, but I want them to know too how it is always the writer's voice, vision, and argument that create the new source. I want my students to see that nothing reveals itself straight out, especially the sources all around them. But I know enough by now that this Emersonian ideal can't be passed on in one lesson or even a semester of lessons.

Many of the students who come to my classes have been trained to collect facts; they act as if their primary job is to accumulate enough authorities so that there is no doubt about the "truth" of their thesis. They most often disappear behind the weight and permanence of their borrowed words, moving their pens, mouthing the words of others, allowing sources to speak through them unquestioned, unexamined.

At the outset, many of my students think that personal writing is writing about the death of their grandmother. Academic writing is reporting what Elisabeth Kübler-Ross has written about death and dying. Being personal, I want to show my students, does not mean being autobiographical. Being academic does not mean being remote, distant, imponderable. Being personal means bringing their judgments and interpretation to bear on what they read and write, learning that they never leave themselves behind even when they write academic essays.

Last year, David Gray came into my essay class disappointed about everything. He didn't like the time of the class, didn't like the reading list, didn't seem to like me. Nothing pleased him. "If this is a class on the essay," he asked the first day, "why aren't we reading real essayists like Addison, Steele, and Lamb?" On the second day, after being asked to read Annie Dillard's "Living Like Weasels," David complained that a weasel wasn't a fit subject for an essay. "Writers need big subjects. Look at Melville. He needed a whale for *Moby-Dick*. A weasel—that's nothing but a rodent." And so it continued for a few weeks.

I kept my equanimity in class, but at home I'd tell my family about this kid who kept testing me, seizing me like Dillard's weasel, and not letting go. I secretly wanted him out of my class. But then again, I sensed in him a kindred spirit, someone else who needed to question authority.

I wanted my students to write exploratory essays about education, so I asked them to think of a time when they had learned something, and then a time when they had tried to learn something but couldn't. I wanted them to see what ideas and connections they could find between these two very different experiences and other essays they were reading for the class. I wanted the various sources to work as catalysts. I wanted my students to find a way to talk back to those other writers. The assigned texts were an odd assortment with few apparent connections. I hoped my students would find the common ground, but also the moments of tension, the contradictions, and the ambiguities in those sources.

David used the assigned texts as a catalyst for his thinking, but as was his way, he went beyond the texts I offered and chose his own. He begins his essay, "Dulcis Est Sapientia," with an account of his high school Latin class, suggesting that he once knew declensions, that he had a knack for conjugations, but has forgotten them. He tells us that if his teacher were to appear suddenly today and demand the perfect subjunctive of *venire,* he would stutter hopelessly.

About that Latin class, David asks, "What is going on here? Did I once know Latin and forget it through disuse? Perhaps I never learned Latin at all. What I learned was a bunch of words which, with the aid of various ending sounds, indicated that Gaius was either a good man delivering messages to the lieutenant or a general who struck camp at the seventh hour. I may have known it once, but I never learned it." The class never gave David the gift of language. There was something awry in the method.

What is learning? That's what David explores in his essay as he moves from his Latin lesson to thinking about surrealist paintings, to thinking about barriers we create, to Plato, to an airplane ride in which he observed a mother teaching her child concepts of color and number, all the time taking his readers along with him on his journey, questioning sources, reflecting, expanding, and enriching his growing sense that learning should stress ideas rather than merely accumulating facts and information.

David draws his essay to a close with an analysis of a joke: A man goes to a cocktail party and gets soused. He approaches his host and asks, "Pardon me, but do lemons whistle?"

The host looks at him oddly and answers, "No, lemons don't whistle."

"Oh dear," says the guest, "then I'm afraid I just squeezed your canary into my gin and tonic."

David reflects about the significance of this joke: "One need not be an ornithologist to get the joke, but one must know that canaries are yellow and that they whistle. . . . What constitutes the joke is a connection made between two things . . . which have absolutely nothing in common except for their yellowness. It would never occur to us to make a comparison between the two, let alone to confuse one with the other. But this is the value of the joke, to force into our consciousness the ideas which we held but never actively considered. . . . This knocking down of barriers between ideas is parallel to the process that occurs in all learning. The barriers that we set . . . suddenly crumble; the boundaries . . . are extended to include other modes of thought." Learning, like joking, David argues, gives us pleasure by satisfying our innate capacity to recognize coherence, to discern patterns and connections.

David's essay, like any essay, does not intend to offer the last word on its subject. The civilizing influence of an essay is that it keeps the conversation going, chronicling an intellectual journey, reflecting conversations with sources. I am confident that when David writes for his philosophy course he won't tell a joke anywhere in his essay. But if the joke—if any of his sources—serves him as a catalyst for his thinking, if he makes connections among the sources that circulate within him, between Plato and surrealism, between Latin lessons and mother-child lessons—the dictionaries of *his* life—then he has learned something valuable about writing.

I say to myself that I don't believe in luck. And yet. Not too long ago Rachel came home speaking with some anxiety about an achievement test that she had to take at school. Wanting to comfort her, I urged her to take my rabbit's foot to school the next day. Always alert to life's ironies, Rachel said, "Sure, Mom, a rabbit's foot will really help me find the answers. And even if it did, how would I know the answer the next time when I didn't have that furry little claw?" The next day, proud of her ease at taking the test, she remained perplexed by the one question that seized her and wouldn't let go. She tried it on me: "Here's the question," she said. "Can you figure out which of these sentences cannot be true?"

(a) We warmed our hands by the fire.

(b) The rain poured in and around the window.

(c) The wind beckoned us to open the door.

Only in the mind of someone who writes achievement tests, and wants to close the door on the imagination, could the one false sentence be "The wind beckoned us to open the door." Probably to this kind of mind, Emerson's sentence "Life is our dictionary" is also not a true sentence.

But life *is* our dictionary, and that's how we know that the wind can beckon us to open the door. Like Emerson, we let the wind blow our pages hither and yon, forcing us to start in the middle, moving from page 8 to page 2, forward to page 7, moving back and forth in time, losing our certainty.

Like Emerson, I love basic units, the words themselves, words like cardamom, coriander, words that play around in my head, swirl around in my mouth. The challenge, of course, is not to be a ventriloquist—not to be a mouther of words—but to be open to other voices, untranslatable as they might be. Being open to the unexpected, we can embrace complexities: canaries and lemons, amulets and autograph books, fathers who want their daughters to be their mothers, and daughters who write notes in Urdu—all those odd, unusual conjunctions can come together and speak through us.

The other day, I called my mother and told her about this essay, told her that I had been thinking about the gold bracelet she took with her as one of her few possessions from Germany—a thin gold chain with three amulets: a mushroom, a lady bug, and, of course, a four-leaf clover. Two other charms fell off years ago—she lost one, I the other. I used to worry over the missing links, thinking only of the loss, of what we could never retrieve. When I look at the bracelet now, I think about the Prussian matriarch, my grandmother, and my whole primordial family drama. I think too of Emerson and the pages that blew in the wind and the gaps that seemed not to matter. The bracelet is but one of many sources that intrigues me. Considering them in whatever order they appear, with whatever gaps, I want to see where they will lead me, what they tell me.

With writing and with teaching, as well as with love, we don't know how the sentence will begin and, rarely ever, how it will end. Having the courage to live with uncertainty, ambiguity, even doubt, we can walk into all of those fields of writing, knowing that we will find volumes bidding *us* enter. We need only be inventors, we need only give freely and abundantly to the texts, imagining even as we write that we too will be a source from which other readers can draw sustenance.

1993

READING, REREADING, AND ANALYSIS

1. Find one or two examples in Sommers's essay that help you to explain or to challenge the idea that "writing is a radical loss of certainty" (pp. 453–454). Write a paragraph summarizing the examples and using them to explain this phrase.

2. Choose one of the personal examples that Sommers uses, such as her experience on the high school's debate team or her wearing of a "QUESTION AUTHORITY" T-shirt in college. Write a short paragraph summarizing the example and relating it to the larger purpose of the essay.

3. Choose one or two of the examples in which Sommers discusses her student David Gray (the high school Latin story or the canary and lemons joke, for instance). What does Sommers learn from these examples? How does her reaction to Gray change over the course of the essay?

4. On page 455, Sommers writes: "I want to understand these living, breathing, primary sources all around me. I want to be, in Henry James's words, 'a person upon whom nothing is lost.'" What kind of person does Sommers want to be, given her use of the quotation from Henry James? Who was Henry James?

5. What are Sommers's attitudes toward Ralph Waldo Emerson? Why is he important to her? Who was Emerson?

6. What does Sommers mean to you when she writes,

> If I could teach my students one lesson about writing it would be to see themselves as sources, as places from which ideas originate, to see themselves as Emerson's transparent eyeball, all that they have read and experienced—the dictionaries of their lives— circulating through them. I want them to learn how sources thicken, complicate, enlarge writing, but I want them to know too how it is always the writer's voice, vision, and argument that create the new source?

RESPONDING THROUGH WRITING:
BUILDING AN INTERPRETATION

7. Write a paragraph analyzing one of the examples Sommers uses involving her own children (for instance, her reactions to her younger daughter's request for pierced ears, "neon nail polish and *real* adult make-up" (p. 455). How does this example compare with the ones involving Sommers's students or her own past? How does this example relate to Sommers's larger purpose in the essay?

8. Write at least two paragraphs that analyze Sommers's attitude toward the following quotations from Ralph Waldo Emerson: "Books are for the scholar's idle time" and "One must be an inventor to read well."

9. Sommers writes:

   > If I could teach my students one lesson about writing it would be to see themselves as sources, as places from which ideas originate, to see themselves as Emerson's transparent eyeball, all that they have read and experienced—the dictionaries of their lives—circulating through them. I want them to learn how sources thicken, complicate, enlarge writing, but I want them to know too how it is always the writer's voice, vision, and argument that create the new source (p. 458).

   Write a letter to Sommers in response.

10. Sommers begins her essay by saying that she stands in her kitchen, wiping spices from her fingers. She goes on to weave comments about writing with comments about her family. Write a short essay that examines why you think Sommers begins her essay on such a personal note. What is the effect on you, the reader? How is her approach different from the approaches in other essays you have read in *Making Sense*?

GOING FURTHER: LEARNING
FROM OTHER SOURCES

11. Using a reference database that includes a range of scholarly sources (such as Academic Search Elite or a similar database recommended by your reference librarian), try the combined search terms "writing and invention" and related keywords from Sommers's essay. Scan the resulting articles to find one or two that relate Sommers's ideas in an interesting or revealing way. Print the articles or their abstracts and bring the results to class.

12. Use a popular search engine such as Google or HotBot to find information about Annie Dillard—a writer included in *Making*

Sense (p. 110)—and her text "Living Like Weasels." What is Dillard's text about? What have reviewers, critics, and scholars said about it? Does your research reveal to you any connections to Sommers?

APPLYING WHAT YOU'VE LEARNED

13. Reflect on Sommers's ideas about learning with Birkerts's ideas about knowledge and wisdom in "The Owl Has Flown," and then imagine if Birkerts and Sommers were to address your composition class. What kind of conversation or debate can you imagine them having? Would they likely agree or disagree with each other and why? Write a five-page paper in which you create a conversation or a debate between Sommers and Birkerts. Be sure to use quotations from both of their essays.

14. Toward the end of her essay, Sommers writes: "The challenge, of course, is not to be a ventriloquist—not to be a mouther of words—but to be open to other voices, untranslatable as they might be. Being open to the unexpected, we can embrace complexities . . ." (p. 461). How might one of the following writers respond: Gloria Anzaldúa ("Chicana Artists: Exploring *Nepantla, el Lugar de la Frontera*"), Ralph Ellison ("The Little Man at Chehaw Station"), or Haunani-Kay Trask ("From a Native Daughter")? Use Sommers's call to be "open to other voices" as a framework for analyzing Anzaldúa's or Ellison's or Trask's essay. In your essay, be sure to discuss potential problems that Anzaldúa or Ellison or Trask identify with trying to be "open to other voices."

15. Write a five-page essay in which you compare one or two of your own most significant educational experiences with Sommers's discussion of her own education and of teaching writing, with Barbara Mellix's discussion of education—particularly her efforts to learn to write academic discourse—in "From Outside, In," and with bell hooks's discussion of her educational experiences both as a student and as a teacher in "keeping close to home: class and education." What are the most significant points of contact between your experience and the experiences of Sommers, Mellix, and hooks? What are the most significant differences or gaps or separations between your experiences and the experiences of any or all three of the essayists? In your paper, also reflect on what you have learned from examining your experience in relation to Sommers's, Mellix's, and hooks's experiences.

SUSAN SONTAG

Susan Sontag (b. 1933) is a novelist and essay writer whose work focuses on the multiple levels of modern culture. Sontag has written essays and reviews on topics related to art, photography, literature, plays, films, and politics. Other topics include the cultural impact of illnesses such as cancer and AIDS and the cultural phenomenon of "camp." Sontag has also written and directed several films. "In Plato's Cave" is the first chapter of her collection, *On Photography* (1977). The title refers to Plato's allegory of the cave in which cave dwellers accustomed to the dark mistake shadows for reality.

To learn more about photography, visit the American Museum of Photography at <http://www.photographymuseum.com/>.

WHAT DO YOU KNOW? WHAT DO YOU EXPECT TO DISCOVER?

Before reading the essay, take a moment to consider the following questions.

1. What topics does Sontag's biography suggest she is interested in? What do you know about those topics? Knowledge can come from personal experience, stories you've heard, other classes you've taken, or other reading you've done.

2. Before reading Sontag's essay, do a Google search on the Internet for the phrase "Plato's Cave," and then think about what you are likely to find in an essay called "In Plato's Cave."

3. Before reading the essay, list all the ways you can think of that we use photographs in our daily lives and in the culture at large.

❧

In Plato's Cave

Humankind lingers unregenerately in Plato's cave, still reveling, its age-old habit, in mere images of the truth. But being educated by photographs is not like being educated by older, more artisanal images. For one thing, there are a great many more images around, claiming our attention. The inventory started in 1839 and since then just about everything has been photographed, or so it seems. This very insatiability of the photographing eye changes the terms of confinement in the cave, our world. In teaching us a new visual code, photographs alter and enlarge our notions of what is worth looking at and what we have a right to observe. They are a grammar and, even more importantly, an ethics of seeing. Finally, the most grandiose result of the photographic enterprise is to give us the sense that we can hold the whole world in our heads—as an anthology of images.

To collect photographs is to collect the world. Movies and television programs light up walls, flicker, and go out; but with still photographs the image is also an object, lightweight, cheap to produce, easy to carry about, accumulate, store. In Godard's *Les Carabiniers* (1963), two sluggish lumpen-peasants are lured into joining the King's Army by the promise that they will be able to loot, rape, kill, or do whatever else they please to the enemy, and get rich. But the suitcase of booty that Michel-Ange and Ulysse triumphantly bring home, years later, to their wives turns out to contain only picture postcards, hundreds of them, of Monuments, Department Stores, Mammals, Wonders of Nature, Methods of Transport, Works of Art, and other classified treasures from around the globe. Godard's gag vividly parodies the equivocal magic of the photographic image. Photographs are perhaps the most mysterious of all the objects that make up, and thicken, the environment we recognize as modern. Photographs really are experience captured, and the camera is the ideal arm of consciousness in its acquisitive mood.

To photograph is to appropriate the thing photographed. It means putting oneself into a certain relation to the world that feels like knowledge—and, therefore, like power. A now notorious first fall into alienation, habituating people to abstract the world into printed words, is supposed to have engendered that surplus of Faustian energy and psychic damage needed to build modern, inorganic societies. But print seems a less treacherous form of leaching out the world, of turning it into a mental object, than photographic images, which now provide most of the knowledge people have about the look of the past and the reach of the present. What is written about a person or an event is frankly an interpretation, as are handmade visual statements, like paintings and drawings. Photographed images do not seem to be statements about the world so much as pieces of it, miniatures of reality that anyone can make or acquire.

Photographs, which fiddle with the scale of the world, themselves get reduced, blown up, cropped, retouched, doctored, tricked out. They age, plagued by the usual ills of paper objects; they disappear; they become valuable, and get bought and sold; they are reproduced. Photographs, which package the world, seem to invite packaging. They are stuck in albums, framed and set on tables, tacked on walls, projected as slides. Newspapers and magazines feature them; cops alphabetize them; museums exhibit them; publishers compile them.

For many decades the book has been the most influential way of arranging (and usually miniaturizing) photographs, thereby guaranteeing them longevity, if not immortality—photographs are fragile objects, easily torn or mislaid—and a wider public. The photograph in a book is, obviously, the image of an image. But since it is, to begin with, a printed, smooth object, a photograph loses much less of its essential quality when reproduced in a book than a painting does. Still, the book is not a wholly satisfactory scheme for putting groups of photographs into general circulation. The sequence in which the photographs are to be looked at is proposed by the order of pages, but nothing holds readers to the recommended order or indicates the amount of time to be spent on each photograph. Chris Markers's film, *Si j'avais quatre dromadaires* (1966), a brilliantly orchestrated meditation on photographs of all sorts and themes, suggests a subtler and more rigorous way of packaging (and enlarging) still photographs. Both the order and the exact time for looking at each photograph are imposed; and there is a gain in visual legibility and emotional impact. But photographs transcribed in a film cease to be collectable objects, as they still are when served up in books.

Photographs furnish evidence. Something we hear about, but doubt, seems proven when we're shown a photograph of it. In one version of its utility, the camera record incriminates. Starting with their use by the Paris police in the murderous roundup of Communards in June 1871, photographs became a useful tool of modern states in the surveillance and control of their increasingly mobile populations. In another version of its utility, the camera record justifies. A photograph passes for incontrovertible proof that a given thing happened. The picture may distort; but there is always a presumption that something exists, or did exist, which is like what's in the picture. Whatever the limitations (through amateurism) or pretensions (through artistry) of the individual photographer, a photograph—any photograph—seems to have a more innocent, and therefore more accurate, relation to visible reality than do other mimetic objects. Virtuosi of the noble image like Alfred Stieglitz and Paul Strand, composing mighty, unforgettable photographs decade after decade, still want, first of all, to show something "out there," just like the Polaroid owner for whom photographs are a handy, fast form of note-taking, or the shutterbug with a Brownie who takes snapshots as souvenirs of daily life.

While a painting or a prose description can never be other than a narrowly selective interpretation, a photograph can be treated as a narrowly selective transparency. But despite the presumption of veracity that gives all photographs authority, interest, seductiveness, the work that photographers do is no generic exception to the usually shady commerce between art and truth. Even when photographers are most concerned with mirroring reality, they are still haunted by

Figure 17 Arthur "Weegee" Fellig, *Top Hats—In Trouble*, 1942. Charles Sodokoff and Arthur Webber Use Their Top Hats to Hide Their Faces, January 27, 1942. New York Daily News Photo. (Weegee/ICP/Liason.)

tacit imperatives of taste and conscience. The immensely gifted members of the Farm Security Administration photographic project of the late 1930s (among them Walker Evans, Dorothea Lange, Ben Shahn, Russell Lee) would take dozens of frontal pictures of one of their sharecropper subjects until satisfied that they had gotten just the right look on film—the precise expression on the subject's face that supported their own notions about poverty, light, dignity, texture, exploitation, and geometry. In deciding how a picture should look, in preferring one exposure to another, photographers are always imposing standards on their subjects. Although there is a sense in which the camera does indeed capture reality, not just interpret it, photographs are as much an interpretation of the world as paintings and drawings are. Those occasions when the taking of photographs is relatively undiscriminating, promiscuous, or self-effacing do not lessen the didacticism of the whole enterprise. This very passivity—and ubiquity—of the photographic record is photography's "message," its aggression.

Images which idealize (like most fashion and animal photography) are no less aggressive than work which makes a virtue of plainness (like class pictures, still lifes of the bleaker sort, and mug shots). There is an aggression implicit in every use of the camera. This is as evident in the 1840s and 1850s, photography's glorious first two decades, as in all the succeeding decades, during which technology made possible an ever increasing spread of that mentality which looks at the world as a set of potential photographs. Even for such early masters as David Octavius Hill and Julia Margaret Cameron who used the camera as a means of getting painterly images, the point of taking photographs was a vast departure from the aims of painters. From its start, photography implied the capture of the largest possible number of subjects. Painting never had so imperial a scope. The subsequent industrialization of camera technology only carried out a promise inherent in photography from its very beginning: to democratize all experiences by translating them into images.

That age when taking photographs required a cumbersome and expensive contraption—the toy of the clever, the wealthy, and the obsessed—seems remote indeed from the era of sleek pocket cameras that invite anyone to take pictures. The first cameras, made in France and England in the early 1840s, had only inventors and buffs to operate them. Since there were then no professional photographers, there could not be amateurs either, and taking photographs had no clear social use; it was a gratuitous, that is, an artistic activity, though with few pretensions to being an art. It was only with its industrialization that photography came into its own as art. As industrialization provided social uses for the operations of the photographer, so the reaction against these uses reinforced the self-consciousness of photography-as-art.

Recently, photography has become almost as widely practiced an amusement as sex and dancing—which means that, like every mass art form, photography is not practiced by most people as an art. It is mainly a social rite, a defense against anxiety, and a tool of power.

Memorializing the achievements of individuals considered as members of families (as well as of other groups) is the earliest popular use of photography. For at least a century, the wedding photograph has been as much a part of the ceremony as the prescribed verbal formulas. Cameras go with family life. According to a sociological study done in France, most households have a camera, but a household with children is twice as likely to have at least one camera as a household in which there are no children. Not to take pictures of one's children, particularly when they are small, is a sign of parental indifference, just as not turning up for one's graduation picture is a gesture of adolescent rebellion.

Through photographs, each family constructs a portrait-chronicle of itself—a portable kit of images that bears witness to its connectedness. It hardly matters what activities are photographed so long as photographs get taken and are cherished. Photography becomes a rite of family life just when, in the industrializing countries of Europe and

America, the very institution of the family starts undergoing radical surgery. As that claustrophobic unit, the nuclear family, was being carved out of a much larger family aggregate, photography came along to memorialize, to restate symbolically, the imperiled continuity and vanishing extendedness of family life. Those ghostly traces, photographs, supply the token presence of the dispersed relatives. A family's photograph album is generally about the extended family—and, often, is all that remains of it.

As photographs give people an imaginary possession of a past that is unreal, they also help people to take possession of space in which they are insecure. Thus, photography develops in tandem with one of the most characteristic of modern activities: tourism. For the first time in history, large numbers of people regularly travel out of their habitual environments for short periods of time. It seems positively unnatural to travel for pleasure without taking a camera along. Photographs will offer indisputable evidence that the trip was made, that the program was carried out, that fun was had. Photographs document sequences of consumption carried on outside the view of family, friends, neighbors. But dependence on the camera, as the device that makes real what one is experiencing, doesn't fade when people travel more. Taking photographs fills the same need for the cosmopolitans accumulating photograph-trophies of their boat trip up the Albert Nile or their fourteen days in China as it does for lower-middle-class vacationers taking snapshots of the Eiffel Tower or Niagara Falls.

A way of certifying experience, taking photographs is also a way of refusing it—by limiting experience to a search for the photogenic, by converting experience into an image, a souvenir. Travel becomes a strategy for accumulating photographs. The very activity of taking pictures is soothing, and assuages general feelings of disorientation that are likely to be exacerbated by travel. Most tourists feel compelled to put the camera between themselves and whatever is remarkable that they encounter. Unsure of other responses, they take a picture. This gives shape to experience: stop, take a photograph, and move on. The method especially appeals to people handicapped by a ruthless work ethic—Germans, Japanese, and Americans. Using a camera appeases the anxiety which the work-driven feel about not working when they are on vacation and supposed to be having fun. They have something to do that is like a friendly imitation of work: they can take pictures.

People robbed of their past seem to make the most fervent picture takers, at home and abroad. Everyone who lives in an industrialized society is obliged gradually to give up the past, but in certain countries, such as the United States and Japan, the break with the past has been particularly traumatic. In the early 1970s, the fable of the brash American tourist of the 1950s and 1960s, rich with dollars and Babbittry, was replaced by the mystery of the group-minded Japanese tourist, newly released from his island prison by the miracle of overvalued yen, who is generally armed with two cameras, one on each hip.

Photography has become one of the principal devices for experiencing something, for giving an appearance of participation. One full-page ad shows a small group of people standing pressed together, peering out of the photograph, all but one looking stunned, excited, upset. The one who wears a different expression holds a camera to his eye; he seems self-possessed, is almost smiling. While the others are passive, clearly alarmed spectators, having a camera has transformed one person into something active, a voyeur: only he has mastered the situation. What do these people see? We don't know. And it doesn't matter. It is an Event: something worth seeing—and therefore worth photographing. The ad copy, white letters across the dark lower third of the photograph like news coming over a teletype machine, consists of just six words: ". . . Prague . . . Woodstock . . . Vietnam . . . Sapporo . . . Londonderry . . . LEICA." Crushed hopes, youth antics, colonial wars, and winter sports are alike—are equalized by the camera. Taking photographs has set up a chronic voyeuristic relation to the world which levels the meaning of all events.

A photograph is not just the result of an encounter between an event and a photographer; picture-taking is an event in itself, and one with ever more peremptory rights—to interfere with, to invade, or to ignore whatever is going on. Our very sense of situation is now articulated by the camera's interventions. The omnipresence of cameras persuasively suggests that time consists of interesting events, events worth photographing. This, in turn, makes it easy to feel that any event, once underway, and whatever its moral character, should be allowed to complete itself—so that something else can be brought into the world, the photograph. After the event has ended, the picture will still exist, conferring on the event a kind of immortality (and importance) it would never otherwise have enjoyed. While real people are out there killing themselves or other real people, the photographer stays behind his or her camera, creating a tiny element of another world: the image-world that bids to outlast us all.

Photographing is essentially an act of non-intervention. Part of the horror of such memorable coups of contemporary photojournalism as the pictures of a Vietnamese bonze reaching for the gasoline can, of a Bengali guerrilla in the act of bayoneting a trussed-up collaborator, comes from the awareness of how plausible it has become, in situations where the photographer has the choice between a photograph and a life, to choose the photograph. The person who intervenes cannot record; the person who is recording cannot intervene. Dziga Vertov's great film, *Man with a Movie Camera* (1929), gives the ideal image of the photographer as someone in perpetual movement, someone moving through a panorama of disparate events with such agility and speed that any intervention is out of the question. Hitchcock's *Rear Window* (1954) gives the complementary image: the photographer played by James Stewart has an intensified relation to one event, through his camera, precisely because he has a broken leg and is confined to a wheelchair; being temporarily immobilized prevents him from acting on what he sees, and makes it even more important to take pictures. Even if incompatible with intervention in a physical sense, using a camera is still a form of participation. Although the camera is an observation station, the act of photographing is more than passive observing. Like sexual voyeurism, it is a way of at least tacitly, often explicitly, encouraging whatever is going on to keep on happening. To take a picture is to have an interest in things as they are, in the status quo remaining unchanged (at least for as long as it takes to get a "good" picture), to be in complicity with whatever makes a subject interesting, worth photographing—including, when that is the interest, another person's pain or misfortune.

"I always thought of photography as a naughty thing to do—that was one of my favorite things about it," Diane Arbus wrote, "and when I first did it I felt very perverse." Being a professional photographer can be thought of as naughty, to use Arbus's pop word, if the photographer seeks out subjects considered to be disreputable, taboo, marginal. But naughty subjects are harder to find these days. And what exactly is the perverse aspect of picture-taking? If professional photographers often have sexual fantasies when they are behind the camera, perhaps the perversion lies in the fact that these fantasies are both plausible and so inappropriate. In *Blowup* (1966), Antonioni has the fashion photographer hovering convulsively over Verushka's body with his camera clicking. Naughtiness, indeed! In fact, using a camera is not a very good way of getting at someone sexually. Between photographer and subject, there has to be distance. The camera doesn't rape, or even possess, though it may presume, intrude, trespass, distort, exploit, and, at the farthest reach of metaphor, assassinate—all activities that, unlike the sexual push and shove, can be conducted from a distance, and with some detachment.

There is a much stronger sexual fantasy in Michael Powell's extraordinary movie *Peeping Tom* (1960), which is not about a Peeping Tom but about a psychopath who kills women with a weapon concealed in his camera, while photographing them. Not once does he touch his subjects. He doesn't desire their bodies; he wants their presence in the form of filmed images—those showing them experiencing their own death—which he screens at home for his solitary pleasure. The movie assumes connections between impotence and aggression, professionalized looking and cruelty, which point to the central fan-

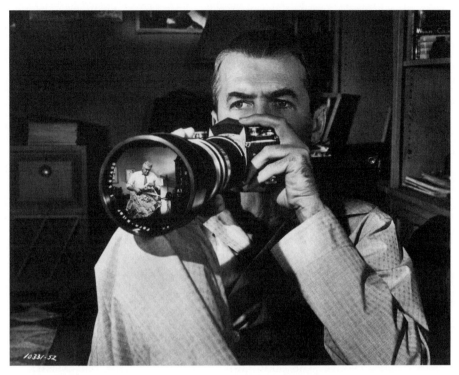

Figure 18 Jimmy Stewart as L. B. Jeffries in *Rear Window,* directed by Alfred Hitchcock. (© Bettman/CORBIS.)

tasy connected with the camera. The camera as phallus is, at most, a flimsy variant of the inescapable metaphor that everyone unselfconsciously employs. However hazy our awareness of this fantasy, it is named without subtlety whenever we talk about "loading" and "aiming" a camera, about "shooting" a film.

The old-fashioned camera was clumsier and harder to reload than a brown Bess musket. The modern camera is trying to be a ray gun. One ad reads:

> The Yashica Electro-35 GT is the spaceage camera your family will love. Take beautiful pictures day or night. Automatically. Without any nonsense. Just aim, focus and shoot. The GT's computer brain and electronic shutter will do the rest.

Like a car, a camera is sold as a predatory weapon—one that's as automated as possible, ready to spring. Popular taste expects an easy, an invisible technology. Manufacturers reassure their customers that taking pictures demands no skill or expert knowledge, that the machine is all-knowing, and responds to the slightest pressure of the will. It's as simple as turning the ignition key or pulling the trigger.

Like guns and cars, cameras are fantasy-machines whose use is addictive. However, despite the extravagances of ordinary language and advertising, they are not lethal. In the hyperbole that markets cars like guns, there is at least this much truth: except in wartime, cars kill more people than guns do. The camera/gun does not kill, so the ominous metaphor seems to be all bluff—like a man's fantasy of having a gun, knife, or tool between his legs. Still, there is something predatory in the act of taking a picture. To photograph people is to violate them, by seeing them as they never see themselves, by having knowledge of them they can never have; it turns people into objects that can be symbolically possessed. Just as the camera is a sublimation of the gun, to photograph someone is a sublimated murder—a soft murder, appropriate to a sad, frightened time.

Eventually, people might learn to act out more of their aggressions with cameras and fewer with guns, with the price being an even more image-choked world. One situation where people are switching from bullets to film is the photographic safari that is replacing the gun safari in East Africa. The hunters have Hasselblads instead of Winchesters; instead of looking through a telescopic sight to aim a rifle, they look through a viewfinder to frame a picture. In end-of-the century London, Samuel Butler complained that "there is a photographer in every bush, going about like a roaring lion seeking whom he may devour." The photographer is now charging real beasts, beleaguered and too rare to kill. Guns have metamorphosed into cameras in this earnest comedy, the ecology safari, because nature has ceased to be what it always had been—what people needed protection from. Now nature—tamed, endangered, mortal—needs to be protected from people. When we are afraid, we shoot. But when we are nostalgic, we take pictures.

It is a nostalgic time right now, and photographs actively promote nostalgia. Photography is an elegiac art, a twilight art. Most subjects photographed are, just by virtue of being photographed, touched with pathos. An ugly or grotesque subject may be moving because it has been dignified by the attention of the photographer. A beautiful subject can be the object of rueful feelings, because it has aged or decayed or no longer exists. All photographs are *memento mori*. To take a photograph is to participate in another person's (or thing's) mortality, vulnerability, mutability. Precisely by slicing out this moment and freezing it, all photographs testify to time's relentless melt.

Cameras began duplicating the world at that moment when the human landscape started to undergo a vertiginous rate of change: while an untold number of forms of biological and social life are being destroyed in a brief span of time, a device is available to record what is disappearing. The moody, intricately textured Paris of Atget and Brassaï is mostly gone. Like the dead relatives and friends preserved in the family album, whose presence in photographs exorcises some of the anxiety and remorse prompted by their disappearance, so the photographs of neighborhoods now torn down, rural places disfigured and made barren, supply our pocket relation to the past.

A photograph is both a pseudo-presence and a token of absence. Like a wood fire in a room, photographs—especially those of people, of distant landscapes and faraway cities, of the vanished past—are incitements to reverie. The sense of the unattainable that can be evoked by photographs feeds directly into the erotic feelings of those for whom desirability is enhanced by distance. The lover's photograph hidden in a married woman's wallet, the poster photograph of a rock star tacked up over an adolescent's bed, the campaign-button image of a politician's face pinned on a voter's coat, the snapshots of a cabdriver's children clipped to the visor—all such talismanic uses of photographs express a feeling both sentimental and implicitly magical: they are attempts to contact or lay claim to another reality.

Photographs can abet desire in the most direct, utilitarian way— as when someone collects photographs of anonymous examples of the desirable as an aid to masturbation. The matter is more complex when photographs are used to stimulate the moral impulse. Desire has no history—at least, it is experienced in each instance as all foreground, immediacy. It is aroused by archetypes and is, in that sense, abstract. But moral feelings are embedded in history, whose personae are concrete, whose situations are always specific. Thus, almost opposite rules hold true for the use of the photograph to awaken desire and to awaken conscience. The images that mobilize conscience are always linked to a given historical situation. The more general they are, the less likely they are to be effective.

A photograph that brings news of some unsuspected zone of misery cannot make a dent in public opinion unless there is an appropriate context of feeling and attitude. The photographs Mathew Brady and his colleagues took of the horrors of the battlefields did not make people any less keen to go on with the Civil War. The photographs of ill-clad, skeletal prisoners held at Andersonville inflamed Northern public opinion—against the South. (The effect of the Andersonville photographs must have been partly due to the very novelty, at that time, of seeing photographs.) The political understanding that many Americans came to in the 1960s would allow them, looking at the photographs Dorothea Lange took of Nisei on the West Coast being transported to internment camps in 1942, to recognize their subject for what it was—a crime committed by the government against a large group of American citizens. Few people who saw these photographs in the 1940s could have had so unequivocal a reaction; the grounds for such a judgment were covered over by the pro-war consensus. Photographs cannot create a moral position, but they can reinforce one—and can help build a nascent one.

Photographs may be more memorable than moving images, because they are a neat slice of time, not a flow. Television is a stream of underselected images, each of which cancels its predecessor. Each still photograph is a privileged moment, turned into a slim object that one can keep and look at again. Photographs like the one that made the front page of most newspapers in the world in 1972—a naked South Vietnamese child just sprayed by American napalm, running down a highway toward the camera, her arms open, screaming with pain—probably did more to increase the public revulsion against the war than a hundred hours of televised barbarities.

One would like to imagine that the American public would not have been so unanimous in its acquiescence to the Korean War if it had been confronted with photographic evidence of the devastation of Korea, an ecocide and genocide in some respects even more thorough than those inflicted on Vietnam a decade later. But the supposition is trivial. The public did not see such photographs because there was, ideologically, no space for them. No one brought back photographs of daily life in Pyongyang, to show that the enemy had a human face, as Felix Greene and Marc Riboud brought back photographs of Hanoi. Americans did have access to photographs of the suffering of the Vietnamese (many of which came from military sources and were taken with quite a different use in mind) because journalists felt backed in their efforts to obtain those photographs, the event having been defined by a significant number of people as a savage colonialist war. The Korean War was understood differently—as part of the struggle of the Free World against the Soviet Union and China—and, given that characterization, photographs of the cruelty of unlimited American firepower would have been irrelevant.

Though an event has come to mean, precisely, something worth photographing, it is still ideology (in the broadest sense) that determines what constitutes an event. There can be no evidence, photographic or otherwise, of an event until the event itself has been named and characterized. And it is never photographic evidence which can construct—more properly, identify—events; the contribution of photography always follows the naming of the event. What determines the possibility of being affected morally by photographs is the existence of a relevant political consciousness. Without a politics, photographs of the slaughter-bench of history will most likely be experienced as, simply, unreal or as a demoralizing emotional blow.

The quality of feeling, including moral outrage, that people can muster in response to photographs of the oppressed, the exploited, the starving, and the massacred also depends on the degree of their familiarity with these images. Don McCullin's photographs of emaciated Biafrans in the early 1970s had less impact for some people than Werner Bischof's photographs of Indian famine victims in the early

1950s because those images had become banal, and the photographs of Tuareg families dying of starvation in the sub-Sahara that appeared in magazines everywhere in 1973 must have seemed to many like an unbearable replay of a now familiar atrocity exhibition.

Photographs shock insofar as they show something novel. Unfortunately, the ante keeps getting raised—partly through the very proliferation of such images of horror. One's first encounter with the photographic inventory of ultimate horror is a kind of revelation, the prototypically modern revelation: a negative epiphany. For me, it was photographs of Bergen-Belsen and Dachau which I came across by chance in a bookstore in Santa Monica in July 1945. Nothing I have seen—in photographs or in real life—ever cut me as sharply, deeply, instantaneously. Indeed, it seems plausible to me to divide my life into two parts, before I saw those photographs (I was twelve) and after, though it was several years before I understood fully what they were about. What good was served by seeing them? They were only photographs—of an event I had scarcely heard of and could do nothing to affect, of suffering I could hardly imagine and could do nothing to relieve. When I looked at those photographs, something broke. Some limit had been reached, and not only that of horror; I felt irrevocably grieved, wounded, but a part of my feelings started to tighten; something went dead; something is still crying.

To suffer is one thing; another thing is living with the photographed images of suffering, which does not necessarily strengthen conscience and the ability to be compassionate. It can also corrupt them. Once one has seen such images, one has started down the road of seeing more—and more. Images transfix. Images anesthetize. An event known through photographs certainly becomes more real than it would have been if one had never seen the photographs—think of the Vietnam War. (For a counter-example, think of the Gulag Archipelago, of which we have no photographs.) But after repeated exposure to images it also becomes less real.

The same law holds for evil as for pornography. The shock of photographed atrocities wears off with repeated viewings, just as the surprise and bemusement felt the first time one sees a pornographic movie wear off after one sees a few more. The sense of taboo which makes us indignant and sorrowful is not much sturdier than the sense of taboo that regulates the definition of what is obscene. And both have been sorely tried in recent years. The vast photographic catalogue of misery and injustice throughout the world has given everyone a certain familiarity with atrocity, making the horrible seem more ordinary—making it appear familiar, remote ("it's only a photograph"), inevitable. At the time of the first photographs of the Nazi camps, there was nothing banal about these images. After thirty years, a saturation point may have been reached. In these last decades, "concerned" photography has done at least as much to deaden conscience as to arouse it.

The ethical content of photographs is fragile. With the possible exception of photographs of those horrors, like the Nazi camps, that have gained the status of ethical reference points, most photographs do not keep their emotional charge. A photograph of 1900 that was affecting then because of its subject would, today, be more likely to move us because it is a photograph taken in 1900. The particular qualities and intentions of photographs tend to be swallowed up in the generalized pathos of time past. Aesthetic distance seems built into the very experience of looking at photographs, if not right away, then certainly with the passage of time. Time eventually positions most photographs, even the most amateurish, at the level of art.

The industrialization of photography permitted its rapid absorption into rational—that is, bureaucratic—ways of running society. No longer toy images, photographs became part of the general furniture of the environment—touchstones and confirmations of that reductive approach to reality which is considered realistic. Photographs were enrolled in the service of important institutions of control, notably the family and the police, as symbolic objects and as pieces of information. Thus, in the bureaucratic cataloguing of the world, many important documents are not valid unless they have, affixed to them, a photograph-token of the citizen's face.

The "realistic" view of the world compatible with bureaucracy redefines knowledge—as techniques and information. Photographs are valued because they give information. They tell one what there is; they make an inventory. To spies, meteorologists, coroners, archaeologists, and other information professionals, their value is inestimable. But in the situations in which most people use photographs, their value as information is of the same order as fiction. The information that photographs can give starts to seem very important at that moment in cultural history when everyone is thought to have a right to something called news. Photographs were seen as a way of giving information to people who do not take easily to reading. The *Daily News* still calls itself "New York's Picture Newspaper," its bid for populist identity. At the opposite end of the scale, *Le Monde,* a newspaper designed for skilled, well-informed readers, runs no photographs at all. The presumption is that, for such readers, a photograph could only illustrate the analysis contained in an article.

A new sense of the notion of information has been constructed around the photographic image. The photograph is a thin slice of space as well as time. In a world ruled by photographic images, all borders ("framing") seem arbitrary. Anything can be separated, can be made discontinuous, from anything else: all that is necessary is to frame the subject differently. (Conversely, anything can be made adjacent to anything else.) Photography reinforces a nominalist view of social reality as consisting of small units of an apparently infinite

Figure 19 Jacob A. Riis, "Room in tenement flat, 1910," from *How the Other Half Lives,* by Jacob A. Riis. (Jacob A. Riis Collection, Museum of the City of New York.)

number—as the number of photographs that could be taken of anything is unlimited. Through photographs, the world becomes a series of unrelated, freestanding particles; and history, past and present, a set of anecdotes and *faits divers.* The camera makes reality atomic, manageable, and opaque. It is a view of the world which denies interconnectedness, continuity, but which confers on each moment the character of a mystery. Any photograph has multiple meanings; indeed, to see something in the form of a photograph is to encounter a potential object of fascination. The ultimate wisdom of the photographic image is to say: "There is the surface. Now think—or rather feel, intuit—what is beyond it, what the reality must be like if it looks this way." Photographs, which cannot themselves explain anything, are inexhaustible invitations to deduction, speculation, and fantasy.

Photography implies that we know about the world if we accept it as the camera records it. But this is the opposite of understanding, which starts from *not* accepting the world as it looks. All possibility of understanding is rooted in the ability to say no. Strictly speaking, one never understands anything from a photograph. Of course, photographs fill in blanks in our mental pictures of the present and the past: for example, Jacob Riis's images of New York squalor in the 1880s are sharply instructive to those unaware that urban poverty in late-nineteenth-century America was really that Dickensian. Nevertheless, the camera's rendering of reality must always hide more than it discloses. As Brecht points out, a photograph of the Krupp works reveals virtually nothing about that organization. In contrast to the amorous relation, which is based on how something looks, understanding is based on how it functions. And functioning takes place in time, and must be explained in time. Only that which narrates can make us understand.

The limit of photographic knowledge of the world is that, while it can goad conscience, it can, finally, never be ethical or political knowledge. The knowledge gained through still photographs will always be some kind of sentimentalism, whether cynical or humanist. It will be a knowledge at bargain prices—a semblance of knowledge, a semblance of wisdom; as the act of taking pictures is a semblance of appropriation, a semblance of rape. The very muteness of what is, hypothetically, comprehensible in photographs is what constitutes their attraction and provocativeness. The omnipresence of photographs has an incalculable effect on our ethical sensibility. By furnishing this already crowded world with a duplicate one of images, photography makes us feel that the world is more available than it really is.

Needing to have reality confirmed and experience enhanced by photographs is an aesthetic consumerism to which everyone is now addicted. Industrial societies turn their citizens into image-junkies; it is the most irresistible form of mental pollution. Poignant longings for beauty, for an end to probing below the surface, for a redemption and celebration of the body of the world—all these elements of erotic feeling are affirmed in the pleasure we take in photographs. But other, less liberating feelings are expressed as well. It would not be wrong to speak of people having a *compulsion* to photograph: to turn experience itself into a way of seeing. Ultimately, having an experience becomes identical with taking a photograph of it, and participating in a public event comes more and more to be equivalent to looking at it in photographed form. That most logical of nineteenth-century aesthetes, Mallarmé, said that everything in the world exists in order to end in a book. Today everything exists to end in a photograph.

1977

READING, REREADING, AND ANALYSIS

1. Sontag's essay gives an account of many historical and current uses of photography. Choose two examples that seem interesting or revealing to you and write a one-paragraph summary of each example in which you cite a key quotation, explain the example, and note why you found it interesting or revealing.

2. Individually or in a group, list all the positive and negative implications of photography that you can find in Sontag's essay. Add your own positives and negatives as they come up in discussion.

3. Sontag says that "photographing is essentially an act of nonintervention," but later in the essay, she argues that cameras are like guns. Look for photos in a magazine that illustrate both claims Sontag makes.

4. In a group, talk about Sontag's discussion of the relationship between the event and the photograph. Choose a passage from Sontag that helps the group explore this question and then prepare a group explanation to present to the class.

5. What does Sontag mean on page 466 when she writes, "Photographs are perhaps the most mysterious of all the objects that make up, and thicken, the environment we recognize as modern. Photographs really are experience captured, and the camera is the ideal arm of consciousness in its acquisitive mood"?

6. Think about technology such as the Internet, digital cameras, camera phones, videotape, and DVDs. What impact have these technologies had on photography? What might Sontag say about these newer technologies and why?

RESPONDING THROUGH WRITING:
BUILDING AN INTERPRETATION

7. Sontag concludes her essay by saying, "The knowledge gained through still photographs will always be some kind of sentimentalism, whether cynical or humanist. It will be a knowledge at bargain prices—a semblance of knowledge, a semblance of wisdom; as the act of taking pictures is a semblance of appropriation, a semblance of rape" (p. 480). Write an essay in which you use examples from "In Plato's Cave" and from outside photographs to explain why Sontag has this seemingly dark vision of photography's impact on our society. To what extent do you share that vision? To what extent do you disagree with some of Sontag's claims or see some alternative implications of photography as a technology?

8. Reread the paragraph on page 476 that begins, "Though an event has come to mean, precisely, something worth photographing, it is still an ideology . . . ." With the aid of your dictionary, summarize Sontag's argument in the paragraph, and then write a one- or two-page response that focuses on the last sentence of the paragraph.

9. Write a three- or four-page essay in which you discuss why Sontag titles her essay on photography "In Plato's Cave."

10. According to Sontag, "Photography implies that we know about the world if we accept it as the camera records it. But this is the opposite of understanding, which starts from *not* accepting the world as it looks" (p. 479). Make a list of examples that illustrate Sontag's suggestive claim that "understanding . . . starts from *not* accepting the world as it looks." Use your examples to write a comparison of your own sense of understanding with Sontag's. Where does your understanding of understanding parallel or intersect with hers? Where does your understanding differ from hers and why?

GOING FURTHER: LEARNING FROM OTHER SOURCES

11. Look through photography books at the library, at photographs used in newspapers, and at photographs displayed on the Internet, in a museum, or in your family album. Use a group of photographs to supply evidence for or against one of Sontag's claims in this essay. For instance, you could use three photos to support or counter Sontag's argument that "to take a photograph is to participate in another person's (or thing's) mortality, vulnerability, mutability"; or her claim that "what determines the possibility of being affected morally by photographs is the existence of a relevant political consciousness"; or her claim that "images transfix. Images anesthetize." Share your findings with your group and create an individual presentation for the class.

12. Use a reference database such as Lexis/Nexis or EBSCO to find articles on and reviews of Sontag's book *On Photography*. What reactions to Sontag's book do you find? How does your own response to "In Plato's Cave" compare with the attitudes expressed in your research?

APPLYING WHAT YOU'VE LEARNED

13. Compare Sontag's discussion of photography as a technology with Sherry Turkle's essay, "The Triumph of Tinkering," which focuses on the varying uses of Internet technology. In each case, do the expectations, assumptions, and perceptions of the users seem to determine the outcome and implications of the technology? To what extent does the technology itself seem to teach its users new uses for the Internet or for photography and new ways of perceiving the world? What are the long-range implications of each technology?

14. Write an essay in which you compare Sontag's analysis of photographs as devices or artifacts for memorializing and monumentalizing people, places, events, and things with Marita Sturken's analysis of memorials and monuments in her essay, "The Wall, the Screen and the Image: The Vietnam Veterans Memorial."

15. In "The Little Man at Chehaw Station," Ralph Ellison talks about the "melting pot" metaphor for United States identity. In one particular example, Ellison discusses a young man who takes a series of photographic self-portraits on "New York's Riverside Drive near 151st Street" (p. 163). Use some of Sontag's key observations about photography to help you analyze Ellison's description of the young man and his photography. In addition, discuss how Sontag's analysis of photography also says something about questions of identity and metaphors such as the "melting pot."

MARITA STURKEN

Marita Sturken (b. 1957) is an Associate Professor at the University of Southern California, where she teaches in the Annenberg School for Communication and the Program in American Studies and Ethnicity. Sturken's four books and numerous articles examine "the ways in which individuals create meaning from cultural products and artifacts, focusing on cultural memory and national identity, images and visual culture, the social function of art, and the cultural effects of technology." She is currently researching the public response to traumatic events such as Columbine, September 11, and the Oklahoma City bombing.

> **To learn more about cultural memory and memorials such as the Vietnam Wall, see Marita Sturken's article "Memorializing Absence" at <http://www.ssrc.org/sept11/essays/sturken.htm>.**

WHAT DO YOU KNOW? WHAT DO YOU EXPECT TO DISCOVER?

Before reading the essay, take a moment to consider the following questions.

1. What does Sturken's title lead you to expect from this essay? Circle keywords in the title. What relations do you see between "Wall," "Screen," and "Image"? Looking up and comparing the definitions of these words can help you make connections.

2. Sturken examines remembrance and cultural memory in this essay. Consider your own understanding of these terms. Think particularly about how you as well as society at large marks or highlights people, places, and events for remembrance. What kinds of people, places, events, and things do you memorialize? How? And Why?

3. Before reading the essay, list all the ways you can think of that we use photographs in our daily lives and in the culture at large.

✗

The Wall, The Screen and the Image
The Vietnam Veterans Memorial

The forms remembrance takes indicate the status of memory within a given culture. In these forms, we can see acts of public commemoration as moments in which the shifting discourse of history, personal memory, and cultural memory converge. Public commemoration is a form of history-making, yet, it can also be a contested form of remembrance in which cultural memories slide through and into each other, merging and then disengaging in a narrative tangle.

With the Vietnam War, discourses of public commemoration are inextricably tied to the question of how war is brought to closure in American society. How, for instance, does a society commemorate a war for which the central narrative is one of division and dissent, a war whose history is still formative and highly contested? The Vietnam War, with its lack of a singular, historical narrative defining clear-cut purpose and outcome, has led to a unique form of commemoration.

Questions of public remembrance of the Vietnam War can be examined through the concept of the screen: a screen is a surface that is projected upon; it is also an object that hides something from view, that shelters or protects. The kinds of screens that converge in the case of the Vietnam Veterans Memorial in Washington, DC both shield and are projected upon: the black walls of the memorial act as screens for innumerable projections of memory and history—of the United States' participation in the Vietnam War and the experience of the Vietnam veterans since the war.

A singular, sanctioned history of the Vietnam War has not coalesced, in part because of the disruption of the standard narratives of American imperialism, technology, and masculinity that the war's loss represented. The history of the Vietnam War is still being composed from many conflicting histories, yet particular elements within the often opposing narratives are uncontested—the divisive effect the war had on American society and the marginalization of the Vietnam veteran. This essay is concerned with how narratives of the war have been constructed out of and within the cultural memory of the Vietnam Veterans Memorial. I shall examine how the screens of the memorial act to eclipse—to screen out—personal and collective memories of the Vietnam War in the design of history, and how the textures of cultural memory are nevertheless woven throughout, perhaps over and under, these screens.

The Status of a Memorial

Although now administered under the aegis of the National Parks Service of the federal government, the impetus for the creation of the Vietnam Veterans Memorial came from a group of Vietnam veterans who raised the funds and negotiated a site on the Washington Mall. Situated on the grassy slope of the Constitutional Gardens near the Lincoln Memorial, the Vietnam Veterans Memorial, which was designed by Maya Lin, consists of a V shape of two walls of black granite set into the earth at an angle of 125 degrees. Together, the walls extend almost 500 feet in length, with a maximum height of approximately 10 feet at the central hinge. These walls are inscribed with 58,196 names of men and women who died in the war, listed chronologically by date of death, with opening and closing inscriptions. The listing of names begins on the right-hand side of the hinge and continues to the end of the right wall; it then begins again at the far end of the left wall and ends at the center again. Thus, the name of the first American soldier killed in Vietnam, in 1959, is on a panel adjacent to that containing the name of the last American killed in 1975. The framing dates of 1959 and 1975 are the only dates listed on the wall; the names are listed alphabetically within each 'casualty day,' although those dates are not noted. Eight of the names on the wall represent women who died in the war. Since 1984 the memorial has been accompanied by a flag and a figurative sculpture of three soldiers, both facing the memorial from a group of trees south of the wall. In 1993 a statue commemorating the women who served in Vietnam was added 300 feet from the wall.

The memorial functions in opposition to the codes of remembrance evidenced on the Washington Mall. Virtually all the national memorials and monuments in Washington are made of white stone and constructed to be seen from a distance. In contrast, the Vietnam Veterans Memorial cuts into the sloping earth: it is not visible until one is almost upon it; if approached from behind, it seems to disappear into the landscape. Although the polished black granite walls of the memorial reflect the Washington Monument and face the Lincoln Memorial, they are not visible from the base of either structure. The black stone creates a reflective surface, one that echoes the reflecting pool of the Lincoln Memorial, and allows the viewers to participate in the memorial; seeing their own image reflected in the names, they are implicated in the listing of the dead. The etched surface of the memorial has a tactile quality, and viewers are compelled to touch the names and make rubbings of them.

Its status as a memorial, rather than a monument, situates the Vietnam Veterans Memorial within a particular code of remembrance. Monuments and memorials can often be used as interchangeable forms, but there are distinctions in intent between them. Arthur Danto writes: 'We erect monuments so that we shall always remember, and build memorials so that we shall never forget.[1] Monuments are not generally built to commemorate defeats; the defeated dead are remembered in memorials. Whereas a monument most often signifies victory, a memorial refers to the life or lives sacrificed for a particular set of values. Memorials embody grief, loss, and tribute. Whatever triumph a memorial may refer to, its depiction of victory is always tempered by a foregrounding of the lives lost.

Memorials are, according to Charles Griswold, "a species of pedagogy' that seeks to instruct posterity about the past and, in so doing, necessarily reaches a decision about what is worth recovering."[2] The Lincoln Memorial is a funeral structure that gains its force from its implicit reference to Lincoln's untimely death. It embodies the man and his philosophy, with his words on its walls. The Washington Monument, by contrast, operates purely as a symbol, making no reference beyond its name to the mythic political figure. The distinction between the two outlines one of the fundamental differences between memorials and monuments: memorials tend to emphasize specific texts or lists of the dead, whereas monuments are usually anonymous.

The Vietnam Veterans Memorial is unmistakably representative of a particular period in Western art. In the uproar that accompanied its construction, it became the focus of a debate about the role of modernism in public sculpture. Just one month prior to the dedication of the memorial in November 1982, Tom Wolfe wrote a vitriolic attack on its design in the *Washington Post,* calling it a work of modern orthodoxy that was a "tribute to Jane Fonda."[3] Wolfe and other critics of modernism compared the memorial to two infamously unpopular, government-funded public sculptures: Carl Andre's *Stone Field Piece* (1980) in Hartford, Connecticut, and Richard Serra's *Tilted Arc* (1981) in downtown Manhattan. Andre's work, which consists of thirty-six large boulders positioned on a lawn near Hartford's city hall, is widely regarded with derision by residents as a symbol of the misguided judgements of their city government.[4] Serra's now notorious *Tilted Arc,* an oppressive, leaning slab of Cor-Ten steel that bisected the equally inhospitable Federal Plaza, inspired several years of intense debate and was dismantled in March 1989 after workers in the Federal Building petitioned to have it removed.[5] In the media, these two works came to symbolize the alienating effect of modern sculpture on the viewing public and people's questioning of the mechanisms by which tax-funded sculpture is imposed upon them.

In situating the Vietnam Veterans Memorial purely within the context of modernism, however, Wolfe and his fellow critics ignore fundamental aspects of this work, an omission which, it might be added, the sketches of the design may have aided. The memorial is not simply a flat, black, abstract wall; it is a wall inscribed with names. When members of the "public" visit this memorial, they do not go to contemplate long walls cut into the earth but to see and touch the names of those whose lives were lost in this war. Hence, to call this a modernist work is to overemphasize its physical design and to negate its commemorative purpose.

Modernist sculpture has been defined by a kind of sitelessness. Yet, the Vietnam Veterans Memorial is a site-specific work that establishes its position within the symbolic history embodied in the national monuments on and around the Washington Mall. Pointing from its axis to both the Washington Monument and Lincoln Memorial, the Vietnam Veterans Memorial references, absorbs, and reflects these classical forms. Its black walls mirror not only the faces of its viewers and passing clouds but the obelisk of the Washington Monument, thus forming a kind of pastiche of monuments. The memorial's relationship to the earth shifts between context and decontextualization, between an effacement and an embracement of the earth; approached from above, it appears to cut into the earth; from below, it seems to rise from it. The site specificity of the Vietnam Veterans Memorial is crucial to its position as both subversive of and continuous with the nationalist discourse of the mall.

It is as a war memorial that the Vietnam Veterans Memorial most distinguishes itself from modernist sculpture. As the first national memorial to an American war built since the Second World War memorials, it makes a statement on war that diverges sharply from the traditional declarations of prior war memorials. The Vietnam Veterans Memorial Fund (VVMF), which organized the construction of the memorial, stipulated only two things in its design—that it contain the names of all of those who died or are missing in action, and that it be apolitical and harmonious with the site. Implicit within these guidelines was the desire that the memorial offer some kind of closure to the debates on the war. Yet, with these stipulations, the veterans set the stage for the dramatic disparity between the message of this memorial and that of its antecedents. The stipulation that the work not espouse a political stand in regard to the war—a stipulation that, in the ensuing controversy, would ultimately appear naive—ensured that in the end the memorial would not glorify war.

The traditional war memorial achieves its status by enacting closure on a specific conflict. This closure contains the war within particular master narratives either of victory or the bitter price of victory, a theme dominant in the "never again" texts of First World War memorials. In declaring the end of a conflict, this closure can by its very nature serve to sanctify future wars by offering a complete narrative with cause and effect intact. In rejecting the architectural lineage of monuments and contesting the aesthetic codes of previous war memorials, the Vietnam Veterans Memorial refuses to sanction the closure and implied tradition of those structures. Yet, it can be said to both condemn and justify future memorials.

The Black Gash of Shame

Before the memorial was completed, its design came under attack not only because of its modernist aesthetics but, more significant, because it violated unspoken taboos about the remembrance of wars. When it was first unveiled, the design was condemned by certain veterans and others as a highly political statement about the shame of an unvictorious war. The memorial was termed the "black gash of shame and sorrow," a "degrading ditch," a "tombstone," a "slap in the face," and a "wailing wall for draft dodgers and New Lefters of the future." These dissenters included a certain faction of veterans and members of the "New Right," ranging from conservative activist Phyllis Schlafly to future presidential candidate Ross Perot, who had contributed the money for the design contest. Many of these critics saw the memorial as a monument to defeat, one that spoke more directly to a nation's guilt than to the honor of the war dead and the veterans.

The criticism leveled at the memorial's design showed precisely how it was being "read" by its opponents, and their readings compellingly reveal codes of remembrance of war memorials. Many saw its black walls as evoking shame, sorrow, and dishonor and others perceived its refusal to rise above the earth as indicative of defeat. Thus, a racially coded reading of the color black as shameful was combined with a reading of a feminized earth connoting a lack of power. Precisely because of its deviation from traditional commemorative codes—white stone rising above the earth—the design was read as a political statement. In a defensive attempt to counter aesthetic arguments, an editorial in the *National Review* stated:

> Our objection . . . is based upon the clear political message of this design. The design says that the Vietnam War should be memorialized in black, not the white marble of Washington. The mode of listing the names makes them individual deaths, not deaths in a cause: they might as well have been traffic accidents. The invisibility of the monument at ground level symbolizes the "unmentionability" of the war . . . Finally, the V-shaped plan of the black retaining wall immortalizes the antiwar signal, the V protest made with the fingers.[6]

This analysis of the memorial's symbolism, indeed a perceptive reading, points to several crucial aspects of the memorial: its listing of names does emphasize individual deaths rather than the singular death of a body of men and women; the relationship of the memorial to the earth does refuse to evoke heroism and victory. Yet these conservative readings of the memorial, though they may have been accurate in interpreting the design, did not anticipate the effects of the inscription of names.

The angry reactions to the memorial design go beyond the accusation of the elite pretensions of abstraction—the uncontroversial Washington Monument itself is the epitome of abstraction. Rather, I believe that the memorial's primary (and unspoken) subversion of the codes of war remembrance is its antiphallic presence. By "antiphallic" I do not mean to imply that the memorial is somehow a passive or "feminine" form, but rather that it opposes the codes of vertical monuments symbolizing power and honor. The memorial does not stand erect above the landscape; it is continuous with the earth. It is contemplative rather than declarative. The V shape of the memorial has been interpreted by various commentators as V for Vietnam, victim, victory, veteran, violate, and valor. Yet one also finds here a disconcerting subtext in this debate in which the memorial is seen as implicitly evoking castration. The V of the two black granite walls, it seems, is also read as a female V. The "gash" is not only a wound, it is slang for the female genitals. The memorial contains all the elements that have been associated psychoanalytically with the specter of woman—it embraces the earth; it is the abyss; it is death.

Indeed, some of the criticism of the memorial was direct in calling for a phallic memorial. James Webb, who was a member of the Fund's sponsoring committee, wrote:

> Watching then the white phallus that is the Washington Monument piercing the air like a bayonet, you feel uplifted. . . . That is the political message. And then when you peer off into the woods at this black slash of earth to your left, this sad, dreary mass tomb, nihilistically commemorating death, you are hit with that message also. . . . That is the tragedy of this memorial for those who served.[7]

To its critics, this antiphallus symbolized this country's castration in an unsuccessful war, a war that "emasculated" the United States. The "healing" of this wound would therefore require a memorial that revived the narrative of the United States as a technologically superior military power and rehabilitated the masculinity of the American soldier.

The person who designed this controversial, antiphallic memorial was unlikely to reiterate traditional codes of war remembrance. At the time her anonymously submitted design was chosen by a group of eight art experts, Maya Ying Lin was a 21-year-old undergraduate at Yale University. She had produced the design as a project for a funerary architecture course. She was not only young and uncredentialed but also Chinese-American and female. Initially, the veterans of the VVMF were pleased by this turn of events; they assumed that the selection of Lin's design would only show how open and impartial

their design contest had been. However, the selection of someone with "marginal" cultural status as the primary interpreter of a
controversial war inevitably complicated matters. Eventually, Maya
Lin was defined, in particular by the media, not as American but as
"other." This otherness became an issue not only in the way she was
perceived by the media and some of the veterans, it became a critical
issue of whether or not that otherness had informed the design itself.
Architecture critic Michael Sorkin wrote:

> Perhaps it was Maya Lin's "otherness" that enabled her to create
> such a moving work. Perhaps only an outsider could have
> designed an environment so successful in answering the need for
> recognition by a group of people—the Vietnam vets—who are
> plagued by a sense of "otherness" forced on them by a country
> that has spent ten years pretending not to see them.[8]

Lin's marginal status as a Chinese-American woman was thus seen as
giving her insight into the marginal status experienced by Vietnam
veterans, an analogy that noticeably erased other differences in race
and age that existed between them.

When Lin's identity became known, there was a tendency in the
press to characterize her design as passive, as having both a female and
an Asian aesthetic. There is little doubt that in its refusal to glorify war,
it is an implicitly pacifist work, and, by extension, a political work. In
its form, the memorial is emphatically antiherioc. Yet as much as it is
contemplative and continuous with the earth, it can also be seen as a
violent work that cuts into the earth. Lin has said, "I wanted to work
with the land and not dominate it. I had an impulse to cut open the
earth . . . an initial violence that in time would heal. The grass would
grow back, but the cut would remain, a pure, flat surface, like a geode
when you cut into it and polish the edge."[9] The black walls cannot con-
note a healing wound without also signifying the violence that created
that wound, cutting into the earth and splitting it open.

Trouble began almost immediately between Maya Lin and the veterans. "The fund has always seen me as a female—as a child," she has
said. "I went in there when I first won and their attitude was—O.K.
you did a good job, but now we're going to hire some big boys—
boys—to take care of it."[10] Lin was situated outside the veterans' discourse, because she was a woman and an Asian-American and because
of her approach to the project. She had made a decision deliberately
not to inform herself about the war's political history to avoid being influenced by debates about the war. According to veteran Jan Scruggs,
who was the primary figure in getting the memorial built,

> She never asked, "What was combat like?" or "Who were your
> friends whose names we're putting on the wall?" And the vets,
> in turn, never once explained to her what words like "courage,"
> "sacrifice," and "devotion to duty" really meant.[11]

In the larger political arena, discourses of aesthetics and commemoration were also at play. Several well-placed funders of the memorial, including Ross Perot, were unhappy with the design, and Secretary of the Interior James Watt withheld its permit. It became clear to the veterans of the VVMF that they had either to compromise or to postpone the construction of the memorial (which was to be ready by November 1982, in time for Veterans Day). Consequently, a plan was devised to erect a statue and flag close to the walls of the memorial; realist sculptor Frederick Hart was chosen to design it. (Hart was paid $330,000, compared to the $20,000 fee that Maya Lin received for her design from the same fund).[12]

Hart's bronze sculpture, placed in a grove of trees near the memorial in 1984, consists of three soldiers—one black, one Hispanic, and one white—standing and looking in the general direction of the memorial. The soldiers' military garb is realistically rendered, with guns slung over their shoulders and ammunition around their waists, and their expressions are somewhat bewildered and puzzled. Hart, one of the most vociferous critics of modernism in the debate over the memorial, said at the time:

> My position is humanist, not militarist. I'm not trying to say there was anything good or bad about the war. I researched for three years—read everything. I became close friends with many vets, drank with them in bars. Lin's piece is a serene exercise in contemporary art done in a vacuum with no knowledge of its subject. It's nihilistic—that's its appeal.[13]

Hart bases his credentials on a kind of "knowledge" strictly within the male domain—drinking with the veterans in a bar—and unavailable to Maya Lin, whom he had on another occasion referred to as "a mere student." She describes the addition of his statue as "drawing mustaches on other people's portraits."[14] Hart characterizes Lin as having designed her work with no "knowledge" and no "research," as a woman who works with feeling and intuition rather than expertise. He ultimately defines realism as not only a male privilege but also an aesthetic necessity in remembering war. Ironically, the conflict over Lin's design forestalled any potential debate over the atypical expression of Hart's soldiers.

The battle over what kind of aesthetic style best represents the Vietnam War was, quite obviously, a battle of the discourse of the war itself. In striving for an "apolitical" memorial, the veterans of the VVMF had attempted to separate the memorial, itself a contested narrative, from the contested narratives of the war, ultimately an impossible task. The memorial could not be a neutral site precisely because of the divisive effects of the Vietnam War. Later, Maya Lin noted the strange appropriateness of the two memorials: "In a funny sense the compromise brings the memorial closer to the truth. What is also memorialized is that people still cannot resolve that war, nor can they separate issues, the politics, from it."[15] However, after Lin's memorial had actually been constructed, the debate about aesthetics and remembrance surrounding its design simply disappeared. The controversy was eclipsed by a national discourse on remembrance and healing. The experience of viewing Lin's work was so powerful for the general public that criticism of its design vanished.

The Vietnam Veteran: The Perennial Soldier

The incommunicability of the experience of the Vietnam veterans has been a primary narrative in Vietnam War representation. This silence has been depicted as a consequence of an inconceivable kind of war, one that fit no prior images of war, one that the American public would refuse to believe. The importance of the Vietnam Veterans memorial lies in its communicability, which in effect has mollified the incommunicability of the veterans' experience.

Though the Vietnam Veterans Memorial most obviously pays tribute to the memory of those who died during the war, it is a central icon for the veterans. It has been noted that the memorial has given them a place—one that recognizes their identities, a place at which to congregate and from which to speak. Vietnam veterans haunt the memorial, often coming at night after the crowds have dispersed. Many veterans regard the wall as a site where they visit their memories. Hence, the memorial is as much about survival as it is about mourning the dead. The construction of an identity for the veterans has become the most conspicuous and persistent narrative of the memorial. The central theme of this narrative is the veterans' initial marginalization, before the memorial's construction generated discussion about them.

Unlike the Second World War veterans, Vietnam veterans did not arrive home en masse for a celebration. Some of the most difficult stories of the veterans' experience are about their mistreatment upon their return, and these incidents serve as icons for the extended alienation and mistreatment felt by the veterans. Many veterans ended up in underfunded and poorly staffed Veterans' Administration Hospitals. They were expected to put their war experiences behind them and to assimilate quickly back into society. That many were unable to do so further exacerbated their marginalization—they were labeled social misfits and stereotyped as potentially dangerous men liable to erupt violently at any moment.

The scapegoating of the veteran as a psychopath absolved the American public of complicity and allowed the narrative of American military power to stand. Implied within these conflicting narratives is the question of whether or not the veterans are to be perceived as victims or complicit with the war. Peter Marin writes, "Vets are in an ambiguous situation—they were the agents and victims of a particular kind of violence. That is the source of a pain that almost no one else can understand."[16] Ironically, their stigma has resulted in many Vietnam veterans' assumption of hybrid roles; they are both, yet neither, soldiers and civilians.

Although the marginalization of the Vietnam veterans has been acknowledged in the current discourse of healing and forgiveness about the war, within the veterans' community another group has struggled against an imposed silence: the women veterans. Eight women military nurses were killed in Vietnam and memorialized on the wall. It is estimated that 11,500 women, half of whom were civilians and many of whom were nurses, served in Vietnam and that 265,000 women served in the military during the time period of the Vietnam War. The experience of the women who served in Vietnam was equally affected by the difference of the war: an unusually large proportion of them, three-quarters, were exposed to hostile fire. Upon their return, they were not only subject to post-traumatic stress like the male veterans but they were also excluded from the veteran community. Many have since revealed how they kept their war experience a secret, not telling even their husbands about their time in Vietnam.

These women veterans were thus doubly displaced, unable to speak as veterans or as women. In response, several women veterans began raising funds for their own memorial, and in November 1993, the Vietnam Women's Memorial was dedicated near the Vietnam Veterans Memorial. The statue, which was designed by Glenna Goodacre, depicts three uniformed women with a wounded soldier. The two women who direct the VWMP, Diane Carlson Evans and Donna Marie Boulay, say that it is Hart's depiction of three men who make the absence of women so visible, and that they would not have initiated the project had Lin's memorial stood alone. Says Evans, "The wall in itself was enough, but when they added the men it became necessary to add women to complete the memorial."[17] Hence, the singular narrative of Hart's realist depiction is one of both inclusion and exclusion.

One could argue that the widespread discourse of healing around the original memorial led women veterans to speak of their memorial as the beginning rather than the culmination of a healing process. Yet the radical message of commemorating women in war is undercut by the conventionality of the statue itself. A contemporary version of the *Pietà*, the statue presents one woman nurse heroically holding the body of a wounded soldier, one searching the sky for help, and one looking forlornly at the ground. Benjamin Forgery, who called this memorial in the *Washington Post* "one monument too many," has criticized the women's memorial for cluttering up the landscape with "blatheringly sentimental sculpture." He wrote that the sculptor's "ambition is sabotaged by the subject and the artist's limited talent—compared with Michelangelo's Christ figure, this GI is as stiff as a board. The result is more like an awkward still from a *M*A*S*H* episode."[18]

The decision to build the women's memorial was not about aesthetics (except in so far as it reaffirms the representational aesthetic of Hart's statue) but about recognition and inclusion. However, by reinscribing the archetypal image of woman as caretaker, one that foregrounds the male veteran's body, the memorial reiterates the main obstacle to healing that women veterans face in recognizing their needs as veterans. Writes Laura Palmer, "After all, these women had *degrees* in putting the needs of others before their own."[19]

The difficulty of adequately and appropriately memorializing the women veterans falls within the larger issue of masculine identity in the Vietnam War. The Vietnam War is depicted as an event in which American masculinity was irretrievably damaged, and the rehabilitation of the Vietnam veteran is thus also a reinscription of American masculinity. This has also taken the form of re-enacting the war at the memorial itself, through the Veterans' Vigil of Honor, which keeps watch there, and the "battles" over its construction and maintenance. As a form of re-enactment, this conflation of the memorial and the war is a ritual of healing, although one that appears to be stuck in its ongoing replay, with a resistance to moving beyond narratives of the war. For the men of the Veterans' Vigil, only the war can provide meaning. In refighting that war every day, they are also reinscribing narratives of heroism and sacrifice. But, for others, there is a powerful kind of closure at the memorial. The one story for which the memorial appears to offer resolution is that of the shame felt by veterans for having fought in an unpopular war, a story that is their primary battle with history.

The Memorial as a Shrine

The Vietnam Veterans Memorial has been the subject of an extraordinary outpouring of emotion since it was built. Over 150,000 people attended its dedication ceremony and some days as many as 20,000 people walk by its walls. It is presently the most visited site on the Washington Mall with an estimated 22 to 30 million visitors. People bring personal artifacts to leave at the wall as offerings, and coffee-table photography books document the experiences of visitors as a collective recovery from the war. It has also spawned the design or construction of at least 150 other memorials, including the Korean War Veterans Memorial, which was dedicated in July 1995.

The rush to embrace the memorial as a cultural symbol reveals not only the relief of voicing a history that has been taboo but also a desire to reinscribe that history. The black granite walls of the memorial act as a screen for myriad cultural projections; it is easily appropriated for a variety of interpretations of the war and of the experience of those who died in it. To the veterans, the wall makes amends for their treatment since the war; to the families and friends of those who died, it officially recognizes their sorrow and validates a grief that was not previously sanctioned; to others, it is either a profound antiwar statement or an opportunity to recast the narrative of the war in terms of honor and sacrifice.

The memorial's popularity must thus be seen in the context of a very active scripting and rescripting of the war and as an integral component in the recently emerged Vietnam War nostalgia industry. This sentiment is not confined to those who wish to return to the intensity of wartime; it is also felt by the news media, who long to recapture their moment of moral power—the Vietnam War was very good television. Michael Clark writes that the media nostalgia campaign,

> healed over the wounds that had refused to close for ten years with a balm of nostalgia, and transformed guilt and doubt into duty and pride. And with a triumphant flourish it offered us the spectacle of its most successful creation, the veterans who will fight the next war.[20]

Though the design of Maya Lin's memorial does not lend itself to marketable reproductions, the work has functioned as a catalyst for much of this nostalgia. The Vietnam Veterans Memorial is the subject of no fewer than twelve books, many of them photography collections that focus on the interaction of visitors with the names. The memorial has tapped into a reservoir of need to express in public the pain of this war, a desire to transfer the private memories of this war into a collective experience. Many personal artifacts have been left at the memorial: photographs, letters, poems, teddy bears, dog tags, combat boots and helmets, MIA/POW bracelets, clothes, medals of honor, headbands, beer cans, plaques, crosses, playing cards. At this site, the objects are transposed from personal to cultural artifacts, as items bearing witness to pain suffered.

Thus, a very rich and vibrant dialogue of deliberate, if sometimes very private, remembrance takes place at the memorial. Of the approximately 40,000 objects that have been left at the wall, the vast majority have been left anonymously. Relinquished before the wall, the letters tell many stories:

> Dear Michael: Your name is here but you are not. I made a rubbing of it, thinking that if I rubbed hard enough I would rub your name off the wall and you would come back to me. I miss you so.

> Dear Sir: For twenty-two years I have carried your picture in my wallet. I was only eighteen years old that day that we faced one another on that trail in Chu Lai, Vietnam. Why you didn't take

FIGURE 20, 21 Vietnam Veterans Memorial, Washington DC (Photos courtesy: Marita Sturken)

my life I'll never know. You stared at me for so long, armed with your AK-47, and yet you did not fire. Forgive me for taking your life, I was reacting just the way I was trained, to kill VC.

Hence, the memorial is perceived by visitors as a site where they can speak to the dead (where, by implication, the dead are present). Many of these letters are addressed not to visitors but to the dead, though intended to be shared as cultural memory. Many of the artifacts at the memorial also represent a catharsis in releasing long-held objects to memory: a can of C-rations, a "short stick," worn Vietnamese sandals, a grenade pin. For those who left these objects, the memorial represents their final destination and a relinquishing of memory.

FIGURE 22, 23 Vietnam Veterans Memorial, Washington DC (Photos courtesy: Marita Sturken)

The National Park Service, which is now in charge of maintaining the memorial, operates an archive of the materials that have been left at the memorial. Originally, the Park Service classified these objects as "lost and found." Later, Park Service officials realized the artifacts had been left intentionally, and they began to save them. The objects thus moved from the cultural status of being "lost" (without category) to historical artifacts. They have now even turned into artistic artifacts; the manager of the archive writes:

> These are no longer objects at the Wall, they are communications, icons possessing a subculture of underpinning emotion. They are the products of culture, in all its complexities. They are

> the products of individual selection. With each object we are in
> the presence of a work of art of individual contemplation. The
> thing itself does not overwhelm our attention since these are
> objects that are common and expendable. At the Wall they have
> become unique and irreplaceable, and, yes, mysterious.[21]

Labeled "mysterious," and thus coded as original works of art, these
objects are given value and authorship. Some of the people who left
them have since been traced. This attempt to tie these objects and
letters to their creators reveals again the shifting realms of personal
and cultural memory. Assigned authorship and placed in an historical
archive, the objects are pulled from cultural memory, a realm in
which they are presented to be shared and to participate in the memories of others.

The memorial has become not only the primary site of remembrance for the Vietnam War, but also a site where people pay homage
to many current conflicts and charged public events. Artifacts concerning the abortion debate, the AIDS epidemic, gay rights, and the Persian
Gulf War have all been left at the memorial. Hence, the memorial's collection inscribes a history not only of the American participation in the
Vietnam War but also of national issues and events since the war. It is
testimony to the memorial's malleability as an icon that both prowar
and antiwar artifacts were left there during the Persian Gulf War.

One of the most compelling features of the Vietnam Veterans
Memorial collection is its anonymity, mystery, and ambiguity. It appears that many of the stories behind a substantial number of artifacts
may never be known, and that the telling of these stories to history
was never the purpose of their being placed at the memorial. Though
couched within an official history and held by a government institution, these letters and offerings to the dead will continue to assert
individual narratives, strands of cultural memory that disrupt historical narratives. They resist history precisely through their obscurity,
their refusal to yield specific meanings.

The Construction of a History

The politics of memory and history of the Vietnam Veterans Memorial shift continuously in a tension of ownership and narrative complexity. Who, in actuality, is being allowed to speak for the experience
of the war? Has the Vietnam Veterans Memorial facilitated the emergence of the voices of veterans and the families and friends of veterans in opposition to the voice of the media and the government?
The process of healing can be an individual process or a national or
cultural process; the politics of each is quite difference.

Much of the current embrace of the memorial amounts to historical revisionism. The period between the end of the war and the positioning of the memorial as a national wailing wall has been long

enough for memories and culpability to fade. Ironically, the memorial allows for an erasure of many of the specifics of history. It is rarely noted that the discussion surrounding the memorial never mentions the Vietnamese people. This is not a memorial to their loss; they cannot even be mentioned in the context of the Mall. Nor does the memorial itself allow for their mention; though it allows for an outpouring of grief, it does not speak to the intricate reasons why the lives represented by the inscribed names were lost in vain.

Thus, remembering is in itself a form of forgetting. Does the remembrance of the battles fought by the veterans in Vietnam and at home necessarily screen out any acknowledgment of the war's effect on the Vietnamese? In its listing of the US war dead, and in the context of the Mall, the memorial establishes Americans, rather than Vietnamese, as the primary victims of the war. For instance, questions about the 1,300 American MIAs are raised at the memorial, yet in that space no mention can be made of the 300,000 Vietnamese MIAs. Does the process of commemoration necessitate choosing sides?

Artist Chris Burden created a sculpture in 1991, *The Other Vietnam Memorial,* in reaction to the memorial's nonacknowledgment of the Vietnamese. Burden's piece consists of large copper leaves, 12 by 8 feet, arranged as a kind of circular standing book, on which are engraved 3 million Vietnamese names to commemorate the 3 million Vietnamese who died in the war. He says: "Even though I feel sorry for the individuals named on [the Vietnam Veterans Memorial], I was repulsed by the idea. I couldn't help but think that we were celebrating our dead, who were aggressors, basically, and wonder where were the Vietnamese names?"[22] Burden's listing of names is not unproblematic; he was unable to get the actual listing of names, so he took 4,000 names and repeated them over and over again. However, Burden's sculpture exposes a fundamental limit of commemoration within nationalism. Why must a national memorial re-enact conflict by showing only one side of the conflict? What is the memory produced by a national memorial?

The memorial's placement on the Washington Mall inscribes it within nationalism, restricting in many ways the kinds of memory it can provide. Its presence indicates both the limitations and the complexity of that nationalist discourse. Lauren Berlant writes:

> When Americans make the pilgrimage to Washington they are trying to grasp the nation in its totality. Yet the totality of the nation in its capital city is a jumble of historical modalities, a transitional space between local and national cultures, private and public property, archaic and living artifacts . . . it is a place of national *mediation,* where a variety of nationally inflected media come into visible and sometimes incommensurate contact.[23]

The memorial asserts itself into this "jumble of historical modalities," both a resistant and compliant artifact. It serves not as a singular statement but a site of mediation, a site of conflicting voices and opposing agendas.

However, the act of commemoration is ultimately a process of legitimation and the memorial lies at the center of a struggle between narratives. It has spawned two very different kinds of remembrance: one a retrenched historical narrative that attempts to rewrite the Vietnam War in a way that reinscribes US imperialism and the masculinity of the American soldier; the other a textured and complex discourse of remembrance that has allowed the Americans affected by this war—the veterans, their families, and the families and friends of the war dead—to speak of loss, pain, and futility. The screens of the memorial allow for projections of a multitude of memories and individual interpretations. The memorial stands in a precarious space between these opposing interpretations of the war.

Notes

1. Arthur Danto, "The Vietnam Veterans Memorial," *The Nation,* August 31, 1985, p. 152.
2. Charles Griswold, "The Vietnam Veterans Memorial and the Washington Mall," *Critical Inquiry,* Summer 1986, p. 689.
3. Tom Wolfe, "Art Disputes War," *Washington Post,* October 13, 1982, p. 134.
4. Kenneth Baker, "Andre in Retrospect," *Art in America,* April 1980, pp. 88 94.
5. See Robert Storr, "'Tilted Arc': Enemy of the People," in Arlene Raven (ed.), *Art in the Public Interest* (Ann Arbor: University of Michigan Press, 1989).
6. "Stop That Monument," *National Review,* September 18, 1981, p. 1064.
7. Quoted in Mary McLeod, "The Battle for the Monument," in Helene Lipstadt. (ed.), *The Experimental Tradition* (New York: Princeton Architectural Press, 1989), p. 125.
8. Michael Sorkin, "What Happens When a Woman Designs a War Monument?" *Vogue,* May 1983, p. 122.
9. Quoted in "America Remembers: Vietnam Veterans Memorial," *National Geographic,* May 1985, p. 557.
10. "An Interview With Maya Lin," in Reese Williams (ed.), *Unwinding the Vietnam War* (Seattle: Real Comet Press, 1987), p. 271.
11. Jan Scruggs and Joel Swerdlow, *To Heal a Nation* (New York: Harper & Row, 1985), p. 79.
12. Mary McLeod, op. cit., p. 127.
13. "An Interview with Frederick Hart," in Reese Williams (ed.), *Unwinding the Vietnam War* (Seattle: Real Comet Press, 1987), p. 274.
14. Quoted in Rick Horowitz, "Maya Lin's Angry Objections," *Washington Post,* July 7, 1982, p. B1.

15. Quoted in Scruggs and Swerdlow, op. cit., p. 133.
16. Peter Marin, "Conclusion," in Harrison Salisbury (ed.), *Vietnam Reconsidered* (New York: Harper & Row, 1984), p. 213.
17. Quoted in Benjamin Forgery, "Battle Won for War Memorials," *Washington Post,* September 20, 1991.
18. Benjamin Forgery, "One Monument Too Many," *Washington Post,* November 6, 1993, p. D7.
19. Quoted in Laura Palmer, "How to Bandage a War," *New York Times Magazine,* November 7, 1993, p. 40.
20. Michael Clark, "Remembering Vietnam," *Cultural Critique* 3, Spring 1986, p. 49.
21. David Guynes, quoted in Lydia Fish, *The Last Firebase* (Shippensburg, Pa.: White Mane, 1987), p. 54.
22. Quoted in Robert Storr, "Chris Burden," *MoMA Members Quarterly,* Fall 1991, p. 5.
23. Lauren Berlant, "The Theory of Infantile Citizenship," *Public Culture* 5, 1993, p. 395.

READING, REREADING, AND ANALYSIS

1. What terms or ideas seem most important to Sturken?

2. What terms or ideas seem most important for people connected to the development of the Vietnam Veterans Memorial?

3. What distinguishes a monument from a memorial?

4. Individually or in a group, make a list of qualities associated with Maya Lin's memorial and a list of qualities associated with Frederick Hart's bronze sculpture of the three soldiers that was placed near the memorial in 1984. What do the differences say about purposes of the memorials?

5. What does Sturken mean on page 493 when she says, "The importance of the Vietnam Veterans Memorial lies in its communicability, which in effect has mollified the incommunicability of the veterans' experience"?

6. In a group, discuss initial negative reactions to Lin's design for the memorial, and come up with at least three explanations for why the memorial has been so much appreciated.

RESPONDING THROUGH WRITING: BUILDING AN INTERPRETATION

7. In a brief essay (one or two pages), discuss Sturken's claim that the Vietnam Veterans Memorial should not simply be understood as "modernist sculpture." What qualities are associated with

modernist art, and what qualities about the Vietnam Veterans Memorial does Sturken emphasize?

8. Using the list you prepared for question 4, write an essay comparing the style of Lin's memorial and of Hart's statue of three soldiers. Which style do you tend to favor or appreciate more and why?

9. In three or four sentences, summarize Sturken's discussion of the politics of the Vietnam Veterans Memorial. Next, write a brief essay (two or three pages) in which you explain relationships you see between your summary and Sturken's discussion of the desires, motives, and effects of creating the additional memorials to the three soldiers and to the nurses.

10. Write a short paper exploring the relationships you see in Sturken's essay between gender issues and traditions of monuments and memorials to commemorate warfare.

GOING FURTHER: LEARNING FROM OTHER SOURCES

11. Use a reference database such as Lexis-Nexis or InfoTrac to find interviews with Lin about the Vietnam Veterans Memorial and to find pictures and information about other sculpture and architecture that Maya Lin has designed. How has Lin's work developed over time? Are there patterns in her work over time, or has she taken a variety of directions in her work?

12. Use a search engine to find out more about the kinds of things people have left at the Vietnam Veterans Memorial. What happens to the objects left? Which objects most catch your attention and why?

APPLYING WHAT YOU'VE LEARNED

13. In "At the Buffalo Bill Museum, June 1988," Jane Tompkins explores her ambivalent reaction to Buffalo Bill Cody as a monument to a conception of American identity. She writes: "I cannot resolve the contradiction between my experience at the Buffalo Bill Historical Center with its celebration of violent conquest and my response to the shining figure of Buffalo Bill as it emerged from the pages of books—on the one hand, a history of shame; on the other, an image of the heart's desire" (p. 523). What relationships do you see between Tompkins's ambivalence and Sturken's analysis of competing reactions to the Vietnam Veterans Memorial?

14. In "Landscape, Drama, and Dissensus: The Rhetorical Education of Red Lodge, Montana," Zita Ingham examines how the use of language affects our desires to find and promote better ways of living. Use Ingham's discussion of rhetoric to analyze Sturken's examination of initial dissensus about the Vietnam Veterans Memorial and subsequent consensus about the memorial. How are issues of language use like the ones Ingham explores reflected in criticisms of the monument and in praise for it?

15. In "The Triumph of Tinkering," Sherry Turkle explores conflicts some women face when experimenting rather than when following a prescribed method of problem solving. Write an essay that applies Turkle's discussion of alternative approaches to problem solving (particularly as they relate to or reflect issues of gender) to Sturken's analysis of Maya Lin's design of the Vietnam Veterans Memorial. Be sure to examine in your paper Sturken's discussion of friction resulting from gender expectations.

JANE TOMPKINS

Jane Tompkins (b. 1940) is Special Assistant to the Provost for Campus Environment at the University of Illinois, Chicago. Before moving to UIC, Tompkins was Professor of English at Duke University. She is the author of *Sensational Designs: The Cultural Work of American Fiction, 1790–1870*, a book widely credited with renewing scholarly interest in the writing of nineteenth-century American women. Tompkins has also written *West of Everything: The Inner Life of Westerns*, from which "At the Buffalo Bill Museum, June 1988," was taken, and *A Life in School: What the Teacher Learned*.

To learn more about the Buffalo Bill Historical Center, visit <http://www.bbhc.org/>.

WHAT DO YOU KNOW? WHAT DO YOU EXPECT TO DISCOVER?

Before reading the essay, take a moment to consider the following questions.

1. What topics does Tompkins's biography suggest she is interested in? What do you know about those topics? Knowledge can come from personal experience, stories you've heard, other classes you've taken, or other reading you've done.

2. Make a list of the images that come to mind when you think about the "wild west." After reading Jane Tompkins's essay, compare the items on your list with the images that she focuses on.

3. Tompkins reflects on several contradictions in her essay, including the discrepancy between praise for Buffalo Bill Cody's inspiring decency and heroism, on the one hand, and blame for Cody's association with the slaughter of the country's buffalo and of the country's imperialist actions against Native Americans on the other. What kinds of attitudes are prevalent in our society or among people you know toward folks in history who have participated in warfare such as the U.S. Civil War, American pioneers or U.S. cavalry battles with Native Americans, or participants in the Mexican-American War? What differences of opinion do you see expressed, and what accounts for the differences in opinions?

❡

At the Buffalo Bill Museum, June 1988

The video at the entrance to the Buffalo Bill Historical Center says that Buffalo Bill was the most famous American of his time, that by 1900 more than a billion words had been written about him, and that he had a progressive vision of the West. Buffalo Bill had worked as a cattle driver, a wagoneer, a Pony Express rider, a buffalo hunter for the railroad, a hunting guide, an army scout and sometime Indian fighter; he wrote dime novels about himself and an autobiography by the age of thirty-four, by which time he was already famous; and then he began another set of careers, first as an actor, performing on the urban stage in wintertime melodramatic representations of what he actually earned a living at in the summer (scouting and leading hunting expeditions), and finally becoming the impresario of his great Wild West show, a form of entertainment he invented and carried on as actor, director, and all-around idea man for thirty years. Toward the end of his life he founded the town of Cody, Wyoming, to which he gave, among other things, two hundred thousand dollars. Strangely enough, it was as a progressive civic leader that Bill Cody wanted to be remembered. "I don't want to die," the video at the entrance quotes him as saying, "and have people say—oh, there goes another old showman. . . . I would like people to say—this is the man who opened Wyoming to the best of civilization."

"The best of civilization." This was the phrase that rang in my head as I moved through the museum, which is one of the most disturbing places I have ever visited. It is also a wonderful place. It is four museums in one: the Whitney Gallery of Western Art, which houses artworks on Western subjects; the Buffalo Bill Museum proper, which memorializes Cody's life; the Plains Indian Museum, which exhibits artifacts of American Indian civilization; and the Winchester Arms Museum, a collection of firearms historically considered.

The whole operation is extremely well designed and well run, from the video program at the entrance that gives an overview of all four museums, to the fresh-faced young attendants wearing badges that say "Ask Me," to the museum shop stacked with books on Western Americana, to the ladies room—a haven of satiny marble, shining mirrors, and flattering light. Among other things, the museum is admirable for its effort to combat prevailing stereotypes about the "winning of the West," a phrase it self-consciously places in quotation marks. There are placards declaring that all history is a matter of

FIGURE 24 Photograph of Buffalo Bill. (Courtesy of the Buffalo Bill Memorial Museum and the Denver Parks and Recreation Department, Denver, Colorado.)

interpretation, and that the American West is a source of myth. Everywhere, except perhaps in the Winchester Arms Museum, where the rhetoric is different, you feel the effort of the museum staff to reach out to the public, to be clear, to be accurate, to be fair, not to condescend—in short, to educate in the best sense of the term.

On the day I went, the museum was featuring an exhibition of Frederic Remington's works. Two facts about Remington make his work different from that of artists usually encountered in museums. The first is that Remington's paintings and statues function as a historical record. Their chief attraction has always been that they transcribe scenes and events that have vanished from the earth. The second fact, related to this, is the brutality of their subject matter. Remington's work makes you pay attention to what is happening in the painting or the piece of statuary. When you look at his work you cannot escape from the subject.

Consequently, as I moved through the exhibit, the wild contortions of the bucking broncos, the sinister expression invariably worn by the Indians, and the killing of animals and men made the placards discussing Remington's use of the "lost wax" process seem strangely disconnected. In the face of unusual violence, or implied violence, their message was: what is important here is technique. Except in the case of paintings showing the battle of San Juan Hill, where white

Americans were being killed, the material accompanying Remington's works did not refer to the subject matter of the paintings and statues themselves. Nevertheless, an undertone of disquiet ran beneath the explanations; at least I thought I detected one. Someone had taken the trouble to ferret out Remington's statement of horror at the slaughter on San Juan Hill; someone had also excerpted the judgment of art critics commending Remington for the lyricism, interiority, and mystery of his later canvasses—pointing obliquely to the fascination with bloodshed that preoccupied his earlier work.

The uneasiness of the commentary, and my uneasiness with it, were nothing compared to the blatant contradictions in the paintings themselves. A pastel palette, a sunlit stop-action haze, murderous movement arrested under a lazy sky, flattened onto canvas and fixed in azure and ochre—two opposed impulses nestle here momentarily. The tension that keeps them from splitting apart is what holds the viewer's gaze.

The most excruciating example of what I mean occurs in the first painting in the exhibit. Entitled *His First Lesson*, it shows a horse standing saddled but riderless, the white of the horse's eye signaling his fear. A man using an instrument to tighten the horse's girth, at arm's length, backs away from the reaction he clearly anticipates, while the man who holds the horse's halter is doing the same. But what can they be afraid of? For the horse's right rear leg is tied a foot off the ground by a rope that is also tied around his neck. He can't move. That is the whole point.

His First Lesson. Whose? And what lesson, exactly? How to stand still when terrified? How not to break away when they come at you with strange instruments? How to be obedient? How to behave? It is impossible not to imagine that Remington's obsession with physical cruelty had roots somewhere in his own experience. Why else, in statue after statue, is the horse rebelling? The bucking bronco, symbol of the state of Wyoming, on every license plate, on every sign for every bar, on every belt buckle, mug, and decal—this image Remington cast in bronze over and over again. There is a wild diabolism in the bronzes; the horse and rider seem one thing, not so much rider and ridden as a single bolt of energy gone crazy and caught somehow, complicatedly, in a piece of metal.

In the paintings, it is different—more subtle and bizarre. The cavalry on its way to a massacre, sweetly limned, softly tinted, poetically seized in mid-career, and gently laid on the two-dimensional surface. There is about these paintings of military men in the course of performing their deadly duty an almost maternal tenderness. The idealization of the cavalrymen in their dusty uniforms on their gallant horses has nothing to do with patriotism; it is pure love.

Remington's paintings and statues, as shown in this exhibition, embody everything that was objectionable about his era in American history. They are imperialist and racist; they glorify war and the

FIGURE 25 *His First Lesson,* by Frederic Remington, 1903. Oil on canvas. (Courtesy of the Amon Carter Museum, Fort Worth, Texas. Accession no. 1961.231.)

torture and killing of animals; there are no women in them anywhere. Never the West as garden, never as pastoral, never as home. But in their aestheticization of violent life, Remington's pictures speak (to me, at least) of some other desire. The maternal tenderness is not an accident, nor is the beauty of the afternoons or the warmth of the desert sun. In them Remington plays the part of the preserver, as if by catching the figures in color and line he could save their lives and absorb some of that life into himself.

In one painting that particularly repulsed and drew me, a moose is outlined against the evening sky at the brink of a lake. He looks expectantly into the distance. Behind him and to one side, hidden from his view and only just revealed to ours, for it is dark there, is a hunter poised in the back of a canoe, rifle perfectly aimed. We look closer; the title of the picture is *Coming to the Call.* Ah, now we see. This is a sadistic scene. The hunter has lured the moose to his death. But wait a moment. Isn't the sadism really directed at us? First we see the glory of the animal; Remington has made it as noble as he knows how. Then we see what is going to happen. The hunter is one up on the moose, but Remington is one up on us. He makes us feel the pain of the anticipated killing, and makes us want to hold it off, to preserve the moose, just as he has done. Which way does the painting cut? Does it go against the hunter—who represents us, after all—or does it go against the moose who came to the call? Who came, to what call? Did Remington come to the West in response to it—to whatever the

FIGURE 26 Frederic Remington, *Coming to the Call*. (Courtesy of Frederic Remington Art Museum, Ogdensburg, N.Y.)

moose represents or to whatever the desire to kill the moose represents? But he hasn't killed it; he has only preserved an image of a white man about to kill it. And what call do we answer when we look at this painting? Who is calling whom? What is being preserved here?

The last question is the one that for me hung over the whole museum.

The Whitney Gallery is an art museum proper. Its allegiance is to art as academic tradition has defined it. In this tradition, we come to understand a painting by having in our possession various bits of information. Something about the technical process used to produce it (pastels, watercolors, woodblock prints, etc.); something about the elements of composition (line and color and movement); something about the artist's life (where born, how educated, by whom influenced, which school belonged to or revolted against); something about the artist's relation to this particular subject, such as how many times the artist painted it or whether it contains a favorite model. Occasionally there will be some philosophizing about the themes or ideas the paintings are said to represent.

The problem is, when you're faced with a painter like Remington, these bits of information, while nice to have, don't explain what is there in front of you. They don't begin to give you an account of why a person would have depicted such things. The experience of a lack of fit between the explanatory material and what is there on the wall is one I've had before in museums, when, standing in front of a painting or a piece of statuary, I've felt a huge gap between the information on the little placard and what it is I'm seeing. I realize that works of art, so-called, all have a subject matter, are all engaged with life, with some piece of life no less significant, no less compelling than Remington's subjects are, if we could only see its force. The idea that art is somehow separate from history, that it somehow occupies a space that is not the same as the space of life, seems out of whack here.

I wandered through the gallery thinking these things because right next to it, indeed all around it, in the Buffalo Bill Museum proper and in the Plains Indian Museum, are artifacts that stand not for someone's expertise or skill in manipulating the elements of an artistic medium, but for life itself; they are the residue of life.

The Buffalo Bill Museum is a wonderful array of textures, colors, shapes, sizes, forms. The fuzzy brown bulk of a buffalo's hump, the sparkling diamonds in a stickpin, the brilliant colors of the posters—the mixture makes you want to walk in and be surrounded by it, as if you were going into a child's adventure story. For a moment you can pretend you're a cowboy too; it's a museum where fantasy can take over. For a while.

As I moved through the exhibition, with the phrase "the best of civilization" ringing in my head, I came upon certain objects displayed in a section that recreates rooms from Cody's house. Ostrich feather fans, peacock feather fans, antler furniture—a chair and a table made entirely of antlers—a bearskin rug. And then I saw the heads on the wall: Alaska Yukon Moose, Wapiti American Elk, Muskox (the "Whitney," the "DeRham"), Mountain Caribou (the "Hyland"), Quebec Labrador Caribou (the "Elbow"), Rocky Mountain Goat (the "Haase," the "Kilto"), Woodland Caribou (world's record, "DeRham"), the "Rogers" freak Wapiti, the "Whitney" bison, the "Lord Rundlesham" bison. The names that appear after the animals are the names of the men who killed them. Each of the animals is scored according to measurements devised by the Boone and Crockett Club, a big-game hunters' organization. The Lord Rundlesham bison, for example, scores 124⅝, making it number 25 in the world for bison trophies. The "Reed" Alaska Yukon Moose scores 247. The "Witherbee" Canada moose holds the world's record.

Next to the wall of trophies is a small enclosure where jewelry is displayed. A buffalo head stickpin and two buffalo head rings, the heads made entirely of diamonds, with ruby eyes, the gifts of the Russian crown prince. A gold and diamond stickpin from Edward VII; a gold, diamond, and garnet locket from Queen Victoria. The two kinds of trophies—animals and jewels—form an incongruous set; the relationship between them compelling but obscure.

If the rest of the items in the museum—the dime novels with their outrageous covers, the marvelous posters, the furniture, his wife's dress, his daughter's oil painting—have faded from my mind it is because I cannot forget the heads of the animals as they stared down, each with an individual expression on its face. When I think about it I realize that I don't know why these animal heads are there. Buffalo Bill didn't kill them; perhaps they were gifts from the famous people he took on hunts. A different kind of jewelry.

After the heads, I began to notice something about the whole exhibition. In one display, doghide chaps, calfskin chaps, angora goathide chaps, and horsehide chaps. Next to these a rawhide lariat and a horsehair quirt. Behind me, boots and saddles, all of leather. Everywhere I looked there was tooth or bone, skin or fur, hide or hair, or the animal itself entire—two full-size buffalo (a main feature of the exhibition) and a magnificent stone sheep (a mountain sheep with beautiful curving horns). This one was another world's record. The best of civilization.

In the literature about Buffalo Bill you read that he was a conservationist, that if it were not for the buffalo in his Wild West shows the species would probably have become extinct. (In the seventeenth century 40 million buffalo roamed North America; by 1900 all the wild buffalo had been killed except for one herd in northern Alberta.) That the man who gained fame first as a buffalo hunter should have been an advocate for conservation of the buffalo is not an anomaly but typical of the period. The men who did the most to preserve America's natural wilderness and its wildlife were big-game hunters. The Boone and Crockett Club, founded by Theodore Roosevelt, George Bird Grinnell, and Owen Wister, turns out to have been one of the earliest organizations to devote itself to environmental protection in the United States. *The Reader's Encyclopedia of the American West* says that the club "supported the national park and forest reserve movement, helped create a system of national wildlife refuges, and lobbied for the protection of threatened species, such as the buffalo and antelope." At the same time, the prerequisites for membership in the club were "the highest caliber of sportsmanship and the achievement of killing 'in fair chase' trophy specimens [which had to be adult males] from several species of North American big game."

The combination big-game hunter and conservationist suggests that these men had no interest in preserving the animals for the animals' sake but simply wanted to ensure the chance to exercise their sporting pleasure. But I think this view is too simple; something further is involved here. The men who hunted game animals had a kind of love for them and a kind of love for nature that led them to want to preserve the animals they also desired to kill. That is, the desire to kill the animals was in some way related to a desire to see them live. It is not an accident, in this connection, that Roosevelt, Wister, and Remington all went west originally for their health. Their devotion to the West, their connection to it, their love for it are rooted in their need to reanimate their own lives. The preservation of nature, in other words, becomes for them symbolic of their own survival.

In a sense, then, there is a relationship between the Remington exhibition in the Whitney Gallery and the animal memorabilia in the Buffalo Bill Museum. The moose in *Coming to the Call* and the mooseheads on the wall are not so different as they might appear. The heads on the wall serve an aesthetic purpose; they are decorative objects, pleasing to the eye, which call forth certain associations. In this sense they are like visual works of art. The painting, on the other hand, has something of the trophy about it. The moose as Remington painted it is about to become a trophy, yet in another sense it already is one. Remington has simply captured the moose in another form. In both cases the subject matter, the life of a wild animal, symbolizes the life of the observer. It is the preservation of that life that both the painting and the taxidermy serve.

What are museums keeping safe for us, after all? What is it that we wish so much to preserve? The things we put in safekeeping, in our safe-deposit boxes under lock and key, are always in some way intended finally as safeguards of our own existence. The money and jewelry and stock certificates are meant for a time when we can no longer earn a living by the sweat of our brows. Similarly, the objects in museums preserve for us a source of life from which we need to nourish ourselves when the resources that would normally supply us have run dry.

The Buffalo Bill Historical Center, full as it is of dead bones, lets us see more clearly than we normally can what it is that museums are for. It is a kind of charnel house that houses images of living things that have passed away but whose life force still lingers around their remains and so passes itself on to us. We go and look at the objects in the glass cases and at the paintings on the wall, as if by standing there we could absorb into ourselves some of the energy that flowed once through the bodies of the live things represented. A museum, rather than being, as we normally think of it, the most civilized of places, a place most distant from our savage selves, actually caters to the urge to absorb the life of another into one's own life.

If we see the Buffalo Bill Museum in this way, it is no longer possible to separate ourselves from the hunters responsible for the trophies with their wondering eyes or from the curators who put them there. We are not, in essence, different from Roosevelt or Remington or Buffalo Bill, who killed animals when they were abundant in the Wild West of the 1880s. If in doing so those men were practicing the ancient art of absorbing the life of an animal into their own through the act of killing it, realizing themselves through the destruction of another life, then we are not so different from them; as visitors to the museum, we stand beside the bones and skins and nails of beings that were once alive, or stare fixedly at their painted images. Indeed our visit is only a safer form of the same enterprise as theirs.

So I did not get out of the Buffalo Bill Museum unscathed, unimplicated in the acts of rapine and carnage that these remains represent.

And I did not get out without having had a good time, either, because however many dire thoughts I may have had, the exhibits were interesting and fun to see. I was even able to touch a piece of buffalo hide displayed especially for that purpose (it was coarse and springy). Everyone else had touched it too. The hair was worn down, where people's hands had been, to a fraction of its original length.

After this, the Plains Indian Museum was a terrible letdown. I went from one exhibit to another expecting to become absorbed, but nothing worked. What was the matter? I was interested in Indians, had read about them, taught some Indian literature, felt drawn by accounts of native religions. I had been prepared to enter this museum as if I were going into another children's story, only this time I would be an Indian instead of a cowboy or a cowgirl. But the objects on display, most of them behind glass, seemed paltry and insignificant. They lacked visual presence. The bits of leather and sticks of wood triggered no fantasies in me.

At the same time, I noticed with some discomfort that almost everything in those glass cases was made of feathers and claws and hide, just like the men's chaps and ladies' fans in the Buffalo Bill Museum, only there was no luxury here. Plains Indian culture, it seemed, was made entirely from animals. Their mode of life had been even more completely dedicated to carnage than Buffalo Bill's, dependent as it was on animals for food, clothing, shelter, equipment, everything. In the Buffalo Bill Museum I was able to say to myself, well, if these men had been more sensitive, if they had had a right relation to their environment and to life itself, the atrocities that produced these trophies would never have occurred. They never would have exterminated the Indians and killed off the buffalo. But the spectacle before me made it impossible to say that. I had expected that the Plains Indian Museum would show me how life in nature ought to be lived: not the mindless destruction of nineteenth-century America but an ideal form of communion with animals and the land. What the museum seemed to say instead was that cannibalism was universal. Both colonizer and colonized had had their hands imbrued with blood. The Indians had lived off animals and had made war against one another. Violence was simply a necessary and inevitable part of life. And a person who, like me, was horrified at the extent of the destruction was just the kind of romantic idealist my husband sometimes accused me of being. There was no such thing as the life lived in harmony with nature. It was all bloodshed and killing, an unending cycle, over and over again, and no one could escape.

But perhaps there was a way to understand the violence that made it less terrible. Perhaps if violence was necessary, a part of nature, intended by the universe, then it could be seen as sacramental. Perhaps it was true, what Calvin Martin had said in *Keepers of the*

Game: that the Indians had a sacred contract with the animals they killed, that they respected them as equals and treated their remains with honor and punctilio. If so, the remains of animals in the Plains Indian Museum weren't the same as those left by Buffalo Bill and his friends. They certainly didn't look the same. Perhaps. All I knew for certain was that these artifacts, lifeless and shrunken, spoke to me of nothing I could understand. No more did the life-size models of Indians, with strange featureless faces, draped in costumes that didn't look like clothing. The figures, posed awkwardly in front of tepees too white to seem real, carried no sense of a life actually lived, any more than the objects in the glass cases had.

The more I read the placards on the wall, the more disaffected I became. Plains Indian life apparently had been not only bloody but exceedingly tedious. All those porcupine quills painstakingly softened, flattened, dyed, then appliqued through even more laborious methods of stitching or weaving. Four methods of attaching porcupine quills, six design groups, population statistics, patterns of migration. There wasn't any glamour here at all. No glamour in the lives the placards told about, no glamour in the objects themselves, no glamour in the experience of looking at them. Just a lot of shriveled things accompanied by some even drier information.

Could it be, then, that the problem with the exhibitions was that Plains Indian culture, if representable at all, was simply not readable by someone like me? Their stick figures and abstract designs could convey very little to an untrained Euro-American eye. One display in particular illustrated this. It was a piece of cloth, behind glass, depicting a buffalo skin with some marks on it. The placard read: "Winter Count, Sioux ca. 1910, after Lone Dog's, Fort Peck, Montana, 1877." The hide with its markings had been a calendar, each year represented by one image, which showed the most significant event in the life of the tribe. A thick pamphlet to one side of the glass case explained each image year by year: 1800–1801, the attack of the Uncapoo on a Crow Indian Fort; 1802–1803, a total eclipse of the sun. The images, once you knew what they represented, made sense, and seemed poetic interpretations of the experiences they stood for. But without explanation they were incomprehensible.

The Plains Indian Museum stopped me in my tracks. It was written in a language I had never learned. I didn't have the key. Maybe someone did, but I wasn't too sure. For it may not have been just cultural difference that made the text unreadable. I began to suspect that the text itself was corrupt, that the architects of this museum were going through motions whose purpose was, even to themselves, obscure. Knowing what event a figure stands for in the calendar doesn't mean you understand an Indian year. The deeper purpose of the museum began to puzzle me. Wasn't there an air of bad faith about preserving the vestiges of a culture one had effectively extinguished? Did the museum exist to assuage our guilt and not for any real educational reason? I do not have an answer to these questions. All I know is that I felt I was in the presence of something pious and a little insincere. It had the aura of a failed attempt at virtue, as though the curators were trying to present as interesting objects whose purpose and meaning even they could not fully imagine.

In a last-ditch attempt to salvage something, I went up to one of the guards and asked where the movie was showing which the video had advertised, the movie about Plains Indian life. "Oh, the slide show, you mean," he said. "It's been discontinued." When I asked why, he said he didn't know. It occurred to me then that that was the message the museum was sending, if I could read it, that that was the bottom line. Discontinued, no reason given.

The movie in the Winchester Arms Museum, *Lock, Stock, and Barrel,* was going strong. The film began with the introduction of cannon into European warfare in the middle Ages, and was working its way slowly toward the nineteenth century when I left. I was in a hurry. Soon my husband would be waiting for me in the lobby. I went from room to room, trying to get a quick sense impression of the objects on display. They were all the same: guns. Some large drawings and photographs on the walls tried to give a sense of the context in which the arms had been used, but the effect was nil. It was case after case of rifles and pistols, repeating themselves over and over, and even when some slight variation caught my eye the differences meant nothing to me.

But the statistics did. In a large case of commemorative rifles, I saw the Antlered Game Commemorative Carbine. Date of manufacture: 1978. Number produced: 19,999. I wondered how many antlered animals each carbine had killed. I saw the Canadian Centennial (1962): 90,000; the Legendary Lawman (1978): 19,999; the John Wayne (1980–81): 51,600. Like the titles of the various sections of the museum, these names had a message. The message was: guns are patriotic. Associated with national celebrations, law enforcement, and cultural heroes. The idea that firearms were inseparable from the march of American history came through even more strongly in the titles given to the various exhibits: Firearms in Colonial America; Born in America: The Kentucky Rifle; The Era of Expansion and Invention; The Civil War: Firearms of the Conflict; The Golden Age of Hunting; Winning the West. The guns embodied phases of the history they had helped to make. There were no quotation marks here to indicate that expansion and conquest might not have been all they were cracked up to be. The fact that firearms had had a history seemed to consecrate them; the fact that they had existed at the time when certain famous events had occurred seemed to make them not only worth preserving but worth studying and revering. In addition to the exhibition rooms, the museum housed three "study galleries": one for hand arms, one for shoulder arms, one for U.S. military firearms.

As I think back on the rows and rows of guns, I wonder if I should have looked at them more closely, tried harder to appreciate the workmanship that went into them, the ingenuity, the attention. Awe and admiration are the attitudes the museum invites. You hear the ghostly march of military music in the background; you imagine flags waving and sense the implicit reference to feats of courage in battle and glorious death. The place had the air of an expensive and well-kept reliquary, or of the room off the transept of a cathedral where the vestments are stored. These guns were not there merely to be seen or even studied; they were there to be venerated.

But I did not try to appreciate the guns. They were too technical, too foreign. I didn't have their language, and, besides, I didn't want to learn. I rejoined my husband in the lobby. The Plains Indian Museum had been incomprehensible, but in the Winchester Arms Museum I could hardly see the objects at all, for I did not see the point. Or, rather, I did see it and rejected it. Here in the basement the instruments that had turned live animals into hides and horns, had massacred the Indians and the buffalo, were being lovingly displayed. And we were still making them: 51,600 John Waynes in 1980–81. Arms were going strong.

As I bought my books and postcards in the gift shop, I noticed a sign that read "Rodeo Tickets Sold Here," and something clicked into place. So that was it. *Everything* was still going strong. The whole museum was just another rodeo, only with the riders and their props stuffed, painted, sculpted, immobilized and put under glass. Like the rodeo, the entire museum witnessed a desire to bring back the United States of the 1880s and 1890s. The American people did not want to let go of the winning of the West. They wanted to win it all over again, in imagination. It was the ecstasy of the kill, as much as the life of the hunted, that we fed off here. The Buffalo Bill Historical Center did not repudiate the carnage that had taken place in the nineteenth century. It celebrated it. With its gleaming rest rooms, cute snack bar, opulent museum shop, wooden Indians, thousand rifles, and scores of animal trophies, it helped us all reenact the dream of excitement, adventure, and conquest that was what the Wild West meant to most people in this country.

This is where my visit ended, but it had a sequel. When I left the Buffalo Bill Historical Center, I was full of moral outrage, an indignation so intense it made me almost sick, though it was pleasurable too, as such emotions usually are. But the outrage was undermined by the knowledge that I knew nothing about Buffalo Bill, nothing of his life, nothing of the circumstances that led him to be involved in such violent events. And I began to wonder if my reaction wasn't in some way an image, however small, of the violence I had been objecting to. So when I got home I began to read about Buffalo Bill, and a whole new world opened up. I came to love Buffalo Bill.

"I have seen him the very personification of grace and beauty . . . dashing over the free wild prairie and riding his horse as though he and the noble animal were bounding with one life and one motion." That is the sort of thing people wrote about Buffalo Bill. They said "he was the handsomest man I ever saw." They said "there was never another man lived as popular as he was." They said "there wasn't a man woman or child that he knew or ever met that he didn't speak to." They said "he was handsome as a god, a good rider and a crack shot." They said "he gave lots of money away. Nobody ever went hungry around him." They said "he was way above the average, physically and every other way."

These are quotes from people who knew Cody, collected by one of his two most responsible biographers, Nellie Snyder Yost. She puts them in the last chapter, and by the time you get there they all ring true. Buffalo Bill was incredibly handsome. He was extremely brave and did things no other scout would do. He would carry messages over rugged territory swarming with hostile Indians, riding all night in bad weather and get through, and then take off again the next day to ride sixty miles through a blizzard. He was not a proud man. He didn't boast of his exploits. But he did do incredible things, not just once in a while but on a fairly regular basis. He had a great deal of courage; he believed in himself, in his abilities, in his strength and endurance and knowledge. He was very skilled at what he did—hunting and scouting—but he wasn't afraid to try other things. He wrote some dime novels, he wrote his autobiography by age thirty-four, without very much schooling; he wasn't afraid to try acting, even though the stage terrified him and he knew so little about it that, according to his wife, he didn't even know you had to memorize lines.

Maybe it was because he grew up on the frontier, maybe it was just the kind of person he was, but he was constantly finding himself in situations that required resourcefulness and courage, quick decisions and decisive action and rising to the occasion. He wasn't afraid to improvise.

He liked people, drank a lot, gave big parties, gave lots of presents, and is reputed to have been a womanizer (Cody, 16). When people came to see him in his office tent on the show grounds, to shake his hand or have their pictures taken with him, he never turned anyone away. "He kept a uniformed doorman at the tent opening to announce visitors," writes a biographer. "No matter who was outside, from a mayor to a shabby woman with a baby, the Colonel would smooth his mustache, stand tall and straight, and tell the doorman to 'show 'em in.' He greeted everyone the same" (Yost, 436).

As a showman, he was a genius. People don't say much about *why* he was so successful; mostly they describe the wonderful goings-on. But I get the feeling that Cody was one of those people who was connected to his time in an uncanny way. He knew what people wanted, he knew how to entertain them, because he *liked* them, was open to them, felt his kinship with them, or was so much in touch with himself at some level that he was thereby in touch with almost everybody else.

He liked to dress up and had a great sense of costume (of humor, too, they say). Once he came to a fancy dress ball, his first, in New York, wearing white tie and tails and a large Stetson. He knew what people wanted. He let his hair grow long and wore a mustache and beard, because, he said, he wouldn't be believable as a scout otherwise. Hence his Indian name, Pahaska, meaning "long hair," which people loved to use. Another kind of costume. He invented the ten-gallon hat, which the Stetson company made to his specifications. Afterward, they made a fortune from it. In the scores of pictures reproduced in the many books about him, he most often wears scout's clothes—usually generously fringed buckskin, sometimes a modified cavalryman's outfit—though often he's impeccably turned out in a natty-looking three-piece business suit (sometimes with overcoat, sometimes not). The photographs show him in a tuxedo, in something called a "Mexican suit" which looks like a cowboy outfit, and once he appears in Indian dress. In almost every case he is wearing some kind of hat, usually the Stetson, at exactly the right angle. He poses deliberately, and with dignity, for the picture. Cody didn't take himself so seriously that he had to pretend to be less than he was.

What made Buffalo Bill so irresistible? Why is he still so appealing, even now, when we've lost, supposedly, all the illusions that once supported his popularity? There's a poster for one of his shows when he was traveling in France that gives a clue to what it is that makes him so profoundly attractive a figure. The poster consists of a huge buffalo galloping across the plains, and against the buffalo's hump, in the center of his hump, is a cutout circle that shows the head of Buffalo Bill, white-mustachioed and bearded now, in his famous hat, and beneath, in large red letters, are the words "Je viens."

Je viens ("I am coming") are the words of a savior. The announcement is an annunciation. Buffalo Bill is a religious figure of a kind who makes sense within a specifically Christian tradition. That is, he comes in the guise of a redeemer, of someone who will save us, who will through his own actions do something for us that we ourselves cannot do. He will lift us above our lives, out of the daily grind, into something larger than we are.

His appeal on the surface is to childish desires, the desire for glamour, fame, bigness, adventure, romance. But these desires are also the sign of something more profound, and it is to something more profound in us that he also appeals. Buffalo Bill comes to the

FIGURE 27 *Je Viens*, c. 1900. Color lithograph. (Courtesy of the Buffalo Bill Historical Center, Cody, Wyoming.)

child in us, understood not as that part of ourselves that we have outgrown but as the part that got left behind, of necessity, a long time ago, having been starved, bound, punished, disciplined out of existence. He promises that that part of the self can live again. He has the power to promise these things because he represents the West, that geographical space of the globe that was still the realm of exploration and discovery, that was still open, that had not yet quite been tamed, when he began to play himself on the stage. He not only represented it, he *was* it. He brought the West itself with him when he came. The very Indians, the very buffalo, the very cowboys, the very cattle, the very stagecoach itself which had been memorialized in story. He performed in front of the audience the feats that had made him famous. He shot glass balls and clay pigeons out of the air with amazing rapidity. He rode his watersmooth silver stallion at full gallop. "Jesus he was a handsome man," wrote e. e. cummings in "Buffalo Bill's Defunct."

"I am coming." This appearance of Buffalo Bill, in the flesh, was akin to the apparition of a saint or of the Virgin Mary to believers. He was the incarnation of an ideal. He came to show people that what they had only imagined was really true. The West really did exist. There really were heroes who rode white horses and performed amazing feats. E. e. cummings was right to invoke the name of Jesus in his poem. Buffalo Bill was a secular messiah.

He was a messiah because people believed in him. When he died, he is reputed to have said, "Let my show go on." But he had no show at the time, so he probably didn't say that. Still, the words are prophetic because the desire for what Buffalo Bill had done had not only not died but would call forth the countless reenactments of the Wild West, from the rodeo—a direct descendant of his show—to the thousands of Western novels, movies, and television programs that comprise the Western genre in the twentieth century, a genre that came into existence as a separate category right about the time that Cody died. Don Russell maintains that the way the West exists in our minds today is largely the result of the way Cody presented it in his show. That was where people got their ideas of what the characters looked like. Though many Indian tribes wore no feathers and fought on foot, you will never see a featherless, horseless Indian warrior in the movies, because Bill employed only Sioux and other Plains tribes which had horses and traditionally wore feathered headdresses. "Similarly," he adds, "cowboys wear ten-gallon Stetsons, not because such a hat was worn in early range days, but because it was part of the costume adopted by Buffalo Bill for his show" (Russell, 470).

But the deeper legacy is elsewhere. Buffalo Bill was a person who inspired other people. What they saw in him was an aspect of themselves. It really doesn't matter whether Cody was as great as people thought him or not, because what they were responding to when he rode into the arena, erect and resplendent on his charger, was something intangible, not the man himself, but a possible way of being. William F. Cody and the Wild West triggered the emotions that had fueled the imaginative lives of people who flocked to see him, especially men and boys, who made up the larger portion of the audience. He and his cowboys played to an inward territory; a Wild West of the psyche that hungered for exercise sprang into activity when the show appeared. *Je viens* was a promise to redeem that territory, momentarily at least, from exile and oblivion. The lost parts of the self symbolized by buffalo and horses and wild men would live again for an hour while the show went on.

People adored it. Queen Victoria, who broke her custom by going to see it at all (she never went to the theater, and on the rare occasions when she wanted to see a play she had it brought to her), is supposed to have been lifted out of a twenty-five-year depression caused by the death of her husband after she saw Buffalo Bill. She liked the show so much that she saw it again, arranging for a command performance to be given at Windsor Castle the day before her Diamond Jubilee. This was the occasion when four kings rode in the Deadwood stagecoach with the Prince of Wales on top next to Buffalo Bill, who drove. No one was proof against the appeal. Ralph Blumenfeld, the London Correspondent for the New York *Herald,* wrote in his diary while the show was in London that he'd had two boyhood heroes, Robin Hood and Buffalo Bill, and had delighted in Cody's stories of the Pony Express and Yellow Hand:

> Everything was done to make Cody conceited and unbearable, but he remained the simple, unassuming child of the plains who thought lords and ladies belonged in the picture books and that the story of Little Red Riding Hood was true. I rode in the Deadwood coach. It was a great evening in which I realized a good many of my boyhood dreams, for there was Buffalo Bill on his white rocking horse charger, and Annie Oakley behind him. (Weybright, 172)

Victor Weybright and Henry Blackman Sell, from whose book on the Wild West some of the foregoing information has come, dedicated their book to Buffalo Bill. It was published in 1955. Nellie Snyder Yost, whose 1979 biography is one of the two scholarly accounts of Cody's life, dedicates her book "to all those good people, living or dead, who knew and liked Buffalo Bill." Don Russell's *The Lives and Legends of Buffalo Bill* (1960), the most fact-filled scholarly biography, does not have a dedication, but in the final chapter, where he steps back to assess Cody and his influence, Russell ends by exclaiming, "What more could possibly asked of a hero? If he was not one, who was?" (Russell, 480).

Let me now pose a few questions of my own. Must we throw out all the wonderful qualities that Cody had, the spirit of hope and emulation that he aroused in millions of people, because of the terrible judgment history has passed on the epoch of which he was part? The kinds of things he stands for—courage, daring, strength, endurance, generosity, openness to other people, love of drama, love of life, the possibility of living a life that does not deny the body and the desires of the body—are these to be declared dangerous and delusional although he manifested some of them while fighting Indians and others while representing his victories to the world? And the feelings he aroused in his audiences, the idealism, the enthusiasm, the excitement, the belief that dreams could become real—must these be declared misguided or a sham because they are associated with the imperialistic conquest of a continent, with the wholesale extermination of animals and men?

It is not so much that we cannot learn from history as that we cannot teach history how things should have been. When I set out to discover how Cody had become involved in the killing of Indians and the slaughter of buffalo, I found myself unable to sustain the outrage I had felt on leaving the museum. From his first job as an eleven-year-old herder for an army supply outfit, sole wage earner for his ailing widowed mother who had a new baby and other children to support, to his death in Colorado at the age of seventy-one, there was never a time when it was possible to say, there, there you went wrong, Buffalo Bill, you should not have killed that Indian. You should have held your fire and made your living some other way and quit the army and gone to work in the nineteenth-century equivalent of the Peace Corps. You should have known how it would end. My reading made me see that you cannot prescribe for someone in Buffalo Bill's position what he should have done, and it made me reflect on how eager I had been to get off on being angry at the museum. The thirst for moral outrage, for self-vindication, lay pretty close to the surface.

I cannot resolve the contradiction between my experience at the Buffalo Bill Historical Center with its celebration of violent conquest and my response to the shining figure of Buffalo Bill as it emerged from the pages of books—on the one hand, a history of shame; on the other, an image of the heart's desire. But I have reached one conclusion that for a while will have to serve.

Major historical events like genocide and major acts of destruction are not simply produced by impersonal historical processes or economic imperatives or ecological blunders; human intentionality is involved and human knowledge of the self. Therefore, if you're really, truly interested in not having any more genocide or killing of animals, no matter what else you might do, if you don't first, or also, come to recognize the violence in yourself and your own anger and your own destructiveness, whatever else you do won't work. It isn't that genocide doesn't matter. Genocide matters, and it starts at home.

1992

Works Cited

Cody, Iron Eyes. *Iron Eyes: My Life as a Hollywood Indian,* as told to Collin Perry. New York: Everest House, 1982.

Russell, Donald B. *The Lives and Legends of Buffalo Bill.* Norman, Okla.: University of Oklahoma Press, 1960.

Weybright, Victor, and Henry Blackman Sell. *Buffalo Bill and the Wild West.* New York: Oxford University Press, 1955.

Yost, Nellie Snyder. *Buffalo Bill, His Family, Friends, Fame, Failure, and Fortunes.* Chicago: Sage Books, 1979.

READING, REREADING, AND ANALYSIS

1. Why does Tompkins label Frederick Remington's paintings and statues "imperialist and racist" (p. 508)?

2. Tompkins asks, "What are museums keeping safe for us, after all?" (p. 513). What is her answer? Put her answer into your own words.

3. Individually or in a group, make a list of explanations for why Tompkins finds the Plains Indian Museum "a terrible letdown" and the Winchester Arms Museum disturbing?

4. How and why does Tompkins come to "love Buffalo Bill"? How does her love of Buffalo Bill affect her understanding of her experience at the Buffalo Bill Museum?

5. In a group, discuss what Tompkins describes as "the blatant contradictions" in the Remington paintings. Use your findings to prepare a ten-minute group oral report to present to your class.

6. When she discusses the apparent contradiction between Cody as a conservationist and Cody as a trophy hunter because of the mounted animal heads in the Buffalo Bill Museum, Tompkins writes: "The combination big-game hunter and conservationist suggests that these men had no interest in preserving the animals for the animals' sake but simply wanted to ensure the chance to exercise their sporting pleasure. But I think this view is too simple; something further is involved here" (p. 512). What is this "something further," according to Tompkins? If you find that her explanation makes sense, then say why. If you are unsure of her explanation, then say why you are uncertain. And, if you do not think that her explanation makes sense, then be able to define the problems with her interpretation.

RESPONDING THROUGH WRITING: BUILDING AN INTERPRETATION

7. Write two paragraphs that summarize why Tompkins finds the Buffalo Bill Museum "disturbing" and "wonderful."

8. Write a letter to Tompkins offering possible answers to or explanations for her questions about the Frederick Remington painting *Coming to the Call*. Particularly, respond to this statement: "And what call do we answer when we look at this painting? Who is calling whom? What is being preserved here?" (p. 510).

9. Tompkins keeps referring to the phrase "the best of civilization," which she hears on a videotaped program playing at the entrance to the Buffalo Bill Museum. What does the phrase mean to you? What does Tompkins think about that phrase and why? Write a short essay that links your own understanding of "the best of civilization" with what you believe to be Tompkins's attitude toward the phrase. Does her attitude change over the course of her essay? If so, how and why? If not, why not?

10. Tompkins says she left the Buffalo Bill Museum "full of moral outrage" (p. 517). Yet, as you know from reading her essay, she comes to believe that Buffalo Bill is wonderful. Someone might argue that her "moral outrage" is an example of responses often

negatively labeled as being "politically correct." Write a four- to five-page essay in which you examine Tompkins's complex attitudes toward Buffalo Bill and toward her museum visit. To what degree, if at all, is Tompkins responding to what might be labeled "political correctness"? What accounts for Tompkins' conclusion that "Buffalo Bill was a person who inspired other people. What they saw in him was an aspect of themselves" (p. 521) and her concluding question, "Must we throw out all the wonderful qualities that Cody had, the spirit of hope and emulation that he aroused in millions of people, because of the terrible judgment history has passed on the epoch of which he was part" (p. 522)? What lesson, if any, has Tompkins learned that she is trying to convey to her readers?

GOING FURTHER: LEARNING FROM OTHER SOURCES

11. Find a book of Frederick Remington's paintings and statues in your library, and find a website that features Remington's work. Take some notes about your reactions to a Remington painting and a Remington statue. Compare your impressions of Remington's work with Tompkins's impressions of his artistry. (Hint: Alternatively, you might use a popular Internet search engine such as AltaVista, search for Remington's work in the "Arts" category, and limit the search to "Images.")

12. See if you can find a website for the Buffalo Bill Museum. Compare the impressions the website gives you of the museum with the impressions of the museum you get from reading Tompkins's essay.

APPLYING WHAT YOU'VE LEARNED

13. Write a three- or four-page essay that compares Tompkins's experience in the Plains Indian Museum with Gloria Anzaldúa's experience in the Denver Museum of Natural History in Anzaldúa's "Chicana Artists: Exploring *Nepantla, el Lugar de la Frontera*."

14. In her essay, "I Stand Here Writing," Nancy Sommers quotes Ralph Waldo Emerson's remark that "one must be an inventor to read well" (p. 458). In "At the Buffalo Bill Museum, June 1988," Tompkins presents readings of artwork and artifacts. Use Sommers's sense of the Emerson quotation to help you analyze Tompkins's acts of reading art and artifacts. How is Tompkins an "inventor" as she interprets museum displays?

15. At the end of her essay, Tompkins discusses genocide and suggests that it is all too easy for us to exhibit the qualities or emotions we might otherwise piously rail against in other people. She writes,

> if you're really, truly interested in not having any more genocide or killing of animals, no matter what else you might do, if you don't first, or also, come to recognize the violence in yourself and your own anger and your own destructiveness, whatever else you do won't work. It isn't that genocide doesn't matter. Genocide matters, and it starts at home (p. 523).

Use this argument as a critical lens for examining "violence," "anger," and "destructiveness" in two other essays in *Making Sense,* such as Gloria Anzaldúa's "Chicana Artists: Exploring *Nepantla, el Lugar de la Frontera,*" Christopher Lasch's "The Lost Art of Argument," Walker Percy's "The Loss of the Creature," Haunani-Kay Trask's "From a Native Daughter," or Susan Willis's "Disney World: Public Use/Private Space." What does Tompkins's perspective help you see in the two essays you choose, and how do arguments in the two essays you examine call into question or complicate Tompkins's argument in her conclusion?

CHRISTOPHER P. TOUMEY

Christopher P. Toumey (b. 1949) is a Professor of Anthropology at the University of South Carolina, where he is also a member of the interdisciplinary team in Nanoscience and Technology Studies. Toumey is the author of *God's Own Scientists: Creationists in a Secular World* and *Conjuring Science: Scientific Symbols and Cultural Meanings in American Life,* from which "Science in an Old Testament Style" was excerpted.

> To learn more about social studies of science, see The Society for Social Studies of Science website at <http://www.4sonline.org/index.htm>.

WHAT DO YOU KNOW? WHAT DO YOU EXPECT TO DISCOVER?

Before reading the essay, take a moment to consider the following questions.

1. What topics does Toumey's biography suggest he is interested in? What do you know about those topics? Knowledge can come from personal experience, stories you've heard, other classes you've taken, or other reading you've done.

2. What relationships do the words "Science" and "Old Testament" in the essay's title suggest to you and why?

3. In the essay that follows, Toumey discusses what he calls the "peculiar role of science in American culture." What do you typically consider the role of science in "American culture"? Why might someone use the word "peculiar" in connection with science's role in U.S. culture?

✄

Science in an Old Testament Style

In 1988, a television commercial for a common drugstore product made an uncommon claim about the endorsement of medical science. An actor from a daytime soap opera appeared on-screen in a white lab coat and declared, "I'm not a doctor, but I play one on TV." Then with those credentials he endorsed the product, recommending it in the authoritative voice of a medical doctor.

Such a commercial would be preposterous if it were generally recognized that there is a real difference between a doctor with genuine credentials and an actor who plays a doctor on TV. After all, the actor who played a doctor was not a doctor, and he candidly declared that he was not.

If a real physician is a symbol of medical science once removed from that kind of abstract institutional authority, and if an actor who pretends to be a doctor, like Robert Young as Marcus Welby, M.D., is a symbol twice removed, then the actor who did not even pretend to be a doctor was thrice removed from medical science. Nevertheless, for the purpose of pitching the product, he was an effective simulacrum of the authority of medical science.

The town of New Madrid, Missouri, devoted itself single-mindedly to emergency preparations for an earthquake in November and December 1990. The city council stockpiled drinking water, the mayor positioned his fire trucks in open fields far from buildings that might collapse, the local elementary school canceled classes for the day the earthquake was expected to hit, and the local insurance business sold many earthquake policies. At nearby St. John Missionary Baptist Church, Sunday school on December 2 began with the invocation to "Bless all of us, oh Father, that are upset about the earthquake."

The reason? Iben Browning, Ph.D., had predicted that a massive earthquake of at least 6.5 Richter had a 50 percent chance of striking New Madrid on December 3, 1990. It was said that Browning had predicted California's 1989 Loma Prieta earthquake. Surely an earthquake warning from someone with credentials and experience like Browning's was serious scientific advice, not to be taken lightly. Indeed, David Stewart, Ph.D., a geophysicist at nearby Southeast Missouri State University, endorsed Dr. Browning's prediction for 1990 in Missouri.

In truth, Iben Browning's Ph.D. was in zoology, not seismology. He had not predicted the Loma Prieta event. His supporter, David Stewart, had previously employed paranormal methods, including the services of psychic Clarissa Bernhard from the *National Enquirer,* to anticipate an earthquake in North Carolina that never happened. The National Earthquake Prediction Evaluation Council, under the auspices of the U.S. Geological Survey, adamantly denounced the faulty logic of Browning's seismological theories.

No matter. Tens of thousands of people in the region around New Madrid changed their plans and their behavior in anticipation of Iben Browning's earthquake. And never mind the skeptical bureaucrats of the U.S. Geological Survey, who seemed indifferent to the worries of the people of New Madrid. Was it not better to choose concerned scientists like Iben Browning and David Stewart as one's friends and advisers?

Tension was as bad as it could be when December 1990 came around. But the earth did not shake.

For many years, the tobacco lobby challenged the conclusion that smoking causes cancer, by drawing a hard distinction between the kind of scientific proof that comes from replicable demonstrations of cause and effect, and the epidemiological conclusions that are drawn from statistical correlations: the absolute proof of test-tube science, so to speak, versus the uncertainty of statistical probability. Then with scientific proof defined in terms of test-tube science, the tobacco advocates argued that scientists have not proven that smoking causes cancer since they have not elucidated the biochemical pathways by which the cause (smoking) leads to the effect (cancer). True, scientists have not, so the tobacco advocates are correct, provided that scientific proof is defined this way.

This logic implicitly compares the value of one form of scientific reasoning with that of another: a statistical conclusion is always inferior to a replicable demonstration of causation since the former is always less than 100 percent certain. More to the point, one can then say that the smoking and cancer connection is *possible* but far from certain, which is enormously useful to smokers who want a reason for not giving up smoking and to those who want to sell them tobacco products.

In June 1993, attorneys for the tobacco industry initiated a lawsuit to reverse the decision of the Environmental Protection Agency (EPA) designating secondhand smoke as a carcinogen. Their legal reasoning centered on the issue of statistical significance. Six of the thirty studies cited by the EPA had confidence levels of 95 percent ($p < .05$) for the conclusion that secondhand smoke causes cancer, but the other twenty-four studies had lower levels, for example, 80 or 85 percent.

Was this really a change in the standards of scientific proof? It seems to have been since the attorneys for the tobacco interests implicitly conceded that epidemiological-statistical methods *might* have scientific merit, provided that they met confidence levels of 95 percent or above (which is entirely reasonable for epidemiological research that has real policy implications). But the weaker studies had an equally important role in this argument. Every scientific study with a confidence level less than 95 percent could be interpreted to impeach all the studies with a level greater than 95 percent. So epidemiological-statistical studies of carcinogenicity can now be legally credible, but only in the sense that weaker studies have the effect of impeaching stronger studies, which is to say that weaker ones are more credible than stronger ones.

This medley of incidents reflects two aspects of the peculiar role of science in American culture. On the one hand, the institutional endorsement of the scientific authority is so greatly respected that the TV doctor, the credentials of Iben Browning, and the august weight of test-tube scientific proof are believed to enhance the worth of drugstore products, disaster preparations, and health regulations. On the other hand, the public understanding of the scientific knowledge and scientific reasoning in which that respect is grounded is so shallow that an *appearance* of scientific authority can be easily conjured from cheap symbols and ersatz images like an actor's white lab coat, a zoologist's credentials in a controversy about seismology, and a definition of scientific proof that makes epidemiological evidence irrelevant to an epidemiological question of carcinogenicity.

In other instances, the raw material for conjuring a semblance of science might be the solemn sounds of Greek or Latin terminology, visual images of shiny laboratory paraphernalia, or graphs and charts that pop up on the monitors of humming computers. Rich and deep is the supply of scientific iconography that can be borrowed for the purpose of cobbling together an image of science.

To understand the strength of popular respect for scientific authority, consider that certain theologians speak of the plenary authority of scripture, meaning that the written word of revelation embodies all the wisdom one needs to answer any of life's questions, big or small, spiritual or secular. We can borrow the term "plenary" to describe the way many citizens feel about science. The prestige of science is so great that it, too, is believed to possess such authority and be able to answer any of life's questions. This is so because science is widely believed to transcend the social forces that obviously shape other human institutions, such as politics or religion. Science is believed to be, in a word, "objective."

Science does not really deserve such awe, nor do most scientists believe such things about it. But many nonscientists do. Thus, to invoke the symbols of science is to make policies sound, commodities desirable, and behavior legitimate. By definition, these things are meritorious when they have the appearance of being scientific.

And yet surrounding the plenary authority of science is a great vacuum of understanding about scientific knowledge and reasoning. Studies of science education and scientific literacy reveal that large portions of the American public do not know such essential scientific concepts as "molecule" or "radiation," cannot comprehend the methods of scientific reasoning, and could not apply either to public issues. Historical surveys of science in America demonstrate that the intangible meanings cherished within the institutional culture of science—the pleasures that make science rewarding to scientists—are alien to most of the American public.

The religion of the Old Testament could be the pattern for this combination of respect without comprehension. The chosen people believed in God, feared Him, and doubted His power only at great risk to themselves; yet they understood God very imperfectly since this being was a distant mystery who made himself known by awesome signs: burning bushes, pillars of fire, dreadful plagues. So it is with science in America today. Instead of comprehending scientific knowledge, scientific methods, or scientific standards, much of the adult population knows science only in terms of certain symbols that stand for science and that stand between people and scientific understanding. An actor who stands for medical science, for example, because he plays a doctor and wears a white lab coat, or a courtroom definition of scientific standards, or a zoologist's credentials in an argument about earthquakes.

This paradox of respect without comprehension can be broken down into three questions. First, what are the historical conditions that have caused the culture of science to be so estranged from other parts of American culture? This is a question of how science is perceived by nonscientists such that the values and meanings of science, as understood by scientists, are not well integrated into the values and meanings of American life. Scientific judgment is one thing, but nonscientists' everyday thinking about science is something else.

Second, how does science fit into American democratic culture today? Even though the values and standards of science are somewhat alien to the rest of American culture, and even though much of the American public is ill-equipped to make informed decisions about scientific issues, decisions affecting science (appropriations, legislation, policy, and the curriculum of public school science education, to name a few) are nevertheless made according to democratic processes. Science in America is strongly affected by extrascientific factors. One consequence of this effect is that various parties can invoke the symbols of science to claim that science endorses their own respective positions and can do so with little or no regard for scientific standards. Because there is too little public understanding of scientific knowledge or reasoning, it is possible to borrow, steal, distort, or manipulate these symbols for causes and ideologies that do not necessarily have anything to do with science.

That, in turn, begs the third question: if the symbols of science are being used to endorse or legitimize certain values and meanings but not the values and meanings of science, then to what exactly do these symbols refer? What do the symbols of science convey, if not the content of science? What are the nonscientific ideas that are being expressed by means of scientific symbols?

. . . By tracing a series of changing notions about science across the last two hundred years, I suggest that science, loosely defined, fit quite comfortably into American democratic culture in the early nineteenth century. Both the empirical content and the intellectual structure of science were relatively simple, so it was easy for the average person to understand science and appreciate it. After the arrival in the United States of modern scientific thinking and methods, however, beginning around the middle of the nineteenth century, a great divergence appeared between science as understood by scientists and science as understood by other Americans.

In the gap between those two ways of understanding science, there arose a certain kind of mischief, namely, the conjuring of science. One could use the common symbols and images of science, as understood by nonscientists, to make it seem that scientists were bestowing the plenary authority of science on various causes and ideologies that had nothing to do with science. By placing this mischief in American history, we can see how and when it arose and how it has been maintained throughout the twentieth century. . . .

. . . Undoubtedly, science occupies an important place in American life by virtue of its authority to bless or curse one commodity or another, one cause or another. But it cannot be taken for granted that the internal values and standards of science will have much effect in a public dispute about science, let alone that they will govern such a dispute. The critical question is not how science influences American culture but rather how American culture treats science. . . . The heart of my anthropological approach is an argument about the cultural conditions that enable various parties to separate the symbols of science from the substantive content of science so as to invoke and deploy those symbols to bestow the plenary authority of science on almost any commodity, ideology, or behavior. . . .

[M]y argument is as follows: In American culture, science is widely believed to possess a plenary authority. But this authority is not really grounded in the values and standards of science because they are estranged from the main themes of American life. Nevertheless, symbols of science are frequently invoked to support claims that science has endorsed a given commodity or cause, which is to say that semblance of scientific authority can be conjured. In which case, it is worth discovering what nonscientific values and meanings do the symbols of science stand for, which is a question of *why* science is conjured, and how it is that those symbols of science serve those nonscientific meanings, which is to ask *how* science is conjured.

I confess that my anthropology of science has very little to do with the methods, the knowledge, or the theories that we point to as the intellectual content of science. Instead, this anthropology is a story about how we borrow bits and pieces of science, loose and jagged, to aid our existential efforts to make sense of our lives. We think we know something about reality or about human existence or about right and wrong, and maybe we do. But our confidence is much enhanced when we think that science endorses or corroborates the things we think we know.

Why do we think so? How do we conclude that science takes sides in moral or existential questions? Why do we believe that a policy is better if it seems that science has blessed it? Why does it appear that one person's behavior is more righteous, or another's less, when a claim is made that science recommends this habit or that? . . .

My argument is that, regardless of the metaphysical status of science, its value in American life is contingent on the cultural values and meanings that frame science. And so I offer a story not about science but about the moralities, the philosophies, the ideologies, and the beliefs that surround science. I ask how the American people attribute the plenary authority of science to those values and meanings by disconnecting the popular symbols of science from its intellectual substance and attaching those symbols to other matters instead. In other words, I ask how we conjure a semblance of science.

1996

READING, REREADING, AND ANALYSIS

1. Look up the word "plenary" in a college-edition dictionary, and compare this definition with the way Toumey uses the term. Why does he describe science in America as having "plenary" authority? Think of at least three different words or phrases that might also describe the attitude Americans have about science.

2. Think of at least three words or phrases other than "plenary" that you could use to describe attitudes Americans have toward science. List the words or phrases you come up with and jot down distinctions you see between those words or phrases and "plenary."

3. In addition to science, list one or two other specialties that exemplify what Toumey calls the "paradox of respect without comprehension," which he discusses in relation to Americans' attitude toward science.

4. Individually or in a group, make a list of examples of "conjuring" that Toumey describes and then make your own list of other possible examples of "conjuring" that would fit with Toumey's argument.

5. Think of the last newspaper story, movie, or book you encountered that referred to or used a difficult scientific term or concept. How was science represented and was the authority of science questioned in any way?

6. What does Toumey mean on page 531 when he says,

   > Even though much of the American public is ill-equipped to make informed decisions about scientific issues, decisions affecting science (appropriations, legislation, policy, and the curriculum of public school science education, to name a few) are nevertheless made according to democratic processes. Science in America is strongly affected by extrascientific factors.

RESPONDING THROUGH WRITING: BUILDING AN INTERPRETATION

7. Use the list you prepared in question 4 to help you write a short essay (one or two pages) about the "conjuring of science." Why does Toumey use the word "conjuring"? Discuss its relation for Toumey to the phrase "an Old Testament Style."

8. Generate an example of a scientist or a doctor as represented by popular culture. You might think of a movie, a television ad or show, or a video game. In two or three pages, discuss the powers granted to the scientist or doctor because of her or his knowledge. Does the scientist or the doctor have powers over others or over nature? What does your example suggest about the way we tend to view scientists?

9. Write a short paper in which you grapple with Toumey's suggestion that we allow representations of science to go unquestioned at our peril. If we are not scientists ourselves, what are we to do about the problems Toumey discusses? What strategies or attitudes might help us overcome this so-called manipulation?

10. In three or four sentences, summarize Toumey's argument that "the values and standards of science . . . are estranged from the main themes of American life."

GOING FURTHER: LEARNING FROM OTHER SOURCES

11. Explore some of Toumey's concepts by looking up some questionable "scientific" practices in books, in magazines, or on websites. (Hint: Try the combined search term "science and magic" in a reference database that includes general-interest and current-events-related magazines, such as MAS Full Text Ultra or a similar database recommended by your reference librarian). In a group, share and analyze your findings: Where do you see science invoked in ways that seem suspicious or misleading to you?

12. The Hubble Space Craft has been sending black-and-white digital photo images back to NASA, where engineers add colors that are supposedly dictated by scientific understanding of cosmic atmosphere. Use an academic search engine to help you research how colors are added to Hubble's black-and-white photos. Is the addition of the colors a version of conjuring? Is it sound science? Is it more embellishment than sound science?

APPLYING WHAT YOU'VE LEARNED

13. Write an essay (four or five pages) in which you compare Toumey's claim that "science in America is strongly affected by extrascientific factors" with Michio Kaku's call for democratic decision making about high-tech science such as the biomolecular revolution in Kaku's essay, "Second Thoughts: The Genetics of a Brave New World?" In your essay, discuss what Toumey might identify as "conjuring" in Kaku's essay and why.

14. In Julie English Early's account of Mary Kingsley, Early tells us that Kingsley courted popularity and created a stir with her unorthodox presentations of scientific materials. Write an essay in which you examine whether Kingsley was guilty of what Toumey calls "conjuring science," or whether she was de-conjuring science with her self-conscious, idiosyncratic style? How did she use, appeal to, and sometimes thwart so-called legitimate scientific authority?

15. In "The Lost Art of Argument," Christopher Lasch argues that there has been a decline in the kind of public debate that is key to a working democracy. As you think about Lasch's explanation for the decline he identifies, think as well about Toumey's discussion of how science has become so estranged from most Americans' everyday lives. Write an essay about the concept of estrangement as it appears in both Lasch's and Toumey's essays. What overlaps do you see in their respective discussions of estrangement, and what possible solutions are available?

HAUNANI-KAY TRASK

Haunani-Kay Trask (b. 1949) is a Hawaiian nationalist, political organizer, poet, and Professor of Hawaiian Studies at the University of Hawaii. She is the coproducer of the award-winning documentary *Act of War: The Over-throw of the Hawaiian Nation* and the author of three books, including *From a Native Daughter: Colonialism and Sovereignty in Hawaii* (1993), in which she offers some political readings of Hawaiian history and, especially, the place of white colonialism in that history. "From a Native Daughter" was published in *The American Indian and the Problem of History* (1987), a collection of essays edited by Calvin Martin.

> To learn more about Hawaiian claims to sovereignty, visit the Hawaii Nation's homepage at <http://www.hawaii-nation.org/>.

WHAT DO YOU KNOW? WHAT DO YOU EXPECT TO DISCOVER?

Before reading the essay, take a moment to consider the following questions.

1. What do you know about Hawaiian culture? Who are the "native" Hawaiians? How would you distinguish between their culture and what Trask calls "Western" culture?

2. Is history more accurate if it is written by the people who have lived through or felt the impact of the historical events? Are there any advantages in being an outsider who is merely learning about or discovering that history?

3. How does one express anger or disappointment in writing? Trask writes for an audience that may feel challenged or even threatened by the assertions she makes. What risks might Trask be taking in being openly critical?

⅍

From a Native Daughter

E noi'i wale mai no ka haole, a,
'a'ole e pau na hana a Hawai'i 'imi loa
Let the haole *freely research us in detail*
But the doings of deep delving Hawai'i
will not be exhausted.

KEPELINO
19th-century Hawaiian historian

A loha kākou. Let us greet each other in friendship and love. My given name is Haunaniokawēkiu o Haleakalā, native of *Hawai'i Nei.* My father's family is from the *'āina* (land) of *Kaua'i,* my mother's family from the *'āina* of Maui. I reside today among my native people in the community of *Waimānalo.*

I have lived all my life under the power of America. My native country, Hawai'i, is owned by the United States. I attended missionary schools, both Catholic and Protestant, in my youth, and I was sent away to the American mainland to receive a "higher" education at the University of Wisconsin. Now I teach the history and culture of my people at the University of Hawai'i.

When I was young the story of my people was told twice: once by my parents, then again by my school teachers. From my *'ohana* (family), I learned about the life of the old ones: how they fished and planted by the moon; shared all the fruits of their labors, especially their children; danced in great numbers for long hours; and honored the unity of their world in intricate genealogical chants. My mother said Hawaiians had sailed over thousands of miles to make their home in these sacred islands. And they had flourished, until the coming of the *haole* (whites).

At school, I learned that the "pagan Hawaiians" did not read or write, were lustful cannibals, traded in slaves, and could not sing. Captain Cook had "discovered" Hawai'i and the ungrateful Hawaiians had killed him. In revenge, the Christian god had cursed the Hawaiians with disease and death.

I learned the first of these stories from speaking with my mother and father. I learned the second from books. By the time I left for college, the books had won out over my parents, especially since I spent four long years in a missionary boarding school for Hawaiian children.

When I went away I understood the world as a place and a feeling divided in two: one *haole* (white), and the other *kānaka* (native). When I returned ten years later with a Ph.D., the division was sharper, the lack of connection more painful. There was the world that we lived in—my ancestors, my family, and my people—and then there was the world historians described. This world, they had written, was the truth. A primitive group, Hawaiians had been ruled by bloodthirsty priests and despotic kings who owned all the land and kept our people in feudal subjugation. The chiefs were cruel, the people poor.

But this was not the story my mother told me. No one had owned the land before the *haole* came; everyone could fish and plant, except during sacred periods. And the chiefs were good and loved their people.

Was my mother confused? What did our *kūpuna* (elders) say? They replied: Did these historians (all *haole*) know the language? Did they understand the chants? How long had they lived among our people? Whose stories had they heard?

None of the historians had ever learned our mother tongue. They had all been content to read what Europeans and Americans had written. But why did scholars, presumably well-trained and thoughtful, neglect our language? Not merely a passageway to knowledge, language is a form of knowing by itself; a people's way of thinking and feeling is revealed through its music.

I sensed the answer without needing to answer. From years of living in a divided world, I knew the historian's judgment: *There is no value in things Hawaiian; all value comes from things haole.*

Historians, I realized, were very like missionaries. They were a part of the colonizing horde. One group colonized the spirit; the other, the mind. Frantz Fanon had been right, but not just about Africans. He had been right about the bondage of my own people: "By a kind of perverted logic, [colonialism] turns to the past of the oppressed people, and distorts, disfigures, and destroys it" (1968:210). The first step in the colonizing process, Fanon had written, was the deculturation of a people. What better way to take our culture than to remake our image? A rich historical past became small and ignorant in the hands of Westerners. And we suffered a damaged sense of people and culture because of this distortion.

Burdened by a linear, progressive conception of history and by an assumption that Euro-American culture flourishes at the upper end of that progression, Westerners have told the history of Hawai'i as an inevitable if occasionally bitter-sweet triumph of Western ways over "primitive" Hawaiian ways. A few authors—the most sympathetic—have recorded with deep-felt sorrow the passing of our people. But in the end, we are repeatedly told, such an eclipse was for the best.

Obviously it was best for Westerners, not for our dying multitudes. This is why the historian's mission has been to justify our passing by celebrating Western dominance. Fanon would have called this missionizing, intellectual colonization. And it is clearest in the historian's insistence that pre-*haole* Hawaiian land tenure was "feudal"—a term that is now applied, without question, in every monograph, in every schoolbook, and in every tour guide description of my people's history.

From the earliest days of Western contact my people told their guests that *no one* owned the land. The land—like the air and the sea—was for all to use and share as their birthright. Our chiefs were *stewards* of the land; they could not own or privately possess the land any more than they could sell it.

But the *haole* insisted on characterizing our chiefs as feudal landlords and our people as serfs. Thus, a European term which described a European practice founded on the European concept of private property—feudalism—was imposed upon a people halfway around the world from Europe and vastly different from her in every conceivable way. More than betraying an ignorance of Hawaiian culture and history, however, this misrepresentation was malevolent in design.

By inventing feudalism in ancient Hawai'i, Western scholars quickly transformed a spiritually-based, self-sufficient economic system of land use and occupancy into an oppressive, medievel European practice of divine right ownership, with the common people tied like serfs to the land. By claiming that a Pacific people lived under a European system—that the Hawaiians lived under feudalism—Westerners could then degrade a successful system of shared land use with a pejorative and inaccurate Western term. Land tenure changes instituted by Americans and in line with current Western notions of private property were then made to appear beneficial to the Hawaiians. But in practice, such changes benefited the *haole,* who alienated the people from the land, taking it for themselves.

The prelude to this land alienation was the great dying of the people. Barely half a century after contact with the West our people had declined in number by eighty percent. Disease and death were rampant. The sandalwood forests had been stripped bare for international commerce between England and China. The missionaries had insinuated themselves everywhere. And a debt-ridden Hawaiian king (there had been no king before Western contact) succumbed to enormous pressure from the Americans and followed their schemes for dividing up the land.

This is how private property land tenure entered Hawai'i. The common people, driven from their birthright, received less than one percent of the land. They starved while huge *haole*-owned sugar plantations thrived.

And what had the historians said? They had said that the Americans "liberated" the Hawaiians from an oppressive "feudal" system. By inventing a false feudal past, the historians justify—and become complicitous in—massive American theft.

Is there "evidence"—as historians call it—for traditional Hawaiian concepts of land use? The evidence is in the sayings of my people and in the words they wrote more than a century ago, much of which has been translated. However, historians have chosen to ignore any references here to shared land use. But there *is* incontrovertible evidence in the very structure of the Hawaiian language. If the historians had bothered to learn our language (as any American historian of France would learn French) they would have discovered that we show possession in two ways: through the use of an "a" possessive, which reveals acquired status, and through the use of an "o" possessive, which denotes inherent status. My body (ko 'u kino) and my parents (ko'u mākua), for example, take the "o" form; most material objects, such as food (ka'u mea'ai) take the "a" form. But land, like one's body and one's parents, takes the "o" possessive (ko'u 'āina). Thus, in our way of speaking, land is inherent to the people; it is like our bodies and our parents. The people cannot exist without the land, and the land cannot exist without the people.

Every major historian of Hawai'i has been mistaken about Hawaiian land tenure. The chiefs did not own the land: they *could not* own the land. My mother was right and the *haole* historians were wrong. If they had studied our language they would have known that no one owned the land. But was their failing merely ignorance, or simple ethnocentric bias?

No, I did not believe them to be so benign. As I read on, a pattern emerged in their writing. Our ways were inferior to those of the West, to those of the historians' own culture. We were "less developed," or "immature," or "authoritarian." In some tellings we were much worse. Thus, Gavan Daws (1968), the most famed modern historian of Hawai'i, had continued a tradition established earlier by missionaries Hiram Bingham (1848) and Sheldon Dibble (1909), by referring to the old ones as "thieves" and "savages" who regularly practiced infanticide and who, in contrast to "civilized" whites, preferred "lewd dancing" to work. Ralph Kuykendall (1938), long considered the most thorough if also the most boring of historians of Hawai'i, sustained another fiction—that my ancestors owned slaves, the outcast Kauwā. This opinion, as well was the description of Hawaiian land tenure as feudal, had been supported by respected sociologist Andrew Lind (1938).[1] Finally, nearly all historians had refused to accept our genealogical dating of A.D. 400 or earlier for our arrival from the South Pacific. They had, instead, claimed that our earliest appearance in Hawai'i could only be traced to A.D. 1100. Thus at least seven hundred years of our history were repudiated by "superior" Western scholarship. Only recently have archeological data confirmed what Hawaiians had said these many centuries (Tuggle 1979).

Suddenly the entire sweep of our written history was clear to me. I was reading the West's view of itself through the degradation of my own past. When historians wrote that the king owned the land and the common people were bound to it, they were saying that ownership was the only way human beings in their world could relate to the land, and in that relationship, some one person had to control both the land and the interaction between humans.

And when they said that our chiefs were despotic, they were telling of their own society, where hierarchy always results in domination. Thus any authority or elder is automatically suspected of tyranny.

And when they wrote that Hawaiians were lazy, they meant that work must be continuous and ever a burden.

And when they wrote that we were promiscuous, they meant that love-making in the Christian West is a sin.

And when they wrote that we were racist because we preferred our own ways to theirs, they meant that their culture needed to dominate other cultures.

And when they wrote that we were superstitious, believing in the *mana* of nature and people, they meant that the West has long since lost a deep spiritual and cultural relationship to the earth.

And when they wrote that Hawaiians were "primitive" in their grief over the passing of loved ones, they meant that the West grieves for the living who do not walk among their ancestors.

For so long, more than half my life, I had misunderstood this written record, thinking it described my own people. But my history was nowhere present. For we had not written. We had chanted and sailed and fished and built and prayed. And we had told stories through the great blood lines of memory: genealogy.

To know my history, I had to put away my books and return to the land. I had to plant taro in the earth before I could understand the inseparable bond between people and *'āina*. I had to feel again the spirits of nature and take gifts of plants and fish to the ancient altars. I had to begin to speak my language with our elders and leave long silences for wisdom to grow. But before anything else, I had to learn the language like a lover so that I could rock within her and lay at night in her dreaming arms.

There was nothing in my schooling that had told me of this, or hinted that somewhere there was a longer, older story of origins, of the flowing of songs out to a great but distant sea. Only my parents' voices, over and over, spoke to me of a Hawaiian world. While the books spoke from a different world, a Western world.

And yet, Hawaiians are not of the West. We are of *Hawai'i Nei,* this world where I live, this place, this culture, this *'aina.*

What can I say, then, to Western historians of my place and people? Let me answer with a story.

A while ago I was asked to share a panel on the American over-throw of our government in 1893. The other panelists were all *haole*. But one was a *haole* historian from the mainland who had just published a book on what he called the American anti-imperialists. He and I met briefly in preparation for the panel. I asked him if he knew the language. He said no. I asked him if he knew the record of opposition to our annexation to America. He said there was no real evidence for it, just comments here and there. I told him that he didn't understand and that at the panel I would share the evidence. When we met in public and spoke, I said this:

There is a song much loved by our people. It was sung when Hawai-ians were forbidden from congregating in groups of more than three. Addressed to our imprisoned Queen, it was written in 1893, and tells of Hawaiian feelings for our land and against annexation. Listen to our lament:

Kaulana na pua a'o Hawai'i	Famous are the children of Hawai'i
Kūpa'a mahope o ka 'āina	Who cling steadfastly to the land
Hiki mai ka 'elele o ka loko 'ino	Comes the evil-hearted with
Palapala 'ānunu me ka pākaha	A document greedy for plunder
Pane mai Hawai'i moku o Keawe	Hawai'i, island of Keawe, answers
Kokua na hono a'o Pi'ilani	The bays of Pi'ilani [of Maui, Moloka'i, and Lana'i] help
Kāko'o mai Kaua'i o Mano	Kaua'i of Mano assists
Pau pu me ke one o Kakuhihewa	Firmly together with the sands of Kakuhihewa
'A'ole a'e kau i ka pūlima	Do not put the signature
Maluna o ka pepa o ka 'enemi	On the paper of the enemy
Ho'ohui 'āina kū'ai hewa	Annexation is wicked sale
I ka pono sīvila a'o ke kānaka	Of the civil rights of the Hawaiian people
Mahope mākou o Lili'ulani	We support Lili'uokalani
A loa'a 'e ka pono o ka 'āina	Who has earned the right to the land
Ha'ina 'ia mai ana ka puana	The story is told
'O ka po'e i aloha i ka 'āina	Of the people who love the land

This song, I said, continues to be sung with great dignity at Hawaiian political gatherings. For our people still share the feelings of anger and protest that it conveys.

But our guest, the *haole* historian, answered that this song, although beautiful, was not evidence of either opposition or of imperialism from the Hawaiian perspective.

Many Hawaiians in the audience were shocked at his remarks, but, in hindsight, I think they were predictable. They are the standard response of the historian who does not know the language and has no respect for its memory.

Finally, I proceeded to relate a personal story, thinking that surely such a tale could not want for authenticity since I myself was relating it. My *tūtū* (grandmother) had told my mother who had told me that at the time of the overthrow a great wailing went up throughout the islands, a wailing of weeks, a wailing of impenetrable grief, a wailing of death. But he remarked again, this too is not evidence.

And so, history goes on, written in long volumes by foreign people. Whole libraries begin to form, book upon book, shelf upon shelf.

At the same time, the stories go on, generation to generation, family to family.

Which history do Western historians desire to know? Is it to be a tale of writings by their own countrymen, individuals convinced of their "unique" capacity for analysis, looking at us with Western eyes, thinking about us within Western philosophical contexts, categorizing us by Western indices, judging us by Judeo-Christian morals, exhorting us to capitalist achievements, and finally, leaving us an authoritative-because-Western record of their complete misunderstanding?

All this has been done already. Not merely a few times, but many times. And still, every year, there appear new and eager faces to take up the same telling, as if the West must continue, implacably, with the din of its own disbelief.

But there is, as there has been always, another possibility. If it is truly our history Western historians desire to know, they must put down their books, and take up our practices. First, of course, the language. But later, the people, the *'āina,* the stories. Above all, in the end, the stories. Historians must listen, they must hear the generational connections, the reservoir of sounds and meanings.

They must come, as American Indians suggested long ago, to understand the land. Not in the Western way, but in the indigenous way, the way of living within and protecting the bond between people and *'āina.*

This bond is cultural, and it can be understood only culturally. But because the West has lost any cultural understanding of the bond between people and land, it is not possible to know this connection through Western culture. This means that the history of indigenous people cannot be written from within Western culture. Such a story is merely the West's story of itself.

Our story remains unwritten. It rests within the culture, which is inseparable from the land. To know this is to know our history. To write this is to write of the land and the people who are born from her.

1987

Notes

1. See also Fornander (1878–85). Lest one think these sources antiquated, it should be noted that there exist only a handful of modern scholarly works on the history of Hawai'i. The most respected are those by Kuykendall (1938) and Daws (1968), and a social history of the twentieth century by Lawrence Fuchs (1961). Of these, only Kuykendall and Daws claim any knowledge of pre-*haole* history, while concentrating on the nineteenth century. However, countless popular works have relied on these two studies which, in turn, are themselves based on primary sources written in English extremely by biased, anti-Hawaiian Westerners such as explorers, traders, missionaries (e.g., Bingham [1848] and Dibble [1909]), and sugar planters. Indeed, a favorite technique of Daws's—whose *Shoal of Time* is the most acclaimed and recent general history—is the lengthy quotation without comment of the most racist remarks by missionaries and planters. Thus, at one point, half a page is consumed with a "white man's burden" quotation from an 1886 *Planter's Monthly* article ("It is better for the colored man of India and Australia that the white man rules, and it is better here that the white man should rule. . . ," etc., p. 213). Daws's only comment is, "The conclusion was inescapable." To get a sense of such characteristic contempt for Hawaiians, one has but to read the first few pages, where Daws refers several times to the Hawaiians as "savages" and "thieves" and where he approvingly has Captain Cook thinking, "It was a sensible primitive who bowed before a superior civilization" (p. 2). See also—among examples too numerous to cite—his glib description of sacred *hula* as a "frivolous diversion," which, instead of work, the Hawaiians "would practice energetically in the hot sun for days on end . . . their bare brown flesh glistening with sweat" (pp. 65–66). Daws, who repeatedly displays an affection for descriptions of Hawaiian skin color, taught Hawaiian history for some years at the University of Hawai'i; he now holds the Chair of Pacific History at the Australian National University's Institute of Advanced Studies.

Works Cited

Bingham, Hiram. *A Residence of Twenty-one Years in the Sandwich Islands.* 2nd ed. New York: Converse, 1848.

Daws, Gavan. *Shoal of Time: A History of the Hawaiian Islands.* Toronto and New York: Macmillan, 1968.

Dibble, Sheldon. *History of the Sandwich Islands.* Honolulu: Thrum, 1909.

Fanon, Frantz. *The Wretched of the Earth.* New York: Grove, Evergreen Edition, 1968.

Kuykendall, Ralph S. *The Hawaiian Kingdom, 1778–1854.* Honolulu: University of Hawaii Press, 1938.

Lind, Andrew. *An Island Community: Ecological Succession in Hawaii.* New York: Greenwood, 1938.

Tuggle, H. David. "Hawaii." In *The Prehistory of Polynesia,* ed. Jesse D. Jennings, pp. 167–199. Cambridge, Mass.: Harvard Univ. Press, 1979.

READING, REREADING, AND ANALYSIS

1. Working individually or in a group, look at the places where Trask describes the difference between the stories she was told by her family and the stories she learned in school. Have you or the other members of your group experienced similar contradictions between the information, messages, and values you learned at home and what you learned in school? Present one or two of your group's examples to the class and explain how they connect to Trask's experience.

2. In a small group, discuss Trask's attitude towards historians of Hawai'i who do not know the Hawaiian language. Why does Trask place so much emphasis on the Hawaiian language? Organize and present at least one example from her text. Summarize the example in your own words, cite a key sentence or passage, and explain how Trask uses the example to build her argument.

3. Why might historians not have accepted Hawaiian songs and oral tradition as valid historical evidence? What is the difference between, on the one hand, the songs and oral histories and, on the other hand, written records? Why have written records traditionally been accorded greater historical weight?

4. What effect does Trask hope to produce with her epigraph from Kepelino (p. 537)? Why does Trask include language that is unfamiliar to most of her readers?

RESPONDING THROUGH WRITING: BUILDING AN INTERPRETATION

5. Use the results of the Library/Internet search described below to write a longer paper in which you agree or disagree with Trask's assessment of mainstream "Western" histories. In the materials you found, is historic Hawai'i presented as it was in Trask's experience—as a barbarian, feudal society that was "civilized" by its colonizers? What differences do you see? What kinds of evidence do these histories use to back up their claims? To what extent do any of these histories support Trask's claim that Hawai'i was a peaceful, egalitarian culture with a "stewardship" relationship to the land that prevented private ownership? Is Trask making too strong a distinction between Western historians and her own approach or is her condemnation of Western historians justified? Explain your answer.

6. Use examples from Trask and from your own experience to make a case for what constitutes "good" evidence. What evidence do

"Western" historians rely on, according to Trask? What kinds of evidence does she accumulate in order to rebut their claims?

GOING FURTHER: LEARNING FROM OTHER SOURCES

7. Trask writes: "Historians, I realized, were very like missionaries" (p. 538). How can historians, who rely on historical, objective facts and arguments, be compared to missionaries, who preach subservience to a religious order? How can Trask argue that the two worldviews, history and religion, work together? Use library or Internet resources to look up some histories of Hawai'i. These can include everything from encyclopedia entries to old and current histories and textbook accounts. Print the results of your search and share your findings in a group. To what extent do these accounts resemble the faulty histories that Trask deplores? To what extent do these accounts resemble Trask's own view of Hawaiian history? Write a one-page paper summarizing your findings.

8. Use a scholarly database such as Academic Search Elite that includes sources from scholarly journals or one such as MAS Full Text Ultra that includes general-interest and current-events-related magazines, to search terms such as "language and racism" or "language and exclusion." List some of the important issues and debates that occur, and print out several articles or abstracts of articles that relate to Trask's ideas in interesting ways.

APPLYING WHAT YOU'VE LEARNED

9. Using Trask's argument about the importance of oral history, consider the narrative offered by Julie Charlip. How does Charlip offer what Trask refers to as "*our* story"? That is, what references do you see in Charlip's narrative that tie her to her background? How do her tone and her choice of words represent her connection to her past? Charlip is, of course, not Hawaiian. What is the "we" she writes of? Do you see any other connections she shares with Trask?

10. In "Chicana Artists: Exploring *Nepantla, el Lugar de la Frontera*," Gloria Anzaldúa argues that "Border art challenges and subverts the imperialism of the United States, and combats assimilation by either the United States or Mexico, yet it acknowledges its affinities to both cultures" (p. 63). Do you think that Trask's brand of history is a kind of "border art"? Can a historian be a border artist? How should a historian truthfully relate extreme differences of opinion?

Yi-Fu Tuan

Yi-Fu Tuan (b. 1930) is professor emeritus of geography at the University of Wisconsin, Madison, and Founding Director of the Center for American Places. Tuan is known as a pioneer of interdisciplinary scholarship, bringing elements of philosophy, psychology, urban planning, anthropology, and landscape architecture into conversation with a geography that incorporates the study of morals. The son of a Chinese diplomat, Tuan attended schools in China, Australia and the Philippines before landing at Oxford University. He earned his Ph.D. from the University of California–Berkeley and spent his scholarly career teaching in the United States. "Earth" is a chapter from *Escapism*.

> **For photographs of Tuan and more information about his life and work, see <http://www.cwu.edu/~geograph/yi_fu.html>.**

WHAT DO YOU KNOW? WHAT DO YOU EXPECT TO DISCOVER?

Before reading the essay, take a moment to consider the following questions.

1. What topics does Tuan's biography suggest he is interested in? What do you know about those topics? Knowledge can come from personal experience, stories you've heard, other classes you have taken, or other reading you've done.

2. The title, "Earth," is general, as is the subtitle of the essay, "Nature and Culture." Make a list of ideas you associate with "Earth," "Nature," and "Culture."

3. Tuan examines the concept of "escapism" in his essay. What does "escapism" mean to you, and what relationships might the term have to "Earth," "Nature," and "Culture"?

✂

Earth
Nature and Culture

"Escapism" has a somewhat negative meaning in our society and perhaps in all societies. It suggests an inability to face facts— the real world. We speak of escapist literature, for instance, and we tend to judge as escapist places such as mega-shopping malls, fancy resorts, theme parks, or even picture-perfect suburbs. They all lack— in a single word—weight.

Suspicion of escapism has many causes. The most obvious is that no animal can survive unless it perceives its environment as it really is. Daydreaming or wishful thinking would not answer. The hard facts cannot be made to go away by shutting one's eyes. But so far as we know, only humans may withdraw, eyes shut, to ponder the nature of a threat rather than confront it directly, muscles tense, eyes open; only they daydream and engage in wishful thinking. Significantly, only humans have culture. By culture I mean not just certain acquired habits, the manufacture and use of certain tools, but a whole world of thought and belief, habits and customs, skills and artifacts. Culture is more closely linked to the human tendency not to face facts, our ability to escape by one means or another, than we are accustomed to believe. Indeed, I should like to add another definition of what it is to be human to the many that already exist: A human being is an animal who is congenitally indisposed to accept reality as it is. Humans not only submit and adapt, as all animals do; they transform in accordance with a preconceived plan. That is, before transforming, they do something extraordinary, namely, "see" what is not there. Seeing what is not there lies at the foundation of all human culture.

Reality and the Real

What do the words "reality" and "real" mean? Although philosophers do not find it easy to agree on an answer, ordinary thinking people have little difficulty using these words in everyday talk, often in conjunction with their opposites, "fantasy" and "unreal." Such talk, when looked at closely, shows how the meaning of "real" shifts, even radically, as the context changes. A common meaning draws on the model of animal life. The idea is that animals live in the real world, respond as best they can to outside forces and their own nature, free of unsettling images and aspirations. Humans can approach that state of existence by also living close to nature, curbing the imagination and jettisoning excess cultural baggage. Nature itself is real. It is indubitably real to humans when they feel it as a blast of cold wind, a sudden shower, or the skin rash caused by contact with poison ivy. So another meaning of "real" emerges: the real as impact. It is not just nature; it is whatever in nature or in society imposes itself on a human being or group, doing so either suddenly or as a consistently felt pressure. "Reality" in this sense is intractable, and it is indifferent to the needs and desires of particular individuals and groups. Facing reality, then, implies accepting one's essential powerlessness, yielding or adjusting to circumambient forces, taking solace in some local pattern or order that one has created and to which one has become habituated. This "local pattern or order" points to another sense of the real: a small and thoroughly humanized world. Far from being shock or impact, the real is the familiar, the predictable, the nurturing and all-enveloping. Home is the prime example. Home is a place to which one is attached by myriad habits of thought and behavior—culturally acquired, of course, yet in time they become so intimately woven into everyday existence that they seem primordial and the essence of one's being. Moving out of home and the familiar, even when this is voluntary and of short duration, can feel like escapism, sojourn in a fantasy world, less real because less dense and all-encompassing.

Does this conclude the list of commonly accepted meanings of "real"? No. For completion, at least one more sense of the word demands to be added. Disconcertingly, it is the opposite of the one I have just given. In this usage, it is daily life, with its messy details and frustrating lack of definition and completion—its many inconclusive moves and projects twisting and turning as in a fitful dream—that is unreal. Real, by contrast, is the well-told story, the clear image, the well-defined architectural space, the sacred ritual, all of which give a heightened sense of self—a feeling of aliveness.

The Earth

The earth is our home. Trips to the moon, another planet, a distant star, have haunted the human imagination and may even become a commonplace reality one day. But they nevertheless have an aura of fantasy about them. Real life is life on earth; it is here that we have our roots and our being. Geographers study the earth as human habitat or home. Interestingly, they discover that the earth is never quite the home humans want it to be; hence the dreams of flying and of a paradise located elsewhere that are common to many cultures. Most people, when they think of the earth, think not of the entire planet but of a part of it—the part they live in. Wherever they happen to be, provided they have been settled there for some time, they consider home. Yet this is not quite the case either, if only because if it were, there would be no story, no *human* story, to tell; people, like other animals, will be "immersed in nature," as G. W. F. Hegel put it. It is the restless activity that produces the story line. Human beings have been and continue to be profoundly restless. For one reason or another, they are not content with being where they are. They move, or if they stay in place, they seek to rearrange that place. Migration and the in situ transformation of the environment are two major themes—*the* two major themes—in human geography. They both reveal a discontent with the status quo, a desire to escape. Geographers have written voluminously on these themes without using "escape" or "escapism" as a guiding concept. What is to be gained by using it now? The gain is that it forces us to reconsider nature and culture, and thereby who we are and what we aspire to, in productive tandem with "real and imagined," "reality and fantasy"—ideas that traditionally are at the core of humanist scholarship and thinking.

Migration

Migration is clearly a type of escape. Animals move out when their home ground starts to deteriorate. Humans have done so since the earliest times; and it now appears that as they acquired certain critical marks of culture—outstandingly, language around sixty thousand years ago—they became better able to organize themselves in complex ways and meet the challenges of the environment by migrating, sometimes over great distances. To overcome great distance, our remote ancestors must have had not only organizational ability, enormously enhanced by language, but also new technical means at their disposal—seaworthy craft, for example. Such people must have been of lively mind and were, I will assume, quite capable of envisaging "greener pastures" elsewhere and making plans as to how best to reach their destination. By the end of the Ice Age, some twelve thousand years ago, human beings had spread into every kind of natural environment, from the Tropics to the Arctic, the major exceptions being ice sheets and the highest mountains.

Much of the human story can be told as one of migration. People move a short distance to a better hunting ground, richer soil, better economic opportunity, greater cultural stimulus. Short-distance movements are likely to be periodic, their paths winding back on themselves with changing circumstance. Over the years such movements become habit, their circuits habitat. Long-distance migrations, by contrast, are likely to be in one direction and permanent. A certain epic grandeur attaches to them, for migrants must be willing to take steps that make life even more difficult than it already is in the hope of future felicity. Before people make a risky move, they must have information about their destination point. What kinds of information are available? To what extent does the need to believe in a better world at the horizon overrule or distort the "hard facts" that people know? Is reality so constraining and unbearable at home that it becomes the seedbed for wild longings and images? And do these images, by virtue of their simplicity and vividness, seem not a dream but more "real" than the familiar world? A great modern epic of migration is the spread of Europeans to the New World. The United States of America proclaims itself a land of immigrants. It would not want to be known as a "land of escapists," yet many did just that: escape from the intolerable conditions of the Old World for the promises of the New.

Nature and Society

Human restlessness finds release in geographical mobility. It also finds release (and relief) in bringing about local change. The circumstances one wishes to change—to escape from—can be social, political, or economic; it can be a run-down urban neighborhood or a ravaged countryside. And it can be nature. In telling a human story, we may start at any point in time, but if we go back far enough we necessarily have nature, untouched nature, as stage: first the swamp, forest, bush, or desert, then . . . then what? Then humans enter, and our story begins.

In the long run, humans everywhere experience, if not forthrightly recognize, nature as home and tomb, Eden and jungle, mother and ogre, a responsive "thou" and an indifferent "it." Our attitude to nature was and is understandably ambivalent. Culture reflects this ambivalence; it compensates for nature's defects yet fears the consequences of overcompensation. A major defect is nature's undependability and violence. The familiar story of people altering nature can thus be understood as their effort to distance themselves from it by establishing a mediating, more constant world of their own making. The story has many versions. Almost all are anguish-ridden, especially early on, when pioneers had to battle nature for a precarious toehold.

A natural environment can itself seem both nourishing and stable to its human habitants. A tropical forest, for example, provides for the modest needs for hunter-gatherers throughout the year, year after year. However, once a people start to change the forest, even if it is only the making of a modest clearing for crops and a village, the forest can seem to turn into a malevolent force that relentlessly threatens to move in and take over the cleared space. Some such experience of harassment is known to villagers all over the world, though perhaps not to the same degree as in the humid Tropics. Villagers are therefore inclined to see nature in a suspicious light. Of course they know that it provides for their needs and are grateful—a gratitude expressed by gestures and stories of respect. But they also know from hard experience that nature provides grudgingly, and that from time to time it acts with the utmost indifference to human works and lives.

Carving a space out of nature, then, does not ensure stability and ease. To the contrary, it can make people feel more than ever vulnerable. What to do? Lacking physical power, the most basic step they can take is to rope nature into the human world so that it will be responsive—as difficult people are—to social pressures and sanctions. If these don't work, they try placatory ritual, and if this in turn fails, they appeal to the higher authority of heaven or its human regents on earth. By one means or another they seek control, with at best only tenuous success. What appears stable to the visiting ecologist, whose discipline predisposes him to focus on long-range people-environment interactions, may be not stable at all but rather full of uncertainty to the local inhabitants struggling to survive from day to day, week to week, one season to another.

Aztec and Chinese

Now, suppose we turn to a more advanced society, one in which the people, unlike isolated and poorly equipped villagers, have the technical and organizational means to make extensive permanent clearings, raise crops, and build monuments, including cities. Won't the exercising of that power and the looming presence of large human works impress on them a sense of their own efficacy and the world's permanence?

The answer is, Not always. The Aztecs of Mexico are a case in point. Here is a people who continued to feel insecure despite the scope and sophistication of their material attainments. Nature's instabilities, made evident by the ominous presence of volcanoes and experienced repeatedly in the wayward behavior of weather, stream flow, and lake level, more than overruled whatever reassurance human artifacts could give. Moreover, in the Aztec civilization the architectural monuments of temple and altar themselves attested more to fear and anxiety than to confidence, for they were built to conduct human sacrifice, with the end in view of sustaining and regulating the enfeebled forces of the cosmos.

Consider another, more confident civilization, the Chinese. The Chinese struggled to regulate nature through physical intervention and by such institutional means as the establishment of public granaries. In these respects the two civilizations, Aztec and Chinese, had something in common. However, unlike the Aztecs, the Chinese managed to sustain over the course of millennia, and in the teeth of abundant contrary evidence, a magnificent model of cosmic harmony. This ability to overlook evidence may earn the Chinese the label of escapists, but without it—without their tenacious hold on the dream of harmony—they would have deprived themselves of optimism and fortitude, psychological advantages that helped them to create an enduring culture. To the Chinese architect-engineer, barriers such as swamp, forest, and hillock could be overcome; they did not have to be accepted as embossed in the eternal order of things. And to the Chinese philosopher—indeed, to the philosopher in any culture—wayward facts and contingencies were not just there to be noted and accepted; rather, they were puzzling pieces of reality that could stimulate one to search for a more comprehensive world-view.

Chinese composure has its source in a number of factors. Tangible architectural and engineering achievements no doubt promoted confidence, as did the memory of extended periods of peace and prosperity during a great dynasty such as the Han, T'ang, or Sung. The Chinese inclination to see the universe as orderly and hence accessible to reason surely also promoted composure. Even more reassuring—more wishful and escapist, from our secularist-modern perspective—is the idea that the universe is moral and hence responsive to moral suasion. China has had its share of natural disasters; these might well have been more devastating and frequent than those that afflicted the Aztec empire. When disasters visited China and could not be alleviated by ordinary means, the emperor took responsibility, for he considered them to be a consequence of his own moral failing. To reestablish order, he "memorialized heaven," imposing a penance on himself on his own and humankind's behalf. As exemplary man, the emperor was the ultimate mediator between heaven and earth; and for this reason he could by his own conduct and sacrifice right wrong, restore harmony throughout the worlds of nature and of people. The emperor was called Son of Heaven rather than Son of Earth. There is no doubt a heavenward tilt in Chinese high culture, as there is in all high cultures. What high culture offers is escape from bondage to earth.

Premodern and Early Modern Europe

Escape from nature's vagaries and violence—except during a blizzard or hurricane—may seem a strange idea to modern Westerners, for whom society rather than nature is unpredictable and violent. How short is their memory! Any full account of life and livelihood in the West from the Middle Ages to the eighteenth century must give a prominent role to weather—that is, if we are more interested in ordinary people than in potentates and their political high jinks. So much misery had its immediate cause in meteorological freakishness. Too much rain or too little, prolonged cold or withering heat, led to crop failure and, all too often—at least locally—to famine and starvation.

Records from the early modern period show how frequently people even in the richest parts of Europe suffered and died from lack of food. In 1597 a citizen of Newcastle wrote of "sundry starving and dying in our streets and in the fields for lack of bread." And this despite importation of foreign grain into the port city. In France, rather than the sort of cosmic stability to be expected from a Sun King, wild swings of lean and fat years seemed more the rule. In 1661–62 much of France was afflicted by bad weather, poor harvests, and famine. Beggars from the countryside flocked to the towns, where citizens formed militias to drive them back. Good weather produced good harvests in 1663; there followed a decade of prosperity. From 1674 onward, however, the times were once more "out of joint." A wet summer curtailed the harvests of 1674; those of 1677, 1678, and 1679 were worse. Yields were again poor in 1681 and catastrophic in some regions in 1684. Between 1679 and 1684 the death toll rose throughout much of France. Good weather prevailed from 1684 to 1689; magnificent harvests made for cheap grain, and the people were, for a change, more than adequately fed. Then came the great famine of 1693–94, the culmination of a succession of cold and wet years. A majority of people in France suffered, though in varying degree. Poor folks resorted to eating "such unclean things as cats and the flesh of horses flayed and cast on to dung heaps," and some starved to death.

In premodern and early modern Europe, uncertainty in both nature and society put a heavy burden on the poor. That hardly surprises us. More difficult for us to imagine now is how uncertainty could haunt the well-to-do, even the rich and the powerful. When uncertainty is so much a fact of life, escape into a make-believe world of perfect order may be excused. Make-believe was one way—an important way—that Renaissance princes coped. They produced elaborate masques in which they themselves sometimes played the roles of gods and goddesses reigning in a pastoral heaven of abundance and peace. If ordinary people sought to exclude unruly weather by putting a roof over their heads, Renaissance rulers did that and far more. By means of the art at their command they produced an alternative heaven: the palace itself and, even more overtly, the theatrical stage of floating clouds, flying chariots, pastures and billowing fields of surpassing fertility.

What was the nature of this art? Shakespeare hinted at it in the magic powers of Prospero. A Renaissance prince was a Prospero—a magician. A magician was not the marginal entertainer we now see him to be. Rather, he was considered a person of deep knowledge—someone who knew how things worked below the surface and so could do wonders. Whereas a prince only purchased such power, a genius like Leonardo da Vinci possessed it in his own person to a remarkable degree. It doesn't seem to me far-fetched to call Leonardo a magician. Indeed, a much later figure, Isaac Newton, has been called a magician, the last one. An important difference, however, separates a Renaissance figure like Leonardo and the outstanding genius of a later time, Newton: Leonardo approached knowledge through art, technique, and technology, skills that would have been necessary to the making of the sort of surrogate heaven that Renaissance princes yearned for. By contrast, Newton showed little interest in the earthbound phenomena such as anatomy and geology that fascinated Leonardo. Nor was he concerned with building a surrogate heaven on earth in the manner of an artist-architect. Rather, his gaze was directed to heaven itself, and his singular contribution to knowledge was through the abstractions of mathematics.

Physical vs. Biological Science: Heaven vs. Earth

Alfred North Whitehead, an outstanding mathematician-philosopher of our time, famously designated the seventeenth century the Century of Genius. He gave twelve names: Bacon, Harvey, Kepler, Galileo, Descartes, Pascal, Huyghens, Boyle, Newton, Locke, Spinoza, and Leibniz. He apologized for the predominance of Englishmen, then noted without apology that he had only one biologist on the list: Harvey. Genius in that century showed itself in celestial mechanics and physics rather than in biology or organic nature, to which humans belong and upon which they depend. At the threshold of the modern age, human helplessness—the recurrent famines and starvation I mentioned earlier—continued to exist even in the developed parts of Europe; on the other hand, the laws of celestial nature were being mapped with unprecedented accuracy. On earth, both nature and human affairs often seemed to verge on chaos; heaven, by contrast, exhibited perfect order. Cosmic order gave the natural philosophers of the seventeenth century confidence, as it has given confidence to priest-kings throughout human history. In premodern times, rulers believed that the regularities discernible above could somehow be brought down below. In early modern Europe, natural philosophers had grounds for hoping that the rigorous method that opened the secrets of heaven could work similar wonders on earth. For two centuries, however, there was hardly any link between the splendid theoretical reaches of the new science and applications that catered to ordinary human needs. Agricultural advances during the eighteenth century had more to do with changes in practice (crop rotation, for example), in a more systematic use of knowledge gained through centuries of trial and error, in changes of land tenure and ownership, and suchlike than with the bright discoveries of an abstract, mechanistic, heaven-inspired science.

To this observation a critic may say, "Well, what do you expect? The challenges of agriculture can be met only by close attention to the intricacies and interdependencies of land and life, to what is happening at our feet and before our eyes rather than in a scientist's playpen (the laboratory), or by seeking models of analysis and conceptualization suited to the world of astronomy and physics. In short, to live well, one needs more down-to-earth realism, not escapism."

This sensible answer has its own difficulties. As we now know, what may be deemed escapism turns out to be a circuitous route to unprecedented manipulative power over organic life, and not just predictive power over the stars. One branch of the route took the scientific and entrepreneurial spirits of the West from the study of general chemistry to the study of soil chemistry, and from there to the manufacture of chemical fertilizers, the use of which led to impressively higher crop yields; another branch took them from the study of genetics to the scientific breeding of plants and animals, which became more and more ingenious, reaching a high peak in the Green Revolution, and onward to genetic engineering. While all this was taking place, the same theoretic-analytic bent of mind produced agricultural machines of increasing power and flexibility, and, one might add, the complex organizational and marketing strategies of advanced farming. Countries that embraced these discoveries and inventions prospered. In the second half of the twentieth century, cornucopia no longer seems just a dream, as it has been for the vast majority of people throughout human time. A substantial number of people in the developed parts of the world encounter it day after day. They have learned to take the supermarket's dazzling pyramids of fruits and vegetables, its esplanades of meat, for granted. And yet a doubt lingers as to whether such abundance is real and can last, whether it is not just an effect of Prospero's magic wand. The upward curve of success in the West has not altogether removed the feeling that technological society must, sooner or later, pay for its arrogation of powers that rightly belong only to nature and nature's God.

Escape to Nature

I have given a brief and sweeping account of "escape from nature," which has taken us from uncertain yields in village clearings to supermarket cornucopia. The escape is made possible by different kinds of power: the power of humans working cooperatively and, deliberatively together, the power of technology, and underlying them, the power of images and ideas. The realities thus created do, however, necessarily produce contentment. They may, on the contrary, generate frustration and restlessness. Again people seek to escape—this time "back to nature."

Escaping or returning to nature is a well-worn theme. I mention it to provide a counterpoint to the story of escaping *from* nature, but also to draw attention to certain facets of the "back to nature" sentiment that have not yet entered the common lore. One is the antiquity of this sentiment. A yearning for the natural and the wild goes back almost to the beginning of city building in ancient Sumer. A hint of it can already be found in the epic of Gilgamesh, which tells of the natural man Enkidu, who was seduced by gradual steps to embrace the refinements of civilization, only to regret on his deathbed what he had left behind: a free life cavorting with gazelles.

The second point I wish to underline is this: Although a warm sentiment for nature is common among urban sophisticates, as we know from well-documented European and East Asian history, it is not confined to them. The extreme artificiality of a built environment is not itself an essential cause or inducement. Consider the Lele of Kasai in tropical Africa. They do not have cities, yet they know what it is like to yearn for nature. What they wish to escape from is the modestly humanized landscape they have made from the savanna next to the Kasai River, for to keep everything there in good order—from social relations to huts and groundnut plots—they must be constantly vigilant, and that proves burdensome. To find relief, the Lele men periodically leave behind the glare and heat of the savanna, with its interminable chores and obligations, to plunge into the dark, cool, and nurturing rain forest on the other side of the river, which to them is the source of all good things, a gift of God.

The third point is that "back to nature" varies enormously in scale. At one end of the scale are such familiar and minor undertakings as the weekend camping trip to the forest and, more permanently, the return to a rural commune way of life. At the other end of the scale is the European settlement of North America itself. It too might be considered a type of "escape to nature." Old Europe was the city; the New World was nature. True, many settlers came from Europe's rural towns and villages rather than from its large cities. Nevertheless, they were escaping from a reality that seemed too firmly set and densely packed to the spaces and simpler ways of life in the New World.

My final point is this: Back-to-nature movements at all scales, including the epic scale of transatlantic migration, have seldom resulted in the abandonment, or even serious depletion, of populations in the home bases—the major cities and metropolitan fields, which over time have continued to gain inhabitants and to further distance themselves from nature.

This last point serves to remind us that "escape to nature" is dependent on "escape *from* nature." The latter is primary and inexorable. It is so because pressures of population and social constraint must build up first before the desire to escape from them can arise; and I have already urged that these pressures are themselves a consequence of culture—of our desire and ability to escape from nature. "Escape from nature" is primary for another reason, namely, that the nature one escapes to, because it is the target of desire rather than a vague "out there" to which one is unhappily thrust, must have been culturally delineated and endowed with value. What we wish to escape to is not "nature" but an alluring conception of it, and this conception is necessarily a product of a people's experience and history—their culture. Paradoxical as it may sound, "escape to nature" is a cultural undertaking, a covered-up attempt to "escape from nature."

Nature and Culture

Nature is culturally defined, a point of view that is by now widely accepted among environmental theorists. Culturally defined? Humanly constituted? Is this the latest eruption of hubris in the Western world? Not necessarily, for the idea can reasonably be coupled with another one, inspired by Wittgenstein, namely this: That which is defined and definable, that which can be encompassed by language or image, may be just a small part of all there is—Nature with a capital *N*. Now, in this chapter I myself have been using the word "nature" in a restricted sense—nature with a small *n*. What do I mean by it? What is the culture that has influenced me? It is the culture of academic geography. The meaning that I give the word is traditional among geographers: Nature is that layer of the earth's surface and the air above it that have been unaffected, or minimally affected, by humans; hence, the farther back we reach in time, the greater will be the extent of nature. Another way of putting it is this: Nature is what remains or what can recuperate over time when all humans and their works are removed.

These ideas of nature are a commonplace in today's world, thanks in part to their popularization in the environmental movement. They seem nonarbitrary, an accurate reflection of a common type of human experience and not just the fantasy of a particular people and time. But is this true? I believe it is. The nature/culture distinction, far from being an academic artifact, is recognized, though in variant forms, in all civilized societies—"civilized" itself being a self-conscious self-designation that postulates an opposite that is either raw and crude or pure and blissful. More generally, the distinction is present—in the subtext, if not the text—whenever and wherever humans have managed to create a material world of their own, even if this be no more than a rough clearing in which are located a few untidy fields and huts. I have already referred to the Lele in Africa. Their appreciation for a pure nature away from womenfolk, society, and culture is as romantic (and sexist) as that of modern American males. Thousands of miles away live the Gimi of New Guinea, another people of simple material means, whose bipolar *kore/dusa* is roughly equivalent to our "nature/culture." *Dusa* is the cultural and social world, opposed to *kore,* which means "wild"—the rain forest with forms of life, plant and animal, that occur spontaneously and hence are "pure."

What about hunter-gatherers, who live off nature and have not carved a permanent cultural space from it? "Nature/culture" is unlikely to be a part of their vocabulary; they don't need it in their intimate, personal, and constant involvement with the individualized, all-encompassing natural elements. But since they undoubtedly feel at home in the midst of these elements, what an outsider calls wild and natural is to them not that at all; rather, it is a world acculturated by naming, storytelling, rituals, personal experience. This familiar world is bounded. Hunter-gatherers are aware that it ends somewhere—at this cliff or that river. Beyond is the Unknown, which, however, is not "nature" as understood by other peoples. It is too underdefined, too far beyond language and experience, to be that.

A current trend in anthropological thinking is to wonder whether the nature/culture dichotomy is not more an eighteenth-century European invention than anything fundamental to human experience. The binary in Western usage has fallen into disfavor because it is considered too categorical or abstract, and because it almost invariably sets up a rank order with women somehow ending at the bottom, whether they be identified with nature or with culture. One may also raise the linguistic conundrum of how far meanings must overlap to justify the use of European-language terms for non-European ones. I now offer one more reason for the declining popularity of the nature/culture binary. It is that one of the two terms has come to be dominant. In our time, culture seems to have taken over nature. Hardly any place on earth is without some human imprint. True, nature in the large sense includes the molten interior of the earth and the distant stars, and these we have not touched. But even they bear our mental imprint. Our minds have played over them; they are, as it were, our mental/cultural constructs. The ubiquity of culture in the life experience of modern people is surprisingly like that of hunter-gatherers, who, as I have indicated, live almost wholly in a cultural world with no nature, separate and equal, to act as a counterweight. There remains what I have called Nature with the capital *N*. But it, like the Unknown of hunter-gatherers, is beyond thought, words, and pictures. Whatever we touch and modify, whatever we see or even think about, falls into the cultural side of the ledger, leaving the other side devoid of content. Culture is, in this sense, everywhere. But far from feeling triumphant, modern men and women feel "orphaned." A reality that is merely a world ("world" derives from *wer* = man) can seem curiously unreal, even if that world is functional and harmonious, which is far from being always the case. The possibility that everywhere we look we see only our own faces is not reassuring; indeed, it is a symptom of madness. In order to feel real, sane, and anchored, we need nature as impact—the "bites and blows [of wind] upon my body . . . that feelingly persuade me what I am" (Shakespeare, *As You Like It* 2.I.8, II); and we may even need nature as that which forever eludes the human mind.

But this hardly exhausts the twists and turns in meaning of nature/culture, real/imaginary. So the real is impact—the unassimilable and natural. But, as I have noted earlier, the opposite can seem more true. The real is the cultural. The cultural trumps the natural by appearing not so much humanmade as spiritual or divine. Thus, the cosmic city is more real than wilderness. The poem is more real than vague feeling. The ritual is more real than everyday life. In all of them there is a psychological factor that enhances the sense of the real and couples it with the divine, namely, lucidity. My own exposition of nature and culture, to the extent that it seems to me lucidly revelatory, is more real to me than whatever confused experiences I have of both. When I am thinking and writing well, I feel I have escaped to the real.

Escape to the Real and the Lucid

I began this chapter by noting that escapism has a somewhat negative meaning because of the common notion that what one escapes from is reality and what one escapes to is fantasy. People say, "I am fed up with snow and slush and the hassles of my job, so I am going to Hawaii." Hawaii here stands for paradise and hence the unreal. In place of Hawaii, one can substitute any number of other things: from a good book and the movies to a tastefully decorated shopping mall and Disneyland, from a spell in the suburbs or the countryside to a weekend at a first-rate hotel in Manhattan or Paris. In other societies and times, the escape might be to a storyteller's world, a communal feast, a village fair, a ritual. What one escapes to is culture—not culture that has become daily life, not culture as a dense and inchoate environment and way of coping, but culture that exhibits lucidity, a quality that often comes out of a process of simplification. Lucidity, I maintain, is almost always desirable. About simplification, however, one can feel ambivalent. If, for example, a people's experience of a place or event is one of simplification, they may soon feel bored and dismiss it—in retrospect, if not at that time—as a thinly constructed fantasy of no lasting significance. Escape into it from time to time, though understandable, is suspect. If, however, their experience has more the feel of clarity than of simplification, they may well regard it as an encounter with the real. Escape into a good book is escape into the real, as the late French president François Mitterrand insisted. Participation in a ritual is participation in something serious and real; it is escape from the banality and opaqueness of life into an event that clarifies life and yet preserves a sense of mystery.

To illustrate the wide acceptance of the idea that whatever is lucid feels real, consider two worlds of experience that superficially have nothing in common: academia and wild nature. Society at large has often called academia "an ivory tower," implying that life there is not quite real. Academics themselves see otherwise; it is their view that if they escape from certain entanglements of "real life," it is only so that they may better engage with the real, and it is this engagement with the real that makes what they do so deeply rewarding. And how do they engage with the real? The short answer is, Through processes and procedures of simplification that produce clarity and a quasi-aesthetic sense of having got the matter under study right. Now, consider wild nature. A sojourn in its midst may well be regarded as an escape into fantasy, far from the frustrations and shocks of social life.

Yet nature lovers see otherwise. For them, the escape into nature is an escape into the real. One reason for this feeling certainly does not apply to academia. It is that the real *is* the natural, the fundament that has not been disturbed or covered up by human excrescences. What academia and nature share—perhaps the only outstanding characteristic that they share—is simplicity. Academic life is self-evidently a simpler organization than the greater society in which it is embedded. As for nature, in what sense is it simple or simpler—and simpler than what? However the answer is given, one thing is certain: People of urban background—and increasingly people are of such background—know little about plants and animals, soils and rock, even if they now live in exurbia or have a home in rural Idaho. Other than the few trained naturalists among them, their images of nature tend to be highly selective and schematic; indeed, for lack of both knowledge and experience, they may well carry reductionism further in the imaging of nature than in the imaging of social life, with the result that nature becomes the more clearly delineated of the two, more comprehensible, and therefore more real.

Middle Landscapes As Ideal and Real

Between the big artificial city at one extreme and wild nature at the other, humans have created "middle landscapes" that, at various times and in different parts of the world, have been acclaimed the model human habitat. They are, of course, all works of culture, but not conspicuously or arrogantly so. They show how humans can escape nature's rawness without moving so far from it as to appear to deny roots in the organic world. The middle landscape also earns laurels because it can seem more real—more what life is or ought to be like—compared with the extremes of nature and city, both of which can seem unreal for contradictory reasons of thinness and inchoateness. Thinness occurs when nature is reduced to pretty image and city is reduced to geometric streets and high-rises; inchoateness occurs when nature and city have become a jungle, confused and disorienting. Historically, however, the middle landscape has its problems serving as ideal habitat. One problem is that it is not one, but many. Many kinds of landscape qualify as "middle"—for example, farmland, suburbia, garden city and garden, model town, and theme parks that emphasize the good life. They all distance themselves from wild nature and the big city but otherwise have different values. The second problem is that the middle landscape, whatever the kind, proves unstable. It reverts to nature, or, more often, it moves step by step toward the artifices of the city even as it strives to maintain its position in the middle.

Of the different kinds of middle landscape, the most important by far, economically, is the land given over to agriculture. People who live on and off the land are rooted in place. Peasant farmers all over the world—the mass of human population until well into the twentieth century—live, work, and die in the confines of their village and its adjoining fields. So the label "escapist" has the least application to them. Indeed, they and their way of life can so blend into nature that to visitors from the city they are nature—elements of a natural scene. That merging into nature is enhanced by another common perception of peasant life: its quality of "timelessness." Culture there is visibly a conservative force. To locals and outsiders alike, its past as a succession of goals, repeatedly met or—for lack of power—renounced, is lost to consciousness. Yet farmers, like everybody else, make improvements whenever they can and with whatever means they have. Their culture has taken cumulative steps forward, though these are normally too gradual to be noticed. Of course, one can find exceptions in the better endowed and politically more sophisticated parts of the world—Western Europe in the eighteenth century, for example. There, science in the broad sense of the systematic application of useful knowledge enabled agriculture to move from triumph to triumph in the next two hundred years, with far-ranging consequences, including one of psychological unease. An "unbearable lightness of being" was eventually to insinuate itself into the one area of human activity where people have felt—and many still feel—that they ought to be more bound than free. Nostalgia for traditional ways of making a living on the family farm is at least in part a wish to regain a sense of weight and necessity, of being subjected to demands of nature that allow little or no room for fanciful choice.

The garden is another middle landscape between wild nature and the city. Although the word evokes the natural, the garden itself is manifestly an artifact. In China one speaks of "building" a garden, whereas in Europe one may speak of "planting" a garden. The difference suggests that the Chinese, unlike Europeans, are more ready to admit the garden's artifactual character. Because artifice connotes civilization to the Chinese elite, it doesn't have quite the negative meaning it has for Europeans brought up on stories of prelapsarian Eden and on Romantic conceptions of nature. European gardens were originally planted to meet certain basic needs around the house: food, medicinal herbs, and suchlike. In early medieval times they were an indiscriminate mixture of the useful and the beautiful, as much horticulture as art. Progressively, however, the gardens of the potentates moved in the direction of aesthetics and architecture. From the sixteenth century onward, first in Renaissance Italy, then in Baroque France, gardens were proudly built to project an air of power and artifice. The technical prowess that made playful foundations and mechanical animals possible, together with the garden's traditional link to the phantasms of theater, resulted in the creation of an illusionary world remote indeed from its humble beginnings close to the soil and livelihood.

A striking example of the pleasure garden in our century is the Disney theme park—a unique American creation that, thanks to modern technology, is able to produce wonder and illusion far beyond that which could be achieved in earlier times. Unique too is the theme park's erasure of the present in favor of not only a mythic past but also a starry future—in favor, moreover, of a frankly designed Fantasyland peopled by characters from fairy tales and from Disney's own fertile imagination. What is more escapist than that? In the spectrum of middle landscapes, a countryside of villages and fields stands at the opposite pole to a Disney park. The one lies closest to nature; the other is as far removed from it as possible without becoming "city." Disney's carefully designed and controlled world has often been criticized for encouraging a childish and irresponsible frame of mind. But again my question is, What if culture *is*, in a fundamental sense, a mechanism of escape? To see culture as escape or escapism is to share a disposition common to all who have had some experience in exercising power—a disposition that is unwilling to accept "what is the case" (reality) when it seems to them unjust or too severely constraining. Of course, their efforts at escaping, whether purely in imagination or by taking tangible steps, may fail—may end in disaster for themselves, for other people, for nature. The human species uniquely confronts the dilemma of a powerful imagination that, while it makes escape to a better life possible, also makes possible lies and deception, solipsistic fantasy, madness, unspeakable cruelty, violence, and destructiveness—evil.

1998

READING, REREADING, AND ANALYSIS

1. What are some of the ways Tuan uses the terms "escapism," "reality," and "the real"?

2. Individually or in a group, explain why Tuan can claim that "daily life is real" and that "daily life is unreal."

3. Individually or in a group, make a list of the contrasts Tuan presents between the Aztecs and the Chinese. How is the contrast Tuan identifies significant to what you see as his larger arguments in his essay?

4. Think about Tuan's claim that "seeing what is not there lies at the foundation of all human culture" (p. 548). Do you agree? Spend twenty minutes freewriting on this topic.

5. Consider Tuan's distinctions between "nature" and "Nature" and between nature and culture. How do these oppositions operate or make sense? Make a list of questions you have about the distinctions Tuan sees and discusses.

6. What does Tuan mean on page 560, when he says, "What one escapes to is culture—not culture that has become daily life, not culture as a dense and inchoate environment and way of coping, but culture that exhibits lucidity, a quality that often comes out of a process of simplification. Lucidity, I maintain, is almost always desirable. About simplification, however, one can feel ambivalent."

RESPONDING THROUGH WRITING: BUILDING AN INTERPRETATION

7. In a brief essay (two or three pages), discuss the following claim from Tuan's essay: "In the long run, humans everywhere experience, if not forthrightly recognize, nature as home and tomb, Eden and jungle, mother and ogre, a responsive 'thou' and an indifferent 'it.' Our attitude toward nature was and is understandably ambivalent" (p. 551).

8. Write an essay in which you demonstrate through examples from your own experience the difference between "escape from" and "escape to." When you think about escaping, where do you imagine yourself going? How would it be different from where you are? Use examples from Tuan's essay as a way of explaining your own examples.

9. Write a short essay that describes a site of escape, such as Disney World, another theme park, or some other location. What fosters escape at the site you describe and why might someone criticize the escape you discuss? You might refer to Tuan's discussion of Disney in your paper.

10. Write a short essay that summarizes and then responds to the following quotation from Tuan's essay: "Human beings have been and continue to be profoundly restless. For one reason or another, they are not content with being where they are. They move, or if they stay in place, they seek to rearrange that place" (p. 550). As you write about the quotation, incorporate your own experience into your response or the experience of a family member or friend.

GOING FURTHER: LEARNING FROM OTHER SOURCES

11. Look up brochures or websites for travel destinations while considering Tuan's ideas about escape. Are the places you see advertised as "escapes"? Look carefully at your examples, and take

notes on how vacations are represented. Find a place in Tuan's essay where he provides an idea or a statement that applies to your example.

12. Search for the term "escapism" using a database of scholarly articles, such as Academic Search Elite, or a database, such as MAS Full Text Ultra, that includes general-interest and current-events-related magazines. Try related searches such as "nature and escapism" or "environment and escape." Scan your findings and print out one or two articles that seem to relate to Tuan's ideas in interesting ways.

APPLYING WHAT YOU'VE LEARNED

13. Compare Tuan's idea of "the real" with Jeanette Winterson's discussion of "reality" in her essay, "Imagination and Reality." Why do both writers seize on "reality" as an idea to be challenged? Do these writers share common ground on the issue? Would either Winterson or Tuan see art as an escape?

14. Write an essay in which you test Tuan's claim that "a human being is an animal who is congenitally indisposed to accept reality as it is" by looking at Witold Rybczynski's discussion of dream houses in "Designs for Escape" and Richard Florida discussion of creativity in "The Transformation of Everyday Life." Although these essays may seem, on the surface, quite different, thinking about a way or ways to connect them can help you test Tuan's claim.

15. Examine Tuan's concept of the "middle landscape," and use it to analyze other potential middle landscapes in the essays you read. For example, does Susan Willis's discussion of Disney World support Tuan's analysis? Is Gloria Anzaldúa's borderland in "Chicana Artists: Exploring *Nepantla, el Lugar de la Frontera*", a middle landscape? What do you learn by applying Tuan's concept of the middle landscape to these two examples?

SHERRY TURKLE

Sherry Turkle (b. 1948) is a licensed clinical psychologist and the Abby Rockefeller Mauze Professor of Social Studies of Science and Technology, and Director of the Initiative on Technology and the Self at the Massachusetts Institute of Technology. Her work in psychology has become increasingly concerned with the impact of technology on the human mind. In addition to three books, Turkle has written numerous articles, book reviews, and commentaries for scholarly and popular audiences. She is a frequent lecturer and a regular guest on both television and radio. "The Triumph of Tinkering" is a section from *Life on the Screen: Identity in the Age of the Internet* (1995).

> To learn more about Turkle and her current research, visit her homepage at <http://web.mit.edu/sturkle/www/>.

WHAT DO YOU KNOW? WHAT DO YOU EXPECT TO DISCOVER?

Before reading the essay, take a moment to consider the following questions.

1. Do you have a "style" of thinking, a personal way of processing information and ideas? How does that style affect the way you read and the way you write?

2. Can computers be used to spur creativity? List all the creative uses of computers that you can think of. In what ways do computers limit creativity? Overall, have computers helped or hindered imagination?

3. Do women and men think or solve problems in different ways? Give at least one specific example to help you establish your position.

❧

The Triumph of Tinkering

In the late 1960s, I studied history and political theory in Paris. In my academic program, all foreigners had to take a French composition class. Over the year, the format of this class never varied. A subject was set, everyone had one week to turn in an outline and two more to write the composition. Then the three-week cycle would begin again with the assignment of a new topic. The format of the composition never varied. Each one had to be written in three parts, with each of these parts further divided into three parts. Although I knew many of my classmates took to this style easily, for me this was a completely alien way of writing. My way had been to read, think, and make notes on little pieces of paper. I would spread these notes out in my room, across my bed, desk, and floor. Then I would immerse myself in their contents, move them around into patterns, scribble in their margins, associate to new patterns, write small bits of text, and frequently rewrite sections. Now, under pressure from the new rules, I developed a technique for getting by. I did my reading and thinking, wrote my notes and bits of text, spread them out in my room, and let my composition emerge—but I did all this in the first week, periodically adjusting the emerging composition so that it would grow with the right number of divisions and subdivisions. After a week of hectic activity, I extracted an outline in three parts. I turned in that outline and put the completed composition in my desk drawer, where it waited two weeks for its turn to be handed in to the instructor.

I am tempted to tell this story in a way that makes it sound like a triumph of my creativity over Gallic rigidity. But that would miss an important aspect of what these French lessons meant to me. Far from increasing my confidence, they undermined it. I wrote my composition before my outline in order to survive, but in the process I came to think of my kind of writing as wrong. My kind of writing was, after all, cheating. The instructor in my 1978 programming class at Harvard—the one who called the computer a giant calculator—described programming methods in universal terms, which he said were justified by the computer's essential nature. But from the very beginning of my inquiries into the computer culture, it became clear that different people approach programming in very different ways. Where my professor saw the necessary hegemony of a single correct style, I found a range of effective yet diverse styles among both novices and experts.

The "universal" method recommended by my Harvard instructor is known as structured programming. A model of the modernist style, it is rule-driven and relies on top-down planning. First you sketch out a master plan in which you make very explicit what your program must do. Then you break the task into manageable subprograms or subprocedures, which you work on separately. After you create each piece, you name it according to its function and close it off, a procedure known as black boxing. You need not bother with its details again. By the 1970s, this structured, planner's method was widely accepted as the canonical style in computing. Indeed, many engineers and computer scientists still see it as the definitive procedure, as simply the way things must be done. They have a powerful, practical rationale for this method. In real organizations, many people have to be able to understand and use any particular piece of software. That means it has to be understandable and fixable (debuggable) long after its programmer has left the research team or business setting.

Others, however, had a style of programming that bore a family resemblance to my associative style of writing, a "soft" style as opposed to a "hard" one. It was bottom-up rather than top-down. It was built up by playing with the elements of a program, the bits of code, much as I played with the elements of my essay, the bits of paper strewn across my room. It is best captured by a word, bricolage, that Claude Lévi-Strauss has used to contrast the analytic methodology of Western science with an associative science of the concrete practiced in many non-Western societies. The tribal herbalist, for example, does not proceed by abstraction but by thinking through problems using the materials at hand. By analogy, problem-solvers who do not proceed from top-down design but by arranging and rearranging a set of well-known materials can be said to be practicing bricolage. They tend to try one thing, step back, reconsider, and try another. For planners, mistakes are steps in the wrong direction; bricoleurs navigate through midcourse corrections. Bricoleurs approach problem-solving by entering into a relationship with their work materials that has more the flavor of a conversation than a monologue. In the context of programming, the bricoleur's work is marked by a desire to play with lines of computer code, to move them around almost as though they were material things—notes on a score, elements of a collage, words on a page.

Through the mid-1980s, soft-style programmers, programming's bricoleurs, received their own discouraging "French lessons" from a mainstream computer culture deeply committed to structured programming. People who did not program according to the canon were usually told that their way was wrong. They were forced to comply with the officially sanctioned method of doing things. Today, however, there has been a significant change. As the computer culture's center of gravity has shifted from programming to dealing with screen simulations, the intellectual values of bricolage have become far more important. In the 1970s and 1980s, computing served as an initiation into the formal values of hard mastery. Now, playing with simulation encourages people to develop the skills of the more informal soft mastery because it is so easy to run "What if?" scenarios and tinker with the outcome.

The revaluation of bricolage in the culture of simulation includes a new emphasis on visualization and the development of intuition through the manipulation of virtual objects. Instead of having to follow a set of rules laid down in advance, computer users are encouraged to tinker in simulated microworlds. There, they learn about how things work by interacting with them. One can see evidence of this change in the way businesses do their financial planning, architects design buildings, and teenagers play with simulation games.

There is something ironic about the computer presence playing a role in nurturing such "informalist" ways of knowing, since for so long, the computer was seen as the ultimate embodiment of the abstract and formal. But the computer's intellectual personality has always had another side. Computational objects—whether lines of codes or icons on a screen—are like abstract and mathematical objects, defined by the most formal of rules. But at the same time, they are like physical objects—like dabs of paint or cardboard cutouts. You can see them and move them, and in some cases you can place one on top of another. Computational objects have always offered an almost-physical access to the world of formal systems. There have always been people whose way of interacting with them had more in common with the style of the painter than with that of the logician.

Consider Lisa, an eighteen-year-old freshman in my Harvard programming course. Lisa's first experiences in the course were very positive. She wrote poetry and found that she was able to approach programming with ways of thinking that she had previously found useful in working with words. But as the term progressed, she came under increasing pressure from her instructors to think in ways that were not her own. Her alienation did not stem from an inability to cope with programming but rather from her preference to do it in a way that came into conflict with the structured and rule-driven style of the computer culture she had entered.

In high school, Lisa had turned away from her own natural abilities in mathematics. "I didn't care if I was good at it. I wanted to work in worlds where languages had moods and connected you with people." She was equally irritated when her teachers tried to get her interested in mathematics by calling it a language. As a senior in high school, she wrote a poem that expressed her sentiments.

> *If you could say in numbers what I say now in words,*
> *If theorems could, like sentences, describe the flight of birds,*
> *If PPL [a computer language] had meter and parabolas had rhyme,*
> *Perhaps I'd understand you then,*
> *Perhaps I'd change my mind. . . .*

But all this wishful thinking only serves to make things worse,
When I compare my dearest love with your numeric verse.
For if mathematics were a language, I'd succeed, I'd scale the hill,
I know I'd understand, but since it's not, I never will.

When she wrote poetry, Lisa knew where all the elements were at every point in the development of her ideas. "I feel my way from one word to another," she said. She wanted her relationship to computer language to be the same. She wanted to tinker, to work as close to the programming code as she did to the words in her poems. When she spoke about the lines of code in her programs, she gestured with her hands and body in a way that showed her moving them and among them. She talked about the elements of her programs as if they were physically graspable.

When Lisa worked on large programs she preferred to write her own smaller subprograms even though she was encouraged to use prepackaged ones available in a program library. She resented that she couldn't tinker with the prepackaged routines. Her teachers chided her, insisting that her demand for hands-on contact was making her work more difficult. They told her that the right way to do things was to control a program by planning. Lisa recognized the value of these techniques for someone else. She herself was reluctant to use them as starting points for her learning. Although her teachers tried to convert her to what they considered proper style, Lisa insisted that she had to work her way if she were ever going to feel comfortable with computers. But two months into the programming course, Lisa abandoned the fight to do things her way and decided to do things their way. She called it her "not-me strategy" and began to insist that it didn't matter because "the computer was just a tool."

Lisa's classmate, Robin, was a pianist with a similar learning style. She wanted to play with computational elements, to manipulate the bits of code, as though they were musical notes or phrases. She, too, was told her way was wrong. Her instructor told her it was "a waste of time."

Lisa and Robin came to the programming course with anxieties about not belonging because they did not see themselves as "computer people." Although both could master the class material intellectually, the course exacerbated their anxieties about not belonging because it insisted on a style of work so different from their own. Both received top grades, but each had to deny who she was in order to succeed. Lisa said that she turned herself "into a different kind of person," and Robin described what she had to do as "faking it."

In the 1970s and 1980s, soft mastery was computing's "different voice." Different and in no way equal. The authorities (teachers and other experts) actively discouraged it, deeming it incorrect or improper. But I found many Lisas and many Robins in schools, universities, and local computer clubs. These were boys and girls, men and women, novices and experts, who reported that they had changed their styles to suit the fashion when they had started to interact with the official computer world. "I got my wrists slapped enough times and I changed my ways," says a college student for whom soft style programming was a passion until he entered MIT and was instructed in the canonical programming style. The cost of such wrist slapping was high. On an individual level, talent was wasted, self-image eroded. On the social level, the computer culture was narrowed.

With the rise of a personal computer culture in the 1980s, more people owned their own machines and could do what they pleased with them. This meant that more people began to experience the computer as an expressive medium that they could use in their own ways. Yet for most, the notion that the computer was a calculator died hard. The idea that the computer was a new medium of expression would not make sense until the 1990s, when large numbers of people owned personal computers with color screens, powerful graphics, and CD-ROMs. In the 1970s through the mid-1980s, the ideology that there was only one right way to "do" computers nearly masked the diversity of styles in the computer culture. In those days top-down thinkers didn't simply share a style; they constituted an epistemological elite.

Discoveries and Denigrations of the Concrete

The elite status of abstract thinking in Western thought can be traced back at least to Plato. Western scientific culture has traditionally drawn a firm line between the abstract and the concrete. The tools of abstraction are propositions; the tools of concrete thinking are objects, and there has always been a right and wrong side of the tracks. The terms "pure science" and "pure mathematics" made clear the superiority of selecting for the pristine propositions and filtering out the messy objects. In the twentieth century, the role of things-in-thinking has had powerful intellectual champions. But, even among these champions there has been resistance to the importance of the bottom-up style of thought preferred by Lisa and Robin. For example, Lévi-Strauss and the noted Swiss psychologist Jean Piaget both discovered ways of reasoning that began with objects and moved to theory, but then they found ways to marginalize them.

In the 1920s and 1930s, Piaget first noticed concrete modes of reasoning among children. Children thought that when you spread three marbles apart there were more marbles than when you moved three marbles close together. Through such observations, Piaget was able to see what others had not: Concrete mapping and manipulation of objects enable children to develop the concept of number, a concept that only gradually becomes a formal sense of quantity. The construction of number, in other words, is born through bricolage.

Piaget fought for the recognition of this kind of concrete thinking, but at the same time he saw it as something to be outgrown. The adult was "beyond" the concrete. For Piaget there was a progression in modes of reasoning that culminates in a final, formal stage when propositional logic liberates intelligence from the need to think with things. So Piaget both discovered the power of the concrete in the construction of the fundamental categories of number, space, time, and causality, and denigrated what he had found by relegating concrete ways of knowing to an early childhood stage of development.

Piaget's discoveries about the processes of children's thinking challenged a kind of cultural amnesia. Adults forget the way they reasoned as children. And we forget very quickly. While Freud discovered the forgetting of infantile sexuality, Piaget identified a second amnesia: the forgetting of concrete styles of thinking. In both, our stake in forgetting is highly charged. In our culture, the divide between abstract and concrete is not simply a boundary between propositions and objects but a way of separating the clean from the messy, virtue from taboo.

Lévi-Strauss, too, both discovered and denied the concrete. He described bricoleur scientists who do not move abstractly and hierarchically from axiom to theorem to corollary but construct theories by arranging and rearranging a set of well-known materials. But the bricoleur scientists he described all operated in non-Western societies. As Piaget had relegated the concrete to childhood, Lévi-Strauss relegated it to the so-called "primitive" and to modern Western humanists. What Lévi-Strauss had a hard time seeing were the significant elements of bricolage in the practice of Western science.

Am I practicing a similar devaluation of the concrete when I characterize the rule-based planner's programming style as hard mastery and Lisa and Robin's style as soft? Our culture tends to equate the word "soft" with unscientific and undisciplined as well as with the feminine and with a lack of power. Why use a term like "soft" when it could turn difference into devaluation? What interests me here is the transvaluation of values. "Soft" is a good word for a flexible, nonhierarchical style, one that allows a close connection with one's objects of study. Using the term "soft Mastery" goes along with seeing negotiation, relationship, and attachment as cognitive virtues. And this is precisely what the culture of simulation encourages us to do.

The soft approach is not a style unique to either men or women. However, in our culture it is a style to which many women are drawn. Among other reasons, we train girls in the component skills of a soft approach—negotiation, compromise, give and take—as psychological virtues, while dominant models of desirable male behavior stress decisiveness and the imposition of will. Boys and girls are encouraged to adopt different relational stances in the world of people. It is not surprising that these differences show up when men and women deal with the world of things.

Through the mid-1980s, a male-dominated computer culture that took one style as the right and only way to program discriminated against soft approaches. Although this bias hurt both male and female computer users, it fell disproportionately on women because they were disproportionately represented in the ranks of the soft masters. But even when women felt free to experiment with soft mastery, they faced a special conflict. Tinkering required a close encounter with the computer. But this violated a cultural taboo about being involved with "machines" that fell particularly harshly on women. When I was a young girl, I assembled the materials to build a crystal radio. My mother, usually encouraging, said, "Don't touch it, you'll get a shock." Her tone, however, did not communicate fear for my safety, but distaste. A generation later, many women were learning to identify being a woman with all that a computer is not, and computers with all that a woman is not. In this cultural construction, computers could be very threatening. In recent years, things have started to change. As the emerging culture of simulation becomes increasingly associated with negotiational and nonhierarchical ways of thinking, it has made a place for people with a wider range of cognitive and emotional styles. In particular, women have come to feel that computers are more culturally acceptable.

The Revaluation of the Concrete

Soft mastery is not a stage, it is a style. Bricolage is a way to organize work. It is not a stage in a progression to a superior form. Richard Greenblatt is a renowned first-generation MIT hacker, a computer culture legend whose virtuoso style of work incorporates a strong dose of bricolage. He has made significant contributions to the development of chess programs as well as systems programming. In the spirit of the painter who steps back to look at the canvas before proceeding to the next step, Greenblatt developed software that put him in a conversation, a negotiation with his materials. He used bricolage at a high level of artistry.

Yet even internationally recognized bricoleur virtuosos such as Richard Greenblatt lived within a dominant computer culture that was scornful of their approach. One of that culture's heroes was the mathematician Edsger W. Dijkstra. Dijkstra, the leading theorist of hard, structured programming, emphasized analytical methods and scientific rigor in the development of programs. In Dijkstra's view, a rigorous planning coupled with mathematical analysis should produce a computer program with mathematically guaranteed success. In this model, there is no room for bricolage. When Dijkstra gave a lecture at MIT in the late 1970s, he demonstrated his points by taking his audience step by step through the development of a short program. Richard Greenblatt was in the audience, and the two men had an exchange that has entered into computer culture mythology. It was a classic confrontation between two opposing aesthetics. Greenblatt asked Dijkstra how he could apply his mathematical methods to something as complicated as a chess program. "I wouldn't write a chess program," Dijkstra replied, dismissing the issue.

In the field of computing, the existence of the bricolage style at virtuoso levels challenged the idea of there being only one correct, mature approach to problem-solving. In the 1980s, this challenge was supported by several currents of research on concrete styles of problem-solving in other domains. Each in its own way called into question the hegemony of the abstract, formal, and rule-driven. Each contributed to a revaluation of the contextual and concrete, in which computers were now playing an unexpected role.

First, psychologists showed the way ordinary people in their kitchens and workplaces make effective use of a down-to-earth mathematical thinking very different from the abstract, formal mathematics they were often so unsuccessfully taught at school. Kitchen mathematics relies on the familiar feel and touch of everyday activities. Second, sociologists and anthropologists demonstrated that in scientific laboratories, there is a time-honored tradition of tinkering first and creating formal rationalizations later. Ethnographers of science showed that bench science often depends on a long, messy process of trial and error followed by the final, frantic scramble to rationalize the results. Similarly, close studies of the way scientific papers are written indicated that successive drafts cover the tracks of messy bricoleurs. Finally, feminist scholars gave evidence for the power of contextual reasoning.

The psychologist Carol Gilligan discerned two voices in the development of moral reasoning. We can hear both in the stories she told about children's responses to moral dilemmas. One well-known story involves a man named Heinz. His wife is dying. He needs a drug to save her. He has no money. What should he do? Gilligan reports that when confronted with Heinz's dilemma, (Should Heinz steal a drug to save a life?), eleven-year-old Jake saw it "sort of like a math problem with humans." Jake set it up as an equation and arrived at what he believed was the correct response: Heinz should steal the drug because a human life is worth much more than money. While Jake accepted the problem as a quantitative comparison of two evils, eleven-year-old Amy looked at it in concrete terms, breaking down the problem's restrictive formal frame, and introducing a set of new elements. In particular, she brought the druggist, who probably had a wife of his own, into the story. Amy proposed that Heinz should talk things over with the druggist, who surely would not want anyone to die.

For Jake, justice was like a mathematical principle. To solve a problem, you set up the right algorithm, put it in the right box, crank the handle, and the answer comes out. In contrast, Amy's style of reasoning required her to stay in touch with the inner workings of her arguments, with the relationships and possibly shifting alliances of a group of actors. In other words, Amy was the bricoleur. Her resemblance to Lisa and Robin is striking. They were all very bright. They were all tinkerers who preferred to stay close to their materials as they arranged and rearranged them. And they were all open to the same kind of criticism. Theorists of structured programming would criticize Lisa and Robin's style for the same kind of reasons that "orthodox" academic psychology would classify Amy at a lower intellectual level than Jake. In both cases, criticism would center on the fact that the bricoleurs were unprepared to take a final step in the direction of abstraction. For orthodox psychology, mature thinking is abstract thinking.

Gilligan argued for equal respect for a line of development that uses concrete, increasingly sophisticated ways of thinking about morality. Some people solved problems contextually, through examples, while others relied on rules and abstractions. Gilligan's work supported the idea that abstract reasoning is not a stage but a style. And contextual, situated reasoning is another. Instead of consigning concrete methods to children, "primitives," and humanists, Gilligan validated bricolage as mature, widespread, and useful.

Bricolage is one aspect of soft mastery. Lisa and Robin showed us a second: a desire to work "close to the object." In a biography of the Nobel Prize-winning geneticist Barbara McClintock, Evelyn Fox Keller wrote about this second aspect of soft mastery. McClintock spoke of her work as a conversation with her materials, a conversation that would have to be held in intimate whispers. "Over and over again," says Keller, McClintock "tells us one must have the time to look, the patience to 'hear what the material has to say to you,' the openness to 'let it come to you.' Above all, one must have a 'feeling for the organism.'"

McClintock related to chromosomes much as Lisa and Robin related to computational objects. The neurospora chromosomes McClintock worked with were so small that others had been unable to identify them, yet the more she worked with them, she said, "the bigger [they] got, and when I was really working with them I wasn't outside, I was down there. I was part of the system. I actually felt as if I were right down there and these were my friends. . . . As you look at these things, they become part of you and you forget yourself."

In the course of her career, McClintock's style of work came into conflict with the formal, hard methods of molecular biology. She was recognized and rewarded by the scientific establishment only when others using the formal approach came independently, and much later, to conclusions that she had derived from her investigations. Many of the things that bricoleur programmers have said to me recalled McClintock's creative aesthetic as well as the resistance to it that she encountered. Lorraine, a computer science graduate student, told me that she used "thinking about what the program feels like inside to break through difficult problems." She added, "For appearances' sake I want to look like I'm doing what everyone else is doing, but I'm doing that with only a small part of my mind. The rest of me is imagining what the components feel like. It's like doing my pottery. . . . Keep this anonymous. It makes me sound crazy." This young woman wanted to downplay her style for the same reasons that McClintock had found hers burdensome. People didn't expect it, they didn't understand it, and they didn't see it as scientific.

In her work on McClintock, Keller remarked on the difficulty people face when they try to understand what it might mean to do science in anything other than the formal and abstract canonical style. In the 1980s, personal computers provided a cultural medium in which ideas about noncanonical styles of science could blossom. Many more people could understand the kind of closeness to a scientific object that McClintock was talking about, because they saw themselves relating to icons or lines of computer code in that very way.

Then and Now

In her late-1970s introduction of the computer culture, Lisa saw computers encouraging social isolation and intellectual regimentation. Not only did she complain that the canonical style constrained her to one way of doing things, but she had contempt for "computer people" who were "always working with their machines. . . . They turn to computers as imaginary friends."

Today, significant changes in the computer culture are responding to both of Lisa's objections. Today's high school students are more likely to think of computers as fluid simulation surfaces for writing and game playing than as rigid machines to program. Or they are likely to think of computers as gateways to communication. When fourteen-year-old Steven describes the importance of his personal computer he says, "It has all the programs that make my modem work." Steven uses his family's account on a commercial online service to chat with net-friends. He borrows his mother's university account to join Internet discussion groups and mailing lists on topics ranging from satanism to *Forrest Gump,* and he participates in Multi-User-Domains, or MUDs, in which he plays a character who inhabits the science fiction world of *Dune.* In MUDs, Steven interacts with other real people, although all of them have created imaginary characters. So the social image of the computer is far more complex than before. It now evokes both physical isolation and intense interaction with other people.

On the issue of intellectual regimentation, there has been an equally dramatic change. In essence, software designers have come to agree with Lisa's concern about computers offering only one way. Instead of rules to learn, they want to create environments to explore.

These new interfaces project the message, "Play with me, experiment with me, there is no one correct path." The new software design aesthetic effectively says that computer users shouldn't have to work with syntax; they should be able to play with shape, form, color, and sound. Computer users shouldn't have to concern themselves with the complexity of a programming language; they should be given virtual objects that can be manipulated in as direct a way as possible. Whether for serious or recreational purposes, simulations should be placed to try out alternatives, to escape from planning into the world of "What if?" In the 1990s, as computing shifts away from a culture of calculation, bricolage has been given more room to flourish.

Today's software programs typically take the form of a simulation of some reality—playing chess or golf, analyzing a spreadsheet, writing, painting, or making an architectural drawing—and try to place the user within it. Children don't learn natural language by learning its rules, but through immersion in its cadences. Similarly, today's most popular software is designed for immersion. One writer described her relationship with wordprocessing software this way: "At first I felt awkward. I was telling the computer what I wanted to write. Now, I think in Microsoft Word." An architect uses similar language to describe his computer design tools: "At first I was not comfortable with the program. There was just so much I had to tell it. . . . But once I got comfortable designing inside of it, I felt so much freer."

People look at a technology and see beyond it to a constellation of cultural associations. When they saw the early computer enthusiasts take the machine and make a world apart, many people felt they did not belong and did not want to belong. Now, the machine no longer has to be perceived as putting you in a world apart. Indeed, it can put you in the center of things and people—in the center of literature, politics, art, music, communication, and the stock market. The hacker is no longer necessarily or only a "nerd"; he or she can be a cultural icon. The hacker can be Bill Gates.

In the emerging culture of simulation, the computer is still a tool but less like a hammer and more like a harpsichord. You don't learn how to play a harpsichord primarily by learning a set of rules, just as you don't learn about a simulated microworld, whether a Macintosh-like graphical interface or a video game, by delving into an instruction manual. In general, you learn by playful exploration. An architect describes how computer tools help him to design housing units: "I randomly . . . digitize, move, copy, erase the elements—columns, walls, and levels—without thinking of it as a building but rather a sculpture . . . and then take a fragment of it and work on it in more detail." In computer-assisted design environments, those who take most advantage of soft-approach skills are often taking most advantage of computing. In the culture of simulation, bricolage can provide a competitive edge.

The computer culture is close to the point where full membership does not require programming skills, but is accorded to people who use software out of a box. Bricoleurs function well here. Recall that they like to get to know a new environment by interacting with it. When all the computer culture offered were programming environments, the bricoleur wanted to get close to the code. Now when dealing with simulation software, the bricoleur can create the feeling of closeness to the object by manipulating virtual objects on the screen. And bricoleurs are comfortable with exploring the Internet through the World Wide Web. Exploring the Web is a process of trying one thing, then another, of making connections, of bringing disparate elements together. It is an exercise in bricolage.

Gender and Computing: Some Special Lessons

From its very foundations, the notion of scientific objectivity has been inseparable from the image of the scientist's aggressive relationship to nature. And from its very foundations, the quest for scientific objectivity was metaphorically engaged with the language of male domination and female submission. Francis Bacon used the image of the male scientist putting female nature on the rack.

Given this, it is not surprising that many women have felt uncomfortable with the language and ways of thinking traditionally associated with science. And computer science has not been exempt. Programs and operating systems are "crashed" and "killed." For years I wrote on a computer whose operating system asked me if it should "abort" an instruction it could not "execute." This is a language that few women fail to note. Women have too often been faced with the choice—not necessarily conscious—of putting themselves at odds either with the cultural meaning of being a scientist or with the cultural construction of being a woman.

For example, when Lisa minimized the importance the computer had for her by insisting that it was "just a tool," it was more than a way of withdrawing because her programming course had forced her into an uncomfortable approach. It was also a way of insisting that what was most important about being a person (and a woman) was incompatible with close relationships to the technology as it had been presented to her.

Lisa was not alone. Through the 1980s, I found many women who vehemently insisted on the computer's neutrality. There was a clear disparity between their message ("It means nothing to me") and their strong emotion. These women were fighting their own experience of the computer as psychologically gripping. I have noted that they were fighting against an element of their own soft approach. Their style of thinking would have them get close to computational objects, but the closer they got, the more anxious they felt. The more they became involved with the computer in the culture of calculation, the more they insisted that it was only a neutral tool and tried to keep their distance from it.

But women do not insist on distance from all tools. Music students live in a culture that, over time, has slowly grown a language for appreciating close relationships with musical instruments. The harpsichord is just a tool. And yet we understand that artists' encounters with their tools will most probably be close, sensuous, and relational. We assume that artists will develop highly personal styles of working with them.

In the mid-1990s, in the culture of simulation, a new "musical" culture of computing is developing. To get to this point has required technical progress that has permitted new cultural associations to grow. Now that computers are the tools we use to write, to design, to play with ideas and shapes and images, to create video sequences and musical effects, to create interactive novels and graphic images, they are developing a new set of intellectual and emotional associations, more like those we apply to harpsichords than to hammers. The culture of personal computing now makes room for ways of knowing that depend on the "concrete" manipulation of virtual paintbrushes and paints, virtual pens and paper. And we shall see that intellectual disciplines such as cognitive science and artificial intelligence, which previously supported hard mastery, are themselves undergoing changes that make it possible for them to support a somewhat more "informalist" intellectual climate.

A classical modernist vision of computer intelligence has made room for a romantic postmodern one. At this juncture, there is potential for a more welcoming environment for women, humanists, and artists in the technical culture. . . .

1995

READING, REREADING, AND ANALYSIS

1. Working in a group, explore Turkle's idea of "bricolage." Give an example of bricolage from the text. Give a few examples of your own. What does Turkle contrast with bricolage?

2. Choose one of Turkle's examples—the story of Lisa, Robin, Carol Gilligan, or Barbara McClintock—and summarize the example in your own words. Then explain the point that Turkle is making in using that example.

3. Working in a group, list the advantages and disadvantages of the planned or structured style of programming versus the bricolage style. In what ways is each style effective? What are the limitations of each? Apply these terms to other activities, such as writing. What does this awareness of style help you see?

4. Working in a group, track down two or three places in the essay where Turkle discusses gender-related language, such as the use of "abort" or the implications of "soft mastery." Prepare a presentation for the class in which you start with a quote, discuss the gender implications, and add an example from your own experience where an approach, an activity, a word or a phrase has similar gendered implications.

5. Paraphrase the final paragraph of the piece. What does Turkle mean by a "romantic postmodern" vision of computer intelligence?

RESPONDING THROUGH WRITING: BUILDING AN INTERPRETATION

6. Use examples from your own experience and from Turkle's essay to show the differences between planned and structured approaches (to programming, writing, or any other activity) and the bricolage approach. What are the effects and limitations of each? Choose one example of your own to discuss in detail. Does your approach to the activity you have chosen to write about depend strongly on one of these styles or does it mix aspects of each? How does your writing for this class fit into these categories? Why?

7. Turkle favors a problem-solving style "that has more the flavor of a conversation than a monologue" (p. 568). How does tinkering (or bricolage) partake of the conversation model? Why is it like a conversation?

GOING FURTHER: LEARNING FROM OTHER SOURCES

8. Use the Internet to test some of Turkle's claims. Choose a topic that you want to learn about and perform two separate Internet searches using a popular search engine. For the first search, follow the planned style by devising a very specific set of goals for your search. Do not follow links or revise your search unless it is part of the original plan. For the second search, become a bricoleur, improvising and following leads wherever and however you can. Take notes on what you see in both searches and on the advantages and disadvantages of each approach.

9. Using a database such as Academic Search Elite that includes a range of scholarly articles, or one such as MAS Full Text Ultra that includes general-interest and current-events-related magazines, try various searches for "computer and gender," "computer and women," or "technology and gender."

APPLYING WHAT YOU'VE LEARNED

10. If Turkle is concerned primarily with the possibility and potential of individual creativity, Lawrence Lessig could be said to focus more on the wider cultural impact such creativity could have. Using his "Introduction to Free Culture: " as support, consider Turkle's claims in light of this growing cultural shift. Is the "concrete style" Turkle champions helping to usher in what Lessig describes as a change in common sense about creativity and ownership? What are the consequences of these evolving ways of imagining the interaction between producers and consumers?

11. Turkle celebrates the "art" of tinkering by comparing creative computer use with the methods of an artist. Comparing the computer to the harpsichord, she argues that "a new 'musical' culture of computing is developing" (p. 529). In "Progress and the Bean," Scott DeVeaux introduces us to Coleman Hawkins, a renowned jazz musician who thinks of himself as a doctor or a scientist of music, working to solve each musical problem as it comes along. Discuss this "cross-pollination" of the arts and the sciences. What are some of the reasons that people who work in one field use analogies from another?

12. Turkle dislikes top-down authority: what she calls the "hegemony" of universal rules (p. 567). Examine the consequence of rules in this essay and in either Susan Willis's analysis of play at Disney World or Gloria Anzaldúa's description of border art. Is bricolage always the better approach? Are there other ways to deal with the hegemony of rules?

Susan Willis

Susan Willis (b. 1946) is an Associate Professor at Duke University, where she teaches courses in minority writing and popular culture. Her research focuses on exposing both the contradictions of capitalism in everyday life and the utopian content in culture. She is the author of *Specifying: Black Women Writing the American Experience* (1987) and *A Primer for Daily Life* (1991). Willis is coauthor of *Inside the Mouse: Work and Play at Disney World* (1995), from which "Disney World: Public Use/Private State" was excerpted.

> **To get the Walt Disney Company's side of the story, visit their corporate website at <http://www.disney.go.com>.**

WHAT DO YOU KNOW? WHAT DO YOU EXPECT TO DISCOVER?

Before reading the essay, take a moment to consider the following questions.

1. Have you ever been to Disney World or Disneyland? Make a list of adjectives that you associate with the Disney theme parks.

2. Willis connects Disney World to the words "public" and "private" in her title. What do those words mean to you? Is Disney World a public place? Is it private?

3. What criticisms have you heard of Disney? Why would anyone care to speak negatively of a place that surely seems designed to please people? Do you see any justification for those critiques?

❧

Disney World
Public Use/Private State

At Disney World, the erasure of spontaneity is so great that spontaneity itself has been programmed. On the "Jungle Cruise" khaki-clad tour guides teasingly engage the visitors with their banter, whose apparent spontaneity has been carefully scripted and painstakingly rehearsed. Nothing is left to the imagination or the unforeseen.

Even the paths and walkways represent the programmed assimilation of the spontaneous. According to published reports, there were no established walkways laid down for the opening-day crowds at Disneyland.[1] Rather, the Disney Imagineers waited to see where people would walk, then paved over their spontaneous footpaths to make prescribed routes.

The erasure of spontaneity has largely to do with the totality of the built and themed environment. Visitors are inducted into the park's program, their every need predefined and presented to them as a packaged routine and set of choices. "I'm not used to having everything done for me." This is how my companion at Disney World reacted when she checked into a Disney resort hotel and found that she, her suitcase, and her credit card had been turned into the scripted components of a highly orchestrated program. My companion later remarked that while she found it odd not to have to take care of everything herself (as she normally does in order to accomplish her daily tasks), she found it "liberating" to just fall into the proper pattern, knowing that nothing could arise that hadn't already been factored into the system. I have heard my companion's remarks reiterated by many visitors to the park with whom I've talked. Most describe feeling "freed up" ("I didn't have to worry about my kids," "I didn't have to think about anything") by the experience of relinquishing control over the complex problem-solving thoughts and operations that otherwise define their lives. Many visitors suspend daily perceptions and judgments altogether, and treat the wonderland environment as more real than real. I saw this happen one morning when walking to breakfast at my Disney resort hotel. Two small children were stooped over a small snake that had crawled out onto the sun-warmed path. "Don't worry, it's rubber," remarked their mother. Clearly only Audio-Animatronic simulacra of the real world can inhabit Disney World. A real snake is an impossibility.

In fact, the entire natural world is subsumed by the primacy of the artificial. The next morning I stepped outside at the end of an early morning shower. The humid atmosphere held the combination of sun and rain. "Oh! Did they turn the sprinklers on?" This is the way my next-door neighbor greeted the day as she emerged from her hotel room. The Disney environment puts visitors inside the world that Philip K. Dick depicted in *Do Androids Dream of Electric Sleep?*—where all animal life has been exterminated, but replaced by the production of simulacra, so real in appearance that people have difficulty recalling that real animals no longer exist. The marvelous effect of science fiction is produced out of a dislocation between two worlds, which the reader apprehends as an estrangement, but the characters inside the novel cannot grasp because they have only the one world: the world of simulacra. The effect of the marvelous cannot be achieved unless the artificial environment is perceived through the retained memory of everyday reality. Total absorption into the Disney environment cancels the possibility for the marvelous and leaves the visitor with the banality of a park-wide sprinkler system. No muggers, no rain, no ants, and no snakes.

Amusement is the commodified negation of play. What is play but the spontaneous coming together of activity and imagination, rendered more pleasurable by the addition of friends? At Disney World, the world's most highly developed private property "state" devoted to amusement, play is all but eliminated by the absolute domination of program over spontaneity. Every ride runs to computerized schedule. There is no possibility of an awful thrill, like being stuck at the top of a ferris wheel. Order prevails particularly in the queues for the rides that zigzag dutifully on a prescribed path created out of stanchions and ropes; and the visitor's assimilation into the queue does not catapult him or her into another universe, as it would if Jorge Luis Borges fabricated the program. The Disney labyrinth is a banal extension of the ride's point of embarkation, which extends into the ride as a hyper-themed continuation of the queue. The "Backstage Movie Tour" has done away with the distinction between the ride and its queue by condemning the visitor to a two-and-a-half-hour-long pedagogical queue that preaches the process of movie production. Guests are mercilessly herded through sound stages and conveyed across endless back lots where one sees the ranch-style houses used in TV commercials and a few wrecked cars from movie chase scenes. Happily, there are a few discreet exit doors, bail-out points for parents with bored children. Even Main Street dictates programmed amusement because it is not a street but a conduit, albeit laden with commodity distractions, that conveys the visitor to the Magic Kingdom's other zones where more queues, rides, and commodities distinguish themselves on the basis of their themes. All historical and cultural references are merely ingredients for decor. Every expectation is met programmatically and in conformity with theme. Mickey as Sorcerer's Apprentice does not appear in the Wild West or the exotic worlds of Jungle and Adventure, the niches for Davey Crockett and Indiana Jones. Just imagine the chaos, a park-wide short circuit, that the mixing of themed ingredients might produce. Amusement areas are identified by a "look," by characters in costume, by the goods on sale: What place—i.e., product—is Snow White promoting if she's arm in arm with an astronaut? The utopian intermingling of thematic opportunities such as occurred at the finale of the movie *Who Framed Roger Rabbit?*, with Warner and Disney "toons" breaking their copyrighted species separation to cavort with each other and the human actors, will not happen at Disney World.

However, now that the costumed embodiment of Roger Rabbit has taken up residence at Disney World, he, too, can expect to have a properly assigned niche in the spectacular Disney parade of characters.

These have been augmented with a host of other Disney/Lucas/Spielberg creations, including Michael Jackson of "Captain EO" and C$_3$PO and R2D2 of *Star Wars* , as well as Disney buyouts such as Jim Henson's Muppets and the Saturday morning cartoon heroes, the Teenage Mutant Ninja Turtles. The Disney Corporation's acquisition of the stock-in-trade of popular culture icons facilitates a belief commonly held by young children that every popular childhood figure "lives" at Disney World. In the utopian imagination of children, Disney World may well be a never-ending version of the finale to *Roger Rabbit* where every product of the imagination lives in community. In reality, the products (of adult imaginations) live to sell, to be consumed, to multiply.

What's most interesting about Disney World is what's not there. Intimacy is not in the program even though the architecture includes several secluded nooks, gazebos, and patios. During my five-day stay, I saw only one kiss—and this a husbandly peck on the cheek. Eruptions of imaginative play are just as rare. During the same five-day visit, I observed only one such incident even though there were probably fifty thousand children in the park. What's curious about what's not at Disney is that there is no way of knowing what's not there until an aberrant event occurs and provokes the remembrance of the social forms and behaviors that have been left out. This was the case with the episode of spontaneous play. Until I saw real play, I didn't realize that it was missing. The incident stood out against a humdrum background of uniform amusement: hundreds of kids being pushed from attraction to attraction in their strollers, hundreds more waiting dutifully in the queues or marching about in family groups—all of them abstaining from the loud, jostling, teasing, and rivalrous behaviors that would otherwise characterize many of their activities. Out of this homogenous "amused" mass, two kids snagged a huge sombrero each from an open-air stall at the foot of the Mexico Pavilion's Aztec temple stairway and began their impromptu version of the Mexican hat dance up and down the steps. Their play was clearly counterproductive as it took up most of the stairway, making it difficult for visitors to enter the pavilion. Play negated the function of the stairs as conduit into the attraction. The kids abandoned themselves to their fun, while all around them, the great mass of visitors purposefully kept their activities in line with Disney World's prescribed functions. Everyone but the dancers seemed to have accepted the park's unwritten motto: "If you pay, you shouldn't play." To get your money's worth, you have to do everything and do it in the prescribed manner. Free play is gratuitous and therefore a waste of the family's leisure time expenditure.

Conformity with the park's program upholds the Disney value system. Purposeful consumption—while it costs the consumer a great deal—affirms the value of the consumer. "Don't forget, we drove twenty hours to get here." This is how one father admonished his young son who was squirming about on the floor of EPCOT's

Independence Hall, waiting for the amusement to begin. The child's wanton and impatient waste of time was seen as a waste of the family's investment in its amusement. If a family is to realize the value of its leisure time consumptions, then every member must function as a proper consumer.

The success of Disney World as an amusement park has largely to do with the way its use of programming meshes with the economics of consumption as a value system. In a world wholly predicated on consumption, the dominant order need not proscribe those activities that run counter to consumption, such as free play and squirming, because the consuming public largely polices itself against gratuitous acts which would interfere with the production of consumption as a value. Conformity with the practice of consumption is so widespread and deep at Disney World that occasional manifestations of boredom or spontaneity do not influence the compulsively correct behavior of others. Independence Hall did not give way to a seething mass of squirming youngsters even though all had to sit through a twenty-minute wait. Nor did other children on the margins of the hat dance fling themselves into the fun. Such infectious behavior would have indicated communally defined social relations or the desire for such social relations. Outside of Disney World in places of public use, infectious behavior is common. One child squirming about on the library floor breeds others; siblings chasing each other around in a supermarket draw others; one child mischievously poking at a public fountain attracts others; kids freeloading rides on a department store escalator can draw a crowd. These playful, impertinent acts indicate an imperfect mesh between programmed environment and the value system of consumption. Consumers may occasionally reclaim the social, particularly the child consumer who has not yet been fully and properly socialized to accept individuation as the bottom line in the consumer system of value. As an economic factor, the individual exists to maximize consumption—and therefore profits—across the broad mass of consumers. This is the economic maxim most cherished by the fast-food industry, where every burger and order of fries is individually packaged and consumed to preclude consumer pooling and sharing.

At Disney World the basic social unit is the family. This was made particularly clear to me because as a single visitor conducting research, I presented a problem at the point of embarkation for each of the rides. "How many in your group?" "One." The lone occupant of a conveyance invariably constructed to hold the various numerical breakdowns of the nuclear family (two, three, or four) is an anomaly. Perhaps the most family-affirming aspect of Disney World is the way the queues serve as a place where family members negotiate who will ride with whom. Will Mom and Dad separate themselves so as to accompany their two kids on a two-person ride? Will an older sibling assume the responsibility for a younger brother or sister? Every ride asks the family to evaluate each of its member's needs for security and independence. This is probably the only situation in a family's visit to Disney World where the social relations of family materialize as practice. Otherwise and throughout a family's stay, the family as nexus for social relations is subsumed by the primary definition of family as the basic unit of consumption. In consumer society at large, each of us is an atomized consumer. Families are composed of autonomous, individuated consumers, each satisfying his or her age- and gender-differentiated taste in the music, video, food, and pleasure marketplace. In contrast, Disney World puts the family back together. Even teens are integrated in their families and are seldom seen roaming the park in teen groups as they might in shopping malls.

Families at Disney World present themselves as families, like the one I saw one morning on my way to breakfast at a Disney resort hotel: father, mother, and three children small to large, each wearing identical blue Mickey Mouse T-shirts and shorts. As I walked past them, I overheard the middle child say, "We looked better yesterday— in white." Immediately, I envisioned the family in yesterday's matching outfits, and wondered if they had bought identical ensembles for every day of their stay.

All expressions of mass culture include contradictory utopian impulses, which may be buried or depicted in distorted form, but nevertheless generate much of the satisfaction of mass cultural commodities (whether the consumer recognizes them as utopian or not). While the ideology of the family has long functioned to promote conservative— even reactionary—political and social agendas, the structure of the family as a social unit signifies communality rather than individuality and can give impetus to utopian longings for communally defined relations in society at large. However, when the family buys into the look of a family, and appraises itself on the basis of its look ("We looked better yesterday"), it becomes a walking, talking commodity, a packaged unit of consumption stamped with the Mickey logo of approval. The theoretical question that this family poses for me is not whether its representation of itself as family includes utopian possibilities (because it does), but whether such impulses can be expressed and communicated in ways not accessible to commodification.

In its identical dress, the family represents itself as capitalism's version of a democratized unit of consumption. Differences and inequalities among family members are reduced to distinctions in age and size. We have all had occasion to experience the doppelgänger effect in the presence of identical twins who choose (or whose families enforce) identical dress. Whether chosen or imposed, identical twins who practice the art of same dress have the possibility of confounding or subverting social order. In contrast, the heterogeneous family whose members choose to dress identically affirms conformity with social order. The family has cloned itself as a multiple, but identical consumer, thus enabling the maximization of consumption. It is a microcosmic representation of free market democracy where the range of choices is restricted to the series of objects already on the shelf. In this system there is no radical choice. Even the minority of visitors who choose to wear their Rolling Stones and Grateful Dead T-shirts give the impression of having felt constrained not to wear a Disney logo.

Actually, Disney has invented a category of negative consumer choices for those individuals who wish to express nonconformity. This I discovered as I prepared to depart for my Disney research trip, when my daughter Cassie (fifteen years old and "cool" to the max) warned me, "Don't buy me any of that Disney paraphernalia." As it turned out, she was happy to get a pair of boxer shorts emblazoned with the leering images of Disney's villains: two evil queens, the Big Bad Wolf, and Captain Hook. Every area of Disney World includes a Disney Villains Shop, a chain store for bad-guy merchandise. Visitors who harbor anti-Disney sentiments can express their cultural politics by consuming the negative Disney line. There is no possibility of an anticonsumption at Disney World. All visitors are, by definition, consumers, their status conferred with the price of admission.

At Disney World even memories are commodities. How the visitor will remember his or her experience of the park has been programmed and indicated by the thousands of "Kodak Picture Spot" signposts. These position the photographer so as to capture the best views of each and every attraction, so that even the most inept family members can bring home perfect postcard-like photos. To return home from a trip to Disney World with a collection of haphazardly photographed environments or idiosyncratic family shots is tantamount to collecting bad memories. A family album comprised of picture-perfect photo-site images, on the other hand, constitutes the grand narrative of the family's trip to Disney World, the one that can be offered as testimony to money well spent. Meanwhile, all those embarrassing photos, the ones not programmed by the "Picture Spots," that depict babies with ice cream all over their faces or toddlers who burst into tears rather than smiles at the sight of those big-headed costumed characters that crop up all over the park—these are the images that are best left forgotten.

The other commodified form of memory is the souvenir. As long as there has been tourism there have also been souvenirs: objects marketed to concretize the visitor's experience of another place. From a certain point of view, religious pilgrimage includes aspects of tourism, particularly when the culmination of pilgrimage is the acquisition of a transportable relic. Indeed, secular mass culture often imitates the forms and practices of popular religious culture. For many Americans today who make pilgrimages to Graceland and bring home a mass-produced piece of Presley memorabilia, culture and religion collide and mesh.

Of course, the desire to translate meaningful moments into concrete objects need not take commodified form. In Toni Morrison's *Song of Solomon*, Pilate, a larger-than-life earth mother if there ever was one, spent her early vagabondage gathering a stone from every place she visited. Similarly, I know of mountain climbers who mark their ascents by bringing a rock back from each peak they climb. Like Pilate's stones, these tend to be nondescript and embody personal remembrances available only to the collector. In contrast, the commodity souvenir enunciates a single meaning to everyone: "I was there. I bought something." Unlike the souvenirs I remember having seen as a child, seashells painted with seascapes and the name of some picturesque resort town, most souvenirs today are printed with logos (like the Hard Rock Cafe T-shirt), or renderings of copyrighted material (all the Disney merchandise). The purchase of such a souvenir allows the consumer the illusion of participating in the enterprise as a whole, attaining a piece of the action. This is the consumerist version of small-time buying on the stock exchange. We all trade in logos—buy them, wear them, eat them, and make them the containers of our dreams and memories. Similarly, we may all buy into capital with the purchase of public stock. These consumerist activities give the illusion of democratic participation while denying access to real corporate control which remains intact and autonomous, notwithstanding the mass diffusion of its logos and stock on the public market. Indeed the manipulation of public stock initiated during the Reagan administration, which has facilitated one leveraged buyout after another, gives the lie to whatever wistful remnants of democratic ownership one might once have attached to the notion of "public" stocks.

Disney World is logoland. The merchandise, the costumes, the scenery—all is either stamped with the Disney logo or covered by copyright legislation. In fact, it is impossible to photograph at Disney World without running the risk of infringing a Disney copyright. A family photo in front of Sleeping Beauty's Castle is apt to include dozens of infringements: the castle itself, Uncle Harry's "Goofy" T-shirt, the kids' Donald and Mickey hats, maybe a costumed Chip 'n Dale in the background. The only thing that saves the average family from a lawsuit is that most don't use their vacation photos as a means for making profit. I suspect the staff of "America's Funniest Home Videos" systematically eliminates all family videos shot at Disney World; otherwise prize winners might find themselves having to negotiate the legal difference between prize and profit, and in a larger sense, public use versus private property. As an interesting note, Michael Sorkin, in a recent essay on Disneyland, chose a photo of "[t]he sky above Disney World [as a] substitute for an image of the place itself." Calling Disney World "the first copyrighted urban environment," Sorkin goes on to stress the "litigiousness" of the Disney Corporation.[2] It may be that *Design Quarterly*, where Sorkin published his essay, pays its contributors, thus disqualifying them from "fair use" interpretations of copyright policy.

Logos have become so much a part of our cultural baggage that we hardly notice them. Actually they are the cultural capital of corporations. Pierre Bourdieu invented the notion of cultural capital with reference to individuals. In a nutshell, cultural capital represents the sum total of a person's ability to buy into and trade in the culture. This is circumscribed by the economics of class and, in turn, functions as a means for designating an individual's social standing. Hence people with higher levels of education who distinguish themselves with upscale or trendy consumptions have more cultural capital and can command greater privilege and authority than those who, as Bourdieu put it, are stuck defining themselves by the consumption of necessity. There are no cultural objects or practices that do not constitute capital, no reserves of culture that escape value. Everything that constitutes one's cultural life is a commodity and can be reckoned in terms of capital logic.

In the United States today there is little difference between persons and corporations. Indeed, corporations enjoy many of the legal rights extended to individuals. The market system and its private property state are "peopled" by corporations, which trade in, accumulate, and hoard up logos. These are the cultural signifiers produced by corporations, the impoverished imagery of a wholly rationalized entity. Logos are commodities in the abstract, but they are not so abstracted as to have transcended value. Corporations with lots of logos, particularly upscale, high-tech logos, command more cultural capital than corporations with fewer, more humble logos.

In late twentieth-century America, the cultural capital of corporations has replaced many of the human forms of cultural capital. As we buy, wear, and eat logos, we become the henchmen and admen of the corporations, defining ourselves with respect to the social standing of the various corporations. Some would say that this is a new form of tribalism, that in sporting corporate logos we ritualize and humanize them, we redefine the cultural capital of the corporations in human social terms. I would say that a state where culture is indistinguishable from logo and where the practice of culture risks infringement of private property is a state that values the corporate over the human.

While at Disney World, I managed to stow away on the behind-the-scenes tour reserved for groups of corporate conventioneers. I had heard about this tour from a friend who is also researching Disney and whose account of underground passageways, conduits for armies of workers and all the necessary materials and services that enable the park to function, had elevated the tour to mythic proportions in my imagination.

But very little of the behind-the-scenes tour was surprising. There was no magic, just a highly rational system built on the compartmentalization of all productive functions and its ensuing division of labor, both aimed at the creation of maximum efficiency. However, instances do arise when the rational infrastructure comes into contradiction with the onstage (parkwide) theatricalized image that the visitor expects to consume. Such is the case with the system that sucks trash collected at street level through unseen pneumatic tubes that transect the backstage area, fully depositing the trash in Disney's own giant compactor site. To the consumer's eye, trash is never a problem at Disney World. After all, everyone dutifully uses the containers marked "trash," and what little manages to fall to the ground (generally popcorn) is immediately swept up by the French Foreign Legion trash brigade. For the consumer, there is no trash beyond its onstage collection. But there will soon be a problem as environmental pressure groups press Disney to recycle. As my companion on the backstage tour put it, "Why is there no recycling at Disney World—after all, many of the middle-class visitors to the park are already sorting and recycling trash in their homes?" To this the Disney guide pointed out that there is recycling, backstage: bins for workers to toss their Coke cans and other bins for office workers to deposit papers. But recycling onstage would break the magic of themed authenticity. After all, the "real" Cinderella's Castle was not equipped with recycling bins, nor did the denizens of Main Street, U.S.A., circa 1910, foresee the problem of trash. To maintain the image, Disney problem solvers are discussing hiring a minimum-wage workforce to rake, sort, and recycle the trash on back lots that the environmentally aware visitor will never see.

While I have been describing the backstage area as banal, the tour through it was not uneventful. Indeed there was one incident that underscored for me the dramatic collision between people's expectations of public use and the highly controlled nature of Disney's private domain. As I mentioned, the backstage tour took us to the behind-the-scenes staging area for the minute-by-minute servicing of the park and hoopla of its mass spectacles such as firework displays, light shows, and parades. We happened to be in the backstage area just as the parade down Main Street was coming to an end. Elaborate floats and costumed characters descended a ramp behind Cinderella's Castle and began to disassemble before our eyes. The floats were alive with big-headed characters, clambering off the superstructures and out of their heavy, perspiration drenched costumes. Several "beheaded" characters revealed stocky young men gulping down Gatorade. They walked toward our tour group, bloated Donald and bandy-legged Chip from the neck down, carrying their huge costume heads, while their real heads emerged pea-sized and aberrantly human.

We had been warned *not* to take pictures during the backstage tour, but one of our group, apparently carried away by the spectacle, could not resist. She managed to shoot a couple of photos of the disassembled characters before being approached by one of the tour guides. As if caught in a spy movie, the would-be photographer pried open her camera and ripped out the whole roll of film. The entire tour group stood in stunned amazement; not, I think, at the immediate presence of surveillance, but at the woman's dramatic response. In a situation where control is so omnipresent and conformity with control is taken for granted, any sudden gesture or dramatic response is a surprise.

At the close of the tour, my companion and I lingered behind the rest of the group to talk with our tour guides. As a professional photographer, my companion wanted to know if there is a "normal" procedure for disarming behind-the-scenes photographic spies. The guide explained that the prescribed practice is to impound the cameras, process the film, remove the illicit photos, and return the camera, remaining photos, and complimentary film to the perpetrator. When questioned further, the guide went on to elaborate the Disney rationale for control over the image: the "magic" would be broken if photos of disassembled characters circulated in the public sphere; children might suffer irreparable psychic trauma at the sight of a "beheaded" Mickey; Disney exercises control over the image to safeguard childhood fantasies.

What Disney employees refer to as the "magic" of Disney World has actually to do with the ability to produce fetishized consumptions. The unbroken seamlessness of Disney World, its totality as a consumable artifact, cannot tolerate the revelation of the real work that produces the commodity. There would be no magic if the public should see the entire cast of magicians in various stages of disassembly and fatigue. That selected individuals are permitted to witness the backstage labor facilitates the word-of-mouth affirmation of the tremendous organizational feat that produces Disney World. The interdiction against photography eliminates the possibility of discontinuity at the level of image. There are no images to compete with the copyright-perfect onstage images displayed for public consumption. It's not accidental that our tour guide underscored the fact that Disney costumes are tightly controlled. The character costumes are made at only one production site and this site supplies the costumes used at Tokyo's Disneyland and EuroDisney. There can be no culturally influenced variations on the Disney models. Control over the image ensures the replication of Disney worldwide. The prohibition against photographing disassembled characters is motivated by the same phobia of industrial espionage that runs rampant throughout the high-tech information industry. The woman in our tour group who ripped open her camera and destroyed her film may not have been wrong in acting out a spy melodrama. Her photos of the disassembled costumes might have revealed the manner of their production—rendering them accessible to non-Disney replication. At Disney World, the magic that resides in the integrity of childhood fantasy is inextricably linked to the fetishism of the commodity and the absolute control over private property as it is registered in the copyrighted image.

As I see it, the individual's right to imagine and to give expression to unique ways of seeing is at stake in struggles against private property. Mickey Mouse, notwithstanding his corporate copyright, exists in our common culture. He is the site for the enactment of childhood wishes and fantasies. for early conceptualizations and renderings of the body, a being who can be imagined as both self and other. If culture is held as private property, then there can be only one correct version of Mickey Mouse, whose logo-like image is the cancellation of creativity. But the multiplicity of quirky versions of Mickey Mouse that children draw can stand as a graphic question to us as adults: Who, indeed, owns Mickey Mouse?

What most distinguishes Disney World from any other amusement park is the way its spatial organization, defined by autonomous "worlds" and wholly themed environments, combines with the homogeneity of its visitors (predominantly white, middle-class families) to produce a sense of community. While Disney World includes an underlying utopian impulse, this is articulated with nostalgia for a small-town, small-business America (Main Street, U.S.A.), and the fantasy of a controllable corporatist world (EPCOT). The illusion of community is enhanced by the longing for community that many visitors bring to the park, which they may feel is unavailable to them in their own careers, daily lives, and neighborhoods, thanks in large part to the systematic erosion of the public sector throughout the Reagan and Bush administrations. In the last decade the inroads of private, for-profit enterprise in areas previously defined by public control, and the hostile aggression of tax backlash coupled with "me first" attitudes have largely defeated the possibility of community in our homes and cities.

Whenever I visit Disney World, I invariably overhear other visitors making comparisons between Disney World and their home towns. They stare out over EPCOT's lake and wonder why developers back home don't produce similar aesthetic spectacles. They talk about botched, abandoned, and misconceived development projects that have wrecked their local landscapes. Others see Disney World as an oasis of social tranquility and security in comparison to their patrolled, but nonetheless deteriorating, maybe even perilous neighborhoods. A recent essay in *Time* captured some of these sentiments: "Do you see anybody [at Disney World] lying on the street or begging for money? Do you see anyone jumping on your car and wanting to clean your windshield—and when you say no, they get abusive?"[3]

Comments such as these do more than betray the class anxiety of the middle strata. They poignantly express the inability of this group to make distinctions between what necessarily constitutes the public and the private sectors. Do visitors forget that they pay a daily use fee (upwards of $150 for a four-day stay) just to be a citizen of Disney World (not to mention the $100 per night hotel bill)? Maybe so—and maybe it's precisely *forgetting* that visitors pay for.

If there is any distinction to be made between Disney World and our local shopping malls, it would have to do with Disney's successful exclusion of all factors that might put the lie to its uniform social fabric. The occasional Hispanic mother who arrives with extended family and illegal bologna sandwiches is an anomaly. So too is the first-generation Cubana who buys a year-round pass to Disney's nightspot, Pleasure Island, in hopes of meeting a rich and marriageable British tourist. These women testify to the presence of Orlando, Disney World's marginalized "Sister City," whose overflowing cheap labor force and overcrowded and under-funded public institutions are the unseen real world upon which Disney's world depends.

1995

Notes

1. Scott Bukatman, "There's Always Tomorrowland: Disney and the Hypercinematic Experience," October 57 (Summer 1991), pp. 55–78.
2. Michael Sorkin, "See You in Disneyland," Design Quarterly (Winter 1992), pp. 5–13.
3. "Fantasy's Reality," *Time*, 27 May 1991, p. 54.

READING, REREADING, AND ANALYSIS

1. What is the true subject of Willis's essay? What is Disney World an example of? What other examples might Willis have used?

2. Throughout this essay, Willis describes Disney's programmed amusement as the opposite of spontaneity and play. As you read, look for clues in the essay that show how she is defining those terms. When you have read through the essay once, go back and find two examples that show the difference between programmed amusement and spontaneous play. Note page numbers for those examples and write a paragraph describing the difference.

3. Working in groups, list everything that gets "commodified" by Disney World, according to Willis. Then go back through your list and choose two examples that show how commodification works. Present your examples to the class. What does Willis want us to think about commodification?

4. Analyze the title of this essay. How is Willis using the term "state"? Identify other terms in the essay that are unfamiliar to you or are used in unfamiliar ways. How do "state" and the other terms used in the title help to categorize the type of language Willis uses in the essay? What does this language tell us about Willis's opinion of Disney World?

RESPONDING THROUGH WRITING: BUILDING AN INTERPRETATION

5. Write a paper based on your computer game or website analysis in response to question 8. Use definitions and examples from Willis's essay to explain her terms as you apply them to aspects of your example. Are there ways to subvert the goals and rules of the program? Are there features of the site that do not fit Willis's terms or that go beyond them? What happens when you think of the rules that order your example as restrictive or limiting? Is there a place for spontaneity within the rules? Explain.

6. Use Willis's essay as a model for creating your own analysis of a commodifying place, such as a chain store, a tourist spot, or a shopping mall. What are the possibilities for planned amusement versus spontaneous play in your example? What is being commodified as compared with Disney World, where Willis argues that the family, memory, and attempted subversion all get commodified? Are there ways to imagine similar spaces but ones that have more room for play? In your writing, design some improvements that would lessen the commodifying effect in the example you've chosen.

7. Write an essay in response to Willis's claim that "what's most interesting about Disney World is what's not there" (p. 585). Read the quotation closely. What does Willis believe is missing? Why does she think its absence is interesting and to whom? Do you agree with her assessment?

GOING FURTHER: LEARNING FROM OTHER SOURCES

8. Because computer games and Internet websites are able to create virtual realities, they may be even more capable than Disney of creating seamless, imaginary worlds. Explore a video game or an appropriate website, and analyze what you see using Willis's terms. How much of the site is structured around amusement? How much spontaneous play is possible? What is being commodified? Are there ways to subvert the commodification? Is the

site preserving a "magic" that could be spoiled by knowing its "backstage" programs?

APPLYING WHAT YOU'VE LEARNED

9. Use Jeanette Winterson's essay, "Imagination and Reality," to test Willis's argument. Is Disney World just an outgrowth of "money culture," of commodification taken to the extreme? Or does Disney World embody some of the aspects of art and imagination that Winterson values? Can money culture and the function of imagination be kept as separate as Winterson implies?

10. Willis seems quite critical of Disney World, and she relies on tough, complex, analytical language throughout her piece. Does her language or her stance as a critic hinder her ability to fully "see" Disney World or to be open to her experience there? Using Walker Percy's consideration of the "spoliation" of experience by theory, examine Willis as an example of "the expert." How does her "theory" about Disney affect her experience of the park?

11. Willis claims that "many visitors . . . treat the wonderland environment as more real than real" (p. 583). What does she mean? How does her use of the word "real" compare with Yi-Fu Tuan's use of it (p. 548)?

12. Look back at Stuart Ewen's essay, "The Marriage Between Art and Commerce." Is Disney World as Willis describes it an example of "consumer engineering"? How do Disney's images relate to Ewen's discussion of style? Ewen claims that style is always being used up. Will Disney's images also be used up? Explain.

JEANETTE WINTERSON

Jeanette Winterson (b. 1959) is an acclaimed writer of creative fiction whose novels include *The Passion, Sexing the Cherry,* and *Written on the Body*. Her most recent work is the novel *Lighthousekeeping*. Among her many jobs, Winterson includes work as a make-up artist at a funeral parlor, an assistant at a mental hospital, and a publisher. She became a full-time writer in 1987. "Imagination and Reality" is a selection from her essay collection, *Art Objects: Essays on Ecstasy and Effrontery*.

To learn more about Winterson, visit her homepage at <http://www.jeanettewinterson.com/>.

WHAT DO YOU KNOW? WHAT DO YOU EXPECT TO DISCOVER?

Before reading the essay, take a moment to consider the following questions.

1. What topics does Winterson's biography suggest she is interested in? What do you know about those topics? Knowledge can come from personal experience, stories you've heard, other classes you've taken, or other reading you've done.

2. We typically understand "imagination" and "reality" as opposites. Think of some examples, however, in which imagination and reality are not necessarily opposites. Is there such a thing as imaginative reality and such a thing as the "reality of the imagination," a phrase Winterson uses in her essay?

3. In the essay that follows, Winterson discusses the roles art plays in our commercial culture and also the roles art could play. What do you consider the role of art to be in your life, in the life of your family, and in the life of United States culture? Make a list of the roles you identify.

⅍

Imagination and Reality

The reality of art is the reality of the imagination.

W̶hat do I mean by reality of art?

What do I mean by reality of imagination?

My statement, and the questions it suggests, are worth consider-ing now that the fashionable approach to the arts is once again through the narrow gate of subjective experience. The charge laid on the artist, and in particular on the writer, is not to bring back visions but to play the Court photographer.

Is this anathema to art? Is it anti-art? I think so. What art pre-sents is much more than the daily life of you and me, and the original role of the artist as visionary is the correct one.

"Real" is an old word, is an odd word. It used to mean a Spanish sixpence; a small silver coin, money of account in the days when the value of a coin was the value of its metal. We are used to notional money but 'real' is an honest currency.

The honest currency of art is the honest currency of the imagination.

The small silver coin of art cannot be spent; that is, it cannot be exchanged or exhausted. What is lost, what is destroyed, what is tarnished, what is misappropriated, is ceaselessly renewed by the min-ing, shaping, forging imagination that exists beyond the conjectures of the everyday. Imagination's coin, the infinitely flexible metal of the Muse, metal of the moon, in rounded structure offers new universes, pri-mary worlds, that substantially confront the pretences of notional life.

Notional life is the life encouraged by governments, mass education and the mass media. Each of those powerful agencies couples an as-sumption of its own importance with a disregard for individuality. Free-dom of choice is the catch phrase but streamlined homogeneity is the objective. A people who think for themselves are hard to control and what is worse, in a money culture, they may be sceptical of product ad-vertising. Since our economy is now a consumer economy, we must be credulous and passive. We must believe that we want to earn money to buy things we don't need. The education system is not designed to turn out thoughtful individualists, it is there to get us to work. When we come home exhausted from the inanities of our jobs we can relax in front of the inanities of the TV screen. This pattern, punctuated by birth, death and marriage and a new car, is offered to us as real life.

Children who are born into a tired world as batteries of new energy are plugged into the system as soon as possible and gradually drained away. At the time when they become adult and conscious they are already depleted and prepared to accept a world of shadows. Those who have kept their spirit find it hard to nourish it and between the ages of twenty and thirty, many are successfully emptied of all resistance. I do not think it an exaggeration to say that most of the energy of most of the people is being diverted into a system which destroys them. Money is no antidote. If the imaginative life is to be renewed it needs its own coin.

We have to admit that the arts stimulate and satisfy a part of our nature that would otherwise be left untouched and that the emotions art arouses in us are of a different order to those aroused by experience of any other kind.

We think we live in a world of sense-experience and what we can touch and feel, see and hear, is the sum of our reality. Although neither physics nor philosophy accepts this, neither physics nor philosophy has been as successful as religion used to be at persuading us of the doubtfulness of the seeming-solid world. This is a pity if only because while religion was a matter of course, the awareness of other realities was also a matter of course. To accept God was to accept Otherness, and while this did not make the life of the artist any easier (the life of the artist is never easy,) a general agreement that there is more around us than the mundane allows the artist a greater licence and a greater authority than he or she can expect in a society that recognises nothing but itself.

An example of this is the development of the visual arts under Church patronage during the late medieval and Renaissance periods in Europe. This was much more than a patronage of money, it was a warrant to bring back visions. Far from being restricted by Church rhetoric, the artist knew that he and his audience were in tacit agreement; each went in search of the Sublime.

Art is visionary; it sees beyond the view from the window, even though the window is its frame. This is why the arts fare much better alongside religion than alongside either capitalism or communism. The god-instinct and the art-instinct both apprehend more than the physical biological material world. The artist need not believe in God, but the artist does consider reality as multiple and complex. If the audience accepts this premise it is then possible to think about the work itself. As things stand now, too much criticism of the arts concerns itself with attacking any suggestion of art as Other, as a bringer of realities beyond the commonplace. Dimly, we know we need those other realities and we think we can get them by ransacking different cultures and rhapsodising work by foreign writers simply because they are foreign writers. We are still back with art as the mirror of life, only it is a more exotic or less democratic life than our own. No doubt this has its interests but if we are honest, they are documentary. Art is not documentary. It may incidentally serve that function in its own way but its true effort is to open to us dimensions of the spirit and of the self that normally lie smothered under the weight of living.

It is in Victorian England that the artist first becomes a rather suspect type who does not bring visions but narcotics and whose relationship to different levels of reality is not authoritative but hallucinatory. In Britain, the nineteenth century recovered from the shock of Romanticism by adopting either a manly Hellenism, with an interest in all things virile and Greek, or a manly philistinism, which had done with sweet Jonney Keats and his band and demanded of the poet, if he must be a poet, that he be either declamatory or decorative. Art could be rousing or it could be entertaining. If it hinted at deeper mysteries it was effeminate and absurd. The shift in sensibility from early to late Wordsworth is the shift of the age. For Tennyson, who published his first collection in 1830, the shift was a painful one and the compromises he made to his own work are clear to anyone who flicks through the collected poems and finds a visionary poet trying to hide himself in legend in order to hint at sublimities not allowed to his own time. Like Wordsworth before him, Tennyson fails whenever he collapses into the single obsessive reality of the world about him. As a laureate we know he is lying. As a visionary we read him now and find him true.

And what are we but our fathers' sons and daughters? We are the Victorian legacy. Our materialism, our lack of spirituality, our grossness, our mockery of art, our utilitarian attitude to education, even the dull grey suits wrapped around the dull grey lives of our eminent City men, are Victorian hand-me-downs. Many of our ideas of history and society go back no further than Victorian England. We live in a money culture because they did. Control by plutocracy is a nineteenth-century phenomenon that has been sold to us as a blueprint for reality. But what is real about the values of a money culture?

Money culture recognizes no currency but its own. Whatever is not money, whatever is not making money, is useless to it. The entire efforts of our government as directed through our society are efforts towards making more and more money. This favours the survival of the dullest. This favours those who prefer to live in a notional reality where goods are worth more than time and where things are more important than ideas.

For the artist, any artist, poet, painter, musician, time in plenty and an abundance of ideas are the necessary basics of creativity. By dreaming and idleness and then by intense self-discipline does the artist live. The artist cannot perform between 9 and 6, five days a week, or if she sometimes does, she cannot guarantee to do so. Money culture hates that. It must know what it is getting, when it is getting it, and how much it will cost. The most tyrannical of patrons never demanded from their protegées what the market now demands of artists; if you can't sell your work regularly and quickly, you can either starve or do something else. The time that art needs, which may not be a long time, but which has to be its own time, is anathema to a money culture. Money confuses time with itself. That is part of its unreality.

Against this golden calf in the wilderness where all come to buy and sell, the honest currency of art offers quite a different rate of exchange. The artist does not turn time into money, the artist turns time into energy, time into intensity, time into vision. The exchange that art offers is an exchange in kind; energy for energy, intensity for intensity, vision for vision. This is seductive and threatening. Can we make the return? Do we want to? Our increasingly passive diversions do not equip us, mentally, emotionally, for the demands that art makes. We know we are dissatisfied, but the satisfactions that we seek come at a price beyond the resources of a money culture. Can we afford to live imaginatively, contemplatively? Why have we submitted to a society that tries to make imagination a privilege when to each of us it comes as a birthright?

It is not a question of the money in your pocket. Money can buy you the painting or the book or the opera seat but it cannot expose you to the vast energies you will find there. Often it will shield you from them, just as a rich man can buy himself a woman but not her love. Love is reciprocity and so is art. Either you abandon yourself to another world that you say you seek or you find ways to resist it. Most of us are art-resisters because art is a challenge to the notional life. In a money culture, art, by its nature, objects. It fields its own realities, lives by its own currency, aloof to riches and want. Art is dangerous.

For Sale: My Life. Highest Bidder Collects.

The honest currency of art is the honest currency of the imagination.

In Middle English, "real" was a variant of "royal".

Can we set aside images of our own dishonoured monarchy and think instead about the ancientness and complexity of the word 'royal'?

To be royal was to be distinguished in the proper sense; to be sin-gled out, by one's fellows and by God or the gods. In both the Greek and the Hebraic traditions, the one who is royal is the one who has special access to the invisible world. Ulysses can talk to Hera, King David can talk to God. Royalty on earth is expected to take its duties on earth seriously but the King should also be a bridge between the terrestrial and the supernatural.

Perhaps it seems strange to us that in the ancient world the King was more accessible to his people than were the priests. Although King and priest worked together, priesthood, still allied to magic, even by the Hebrews, was fully mysterious. The set-apartness of the priest is one surrounded by ritual and taboo. The priest did not fight in battle, take concubines, hoard treasure, feast and riot, sin out of hu-manness, or if he did, there were severe penalties. The morality of the priesthood was not the morality of Kingship and whether you read *The Odyssey* or The Bible, the difference is striking. The King is not better behaved than his subjects, essentially he was (or should have been) the nobler man.

In Britain, royalty was not allied to morality until the reign of Queen Victoria. Historically, the role of the King or Queen had been to lead and inspire, this is an imaginative role, and it was most perfectly fulfilled by Elizabeth the First, Gloriana, the approachable face of God-head. Gloriana is the Queen whose otherness is for the sake of her peo-ple, and it is important to remember that the disciplines she laid upon her own life, in particular her chastity, were not for the sake of exam-ple but for the sake of expediency. The Divine Right of Kings was not a good conduct award it was a mark of favour. God's regent upon earth was expected to behave like God and anyone who studies Greek or He-brew literature will find that God does not behave like a Christian schoolmistress. God is glorious, terrifying, inscrutable, often capricious to human eyes, extravagant, victorious, legislative but not law-abiding, and, the supreme imagination. "In the beginning was the Word."

At its simplest and at its best, royalty is an imaginative function; it must embody in its own person, subtle and difficult concepts of Otherness. The priest does not embody these concepts, the priest serves them. The priest is a functionary, the King is a function.

Shakespeare is preoccupied with Kingship as a metaphor for the imaginative life. Leontes and Lear, Macbeth and Richard II, are stud-ies in the failure of the imagination. In *The Winter's Tale*, the redemp-tion of Leontes is made possible through a new capacity in him; the capacity to see outside of his own dead vision into a chance as vibrant as it is unlikely. When Paulina says to him, "It is required you do awake your faith" she does not mean religious faith. If the statue of Hermione is to come to life, Leontes must believe it *can* come to life. This is not common sense. It is imagination.

In the earliest Hebrew creation stories Yahweh makes himself a clay model of a man and breathes on it to give it life. It is this supreme confidence, this translation of forms, the capacity to recognise in one thing the potential of another, and the willingness to let that potential realise itself, that is the stamp of creativity and the birthright that Yahweh gives to humans. Leontes' failure to acknowledge any reality other than his own is a repudiation of that birthright, a neglect of humanness that outworks itself into the fixed immobility of his queen. When Hermione steps down and embraces Leontes it is an imaginative reconciliation.

I hope it is clear that as I talk about King and priest I am dealing in abstracts and not actualities. I do not wish to upset republicans anywhere. What I do want to do is to move the pieces across the chessboard to see if that gives us a different view.

By unraveling the word "real" I hope to show that it contains in itself, and without any wishful thinking on my part, those densities of imaginative experience that belong to us all and that are best communicated through art. I see no conflict between reality and imagination. They are not in fact separate. Our real lives hold within them our royal lives; the inspiration to be more than we are, to find new solutions, to live beyond the moment. Art helps us to do this because it fuses together temporal and perpetual realities.

To see outside of a dead vision is not an optical illusion.

The realist (from the Latin *res* = thing) who thinks he deals in things and not images and who is suspicious of the abstract and of art, is not the practical man but a man caught in a fantasy of his own unmaking.

The realist unmakes the coherent multiple world into a collection of random objects. He thinks of reality as that which has an objective existence, but understands no more about objective existence than that which he can touch and feel, sell and buy. A lover of objects and of objectivity, he is a fact caught in a world of symbols and symbolism, where he is unable to see the thing in itself, as it really is, he sees it only in relation to his own story of the world.

The habit of human beings is to see things subjectively or not to see them at all. The more familiar a thing becomes the less it is seen. In the home, nobody looks at the furniture, they sit on it, eat off it, sleep on it and forget it until they buy something new. When we do look at other people's things, we are usually thinking about the cachet, their value, what they say about their owner. Our minds work to continually label and absorb what we see and to fit it neatly into our own pattern. That done, we turn away. This is a sound survival skill but it makes it very difficult to let anything have an existence independent of ourselves, whether furniture or people. It makes it easier to buy symbols, things that have a particular value to us, than it does to buy objects.

My mother, who was poor, never bought objects, she bought symbols. She used to save up to buy something hideous to put in the best parlour. What she bought was factory made and beyond her purse. If she had ever been able to see it in its own right, she could never have spent money on it. She couldn't see it, and nor could any of the neighbours dragged in to admire it. They admired the effort it had taken to save for it. They admired how much it cost. Above all, they admired my mother; the purchase was a success.

I know that when my mother sat in her kitchen that had only a few pieces of handmade furniture, she felt depressed and conscious of her lowly social status. When she sat in her dreadful parlour with a china cup and a bought biscuit, she felt like a lady. The parlour, full of objects unseen but hard won, was a fantasy chamber, a reflecting mirror. Like Mrs. Joe, in *Great Expectations*, she finally took her apron off.

Money culture depends on symbolic reality. It depends on a confusion between the object and what the object represents. To keep you and me buying and upgrading an overstock of meaningless things depends on those things having an acquisitional value. It is the act of buying that is important. In our society, people who cannot buy things are the underclass.

Symbolic man surrounds himself with objects as tyrants surround themselves with subjects: "These will obey me. Through them I am worshipped. Through them I exercise control." These fraudulent kingdoms, hard-headed and practical, are really the soft-centre of fantasy. They are wish fulfillment nightmares where more is piled on more to manufacture the illusion of abundance. They are lands of emptiness and want. Things do not satisfy. In part they fail to satisfy because their symbolic value changes so regularly and what brought whistles of admiration one year is next year's car boot sale bargain. In part they fail to satisfy because much of what we buy is gadgetry and fashion, which makes objects temporary and the need to be able to purchase them, permanent. In part they fail to satisfy because we do not actually want the things we buy. They are illusion, narcotic, hallucination.

To suggest that the writer, the painter, the musician, is the one out of touch with the real world is a doubtful proposition. It is the artist who must apprehend things fully, in their own right, communicating them not as symbols but as living realities with the power to move.

To see outside of a dead vision is not an optical illusion.

According to the science of optics, if an image consists of points through which light actually passes, it is called real. Otherwise it is called virtual.

The work of the artist is to see into the life of things; to discriminate between superficialities and realities; to know what is genuine and what is a make-believe. The artist through the disciplines of her work, is one of the few people who does see things as they really are, stripped of associative value. I do not mean that artists of whatever sort have perfect taste or perfect private lives, I mean that when the imaginative capacity is highly developed, it is made up of invention and discernment. Invention is the shaping spirit that re-forms fragments into new wholes, so that even what has been familiar can be seen fresh. Discernment is to know how to test the true and the false and to reveal objects, emotions, ideas in their own coherence. The artist is a translator; one who has learned how to pass into her own language the languages gathered from stones, from birds, from dreams, from the body, from the material world, from the invisible world, from sex, from death, from love. A different language is a different reality; what is the language, the world, of stones? What is the language, the world, of birds? Of atoms? Of microbes? Of colours? Of air? The material world is closed to those who think of it only as a commodity market.

> How do you know but every bird that cuts the airy way
> Is an immense world of delight closed by your senses five?
>
> William Blake,
> *The Marriage of Heaven and Hell* (c. 1790)

To those people every object is inanimate. In fact they are the ones who remain unmoved, fixed rigidly within their own reality.

The artist is moved.

The artist is moved through multiple realities. The artist is moved by empty space and points of light. The artist tests the image. Does light pass through it? Is it illuminated? It is sharp, clear, its own edges, its own form?

The artist is looking for real presences. I suppose what the scientist Rupert Sheldrake would call "morphic resonance"; the inner life of the thing that cannot be explained away biologically, chemically, physically. In the Catholic Church "real presence" is the bread and wine that through transubstantiation becomes the living eucharist; the body and blood of Christ. In the Protestant Church the bread and wine are symbols only, one of the few places where we recognise that we are asking one thing to substitute for another. For the average person, this substitution is happening all the time.

The real presence, the image transformed by light, is not rare but it is easily lost or mistaken under clouds of subjectivity. People who claim to like pictures and books will often only respond to those pictures and books in which they can clearly find themselves. This is ego masquerading as taste. To recognise the worth of a thing is more than recognising its worth to you. Our responses to art are conditioned by our insistence that it present to us realities we can readily accept, however virtual those realities might be. Nevertheless art has a stubborn way of cutting through the subjective world of symbols and money and offering itself as a steady alternative to the quick change act of daily life.

We are naturally suspicious of faculties that we do not ourselves possess and we do not quite believe that the poet can read the sermons in stones or the painter know the purple that bees love. Still we are drawn to books and pictures and music, finding in ourselves an echo of their song, finding in ourselves an echo of their sensibility, an answering voice through the racket of the day.

Art is for us a reality beyond now. An imaginative reality that we need. The reality of art is the reality of the imagination.

The reality of art is not the reality of experience.

The charge laid on the artist is to bring back visions.

In Shakespeare's *Othello,* we find that the Moor wins Desdemona's heart by first winning her imagination. He tells her tales of cannibals and of the Anthropophagi whose heads grow beneath their shoulders. What he calls his "round unvarnished tale" is a subtle mixture of art and artfulness. When a Shakespearean hero apologises for his lack of wit we should be on our guard. Shakespeare always gives his heroes the best lines, even when the hero is Richard II.

Othello's untutored language is in fact powerful and wrought. He is more than a master of arms, he is a master of art. It is his words that win Desdemona. She says "I saw Othello's visage in his mind." His face, like his deeds, belongs to the world of sense-experience, but it is his wit that makes both dear to her. For Desdemona, the reality of Othello is his imaginative reality.

OTHELLO   she thank'd me,
                    And bade me, if I had a friend that lov'd
                                                              her,
                    I should but teach him how to tell my story,
                    And that would woo her.

The clue here is not the story but the telling of it. It is not Othello the action man who has taught Desdemona to love him, it is Othello the poet.

We know that Shakespeare never bothered to think of a plot. As a good dramatist and one who earned his whole living by his work, he had to take care to make his historical ransackings stage-satisfactory. The engineering of the plays gives pleasure even to those who are not interested in the words. But the words are the thing. The words are what interested Shakespeare and what should closely interest us. Shakespeare is a dramatic poet. He is not a chronicler of experience.

I have to say something so obvious because of the multitude of so called realists, many making money out of print, who want art to be as small as they are. For them, art is a copying machine busily copying themselves. They like the documentary version, the "life as it is lived." To support their opinions they will either point to Dickens or Shakespeare. I have never understood why anyone calls Dickens a realist, but I have dealt with that myth elsewhere. . . . As for Shakespeare, they will happily disregard the pervading spirit behind the later plays, and quote *Hamlet* Act III, Scene II "the purpose of playing . . . is, to hold, as 'twere, the mirror up to nature."

But what is nature?

From the Latin *Natura*, it is my birth, my characteristics, my condition. It is my nativity, my astrology, my biology, my physiognomy, my geography, my cartography, my spirituality, my sexuality, my mentality, my corporeal, intellectual, emotional, imaginative self. And not just my self, every self and the Self of the world. There is no mirror I know that can show me all of these singularities, unless it is the strange distorting looking-glass of art where I will not find my reflection nor my representation but a nearer truth than I prefer. *Natura* is the whole that I am. The multiple reality of my existence.

The reality of the imagination leaves out nothing. It is the most complete reality that we can know. Imagination takes in the world of sense experience, and rather than trading it for a world of symbols, delights in it for what it is. The artist is physical and it is in the work of true artists in any medium, that we find the most moving and the most poignant studies of the world that we can touch and feel. It is the writer, the painter, and not the realist, who is intimate with the material world, who knows its smells and tastes because they are fresh in her nostrils, full in her mouth. What her hand touches, she feels. R. A. Collingwood said that Cézanne painted like a blind man (critics at the time agreed though for different reasons). He meant that the two-dimensional flimsy world of what is overlooked by most of us, suddenly reared out of the canvas, massy and tough. Cézanne seems to have hands in his eyes and eyes in his hands. When Cézanne paints a tree or an apple, he does not paint a copy of a tree or an apple, he paints its nature. He paints the whole that it is, the whole that is lost to us as we pass it, eat it, chop it down. It is through the painter, writer, composer, who lives more intensely than the rest of us, that we can rediscover the intensity of the physical world.

And not only the physical world. There is no limit to new territory. The gate is open. Whether or not we go through is up to us, but to stand mockingly on the threshold, claiming that nothing lies beyond, is something of a flat earth theory.

The earth is not flat and neither is reality. Reality is continuous, multiple, simultaneous, complex, abundant and partly invisible. The imagination alone can fathom this and it reveals its fathomings through art.

The reality of art is the reality of the imagination.

1996

READING, REREADING, AND ANALYSIS

1. According to Winterson, what is "the charge laid on the artist" (p. 598)?

2. Look up the words "reality" and "imagination" in the dictionary. Does Winterson's use of these words follow those definitions? What new or unexpected elements does she add to these terms?

3. Winterson gives an example of her mother's perception of and relationship to her furniture. Working in a group, explain the author's example. Then read the paragraphs before and after the example to look for clues about Winterson's larger point. What is Winterson trying to explain about our subjective relationship to the things around us?

4. In the paragraph beginning "The work of the artist . . ." (p. 604), Winterson tries to describe the artist's relationship to things. How is that relationship different from the relationship of her mother to her furniture?

5. What does "money culture" mean for Winterson? What are her criticisms of it and are they well founded from your perspective? Why and how is art an alternative to "money culture"?

6. What does Winterson mean on page 605 when she writes,

> The artist is a translator; one who has learned how to pass into her own language the language gathered from stones, from birds, from dreams, from the body, from the material world, from the invisible world, from sex, from death, from love. A different language is a different reality; what is the language, the world, of stones?

RESPONDING THROUGH WRITING:
BUILDING AN INTERPRETATION

7. In two paragraphs, discuss whether Winterson's essay fulfills her definition of "art." Respond not only to specific passages from Winterson's essay but also to the form of it. How and why does Winterson attempt to connect the content of the essay—her ideas—with the form of the essay—its appearance and style?

8. Assume that you read Winterson's essay in your campus newspaper. Write a letter to the editor that responds to Winterson's discussion of "money culture" and her provocative claim that "the education system is not designed to turn out thoughtful individualists, it is there to get us to work" (p. 599).

9. Write an essay describing your sense of who "uses" art and who does not. Connect quotations from Winterson's essay with examples from your own experience. Your essay should include your response to some of the following questions: Which of Winterson's details, examples, or references suggest that she imagines her readers to be well educated? Where does art fit into Winterson's understanding of what it means to be well educated? What have been your experiences with art? Where do you see art fitting into your college education? If your campus has an art museum, have you been to it? If you have, what did you see? Did you like what you saw? If you have not visited, why not?

10. Winterson defines several terms in her essay. Make a list of the definitions you see in her text, and write an essay in which you discuss and analyze her use of definitions. In your paper you might respond to some of the following questions: How do her definitions relate to her thesis or main argument? What did you learn from her definitions? Which definitions seem the most important or interesting or puzzling, and why? How do the definitions help her structure her writing (the essay's form or arrangement) and help her support her larger argument? Do you find her use of definitions helpful or problematic, eloquent or hard to follow, and why?

GOING FURTHER: LEARNING
FROM OTHER SOURCES

11. Find a painting or visual image in a book or on the Internet that you consider to be art (Hint: Try a popular search engine such as AltaVista, limit your search to images, and search in the "Arts" category.) You could even choose a work by Cézanne, an artist Winterson clearly admires. Copy or print out this image, and bring it to class to discuss in the context of Winterson's claims about art. Begin thinking about this by asking yourself what your example suggests about two of Winterson's key terms, "imagination" and "reality." What makes this image "art"?

12. Search for the combined term "art and money" using a database of scholarly articles, such as Academic Search Elite, or a database that includes general-interest and current-events-related magazines such as MAS Full Text Ultra. Scan the resulting articles for

overlaps between the worlds of "money culture" and "art and imagination" that might help you to question or challenge Winterson's ideas about the split between these worlds.

APPLYING WHAT YOU'VE LEARNED

13. Use Winterson's ideas about the imagination, money culture, and symbolic reality to analyze an example from Stuart Ewen's "The Marriage Between Art and Commerce" (p. 178). Ewen discusses how styles affect marketing and sales. How does Ewen's argument fit into Winterson's ideas about the link between imagination and money? You might consider the following quotation from Ewen as a point of entry: "Styling, it was increasingly argued, must speak to the unconscious, to those primal urges and sensations that are repressed in the everyday confines of civilization."

14. Use Winterson's idea about the artist as "visionary" to test Ralph Ellison's definition of the particular requirements of an "American" art as outlined in "The Little Man at Chehaw Station." Does Winterson's idea of the artist's role support or resist Ellison's sense of how American artists are always up against "the little man behind the stove"? Does the United States as Ellison imagines it present an artistic environment that is impoverished by the "money culture" that Winterson decries? What do you think Winterson, who is British, would say about Ellison's idea of America?

15. Use Winterson's discussion of the tensions between "imagination" and "money culture" as a critical lens to help you view in some new ways the theses or main arguments in one or two of the following texts: Gloria Anzaldúa's "Chicana Art: Exploring *Nepantla, el Lugar de la Frontera*," Scott DeVeaux's "Progress and the Bean," Walker Percy's "The Loss of the Creature," Susan Sontag's "In Plato's Cave," and Susan Willis's "Disney World: Public Use/Private State." In your paper, be sure to discuss the following claim in Winterson's essay: "I do not think it an exaggeration to say that most of the energy of most of the people is being diverted into a system which destroys them. Money is no antidote. If the imaginative life is to be renewed it needs its own coin" (p. 599).

Part III

Assignment Sequences

Assignment Sequences

SUCCESSFUL WRITING IS AN ACT of both reconsideration of established ideas (revision) and discovery of fresh paths (exploration). Therefore, we prefer writing assignments that draw on earlier work while enabling new thinking, assignments that ask for both revision and exploration. The following assignment sequences offer clusters of writing assignments and examples of ways to imagine just a few of the conversations that the readings in *Making Sense* engender. You will probably see other connections between texts and even more ideas for essays as you read through *Making Sense*—and, indeed, our Applying What You've Learned questions at the end of each reading selection offer additional assignment ideas. But we provide these sequences here as examples of the kind and range of writing that is possible with *Making Sense* and to demonstrate that multiple readings and linked assignments can provide richness and depth that is often less possible in courses with several discrete "units" and varying course content.

By "sequences" we mean groupings of assignments that build on one another by adding elements, raising related questions, and asking for dialogue between texts. The assignments are "in sequence" because each new assignment depends upon the previous assignment or assignments. Each new reading, then, enters a context, and the subsequent discussion and writing both works out of and revises that context. In essence, the sequences allow student writers to establish some authority and some common language for grappling with the evolving course content.

The sequences do more than provide "themes" on which to write, however. Indeed, many of these sequences offer unexpected linkages intended to challenge received ideas about how a text might be used. We do not always, for example, group pieces with a scientific emphasis with other science-oriented selections. You will see that each selection is used in more than one sequence and in more than one way. We are as interested in the framing ideas of each piece and in *how* it says what it says as much as, simply, its content or theme.

Sequencing assignments allows for a revision of an earlier idea but without the static experience of revising one paper over and over. Call it "revision through revisiting." In other words, a second assignment will build on the first without repeating its exact goals. It may, in fact, ask for a substantial reexamination of previous assumptions or claims. Later assignments use some of the same texts and ask similar (but developing) questions, and student writers can then refer back to the first assignment and "revisit" some of the same questions and problems but now with added materials and insight. They can access the best parts of their previous writing but also leave the lesser aspects behind.

Sequenced assignments offer these advantages:

- Working with multiple texts over a sustained period of time
- Revising one's writing without repeating one's work
- Echoing the academic practice of finding ideas for writing amid ongoing debate
- Seeing published writers as contributors to a discussion but not necessarily stable, unassailable authorities
- Increasing the scale and depth of what is possible in a single semester

Note: Our sequences are not exhaustive, and we have deliberately left out such details as page lengths, paper formatting, and schedule information. We expect that each writing class will have its own rhythms and its own requirements, and these sequences are meant to complement a wide range of classroom practices.

SEQUENCE 1: *Challenging the Inertia of Old Ideas*

Readings: Toumey, Percy, Lessig, Hochschild

Assignment 1

Both Toumey and Percy have great concerns about what Percy calls the "predicament" of our "modern technical society" (p. 409). Specifically, both authors address the consequences of influence by forces that are sometimes hard to see or recognize. What, in their terms, is this "predicament" exactly, and how can we overcome or lessen its negative impacts on our lives? In an essay that uses both Toumey and Percy, develop one example or situation (real or hypothetical), and use it to comment on the issues at hand. Stay specific and focused on your example as you apply concepts, keywords, or ideas from Toumey and Percy. Ultimately, your paper should explore an aspect (only an aspect) of the topic in a manner that leads you to purposeful argument about the predicament your example entails.

This first essay should demonstrate your ability to understand and apply concepts and examples from critical sources. You'll be using one or more of Toumey's and Percy's concepts to help you describe and explore an idea you have about authority and experience (or something else). You needn't always agree with Toumey and Percy, but you must use their ideas to *frame* your discussion. Also, keep in mind that Toumey and Percy are not saying the same things, so a nuanced response will also account for the *differences* between the two pieces.

ASSIGNMENT 2

Lawrence Lessig seems eager to encourage new ways of thinking about technology. In many ways, he seems sympathetic to Percy's calls for discovery and innovation and Toumey's frustration with complacent acceptance. Using Percy or Toumey as an organizing "frame" for your discussion (as a source that provides concepts, ideas, and terminology for your analysis), write an essay that considers Lessig's challenge to the concept of "ownership," of "creativity," or of "freedom." You may look at more than one of these terms, but be sure to look closely at what Lessig says about *how* technology changes our understanding of these concepts. What do his examples show about the challenges of the digital age?

ASSIGNMENT 3

Arlie Russell Hochschild writes to show how two of the most revered things in America—work and family—can conflict. She describes this tension as a crisis in values and pressures: "Increasingly, our belief that family comes first conflicts with the emotional draw of both workplace and mall" (p. 217). Write an essay that develops her suggestions about what's at stake when capitalism becomes, in a sense, a religion. Look to your previous papers for important supplementary material. Draw on at least one of the previous texts (Percy, Toumey, or Lessig) to help you explore the question of just what compels people to change their ways, to alter their behavior. Are we simply the products of the ideas we inherit and learn through television and newspapers, or do we have the will and the tools to invent new and better ways of living? Why are new ideas so challenging for many people?

SEQUENCE 2: *Seeing and Knowing*

Readings: Percy, Winterson, Dillard

ASSIGNMENT 1

Write an essay that analyzes the link Walker Percy makes between "experts" and "theory" in the second half of "The Loss of the Creature." In your essay, you may want to look at the relationship

Percy sees between "experts" and "theory" with respect to his ideas of "sovereignty" and the "preformed symbolic complex." What is Percy trying to say about experts and what they know? Develop an example of your own to explore Percy's claims. Does Percy think we should avoid experts? Is he himself an expert who uses theory? Your essay should draw on these questions, but remember to explore the *consequences* of the positions you see Percy taking. Your writing should not only *report* on Percy but also convey your own response to the issues.

ASSIGNMENT 2

This new assignment allows you to extend and revise your understanding of Walker Percy's essay, "The Loss of the Creature." Think about the relationships you see between Percy's idea of "sovereignty" and Jeanette Winterson's understanding of the artist in her essay, "Imagination and Reality." Write an essay that examines whether Percy's "sovereign" person is a type of artist—a "visionary"—in Winterson's terms. As you begin to draft your essay, you might think about some of the following questions: What are Winterson's and Percy's attitudes toward "imagination"? What would Percy likely say in response to Winterson's claim that "the more familiar a thing becomes the less it is seen?" How does Percy define or characterize artists in his essay? Your essay should develop an idea about the consequences of the connections you see. Can we think of travel, schoolwork, or even conversation as an "art"?

ASSIGNMENT 3

In "Seeing," Annie Dillard discusses Marius von Senden's book, *Space and Sight,* which analyzes the spatial perception of the "newly sighted." The "newly sighted" are people who once were blind; they are given sight after successful cataract operations. "In general," Dillard writes, "the newly sighted see the world as a dazzle of color patches," and "many newly sighted people . . . teach us how dull is our own vision" (p. 121). Use Dillard's discussion of the "newly sighted" to help you assess the most significant arguments about "vision" in Walker Percy's "The Loss of the Creature" and Jeanette Winterson's "Imagination and Reality." Does Dillard's discussion of the "newly sighted" help you produce a re-vision of your previous understanding of Percy's or Winterson's main arguments about sight and insight? What does the comparison reveal?

SEQUENCE 3: *Reading Art and Culture*

Readings: Tompkins, Anzaldúa, Birkerts, Ewen

ASSIGNMENT 1

Jane Tompkins's "At the Buffalo Bill Museum" recounts her experience of the four museums in the Buffalo Bill Historical Center. Gloria Anzaldúa, in "Chicana Artists: Exploring *Nepantla, el Lugar de la Frontera*," writes of a similar experience at the Denver Museum of Natural History. Write an essay in which you consider the reactions that both authors have to the exhibits they encounter. What pieces do they respond to and why? How, in each case, does the exhibit lead the author to wider reflections? What topics do they proceed to consider?

ASSIGNMENT 2

Use Sven Birkerts's discussion of vertical and horizontal consciousness in "The Owl Has Flown" to analyze Gloria Anzaldúa's "reading" of "Aztec: The World of Moctezuma," the exhibition at the Denver Museum of Natural History. In what ways are Birkerts's discussions of reading and wisdom similar to Anzaldúa's experience of attending the exhibition (and in what ways do they differ)? Why might Anzaldúa object to your use of Birkerts's terminology as a framework for interpreting her arguments? Do you find Birkerts's discussions helpful or unhelpful in analyzing Anzaldúa's text?

ASSIGNMENT 3

Create a conversation between Gloria Anzaldúa and Stuart Ewen about art in America as a way to consider the effects of culture on identity. Think about key terms such as "border art" for Anzaldúa and the "marriage between art and commerce" for Ewen. How might Anzaldúa respond to Ewen's characterization of the "marriage between art and commerce"? Is art a tool for positive change or just a partner of commerce? In your response, you might look closely at the following assertions by Anzaldúa:

> The dominant culture consumes, swallows whole the ethnic artist, sucks out her vitality, and then spits out the hollow husk along with its labels (such as Hispanic). The dominant culture shapes the ethnic artist's identity if she does not scream loud enough to name herself. Until we live in a society where all people are more or less equal, we need these labels to resist the pressure to assimilate. (p. 64)

Does Ewen, in your view, subscribe to a similar view of the dominant culture? What might he say about Anzaldúa's claims?

To respond to this assignment, you need to quote from both texts to support your interpretation of how Ewen and Anzaldúa might respond to one another's work. Be sure to provide a shaping idea to your essay that tells your reader how *you* see this conversation.

ASSIGNMENT 4

In "Chicana Artists: Exploring *Nepantla, el Lugar de la Frontera*," Gloria Anzaldúa laments the fact that "border art" is "becoming trendy" and that it is being "misappropriated by pop culture" (p. 63).

What danger does Anzaldúa see? Is her anxiety justified? Is she overreacting? Use Stuart Ewen's discussion of "the style market" in "The Marriage Between Art and Commerce" or Sven Birkerts's argument about losing touch with depth and wisdom in our culture of superabundance to help you analyze the potential consequences, both positive and negative, of popular culture's appropriation of border art.

SEQUENCE 4: *Using Oneself as a Source*

Readings: Rodriguez, McGraw, Allison, Sommers

ASSIGNMENT 1

Erin McGraw begins her essay account of her failing eyes with a statement of her writing practice: "The subject veers almost uncontrollably toward metaphor, but I mean to take it literally" (p. 371). McGraw seems intent on offering a "literal," objective account, and yet her piece includes scores of examples of metaphors and other figurative language. For this paper, begin by reviewing the basic categories of figurative language and find as many examples as you can in "Bad Eyes." Write a paper that draws on some of those examples and develop an argument about why McGraw betrays her opening statement. How does the "poetic" use of language help McGraw communicate with readers? Finally, is this really an essay about blindness? Might her "bad eyes" be a metaphor for something else?

ASSIGNMENT 2

Richard Rodriguez's discussion of race and identity draws much of its strength from his self-deprecating account of his own confusion about his ethnic identity. He challenges perceived categories by showing us repeatedly how inadequate those categories are. For this assignment, think about his text in relation to McGraw's. What "kind" of writing is this? Do these pieces have arguments? How are these writers using personal experience to uncover and demonstrate insights? Write an analytical essay that offers an argument about the ways that personal knowledge or experience can be used to convey meaning. Do not forget to consider the limitations of personal experience. Why do many essays (and most academic essays) avoid using the personal?

ASSIGNMENT 3

Dorothy Allison is another writer drawing on personal experience, but in many ways her tone and approach seem quite distinct from either McGraw's or Rodriguez's. She privileges discord and confrontation and claims for art a role in "transgressing" everyday reality. Would McGraw or Rodriguez agree? In an essay that draws on McGraw and Rodriguez for contrast and support, examine Allison's claim that "the world is meaner than we admit, larger and more astonishing" (p. 49). How does her piece provide evidence and support for this claim and where does this thinking lead her?

ASSIGNMENT 4

This fourth essay assignment is a place to expand our definition of what an "essay" can be. In particular, you should feel that the subject of this assignment is broader than those of the first three. You can write about anything for this paper, but look carefully at how you write about this "anything."

Consider Nancy Sommers's comments from her essay, "I Stand Here Writing":

> I know that I can walk into text after text, source after source, and they will give me insight, but not answers. I have learned too that my sources can surprise me. Like my mother, I find myself sometimes surrounded by a field of four-leaf clovers, there for the picking, waiting to see what I can make of them. But I must be an inventor if I am to read those sources well, if I am to imagine the connections. (p. 458)

Write an essay on a "text" or "source" of your choosing that enables you to provide "insight, but not answers." What this means is that you should find something that you can interpret and explore and then follow your thinking through to new insights. Your reader may not be familiar with what you write about and you yourself may begin in uncertainty, but your goal should be to "translate" your topic into an idea that "makes sense" to you and your reader. Be as specific as possible about the thing you choose to write about, and remember to think of your paper as in many ways like the previous papers. You must still introduce, quote, analyze, and interpret your sources.

You might choose one of these sources:

Something you know a great deal about (music, movies, a book, a saying)

A "text" that has entered your life in some way (as in the short assignment)

Something small that you can connect to something else

You do not need to use any of the texts you've used this semester, but you may *choose* to do so if it helps you with the writing of this paper. You could, for example, respond directly to Sommers's claims about writing if you feel more comfortable beginning that way.

SEQUENCE 5: *Contradictions in Class and Classroom*
Readings: hooks, Charlip, Ellison

ASSIGNMENT 1

In "keeping close to home: class and education," bell hooks writes that she seeks "resolution and reconciliation" (p. 229) of the contradictions she finds in being a scholar from a working-class background. What does she discover about her schooling that creates those contradictions? In an essay that identifies at least one key contradiction, develop a presentation of and a response to hooks's ideas. How does she hope to "resolve" these problems?

ASSIGNMENT 2

Julie Charlip adds to our discussion of class and education by presenting a personal narrative that differs in some key ways from hooks's account of her experience. In an essay that revisits hooks's claims about the transforming (and disturbing) effects of education, look closely at Charlip's example. Do Charlip's experiences and her conclusions about those experiences bear out hooks's ideas? In your essay, be sure to connect an analysis of at least one of Charlip's anecdotes to a specific statement from hooks about social class.

ASSIGNMENT 3

Like hooks and Charlip, Ralph Ellison begins his essay with an account of his own experience of class distinctions in America. But where hooks and Charlip are primarily interested in addressing the injustices of class bias, Ellison turns his attention to the creative, artistic dimension of life in America. How does Ellison's approach to creativity and "American-ness" reframe the discussion that hooks and Charlip have set up? Does he come to conclusions similar to theirs? In your essay, be sure to reflect on the role artistic expression plays in our understanding of people and places.

SEQUENCE 6: *History and Memory*
Readings: Trask, Tompkins, Sturken

ASSIGNMENT 1

In "From a Native Daughter," Haunani-Kay Trask describes her realization that the historians of her homeland, Hawai'i, present a version of Hawai'i's history that conflicts with the history many Hawaiians have experienced: "This world, they had written, was the truth. . . . But this was not the story my mother told me" (p. 538). Why do you suppose such discrepancies of history and memory occur? What does

Trask suggest is the reason for the differences? In an essay that explores Trask's argument, develop an idea about the proper goal of history. What should a historian aim to do? How might she or he avoid the problems Trask details?

ASSIGNMENT 2

In "At the Buffalo Bill Museum, June 1988," Jane Tompkins looks at how the presentation of one figure from history, Buffalo Bill Cody, speaks to a range of still-active ideas about America, the West, and our collective responsibility for the history we make and preserve. The Buffalo Bill Museum is for Tompkins "a kind of charnel house that houses images of living things that have passed away but whose life force still lingers around their remains and so passes itself on to us" (p. 513). Remembering your first essay's claims about the purpose of history, write a new essay that examines the role museums play in keeping that history alive and active. What does Tompkins find that is so disturbing about museums? Does the museum offer something that Trask's history books do not? What is a museum supposed to do for us (or to us)?

ASSIGNMENT 3

We have looked at history books and museums. Marita Sturken's "The Wall, the Screen and the Image: The Vietnam Veterans Memorial" offers an excellent discussion of yet another way to represent the past: memorials. Sturken seems particularly interested in the debates about representation and meaning that go into the construction of a memorial. As she details the process through which the Vietnam Veterans Memorial came together, she provides an account, too, of the competing ideas of memory and imagination that swirl around such a project. Taking "history and memory" as your topic, write an essay that examines a similar project, such as the proposed World Trade Center Memorial or the World War II Memorial. Represent at least two competing ideas about what is "proper" for this memorial and what the final design communicates about our current attitudes toward cultural memory.

SEQUENCE 7: *Democracy and Debate*
Readings: Lasch, Ingham, Hochschild

ASSIGNMENT 1

In "The Lost Art of Argument," Christopher Lasch claims that there has been a decline in the kind of public debate that is the key to a working democracy. This assignment asks you to test Lasch's argument using examples from the press coverage of a current political issue. Choose a newspaper article as the basis for your analysis. Does the article have an "aura of objectivity," does it present information, or does it openly argue an "opinion"? Are you getting a "painstaking analysis of complex issues"? Are you getting more than one side of the issue? Do you see evidence of a public debate or a way in which public debate might reshape this political issue? Which of the historical factors that Lasch mentions would best explain the way the article is written? Even if you end up disagreeing with Lasch, demonstrate an understanding of his examples and his point of view.

ASSIGNMENT 2

In your first paper, you reflected on whether public debate can help to build a working democracy. Zita Ingham's article, "Landscape, Drama, Dissensus: The Rhetorical Education of Red Lodge, Montana," gives us a test case for analyzing how the people of Red Lodge used public debate to try to change their community. Would Lasch see Red Lodge as a working democracy? Do the strategies of "dissensus" or "deferred consensus" used by the people of Red Lodge have any connection to the historical uses of public debate that Lasch describes? Does the role of the Sonoran Institute, the "outsiders" who in some ways prompted the debate, affect the democratic significance of this community? Use this second paper to illustrate the connections you see between Lasch and Ingham.

ASSIGNMENT 3

In "From the Frying Pan into the Fire," Arlie Russell Hochschild provides some "unconventional wisdom" about the value system that has emerged in response to capitalism. She writes to reveal what she calls contradictions and conflicts in what is often represented as a seamless cultural fabric. What is the purpose of arguments such as this one that criticize common ways of life? Use Hochschild as an example to test some of Lasch's and Ingham's conclusions about the way communities and democracies can and should function and the role that writers and thinkers play in this work. Is Hochschild a good example of someone with a democratic impulse? Do the advertisements and messages she criticizes encourage debate and reflection? In thinking through your response to these questions, be sure to access the terms and ideas from Lasch and Ingham. Also, think about whether the writing you do for this course is in any sense "democratic."

SEQUENCE 8: *Imagination, Possibility, and Control*

Readings: Winterson, Mosley, Willis, Toumey

ASSIGNMENT 1

Jeanette Winterson concludes her essay, "Imagination and Reality," with the following statement: "The earth is not flat and neither is reality. Reality is continuous, multiple, simultaneous, complex, abundant and partly invisible. The imagination alone can fathom this and it reveals its fathomings through art. . . . The reality of art is the reality of the imagination" (p. 608). Winterson's conclusion requires interpretation; it is not immediately clear what she means. In fact, Winterson's entire essay develops an idea of imagination that is slippery and diffuse and that seems designed to be itself "continuous, multiple, simultaneous," and so on. Winterson, you could say, approaches writing both as an act of imagination and as art.

Consider the implications of imaginative and artful writing. How does Winterson's essay differ from other, more conventional essays you have read or from essays you have written? List some of those differences; then describe as best you can Winterson's writing strategy. Why is she writing in this way? How does her own writing demonstrate the qualities of imagination that she admires?

Assignment 2

Walter Mosley is a novelist who advises fellow writers to be wary of surrendering to what he calls "reality": "Reality fights against your dreams, it tries to deny creation and change. The world wants you to be someone known, someone with solid ideas, not blowing smoke. Given a day, reality will begin to scatter your notions; given two days, it will drive them off" (p. 398). What do you suppose Mosley means by reality? How or why should we escape it? What other words might be used to describe this reality? Why is Mosley suspicious of "solid ideas"?

Write an essay that compares Mosley's sense of reality with Winterson's. Pay close attention to the things they associate with reality. What forces or attitudes are they struggling against? How does writing, for both of them, offer a challenge to reality? Are there dangers in resisting reality?

Assignment 3

Apply your understanding of Winterson's "Imagination and Reality" to the example of Disney World. In "Disney World: Public Use/Private State," Susan Willis complains about the "erasure of spontaneity" at Disney World and argues that Disney functions by limiting the possibilities of "play." In your essay, use your ideas about imagination to analyze the Disney World of Willis's essay. How, in your estimation, does Disney *sell* amusement to consumers? Why might Disney seek to control the experiences of those who come to Disney World? Does this control eliminate or smother imagination? Explore at least one example in detail. You might consider the role of what Winterson calls "money culture" in the realm of entertainment. Does what we call the "entertainment industry" promote or curb imagination?

ASSIGNMENT 4

In "Science in an Old Testament Style," Christopher P. Toumey argues that science has "plenary authority" in American society. That is, Toumey argues that most Americans view anything associated with science with an attitude of "respect without comprehension" (p. 530). In an essay that draws on your reading of Winterson, Mosley, and Willis, discuss the problems with allowing *anything* to have unquestioned authority. How do the examples Toumey uses demonstrate the dangers of unimaginative obedience? What can happen if authority remains unquestioned?

SEQUENCE 9: *Escapes*

Readings: Tuan, Rybczynski, Solnit

ASSIGNMENT 1

Geographer Yi-Fu Tuan suggests in "Earth: Nature and Culture" that "escapism" is a uniquely human response to uncertainty. He writes, "By one means or another [humans] seek control, with at best only tenuous success" (p. 552). Looking closely at Tuan's argument, develop your own idea about why people spend so much time and energy thinking about escaping from their lives. Does any good come of imagining that life could be better, smoother, or less uncertain?

ASSIGNMENT 2

Witold Rybczynski's "Designs for Escape" tells the story of a couple—Danièle and Luc—who are anxiously building a weekend house. Use the couple as a test case for the ideas you pursued in Assignment 1. What are they trying to ensure or confirm with their new house, and why does Rybczynski have different ideas? What does he want us to see about the relationship between fantasy and architecture? Why do you suppose that Danièle is so interested in getting Rybczynski's approval? Be sure to use a passage from Tuan to support your interpretation of Danièle and Luc's motivation.

ASSIGNMENT 3

Rebecca Solnit, in "Aerobic Sisyphus and the Suburbanized Psyche," explains that much of the contemporary fascination with physical fitness is a perverse response to the fact that modern living no longer requires much physical strength. "That muscles have become status symbols signifies that most jobs no longer call upon bodily strength: like tans, they are an aesthetic of the obsolete" (p. 446). Compare that idea with Tuan's notion that "Nostalgia for traditional ways of making a living on the family farm is at least in part a wish to regain a sense of weight and necessity, of being subjected to demands of nature that allow little or no room for fanciful choice" (p. 562).

Write an essay that considers the place of nostalgia in the mind-set of one who exercises. Why do so many modern exercise machines replicate the work activities of an earlier period—lifting, rowing, climbing, and walking? What might Tuan say about the desires of the people who engage in these activities? What role does discipline have in this phenomenon?

SEQUENCE 10: *Fragility and Fruition*
Readings: DeVeaux, Mosley, McCloud

ASSIGNMENT 1

In "Progress and the Bean," Scott DeVeaux discusses changing reputations in the development of jazz music by examining the case of Coleman Hawkins, one of the founders of jazz. To make sense of Hawkins's career, DeVeaux draws on analogies between art and science. Write a paper in which you assess DeVeaux's thesis and approach. How persuasive is DeVeaux's explanation? Does the analogy with science make sense? Why or why not? Your paper needs a specific thesis about De-Veaux's thesis, and your argument should be developed by focusing on two or three particular examples from DeVeaux's essay.

ASSIGNMENT 2

In "For Authors, Fragile Ideas Need Loving Every Day," Walter Mosley argues that would-be writers need to "write every day." Compare Mosley's advice and picture of the writer as artist to De-Veaux's analysis of "progress" as it relates to Coleman Hawkins and Charlie Parker. You might explore possible relations between Mosley's claim that "writing a novel is gathering smoke" and De-Veaux's characterization of Hawkins's and Parker's artistry. What are the links between Mosley's argument and DeVeaux's discussion of progress and changing styles? Is Mosley's writer like a jazz musician? What relationships do you see between yourself as a composition student, the musicians DeVeaux examines, and the writer Mosley describes?

ASSIGNMENT 3

Consider Scott McCloud's "Setting the Record Straight" as an example of an artist justifying and defending his work. Why might Mc-Cloud be protective or somewhat "fragile" in his defense of comics? Drawing on your previous discussions of either DeVeaux or Mosley, develop an argument about McCloud's project and how successful you think he is in making his case. You might want to reflect on why each of these writers comments on the resistance and misunderstanding artists sometimes encounter. Why is producing something imaginative so difficult?

SEQUENCE 11: *Self-Reflection and Making Sense*
Readings: Tompkins, hooks, Mellix

ASSIGNMENT 1

In "At the Buffalo Bill Museum, June 1988," Jane Tompkins discusses contradictions she grapples with as a result of visiting the four museums at the Buffalo Bill Historical Center: the Whitney Gallery of Western Art, the Buffalo Bill Museum, the Plains Indian Museum, and the Winchester Arms Museum. In an essay, define what Tompkins sees as the most significant contradictions and analyze her responses and sense of resolution. She left the museum "full of moral outrage," yet her essay does not justify her anger. Rather, through self-reflection she complicates her response and explores alternatives to her "outrage." In your paper, assess her decision to praise Buffalo Bill rather than blame him for participating in many of the wrongs of his historical epoch. Why does she not simply condemn the museum?

ASSIGNMENT 2

In "keeping close to home: class and education," bell hooks explores a series of contradictions resulting from the tensions between her life as an academic and her identity as a working-class black southern woman. She writes:

> It is difficult for me to talk about my parents and their impact on me because they have always felt wary, ambivalent, mistrusting of my intellectual aspirations even as they have been caring and supportive. I want to speak about these contradictions because sorting through them, seeking resolution and reconciliation has been important to me both as it affects my development as a writer, my effort to be fully-self-realized, and my longing to remain close to the family and community that provided the groundwork for much of my thinking, writing, and being. (p. 230)

Write an essay that compares hooks's and Tompkins's approaches to dealing with the contradictions they foreground in their respective essays. Although these texts may appear completely different, careful reflection can reveal significant points of contact between them, contacts that can enable you to develop an argument about their approaches to contradictions and their means of resolution.

ASSIGNMENT 3

In "From Outside, In," Barbara Mellix details her struggles to become a comfortable, fluent writer of standard English. Mellix notes her ambivalence toward English: She both scorned it and needed it. Her struggles to master standard English in her college writing reveal heightened contradictions in her sense of self. Indeed, she writes, "I wanted those sentences—and the rest of the essay—to convey the anguish of yearning to, at once, become something more and yet remain the same. I had the sensation of being split in two, part of me going into a future the other part didn't believe possible" (p. 390). Write an essay in which you evaluate "the consequence of [Mellix's] education," a phrase from page 392, and develop an argument about the effects of education on personal development. Compare the methods used by bell hooks and Jane Tompkins to deal with contradictions with Mellix's strategies to help you analyze Mellix's situation and what she learns. In your paper, discuss what you think hooks and Tompkins might say about "the consequences of [Mellix's] education."

SEQUENCE 12: *Technology and Change*
Readings: Sontag, Turkle, Kuhn, Lessig

ASSIGNMENT 1

Susan Sontag concludes her essay, "In Plato's Cave" as follows:

> The knowledge gained through still photographs will always be some kind of sentimentalism, whether cynical or humanist. It will be a knowledge at bargain prices—a semblance of knowledge, a semblance of wisdom; as the act of taking pictures is a semblance of appropriation, a semblance of rape. . . . The omnipresence of photographs has an incalculable effect on our ethical sensibility. By furnishing this already crowded world with a duplicate one of images, photography makes us feel that the world is more available than it really is. (p. 480)

Look through photography books at the library, at photographs used in newspapers, or at photographs displayed on the Internet, in a museum, or in your family album. Use a group of photographs to supply evidence for or against Sontag's seemingly dark vision of photography's impact on our society. To what extent do you share that vision? To what extent do you disagree with Sontag's claims or see alternative implications of photography as a technology? Be specific and direct about the connections you see between your ideas and Sontag's.

ASSIGNMENT 2

Compare Sontag's discussion of photography as a technology with Sherry Turkle's essay on the varying uses of Internet technology. In each case, do the expectations, assumptions, and perceptions of the users seem to determine the outcome and implications of the technology? In other words, how does the "tool" of technology affect the outlook of those who use it? To what extent does the technology it-self seem to teach its users both new ways of using it and new ways of perceiving the world? What are the long-range implications of each technology?

ASSIGNMENT 3

Use Thomas Kuhn's discussion of scientific change to analyze Sherry Turkle's description of developments in the field of computer pro-gramming. What were the reigning ideas in the field and to what ex-tent have they been successfully challenged or replaced? Which "anomalies" have become the new laws in the field? How did these new "discoveries" alter the direction of computer science? If you can think of recent technological developments that may have an impact on this evolution of ideas, be sure to refer to them.

ASSIGNMENT 4

If, as Lawrence Lessig argues in "Introduction to *Free Culture*," tech-nological advances have necessitated changes in common sense, does it follow that technology is a key part of our culture or, in a sense, a modern art form? Reflecting on the arguments about technology in Sontag and Turkle, write an essay that examines Lessig's claim that "the Internet has unleashed an extraordinary possibility for many to participate in the process of building and cultivating a culture that reaches far beyond local boundaries" (p. 320). Use a specific illustrat-ing example to help you establish your argument.

SEQUENCE 13: *Parts and Wholes*
Readings: Lasch, Anzaldúa, Rodriguez

ASSIGNMENT 1

In "The Lost Art of Argument," Christopher Lasch argues that we must be wary of the effects of our "information age." For Lasch, pub-lic debate is the key to a functioning democracy and only real, sus-tained public debate can help us to synthesize and make productive use of the information we're bombarded with. Is Lasch's piece hope-ful about democracy? We know that "information" will continue to proliferate. How can we best prepare for this constant increase of im-ages, words, and ideas?

In particular, Lasch seems suspicious of the "aura of objectivity" that has become a part of the modern press, and he suggests that the press has actually helped us "lose" the "art of argument." How can he argue that public debate actually *declined* with the rise of "objec-tive," "impartial," and more professional press? This assignment asks you to test Lasch's claims by examining his position and responding to it with your own argument. Look closely at Lasch's contrasting of the two possible roles for the press, "circulat[ing] information" or "encourag[ing] debate" (p. 308), and use his analysis of that distinction to help you formulate your response. You might choose to explore one or two of his historical examples in some detail. Or you might use an example from a newspaper or a website or from your own experience. Whatever strategy you use, be specific and be clear about your terms.

Assignment 2

In the first assignment, we looked at Christopher Lasch's ideas about what he calls the "lost art of argument." This second assignment asks you to use ideas and examples from Gloria Anzaldúa's essay to help you reconsider Lasch's claims and to build an argument that relates these claims to relates detailed examples from one of the following themes, control, art, power, debate, passivity, identity, assimilation, or America. Your paper must address both essays in some detail.

Some questions you might consider: What goals or points of view do these writers share? What accounts for their differences? How does the *way* each writer writes influence the message of the writing? What examples does either writer offer that might help you add details and specifics to your own argument?

Do not write an essay that simply argues that Anzaldúa and Lasch are saying the same things. Rather, use the two to illustrate aspects of a multi-faceted discussion. Find connections or distinctions that allow you to develop and explain your idea most fully.

Assignment 3

In "'Blaxicans' and Other Reinvented Americans" Richard Rodriguez writes about the problems of assimilation. For this third paper, consider how Rodriguez's argument relates to ideas in your first two essays. Is Anzaldúa a "reinvented" American? How is Rodriguez representing (and participating in) what Lasch calls the "art of argument"? For this paper, use Rodriguez and at least one of the other texts to help you develop an idea that has been emerging in your work. Remember to account for the distinctions you see between the texts and your own ideas.

SEQUENCE 14: *Writing on Writing*
Readings: Sommers, Mellix, Early

Assignment 1

Write a short paper comparing some of Nancy Sommers's ideas and examples about writing in "I Stand Here Writing" with your own observations and experiences involving writing. For instance, what does Sommers mean when she says that writing involves "a radical loss of certainty," and to what extent has that been your experience (p. 454)? What does Sommers learn from Emerson's statement, "One must be an inventor to read well," and to what extent does that apply to your experience (p. 458)? What is something you have learned about writing that you would want to communicate to a classmate or student of your own?

ASSIGNMENT 2

Write a longer paper assessing how well Sommers's ideas about writing apply to Barbara Mellix's experiences in "From Outside, In" and to your own experiences as a writer. To what extent does Mellix experience a "radical loss of certainty," or learn to "be an inventor"? Does Mellix learn things that challenge, contradict, or go beyond Sommers's ideas about writing? Do the ideas and experiences of either writer help you to define yourself as a writer?

ASSIGNMENT 3

Julie English Early's "The Spectacle of Science and Self: Mary Kingsley" offers an example of a woman fashioning a persona through her publicly acclaimed writing and speaking. Mary Kingsley, a 19th-century woman with little formal education (but plenty of "real world" experience and independent reading), wrote about science and exploration in a direct popular voice that was highly unusual for its time. Indeed, her publishers and some scientists and ethnographers felt the "threat of Kingsley's eclectic self-performance" regularly challenged her way of expressing herself.

Using your discussion in previous essays of the way that writing challenges accepted practices, examine the historical example of Mary Kingsley and develop an argument about how writing served her. What does Early suggest makes Kingsley such an interesting example? How do writers such as Sommers and Mellix carry on the "tradition" of Kingsley's "spectacle"?

SEQUENCE 15: *The Art of "Reality"*

Readings: Winterson, Sturken, Kaku, Allison

ASSIGNMENT 1

In "Imagination and Reality," Jeanette Winterson begins by asking the question, "What do I mean by the reality of art" (p. 598)? Write an essay that explores your interpretations of Winterson's answer to her question. Trace how she defines and redefines "reality" and "the real." Piece together the examples and the definitions from her essay that best help you explain what she means. You might choose to bring in a photograph, a painting, a poem, or some other art object that helps you exemplify or interpret Winterson's point. (If you do so, attach a photocopy of the art object to the paper).

Thinking about and writing preliminary responses to one or more of the following questions can help you to construct a rough draft. How is "the real" related to the goal of art and the imagination? How is it related to the goal of science? How is it opposed to the pressure of "money culture"?

ASSIGNMENT 2

Marita Sturken, in "The Wall, the Screen and the Image: The Vietnam Veterans Memorial," claims that "the Vietnam Veterans Memorial is unmistakably representative of a particular period in Western art" (p. 487). Use Sturken's analysis of the memorial to help you explain Winterson's comment that "art is not documentary . . . its true effort is to open to us dimensions of the spirit and of the self that normally lie smothered under the weight of living" (p. 600). How does the memorial symbolize the American involvement in Vietnam? How does it go beyond the "documentary"? In what ways has the memorial's designer, Maya Lin, used imagination to comment on reality?

ASSIGNMENT 3

In "Second Thoughts: The Genetics of a Brave New World?" Michio Kaku explores some of the positive and negative possibilities of scientific research. He says, "the awesome scientific knowledge that will be unveiled early in the next century must be tempered by the enormous ethical, social, and political questions that it raises" (p. 265). Choose two of the scientific goals that Kaku presents that you think will require the public to ask serious "ethical, social, and political questions," then use two key ideas from Jeanette Winterson's "Imagination and Reality" to help you write an essay that analyzes them.

In planning your argument, you might consider the following questions. What is the role of imagination in Kaku's essay? Is the pressure of "money culture" operating in the debates over cloning? To what extent are the goals of science "fus[ing] together temporal and perpetual realities" in the future that Kaku envisions, and to what extent are they constrained by "money culture"?

ASSIGNMENT 4

In "This Is Our World," Dorothy Allison argues that art is documentary: "Art is not meant to be polite, secret, coded, or timid. Art is the sphere in which that impulse to hide and lie is the most dangerous" (p. 50).

She provides an array of examples from her own experience that illustrate her conception of art's relation to reality. Look closely at your earlier essays, then write a new essay that explores the pieces of Allison's essay as attempts to "imaginatively" present reality. How does your understanding of Winterson, Sturken, and Kaku shed light on this topic? How has your understanding of Winterson or Sturken or Kaku changed as a result of reading and writing about Allison's ideas?

SEQUENCE 16: *The Arts and Sciences*
Readings: Toumey, Kuhn, Winterson, Ellison

ASSIGNMENT 1

Compare Thomas Kuhn's discussion of the processes of scientific discovery in "The Historical Structure of Scientific Discovery" with Christopher P. Toumey's discussion of public acceptance of science in "Science in an Old Testament Style." What connections do you see between Kuhn and Toumey? What gives a new idea in science its authority? What forces resist change and why?

ASSIGNMENT 2

In "Imagination and Reality," Jeanette Winterson identifies the artist as a "visionary." Write an essay that explores some of the significant intersections you see between Winterson's view of the artist and Kuhn's more general discussion of art and science. Are scientists, as Kuhn describes them in "The Historical Structure of Scientific Discovery," visionary as well? In your essay, be sure to define "visionary."

ASSIGNMENT 3

Select a key moment in Ralph Ellison's account of his developing understanding of art and identity in America in "The Little Man at Chehaw Station." Use Jeanette Winterson's discussion of "the charge laid on the artist" (598) and Thomas Kuhn's discussion of "anomaly" to help you analyze the Ellison moment that you select for analysis. In what ways does Ellison's discovery involve what Kuhn describes as "transformations," "revolutions," and "readjustments"? In what ways does it exemplify the "visionary" qualities that Winterson ascribes to the artist? Be specific about the connections you find.

ASSIGNMENT 4

Write an essay that applies Ellison's ideas to Jeanette Winterson's views of art. Would Ellison likely applaud her views? Or would he protest like the "little man" he describes in his essay? As you write, consider the consequences of the position you take. What does Ellison enable you to see about Winterson?

SEQUENCE 17: *Technology and Understanding*
Readings: Sontag, Lasch, Turkle

ASSIGNMENT 1

Although Susan Sontag writes of the "promise" of photography "to democratize all experiences by translating them into images" (p. 469), she soon seems suspicious of that promise. She writes, "taking photographs has set up a chronic voyeuristic relation to the world which levels the meaning of all events" (p. 471). What is the difference between democratizing and leveling? What does photography *do* to experience to make Sontag suspicious? If a photograph can be said to establish authority (as in photographic evidence), can this authority be abused? How? What is the place of power or control in photography? Why might this work against the goals of democracy?

Write an essay that uses Sontag's text as a point of departure for discussing the differences between the democratizing and leveling consequences of technology. How does technology transform the world or at least our understanding of it? You will need to consider at least one of her examples in some detail. You might also find it useful to discuss a photographic object, such as a family photo, a newspaper photo, or an ad. Discuss the "way of seeing" the object seeks to promote. You might consider using or analyzing some of the following concepts to help you make your argument: objectivity, voyeurism, surveillance, evidence, cataloguing, compulsion, or art.

ASSIGNMENT 2

In "The Lost Art of Argument," Christopher Lasch argues that the art of argument has suffered in the information age, as scientific observation and objective press coverage "provide us with a copy of reality that we can all recognize" (p. 309). He believes that only real, sustained public debate can help us to synthesize and make productive use of the information we are bombarded with.

Test Lasch's claims by examining them in the terms of Sontag's example of photography. Look closely at Lasch's contrasting of the two possible roles for the press—"circulat[ing] information" or "encourag[ing] debate." Use his analysis of that distinction to help you formulate a response to Sontag that addresses her claim that "in these last decades, 'concerned' photography has done at least as much to deaden conscience as to arouse it" (p. 477). Does Lasch's critique carry with it hope for a successful democracy? We know that "information" will continue to proliferate. How can we best prepare for this constant increase of images, words, and ideas?

ASSIGNMENT 3

Sherry Turkle's "The Triumph of Tinkering" describes a technologically driven shift similar to the histories of change narrated by Sontag and Lasch. Turkle's tone, however, is almost completely different. Why? Where Sontag and Lasch see manipulation and abuse, Turkle sees progress and opportunity. She writes to persuade us to take advantage of these positive events: "A classical modernist vision of computer intelligence has made room for a romantic, postmodern one. At this juncture, there is potential for a more welcoming environment for women, humanists, and artists in the technical culture" (p. 579). Turkle speaks here of "room" being "made" to allow for voices and ideas that had been traditionally silenced. She is specifically interested in opportunities for women. How does Turkle's more specific audience and more detailed example allow her to emphasize potential over abuse? How does Turkle's approach differ from Sontag's and Lasch's?

Write an essay that treats Turkle's text as an extended example for your analysis of the possibilities and problems that come with technological expansion. How does what Turkle describes as a change in the "center of gravity" of computer programming—a change in which the experimental methods of *bricolage* and simulation helped undermine the authority of traditional formal methods—relate to changes *outside* the immediate sphere of the computer field? How does this example extend or complicate your previous discussion of democracy and its values? What other examples can you think of?

SEQUENCE 18: *Images and Words*

Readings: Hochschild, Florida, Tuan, Charlip

ASSIGNMENT 1

Arlie Russell Hochschild begins her essay, "From the Frying Pan into the Fire," by presenting a close reading of a breakfast advertisement for Quaker Instant Oatmeal. Reread Hochschild's analysis of the advertisement, and list the features she focuses on. Think about Hochschild's process of argument. How does she get from the list of features to her interpretation of the ad? Likewise, how does her interpretation of the ad relate or connect to her larger argument in the essay? Find an ad for breakfast, lunch, or dinner foods, and perform your own written analysis of it. Next, write an essay in which you look at the ad you selected within the terms of Hochschild's larger argument about how workplace agendas are transforming home life in subtle and not-so-subtle ways.

ASSIGNMENT 2

Write an essay that compares Richard Florida's discussion in "The Transformation of Everyday Life" of "dizzying social and cultural changes" since the 1950s with Hochschild's discussion of social and cultural transformations spawned by the encroachment of workplace norms and standards on the home. Do Florida's and Hochschild's attitudes toward transformation tend to be similar or different? What do you think accounts for each writer's orientation?

ASSIGNMENT 3

What would be the perfect place of escape for you? Use key examples from Hochschild's essay, from Florida's essay, and from Yi-Fu Tuan's essay, "Earth: Nature and Culture," to help you discuss and analyze desires for escape, particularly escape from the pressures of work at home. In your essay, be sure to discuss possible relationships between Tuan's examination of nature and culture, on the one hand, and Hochschild's and Florida's analyses of pressures and desires for escape, on the other.

ASSIGNMENT 4

Think about the images of home and self that Julie Charlip presents in "A Real Class Act: Searching for Identity in the Classless Society." How are class notions of entitlement reflected in Charlip's claims about appearance versus reality (particularly in terms of the suburbs)? In an essay, examine Charlip's analysis of home and sense of self by using some key ideas from one or two of the essays you have already read for this sequence. The key ideas you turn to might include but are not limited to the following: work and family, creativity and individuality, escape and culture.

SEQUENCE 19: *Applying Arguments and Concepts*
Readings: Ewen, Willis, Percy

ASSIGNMENT 1

In "The Marriage Between Art and Commerce," Stuart Ewen presents an account of what he sees as a crucial cultural shift. In an essay that looks closely at his claims, use Ewen's history of the concept of style to help you examine something "stylish" from our own time. How does the item (or event or phenomenon) support or challenge Ewen's claims? What forces seem to be at work and why?

Your paper will need to show a balance between careful analysis of Ewen's text and a thoughtful exposition of your own ideas. You needn't completely agree or disagree with Ewen, but you should use your detailed discussion of one or two of his points to help you set up your example. A successful paper will integrate the materials by creating a dialogue between them.

ASSIGNMENT 2

In "Disney World: Public Use/Private State," Susan Willis contrasts Disney World's "programmed amusement" with the values of play and spontaneity. As she puts it, "Amusement is the commodified negation of play" (584). What is the difference between amusement and play and why would Willis prefer one to the other? In an essay that takes her example of Disney World as a chief illustration, examine something else (e.g., another place, an event, or an entertainment) in Willis's terms and through Willis's examples. What does the "lens" Willis provides help you see in your topic? How does it help you think about style as it relates to Disney World and your own example?

ASSIGNMENT 3

In "The Loss of the Creature," Walker Percy offers a series of strategies for dealing with what he calls the "predicament" of our "modern technical society" (p. 413). In an essay that clearly explores Percy's strategies, develop an "answer" to the problems and/or questions raised by Stuart Ewen or Susan Willis in their respective essays. Your paper should investigate an aspect of the topic in a manner that leads you to purposeful, directed comments.

This third essay should demonstrate your ability to understand and apply concepts and examples from critical sources. In this case, you'll be using one or more of Percy's concepts to help you describe and explore an idea that emerged in your reading of Ewen and Willis. You needn't always agree with Percy, of course, but you must use his ideas to frame your discussion. And don't oversimplify. There are several places where these writers do not agree or where there are key differences. You may indeed find yourself using one text against another in some ways. That is fine. Just be sure to "orchestrate" these voices in a way that makes sense to your reader.

SEQUENCE 20: "Progress" in Art and Technology
Readings: DeVeaux, Ewen, Birkerts

ASSIGNMENT 1

In "Progress and the Bean," Scott DeVeaux shows that one of the "sense-making" concepts of the sciences, the idea of progress, does not fully explain the process of innovation and change in an artistic field such as music. He writes:

> In particular, it is grating to find notions of progress applied to the arts. To claim progress in the fields of science and technology is one thing. Some may argue whether such "advances" actually improve life, but few disagree that new solutions to old problems have rendered previous efforts obsolete. . . . In the arts, however, such wholesale dismissal of the past seems unthinkable. As museums attest, the old retains its power and actively shapes the sensibilities of the present. (p. 102)

Unlike technological progress, artistic "advances" do not make past achievements obsolete. We do not hand-crank our car's engine anymore, nor do we travel across the ocean by boat, but we may still be deeply interested in Impressionist painting or Shakespeare's plays. Why do artistic creations sometimes become "classics" while scientific or technological precedents are discarded or described as just plain wrong?

In an essay, develop your own ideas about the place of "progress" and "obsolescence" in the arts and sciences. Consider why DeVeaux thinks that speaking of progress in the arts is "grating." Do you think that artistic creations—for example, books, movies, and music—should be thought of as part of a progression? Keep in mind: Coleman Hawkins thought that his music *was* progressive. Conversely, why do you suppose science and technology so readily scrap the achievements of the past? Is there a danger of losing track of what has come before?

Assignment 2

Stuart Ewen gives a history of the development of style in industry in "The Marriage Between Art and Commerce." In many ways, Ewen's essay speaks to the concerns of your previous essay by showing a "marriage" of technological and artistic goals in the form of advertising and marketing. Ewen refers to this as "the instrumental use of style as a business device" (p. 179). In your second essay, apply your ideas about "progress" and "obsolescence" to the historical narrative that Ewen provides. What factors allowed the "marriage" to occur? What *unsatisfying* effects came out of that transformation? Does the market provide a suitable arena for the cooperation of art and technology, or are the sacrifices that must be made too great?

Assignment 3

In "The Owl Has Flown," Sven Birkerts laments the destructive consequences of the information age and argues that in our time one technological development—the profound increase in the availability of information—has affected the ways in which our minds actually work. Birkerts describes the replacement of "intensive reading" with a broader (and more superficial) "extensive reading." How does this categorization of a dramatic cultural shift affect the lives that we live? Do you agree with Birkerts that our period is marked by a profound "loss of depth"? Are there advantages to having "extensive" knowledge? In an essay that incorporates your ideas from the previous two assignments, construct an argument that responds to Birkerts's claim that we have almost wholly forsaken "wisdom." Why do you suppose he locates art as the place where depth survives?

SEQUENCE 21: *Rhetorical Education*
Readings: Ingham, Florida, Martin et al.

ASSIGNMENT 1

Zita Ingham represents the debate over the future of Red Lodge, Montana, as an account of competing stories in her essay, "Landscape, Drama, and Dissensus: The Rhetorical Education of Red Lodge, Montana." She shows how the success of the Red Lodge discussion hinged on a series of presentations organized to provide the "rhetorical education" of the citizens and draw them into a dialogue about the possibilities and consequences of their decisions. In an analytical essay, look into at least two key moments in the text and develop an argument about the role that words play in solving problems. That is, your paper should focus more on *how* the positions are represented than on what those positions are. In doing this, your paper should further define Ingham's concept of "rhetorical education" by explaining it through these examples and in your own terms.

ASSIGNMENT 2

In "The Transformation of Everyday Life," Richard Florida describes pervasive changes in lifestyles and world-views in the United States since the 1950s. Write an essay that explores Florida's text as an attempt at what Ingham calls "rhetorical education." Who is the "hero" in Florida's "script" and why? What is the place of "dissensus" in Florida's exposition of the changes he identifies? How persuasive do you find Florida to be and why?

ASSIGNMENT 3

Using the ideas about rhetoric, creativity, and social transformations that have emerged in your work with Ingham and Florida, consider the problem of scientific literacy as a rhetorical problem. Look carefully at Martin et al.'s "Scientific Literacy, What It Is, Why It's Important, and Why Scientists Think We Don't Have It: The Case of Immunology and the Immune System." What do the examples in this piece share with the struggle for a plan in Red Lodge, Montana? How might a "rhetorical education" of scientists (and of those who seek to understand or draw on science) improve the situation?

SEQUENCE 22: *What is Scientific Literacy?*

Readings: Martin et al., Toumey, Kaku

ASSIGNMENT 1

Write a paper in which you explore the relationship between "facts" and "local knowledge" that Emily Martin et al. use in "Scientific Literacy, What It Is, Why It's Important, and Why Scientists Think We Don't Have It: The Case of Immunology and the Immune System" (p. 343). What does it mean "to know" something? Is knowledge the same for everyone? Use examples from Martin to help you illustrate the ways that individuals or small, "local" environments sometimes invent new ways to represent facts.

ASSIGNMENT 2

In "Science in an Old Testament Style," Christopher P. Toumey warns against the ways that science is "conjured" by the mainstream media. He argues that "science is widely believed to transcend the social forces that obviously shape other human institutions, such as politics or religion" (530). How might the ideas of "scientific literacy" explored in Martin help to alleviate or improve the problem that Toumey points out? Use the arguments in Martin to comment on the examples in Toumey's piece. What is revealed?

ASSIGNMENT 3

In "Second Thoughts: The Genetics of a Brave New World?" Michio Kaku expresses concerns similar in many ways to Toumey's. He stresses the importance of public involvement in scientific questions: "Ultimately, society must make democratic decisions on whether or not to restrict certain kinds of technology" (p. 283). And yet, given the complexity of many scientific issues, it may be tricky to establish this "democratic" practice. How might the ideas in the Martin and Toumey pieces contribute to this hope for a stable, peaceful modern world?

ASSIGNMENT 4

If we reread "Scientific Literacy" as representative of its authors' work, what can we say about them and about their approach to knowledge? What is their purpose in writing the article? Martin and her co-authors are sometimes called "social scientists." Write a paper in which you construct a preliminary definition of a social scientist based on your analysis of the authors' work in this article. (Keep in mind that we are looking at only a small sample of their work.)

SEQUENCE 23: *Visual Literacy*
Readings: Sontag, McGraw, McCloud

ASSIGNMENT 1

Collect your own "anthology of images," including several photographs that interest you, and use them to write an essay explaining and testing some of Susan Sontag's claims in "In Plato's Cave." What are some of the problems with photography that Sontag identifies? Do the images you have chosen tend to support, contradict, or go beyond her arguments in this essay? Be specific about which passages in Sontag you are responding to.

ASSIGNMENT 2

In "Bad Eyes," Erin McGraw describes some of the ways in which her vision affected how she behaved and how she thought about herself. Write an essay using ideas and examples from Sontag and McGraw to develop your own theory about the connection between vision and identity, between how we see and how we think about ourselves.

ASSIGNMENT 3

In "Setting the Record Straight," Scott McCloud creates a comic self-portrait. What does McCloud's self-portrait suggest about how he sees himself? Find photographs of McGraw and McCloud online. Compare McGraw's photograph to the word portrait she creates in her essay, "Bad Eyes." Compare McCloud's photograph to his comic self-portrait in "Setting the Record Straight." What do these four "images" suggest about portraits that are taken and portraits that are made? Use Sontag's essay to help you construct your response.

SEQUENCE 24: *The Ways That Thinking Happens*
Readings: Birkerts, Turkle, Solnit

ASSIGNMENT 1

In "The Owl Has Flown," Sven Birkerts asks us to consider the consequences of the "shift from intensive to extensive reading" (p. 72). Birkerts seems to say that, for a variety of reasons, our current cultural climate discourages "vertical consciousness" (p. 74). What do you suppose he means by that? Do you think there are ways for us to reclaim "wisdom" and "depth"? Are there aspects of the culture that Birkerts overlooks or misrepresents?

Write an essay that takes on this question of "vertical consciousness." Using Birkerts's text as a touchstone, develop an argument that explores an idea you have about these issues. You do not need to agree with Birkerts, but you should use some of his key concepts or ideas to set up or frame your ideas. In other words, you should be quoting Birkerts occasionally and responding to those quotations. You might choose to develop your own example or illustration. But don't just look for a "right" answer. Try to be creative, thoughtful, and engaged.

ASSIGNMENT 2

We have been examining Sven Birkerts's concept of "vertical consciousness" and responding to his claims that our culture has become too "horizontally" oriented. It would be equally easy to side with Birkerts and level charges against our complacent culture or to reject Birkerts and praise our diverse and multi-faceted culture. These approaches are a start, but they are rather limited. It's probably best to seriously consider the implications of the ideas you address by spending time looking closely at one or two points and reflecting on their consequences. One needn't agree or disagree with Birkerts' conclusions to *use* his ideas in some way. After all, your final draft should take you *beyond* these texts and into your own ideas.

This second paper adds Sherry Turkle's "The Triumph of Tinkering" to your ongoing exploration of the way that thinking happens (or, if you prefer, how the modern mind works). Turkle provides a series of examples to illustrate a couple of main ideas that she returns to throughout the essay. Her argument centers on styles of learning and, more specifically, on ramifications of technological advances. But she touches on a number of other things as well. In a paper at least four pages in length, use Turkle and Birkerts as material for a fresh look at a topic that has emerged from your reading of their essays. You can use the essays in any number of ways, but be sure to have a few moments of "close reading" so that you are fully illustrating each text's point. Then, move back into your own applications of that point. Use at least one example to give your idea specificity and to make it concrete. You do not need to pit Turkle against Birkerts or to show them in perfect agreement. They can serve different phases or aspects of your idea.

ASSIGNMENT 3

Rebecca Solnit's essay, "Aerobic Sisyphus and the Suburbanized Psyche," seems to be an appeal to her audience to develop a heightened awareness of the world that surrounds us—to preserve that "ancient and profound relationship between body, world, and imagination" (p. 435) that Solnit fears may otherwise disappear. With that awareness comes an understanding of the "strangeness" (p. 447) of even the most commonplace forms of technology or expert "planning." In fact, it is the "making strange" of the familiar that can lead to independence of mind and awareness of choices rather than mere following of cultural scripts.

Write an essay that engages with Solnit's thesis about the important interrelationship of "body, world, and imagination" and demonstrates a "heightened awareness" of the world around you. Incorporating your reading of Birkerts's and Turkle's essays, consider the impact of our thinking on our physical experience of the world (and vice versa).

SEQUENCE 25: *Status, Self, and Authority*
Readings: Anzaldúa, Trask, Early

ASSIGNMENT 1

In gaining experience in a particular field, one often learns to recognize one's own personal experience within the accepted categories of the world of experts. That is, as we learn to associate ourselves with specific groups (in terms of national origin, gender, race, political affiliation), we see our experience as *linked* in some way to that of others. Academic disciplines such as history, sociology, and linguistics exist, in part, to identify and categorize such group behaviors. Gloria Anzaldúa and Haunani-Kay Trask are troubled by the boundaries drawn by the world of experts; they *do not* recognize themselves in the histories they read. For them, the authorities that speak and write about the Chicana and the Hawaiian experience, respectively, do not "make sense." As a result, both Anzaldúa and Trask write in order to force scholars and others to re-examine the ways in which Chicana and Hawaiian experience have been categorized.

In "Chicana Artists: Exploring *Nepantla, el Lugar de la Frontera*," Anzaldúa introduces a word to help define the place where personal identity meets these established social categories: "*Nepantla* is the Nahuatl word for an in-between state, that uncertain terrain one crosses when moving from one place to another, when changing from one class, race, or gender position to another, when traveling from the present identity into a new identity" (p. 60). Anzaldúa wants us to see how uncertainty about labels and categories can actually be productive and can foster new ways of seeing.

In an essay of at least three pages, use Anzaldúa's word "Nepantla" to explain Trask's argument in "From a Native Daughter." How does "border art" help us to "make sense" of the world differently than the traditional history that Trask describes? You might choose to look closely at how both writers use language to express identity. You might also choose to examine one or more of the examples from the essays. In any case, be sure to look carefully at the ways these writers use their own experience as evidence.

Assignment 2

Build on the paper that you wrote for your first assignment by selecting and analyzing an example from your own personal history. Are Anzaldúa's and Trask's arguments valid only because they are writing from historically marginalized points of view, or is there a way in which anyone can use personal experience to problematize or refine established categories? Become a historian of your own life for this assignment and describe an "in-between state" that you have passed through or are currently in. How does your experience contribute to your understanding of "Nepantla"? Does your argument from your first paper apply to the example you choose? What aspects of your own example cannot be neatly compared with those offered by Anzaldúa and Trask? Why? Finally, what does your comparison tell you about the importance of documenting and examining personal history?

Assignment 3

Because of her status as a woman in the nineteenth century, Mary Kingsley could not gain full admittance to the scientific community of her time. She wrote popular treatments of scientific phenomena and gave lectures that drew people as much for their entertainment value as for their scientific content. And yet, in "The Spectacle of Science and Self," Julie English Early wants us to consider Kingsley as a legitimate, if unorthodox, voice of nineteenth-century science. What makes Kingsley's contributions to scientific discourse especially worthy to Early? Drawing on your previous two essays, use Kingsley as an example of a "border artist" whose commitment to her own personal style makes her an interesting case today. Why do you suppose there is renewed interest in Kingsley's writings? Kingsley lived a privileged life among some of the wealthiest people in the world. Can we equate her situation with the violent struggles that Anzaldúa and Trask describe?

$\mathscr{A}$

Appendix A

Making Sense
Through Research

For some of us, the word "research" conjures up images of laboratories, men and women in white coats, and highly technical equipment; for others, students at library tables surrounded by books, or people at computer terminals mining data. All those images are accurate, but they present only a partial picture of how research is done today, and they suggest nothing at all about why research is done. In fact, all too often research is mistakenly understood as simply a deferring to experts, as a transparent gathering of already-known proofs and evidence. It is not surprising, then, that some writers blanch when they are assigned to prepare a researched essay.

But the research process includes much more than the time-consuming act of locating and reading other people's work. Research is also a dynamic interaction with the ideas and problems that swirl around a topic. Understood as an active, empowering engagement with concepts, proposals, and examples, research is less an arcane task than simply a natural way to extend the reach of one's "making sense" process. Research needn't be a lonely, academic exercise; it can be a way to find unexpected connections and a common language with people who have related goals and purposes.

In this text, "research" means using reference or other sources found in the library or on the Internet to learn more about a particular person, place, thing, or idea for the purpose of developing a better understanding of your reading and stimulating fresh ideas about a topic. But this learning is not a one-way street. Research is fundamentally interactive. It is in a sense a collaborative exchange with other writers. By "inviting" these sources into your work, you provide a forum for the illustration and testing of your ideas.

Doing some preliminary research on a topic addressed in your reading benefits you in several ways.

- You gain better access to the assigned reading, because the outside sources and examples you find actually help you see it better.

- You gain a more expert knowledge of some aspect of the assigned reading, or a new perspective on the reading as a whole.

- You develop your own position on issues raised in the assigned reading by testing its major claims against the sources and examples you find.

- You practice research skills in a manageable, focused area that prepares you for a more intensive use of those same skills in a full-length research paper.

In short, research is a way of learning. It allows you to extend your exploration of a general subject area in a particular direction, to develop a specific topic or issue that interests you, or to expand your knowledge base on that topic.

Suggestions for Additional Research with the Assigned Readings

The essays in *Making Sense* offer many interesting possibilities for research. We have tried to outline some of those possibilities by including a suggestion for Internet research in the headnote to each reading and one or more "Going Further: Learning from Other Sources" questions after each reading. In this section, we will describe in more detail techniques and strategies for pursuing text-based research in the university.

In most libraries today, students have access to online search tools. The sources revealed through your search may be books or articles that you can then find on the library shelves, or they may be books, articles, or other forms of information available only online. Whether your source is hard copy or electronic, finding it through online searching requires many of the same skills and strategies.

Your first step in any research project should be a tour of the library at your college or university. Just as different libraries subscribe to different magazines and newspapers, they also subscribe to different electronic databases. It is important to know what your library has available for you. If a tour is not appropriate, visit the library reference desk or its homepage on the university website. At most libraries and on many library homepages, you will find important information prepared by your reference librarian on how to use the research tools available at your library. (See Resource 1 on the next pages for an example.) The job of reference librarians is to help you find the information you need. Do not be afraid or embarrassed to ask them for help.

To learn what various reference resources can do for you, try the following experiment. Choose a search term such as an author's name, the title of a book or article, or a keyword referred to in the reading. Use that term in a reference database, such as Academic Search Elite, that gives you access to scholarly journals from the social sciences, the humanities, the general sciences, and education. Then try the same keyword searches using a database, such as Lexis/Nexis, that gives you access to a broader collection of magazines, journals, and newspapers. Using the more general database will result in a wider field of examples and case studies related to your topic, but you will have to be more careful about *evaluating* those sources. Finally, try using the same keywords in an Internet search engine such as Google. You will find that your search results cover a much broader area; they will include images and products for sale as well as a list of all the websites that may relate to your topic. Exploring some of those websites can help you to think about an assigned reading from a fresh perspective and can lead you to a related research topic of your own; however, it will also involve weeding out a great deal of unreliable and unusable information.

Experiment with the following suggestions for online searching until you find the one that works best for you.

- Try searching for the author of the assigned reading using his or her full name as your search term. This will give you access to other writings by the same author, reviews of the author's books, and related subject areas, which you can then use as the keywords for an expanded search or ideas for a research paper topic of your own. For example, using "Annie Dillard" as the search term in a scholarly database will not only enable you to learn more about her as a writer but also link you to critics' reactions to her work and to topics related to her work, such as "nature writing" or "belief and doubt." Using her name as a keyword in a general search engine such as Google will open up dozens of entries, including useful items, such as interviews with Annie Dillard, and less reliable items, such as personal homepages or publicity from booksellers.

- Try using the key terms from the assigned essay as your search terms. For example, the keywords "scientific literacy" from Emily Martin's article, "Scientific Literacy, What It Is, Why It's Important, and Why Scientists Think We Don't Have It'" when

Resource 1

Database Searching

Some Advantages of Database Searching

1. The ability to search through several years of published sources at once
2. The ability to search using your own terms ("keyword searching")
3. The ability to combine terms by using "and," "or," or "not" ("Boolean searching")
4. The ability to retrieve precise information quickly

Some Disadvantages of Database Searching

1. A lot of relevant information has not been digitized (put in a computer database).
2. Use an incorrect term or misspell a term, and you miss things that are in the database.

Three Basic Ways to Conduct a Database Search

1. Use a keyword search.
2. Use a keyword search to find subject headings to refine or focus your search.
3. Use a database thesaurus or index to focus your search from the start.

In any database search, find out what subject headings the database uses for your keywords. For example, your keyword is "toddler" but the subject heading used is "child, preschool."

Expanding or Limiting a Database Search

When you want to

- get more information, or
- retrieve as much information as possible, you need to broaden or expand your search.

Ways to expand your search

1. Use broader or related terms.
2. Use a truncation symbol: *.
3. Use the term "or."

When you want to

- limit the amount of information, or
- retrieve very precise information, you must limit or narrow your search.

Ways to limit your search

1. Use narrower terms or subject subheadings.
2. Use the fields that the database provides to narrow your search.
3. Combine terms or set numbers with the term "and."
4. Use the term "not."

Remember, different computer databases

- use different types of searches
- limit or expand in different ways
- provide (or do not provide) an index or thesaurus
- provide (or do not provide) some form of truncation or wildcard symbol
- allow (or do not allow) Boolean searches

In general, however, computers usually will let you expand or limit your search in at least a few ways.

Basic Research Steps for Journal Articles

1. Choose the appropriate databases.
2. Have a list of keywords.
3. Find out how the database classifies your keywords.
4. Limit or expand your search as needed.
5. Evaluate what you find.
6. Use what you find to get other resources.
7. Use only one documentation style.

Source: Mark van Lummel, Indiana University, South Bend.

used in a scholarly database will give you access to over one hundred related articles. If you make the search more general by expanding the keywords to "science and literacy," you will find an even broader pool of results. It will help to try out several of the key terms from an essay.

- Try using one key term from the assigned reading combined with a topic that interests you. For example, when reading Arlie

Russell Hochschild's "From the Frying Pan into the Fire," enter the search term "capitalism" in a scholarly database. The result will be several hundred articles related to capitalism. However, if you have a particular interest in following up on the way the values of capitalism insinuate themselves into family life, searching for "capitalism and family" will result in a more manageable collection of articles that are more specifically related to that aspect of the topic.

- Try collecting a number of case studies or examples related to the assigned reading. (Here, using a database such as Lexis/Nexis or a similar research tool that gives you access to newspapers will be helpful.) For example, when reading about Susan Willis's reaction to Disney World, collect a series of articles from popular magazines and newspapers that demonstrate other public reactions to Disney World. Are people gaining emotional satisfaction from these vacation sites that Willis does not acknowledge? Do their testimonies reveal the language of consumption or any other of the prepackaged beliefs that Willis claims Disney World is selling?

- Think of practical ways to negotiate the immense quantity of materials available through Internet search engines. For example, use the Internet as a way to find non-Internet sources. That's right. Some of the best Web discoveries are, in fact, bibliographies that come from academic websites and course pages (often syllabi and reading lists). Using Google to search for the word "bibliography" plus whatever topic you are researching will often turn up some great lists of relevant books and articles. This techniques helps you find sources that have been "endorsed" by other writers and academics, pieces that are "in circulation" in the world of ideas. When reading Scott McCloud's "Setting the Record Straight," for example, try searching "bibliography comics" in Google. You will find a "comics research bibliography" as one of the first items on the list of hits.

You may need to use one or more of these techniques each time you do a search. Although it is obvious that some reference databases include information sources that others do not, it is less obvious but equally true that Internet search engines index different information sites. Using the same search terms with a different search engine will most likely yield different results. To learn more about the differences between subject guides and search engines, go to the Tool Kit for the Expert Web Searcher developed and maintained by Pat Ensor for the American Library Association, <http://www.lita.org/committee/toptech/toolkit.htm>.

So far, we have discussed how to search for information to help you better understand your reading. As we have mentioned in other sections, however, writing about what you read is one of the best ways to make sense of what you read. The same is true with research.

Writing a Research Paper

Writing a research paper combines the writing skills we describe in Chapters 1 and 2 with the research skills described above. The process of writing a research paper, then, requires you to perform the following steps:

1. **Collect** additional sources (readings, data, case studies, and examples) that relate to your chosen subject area or that provide an angle or approach that might be applied to your subject.

2. **Develop** a topic by choosing a particular problem, issue, or idea you see in that subject area.

3. **Evaluate** your sources by deciding how reliable they are, whether they are scholarly or popular, and if they are useful for your project.

4. **Read** and **synthesize** the information contained in the sources you plan to use.

5. **Determine** the role that each of your sources will have in the paper by thinking about whether it provides a conceptual framework, illustrating examples, or contrasting ideas, or whether it serves a smaller, supporting role.

6. **Establish** your own position on that topic or issue in relation to the readings you have chosen.

Although research assignments differ from discipline to discipline and from course to course, following these steps will help you to produce a strong college research paper. Be sure to review your assignment carefully and to check with your instructor if you have any questions about the purpose, persona, audience, or argument required for the paper. See Resource 2 (p. 652) for examples. Different disciplines also require different methods of citing sources, which we discuss on page 658.

Collecting Sources and Developing a Topic

Instead of picking a research topic out of thin air, such as "baseball," "world hunger," or "race-car driving," try developing a topic that relates to the assigned reading you have been doing in *Making Sense*.

Resource 2
_____

Questions for a Research Proposal

To help yourself focus your research, write a one-page proposal that answers the following questions.

1. What subject area interests you?
2. Which of your readings or papers will you use to generate your topic?
3. What narrower topics, issues, or problems could you focus on using that reading or paper?
4. What sources beyond those in *Making Sense* do you hope to find or plan to use?
5. What databases and search engines could you try?
6. What search terms are you planning to try? These might include key terms from the *Making Sense* writer you are using and terms related to your subject area.
7. What additional readings from *Making Sense* might be relevant?
8. What concepts from those readings could you use?
9. What examples from those readings could you use?
10. What examples or case studies are you hoping to find?
11. What key quotes from the readings could you use (include page numbers)?

That will give you two huge advantages. First, you can use the assigned essay to generate key terms for your research, to help focus your topic, and to provide a framework for analyzing your sources in the actual paper. Second, if you have already discussed and written about the assigned essay for an earlier paper in the class, you will be able to build on some of that earlier work and even revise some of the earlier ideas you had about that reading in relation to your research topic. Although your additional research will help you approach the assigned essay from a fresh perspective, the assigned reading will also help you bring a perspective or a set of questions to bear on the new sources. For example, the short paper you wrote using bell hooks to talk about the sacrifices involved in conforming to professional and educational institutions could lead to a research paper in which you explore the ways that schools have tried to be more inclusive of people from a range of backgrounds. Richard Rodriguez's work might help you to think about what the concept of "inclusive" really means. Think about it this way: Scholars in the various disciplines almost *never* approach a brand-new topic from scratch; they are always building on knowledge they already have, reading they have already done, or expertise they have already accumulated in a related topic area. Building on one or more of the assigned readings for your research topic, and on your previous papers in developing your research paper, gives you the same advantage of using the familiar to help you make sense of the new sources you collect.

Building on an assigned reading, however, does not stop you from exploring an area of real interest. For example, say you have an interest in baseball. Rather than looking through the essays you have read for specific references to baseball, look for ideas or key terms that could be applied in the subject area of baseball. For example, could Walker Percy's claims about the "symbolic packaging" that prevents us from really experiencing the Grand Canyon hold true for baseball games as well? What effect do baseball cards, announcers, or advertisements really have on how we approach the game? Can Lawrence Lessig's essay help you to analyze the issue of public subsidies for stadium construction? Could you use McGraw and Dillard to talk about learning to "see" the game of baseball through the eyes of the "lover" and the "knowledgeable"? Might Scott DeVeaux's discussion of progress and jazz be used to open up a discussion of the difference between Ted Williams and Barry Bonds? Whatever connections you pursue, it is crucial to realize that not all your sources will be "on your topic" in an absolute, direct way. Actually, it is this creative linking and shaping that typifies the most rewarding and valuable research projects.

However you begin, the two stages of collecting sources and developing a topic work especially well together. Rather than going into the library with a perfectly narrowed topic in mind, you can use some early searches in a general topic area to help you define a particular focus. If, for example, you want to follow up on Barbara Mellix's ideas about how we learn to translate our private, family languages into public, academic writing, you might begin searching the index to popular magazines for the terms "standard English," "code-switching," or "language and power" (all key terms from Mellix). Among the articles that appear, you might find one on the problems of communication that come up in intercultural businesses, such as the advertisements that do not translate from one culture to another or the misunderstandings that occur when people from different cultures transact business. If this general topic interests you, you might consider pursuing the slightly narrower topic of the problems of intercultural communication in the computer industry. This topic would still allow you to use Mellix's thoughts about code-switching or to bring in some of Turkle's ideas to show how styles of communication affect our use of technology. You could also return to the library to collect more sources on communication in the computer industry and on intercultural communication in general. As you piece several of the sources together, you might see a pattern emerging: Several writers argue that the technology itself will help with communication because it draws so many people together into a global marketplace, but others argue that this globalizing effect creates huge communication problems.

As long as you *give yourself time,* the process of choosing a subject area and collecting sources that help you focus on a particular topic or issue can be an extremely exciting and creative one. Through the research process, you are extending the familiar activities of summarizing, analyzing, and piecing together ideas and examples within one reading; now, you are piecing together ideas and examples from a number of readings, creating relationships between sources that have not been thought of before. You are using the key terms of your essay to stitch together a patchwork of disparate examples and to develop the patterns that link them together.

Evaluating Your Sources

Because we are surrounded—sometimes bombarded—with all kinds of information from all kinds of sources, we gradually learn to categorize and sift through the data and to make sense of what we are hearing in relation to what we already know. As you are collecting sources for a research paper, you are performing a similar evaluative process. To convince your readers that you are presenting trustworthy and valuable ideas, you must show them that those ideas come from reliable sources; and if you include less-reliable material, you must let your readers know about the source of that information so that they can make judgments about how much of it to accept. If you are using Michio Kaku to analyze popular reactions to cloning, for example, a series of outlandish articles from *The National Enquirer* "reporting" secret human cloning experiments might offer some useful testimony about extreme public fears and superstitions related to this issue. At the same time, it would be important to identify the unreliable nature of the source and to balance that information by building in some evidence from more reliable medical journals about actual current uses of cloning technology. As you collect research materials, then, it is important to evaluate them for reliability, to determine whether they are popular or scholarly, and to test their usefulness for your particular topic.

How do you determine the reliability of a source, especially one found on the Internet? Keep careful records of how and where you found the source. (This will be crucial for bibliographic citation format as well.) If you know where the information came from, you can deduce a great deal about its reliability: A personal homepage or a for-profit business site will probably be less reliable than an educational site, for example, but you still want to find out who produced that educational site. If the information is provided by an organization, find out more about that organization and its agenda; if the source has an author, find out more about that person—what are his or her credentials? (See Resource 3 on the next page for questions you can use to evaluate information found on the Internet.)

Many college instructors will require that the majority of your information come from scholarly sources. Scholarly sources are considered more reliable than popular sources. A scholarly book or journal article has been researched and written in relation to the knowledge that has already accumulated in that field. Like you, the scholarly author is responsible for keeping to certain professional standards, for presenting evidence for his or her claims, for determining the reliability of his or her sources, and for citing them carefully so that readers can make their own judgments. By contrast, an article in a popular magazine can be an unresearched account of the writer's experience or a simple declaration of the writer's opinion with little or no evidence to back it up.

The best way to decide whether a source is popular or scholarly is to check for footnotes, endnotes, or some other form of bibliographic citation. Scholarly sources must show how their ideas relate to other ideas in the field, so they almost always have some form of bibliographic citation. Popular sources often have few or no citations. Popular sources (from newspapers and magazines, for example) can be useful for gaining very general information about a topic, for demonstrating public responses, or for documenting what information about a topic is publicly available. For example, if you are writing a paper using Martin's examples of how different people understand the immune system and you want to explore some ways in which the general public tends to hear about those issues, you might look in *Time* or *Newsweek* or do a search of the major newspapers for those topics—all popular sources. However, if you want to discuss the findings of the medical community on those issues, you might check the scholarly sources *New England Journal of Medicine* and *American Journal of Public Health*.

Only you can determine the usefulness of a particular source for your topic. As with the issue of reliability, it helps to approach prospective sources with a balance between critical judgment and open-mindedness. It may seem at first that the article you have discovered on the cost of mounting museum exhibits does not exactly connect with the topic you had developed using ideas from Gloria Anzaldúa and Jane Tompkins: a study of the challenges that minority women artists face in presenting their work to mainstream audiences without selling out. A second reading, however, may reveal that the article contains a small but key portion of your argument. For example, you might show that *because* of the high cost of museum and gallery exhibits, women and minority artists, who have less access to

Resource 3

Questions to Ask About Information Found on the Internet

1. **Who?**
   Who wrote what I am reading?
   Who maintains the Internet site?
   Who would accept this information as authoritative (my professor, my friends, my mom, etc.)?
2. **What?**
   What kind of organization owns the Internet site: educational (.edu), commercial (.com), nonprofit (.org), governmental (.gov)? Or does an individual own it (personal home page)?
   What exactly am I reading (a research article, an editorial, some gossip, etc.)?
   What information from this Internet source do I include in a bibliographic citation?
3. **Where?**
   Where exactly did I find this information, and can I get back there?
   Where are the credentials of the author or of the people responsible for the Internet site (that is, are they included on the site)?
4. **When?**
   When was the information originally written?
   When was the last time this Internet site was updated?
   When I go back to find this Internet site again, is it there?
5. **Why?**
   Why was the information originally written?
   Why was this specific information put on the Internet (to provide general information, to sell a product, to enlist support, etc.)?
   Why was searching the Internet better than using print sources?
6. **How?**
   How can I cite this information?
   How accurate and up-to-date is the information?
   How well organized and written is the information?
   How can I repeat this search quickly and efficiently if I need this information again?

Source: Mark van Lummel, Indiana University, South Bend.

funding, also have less access to those spaces to show their work unless they can appeal to mainstream interests. Sometimes a seemingly unusable article can offer one useful example or one bit of useful data. On the other hand, you want to be careful not to let a trail of sources lead you away from your topic or broaden it too much. A key step in the evaluation of sources is asking yourself, how can I use *this* information in *this* paper.

Synthesizing Sources and Establishing Your Own Position in Relation to Them

In the course of college writing, you have probably practiced the skills of paraphrase, summary, and analysis. Those three terms identify three levels at which writers engage with a reading: by restating it in their own words (paraphrase); by giving a condensed account of an important point in a reading (summary); and by further exploring the implications of the reading, testing its limitations or usefulness for their own purposes, or demonstrating its larger significance (analysis). Once you have performed these operations with two or more readings by showing the significance of one writer's ideas in relation to the work of another writer, you have begun the process of synthesis.

Synthesis is the operation of piecing together ideas and examples from a number of readings with the aim of producing a meaningful whole. In synthesis, you are using all the skills you have already practiced (paraphrase, summary, and analysis) to build connections between sources. You create relationships between sources by paying attention to the connections, the overlaps, and the differences that already exist between those sources.

The process of synthesizing sources will also help you to develop your own position or argument in relation to the sources. Once you have developed the connections between sources, you have often developed your thesis statement as well. For example, if your research paper involved an investigation into how the idea of the common good is used in the current debate between the logging industries and "old growth forest" environmentalists, you might collect ideas, examples, case studies, and data from the following sources: from Zita Ingham, the concept of "dissensus" as a means of maintaining community; and from government documents, the policy protecting public parks from logging. You might use a scholarly source documenting the difficulty of regrowing forests; a scholarly source documenting the impact of job losses on the logging community's quality of life; a scholarly source showing how environmentalists use illegal tactics as well as laws protecting endangered species, such as the "spotted owl," to stop logging; and several newspaper accounts quoting the opinions of loggers and environmentalists on the issue. You might weave together many of these ideas and examples to show how both sides have used inflammatory rhetoric to defend their interests; or, on the basis of the evidence collected, you might end up strongly supporting the loggers' case or the environmentalists'. You might end up arguing that by using the process of "dissensus" and community-building described in Ingham's article, the two sides could negotiate a reasonable compromise; or, you might argue in the end that Ingham's proposal would probably have no power to create a peaceful solution in a situation this complex.

In the process of synthesis, you have generated an organizational structure that links those sources into a coherent pattern for a meaningful purpose; you have created an argument about how those sources connect and what they mean. The argument you make is an interpretation of those sources, but it builds from the evidence and uses the evidence to demonstrate and explore its claims.

Once you have collected your sources, you can synthesize them by following one of these procedures:

- Comparing and contrasting the positions of several writers in relation to an issue, using the examples and case studies to help you show the overlaps and differences in their positions

- Testing one of the main theories held by one or two writers on the issue by using their key terms of analysis to explain several of the examples and case studies you have collected

- Developing your own theory about the issue by showing how a number of readings can connect to help us think about that issue in a new or interesting way (that is, by combining key terms from one or two readings with examples and case studies from several sources in a way that reveals something new or interesting about those sources)

However you proceed, the process of synthesis itself will help you develop an argument and establish your own position in relation to the material you have collected. For instance, if you have shown that several writers are debating a particular issue, you might want to show where you stand in that debate. Establishing your own position requires more than stating your opinion: it means demonstrating how your opinion has been developed and tested through a thoughtful interaction with the readings.

Citing and Documenting Sources

When you are citing sources, you must include two components. The first and most important thing to include is a brief citation for each quotation you use in the body of the paper. The second component is a documentation page placed at the end of your paper that lists full information for all the sources used. In the body of your paper, you give the reader only enough information to find each source in the list at the end of your paper; in the bibliographic list at the end of your paper, you give full information about where your reader can find each source. The rules for presenting this information, the "styles" of citation, vary from discipline to discipline and sometimes from course to course. In this section of the book, we provide some basic information for two of the most commonly used styles of citation and documentation: the Modern Language Association (MLA) style and the American Psychological Association (APA) style. Other styles of citation include the University of Chicago Press style, frequently preferred by history instructors, and the Council of Science, formerly Biology, Editors (CSE) style, preferred by some science instructors. Ask your instructor about which system of documentation he or she prefers.

> For more information about MLA style, go to <http://www.mla. org/> and click on "MLA Style" and then on "Frequently Asked Questions about MLA Style."

MLA Style

CITING SOURCES IN THE TEXT   Whenever you use a quotation, provide in parentheses at the end of the sentence the author's name and the page number on which the quotation appears. Because you are integrating that citation into your sentence, the punctuation mark that ends your sentence should always follow the final parenthesis of the citation.

> *Example 1*
>
> Many individuals in this century would not be interested in having their portraits painted, partly because photography creates a more accurate likeness; in this sense, photography "raised our standards for judging how much an informative likeness should include" (Berger 60).

If you use the author's name in the sentence that introduces the quotation, do not restate it in the parenthetical citation.

> *Example 2*
>
> Berger believes that photography "raised our standards for judging how much an informative likeness should include" and, in doing so, contributed to the decline in portrait painting in this century (60).

By using these citations in the body of your paper you give your readers information about where the quotations come from and who first said them in case they would like to track down the original sources. Your goal is to give clear but concise information about each quotation. Notice in Example 2 that this information *always* comes at the end of your sentence, even if the quote itself falls at the beginning. This holds true unless you are citing works by more than one author and need to incorporate the citation earlier to avoid confusion.

Do not cite the title of a work unless your paper quotes from two different works written by the same author (in which case you would include the title in your sentence or in the final parentheses to avoid confusing your reader). However, as a matter of quotation etiquette, it is customary to fully introduce an essay by title and author the *first* time that the essay is mentioned in a paper.

Example 3

In "The Changing View of Man in the Portrait," John Berger argues that the decline in portrait painting is explained in part by larger historical transformations in "the nature of individual identity" (66).

"WORKS CITED" PAGE   In a research paper, it is important to include a "Works Cited" page that gives your readers further information about where to find your sources. The "Works Cited" page should be the last page of your paper, with the accompanying heading giving your last name and the page number, and should give full citations for each source (see sample "Works Cited" on the opposite page). As you collect sources for the research paper, keep careful track of these four elements:

1. Names (the author or authors, editors of collections, sometimes the group or organization responsible for the source)

2. Titles (titles of the source itself, and of the book, journal, newspaper, or website in which it appeared)

3. Dates of publication (including month, volume number, and issue number for articles, the specific day of the month and particular edition for newspapers, and, for Internet sources, both the date of publication and the date you accessed the information)

4. Page numbers for the source and, for Internet sources, the Web addresses and databases involved in finding the source

APA Style

For more information about APA Style, go to <http://www.apa.org/journals/acorner.html> and click on "Frequently Asked Questions" under "Publication Manual (5th ed.)."

For more details about citing electronic sources, go directly to <http://www.apa.org/journals/webref.html>.

Works Cited

Berger, John. "The Changing View of Man in the Por-
    trait." *Making Sense: Constructing Knowledge in the
    Arts and Sciences.* Ed. Bob Coleman, Rebecca Brit-
    tenham, Scott Campbell, and Stephanie Girard.
    Boston: Houghton Mifflin, 2002. 59–68.

Fitzpatrick, John. "Portraiture and the Problem of His-
    tory." *Art Journal* 49 (1990): 323–43.

Kiernan, Vincent. "Study Finds Errors in Medical Infor-
    mation Available on the Web." *Chronicle of Higher
    Education* 12 June 1998: A25.

Lorh, Steve. "Now Playing: Babes in Cyberspace." *The
    New York Times* 3 Apr. 1998, late ed.: C1+.

Martin, Emily, et al. "Scientific Literacy, What It Is, Why
    It's Important, and Why Scientists Think We Don't
    Have It: The Case of Immunology and the Immune
    System." *Making Sense: Constructing Knowledge in
    the Arts and Sciences.* Ed. Bob Coleman, Rebecca
    Brittenham, Scott Campbell, and Stephanie Girard.
    Boston: Houghton Mifflin, 2002. 340–56.

Miller, Rachel. "Why Your Immune System Matters."
    South Bend Tribune Online 13 April 1999, 5 Nov.
    2000 <http://www.southbendtribune.com/>.

Richmond, Caroline. "British girl recovering after forced
    heart transplant." *CMAJ: Canadian Medical Associ-
    ation Journal* 161.6 (21 Sept. 1999): 680. *Ebsco-
    host.* Schurz Library, Indiana University South
    Bend. 25 Oct. 1999 <http://search.epnet.com/>.

CITING SOURCES IN THE TEXT Whenever you use a quotation, provide in parentheses at the end of the sentence the author's name, the date the source was published, and the page number on which the quotation appears. (Note that APA style uses "p." or "pp." before page numbers.) Because you are integrating that citation into your sentence, the punctuation mark that ends your sentence always follows the final parenthesis of the citation.

> *Example 1*
>
> Many individuals in this century would not be interested in having their portraits painted, partly because photography creates a more accurate likeness; in this sense, photography "raised our standards for judging how much an informative likeness should include" (Berger, 2002, p. 60).

If you use the author's name in the sentence that introduces the quotation, add the date of the source immediately after the name. Because you have already supplied this information, do not restate the author's name or give the date in the parenthetical citation at the end of the sentence.

> *Example 2*
>
> Berger (2002) believes that photography "raised our standards for judging how much an informative likeness should include" and, in doing so, contributed to the decline in portrait painting in this century (p. 60).

By using these citations in the body of your paper you give your readers information about where the quotations come from, when they were published, and who first said them in case they would like to track down the original source. Your goal is to give clear but concise information about each quotation.

If you are citing a general concept rather than a specific quotation, do not cite a page number.

> *Example 3*
>
> Two of the essays (Berger, 2002; Sontag, 2002) demonstrate that photography has significantly changed the way we think about individual identity.

"REFERENCES" PAGE In a research paper, it is important to include a "References" page that gives your readers further information about where to find your sources. This list of references should be the last page of your paper, with the accompanying heading giving your last name and the page number, and should give full citations for each source (see sample "References" on page 663). As you

References

Berger, J. (2002). The changing view of man in the portrait. In B. Coleman, R. Brittenham, S. Campbell, &
S. Girard (Eds.), *Making sense: Constructing knowledge in the arts and sciences* (1st ed.) (pp. 59–68).
Boston: Houghton Mifflin.

Fitzpatrick, J. (1990). Portraiture and the problem of
history. *Art Journal, 49,* 323–43.

Jacobson, J. W., Mulick, J. A., & Schwartz, A. A. (1995).
A history of facilitated communication: Science,
pseudoscience, and antiscience: Science working
group on facilitated communication. *American Psychologist, 50,* 750–765. Retrieved January 25,
1996, from the World Wide Web <http://
www.apa.org/journals/jacobson.html>.

Kiernan, V. (1998, June 12). Study finds errors in medical information available on the Web. *Chronicle of
Higher Education,* p. A25.

Lohr, Steve. (1998, April 3). Now playing: Babes in cyberspace. *The New York Times,* pp. C1+.

Martin, E., Claeson, B., Richardson, W., Schoch-Spana,
M., & Taussig, K. (2002). Scientific literacy, what it
is, why it's important, and why scientists think we
don't have it: The case of immunology and the
immune system. In B. Coleman, R. Brittenham,
S. Campbell, & S. Girard (Eds.), *Making sense:
Constructing knowledge in the arts and sciences*
(pp. 000–00). Boston: Houghton Mifflin.

collect sources for the research paper, keep careful track of these four elements:

1. Names (the author or authors, editors of collections, sometimes the group or organization responsible for the source)

2. Titles (titles of the source itself, and of the book, journal, newspaper, or website in which it appeared); capitalize only the first word of the title or subtitle

3. Dates of publication (including month, volume number, and issue number for articles, the specific day of the month and particular edition for newspapers, and, for Internet sources, both the date of publication and the date you accessed the information)

4. Page numbers for the source and, for Internet sources, the Web addresses and databases involved in finding the source

❦

Appendix B

Writing in the Disciplines

❦

Writing in the Disciplines

Your first-year composition course is preparing you and the other students in your classroom for any number of majors or professions. The skills you learn in the writing classroom must be adaptable to the differing demands of the other courses you go on to take, whether they are in sociology, history, accounting, political science, biology, English, or a foreign language. To better address what those differing demands might be, we asked people in a range of disciplines to consider the role of writing in their fields, the kinds of writing assignments you might expect in their classes, and the ways those assignments function as preparation for further work in that field.

As you read these essays, you will notice that different disciplines have different expectations. In biology, for example, you probably will not be asked to work with direct quotation, but you probably will be asked to summarize your data in a table, graph, or picture; to explain that graphic clearly; and to show logically how it supports your conclusions. An assignment in political science might require you to interpret a political speech by using quotations as evidence and including explanations and interpretations of the quotations to support your thesis statement and argument. In foreign-language classes you might be asked to fill out government or other forms in the language you are learning. In accounting, you might need to summarize "a page of numbers in a sentence or two" (Scofield, p. 673), whereas in sociology you might be asked to go beyond "a bland summary of the text" when writing about your reaction to an assigned reading (McClelland, p. 681). One assignment might ask for your perspective on the material, and another might ask you to synthesize literature in the field without giving your own opinion.

The commonalities are more important than the differences, however, when it comes to the varied expectations about writing among disciplines, instructors, and assignments. One commonality that becomes apparent is this: Assignments in college courses almost always depend on the ability to *respond to material in that field, whether that material involves readings or numerical or statistical* data. College writing is almost never done in isolation from the materials in that field. Thus, for example, you probably will be asked to write personal narratives or creative pieces only in creative writing courses, where personal expression is part of the subject matter, or in foreign-language courses, where personal or creative writing can help you to gain fluency in another language (Lomangino, p. 683). Other commonalities include

- Clarity of presentation, including grammar and mechanics, and correct citation form
- Logical organization and progression of ideas
- Accurate paraphrase, summary, and analysis of evidence
- Interpretation of evidence or data to demonstrate how it supports arguments or conclusions
- Adaptation of ideas or information for a particular audience

The greatest commonality, however, is the importance all professionals place on writing. Accounting professor Barbara Scofield notes that "Big 5 accounting firms require interviewees to complete written questions *during the interview* to evaluate applicants' skills" (p. 673). Or, as German Professor Heide R. Lomangino puts it, writing "consolidates and reinforces grammar and vocabulary learning and promotes the development of listening, speaking, and reading skills" (p. 683). That is true of all classroom and learning situations. Writing helps you to make sense of unfamiliar arenas of knowledge, to develop your own ideas and abilities in relation to that knowledge, and to communicate those ideas to others.

Disciplinary Table of Contents

BARBARA SCOFIELD
University of Texas at the Permian Basin

❧

Writing in Accounting

As technology takes on more and more of the work of gathering, recording, and summarizing information, an accountant's competitive advantage is the ability to analyze and communicate financial information. Consider the following scenario.

The printout for the profit for this year states:

	2001	2002
Sales	$40,000,000	$60,000,000
Net Income	$4,000,000	$5,000,000

Based on the figures alone, management is in a quandary. Then the accountant's report arrives:

> Although sales increased 50%, net income only increased 25%, suggesting that there is a steep cost to expanding sales internationally. As the company moves into markets even further from its base customers, the company must increase the efficiency of its selling costs or profit growth will continue to lag.

Or perhaps . . .

> The company achieved its target 25% growth in profit by broad market expansion internationally that saw sales increase 50%. Much of the initial advertising expenses in entering new markets will pay off next year when the company expands in each of these new markets, boosting profit margins.

The accountant decided whether the numbers were good news or bad news and turned these numbers into information that could be used in making business decisions.

In creating information from data, accountants need to summarize information succinctly. Two years of data is communicated by the percentage change. Numbers that are accurate to the penny appear to the nearest million. Sales from the best and worst districts merit a line in reports, but the normal and the routine do not appear. The precision required in preparation of the financial information can obscure the point in narrative form. Beginning accounting students are asked to explain why a company is profitable or unprofitable based on their own computations of net income, an assignment that requires them to summarize a page of numbers in a sentence or two.

Accountants connect evidence with conclusions. Typically accountants have supporting charts or tables for assertions they make. But every chart and table must have written titles, legends, and footnotes that allow the graphic to communicate without an accompanying narrative, and the narrative must provide a clear enough verbal picture so that the graphic is optional. The first step for accounting students is writing footnote disclosures that provide the context for the specific debits and credits used in journal entries.

Accountants organize logically but in a manner that sometimes seems upside down to nontechnical writers. Building suspense is anathema. The best report provides its conclusion in the first paragraph and uses the body of the report to persuade the audience. No one wants to know how the author developed his or her own opinion. Explanations of the process of gathering evidence are placed in appendices, if included at all. A typical research assignment for a new accounting student teaches this organizational skill by having the student gather financial information about a consumer-oriented company and providing a "Buy," "Sell," or "Hold" recommendation on its stock.

Accountants match vocabulary to the expertise of the audience. Some accounting writings are workpapers that are used only by successor accountants. A common, technical vocabulary (e.g., "accruals") and routine abbreviations (AJE) are appropriate. Some accounting writings communicate within a company. No business executive mistakes the meaning of "net income" and "revenues." Some accounting writing communicates with suppliers and clients outside of a company. "The value of all goods delivered to customers during the year" distinguishes what is meant by "revenues" from cash received from customers or value of goods available for sale. Reports are customized to the needs of the audience. A typical audience for an entering student is fellow students. Can you explain accounting terminology so that another fresman can understand it?

How important is writing in the field of accounting? Big 5 accounting firms require interviewees to complete written questions *during the interview* to evaluate applicants' skills. The Certified Public Accounting examination grade is based on writing skills as well as technical skills. The Securities and Exchange Commission identifies good writing as an essential part of its investor protection program (see *A Plain English Handbook* at <http://www.sec.gov/pdf/handbook.pdf>). So you want to be an accountant? Start writing!

STEVEN GERENCSER
Indiana University, South Bend

❧

Writing in Political Science

Writing for a course in political science offers many opportunities and, of course, many challenges. The student of political science might need to write an interpretation of the classical philosopher Plato's conception of the ideal political regime for one class and an analysis of statistical polling data for another. Some assignments will ask students to write about their response to an argument they have read or a film they have seen; others will ask them to avoid putting their personal opinions into their analyses. Some instructors will ask a student to write about an assignment that all students have read for class; others will require a student to do individual research about anything from the various electoral systems of countries around the world to how congressional subcommittees develop policies. Given this range of writing, what, if anything, ties together writing for political science?

Good writing in political science shares with good writing in all disciplines an attention to the mechanics of good grammar and syntax. Accurate spelling, correct punctuation, proper sentence structure, and good paragraph organization are not only important for English composition courses, but also for clear writing in political science. But the variety of writing assignments mentioned above means that more than attention to good mechanics is important.

Most important is to convey immediately and directly to the reader what the writer is attempting to accomplish in the piece. What is the thesis of the argument, the significance of the explanation, or the point of the interpretation? What is the purpose of the writing? Is it to persuade? To interpret? To inform? To argue? Who is the audience for this writing? Should the writer assume the reader knows as much as the political science instructor? Another student in the class? Someone with no knowledge of the subject matter? Of course, to convey his or her intentions to the reader, the writer must know what he or she is trying to accomplish. Is he, for example, trying to argue that Plato's ideal city is fundamentally problematic? If so, the writer might start by declaring, "In this paper I will argue that Plato's favorite political regime is flawed because it makes accidental differences between people the basis of political inequality." Is the writer instead trying to interpret and explain a feature of Plato's discussion? In that case, the writer might state her thesis as "Plato's suggestion that the best city would be ruled by a philosopher might sound odd, but I will show how it is based upon his theory of knowledge." These two sentences indicate quite different papers, but each thesis statement makes it clear what the writer is attempting. Each statement assumes that the reader is aware of Plato's conception of the ideal city and knows some of its features.

A student could also be asked to provide a narrative that makes sense of the numbers in a statistical survey or to construct an argument that uses those numbers to persuade the reader to pursue a particular course of action. Again, the thesis statement makes the paper's direction clear to the reader. In the first case, the writer might begin by informing the reader, "This paper will attempt to explain the complex responses to a recent healthcare survey by discussing how the survey was taken, what questions were asked, and how the answers changed depending on the order in which those questions were asked." The writer of the second paper might announce, "I will contend in this paper that the results of a recent healthcare survey clearly show this country is ready to extend healthcare to all its citizens." Each of these thesis statements indicates that the reader is not required to know anything about the healthcare survey; the writer will explain what is necessary. Before beginning any writing assignment, of course, it is important to ask for clear directions from the instructor. The student can then use the instructor's guidelines to consider the topic of the assignment before developing an approach to writing it.

One of the most important and difficult aspects of learning to write in political science is knowing how to use evidence to support the argument, explanation, or interpretation. Whether it is the text of a philosophical treatise or a political speech, the data from a statistical survey or the Gross National Product of a Third World country, the evidence never speaks for itself. The writer needs to use the data or text to support his or her argument, explanation, or interpretation, but he cannot simply assemble a puzzle of pieces of data or quotes. This is a tricky task. The writer must be able to point to specific data or quotations from a text and explain or interpret what she thinks they mean. Again, it is important to ask the instructor assigning a paper how she expects the writer to refer to the evidence. Does she want direct quotations? Should statistical figures be brought into the text directly or left for footnotes?

Asking how best to use quotations or data raises the question of how to cite the sources the writer uses. As a general recommendation, it is a good idea to write down the bibliographic information for any source used at any stage of writing, even if it is unclear if it will make it into a final draft; this way, a writer does not have to scurry back to the library to find that information, risking the possibility that the source is being used by someone else. There are many different styles used in many different political science publications, so again, consult with the instructor to determine which style he or she prefers.

ANN GRENS, DEBORAH MARR, AND
ANDREW SCHNABEL
Indiana University, South Bend

✗

Writing in the Sciences

Writing is a central part of being a professional scientist. Scientists write the results of their research for publication, write proposals to obtain funding for research, and write reviews to present new ideas that are emerging from the results of many experiments. One of the major goals of writing in undergraduate science classes is to develop skills in two major categories: research papers and literature reviews.

Both research papers and literature reviews are structured in a fundamentally similar way, which reflects the scientific process. In all cases, a scientific paper begins with an introduction to the hypothesis to be tested and a brief review of relevant background information. In research papers, but typically not in literature reviews, the introduction is followed by a detailed description of the methods and materials used to conduct the study. The true heart of any scientific paper, however, is the presentation of observations or experimental results, which are often in the form of quantitative data. In a research paper, the author reports the results he or she generated, while in a review the author summarizes results from previously published work. Finally, the author presents his or her conclusions and explains how the experimental evidence supports those conclusions.

Because the primary purpose of writing in the sciences is to convey factual information, the key skills for success are clear presentation and the ability to develop a logical argument. Conveying accurate meaning to the reader requires correct spelling, punctuation, and grammar. Sloppiness, in the form of imprecise wording or inaccurate phrasing, can lead a reader to misunderstand how or why an experiment was performed or what results were obtained. If the reader is unable to determine precisely what was done, he or she is unlikely to accept the results as reliable. Thus, accuracy is of greater importance than originality; it is far preferable to use a term repeatedly that conveys the precise meaning intended than to lose clarity or accuracy by substituting nearly synonymous terms for the sake of variety. Accuracy in wording also requires clearly distinguishing between fact and possibility. For example, compare these two statements:

1. Species A cannot tolerate temperatures above 30°C.

2. Our data suggest that species A cannot tolerate temperatures above 30°C.

The first statement is factual, whereas the second is an interpretation of the data.

The logic by which the author has drawn conclusions from experimental results must also be clearly presented and supported both with examples from previously published work and by reference to the data contained in earlier portions of the paper. The author must explain his or her conclusions, discuss how those conclusions were reached, and convincingly demonstrate that alternative explanations are unlikely to explain the observed results. Finally, the author should resist overinterpretation and should limit conclusions to those that can be logically supported by the available data. Consider the conclusions a student could make from an experiment that involved measuring light absorption for various plant pigments. The first student states that the plant pigments absorbed primarily blue and red wavelengths, and predicts that blue and red wavelengths promote the greatest amount of plant growth because capturing light is critical for plant growth. The second student makes the same statement, but then predicts that blue and red wavelengths are best for promoting growth of all photosynthetic organisms. The first statement is a logical extension of the results, whereas the second conclusion overinterprets the results because many photosynthetic organisms are not plants and have different pigments.

Most writing in the sciences is related to qualitative or quantitative results generated by testing hypotheses. Students therefore also must develop the ability to present such information accurately and clearly. Little scientific information lends itself well to narrative description. Instead, most research results are best summarized in a figure, such as a table, graph, or picture. This is especially true for numerical data, which is the most common type of information presented in scientific studies. The author must construct appropriate figures that present the relevant information and must explain the figures in such a manner that the reader can easily extract that information. The reader should be led through a figure, with specific results of interest clearly indicated. The author should not simply include the figure and trust that the reader will interpret it correctly.

Figure 1, for example, shows data on human survivorship that were collected by students in an introductory biology class. A student writing a lab report about human survivorship based on these data would need to refer to the figure in the results section of the paper and explain the main points of the graph. Suppose the explanatory text accompanying the figure states, "Figure 1 shows that females had high survival through the early and middle years and began to suffer high mortality rates only in older age classes." This text helps ensure that the reader understands the information that is being presented. It also makes it easier for the author to refer to the figure in support of his or her conclusions. In the discussion section of the report, for example, the student might argue, "The high survivorship of each individual offspring, as shown in Figure 1, reflects important aspects of human life history that are similar to those of many other mammals, such as large energetic investment in producing offspring, having small numbers of offspring per reproductive episode, and investing heavily in parental care of the young."

The final part of the scientific paper presents complete bibliographic information for each source used to support statements in the text. The precise format for presenting bibliographic information varies depending on the scientific discipline and journal, but there are two general rules that apply across virtually all forms of scientific writing. First, and most importantly, an accurate citation must be given for any results or ideas that are not the author's original work. Second, direct quotes are extremely rare; the author generally paraphrases hypotheses, experimental results, and interpretations that originated elsewhere. A citation in the format required by the journal (or the instructor, in the case of class assignments) should immediately follow the paraphrase and should refer the reader to a complete reference for the original source in the "Works Cited" or "References" section of the paper.

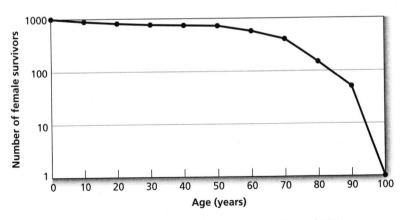

FIGURE 1 Survivorship curve for females born between 1850 and 1869

In summary, the general rules of basic composition apply in scientific writing as much as in any other discipline. Writing in the sciences is somewhat different from writing in many other fields, however, because of a difference in emphasis and intention. Scientific writing aims to convey factual information accurately and precisely, whether communicating novel results of new experiments performed by the author or a summary of previously published results in a literature review. In either case, clarity of presentation is considered to be of far greater importance than literary style. As discussed here, most scientific writing follows a basic structure that mirrors the scientific process of observation, hypothesis testing, and analysis and interpretation of quantitative data. Students who become skilled at the clear presentation and explanation of scientific methods and results will have a distinct advantage in their science courses.

KENT MCCLELLAND

Grinnell College

Writing in Sociology

As a sociology student, you are likely to get paper assignments asking for your reactions to assigned readings. For example, you might be asked to write an essay discussing the "sociological imagination" (Mills 1959:3–24). Such papers too often end up as little more than a bland summary of the text. To avoid this pitfall and to make your paper more interesting, imagine your essay as a three-way conversation among the author of the text, your readers, and you. If you hope to write a really good essay, you cannot hide behind the author whose work you are analyzing. Instead you must stake out your own position in the conversation.

The first side of the three-way conversation in a good essay links the author of the text with the readers of the paper, whom you should think of as intelligent students who have not yet read the text. In this part of the conversation, you convey to your readers what this author is saying. The second conversation connects you personally with these readers, as you tell them what interests you most about these ideas. The third and most important conversation requires you to confront the author directly by engaging in a critical analysis and appreciation of the text. Since these conversations cannot all occur at once, knowing when to hold each can help you to structure your paper.

A well-written introduction gets all three of the conversations under way. You start the first conversation by introducing your readers to the author and the central ideas under discussion. In almost the same breath, you can begin the second conversation, the one between you and your readers, by finding a way to catch your readers' interest. You might hook your readers, for example, by showing how the chosen text creates an apparent contradiction or a problem to be solved. Your introduction must also initiate the crucial third conversation by stating your thesis, the main point of your critical comments on the author's ideas. Many introductions end by quickly returning to the conversation between you and your readers, as you forecast the direction the paper will take.

In the middle paragraphs, or body of the essay, you focus on the two conversations involving the author of the text. While it is tempting to devote most sentences in these paragraphs to the first conversation—the one conveying the author's ideas to your readers—you should not neglect the even more important exchange—the one between you and the author. Which of the author's ideas do you believe are on the right track and which off course? Which ideas can be extended or applied? This critical commentary constitutes your essay's *argument,* and readers expect to find it in the transitional sentences at the beginnings and ends of these paragraphs.

Your essay's concluding paragraph ordinarily sums up the highlights of your argument, but the conclusion also offers you a chance to turn to your readers and renew your conversation with them by putting things in perspective. Where should we go with the new insights developed here? What might it all mean in the scheme of things?

With all these conversations going on, readers may need help in keeping them straight. Thus, careful citation is crucial. Citations enable you to separate your own voice from the voice of the author. You can also clarify the separation of voices by not trying to sound like the original author. As a college student, you need not pretend that you have already earned a Ph.D., and, in fact, such pretension risks making you sound foolish. Readers want to hear your perspective on the material in your own words as you add your voice to the ongoing discourse of academic scholarship.

References

Mills, C. Wright. 1959. *The Sociological Imagination.* New York: Grove Press.

Heide R. Lomangino

University of South Alabama

❧

Writing in Foreign Languages

Students write a lot in foreign language classes. Some assignments are similar to those required in other disciplines, but others are quite different and unique to foreign language learning. Unless students advance to the third and fourth year of college-level study, they generally are not required, nor able, to produce research papers or other formal writing in the target language. Writing in another language is a complex skill that must be developed and practiced thoroughly. The overall objective of writing instruction is to enable students to express their ideas in written form and produce messages that are comprehensible and acceptable to native speakers. This, however, does not imply native speaker proficiency, because it is rare that nonnative speakers, even after many years of language study, are able to write as well as educated native speakers.

Writing fulfills two basic roles in foreign language acquisition. First, it consolidates and reinforces grammar and vocabulary learning and promotes the development of listening, speaking, and reading skills. In this case, writing functions as a support skill. Second, writing is an important mode of communication as, for example, in correspondence of all kinds: notes, forms, reports, essays, and creative writing.

The writing activities in foreign language courses reflect the many skills that are involved in the writing process. If the writing system is different from English as, for example, in Russian, Arabic, or Japanese, students initially may spend considerable time practicing how to write the new symbols.

To help students learn the spelling rules of the new language, early writing activities may consist of copying written texts or writing down words and phrases that students have heard or spoken. These exercises involve noting and remembering the choice of letters and their sequence. It also means associating speech sounds with graphic symbols and recognizing instances of unsounded letters. Students must also learn to use grammar according to target language norms. In addition, they must acquire skill in selecting and using words and phrases that convey the meanings they wish to express.

Other writing activities on the beginning level are listing, labeling, matching, filling out forms, and answering questions on simple readings. In addition, students begin to create their own texts by writing brief descriptions of people and places, short messages for postcards and letters, and dialogue journals.

On the intermediate level, roughly the second year of language study in college, students are able to produce longer sentences and short connected texts. Writing is still used to consolidate the learning of vocabulary and grammar, but also to promote personal expression that includes the composing of notes, letters, descriptions, guided and free compositions, advertisements, daily journals, and simple poems.

On the advanced level, students generally are required to take several specialized courses in literature, language, and culture. There they engage in a variety of demanding writing tasks. The content of these courses is drawn from a number of diverse disciplines and fields of inquiry, such as literary criticism, history, politics, art, music, and business. Consequently, students must not only develop skill in organizing their ideas effectively and creating texts coherently, they also must learn how to use subject-specific language appropriately.

In some upper-level composition courses, students are systematically introduced to the composing process. The different steps, from prewriting to revising, are practiced in a variety of formats. Writing projects may include research papers and reports, letters, essays, compositions, journals, poetry, and translation. Expressive writing usually is graded holistically or analytically. Holistic evaluation is done quickly and impressionistically, and a single grade is assigned based on the overall impression of the clarity and effectiveness of the work and its linguistic and organizational quality. In analytical evaluation, significant elements of a composition are separated into components for scoring purposes, for example, grammar, vocabulary, spelling, stylistic technique, organization, and content. Based on the nature of the writing activity, each component is assigned a certain weight and value, and thus students are given an accurate diagnosis of the strengths and weaknesses of their written work.

Foreign language learners have access to many tools and resources to assist them with their writing. Dictionaries are available in book form, on CD-ROMs, and on the Internet. Most writing instructors have definite preferences in respect to dictionaries and other reference works. Bilingual or learners' dictionaries generally are not recommended because the excessive use of bilingual dictionaries tends to encourage translation from the native to the target language, a practice that can be detrimental to the development of natural and fluent expression.

Computer-assisted instruction is now popular in foreign language education, and word processing programs, electronic mail, and computer conferencing systems are being used to promote writing skills. In addition, special writing assistant programs have been designed to facilitate the writing process. These contain guided composing activities as well as bilingual dictionaries, verb conjugators, and vocabulary, grammar, and phrase indexes.

Learning to write in a second language is a demanding but rewarding process. It requires continuous practice. Extensive reading in the target language is one of the best ways to maintain and expand this skill. Fortunately, traditional and modern media offer an abundance of suitable reading material to the foreign language learner.

RICHARD FLORIDA Pages 1–17 from *The Rise of the Creative Class: And How Its Transforming Work, Leisure, Community, and Everyday Life* by Richard Florida, copyright © 2002 by Richard Florida. Reprinted by permission of Basic Books, a member of Perseus Books, L.L.C.

ARLIE RUSSELL HOCHSCHILD "From the Frying Pan Into the Fire" from *The Commercialization of Intimate Life: Notes from Home and Work.* Copyright © 2003 by Arlie Russell Hochschild, reprinted with permission of the Regents of the University of California and the University of California Press.

BELL HOOKS "Keeping Close to Home: Class and Education." from *Talking back: thinking feminist, thinking black* by Bell Hooks, copyright © 1989, reprinted by permission of South End Press.

ZITA INGHAM "Landscape, Drama, and Dissensus: The Rhetorical Education of Red Lodge, Montana" from *Green Culture: Environmental Rhetoric in Contemporary America* by Carl G. Herndl and Stuart C. Brown, copyright © 1996. Reprinted by permission of The University of Wisconsin Press.

MICHIO KAKU "Second Thoughts: the Genetics of a Brave New World?" from *Visions: How Science Will Revolutionize the 21st* Century by Michio Kaku, copyright © 1997 by Michio Kaku. Used by permission of Doubleday, a division of Random House, Inc.

THOMAS KUHN "The Historical Structure of Scientific Discovery." *International Encyclopedia of Unified Science.* vol 2 by Thomas Kuhn, copyright © 1988 by AAAS, reprinted with permission.

CHRISTOPHER LASCH Christopher Lasch, "The Lost Art of Argument," in *The Revolt of the Elites and the Betrayal of Democracy.* New York: W.W. Norton, 1996. This essay was originally published as "Journalism, Publicity, and the Lost Art of Argument" in the Spring 1990 issue of *Media Studies Journal* and is reprinted by permission of the Freedom Forum.

LAWRENCE LESSIG "Introduction" from *Free Culture: How Big Media Uses Technology and the Law to Lock Down Culture and Control Creativity* by Lawrence Lessig, copyright © 2004 by Lawrence Lessig. Used by permission of The Penguin Press, a division of Penguin Group (USA) Inc.

EMILY MARTIN, BJORN CLAESON, WENDY RICHARDSON, MONICA SCHOCH-SPANA, AND KAREN-SUE TAUSSIG "Scientific Literacy, What It Is, Why It's Important, and Why Scientists Think We Don't Have It: The Case of Immunology and the Immune System" from *Naked Science: Anthropological Inquiry into Boundaries, Power, and Knowledge* edited by Laura Nader, copyright © 1996, Reproduced by permission of Routledge/Taylor & Francis Books, Inc.

SCOTT McCLOUD "Setting the Record Straight" [pp. 2–23] from *Understanding Comics* by Scott McCloud, copyright © 1993, 1994 by Scott McCloud. Reprinted by permission of HarperCollins Publishers, Inc.

ERIN McGRAW Erin McGraw, "Bad Eyes," *The Gettysburg Review.* Copyright © 1998 by Erin McGraw. Reprinted by permission of the author.

BARBARA MELLIX "From the Outside, In." originally appeared in The Georgia Review, vol. XLI, No. 2 (Summer 1987), copyright © 1987 by The University of Georgia / copyright © 1987 by Barbara Mellix. Reprinted by permission of Barbara Mellix and The Georgia Review.

WALTER MOSLEY "For Authors, Fragile Ideas Need Loving Every Day" by Walter Mosley, which appeared in The New York Times, July 3, 2000. Copyright © 2000 by The New York Times Co. Reprinted with permission.

WALKER PERCY "The Loss of the Creature" from The Message in the Bottle: How Queer Man Is, How Queer Language Is, and What One Has to Do With the Other by Walker Percy. Copyright © 1975 by Walker Percy

Author and Title Index